Learning Media Design with Adobe® CS5
Illustrator®, Photoshop®, InDesign®

Catherine Skintik

Prentice Hall

Boston • Columbus • Indianapolis • New York • San Francisco • Upper Saddle River
Amsterdam • Cape Town • Dubai • London • Madrid • Milan • Munich • Paris • Montreal • Toronto
Delhi • Mexico City • Sao Paulo • Sydney • Hong Kong • Seoul • Singapore • Taipei • Tokyo

Editor in Chief: Michael Payne
Associate VP/Executive Acquisitions Editor, Print: Stephanie Wall
Product Development Manager: Eileen Bien Calabro
Editorial Assistant: Nicole Sam
Director of Marketing: Kate Valentine
Marketing Manager: Tori Olson Alves
Marketing Coordinator: Susan Osterlitz
Marketing Assistant: Darshika Vyas
Senior Managing Editor: Cynthia Zonneveld
Associate Managing Editor: Camille Trentacoste
Production Project Manager: Mike Lackey
Operations Director: Alexis Heydt

Senior Operations Specialist: Diane Peirano
Senior Art Director: Jonathan Boylan
Text and Cover Designer: Vanessa Moore
AVP/Director of Online Programs, Media: Richard Keaveny
AVP/Director of Product Development, Media: Lisa Strite
Media Project Manager, Editorial: Alana Coles
Media Project Manager, Production: John Cassar
Full-Service Project Management: Emergent Learning, LLC
Composition: Vanessa Moore
Printer/Binder: Edwards Brothers
Cover Printer: Lehigh-Pheonix Color
Text: 10/12 Helvetica

Microsoft® and Windows® are registered trademarks of the Microsoft Corporation in the U.S.A. and other countries. Screen shots and icons reprinted with permission from the Microsoft Corporation. This book is not sponsored or endorsed by or affiliated with the Microsoft Corporation.

10 9 8 7 6 5 4 3 2 1

ISBN-10:   0-13-138408-2
ISBN-13: 978-0-13-138408-8

Table of Contents

Exercise 98

Exercise 99

END OF LESSON PROJECTS

Exercise 100

Exercise 101

Exercise 102

Exercise 103

Lesson 11: Assemble and Print Publications 515

Exercise 104

Exercise 105

Exercise 106

Exercise 107

Exercise 108

Exercise 109

Introduction

Learning Media Design with Adobe CS5 shows you how to use Adobe Illustrator, Adobe Photoshop, and Adobe InDesign to create high-quality illustrations, images, and documents for print, Web, and devices. In this book, you learn to design and create attention-getting products for a wide variety of media needs.

WHO SHOULD READ THIS BOOK?

- *Learning Media Design with Adobe CS5* is written for beginning designers, graphic artists, and page layout specialists. The book assumes the reader has a working knowledge of basic design elements, common Windows navigation, and word processing skills.

- This book is for everyone who needs to know how to create illustrations, work with digital images, and lay out documents that include both text and graphics. You can use this book as an exercise-by-exercise tutorial on many Illustrator, Photoshop, and InDesign features or refer to it on an as-needed topical basis.

- You should read this book if you need to design any kind of document for the print market, from simple flyers to four-color magazine spreads, and want to learn sophisticated illustration and image techniques, as well as learn to prepare a document for printing. The content of this book will also be valuable for designers who are creating or modifying illustrations for use on Web pages or digital devices.

WHAT YOU NEED

To gain the most from this book, you will need:

- Knowledge of fundamental Windows navigation and terminology.

- 2GHz or faster processor.Intel® Pentium® 4 or AMD Athlon® 64 processor.

- Microsoft® Windows® XP with Service Pack 2 3 (Service Pack 3 is recommended); or Windows Vista™ ® Home Premium, Business, Ultimate, or Enterprise with Service Pack 1 (certified for 32-bit editionsService Pack 2 recommended); or Windows 7.

- 1GB of RAM or more recommended.

- 7.7GB of available hard-disk space (additional free space required during installation).

- At least 1,024 × 768 monitor resolution with 16-bit video card.

- Adobe CS5 Design Standard or Premium, including Illustrator, Photoshop, InDesign, and Acrobat.

INTEGRATED APPROACH

■ Because Adobe CS5 Design is a suite of powerful applications—Adobe Illustrator CS5, Adobe Photoshop CS5, and Adobe InDesign CS5—this course includes exercises that incorporate tasks and features from each of the three programs to give you a comprehensive understanding of the suite.

■ Each application is covered in one of this book's three parts. As you work in each part, you may use other applications or resources prepared in other applications. In the Illustrator section, for example, you may place files for tracing that were prepared in Photoshop. In the InDesign section, you may insert in a document both Illustrator illustrations and Photoshop images. This integrated approach helps you get the feel for the different programs and learn to use them together easily.

■ Though the InDesign portion of the book gives it a slant toward print documents, several exercises in each section of the book provide practice in creating objects for use in other media. You learn how to create objects in Illustrator that may be used as buttons on a Web page. In the Photoshop section, you learn how to optimize images for use on Web pages or devices. The InDesign section shows you how to create interactive documents that can readily be exported as PDFs or Flash files.

HOW THIS BOOK IS ORGANIZED

This book is organized in three parts. Each part is dedicated to one of the three applications used in the text: Illustrator, Photoshop, and InDesign. Within the three parts are eleven lessons that cover the skills of the three applications, from simple basics to more advanced features. In addition, an introductory lesson covers basic Adobe features.

■ **Adobe CS5 Basics.** This lesson covers aspects of the Adobe interface and standard procedures that are the same in all three applications used in the book. You learn how to start and exit an application, open and close an application file, use menus and panels, change views and magnification, change preferences, and restore the default workspace. You also learn how to use Adobe Bridge, an application that helps you organize and work with the many files you will use and create in this course, and how to find help using Adobe's help system.

■ **Lesson 1—Work with Basic Graphic Tools in Illustrator CS5.** This lesson introduces Adobe Illustrator and its workspace and tools and teaches basic drawing techniques. You learn how to create a new drawing; select objects; use common drawing tools such as Pencil, Paintbrush, Rectangle, and Ellipse; apply fill and stroke color; and align, group, position, and arrange objects. You also learn how to create new shapes by cutting objects; how to reshape and rotate objects; how to work with multiple artboards in the same illustration; and how to insert text in an illustration.

■ **Lesson 2—Work with Paths and Layers.** In this lesson, you learn additional selection techniques, such as how to select one object from a group or how to select a single anchor point or side of an object. This lesson focuses on more advanced drawing skills: using the Pen tool to draw both straight and curved lines and using the Paintbrush tool with a variety of brush settings. You learn how to use the new Width tool and the Draw Inside and Draw Behind modes. You learn how to place a file and trace a drawing using Live Trace. Finally, you learn how to use layers in Illustrator to organize and arrange objects in an illustration.

■ **Lesson 3—Work with Colors, Effects, and Styles.** This lesson concentrates on features that allow you to fine-tune a graphic by adjusting color, applying effects, and creating graphic styles. You learn about the color models available in Illustrator and when each is appropriate, and you use the Swatches panel to manage colors and groups of colors in an illustration. You learn how to change opacity and blending mode to control how colors of various objects interact with each other. You use the new Shape Builder tool to create complex objects by combining shapes. You use Live Paint and Live Color to flow paint into areas of an illustration and edit color interactively. You use Illustrator's gradient feature to blend colors, and apply commonly used Illustrator effects to give objects special appearances. You learn how to create graphic styles that can be easily applied and modified throughout an illustration and use the Appearance panel to modify and manage appearance attributes.

- **Lesson 4—Work with Drawing and Selecting Tools in Photoshop CS5.** This lesson introduces Adobe Photoshop and its workspace and tools. You create a new image and learn how to select foreground and background colors, how to select a drawing mode, and how to use the Brush and the new Mixer Brush to apply color. You are introduced to the Photoshop Layers panel and learn how it differs from the Illustrator Layers panel. This lesson also covers essential Photoshop skills such as erasing image content and the many options for selecting areas and objects in an image. You use selection marquee tools, Lasso tools, the Magic Wand, and Photoshop's Quick Selection tool. You manipulate selections by applying fill and stroke color, using transform options, and feathering. You also learn how to refine a selection, add to or subtract from a selection, save a selection, and load a previously saved selection.

- **Lesson 5—Correct and Modify Images.** This lesson teaches techniques for correcting images. You learn how to apply automatic corrections that can quickly adjust levels, color, and contrast, and you are also introduced to the Adjustments panel, where you can select nondestructive options to correct color balance, brightness and contrast, tone levels, and hue and saturation. You also experiment with photo filters, correct exposure problems, modify vibrance, and adjust shadows and highlights to improve a picture. You learn how to fix problems in an image using tools such as Red Eye, Healing Brush and Spot Healing Brush, and Patch, and you copy an image area using the Clone Stamp tool. You learn how to use the new content-aware fill feature to remove portions of an image and replace them with surrounding content. You use tools such as Dodge, Burn, Sponge, and Blur to correct an image or create special effects in an image. This lesson also shows you how to crop an image, rotate the canvas and adjust canvas size, and change image dimensions and resolution. You are introduced to the content-aware scaling feature that allows you to modify image size without changing the size or appearance of important content in the image. Finally, you have a chance to work with the new Puppet Warp feature that allows you to distort or transform an image by dragging areas into new locations.

- **Lesson 6—Explore Advanced Image Techniques.** In this lesson, you learn about Photoshop path techniques. You create paths using shape tools and the Pen tool and add strokes and fills to paths. This lesson shows you alternate ways to modify an image's appearance by using adjustment layers, layer blending, layer styles, and filters. You apply several kinds of masks, including type masks, layer masks, clipping masks, and vector masks, and manipulate them using the Masks panel. An exercise on optimization gives you the chance to adjust images for best appearance on the Web and devices. This lesson also includes very important information about color management systems and color profiles and how to convert images from Photoshop's default RGB color model to the CMYK model required for printed output.

- **Lesson 7—Work with Basic Layout Tools in InDesign CS5.** This lesson introduces Adobe InDesign and its workspace and tools. You create a new document, add guides to help you align content, and insert text and graphic frames. You can draw in InDesign with tools identical to those you mastered in Illustrator to add basic shapes to pages. In this introductory lesson, you learn the basics of typing and placing text in a text frame, as well as placing and adjusting a graphic in a graphic frame. You learn how to apply fill and stroke color in InDesign, adjust corner rounding using Live Corners, and wrap text around a graphic. You add and delete pages in a simple document and insert elements on master pages that will display on every page of a document. You also work with the InDesign Layers panel, improved in CS5, to organize and arrange shapes and frames in a document.

- **Lesson 8—Work with Objects, Colors, and Masters.** This lesson gives you a more in-depth view of working with objects such as frames and shapes in InDesign. You review techniques that allow you to reshape, transform, align, distribute, and group objects, jobs that are easier when you use Smart Guides and tools such as the new Gap tool. You spend more time with the InDesign Swatches panel and explore InDesign's transparency effects and special formats for strokes and corners. You also learn how to create and apply object styles and how to quickly find and change objects using their style attributes. You also learn more about how to create, apply, and modify master pages.

- **Lesson 9—Work with Type and Styles.** In this lesson, you explore InDesign's sophisticated text features. After learning additional techniques for placing text in a document, you work with the Story Editor, learn how to find and change text, and check spelling. Then you move on to learn more about fonts, font styles, and font sizes, as well as features such as text scaling, tracking, kerning, and leading that allow you to control text appearance and spacing. The lesson covers InDesign's special text options, such as glyphs that allow you to insert many special characters and alternate versions of standard text characters, and OpenType options that allow you to insert ligatures, fractions, alternate number formats, and other special character formatting. From character formats you proceed to paragraph formats such as alignment, indents, and space above and below paragraphs. You explore special paragraph formatting such as drop caps, paragraph rules, and bulleted and numbered lists. You learn how to control text using tabs, adjust paragraph breaks, and turn hyphenation on and off. InDesign's conditional text feature allows you to create documents that can be customized for a particular use; the smart text reflow feature adjusts story length automatically as conditional text is hidden or displayed. This lesson also teaches you how to create both character and paragraph styles that allow you to quickly apply formats throughout a document.

■ **Lesson 10—Work with Tables and Graphics.** In this lesson, you learn how to create tables from scratch or convert tabular text to create a table, as well as how to modify table structure by inserting and deleting columns and rows or merging and splitting table cells. You create both cell and table styles to apply stroke and fill formats to areas of a table. You learn more about placing graphic files, including using the option for placing multiple files, and develop an understanding of how graphic files are linked in InDesign. You work with graphics that have multiple layers and use InDesign features to display or hide layers, use paths or channels that have been saved with a graphic, and fine-tune text wrap based on a path or channel. You learn how to place one or more images from an Illustrator file that uses multiple artboards. You also explore some fun ways to use text to create graphic interest in a document.

■ **Lesson 11—Assemble and Print Publications.** This lesson gives you more information on how to handle common chores associated with longer documents, such as rearranging pages, creating sections to apply different page numbering options, organizing sections in the Pages panel using color labels, inserting jump lines, and using text variables. You learn how to create a book to manage multiple documents so that styles can be applied consistently and document pages can be numbered consecutively. You also create a table of contents. This lesson provides valuable information on preparing a document for final printed output by covering issues such as overprinting and trapping, preflight checks, and color separation preview, and it also covers in depth settings you can choose before sending a job to print. You also learn how to print color separations, package a document for distribution, and export a document in PDF or EPS format. Interactive features such as cross-references, sample buttons, hyperlinks, the new Preview panel, and page transitions are also covered.

Learning Media Design with Adobe CS5 is designed to make your learning experience easy and enjoyable. Lessons are comprised of short exercises designed to help you learn how to use Adobe CS5 in real-life business settings. Every application exercise is made up of eight key elements:

■ **Software Skills.** Each exercise starts with a brief description of how you would use the features of that exercise in the workplace.

■ **Design Skills.** Good design is essential for creating effective and attractive print materials. Important design skills are outlined before you begin the exercise.

■ **Application Skills.** A scenario is set to put the program features into context.

■ **Terms.** Key terms are included and defined at the start of each exercise, so you can quickly refer back to them. The terms are then highlighted in the text.

■ **Notes.** Concise notes aid in learning the computer concepts.

■ **Procedures.** Hands-on mouse and keyboard procedures teach all necessary skills.

■ **Application Exercise.** Step-by-step instructions put your skills to work.

■ **On Your Own.** Each exercise concludes with a critical-thinking activity that you can work through on your own. You are frequently challenged to provide your own content. The "On Your Own" sections can be used as additional reinforcement, for practice, or to test skill proficiency.

In addition to these elements, you may see Design Suite Integration boxes that inform you of similar features in other Design Suite applications, as well as Extra boxes that tell you about additional related features you may want to explore on your own.

Enhanced End-of-Lesson material puts skills to the test:

■ **Summary Exercise.** Comprehensive exercises that touch on most skills covered in the lesson. Step-by-step directions guide you through the exercises.

■ **Application Exercise.** The level of difficulty starts to ramp up with the application exercises. These exercises do not contain detailed steps.

■ **Curriculum Integration.** Integrate other subject areas into the computer course with the Curriculum Integration exercises. Topics include math, English, social studies, and science.

■ **Portfolio Builder.** These challenging exercises are scenario-based—no specific steps are given. Use these exercises to create illustrations and documents you can add to a portfolio.

WORKING WITH DATA AND SOLUTION FILES

As you work through the exercises in this book, you'll be creating, opening, and saving files. You should keep the following instructions in mind:

- You will create many illustrations, images, and documents on your own, but a number of data files are included to allow you to focus on specific features without having to create every aspect of the illustration or document. Data files include partially completed illustrations, graphic files in formats such as JPEG and GIF, digital images, and document text that would be very time consuming to type.

- When the application or On Your Own exercise includes a file name and a CD icon ⊙, you can open the file provided on the CD that accompanies this book.

- The Directory of Files below lists the exercise file (from the CD-ROM) you need to complete an exercise. Unless the book instructs otherwise, use the default settings when creating a file.

- When you see _xx in any instruction in this book, it means that you should type an underscore followed by your own initials—not the actual text "_xx". This will help your instructor identify your work.

COPY DATA FILES

You can copy data files from the CD-ROM to a hard drive.

1. Open Windows Explorer. (Right-click the **Start** button and click **Explore**.)
2. Be sure that the CD is in your CD-ROM drive. Select the CD-ROM drive letter from the All Folders pane of the Explorer window.

3. Click to select the **Data** folder in the Contents of (CD-ROM drive letter) pane of the Explorer window.
4. Drag the folder onto the letter of the drive to which you wish to copy the data files (usually C:) in the All Folders pane of the Explorer window.

DIRECTORY OF FILES ON CD

Use the following table to locate the files you use in exercises throughout this book. You are prompted in the text when to open the needed files from the CD.

EXERCISE	FILE NAME	PAGE	EXERCISE	FILE NAME	PAGE
2	02Park.ai	13	18	18Global.ai	107
	OYO02.psd	14		OYO18.ai	108
3	03Cat.jpg	20, 21	19	19Australia.ai	113
5	05MP3.ai	34		OYO19.ai	114
6	06Park.ai	41	20	20Bowling.ai	115
	OYO06.ai	43	21	21Violin.ai	117
7	07Park.ai	49		21Violin.gif	117
	OYO07.ai	51	24	24Wave.ai	129
8	08Park.ai	58	25	25Earthtone.ai	135
	OYO08.ai	60		OYO25.ai	136
13	13Picnic.ai	74	26	26Toys.ai	141
14	14Picnic	82		OYO26.ai	142
15	15Greenwood.ai	89	27	27Newfound.ai	149
	OYO15.ai	90		OYO27.ai	151
16	16Picnic.ai	94	28	28Greenwood.ai	158
	OYO16.ai	96		OYO28.ai	159
17	17Australia.gif	101	29	29Players.ai	165
	OYO17_earth.gif	102		OYO29.ai	166

Adobe CS5 Basics

Exercise | 1

Skills Covered

- **The Creative Suite Applications**
- **Start and Exit Adobe CS5 Applications**
- **The Adobe Design Interface**
- **Work with Multiple Documents**
- **Use Menus**
- **Work with Panels**
- **Save and Close a Document**

Software Skills   The Adobe CS5 applications make it easy to create professional print documents that include drawings, photos, and text. Workspaces, tools, and commands are consistent across all applications in the Adobe Design suites.

Application Skills   In this exercise, you learn about the Creative Suite Design Standard applications and their similarities. You explore workspaces, menus, and panels and learn how to start and exit an application.

TERMS

Context menu   A menu that displays when you right-click the screen, displaying commands that relate to your current task.

Dock   A location in the application window where a panel or panels are secured so they do not float.

Panel   A group of related commands and options.

NOTES

The Creative Suite Applications

- The Adobe Creative Suites combine some of the most popular and widely used design tools on the market. The applications in these suites can be used to create sophisticated documents for a wide range of end products.
- This book uses the applications in the Creative Suite 5 Design family and focuses on creating design documents. Adobe offers two levels of Design suites:
  - Adobe Creative Suite 5 Design Standard includes Adobe Illustrator CS5, Adobe Photoshop CS5, Adobe InDesign CS5, and Adobe Acrobat 9 Professional.
  - Adobe Creative Suite 5 Design Premium includes Adobe InDesign CS5, Adobe Photoshop CS5 Extended, Adobe Illustrator CS5, Adobe Flash CS5 Professional, Adobe Flash Catalyst CS5, Adobe Dreamweaver CS5, Adobe Fireworks CS5, and Adobe Acrobat 9 Professional.

- This book has been created using applications available in the Design Standard version, but you can perform the exercises using either version.
- Both versions include some shared programs such as Adobe Bridge CS5 and Adobe Device Central CS5.

Start and Exit Adobe CS5 Applications

- Use any of the following options to start a Design suite application:
  - Select the program from the Adobe Design Standard or Premium CS5 folder on the All Programs menu in Windows.
  - Click a program icon on the Start menu if it has been used recently.
  - Double-click a program shortcut icon on the desktop if one is available.
- Some applications, such as Illustrator and InDesign, display a Welcome screen after opening that allows you to select a type of document to create or open a document you have previously worked on.

2

■ When you have finished using an application, close all open documents (saving them first if necessary) and click the program Close button 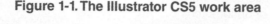 on the title bar or click File > Exit.

The Adobe Design Interface

■ The work area, or interface, of each Creative Suite Design application looks similar, making it easy to work with all applications after you have become familiar with any one of them.

■ As you open each application, you will notice that features such as the Application bar, Tools panel, and other panels are arranged in much the same way in all applications. Figure 1-1 shows the Illustrator CS5 work area with common features labeled.

✓ *The illustrations in this book have been created on a Windows 7 system. If you are using Windows XP or Vista, your screen will look slightly different.*

■ The Application bar combines the menu bar with control buttons that allow you to perform tasks such as arranging multiple documents or changing the workspace view. You can also find a search box on the Application bar that you can use to get help in most applications.

■ The central portion of the window is the area in which you work on the current document. In Illustrator, this area is called the *artboard*. In Illustrator and InDesign, the document area is surrounded by space called the *scratch area* in Illustrator and the *pasteboard* in InDesign that you can use to store objects you are not currently working with.

Figure 1-1. The Illustrator CS5 work area

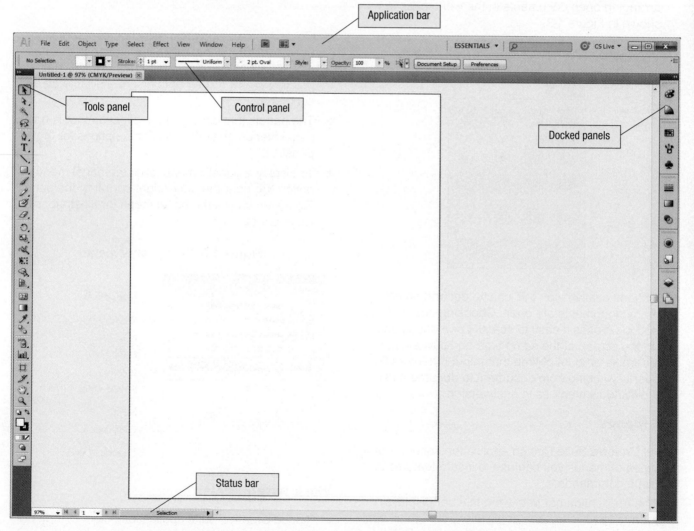

Work with Multiple Documents

- The CS5 Design Standard applications display open documents as tabbed document windows. A document's tab displays its name and other important information, as shown in Figure 1-2. The active document's tab is light gray; inactive document tabs are darker gray.

Figure 1-2. Document tabs in the Illustrator workspace

- Click the Arrange Documents button  on the Application bar to see a palette of options for arranging open documents in the workspace, as shown in Figure 1-3.

Figure 1-3. Arrange Documents palette

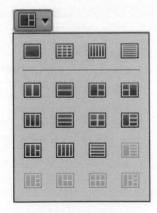

- Options available on this palette depend on how many documents are open. Choosing one of these options makes it easy to see all open documents on the screen at the same time and saves a considerable amount of time that might otherwise be spent switching from document to document using the Window menu as in past versions.

Use Menus

- All Creative Suite Design applications offer several types of menus you can use to locate features and issue commands.
- The Application bar below the title bar displays menus specific to each application, though all applications share some menus, such as File, Edit, View, Window, and Help. Click a menu name to see the options available on that menu.

- You can find commands that relate to your current task by right-clicking on an object or area of the screen. This displays a **context menu** such as the one shown in Figure 1-4.

Figure 1-4. Illustrator context menu

- Context menus provide a selection of commonly used commands that might be applied in the current situation. If a menu command displays a right-pointing arrow, further options are available on a submenu.
- The panels that contain an application's tools have panel menus that offer additional options for that panel.
- To display a panel's menu, click the panel menu button near the upper-right corner of the panel. Figure 1-5 shows the panel menu for Illustrator's Color panel.

Figure 1-5. Color panel menu

Work with Panels

- Adobe Creative Suite applications store commonly used tools and settings on **panels** such as the Color panel shown in Figure 1-5.

■ Panels appear in three areas in the application window:

- The Control panel displays just below the Application bar and extends the full width of the application window. The Control panel options adjust according to your current task. If you are using the Horizontal Type tool in Photoshop, for example, the Control panel displays the Set the font family, Set the font style, and Set the font size options to allow you to adjust the appearance of type.

✓ *In Photoshop, the Control panel is called the* options bar.

- The Tools panel displays at the left side of the window. This panel organizes tools you use to draw, select, insert type, magnify the screen content, and so on.

- A panel **dock** at the right side of the window organizes groups of panels. Groups of panels are organized according to the current workspace. For example, panels that display for Illustrator's Painting workspace include the Navigator, Color, Color Guide, Brushes, and Layers panels. The panels that display for the Typography workspace are shown in Figure 1-6.

✓ *You learn more about workspaces in the next exercise.*

■ In some cases, as in Figure 1-6, the right panel dock actually has two levels of panels. The panels at the far right are expanded, and the panels to the left of the expanded ones are collapsed. To open a collapsed panel, click on its icon.

■ The current screen size can affect the appearance of the Control panel. If the screen is not wide enough to display all options, groups of options are dropped from the Control panel. Your Control panel may display more or fewer options than shown in this book's figures.

■ By default, all panels are docked at their locations; that is, they are "attached" so they do not move as you work with them.

■ You can undock the Control panel to move it out into the application window by dragging the gripper bar at the left side of the panel. When it is not docked, a panel is said to be *floating*.

■ To redock the Control panel at the top or bottom of the screen, move it toward the dock location until you see a heavy horizontal blue bar, then release the mouse button. The panel is once again docked.

■ In addition to moving the Tools panel to any location on the screen, you can customize it by adjusting the display from a single column of tools to a double column by clicking the double right-pointing arrows ■ at the top of the panel.

Figure 1-6. Illustrator Typography panels

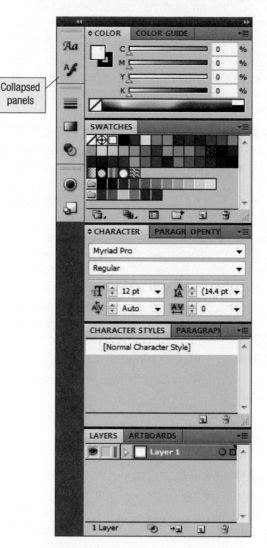

Collapsed panels

■ If panels at the right side of the window are collapsed, you can expand them by clicking the left-pointing Expand Dock arrows ■ at the top of the panel group.

■ After the dock is expanded, the Expand Dock arrows change to right-pointing Collapse to Icons arrows ■ so you can neatly store the panels again when you are not using them.

■ The panels in the right dock are arranged in groups. In Figure 1-6, for example, you see that the first group contains the Color and Color Guide panels.

■ To work with any panel in a group, click its tab to bring the panel to the front of the group.

- If the panels are collapsed to display only icons, when you click an icon that panel flies out so you can use it. Clicking an icon for a panel in another group will close the open panel and open the panel you selected.

  ✓ *If you can't identify the panel name from the icon, rest the mouse pointer on the icon to see a tool tip giving the panel name.*

- You will sometimes want to work with more than one panel in a group. For example, it is common to need to see both the Color and Swatches panels.

- To see both panels at the same time, drag a panel out of the group by its tab to float in the work area. You can float any panel from any group.

- To restore a panel to its group, drag it back on top of the group until you see a heavy blue border around the group. Release the mouse button to drop the panel in the group.

- The panel dock does not show all panels available in an application. You can find other panels listed on the Window menu of the application. Click a panel name to open it in the work area.

  ✓ *You will learn more about adjusting panel display in Exercise 2.*

Save and Close a Document

- All Creative Suite Design documents are saved in the same way.

- Click the Save or Save As (if saving for the first time) command on the File menu to open the Save As dialog box. Navigate to the location where you want to save the file, type a file name and select a format type if necessary, and then click the Save button.

- After you click the Save button, some applications, such as Illustrator and Photoshop, display a further dialog box that allows you to specify additional settings.

- When you have finished working with a program, close it to free up working space. You can click the document Close button ⊠ on a document tab or use a menu command to close a document.

- After you have closed a document, the program remains open so that you can start or open another document.

PROCEDURES

Start a Creative Suite Application

1. Click the **Start** button on the Windows taskbar .... CTRL + ESC
2. Click **All Programs**.
3. Click the **Adobe Design Standard CS5** folder.

   ✓ *If you are using the Design Premium suite, the folder name changes accordingly.*

4. Click the desired application.

   OR

1. Click the **Start** button on the Windows taskbar .... CTRL + ESC
2. Click the application name pinned to the Start menu.

   OR

- Double-click an application icon on the desktop.

Exit an Application *(Ctrl + Q)*

- Click the program **Close** button ✗ at the right end of the program's title bar.

  OR

1. Click **File** .... ALT + F
2. Click **Exit** X

Display Multiple Open Documents

1. With multiple documents open, click **Arrange Documents** tool ▦ ▾ in Application bar.
2. Select desired arrangement from palette.

Use Menus

- Click a menu name in the menu bar below the title bar, then select the desired command.

  ✓ *If the command has a right-pointing arrow, point to the command to see a fly-out submenu of further choices for that option.*

  OR

- Right-click on an object or area of the screen to display a context menu.

  OR

1. Click a panel's panel menu button ▦.
2. Select an option on the panel menu.

Work with Panels

To move the Control panel:

- Drag the Control panel by the gripper bar at the left side of the panel.

To redock the Control panel:

1. Drag the Control panel by its gripper bar toward the top or bottom of the window.
2. When a heavy blue horizontal line appears, release the mouse button.

   OR

1. Click the Control panel's panel menu icon ▾≣.
2. Click **Dock To Top**.

   OR

   Click **Dock To Bottom**.

To adjust the width of the Tools panel:

- Click the expand arrows ▸▸ at the top of the Tools panel to expand the panel to two columns.
- Click the collapse arrows ◂◂ to return the panel to one column.

To adjust the panel dock display:

- Click the Expand Dock arrows ◂◂ at the top of the panel dock to expand the panels in all docked groups.
- Click the Collapse to Icons arrows ▸▸ to minimize the panels to icons.

To display a hidden panel in a group:

- Click the panel's tab to bring it to the front of a group.

To float a panel away from a group:

- Click a panel's tab and drag it out of the group.

To restore a floating panel to its group:

1. Drag the floating panel by its tab and position it on top of its group.
2. When a heavy blue outline displays around the group, release the mouse button.

To display any panel not visible in a dock:

1. Click **Window** .... ⌐ALT⌐ + ⌐W⌐
2. Click the name of the panel you want to display.

   ✓ If a checkmark displays to the left of the panel name, it is already open.

Save a Document *(Ctrl + S)*

1. Click **File** .... ⌐ALT⌐ + ⌐F⌐
2. Click **Save** .... ⌐S⌐

   OR

   Click **Save As** .... ⌐A⌐

3. Click **Save in** drop-down arrow .... ⌐ALT⌐ + ⌐I⌐
4. Select drive and folder.
5. Double-click **File name** box .... ⌐ALT⌐ + ⌐N⌐
6. Type file name.
7. Click **Save** .... ⌐ALT⌐ + ⌐S⌐

Close a Document *(Ctrl + W)*

- Click the document **Close** button ⌐×⌐.

   ✓ If the document is not maximized, the document Close button looks the same as the program Close button.

   OR

1. Click **File** .... ⌐ALT⌐ + ⌐F⌐
2. Click **Close** .... ⌐C⌐

EXERCISE DIRECTIONS

1. Start Illustrator.
2. In the Welcome screen, click Print Document to start a new document, then click OK to accept default settings.
3. Move the Control panel from the top of the screen to the bottom of the screen.
4. Expand the panel dock.
5. Adjust the Tools panel to display its tools in two columns.
6. Open another new document and use the Arrange Documents palette to tile the documents vertically.
7. Use the Window menu to open the Pathfinder panel.
8. Start InDesign.
9. In the Welcome screen, click Document to start a new document, then click OK to accept default settings.
10. Expand the panel dock. In the first panel group, click the Pages tab if necessary to bring the Pages panel to the front in the group.
11. Drag the Pages panel out of the group to float in the work area.
12. Drag the Pages panel back to its group.
13. Close the InDesign document without saving changes, and then exit InDesign.
14. Close the Untitled-2 Illustrator document without saving. Save the Untitled-1 document as *01Myspace_xx*, where *xx* stands for your initials. Click OK to accept default Illustrator settings.
15. Exit Illustrator.

ON YOUR OWN

1. Start Photoshop.

2. On the File menu, click New to open a new document. Make sure the Preset box shows Default Photoshop Size and then click OK.

3. Drag both the Color panel and the Swatches panel out onto the work area.

4. Display the Color panel menu and click Lab Sliders to change the panel display.

5. Right-click on *Background* in the Layers panel to display a context menu.

6. Click Duplicate Layer and then click OK to accept the default name for the new layer.

7. Collapse the right panel dock.

8. Close the document without saving changes and exit Photoshop.

Exercise | 2

Skills Covered

- **Adjust Panel Display**
- **Save and Load a Workspace**
- **Change Magnification**
- **Toggle Views**
- **Open a Document**

Software Skills The Adobe Creative Suite applications allow you to adjust panel display or create your own groups of panels. You can save a workspace after you have customized it to your satisfaction and reload it or any of an application's other workspaces. Change magnification or choose a different view to make it easier to work with a document.

Application Skills In this exercise, you learn more about how to adjust panel display by minimizing or maximizing a panel and creating custom panel groups. You save a custom workspace and learn how to reload the workspace. Finally, you learn how to change the document view by adjusting magnification or selecting a different view and explore options for opening existing documents.

TERMS

Marquee Rectangle drawn around an object with a tool, to select an area.

Workspace A saved set of panel arrangements and tool settings.

NOTES

Adjust Panel Display

- In the previous exercise, you learned some ways to change the default display of docked panels by expanding the panel dock or moving a panel to float in the work area.
- You have some additional options for adjusting the way panels display.
- Some panels include small triangles to the left of the panel name, as shown in Figure 2-1. Clicking the double triangles cycles the panel through three display sizes: the full panel size that shows all options, a reduced size that shows only the most often-used option, and a minimized size that shows only the panel name tab (see Figure 2-1).

Figure 2-1. Three display sizes for a panel

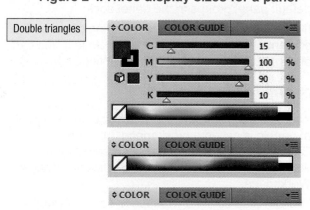

- Some panels can also be resized by simply dragging the size box at the lower-right corner to enlarge or reduce the panel.

- You can create your own groups by stacking or docking floating panels.

- Stacked panels display as a unit, one on top of another. To stack panels, drag a panel to the bottom of another panel until the heavy blue horizontal bar displays, as shown in Figure 2-2. The heavy blue bar indicates the *drop zone* where one panel snaps to another.

Figure 2-2. Stacking two panels

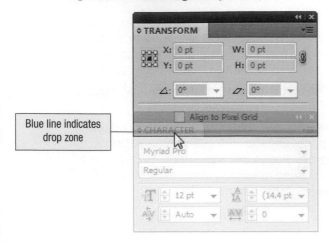

- The stacked panels move as a group when you drag by the dark gray horizontal bar at the top of the group. If you drag by one of the panel tabs, you will move the panel out of the stack.

- To dock one panel with another, drag the panel on top of another panel until the blue outline appears. The two panels are then grouped just like the default panel groups in the panel dock.

- If you no longer need to see a floating panel on the screen, click its Close button ☒ to close it. You can always redisplay a panel from the Window menu.

Save and Load a Workspace

- An application window with a specific arrangement of panels is called a **workspace**. All Adobe Creative Suite applications offer a selection of workspaces that you can view by clicking Window > Workspace.

- You can also select a workspace using the workspace switcher in the Application bar, shown in Figure 2-3. The Essentials workspace is selected by default in Illustrator, Photoshop, and InDesign.

  ✓ *In Photoshop, the Live Workspace switcher displays several workspace choices on the options bar.*

Figure 2-3. Click workspace switcher to see a list of available workspaces

✓ *Illustrator's workspace switcher, shown in Figure 2-3, lets you arrange the workspace to resemble that of other applications such as Photoshop or InDesign.*

- You can load any other workspace by simply clicking it. Panels may rearrange themselves and other changes may also be made to shortcuts and menu options.

- InDesign and Photoshop allow you to select a Reset option on the workspace menu to restore the appearance of a workspace after you have made changes to the position of panels.

- If you do not find a workspace that arranges the work area the way you want it, you can create your own workspace and then save it.

- Use the Save Workspace or New Workspace command on the Window > Workspace submenu to open a dialog box similar to the one shown in Figure 2-4.

Figure 2-4. InDesign New Workspace dialog box

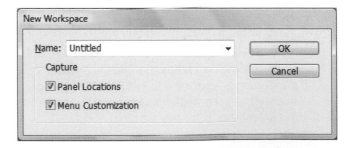

- Options available in this dialog box vary by application. Illustrator, for example, does not give you a choice of panel locations or menu customization, and in Photoshop you can also choose to save keyboard shortcuts and menus you have customized as part of the workspace.

- Your saved workspace displays in the Workspace submenu and in the workspace switcher menu along with the other default workspace options.

Change Magnification

- As you work with documents, you will sometimes need to change magnification to be able to see more detail of a drawing or text frame. All of the Creative Suite applications offer several options for adjusting magnification.

- Use the Zoom tool 🔍 to enlarge a specific area of a document.

- Click the Zoom tool once on the document to increase magnification by a set interval (the interval varies by application). To reduce magnification, hold down Alt while clicking the tool on the document.

  ✓ *Zoom In and Zoom Out commands are also available on the View menu.*

- Double-click on the Zoom tool in the Tools panel to display the document at 100% size.

- To zoom in on a specific area, use the Zoom tool to drag a **marquee** around the area, as shown in Figure 2-5.

Figure 2-5. Drag a marquee with the Zoom tool

- The closer around an object you draw the marquee, the greater will be the magnification.

- Another way to adjust magnification is to use the Navigator panel in Illustrator or Photoshop.

- As shown in Figure 2-6, the Navigator panel allows you to use a slider or buttons to adjust magnification. You can drag the red view box over an area of the document in the panel to bring that area into view in the document.

Figure 2-6. Use the Navigator panel to zoom in on an area

- All of the Creative Suite applications also allow you to change the zoom level by selecting from a list of levels. You can find the zoom level list in the Illustrator status bar; the zoom level option displays in the Application bar in Photoshop and InDesign. In any application, you can select the current zoom level and type a new level.

Toggle Views

- Adobe Creative Suite applications offer a number of standard views that you can switch among as you work with your documents. These views modify the screen display to allow you to work with fewer distractions or see how your final document will look.

- You find the tool to control views on the Tools panel (Illustrator) or on the Application bar (Photoshop and InDesign). In Illustrator and Photoshop, you can choose among the following screen modes:

  - Normal or Standard Screen Mode shows the document in a standard window, with the Application bar, Control panel, and scroll bars.

  - Full Screen Mode with Menu Bar shows the document in a full-size window. The Application bar and Control panel display, but document tabs and vertical scroll bar do not appear. In Photoshop, the horizontal scroll bar and Windows task bar do not display either.

  - Full Screen Mode shows the document in a full-size window that does not have an Application bar, scroll bars, document tabs, or the Windows task bar.

- You can click the F key repeatedly to cycle through these views.

- InDesign calls its view options *screen modes* and offers five different modes:
  - Normal mode shows the document with all grids and guides displayed, as well as nonprinting objects.
  - Preview mode shows the document the way it will look when printed, hiding all grids, guides, and nonprinting objects.
  - Bleed mode shows the document the same way as Preview mode, but displays everything that will print in the bleed area (the area specified to allow objects to run off the page during printing).
  - Slug mode shows the document the same way as Preview mode, but displays the specified slug area, which is often used to print notes or sign-off boxes. (The slug area is usually trimmed away after printing.)
  - Presentation mode is new in InDesign CS5 and allows you to see a document in full-screen view as a presentation. You can move through the document one spread at a time. While in Presentation mode, the document looks as it would in Preview mode, with guides and grids hidden.

- View options are usually also available on an application's View menu, along with other helpful options such as Fit in Window or Fit Spread in Window.

Open a Document

- The process of opening an existing document is the same in all Creative Suite applications. You can use any of the following procedures:
  - If the application displays a Welcome screen when it starts, you may be able to click a previously opened document in the Open a Recent Item list on the Welcome screen. Or, you can click the Open button to display the Open dialog box.
  - If the application is already open, or if it does not display a Welcome screen when starting, use the File > Open command to display the Open dialog box.
  - In any application, use the File > Open Recent or Open Recent Files command to see a list of files you have worked with recently. Select a file name to open the file.

PROCEDURES

Adjust Panel Display

To change panel display size:

- Click the double triangles to the left of a panel's name to cycle through all three display sizes.

  OR

- Drag the size box at the lower-right corner of the panel to adjust height and width.

To create stacked panels:

1. Float the panels you want to stack on the work area by dragging them from their current groups.
2. Choose one of the panels to be the first in the stack.
3. Drag the panel that will be next in the stack toward the bottom of the first panel.
4. When the heavy blue drop zone line displays, release the mouse button.

To create a docked panel group:

1. Float the panels you want to dock on the work area by dragging them from their current groups.
2. Drag one of the panels on top of another.
3. When the blue border drop zone outline displays, release the mouse button.

To close a panel:

- Click the panel's **Close** button ✕.

Save a Workspace

In any application:

1. Click **W**indow .... ALT + W
2. Point to **Workspace**.

   ✓ *Shortcut keys vary for this command in different applications.*

3. Click **S**ave **Workspace** in Illustrator .... S

   OR

   Click **N**ew **Workspace** in InDesign or Photoshop .... N

4. Type a name for the workspace.
5. Select options to include in the workspace, if available.
6. Click **OK** .... ENTER

   OR

   Click **S**ave in Photoshop .... ALT + S

Load a Workspace

In any application:

1. Click **W**Indow .... ALT + W
2. Click **Workspace**.

   ✓ *Shortcut keys vary for this command in different applications.*

3. Click the desired workspace to load it.

   OR

- Click workspace switcher in Application bar and select the desired workspace.

Change Magnification

To use the Zoom tool:

1. Click the **Zoom** tool in the Tools panel................ Z
2. Click the tool on the document to enlarge by a set percentage.

   OR

   Hold down ALT while clicking to reduce the magnification by a set percentage.

   OR

   Drag an outline around the area to enlarge.

   OR

   ■ Double-click the Zoom tool to change magnification to 100%.

To use menu commands:

1. Click **View**................ ALT + V
2. Click **Zoom In**.

   OR

   Click **Zoom Out**.

   ✓ Each time you issue a menu command, the zoom changes by a set interval. Shortcut keys vary for these commands.

To use the Navigator panel:

1. Drag the zoom slider to change magnification.
2. Drag the view box to a specific area of the document to see the magnified view in the document area.

To use the zoom level setting:

1. Click the Zoom box's list arrow on the status bar or Application bar.
2. Select the desired magnification from the pop-up menu.

   OR

1. Select the current zoom level.
2. Type a new zoom percentage.

Toggle Views

1. Click the **Change Screen Mode** tool on the Illustrator Tools panel or **Screen Mode** tool on the Application bar (Photoshop and InDesign).
2. Select the desired view.

   OR

1. Click **View**................ ALT + V
2. Click the desired view on the View menu.

Open a Document (Ctrl + O)

To open a file from the Welcome screen:

■ Click a file name in the Open a Recent Item list on the Welcome screen.

   OR

■ Click the **Open** folder on the Welcome screen to display the Open dialog box.

   ✓ See instructions below for using the Open dialog box to open a file.

To use File menu commands:

1. Click **File**................ ALT + F
2. Click **Open**................ O
3. Click **Look in** arrow .... ALT + I , ↓
4. Select drive or folder.
5. Click file name to select.
6. Click **Open** .... ALT + O

EXERCISE DIRECTIONS

1. Start Illustrator and create a new print document with default settings. If no one has used the program since you completed Exercise 1, your screen should show the Control panel docked at the bottom of the window and the Pathfinder panel floating in the work area.
2. If your screen does not match this description, move the Control panel and open the Pathfinder panel.
3. Select the Transform panel from the Pathfinder group and drag it out of the group. Then close the Pathfinder group.
4. Change the display size of the Stroke panel to display the minimum panel size.
5. Drag the Stroke panel out of its group and stack it to the bottom of the Transform panel. Minimize the Stroke panel if necessary after stacking so that only the Weight option displays.
6. Collapse the panel dock to icons and then move the stacked panels to the top of the screen near the panel dock.
7. Save the current workspace with the name 02Myspace_xx, where xx stands for your initials.
8. Use the workspace switcher to load the Painting workspace.
9. Open 02Park.ai from the data files for this lesson.
10. Load the 02Myspace workspace. Your screen should look similar to the one shown in Illustration A.
11. Use the Zoom pop-up menu to change the magnification to 200%.
12. Double-click on the Zoom tool in the Tools panel to change magnification to 100%.
13. Display the Navigator panel from the Window menu and use the zoom slider in the panel to change magnification to about 300%.

14. Move the red view box to surround the Greek temple so you get a close-up view of the structure.

15. Use any method to change magnification to 25%.

16. Use the Zoom tool to draw a marquee around the stars and the text at the lower left to enlarge the view.

17. Change to Full Screen Mode with Menu Bar, then return to Normal Screen Mode.

18. Reload the Essentials workspace, and then close the file without saving changes.

19. Exit Illustrator.

Illustration A

ON YOUR OWN

1. Start Photoshop.

2. Open ⊚OYO02.psd from the data files for this lesson.

3. Cycle through the different screen modes using the Screen Modes tool on the Application bar.

4. Return to Standard Screen Mode.

5. Stack together the Layers panel and the Swatches panel and position the stack near the bottom-right corner of the screen.

6. Create a new workspace with a name such as 02Workspace_xx, accepting the default selections in the Save Workspace dialog box, and then load the Essentials workspace.

7. Use the Zoom tool to draw a marquee around the flower so you can see it close up.

8. Choose 50% from the Zoom level list on the Application bar to reduce the size of the image.

9. Double-click the Zoom tool to restore the image to 100%.

10. Close the document without saving changes and then open a new document using default settings.

11. Apply your saved workspace to the new document. Then restore the Essentials workspace.

12. Close the document without saving and exit Photoshop.

Exercise | 3

Skills Covered

- **Understand File Formats**
- **View Preferences**
- **Use Adobe Bridge**
- **Get Help**

Software Skills Creative Suite applications save files in standard formats and can work with other graphic file formats that you should be familiar with. The Preferences dialog box allows you to customize an application's options. Use Adobe Bridge to organize and manage images. Getting help on Adobe applications is fast and easy.

Application Skills In this exercise, you learn about the file formats you will be working with in this course. You also learn how to restore default settings and specify preferences for each application. You are introduced to Adobe Bridge, one of Adobe's shared programs, and, finally, you view the help options.

TERMS

No new terms in this exercise.

NOTES

Understand File Formats

- As you complete the exercises in this course, you will be working with a number of file formats. The native file formats for each of the Creative Suite applications you will be using are as follows:
  - Illustrator files are saved by default with the .ai extension.
  - InDesign files are saved with the .indd extension.
  - Photoshop files are saved with the .psd extension.
- Although you will not be creating templates, each of these applications has a file extension specifically for templates, such as .ait for Illustrator templates or .indt for InDesign templates.
- You may save some documents in different file formats, such as:
  - PDF (Portable Document Format), an Adobe file format that allows a user to display formatted information and graphics just as they would print. All of the Design Creative Suite applications can save or export to the PDF format.

- EPS (Encapsulated PostScript), a file format that can be used to store image and page layout information so that it can easily be shared with a variety of applications and devices. All of the Design Creative Suite applications can save or export to the EPS format.
- In addition to the Creative Suite files, you will be working with several other graphic file formats:
  - GIF (Graphics Interchange Format), a format used for graphics that have a limited number of colors (up to 256). This format can include transparent areas.
  - JPG or JPEG (Joint Photographic Experts Group), a format used for continuous tone images such as photos or graphics that contain gradients or color blends. JPG is a compressed format that keeps file sizes low by discarding some image data when the image is saved.
- When working with InDesign, you will be importing text on occasion; text files are saved in Microsoft Word's .doc format.

View Preferences

- All of the Creative Suite applications allow you to customize settings in a number of categories, such as units used in documents or type settings. Use the Edit > Preferences command to display a list of preference categories on a submenu. Selecting any of these items opens the Preferences dialog box.

  ✓ *In Illustrator, you can also click the Preferences button on the Control panel to open the Preferences dialog box.*

- The Preferences dialog box, shown for InDesign in Figure 3-1, displays a list of categories at the left side with settings for each category in the main pane of the dialog box. In Illustrator, the categories appear on a drop-down list at the top of the dialog box.

- To make sure the preference will apply to all new documents, make the change in the Preferences dialog box while no document is open. If you make a change while a document is open, it will apply only to that document.

- You will work with some preferences in the Design applications covered in this course, but you are encouraged to explore these options on your own to learn how you can adjust application settings to customize your work environment.

- Creative Suite applications store preferences in a file such as Illustrator's AIPrefs file or Photoshop's Adobe Photoshop CS5 Prefs file. These preference files are hidden by default in application folders stored in the current user profile.

- Depending on your operating system, you may be able to easily reset preferences to their default settings by simply holding down Alt+Shift+Ctrl as you start an application from the Start menu. This shortcut works for Illustrator, Photoshop, and InDesign.

- Depending on the application, you may see a dialog box that asks if you want to delete the settings file, such as the one shown in Figure 3-2. Clicking Yes in this dialog box throws away the preferences file, allowing the application to build a new preferences file using default settings.

Figure 3-1. Preferences dialog box

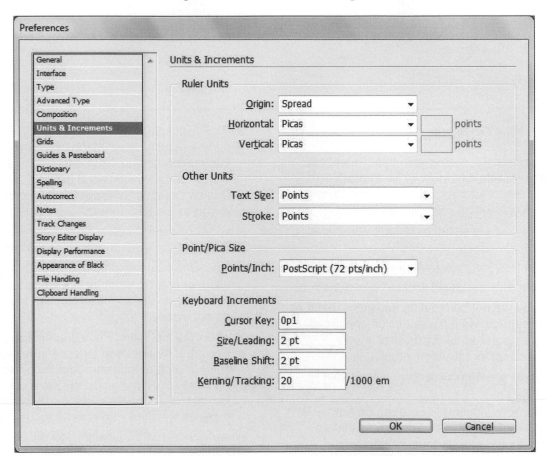

Figure 3-2. Deleting Photoshop settings

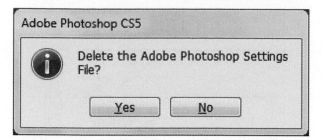

■ If you are working in Windows 7 or Windows Vista in a user account that does not have administrator privileges, pressing Alt+Ctrl+Shift may trigger a dialog box asking you to supply an administrator password to complete the action. This interruption can make it difficult to carry out the command to delete preferences. Your best option in this situation is to manually delete the preferences file for the application you want to restore to default settings.

✓ *For information on how to manually reset preferences, see your instructor or check your application's user guide.*

■ There is a down side to deleting settings. You lose links to previously created documents, and you may also lose custom settings you have defined for some tools. So, while deleting preferences can help you restore out-of-the-box settings, you may want to take this step only when your application is not responding the way you think it should.

Use Adobe Bridge

■ Adobe Bridge is one of the shared programs installed along with the Creative Suite applications. It is a file management utility similar to Windows Explorer, but it has some advantages over Windows Explorer, such as the capability to show thumbnail images of a wide variety of content.

■ You can access Adobe Bridge from any Creative Suite application by clicking the Bridge button [Br] on the application's Application bar or by using the Browse in Bridge command on the application's File menu.

■ The Adobe Bridge interface, shown in Figure 3-3, allows you to access folders that contain the files you want to work with.

Figure 3-3. Adobe Bridge displaying files in a folder

- Navigate to a folder using the directory tree in the left pane. The contents of the selected folder display in the Content pane. When you select an item in the Content pane, you see a preview in the Preview pane and information about the file in the Metadata pane.

- You can use the options on the Filter tab to show files of a specific type, such as all JPEGs, or sort the files by name. You can also apply a rating to each file (from one to five stars) and then filter to show only specific ratings.

- You can use the Open With command on the File menu or the context menu that displays when you right-click an image to select an application to open the file. As you work through the exercises in this course, you may want to open files from Bridge rather than use the application Open dialog boxes.

- If space allows on your desktop, you can position Bridge on top of a Creative Suite application and drag a file directly from Bridge to the application. This is a fast and accurate way to place a file.

- Bridge can be used to adjust settings for all Creative Suite applications. The Edit > Creative Suite Color Settings command, for example, opens a dialog box that allows you to synchronize color settings for all applications in the suite. Synchronized settings make it easier to integrate the content of the Design applications.

  ✓ *You will learn more about color settings later in this course.*

- Bridge can be customized and adjusted in a number of ways to fit your working style. You are encouraged to explore this application to make the most of its many features.

- Photoshop CS5 and InDesign CS5 offer the Mini Bridge panel that gives you a quick way to work with your files. Mini Bridge, shown in Figure 3-4, is a panel that you can dock in your application so you don't have to leave it to work with Bridge features.

- As in Bridge, you can use this panel to navigate to files and preview them right in the panel. You can also drag a file from the panel into the document you are working on.

Get Help

- The CS5 applications give you easy access to a variety of help options in a Web environment. Clicking the first help option on the Help menu for an application (such as Illustrator Help) opens a screen such as the one shown in Figure 3-5 on the next page for Illustrator.

Figure 3-4. Mini Bridge panel

- You can browse through reference topics in the right pane by expanding each topic (such as Workspace or Painting) to see the subtopics beneath it. This opening page also gives you helpful links to support, tutorials, and forums.

- Or, you can type a search phrase in the Search box in the left pane to display a list of matching search results in the left pane. Click the search result to see full information in the right pane.

- For more information on an application, click the second command on the Help menu, such as Photoshop Support Center, to open the Web support center for that application. The support center gives you access to support information, forums, developer content, and so on.

Figure 3-5. Online support for Illustrator

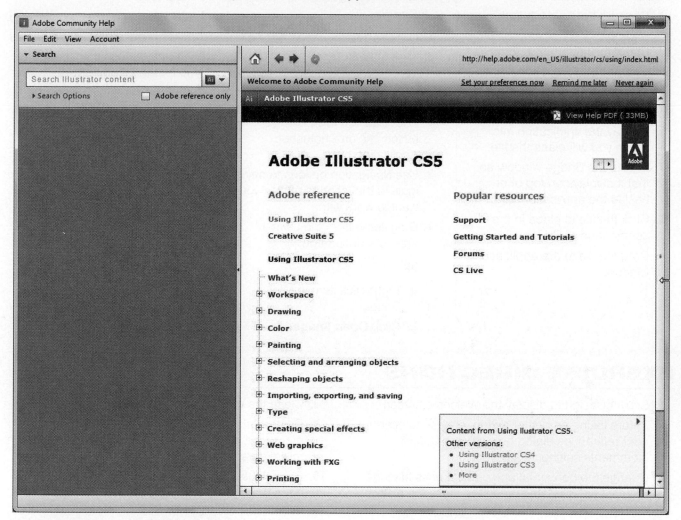

PROCEDURES

View Preferences *(Ctrl + K)*

1. Click **Edit** .... `ALT` + `E`
2. Click **Preferences** .... `N`
3. Select a category from the submenu or drop-down list.
4. Change settings as desired from options listed in the main pane.
5. Click **OK** .... `ENTER`

Restore Default Settings

Applications should be closed when you begin the process of restoring defaults.

To restore defaults in Photoshop or InDesign:

1. Hold down `CTRL` + `SHIFT` + `ALT`.
2. Start Photoshop or InDesign from the Start menu and keep the keys pressed until the dialog box displays.
3. Click **Yes** .... `ALT` + `Y`

To restore defaults in Illustrator:

1. Hold down `CTRL` + `SHIFT` + `ALT`.
2. Start Illustrator and keep the keys pressed until the Welcome screen displays.

Use Adobe Bridge *(Alt + Ctrl + O)*

To open Bridge:

In any application:

■ Click `Br` on the Application bar.

OR

1. Click **File** .... `ALT` + `F`
2. Click **Browse in Bridge**.

   ✓ *Shortcut keys vary by application.*

To display files in a folder:

1. Click the **Folders** tab in the top left pane.
2. Use the directory tree to navigate to the folder that contains the files to view.

To place a file from Bridge into an application:

1. Display the application into which you will place the file.
2. Resize the Bridge window so that it displays on top of or beside the application window.
3. Click the file to place in the center pane of Bridge.
4. Drag the file to the application window.

To work with Mini Bridge:

In InDesign:

1. Click **Window** .... ALT + W
2. Click **Mini Bridge**.

   OR

   In Photoshop:

   Click **Launch Mini Bridge** button Mb on Photoshop Application bar.
3. Use Navigation options to navigate to the location of files you want to work with.
4. Drag items from the Content area to a document.

   OR

   a. Right-click item in Mini Bridge.
   b. Click **Open Image**.

Get Help (*F1*)

1. Click **Help** .... ALT + H
2. Click *[application]* **Help** .... H
3. Click a topic in the main pane to expand it and show subtopics; browse through subtopics as desired.

   OR

   a. Click in the Search pane and type a search term.
   b. Click any of the search results to display more information in the main pane.

EXERCISE DIRECTIONS

1. Start InDesign to display the Welcome screen.
2. Before taking any other action, choose to open the Preferences dialog box with the Units & Increments settings displayed.
3. Change the horizontal and vertical units of measurement to Millimeters and then close the dialog box.

   ✓ *Because you changed this setting when no document was open, it becomes the new default.*

4. In the Welcome screen, choose to create a new document. Note that the measurements in the New Document dialog box are all in millimeters (mm). Click OK to accept the defaults.
5. Open Bridge and navigate to the Data folder for this lesson. If necessary, arrange both InDesign and Bridge so that you can see both applications.
6. Drag the ⊙ 03Cat.jpg file from the Data folder to the InDesign document and click the left mouse button to place the file. The top of your InDesign document should look similar to Illustration A on the next page after you have placed the file.
7. Save the document as 03Cat_xx.

8. Close the document and then exit InDesign.
9. Restart InDesign. Choose to create a new document, and notice that the measurements are still in millimeters, the new default setting.
10. Cancel the New Document dialog box and open the Preferences dialog box with Units & Increments settings displayed. Change the horizontal and vertical units of measurement back to Picas.
11. Now create a new document and notice the measurements are back to picas. Then open the 03Cat_xx.indd file that you saved in step 7. Note that the measurements are still in millimeters for this file.
12. Click InDesign Help on the Help menu.
13. Click the plus sign to the left of Workspace in the outline, then click the plus sign next to Workspace basics, and finally click Workspace overview and read about the InDesign workspace.
14. Close the browser and then close both files without saving changes.
15. Exit InDesign and Bridge.

Illustration A

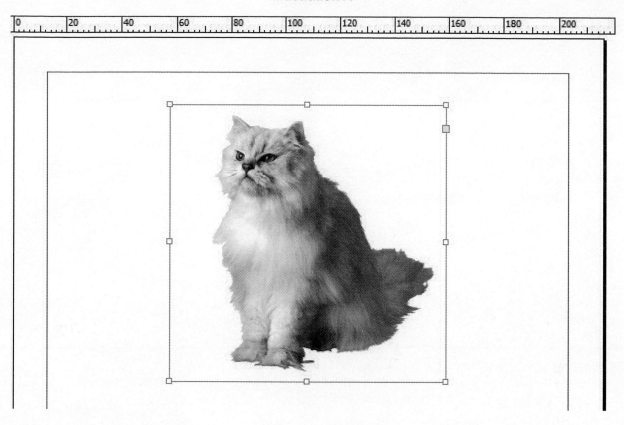

ON YOUR OWN

1. If your operating system allows you to, throw away preferences as you start Photoshop.

2. With no image open, display the Preferences dialog box to determine the default unit of measurement for the rulers.

3. Change the unit of measurement to another option, such as centimeters (cm).

4. Start Mini Bridge, and then navigate to the location of your data files. Right-click the 03Cat.jpg image. Click Open Image.

5. Display the rulers by clicking View > Rulers. You should see the rulers display in centimeters (or the measurement you chose).

6. Close the image file and exit Photoshop.

7. Once again delete the settings file as you start Photoshop if your operating system allows this change.

8. Open the 03Cat.jpg file again from Mini Bridge and display rulers. Note that they now show measurements in inches.

9. Close the document without saving. If you could not delete the setting file in step 7, go to the Preferences dialog box and restore the default unit of measurement for the rulers, inches. Then exit Photoshop.

Lesson | 1

Work with Basic Graphic Tools in Illustrator CS5

Exercise | 4

Skills Covered

- About Adobe Illustrator
- Create a New Drawing
- Illustrator Tools
- Basic Drawing Techniques
- Display Rulers, Grid, and Guides
- Use Smart Guides

Software Skills   Adobe Illustrator is a software program that enables you to create vector graphics for a wide variety of media, including print applications and Web pages. Use similar drawing techniques to create simple objects. Use rulers, a grid, and guides to keep track of dimensions and provide guidelines for drawing.

Design Skills   As a designer, you need to become familiar with Illustrator's tools and workspace. Learning basic drawing techniques will help you master many of Illustrator's features.

Application Skills   You work in the illustration department for a small graphic services firm. A standardized testing center has asked you to create a poster to let test-takers know they are not allowed to use their MP3 players during tests. In this exercise, you will practice using basic drawing tools and techniques you will need to create the illustration.

TERMS

Artboard   Printable portion of the work area, where illustrations can be finalized.

Bitmap images   Images created using a grid of small squares called *pixels*. Also called *raster images* or *pixel images*.

CMYK model   The color model used for printed output. Cyan (C), magenta (M), yellow (Y), and black (K) inks are combined to create the desired colors.

Color mode   Determines the color model used to display and print the Illustrator file.

Guides   Nonprinting lines that can be used to create boundaries or guidelines in a drawing.

Picas   Measurement system frequently used in graphic design. There are six picas to an inch.

Pixel   Term that stands for *picture element*, a single point on a computer monitor screen.

Points   Measurement system frequently used in graphic design. A point is 1/72nd of an inch.

Resolution   The number of dots or pixels per linear unit of output. For example, a monitor's resolution is usually 72 dots per inch.

RGB model   The color model used for illustrations to be viewed on monitors or digital devices. Red (R), green (G), and blue (B) values are combined to create the final color.

Vector graphics   Drawings made up of lines and curves that are defined by *vectors*.

Vectors   Mathematical concept that describes a graphic according to geometric characteristics.

NOTES

About Adobe Illustrator

■ Adobe Illustrator is a professional-level software program that can be used to create graphical illustrations for a wide variety of uses.

■ Graphic designers can use Illustrator to prepare illustrations for printed output, such as corporate marketing materials, technical illustrations, informational illustrations, packaging, and so on. Illustrator can also be used to create illustrations that will be used with other media, such as Web pages, electronic devices, and video.

■ Illustrations produced in drawing or painting programs create either **vector graphics** or **bitmap images**.

■ Illustrator illustrations are vector graphics. Vector graphics are created using mathematical expressions called **vectors** and retain their detail and clarity if the graphic is resized.

■ Bitmap images, on the other hand, are formed of tiny squares called **pixels**. Pixels remain the same size when a bitmap image is resized.

■ As a result, a bitmap image's edges can appear jagged when the image is enlarged or reduced in size.

■ Figure 4-1, shown at top right, shows a vector graphic and a bitmap image viewed at 300% of the original size. The vector graphic on the left has a smooth curve. The bitmap image on the right shows the small square pixels used to create the image.

■ File sizes for vector graphics tend to be much smaller than file sizes for bitmap images.

Figure 4-1. Vector graphic and bitmap image at 300%

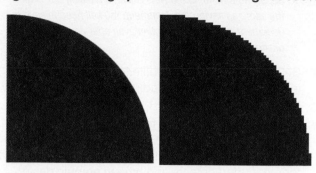

■ A vector graphic stores mathematical formulas for producing the elements of the drawing, while a bitmap image must store information about every single pixel used in the drawing.

■ When displayed on a computer monitor, vector graphics are shown using the monitor's **resolution**, usually 72 dots (pixels) per inch.

■ The monitor's low resolution may give a slightly jagged appearance to an Illustrator graphic, but this jaggedness does not increase when the graphic is enlarged; and it may not display at all if the illustration is printed at a higher resolution.

Create a New Drawing

■ Start a new drawing in Illustrator using the Welcome screen or the File > New command. Illustrator displays the New Document dialog box shown in Figure 4-2. This illustration shows the dialog box with all options (including advanced options) displayed.

Figure 4-2. New Document dialog box

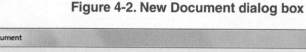

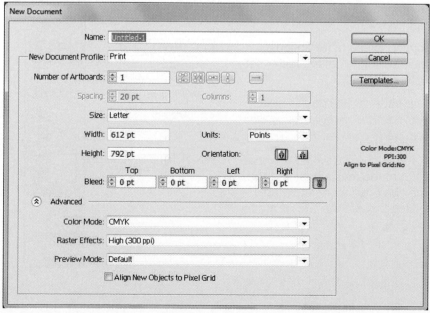

- In this dialog box, you can supply a name for the new illustration.

  ✓ *Supplying a name in the New Document dialog box is not the same as saving the document. You still need to save the document to a specific location even after naming it in this dialog box.*

- Selecting a document profile in this dialog box (or in the Welcome screen) adjusts settings in the New Document dialog box for that profile.

- When you choose Print, for example, the **color mode** changes to CMYK, the page size defaults to Letter, and units are set to **points**, the standard unit for measuring objects and type in graphic design. One point is 1/72nd of an inch.

- Choosing the Web document profile sets the color mode to RGB and adjusts the size to 800 × 600 pixels, a standard screen size used in Web site development. The Align New Objects to Pixel Grid option is also selected for this profile, allowing you to align objects precisely to pixels for graphics that will look sharp and clean when viewed on a Web page.

- Even after selecting a document profile, you may change settings in the New Document dialog box. You can select a different size from those listed on the Size drop-down menu, change width and height of the **artboard**, and select a new unit of measurement, such as **picas**, inches, millimeters, centimeters, or pixels. You can also change the orientation of the page from the default portrait to landscape.

- Note that you can choose to create more than one artboard at a time. You will work with multiple artboards in Exercise 8.

- You can also specify the *bleed* settings. Bleed is a space outside the specified page size into which you extend objects so that they appear to run off the page when printed.

- Click the Advanced button to see more options, such as the color mode setting, a default raster setting, and the preview mode.

  ✓ *Raster setting comes into play when you convert a vector object to a bitmap object. The higher the raster setting, the more refined the bitmap object's edges will be.*

- As discussed above, the document profile automatically specifies the color mode that is best for that type of document. The two color modes available for selection in this dialog box are the CMYK model and the RGB model.

- In the **CMYK model**, the letters C, M, Y, and K stand for cyan (blue), magenta (dark pink), yellow, and the key color (the color to which the other colors are keyed, or registered, on the press), and black. This model is used when an illustration will be printed in full color. Combinations of cyan, magenta, yellow, and black ink produce the desired colors on paper.

- In the **RGB model**, the letters R, G, and B stand for red, green, and blue. This model is most often used for graphics that will ultimately be displayed on a computer monitor as Web content, on a mobile device, or as a video or film illustration.

  ✓ *You will learn more about colors and color models in Lesson 3, Exercise 24.*

Illustrator Tools

- The tools in the Illustrator Tools panel, shown in expanded form in Figure 4-3, are used for a variety of tasks, including selecting, drawing, modifying or transforming, navigating, and applying color.

Figure 4-3. Illustrator Tools panel

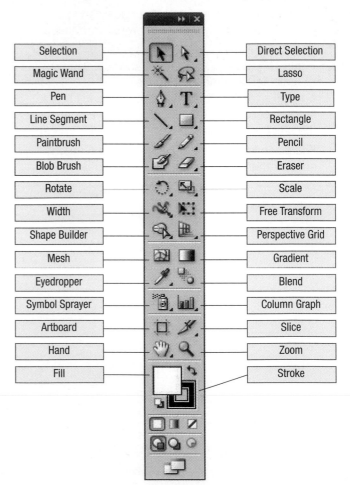

Selection	Direct Selection
Magic Wand	Lasso
Pen	Type
Line Segment	Rectangle
Paintbrush	Pencil
Blob Brush	Eraser
Rotate	Scale
Width	Free Transform
Shape Builder	Perspective Grid
Mesh	Gradient
Eyedropper	Blend
Symbol Sprayer	Column Graph
Artboard	Slice
Hand	Zoom
Fill	Stroke

- Many tools with similar functions are grouped on toolbars beneath the tool displayed on the Tools panel. Only one tool from the group shows at a time in the Tools panel. Small triangles at the bottom right of a tool indicate the presence of a hidden toolbar.

- To display a hidden toolbar, click on a tool that shows a triangle and hold down the mouse button. The hidden toolbar displays as shown in Figure 4-4.

Figure 4-4. Display a hidden toolbar

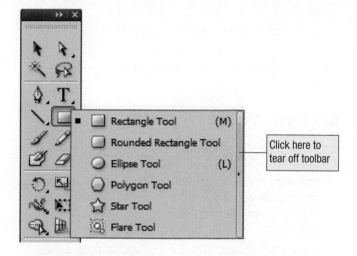

- Click and release while on the arrow at the right side of the toolbar to detach it from the Tools panel (the tool tip reads "Tearoff"). This makes it easy to access related tools.

  ✓ *A detached toolbar displays a close box that can be used to close the toolbar.*

- Illustrator's many tools can be identified not only by the graphic on the tool but by the names that pop up when the pointer is placed on the tool.

- Each tool in the Tools panel has a shortcut key assigned to it that displays in parentheses with the tool's name, as shown in Figure 4-5.

Figure 4-5. Tool names and shortcuts pop up

- Some tools on hidden toolbars may have shortcut keys assigned to them. Other hidden tools can be accessed only by displaying the hidden toolbar and selecting them directly.

- When a tool is selected, the pointer often changes shape to a crosshair or other shape specific to a tool.

- When you choose a tool from a hidden toolbar, that tool displays in the Illustrator Tools panel in place of the default tool.

Design Suite Integration

Tools

Many of the tools you learn about in Illustrator are used in other Creative Suite Design applications. All applications, for example, offer a Selection, Direct Selection, Pen, Type, Hand, and Zoom tool, and these tools work in similar ways in each application.

Basic Drawing Techniques

- Drawing objects with basic Illustrator shape tools such as Rectangle and Ellipse is the same as using the drawing tools in programs such as Microsoft Word or Windows Paint.

- Select the desired tool, hold down the left mouse button, and drag until the shape or line is the desired size, then release the mouse button.

- Illustrator allows you to adjust or modify shapes in a number of ways while drawing by using modifier keys: Shift, Ctrl, and Alt.

  ✓ *You will learn how to use modifier keys with tools as you are introduced to tools in subsequent exercises.*

- If the shape or line is not as desired, you can use the Edit > Undo command to reverse the action.

- To undo a whole series of actions, continue to issue this command or its keyboard shortcut, Ctrl + Z. Use the Edit > Redo command to reverse an undo.

Display Rulers, Grid, and Guides

- Illustrator's rulers can help you keep an eye on the overall size of an illustration.

- Display the rulers using the View > Rulers > Show Rulers command. Rulers display at the top and left side of the work area, using the current measurement system.

- The horizontal (top) ruler measures from left to right, with 0 at the left edge of the artboard. The vertical (left) ruler measures from top to bottom, with 0 at the top of the artboard (see Figure 4-6).

Figure 4-6. Display rulers at top and left of work area

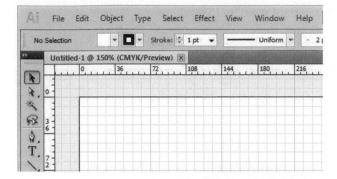

- Labels are provided at intervals depending on the measurement system. On the horizontal ruler, labels are to the right of the tall tick marks. On the vertical ruler, labels are above their corresponding tick marks.

  ✓ *Illustrator CS5 allows you to specify either global rulers or artboard rulers. You will read more about this in Exercise 8.*

- You can display a grid that looks like graph paper over the entire artboard, as shown in Figure 4-6, as further aid in sizing and positioning objects.

- The default grid displays light gray lines, with a heavier gray line every 72 points. You can change these defaults in the Preferences dialog box's Guides & Grid settings.

- If you select the View > Snap to Grid command, objects that you draw will automatically align with the grid as you draw and move them.

  ✓ *The Perspective Grid, an advanced Illustrator CS5 feature, allows you to display a grid on the screen that shows perspective lines in three dimensions to help you create objects that diminish in size or vanish toward distant points.*

- With rulers displayed, you can easily add **guides** to an illustration to provide boundaries or guidelines for positioning objects.

- To display a horizontal guide, click on the horizontal ruler and drag downward to display the guide and then drag the guide into position as shown in Figure 4-7. Display a vertical guide by dragging it from the vertical ruler.

- Use commands on the View > Guides submenu to work with guides. You can lock guides to keep them from moving, turn guides into line objects, create a guide from any object, or remove all guides from an illustration.

Figure 4-7. Drag a guide from a ruler

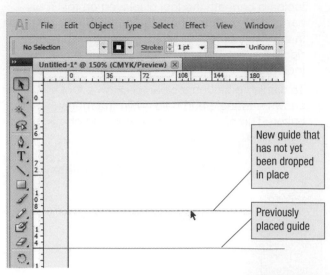

Use Smart Guides

- Smart Guides are temporary guides that display when a user moves the pointer over an object in the work area. Smart Guides give information about objects as you draw them, such as size and how they align or intersect with other objects on the artboard.

- Figure 4-8 shows how Smart Guides help a user insert a straight line that intersects with the center of a circle and the corner of a rounded rectangle.

Figure 4-8. Smart Guide information about a new line

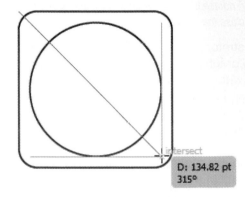

- Note in Figure 4-8 the green guidelines and text that indicate the point of intersection with the side and bottom of the ellipse. The gray pop-up box attached to the crosshair pointer indicates the current length of the line (the D value) and the angle at which the line is being drawn.

- Smart Guides are on by default but may be turned off if desired. You can customize Smart Guide behavior by adjusting options in the Preferences dialog box's Smart Guides settings.

PROCEDURES

Start a New Drawing (Ctrl + N)

In the Welcome screen:

■ Click the type of document to create in the Create New list.

While working in Illustrator:

1. Click **File**................... ALT + F
2. Click **New** .... N

In the New Document dialog box:

3. Click **Name** and type a name for the file if desired.... ALT + N
4. Click **New Document Profile** and select a default document profile.................. ALT + P , ↓
5. Make any desired adjustment to artboard size or units.
6. Click **OK** .... ENTER

Display Tools Panel Tool Names

■ Move pointer over tool and view name and shortcut key in pop-up tip.

Display Hidden Toolbar Tools

1. Click on tool that shows a small triangle at bottom right.
2. Hold down mouse button until hidden toolbar displays.
3. Click toolbar arrow if desired to detach toolbar.
4. Close toolbar by clicking close button.

Show/Hide Rulers (Ctrl + R)

1. Click **View**................ ALT + V
2. Point to **Rulers** .... R
3. Click **Show Rulers** .... R

OR

Click **Hide Rulers**.............. R

Show/Hide Grid (Ctrl + ")

1. Click **View**................ ALT + V
2. Click **Show Grid**............... G

OR

Click **Hide Grid**.................. G

Turn on Snap to Grid (Shift + Ctrl + ")

1. Click **View**................ ALT + V
2. Click **Snap to Grid**.

   ✓ *Repeat these steps to turn off Snap to Grid.*

Display Guides

■ Drag guide down or right from appropriate ruler to desired position and release mouse button.

To remove guides:

1. Click **View**................ ALT + V
2. Point to **Guides** .... U
3. Click **Clear Guides**............. C

Show/Hide Smart Guides (Ctrl + U)

1. Click **View**................ ALT + V
2. Click **Smart Guides** I

   ✓ *Repeat these steps to turn off Smart Guides.*

EXERCISE DIRECTIONS

1. Start Adobe Illustrator CS5.
2. Start a new Illustrator print document, accepting all the defaults in the New Document dialog box.
3. Display the rulers and the grid. Turn on Snap to Grid if necessary.
4. Drag a vertical guide from the vertical ruler to the 216-pt marker on the horizontal ruler and a horizontal guide from the horizontal ruler to the major tick mark below 216 on the vertical ruler.
5. Display the hidden toolbar beneath the Rectangle tool and tear (detach) this toolbar from the Tools panel.
6. Press l (the letter el) to activate the Ellipse tool. With the crosshair at the intersection of the two guides (the Smart Guides will tell you when the crosshair is over the intersection), draw an oval of any size. Watch the Smart Guide's size information as you draw.
7. Click the Rounded Rectangle tool. With the crosshair on the vertical guide below the oval, draw a rectangle of any size that snaps to major gridlines.
8. Close the open Rectangle toolbar.
9. Click the Line Segment tool and drag to draw a horizontal line below the rectangle, beginning at the guide. Your screen should look similar to Illustration A on the next page.
10. Save the file as 04MP3_xx. Accept the default file formats.
11. Close the file and exit Illustrator.

Illustration A

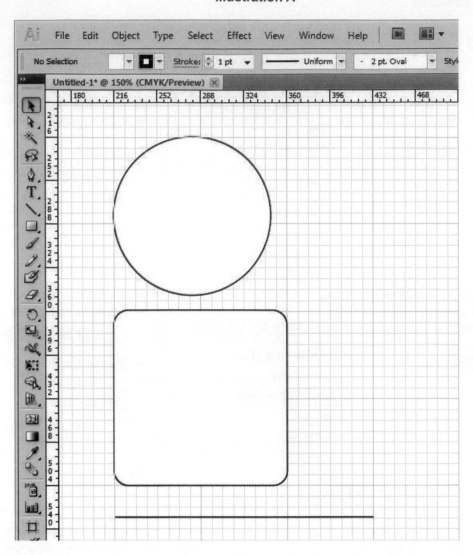

ON YOUR OWN

1. Start Illustrator and create a new print document.

2. Practice using drawing tools from the Tools panel to create rectangles, ellipses, rounded rectangles, and lines.

3. Open a new document and practice drawing with tools you have not already used. Use Smart Guides to help you line up objects.

4. Use the Help system to find out what some of the Tools panel tools are for, if you don't understand their use.

5. Close both files without saving and exit Illustrator.

Skills Covered

- Select Objects
- Move and Delete Objects
- More Drawing Techniques
- About Paths and Anchor Points

Software Skills   Use the Selection tool to select objects so that they can be moved, modified, or deleted. Besides dragging a tool to draw an object, you can use a dialog box to set precise dimensions. Modifier keys such as Alt and Shift can be used to constrain an object to a particular shape or draw it from the center outward. Tools may draw open or closed paths, and the anchor points on an object can be used to modify or group objects.

Design Skills   When working with an illustration, a designer often needs to select and reposition objects to follow principles of good design. Illustrator's tools allow you to perform some of the sizing and appearance chores as you draw.

Application Skills   In this exercise, you will create the MP3 illustration required for the testing center. You will select and delete the objects you created in the last exercise and draw objects to precise measurements. You will move objects to assemble the MP3 player. Finally, you will create a barred circle to indicate that use of the object is forbidden.

TERMS

Anchor point   A point on a path that indicates a change of direction.

Bounding box   A temporary frame around a selected object that shows the object's outer dimensions.

Constrain   To force an object to take a certain form. Use modifier keys to constrain objects.

Corner point   An *anchor point* where a path changes direction in an angle rather than smoothly.

Path   The line that forms the shape of an object.

Smooth point   An *anchor point* that connects path segments in a smooth curve.

NOTES

Select Objects

- Before objects can be modified, moved, or deleted, they must be selected.

- Illustrator offers a number of selection tools to simplify the process of selecting single objects, similar objects, or parts of objects.

- The most basic of these tools is the ![Selection tool icon] Selection tool, located at the upper-left corner of the Tools panel.

- To select an object with the Selection tool, point to the object with the selection pointer and click the mouse. If the object is a line or is not filled, click on the object's path.

  ✓ *You will read more about paths later in this exercise.*

- By default, a selected object displays a **bounding box** around the object.

- If an object is rectangular, the bounding box is the same dimensions as the object. For an ellipse, line, or irregular object, the bounding box creates a frame around the object as shown in Figure 5-1.

Figure 5-1. Bounding boxes for rectangle and ellipse

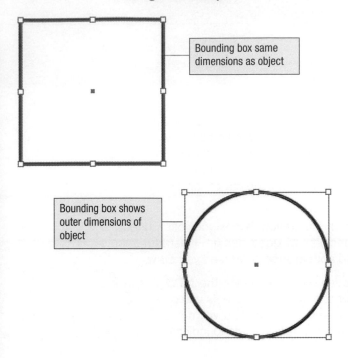

- A selected bounding box is blue by default and displays hollow selection handles at intervals.
- Bounding boxes for objects in an illustration may be turned off, if desired.
- When bounding boxes are hidden, a selected object shows a colored path and small colored squares called **anchor points**, as shown in Figure 5-2.

✓ *The path and anchor points have been changed to yellow in this figure to make them easier to see.*

Figure 5-2. Selected objects with hidden bounding boxes

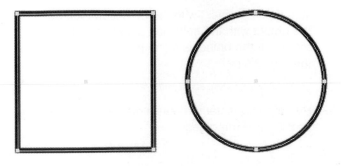

✓ *You will read more about anchor points later in the exercise.*

- The Selection tool pointer changes its shape depending on what it is pointing to.
  - When pointing to an unselected object, the pointer has a small black square to the right: [�]
  - When pointing to a selected object or path, the pointer shows only the arrowhead: [▶]
  - When pointing to an anchor point, the pointer shows a hollow square to the right: [�] (when pointing to an unselected anchor point) or [▶] (when pointing to a selected anchor point with the object's bounding box hidden).
- Paying attention to the pointer shape can help you select paths and anchor points that may be partially obscured by other objects.
- You will often need to select more than one object at a time when modifying a drawing. Techniques for selecting multiple objects are covered in Exercise 7.

Move and Delete Objects

- Once an object has been selected, you can easily move it by simply dragging the object with the Selection tool.
- For a filled object, click anywhere in the object to select it and drag it. For a line, click on the line's path to select and drag it.
- To keep the same vertical or horizontal orientation while moving, hold down the Shift key.
- In Figure 5-3, for example, holding Shift while dragging the circle to the right will ensure that the bottom of the circle is on exactly the same horizontal line as in its original location.

Figure 5-3. Hold Shift while moving

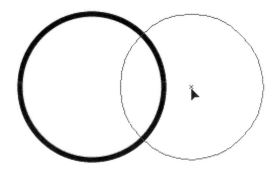

- Deleting an object is easy: Simply select it and press the Backspace or Delete key.
- If an object is deleted accidentally, use Undo to restore it.

More Drawing Techniques

- Dragging a tool pointer is perhaps the simplest way to create an object. Illustrator offers a number of other drawing techniques, however, to give you more control over the shape and size of the object.

Display a Tool's Dialog Box

- Rather than size an object as you draw it using the Smart Guide size information (or guesswork), you can display a dialog box and specify measurements and in some cases other options for the object.

- Display a tool's dialog box, such as the one shown in Figure 5-4, by selecting the tool and then clicking in the work area.

Figure 5-4. Rectangle dialog box

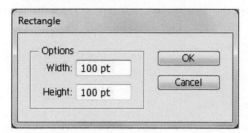

- You can insert another object of the same type by simply clicking again in the work area to open the dialog box. Accept the same measurements or adjust measurements as desired.

Use Modifier Keys to Constrain Objects

- Pressing a modifier key—Ctrl, Shift, or Alt—can **constrain** an object to take a certain form or direction.

- When drawing an ellipse or rectangle, hold down Shift to create a perfect circle or square.

- When drawing a line with the Line Segment tool or the Pen tool, hold down Shift to create a straight horizontal, vertical, or diagonal line.

- When drawing a circle or other closed object, hold down Alt to draw outward from the center. This technique makes it easy to center objects on existing objects.

- Hold down Alt when drawing a line to extend the line in either direction from its center.

  ✓ *You learn how to use the Ctrl key when drawing objects in Exercise 7.*

About Paths and Anchor Points

- The line that forms the shape of an object is its **path**. Note that you only see the object's path if formatting has been applied to it. Without that formatting, the path would not display. You can see the actual path of an object when it is selected.

- A path may be open or closed. Figure 5-5 shows both an open path (the line created with the Pencil tool on the left) and a closed path (the circle on the right).

Figure 5-5. Open and closed paths

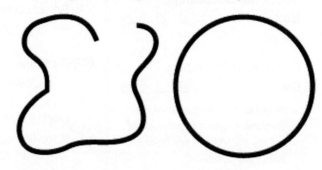

- Paths are created from a series of straight or curved segments. At the beginning and end of each segment is an anchor point. By adjusting the anchor points, you can modify the direction of the path.

- Figure 5-6 shows the anchor points for the open path shown in Figure 5-5. An open path also has two *endpoints* at the beginning and end of the path.

Figure 5-6. Endpoints and anchor points for open path

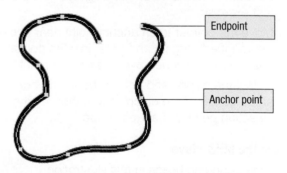

- Notice in Figure 5-6 that the anchor points display at the start or end of a change of direction in the path.

- Anchor points may be **smooth points** or **corner points**. Smooth points, such as those shown in the illustration above, join segments in a smooth curve. Corner points indicate where a path changes direction abruptly.

PROCEDURES

Select Objects
1. Click **Selection** tool ![cursor] V
2. Click anywhere in a closed object, or click the path of a closed or open object.

Hide/Show Bounding Box
(Shift + Ctrl + B)
1. Click **View** .... ALT + V
2. Click **Hide Bounding Box** .... X, X, ENTER

   OR

   Click **Show Bounding Box** .... X, X, ENTER

   ✓ *Note that two commands on the View menu have a shortcut key of x. Click the shortcut key twice to select this command.*

Move Objects
1. Select object to move.
2. Using **Selection** tool ![cursor], hold down mouse and drag object to new location.
3. Press SHIFT while dragging to maintain horizontal or vertical orientation.

Delete Objects
1. Select object to delete.
2. Press BACKSPACE or DEL.

Display a Tool's Dialog Box
1. Click desired tool in Tools panel.
2. Click anywhere in work area to display dialog box.
3. Specify measurements and any other options.
4. Click **OK**.
5. Click again in work area to display dialog box again.

Use Modifier Keys to Constrain Objects
- Use SHIFT:
  - When drawing a rectangle or ellipse to create a perfect square or circle.
  - When drawing a line to create a straight vertical, horizontal, or diagonal line.
- Use ALT:
  - When drawing a closed object to draw outward from the center.
  - When drawing a line to extend the line in either direction from the center.

EXERCISE DIRECTIONS

1. Start Adobe Illustrator.
2. Open 📟04MP3_xx, or open 💿05MP3.
3. Save the file as 05MP3_xx.
4. Turn off Snap to Grid if necessary. Click the Selection tool and move the Selection pointer over the path of the rounded rectangle you drew in the last exercise.
5. Move the pointer to an anchor point near one of the rounded corners and note how the pointer changes shape when over the anchor point.
6. Select the ellipse and note its bounding box. Point at the center of the object to see the way the selection pointer changes shape.

Create the MP3 Player
1. Hide bounding boxes in this illustration.
2. Select each object you created in the last exercise and delete it.
3. Starting from the intersection of the top and left guide, draw a rounded rectangle for the MP3 player body as shown in Illustration A. The rounded rectangle should be about **216** points wide by **360** points high.

Illustration A

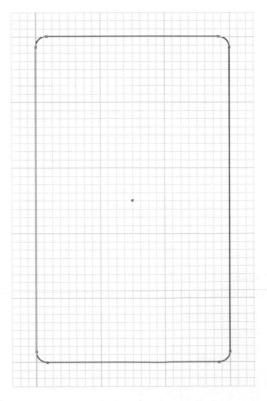

4. Choose the Rectangle tool and click in the player object to display the Rectangle dialog box.

5. Specify a width of **180** points and a height of **144** points and click OK. This rectangle will be the display area of the player.

6. Use the Selection tool to move the rectangle into the upper half of the player. (See Illustration B.)

7. Choose the Ellipse tool. Position the crosshair in the center of the area below the display area rectangle. (See Illustration B.) Then draw a perfect circle for the click wheel from the center outward until the circle is about **126** points in both dimensions.

   ✓ Hint: Hold down Alt and Shift while drawing the circle.

8. Click anywhere on the artboard to display the Ellipse dialog box. It will show the width and height of the circle you just drew.

9. Change the measurements to be **60** points in width and height and click OK.

10. Select the new, smaller circle and place the selection pointer over its center mark. Drag the circle on top of the first, larger circle until their center points overlap.

Create the "Forbidden" Circle and Slash

1. Locate the center of the rounded rectangle by selecting the rectangle and noting the location of the small blue x center point. Draw another perfect circle from the center of the player outward to overlap the player as shown in Illustration B.

2. If the object has a fill, it will obscure the player body. If necessary, click the Fill box in the Tools panel and then click the None box in the Tools panel to remove the fill from the large circle.

   ✓ You will learn more about stroke and fill options in the next exercise.

3. Choose the Line Segment tool. Draw a straight diagonal line through the center of the large circle from the top right to the bottom left of the large outer circle. (See Illustration B.)

4. Save your changes, close the file, and exit Illustrator.

   ✓ You will have a chance to improve this illustration in the next exercise.

Illustration B

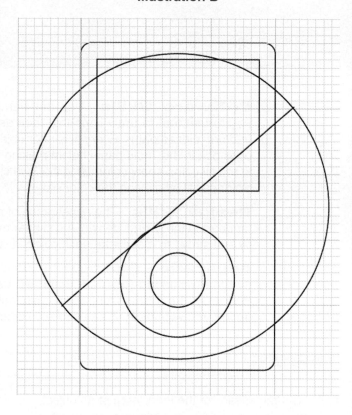

ON YOUR OWN

1. Start Illustrator.

2. Open a new Illustrator document, using default settings.

3. Practice using the tools and features you have learned about in this exercise.

4. You may simply draw shapes or create a simple drawing similar to the one in the exercise.

5. Select and move objects to different locations.

6. Practice using the modifier keys to constrain objects as you draw them.

   ✓ The more familiar you become with keyboard shortcuts for modifying objects, the quicker you will master Illustrator.

7. As you select the objects you create, identify their bounding boxes, paths, anchor points, and endpoints.

8. Close the file without saving and exit Adobe Illustrator.

Skills Covered

- **Pencil Tool Basics**
- **Paintbrush Tool Basics**
- **Use the Blob Brush Tool**
- **Understand Fill and Stroke**

- **Apply Fill and Stroke Color**
- **Change Stroke Weight**
- **Adjust a Color Using the Color Panel**

Software Skills Use the Pencil tool to draw freeform lines and the Paintbrush tool to draw lines that look as if brushed. The Blob Brush tool paints freeform closed paths. Every Illustrator object has a stroke and a fill. Select the stroke or fill box in the Tools panel before making changes to the stroke's weight or color or to the fill color. Apply color using the Swatches panel, or create a specific color in the Color panel by moving the color sliders.

Design Skills The appearance of an illustration's objects can play an important part in the overall design. A designer must know how to apply attributes to object fill and stroke to make sure each object displays as desired.

Application Skills In this exercise, you will begin work on an illustration that the Richmond City Park Board will use for several purposes. You will use the Pencil tool, Blob Brush tool, Paintbrush tool, and other tools to create a stylized illustration. You will adjust fill and stroke color and stroke weight for some objects.

TERMS

Fill   Characteristics of the inner area of an object, such as the color, pattern, style, etc., inside an object.

Stroke   Characteristics of the outline of an object, such as its weight, color, style, etc.

NOTES

Pencil Tool Basics

- Use the Pencil tool ![pencil icon] to draw a freeform path. Drawing with the Pencil tool in Illustrator is just like drawing with a pencil on a piece of paper.

- Because the mouse is used like a pencil, the better the mouse, the easier it will be to draw.

  ✓ *Illustrator also accepts input from graphic tablets and graphic pens.*

- As you draw with the Pencil tool, Illustrator adds anchor points where the line changes direction. You can see the anchor points after you release the mouse button, as shown in Figure 6-1.

Figure 6-1. Path drawn with Pencil tool

- The Pencil tool can be used to create either open or closed paths. The default option is to draw an open path, indicated by the small *x* to the right of the pencil pointer.

- Create a closed path by holding down Alt after you start drawing. Illustrator automatically closes the path as soon as you release the mouse button.

- Illustrator displays a small *o* next to the pointer while Alt is pressed to indicate the path will close when the mouse button is released.

- Illustrator smooths the pencil path after you release the mouse button. If you are not happy with the path, you can go back to any point on the path and begin drawing again to adjust the path as shown in Figure 6-2.

Figure 6-2. Change the path of the pencil line

- You can also delete a portion of the pencil path using the Path Eraser tool ![icon], on the hidden toolbar beneath the Pencil tool.

  ✓ *Do not confuse the Path Eraser and Eraser tools. The Eraser tool removes all pixels in a given area.*

- Drag the Path Eraser tool along the selected pencil path to delete that portion of the path.

- Illustrator allows you to specify preference settings for how smooth a pencil path will be when drawn and offers a Smooth tool ![icon] to speed the process of smoothing a pencil line.

- To use the Smooth tool, drag it over a path. This tool removes anchor points to make a path less "bumpy."

Paintbrush Tool Basics

- Use the Paintbrush tool ![icon] to draw a line that looks as if it has been brushed. Paintbrush paths can have thick and thin areas such as those that would be created by a paintbrush, as shown in Figure 6-3.

Figure 6-3. Paintbrush path

- Unlike a pencil path, a paintbrush path does not remain selected by default.

- You can adjust settings so that paintbrush paths remain selected. When this setting is selected, it is easy to redraw a paintbrush path if you need to change its appearance.

- Double-click the Paintbrush tool in the Tools panel to display the Paintbrush Tool Options dialog box shown in Figure 6-4.

Figure 6-4. Paintbrush Tool Options dialog box

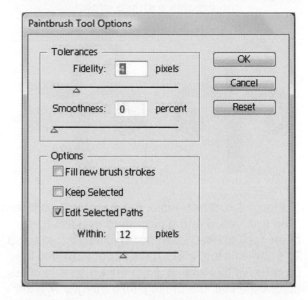

- Check the Keep Selected option if you want the paintbrush line to stay selected after you draw it. When Edit Selected Paths is selected, any new paintbrush stroke you make modifies a selected path, rather than creating a new line.

  ✓ *The Pencil Tool Options dialog box also has an Edit Selected Paths option that can be deselected to allow you to add to a pencil path rather than redraw it.*

- You can use the Paintbrush tool to draw many types of paths other than plain brushed lines. Illustrator offers five different types of brush patterns that can add special touches to an illustration. You will find a small selection of brushes in the Brushes panel, but many more are available in libraries.

- To quickly access the Brushes panel and choose a different brush, click the Brush Definition list arrow on the Control panel, or click the Brushes panel in the panel dock.

  ✓ *You will work with the Brushes panel and the Paintbrush tool more extensively in Lesson 2, Exercise 16.*

Use the Blob Brush Tool

- You use the Blob Brush tool ![icon] in the same general way you use the Paintbrush tool, but the result is a closed shape, as shown in Figure 6-5 on the next page.

- The Blob Brush tool is useful for creating freeform shapes. After completing the shape, you can use the Smooth tool to adjust the anchor points for a smoother shape outline.

- The Blob Brush tool can also be used to create objects that intersect with other objects, sharing attributes such as fill and effects.

Figure 6-5. Blob Brush tool paints like a brush (left) and creates a shape (right)

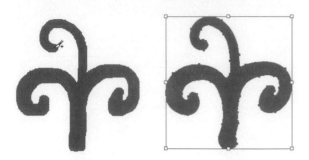

- In Figure 6-6, for example, the star shape has been filled with yellow and a drop shadow effect has been applied. (You learn about effects in Lesson 3.) The same fill and effect have been applied to the Blob Brush tool so that when the brush is stroked across the star, the brush stroke merges with the star shape and displays the same fill and effect.

Figure 6-6. Blob Brush stroke merges with an existing object

- Double-click the Blob Brush tool to display the Blob Brush Options dialog box, where you can modify tool settings if desired.

Understand Fill and Stroke

- Every object drawn in Illustrator has both a stroke and a fill by default.
- The **stroke** of an object consists of the characteristics of the object's outline. For example, the weight of the line and the color of the line would be stroke characteristics.

- The **fill** of an object consists of the characteristics of the inner area of an object. Color, pattern, and style are fill characteristics.
- Though you may consider that only objects with closed paths can have a fill, Illustrator in fact can apply a fill to any object, including lines drawn by the Pencil, Paintbrush, and Pen tools.
- Default settings use black for stroke and white for fill. You can change stroke and fill color for any object. In addition, you can specify that an object have no stroke or fill.

Apply Fill and Stroke Color

- To change fill and stroke color, you must first select the fill or stroke for an object and then select a color from a color panel.
- When working with drawing and painting tools such as the Pencil, Paintbrush, and Blob Brush, you may find it helpful to switch to the Painting workspace. This workspace gives you easy access to the Color, Swatches, and Color Guide panels.

    ✓ You will learn about the Color Guide panel in a later exercise.

Select Fill or Stroke

- The Tools panel displays Fill and Stroke boxes that make it easy for you to select fill and stroke.
- The Fill box is the upper-left box in the Tools panel as shown in Figure 6-7. The Stroke box, which looks like a frame, is the lower-right box.

Figure 6-7. Fill and stroke options

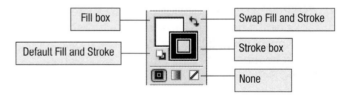

- Selecting one of these boxes causes it to come to the front, so you know it is active.
- You can restore default colors for fill and stroke by clicking the Default Fill and Stroke icon.
- If you have applied to the stroke a color or pattern meant for the fill, you can click the Swap Fill and Stroke icon to switch fill and stroke characteristics.
- To eliminate the fill or stroke color, activate the appropriate box and click the None button.

    ✓ There is a difference between a white fill or stroke and no fill or stroke, though both may look the same on the Illustrator screen.

Use the Swatches Panel

- One way to apply color to a fill or stroke is to use the preset colors in the Swatches panel, shown in Figure 6-8.

Figure 6-8. Swatches panel

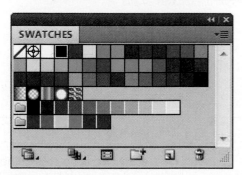

- The Swatches panel's colors are created from percentages of the colors specified by the default color model.

- For example, the darker red swatch in the first row of colors is made up of 15% cyan, 100% magenta, 90% yellow, and 10% black. Swatches are named using their percentages of colors.

  ✓ *Rest the pointer on a swatch to see its color percentages.*

- To apply a swatch color to the fill or stroke, select the appropriate box in the Tools panel and then click the swatch color.

- You can also drag the swatch color to the Fill or Stroke box or drag the swatch onto the object itself. If dragged to the object, the swatch will color either the stroke or fill, depending on which is selected in the Tools panel.

- The Swatches panel also displays *gradients* and *patterns* that can be applied to objects the same way as colors.

  ✓ *You will work more extensively with the Swatches panel in Lesson 3, Exercise 24. You will work with gradients in Exercise 28.*

Use the Control Panel

- The Control panel can also be used to apply fill and stroke colors. Click the list arrow to the right of the current Fill color or Stroke color to display a Swatches panel identical to the one in the panel dock. Click a color from the panel to apply it.

- Colors applied to the fill and stroke become default settings for all new objects. With the colors displayed prominently in the Control panel, it's easy to keep track of the current defaults.

Change Stroke Weight

- By default, stroke weight—that is, the thickness of the stroke—is set at 1 point.

- Use the Stroke panel, shown in Figure 6-9, to change stroke weight.

Figure 6-9. Stroke panel

- Type a weight in the Weight box, click the up or down spin arrows to increase or decrease the stroke weight by 1-point increments, or click the list arrow to display a list of weights to choose from, from 0.25 pt to 100 pt.

- The stroke weight box is also available on the Control panel.

- After you set the stroke weight, that weight becomes the new default setting for objects in the illustration.

- Expanding the Stroke panel to its full size displays other stroke formatting. You can specify end and corner options, control how the stroke displays in relation to the path, create custom dashed lines, and apply arrowheads to either or both ends of the stroke.

- The new Variable Width Profile settings in the Control panel and the expanded Stroke panel allow you to apply different profiles to a stroke to vary its thickness from start to end of the stroke.

- To display the expanded Stroke panel from the Control panel, click the Stroke link on the Control panel. The Stroke panel drops down below the Control panel to give you access to all stroke options.

  ✓ *You will work with stroke formats in Lesson 2, Exercise 13.*

Adjust a Color Using the Color Panel

- Using a swatch from the Swatches panel is a quick way to apply a color to an object. You may, however, want to adjust a color that you applied as a swatch.

- Use the Color panel in Figure 6-10 to adjust colors.

  ✓ *You can display this panel from the Control panel by holding down Shift while clicking the Fill or Stroke color list arrow.*

Figure 6-10. Color panel

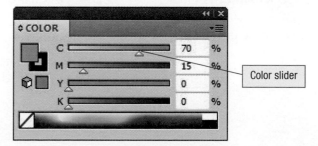

- Adjust percentages of colors by dragging the sliders for each color. Percentages are shown at the right of the color bars to make it easy to achieve precision.

  ✓ *You can also type the desired percentages right in the percent boxes. Use Tab to move from box to box.*

- Notice in Figure 6-10 that the Color panel includes Fill and Stroke boxes the same as those that appear in the Tools panel. Make sure the correct box is selected before changing a color.

- The Color panel also has a None box at the bottom left of the panel and solid black and white areas at the bottom right of the panel. These choices make it easy to eliminate stroke or fill or select solid black or white for a stroke or fill.

  ✓ *You will work more extensively with the Color panel in Lesson 3, Exercises 24 and 25.*

PROCEDURES

Use Pencil Tools
1. Click **Pencil** tool 🖉 .... Ⓝ
2. Drag to create pencil path.

To reshape the path:
- While the Pencil tool is still selected, redraw path from any point to change path.

To create a closed path:
- Hold down ALT while dragging path to create closed path.

  ✓ *First start drawing and then select Alt.*

To delete part of the path:
1. Click **Path Eraser** tool 🖉 from the hidden toolbar beneath Pencil tool.
2. Drag over the portion of the selected path to erase.

To smooth a path:
1. Click **Smooth** tool 🖉 from the hidden toolbar beneath Pencil tool.
2. Drag over the portion of the selected path to erase.

Use Paintbrush Tool
1. Click **Paintbrush** tool 🖌 .... Ⓑ
2. Drag to create brushed path.

To select a different brush from the Brushes panel:
1. Click the Brushes panel docked in the panel dock.

  OR

  Click the Brush Definition list arrow on the Control panel.
2. Select the desired brush.

Use Blob Brush Tool
1. Click **Blob Brush** tool 🖌 .... SHIFT + Ⓑ
2. Drag to create desired shape.

Select Fill or Stroke
- Click Fill box or Stroke box in Tools panel.
- Click 🔲 to restore default fill and stroke settings.
- Click ↰ to swap current fill and stroke settings.

Apply Color from Swatches Panel
1. Select Fill or Stroke box in Tools panel, as appropriate.
2. Click swatch in Swatches panel.

  OR

  Drag swatch to appropriate box (Fill or Stroke) in Tools panel.

  OR

  Drag swatch directly to selected object.

OR
1. Click the list arrow to the right of the current Fill or Stroke color in the Control panel.
2. Select a fill or stroke color from the drop-down Swatches panel.

Change Stroke Weight
1. Select object to change.
2. Make sure Stroke box is selected in Tools panel.
3. Type desired stroke weight in Weight (or Stroke) combo box, either in the Stroke panel or on the Control panel.

  OR

  Click up or down spin arrow to increase or decrease stroke weight by 1-point increments.

  OR

  Click list arrow to display list of weights and click a weight to select it.

Adjust Color Using the Color Panel
1. Select stroke or fill to modify.
2. Drag color sliders in Color panel to achieve desired color.

  OR

  Type desired percentages in percent boxes in Color panel.

EXERCISE DIRECTIONS

1. Open ⊙06Park. Use the workspace switcher to display the Painting workspace.
2. Save the file as 06Park_xx.

Draw the Remaining Objects

✓ *This data file contains several objects that have already been drawn for the brochure. You need to draw a few more objects for the illustration.*

1. With Fill and Stroke set to default appearance, use the Pencil tool to draw the following shapes shown in white in Illustration A:

   ■ Draw the bank to the left of the lake object.

   ✓ *Remember to hold down Alt as you return to the beginning of the shape to create a closed shape.*

   ■ Add the tree leaves object

2. Select the Blob Brush tool and create the tree trunk and branches, similar to the tree shown in Illustration B. You may make multiple strokes with the Blob Brush to thicken the trunk of the tree.
3. Display the Brushes panel and choose the **5 pt Flat** brush in the top row.
4. Use the Paintbrush tool to draw some smaller limbs as shown in the picture in Illustration B. You may also change to any of the other brushes to add additional limbs.
5. Use the Line Segment tool to draw three straight vertical lines near the edge of the lake. These will be cattail stems. Your drawing should resemble Illustration B at this point.

   ✓ *Your drawing will not display the gray shading on the pre-drawn areas that is shown in Illustration A.*

Change Colors and Strokes

1. Apply fill and stroke colors and formats as follows. Refer to the labels on Illustration A for the names of the objects.

   ✓ *You may want to drag the Color panel out onto the work area so that you can see both the Color and Swatches panels at the same time to make it easier to select and adjust colors.*

a. Select the bank object that you drew and remove the stroke. Apply the **CMYK Green** swatch color as the fill. Then, in the Color panel drag the C slider back to **C = 65**. (Expand the Color panel if necessary to see the sliders.)
b. Select the lake object. Change the stroke to None and use the Control panel to apply the **C = 85, M = 50, Y = 0, K = 0** swatch color as the fill.
c. Select the lawn object. Change the stroke to None on the Tools panel and apply the **C = 85, M = 10, Y = 100, K = 10** swatch color as the fill.
d. Select the Blob Brush tree trunk and apply the **C = 40, M = 70, Y = 100, K = 50** swatch color as the fill.
e. Select each of the tree branch brush strokes and apply the same brown color as a stroke. Set the fill for the brush strokes to None.
f. Select the tree leaves object and remove the stroke. Apply the **C = 0, M = 80, Y = 95, K = 0** swatch color as the fill.
g. Select the mountain object that is directly above the lawn. Change the stroke to None and apply the **C = 0, M = 35, Y = 85, K = 0** swatch color as the fill.
h. Select the second mountain object. Change the stroke to None and apply the **C = 40, M = 65, Y = 90, K = 35** swatch color as the fill.
i. With the mountain object still selected, adjust the colors in the Color panel as follows: **C = 20, M = 65, Y = 95, K = 6**.

2. Select each of the cattail stems and use the Stroke box in the Control panel to change the stroke weight to **2** pt. Apply the **C = 50, M = 70, Y = 80, K = 70** swatch color to the stroke. Adjust the position of the cattail stems to stand in the water if necessary after changing the stroke weight.
3. Save your changes, close the file, and exit Illustrator.

Illustration A

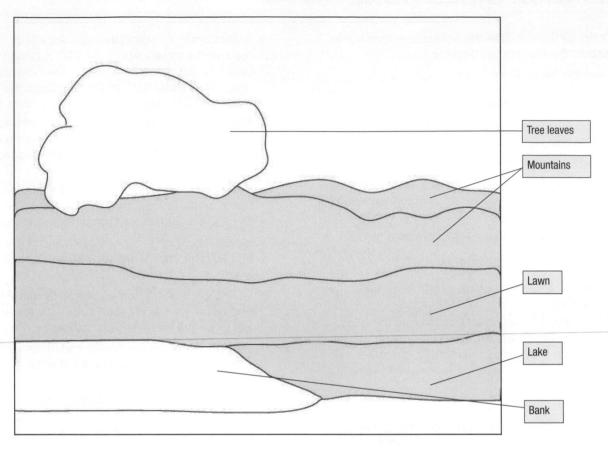

Tree leaves

Mountains

Lawn

Lake

Bank

Illustration B

ON YOUR OWN

1. Start Illustrator.

2. Open 05MP3_xx or OYO06.

3. Save the file as OIL06_xx. Display the Painting workspace, if necessary.

4. Select the player body and apply a gray fill such as **K = 80**.

   ✓ *You can find a selection of grays at the bottom of the Swatches panel.*

5. Select the innermost circle of the click wheel and apply a gray fill such as **K = 30**. Modify the gray fill to **C = 0, M = 0, Y = 10, K = 35**.

6. Select the outermost click wheel circle and apply a gray fill such as **K = 10**. Add 10% yellow to this color.

7. Remove the stroke from the display area rectangle and fill with a color of your choice.

8. Select the large "forbidden" circle and change its stroke weight to **30** pt. Change the fill to None and apply a bright red color to the stroke.

9. Select the diagonal path and apply the same red color and stroke weight.

10. Clear the guides and turn off the grid. Your illustration should look similar to Illustration C.

11. Save your changes, close the file, and exit Illustrator.

Illustration C

Exercise | 7

Skills Covered

- Adjust Shapes While Drawing
- Copy Objects
- Select Multiple Objects
- Align and Distribute Objects
- Group Objects
- Position Objects
- Change Stacking Order

Software Skills Some Illustrator tools, such as the Star and Polygon, allow you to adjust the final shape during the drawing process. Copying, selecting multiple objects, aligning objects, and grouping objects save time when creating or modifying a drawing. Use Transform settings and the nudge feature for fine positioning. Change stacking order to control how objects appear in relation to each other.

Design Skills A coherent and attractive design often requires that objects be grouped, aligned, and arranged in specific ways. A designer can speed the process of creating a complex illustration by learning to manipulate multiple objects and groups of objects.

Application Skills In this exercise, you will continue to work on the Richmond Parks illustration. You will add details to the drawing such as spiral-shaped clouds and several stars, insert a stylized gazebo structure, and add the sky. You will select, align, and group multiple objects, position objects, and change stacking order.

TERMS

Align Line up objects at their tops, bottoms, edges, or centers.

Distribute Space objects evenly, either vertically or horizontally.

Polygon Any object with three or more straight sides.

Spiral An open shape that consists of a number of *winds* around a central point.

Winds Complete revolutions around the center point in a spiral. Each wind consists of four segments.

NOTES

Adjust Shapes While Drawing

- You have already learned about constraining simple shapes such as rectangles and ellipses using the Shift key.

- You can change the appearance of other shapes using the keyboard's arrow keys and modifier keys.

- For example, press the up or down arrow while drawing a rounded rectangle to adjust the roundness of the corners.

- More complex shapes, such as stars, polygons, and spirals, can also be adjusted during the drawing process.

- For example, when drawing a star using the Star tool, you can adjust its shape by:
  - Moving the crosshair pointer left or right to rotate the star.
  - Pressing the up or down arrow key to increase or decrease the number of points on the star.
  - Holding down Shift to keep one point of the star straight up.
  - Holding down Ctrl to keep the inner points in the same position while lengthening the outer points (see Figure 7-1).
  - Holding down Alt to keep the sides of the star straight (see Figure 7-1).

Figure 7-1. Adjust star points with Ctrl or Alt

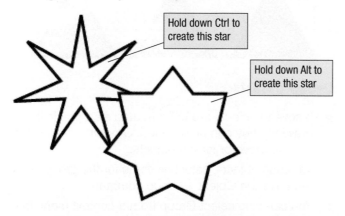

Hold down Ctrl to create this star

Hold down Alt to create this star

- You can use some of the same techniques to adjust shapes such as polygons and spirals.

- A **polygon** is an object with three or more straight sides, such as a triangle, rectangle, hexagon, and so on.

- A **spiral** is an open shape that consists of a number of **winds** around a central point.

- For more control over shapes such as stars, polygons, and spirals, specify settings in the shape's dialog box, which you can display by selecting the tool and clicking on the artboard.

Copy Objects

- If a drawing contains a number of similar objects, you can save a great deal of time by copying one object and pasting as many versions of it as required.

- The traditional method for copying and pasting uses the Edit > Copy and Edit > Paste commands. Using Edit > Paste places the copied object in the middle of the screen.

  ✓ *The Paste in Front, Paste in Back, and Paste in Place commands can be used to position a copied object more precisely. You will learn about these commands in later exercises.*

- Illustrator also offers an easy keyboard shortcut for copying an object. Select the object and hold down Alt while dragging the object.

- The pointer changes from a single arrowhead to a double arrowhead to show a copy is being created, as shown in Figure 7-2.

Figure 7-2. Copy an object by dragging

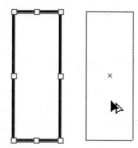

- When dragging a copy, it is a good idea to hold down Shift as well as Alt if the copied item is to align at the bottom or side with the original.

Select Multiple Objects

- Editing an illustration often requires selecting a number of objects to format in the same way or to move easily.

- Use the Selection tool to select multiple objects using either of these methods:
  - Click on the first object, hold Shift, and click additional objects.
  - Use the Selection tool to drag a marquee that touches all items to be selected. The marquee does not have to surround the objects, merely intersect them at some point, as shown in Figure 7-3 on the next page.

Figure 7-3. Drag a marquee to select objects

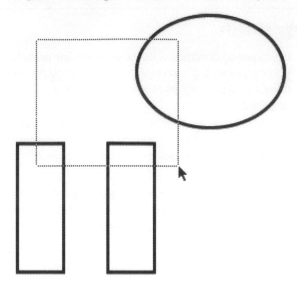

- All selected objects are surrounded by one selection outline.

- These methods may also be combined to add objects to the selection outline: Drag the selection marquee, then hold down Shift and click additional items to add them.

  ✓ *Use the same method to remove an item from the selection outline.*

Align and Distribute Objects

- Creating a drawing often requires you to **align** or **distribute** multiple objects. Align objects to line them up by some common aspect, such as their tops or centers. Distribute objects to space them evenly.

- When you select more than one object, the align and distribute options become active in the Control panel. You can also display the Align panel, shown in Figure 7-4, to select alignment options.

Figure 7-4. Align panel

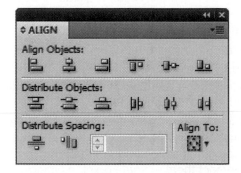

- Selected objects can be aligned on their left or right edges or centered horizontally on each other. Or, they can be aligned by their tops, centers, or bottoms.

- Selected objects can be distributed vertically according to their tops, centers, or bottoms, or horizontally from the left, center, or right.

- You can choose what to align selected objects to: the current selection, the artboard, or a *key object*. A key object is one item in the selected group with which other items should align.

- At the top of Figure 7-5, for example, three objects have been selected and the middle triangle has been designated as the key object. Note the bright blue border that indicates it is the key object. The bottom part of the figure shows how the other two triangles have been aligned at bottom with the key object.

Figure 7-5. Aligning using a key object

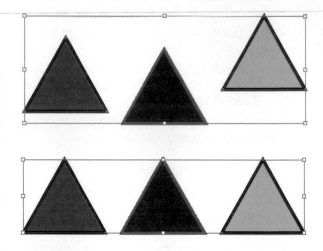

Group Objects

- If several objects are to be treated as a unit in the drawing, they can be grouped. Grouping makes it easy to move or format objects.

- To group objects, select all items for the group and then use the Object > Group command.

- You can also select Group from a context menu by right-clicking on the selected objects.

- A group can be restored to individual objects using the Object > Ungroup or context menu Ungroup command.

  ✓ *Illustrator provides a tool for selecting an individual item in a group: the Group Selection tool. You will learn how to use this tool in Lesson 2, Exercise 14.*

Position Objects

- You have several options for positioning an object exactly. The easiest way is to drag the object to its approximate final location and then use the arrow keys on the keyboard to "nudge" the object into place.

- By default, each press of an arrow key moves the object 1 point in the arrow's direction.

  ✓ *You can change this keyboard increment in the General Preferences dialog box.*

- If you need to move an object some distance, or need to specify an exact location, use the X and Y boxes that display in several Illustrator panels (and on the Control panel if your monitor is wide enough to display the full panel).

- The X and Y boxes show the X and Y coordinates of the selected object.

- The X coordinate measures the distance from the left edge of the artboard. The Y coordinate measures the distance from the top of the artboard.

- You can use the Info panel, shown in Figure 7-6, to see X and Y coordinates as you move the pointer on the artboard. This panel also shows you width and height of an object as you draw it, and it can also tell you the distance you have moved an object and the angle of the move relative to the original position.

Figure 7-6. Info panel

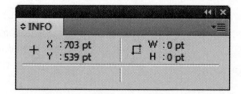

- The Info panel does not allow you to specify a location or a width or height. If you need to indicate a precise location or size, you can use the Transform panel.

- You can open this panel (Figure 7-7) from the Window menu. You may also see the Transform boxes on the Control panel, or a Transform link that allows you to drop the Transform panel from the Control panel.

- The Transform panel is one of Illustrator's most useful panels. Not only can you specify an exact position for an object, you can specify an exact size, adjust its rotation, and shear the object (slant it a set amount).

Figure 7-7. Transform panel

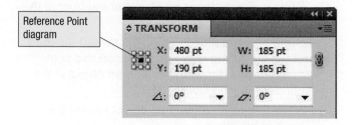

- When positioning an object using either the Info panel or the Transform panel, Illustrator measures from the center of the object by default. You can change the point from which to measure by selecting a location on the Reference Point diagram to the left of the X and Y boxes (see Figure 7-7). Click one of the small open squares at the center, corners, or sides of the diagram to set the reference point. It will become black to indicate that Illustrator will measure from that location.

- Note that if you have Smart Guides displayed, you will also see positioning information displayed as you move an object. The gray information box attached to the pointer shows you the distance you have moved an object relative to its original position.

Change Stacking Order

- As objects are drawn in an illustration, they stack up in the order they were created. The first object drawn is at the bottom or back of the stack; the last object is on the top or at the front of the stack.

- In Figure 7-8, for example, the square was drawn first, the triangle second, and the circle last. The square is at the back of the stack and the circle is at the front.

Figure 7-8. Stacked objects

- Often, you will need to adjust the stacking order to reveal or obscure some objects in a drawing.

- To adjust stacking order, use the Object > Arrange command.

  ✓ *Or display the context menu and select the Arrange command.*

- The Arrange command provides four options:
  - Bring to Front places an object at the front of the stack.
  - Bring Forward moves an object toward the front of the stack. You may need to issue this command several times to position an object in the correct stacking layer.
  - Send Backward moves an object toward the back of the stack.
  - Send to Back moves an object to the back of the stack.

- You have another option for adjusting stacking order: You can move items in the Layers panel. You will work with the Layers panel in Lesson 2.

- Once you have begun stacking shapes on top of one another, it can be difficult to select some objects. You can use Outline mode to see all objects in a drawing as outlines rather than filled shapes, making it easy to view and select them.

PROCEDURES

Adjust Rounded Rectangle

1. Select **Rounded Rectangle** tool [□], and begin drawing object.
2. Press ⬇ or ⬆ to adjust roundness of corners.

Draw Star

1. Select **Star** tool [☆] from toolbar beneath Rectangle tool.
2. Click in work area to open Star dialog box.
3. Specify Radius 1 (radius of inner points), Radius 2 (radius of outer points), and number of points.
4. Click **OK** .... [ENTER]

OR

1. Select **Star** tool [☆] from toolbar beneath Rectangle tool.
2. Drag crosshair to draw and while drawing:
   - Drag the pointer in an arc to rotate star.
   - Press ⬇ or ⬆ to adjust number of points.
   - Press [SHIFT] to keep one point straight up.
   - Press [CTRL] to keep inner points at same radius while outer points increase in size.
   - Press [ALT] to keep sides straight.

Copy Objects (Ctrl + C, Ctrl + V)

1. Select object to copy.
2. Click **Edit** .... [ALT] + [E]
3. Click **Copy** .... [C]
4. Click **Edit** .... [ALT] + [E]
5. Click **Paste** .... [P]

OR

1. Select object to copy.
2. Hold down [ALT] while dragging copy to new location.

Draw Spiral

1. Select **Spiral** tool [◎] from toolbar beneath Line Segment tool.
2. Click in work area to open Spiral dialog box.
3. Specify radius, decay (percent decrease in relation to previous wind), number of segments, and clockwise or counterclockwise style.
4. Click **OK** .... [ENTER]

OR

1. Select **Spiral** tool [◎] from toolbar beneath Line Segment tool.
2. Drag crosshair to draw and while drawing:
   - Drag pointer in an arc to rotate spiral.
   - Press ⬇ or ⬆ to specify number of winds.

Select Multiple Objects

1. Select first item.
2. Hold down [SHIFT] and select additional items.

OR

- Use **Selection** tool [▸] to draw marquee that intersects all items to select.

Align and Distribute Objects

To align objects:

1. Select objects to align.
2. Display Align panel if align options do not display on Control panel .... [SHIFT] + [F7]
3. Select appropriate tool to align horizontally at right, center, or left, or vertically at top, center, or bottom.

To distribute objects:

1. Select objects to distribute.
2. Display Align panel if align options do not display on Control panel .... [SHIFT] + [F7]
3. Select appropriate tool to distribute objects vertically according to the top, center, or bottom, or horizontally from the left, center, or right.

To align relative to a key object:

1. Select objects to distribute.
2. Click one of the selected objects to become the key object.

   ✓ *A bright blue outline appears around the key object.*

3. Display Align panel if align options do not display on Control panel .... SHIFT + F7
4. Click list arrow of Align to Selection button ▦▾ and select **Align to Key Object**.
5. Choose desired alignment option.

Group Objects (Ctrl + G)

1. Select all objects to group.
2. Click **Object** .... ALT + O
3. Click **Group** .... G

   OR

1. Select all objects to group.
2. Right-click to open context menu.
3. Click **Group**.

To ungroup objects:

1. Click **Object** .... ALT + O
2. Click **Ungroup** .... U

Position Objects

To nudge objects:

1. Select object to position.
2. Nudge object into place by pressing ↓, ↑, ←, or →.

To determine position using the Info panel:

1. Click **Window** .... ALT + W
2. Click **Info** .... CTRL + F8
3. Watch X and Y measurements as you move pointer on the artboard.

To position exactly using the Transform panel:

1. Select object to position.
2. Display the Transform panel if Transform settings do not display in Control panel .... SHIFT + F8
3. Type desired coordinates in X and Y boxes, or use spin arrows to set values if using Control panel boxes.

Change Stacking Order

1. Select object to arrange.
2. Click **Object** .... ALT + O
3. Point to **Arrange** .... A
4. Select an option:
   - **Bring to Front** .... F
     or SHIFT + CTRL +]
   - **Bring Forward** .... O
     or CTRL +]
   - **Send Backward** .... B
     or CTRL + [
   - **Send to Back** .... A
     or SHIFT + CTRL + [

   OR

1. Select object to arrange.
2. Right-click to open context menu.
3. Click **Arrange**.
4. Click desired arrangement option.

Use Outline View (Ctrl + Y)

1. Click **View** .... ALT + V
2. Click **Outline** .... O

To return to Preview mode:

1. Click **View** .... ALT + V
2. Click **Preview** .... P

EXERCISE DIRECTIONS

✓ *Display the Painting workspace after starting Illustrator.*

1. Start Adobe Illustrator.
2. Open ⌨ 06Park_xx or open 💿 07Park.
3. Save the file as 07Park_xx.

Modify the Cattails and Create Clouds

1. Add a long, rounded rectangle near the top of one of the cattail stems, controlling the corner roundness as you draw. (See Illustration A.)
2. Remove the stroke from the cattail rectangle and fill with the **C = 35, M = 60, Y = 80, K = 25** swatch color.
3. Copy the cattail rectangle using any means and position the copies over the other two stems.
4. Select all objects that make up the cattails and group the objects.

5. Use the Spiral tool with no fill and a black stroke to draw a spiral in the sky area above the tree leaves. (See Illustration A.) Try adjusting winds and rotation as you draw.
6. When you are happy with the spiral you have drawn, copy it twice using any means and arrange the spirals to represent clouds. Group the spirals.

Begin the Gazebo

1. Create a rectangle that is **17** pts wide by **93** pts high. Fill with white and remove the stroke, if necessary.
2. Position the rectangle on the lawn above the lake.
3. Use Copy and Paste to paste two copies of the rectangle.

4. Move the two copies near the original rectangle. Align the three objects by their tops, and distribute them horizontally by their centers. They should look similar to the ones in Illustration A.

5. Group the rectangles.

Add Stars and Sky

1. Use the Star tool to draw a small star in the bank area. Reduce the points as you draw to create a four-pointed star, and hold down Ctrl to lengthen the star points. Remove the stroke and fill the star with white.

2. Use the Transform panel to adjust the star size to **45** pts high and wide and to position the star so that, when selected, its center coordinates are approximately **X = 31** and **Y = 452**.

   ✓ *You can type these values directly in the X and Y boxes if you see them on your Control panel.*

3. Create two copies of the star and align and distribute them as shown in Illustration A. Group the stars.

4. Create a large rectangle that covers the "sky" area above the mountain range. The rectangle should extend from the top line of the artboard to below the top of the first mountain range, and from side to side of the artboard.

5. Fill the rectangle with the **C = 70, M = 15, Y = 0, K = 0** color swatch and remove the stroke if necessary.

6. Send the blue sky rectangle to the back.

7. Select the group of spirals and change the stroke to white. Your illustration should resemble Illustration A.

8. Save your changes, close the file, and exit Illustrator.

Illustration A

ON YOUR OWN

1. Start Adobe Illustrator.
2. Open ⌨ OIL06_*xx* or 💿OYO07.
3. Save the file as OIL07_*xx*.
4. Select the outer red circle and the red diagonal line.
5. Group these objects and then send the grouped object to the back.
6. Select the two click wheel circles and make sure they are aligned using the Vertical Align Center option. Group the two circles.

7. With the click wheel group still selected, add the player body and the display area to the selection border and group all selected items.

   ✓ *Hold Shift and click the player body and then the display area.*

8. Switch to Outline view to see all objects as outlines.
9. Switch back to Preview mode. Send the grouped player body to the back.
10. Save your changes, close the file, and exit Illustrator.

Skills Covered

- **Work with Multiple Artboards**
- **Resize Objects**
- **Use Cutting Tools**

- **Reshape Objects**
- **Rotate Objects**
- **Insert Text**

Software Skills   You can add multiple artboards to a document to work on more than one illustration at a time in the same document. In the course of editing an illustration, objects may need to be resized, reshaped, or rotated. Use cutting tools to divide objects into parts. Use the Type tool to add text to an illustration.

Design Skills   Even simple designs can require a designer to manipulate objects in many ways. Cutting and reshaping tools, for example, can be used to transform simple shapes into more complex shapes that would be difficult or impossible to draw. Text is often a part of an illustration, and a designer needs to understand how to select appropriate type formats and add text to a design.

Application Skills   In this exercise, you will continue to work on the Richmond Parks illustration. You will create a crescent moon from half of an ellipse and rotate objects to finish the gazebo. You will add text to the drawing, and then you will add new artboards to the illustration to create a program cover and a postcard for the play to be held in the park.

TERMS

Font   A design of type.

Font style   Appearance changes to a font such as **bold** or *italic*.

Point of origin   The point on which an object rotates or transforms. The point of origin may be within the object or outside it.

NOTES

Work with Multiple Artboards

- Illustrator allows you to add multiple artboards to an illustration. Each artboard represents a printable area that you can specify when you output the job.

    ✓ *You can also specify the desired artboard when importing Illustrator documents into InDesign.*

- Figure 8-1 shows a workspace with three artboards. Each artboard can be separately selected and the size adjusted by dragging handles. Note that each artboard is numbered in the upper-left corner.

- Multiple artboards allow you to prepare several different illustrations in the same document.

- In Figure 8-1, for example, a designer might create a full-page size illustration in artboard 01, move several of the illustration's elements to the envelope-sized artboard 02, and create yet another version of the illustration on the postcard-sized artboard 03. All three illustrations can be output at the same time with one command.

- You can insert an artboard within an artboard to create a crop area to output only a portion of an illustration.

- Working with multiple artboards can save a great deal of time and ensure consistency among versions of an illustration.

Figure 8-1. Multiple artboards in a document

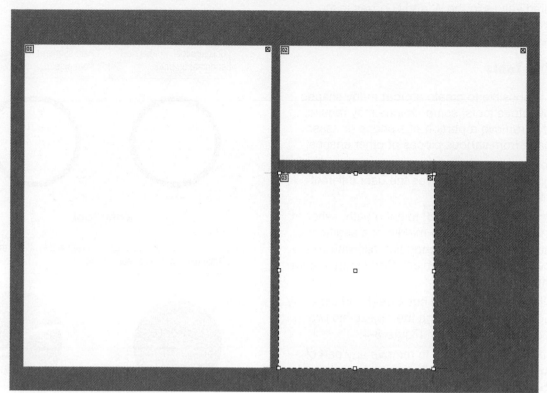

- Illustrator CS5 introduces the Artboards panel (Figure 8-2) that you can use to work with artboards.

Figure 8-2. Artboards panel

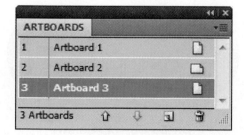

- Each artboard is listed with a thumbnail of the artboard shape. Click the artboard name to make that artboard active.

- Use the tools at the bottom of the panel to adjust the order of an artboard in the list (adjusting order also changes the artboard number), add a new artboard, or delete a selected artboard.

- You can choose to apply Illustrator's rulers to your artboards so that you are always starting from 0 at the upper-left corner of the currently selected artboard. Select View > Rulers > Change to Artboard Rulers to use artboard rulers, or View > Rulers > Change to Global Rulers to switch back to rulers that start at the upper-left corner of the document, regardless of which artboard is active.

Resize Objects

- Objects very often need to be resized in the course of creating an illustration.

- The easiest way to resize an object is to drag a selection handle on the object or its bounding box using the Selection tool.

- When you position the Selection tool over a handle, the pointer becomes a double-pointed arrow.

- Hold down the mouse button and drag in the direction to resize, as shown in Figure 8-3. Illustrator displays a light blue outline during the resize process to help you visualize the object's new size.

Figure 8-3. Resize an object

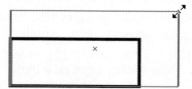

- Dragging a side or top or bottom handle resizes in one direction only. To maintain the original proportions of the object, drag a corner handle or hold down Shift while dragging.

- To resize an object to precise measurements, type the desired values in the W and H boxes in the Transform panel. Or, watch the Smart Guides measurement label as you drag a corner.

Use Cutting Tools

- While it is possible to create a great many shapes from Illustrator's tools, some shapes may require the user to remove a portion of a shape or assemble a shape from various pieces of other shapes.
- Illustrator's cutting tools make it easy to cut objects into segments. Each tool gives the user different options for cutting:
  - Use the Scissors tool ✂ to cut a path, either at an anchor point or in the middle of a segment. The tool creates a new endpoint, allowing you to remove portions of the object. See Figure 8-4 for a sample result.
  - Use the Knife tool 🔪 to cut a freehand path through an object, dividing the object into two filled objects as shown in Figure 8-4.
  - Use the Eraser tool 🧽 to remove any part of an object or a drawing. When you erase through an object, Illustrator creates filled, stroked objects from the portions that are left, as shown in Figure 8-4. If you select the object before erasing on it, you will erase only that object, allowing any objects below to show through. If you do not select an object before erasing, the Eraser tool erases all the way down to the artboard.
- Illustrator also offers a menu command for cutting objects. The Object > Path > Divide Objects Below command uses an object on top of another object as a guide to cut the object below.
- A line across a circle, for example, can be used to cut the circle into two parts, as shown in Figure 8-4. The line object is eliminated during this process.

Reshape Objects

- You may need to change the actual shape of an existing object, as opposed to simply resizing it.
- To reshape an object, you can drag individual anchor points along the object's path.
- Use the Direct Selection tool ➤ to select and modify a single anchor point on a path.
- If you click anywhere on the path with the Direct Selection tool, you select the entire object the same way as with the Selection tool.
- To select only a single point, deselect the object and then use the Direct Selection pointer to locate the anchor point. When the pointer is over an anchor point, a hollow square appears at the right of the pointer.

Figure 8-4. Ways to cut objects into sections

Scissors tool

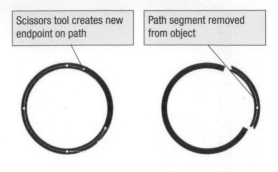

Scissors tool creates new endpoint on path

Path segment removed from object

Knife tool

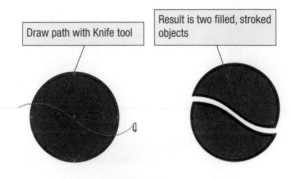

Draw path with Knife tool

Result is two filled, stroked objects

Eraser tool

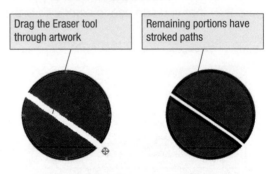

Drag the Eraser tool through artwork

Remaining portions have stroked paths

Divide Objects Below

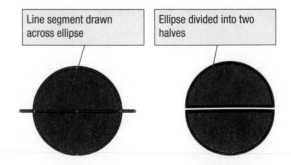

Line segment drawn across ellipse

Ellipse divided into two halves

✓ *If Smart Guides are active, a green anchor label displays when the pointer is over the anchor.*

■ You can add anchor points to a path if necessary to provide more options for reshaping an object.

■ Use the Object > Path > Add Anchor Points menu command to add points halfway between the object's default anchor points.

 ✓ *You will learn in a later exercise how to add anchor points anywhere on a path using the Add Anchor Point tool on the menu beneath the Pen tool.*

■ You can also add a point anywhere on a path using the Reshape tool, located on the toolbar beneath the Scale tool.

■ Dragging an ordinary anchor point on a straight path with the Direct Selection tool maintains straight lines from the selected anchor point to other anchor points (see Figure 8-5, left).

■ Dragging an anchor point inserted with the Reshape tool on a straight path allows the path to curve away from the selected anchor point (see Figure 8-5, right).

Figure 8-5. Dragging a single point

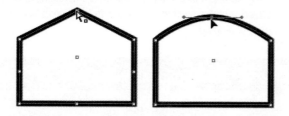

 ✓ *The small lines extending from the point in the right illustration are called direction handles. You will learn more about reshaping objects using direction handles in Lesson 2, Exercise 15.*

Rotate Objects

■ You often need to rotate objects in a drawing to present them in the desired orientation.

■ As with most Illustrator features, there are a number of ways to rotate an object. The simplest is to position the Selection tool near any selection handle of a selected object.

■ The pointer changes shape to the rotate pointer. Hold down the mouse button and drag the pointer up or down to rotate the object, as shown in Figure 8-6.

■ By default, the object rotates around its center point, no matter which corner you use to start the rotation.

 ✓ *Hold down the Shift key while rotating to rotate in increments of 45°.*

Figure 8-6. Rotate an object using the pointer

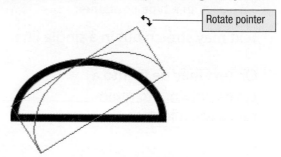

Rotate pointer

■ You can also use the Rotate tool on the Tools panel to rotate an object. Clicking the tool when an object is selected places the **point of origin** in the center of the object by default. Use the pointer to drag the object around the point of origin.

■ You can click with the Rotate tool to set the point of origin outside an object if desired for a different type of rotation effect and also use the Rotate dialog box to set a precise degree of rotation. Figure 8-7 shows an object rotating around a point of origin that is not in the center of the object.

Figure 8-7. Rotating around a point of origin

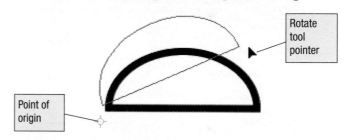

Rotate tool pointer

Point of origin

Insert Text

■ Illustrations often require text to complete the drawing. The text may be a company name, one or more labels to identify portions of the drawing, or even columns of informational text.

■ Use the Type tool to insert text in an illustration.

 ✓ *Beneath the Type tool is a toolbar that offers some other Type tool options, such as the Area Type tool, the Type on a Path tool, and the Vertical Type tool. You will work with some of these tools later in the course.*

■ You have two options for inserting text with the Type tool:

 ● Click to place an insertion point (a blinking vertical line) and begin typing. Text entered this way will appear on one line that is as long as the text (see Figure 8-8).

 ● Drag with the Type tool to create a type container. Text inserted in the container stays inside the container's border (see Figure 8-8).

Figure 8-8. Insert text in a line or in a type container

Text may stretch out in a single line.

Or, text may be fit into a
type container to main-
tain a specific shape.

- Text inserted with the Type tool uses a default **font**, Myriad Pro. When the Type tool is active, you can choose a new font by clicking the Font list arrow on the Control panel to display available fonts and then selecting one.

- Figure 8-9 shows the Font list displayed and the other character formatting options on the Control panel.

  ✓ *You can also use the Type > Font command to see available fonts or use the Character panel. You will work with the Character panel in the InDesign section of the course.*

Figure 8-9. Font list

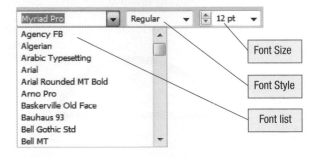

- Fonts are measured in points. A font size of 12 points will be 12 points from the top of the tallest letter to its base.

- To change font size, click the Font Size list arrow on the Control panel (see Figure 8-9) to display a list of sizes from which to choose, or type the desired font size in the Font Size box.

  ✓ *You can also choose the Type > Size menu command to display a pop-out menu of sizes.*

- **Font styles** are appearance changes such as bold-face or italics applied to a font. Use font styles to add emphasis to type.

- Apply a font style by clicking the Font Style list arrow on the Control panel (see Figure 8-9) to see a list of font styles supported for the current font.

- The Control panel also offers three paragraph alignment options for left aligning, centering, or right-aligning text within the text bounding box.

- A type object may be selected like any other Illustrator object using the Selection tool. Select a type object if you want to move it to a new location.

- To select the text itself, use the Type tool to click in the text, or double-click the text. This places an insertion point in the text, just like the one in a word processing program.

- With the insertion point in place in the text, use the Backspace or Delete key to remove text, or type to insert new text.

- Type objects have stroke and fill like other Illustrator objects. By default, the stroke is set to None. To change the text color, select a new swatch color or create a color in the Color panel.

  ✓ *Select different stroke and fill colors for interesting special effects, but use such effects only with large point sizes for ease of reading.*

Design Suite Integration

Working with Type

Illustrator, Photoshop, and InDesign all offer character and paragraph formatting options on the Control panel as well as on the Character and Paragraph panels. You will work extensively with type in the InDesign section of this course.

PROCEDURES

Work with Multiple Artboards

To insert more than one artboard:

When creating a new illustration:

1. In New Document dialog box, click **Number of Artboards** .... `ALT` + `M`
2. Type the desired number of artboards, or use the spin arrows to select the desired number.
3. Select the desired layout for the artboards and make any other selections in the dialog box.
4. Click **OK** .... `ENTER`

Add an artboard to an existing illustration:

1. Click **Artboard** tool `□` in Tools panel .... `SHIFT` + `O`
2. Scroll in the workspace to the point where the new artboard should appear.
3. Use the Artboard tool to draw the artboard the desired size.

To work with existing artboards:

1. Click **Artboard** tool `□` in Tools panel .... `SHIFT` + `O`
2. Click on any artboard to select it.
3. Modify the artboard as desired:
   - Resize the artboard by dragging handles.
   - Move the artboard by dragging with the four-headed arrow.
   - Change artboard options by double-clicking on the Artboard tool to open the Artboard Options dialog box.
   - Delete the artboard by pressing `DEL`.

To return to Preview view:

Press `ESC` to restore normal view.

To work with the Artboards panel:

1. Click **Window** .... `ALT` + `W`
2. Click **Artboards**.
3. Use the panel tools:
   - Click an artboard name to activate that artboard.
   - Click the **Move Up** `⇧` or **Move Down** `⇩` button to rearrange artboard order.
   - Click the **New Artboard** button `⊡` to insert a new artboard.
   - Click the **Delete Artboard** button `🗑` to remove the selected artboard.

Resize Objects

1. Select object to resize with **Selection** tool `▶`.
2. Position Selection tool pointer on corner or side selection handle.
3. Drag inward or outward to resize.
4. Press `SHIFT` to maintain original proportions of height to width.

   OR

1. Select the existing measurement in the W box on the Control panel or in the Transform panel.
2. Type a new value and press `ENTER`.
3. Select the existing measurement in the H box.
4. Type a new value and press `ENTER`.

Use the Scissors Tool

1. Select **Scissors** tool `✂` from toolbar beneath Eraser tool .... `C`
2. Position tool directly on path and click to cut path.

3. Use Selection tool to drag cut object apart.

Use the Knife Tool

1. Select **Knife** tool `🔪` from toolbar beneath Eraser tool.
2. Drag crosshair across object to cut.
3. Use Selection tool to drag cut objects apart.

Use the Eraser Tool

1. Select **Eraser** tool `✐` .... `SHIFT` + `E`
2. Drag eraser pointer across object to erase.

Use Divide Objects Below

1. Draw first object, the object that will be cut.
2. Draw object to use as pattern for cut on top of first object.
3. Select top object.
4. Click **Object** .... `ALT` + `O`
5. Point to **Path** .... `P`
6. Click **Divide Objects Below** .... `D`

Use Direct Selection Tool

1. Select **Direct Selection** tool `▶` .... `A`
2. Move Direct Selection pointer near anchor point of unselected object until pointer displays hollow square to right: `▶□`
3. Click to select single anchor point.
4. Drag anchor point to reshape path.

Add Anchor Points

1. Select object to add anchor points to.
2. Click **Object** .... `ALT` + `O`
3. Point to **Path** .... `P`
4. Click **Add Anchor Points** ... `A`

Use Reshape Tool

1. Select **Reshape** tool 🖾 from toolbar beneath Scale tool.
2. Click on path of object to insert reshape anchor point.
3. Deselect the path by clicking outside it.
4. Use Direct Selection tool to point at the reshape anchor point, then drag reshape anchor point to reshape path.

Rotate Objects

1. Select object to rotate.
2. Position Selection tool pointer near any selection handle so the pointer changes to the rotate pointer.
3. Drag the pointer up or down to rotate object.

   ✓ *Hold down the Shift key to rotate in 45° increments.*

   OR

1. Select object to rotate.
2. Select **Rotate** tool 🔄 .... R
3. Drag pointer to rotate object.

   OR

1. Select object to rotate.
2. Select **Rotate** tool 🔄 .... R
3. Click to set the rotate origin.
4. Drag pointer to rotate object.

Insert Text

1. Select **Type** tool T .... T
2. Click at desired location to place insertion point and begin typing.

   OR

   Drag Type tool I-beam to create type container to hold text and begin typing.

To move a type object:

1. Select type object with Selection tool.
2. Drag the object to a new location.

Apply Character Formats to Text

   ✓ *If desired, select character formats before creating text object.*

To change font:

1. Select type object.
2. Click Font list arrow on Control panel.
3. Select desired font from list.

   OR

1. Select type object.
2. Click **Type** .... ALT + T
3. Click **Font** .... F
4. Select desired font, or click list arrow until desired font is shown on menu.

To change font size:

1. Select type object.
2. Click Font Size list arrow on Control panel.
3. Select desired size from list.

   OR

   Click up or down spin arrow to change font size by 1 point increments.

   OR

   Type desired font size in Font Size box.

   OR

1. Select type object.
2. Click **Type** .... ALT + T
3. Click **Size** .... Z
4. Select desired size from pop-out menu.

To change font style:

1. Select type object.
2. Click Font Style list arrow on Control panel.
3. Select desired font style from list.

   ✓ *Available font styles vary by font.*

EXERCISE DIRECTIONS

   ✓ *Display the Painting workspace after you start Illustrator.*

1. Start Illustrator and open 🖾07Park_xx or open 💿08Park.
2. Save the file as 08Park_xx.

Complete the Gazebo

1. Ungroup the three gazebo columns and copy one of the columns. Paste the copy and then drag it to the scratch area to the right of the illustration. Group the columns again.
2. Rotate the column in the scratch area 90° so that it is horizontal rather than vertical.

   ✓ *Hold down the Shift key while rotating.*

3. Drag the horizontal column to the top of the three vertical columns.

   ✓ *If the vertical columns are too far apart to allow for an overlap as shown in Illustration A, ungroup the columns and move them closer together, then regroup them.*

4. Specify default fill and stroke. In the scratch area to the right of the illustration, create an ellipse that is **80** pts wide and high.

   ✓ *Remember, select the tool and then click in the work area to display the dialog box to set precise measurements.*

5. With the ellipse still selected, use the Line Segment tool to draw a straight horizontal line through the middle of the ellipse.

   ✓ *Position the Line Segment crosshair on the left-most anchor point and hold Shift while you drag the crosshair to the other side of the ellipse.*

6. Select the line segment, if necessary, and use the Divide Objects Below command to cut the ellipse into two halves.

7. Deselect the object, then use the Selection tool to drag the bottom ellipse half down from the top ellipse half.

8. Drag the top ellipse half to perch on top of the gazebo, like a dome. Remove the stroke.

9. Select all three gazebo objects and use the Horizontal Align Center alignment option to make sure they are centered on each other. Group the objects that make up the gazebo.

Add the Moon Object

1. Select the bottom ellipse half in the scratch area. Use the Reshape tool to add an anchor point to the center of the half ellipse's straight line.

2. Deselect the object. Use the Direct Selection tool to click the reshape anchor point and drag it downward to create a crescent shape.

   ✓ *With the shape deselected, you will not be able to see exactly where the reshape point is. Move the Direct Selection tool near where you think the point is. When the dark square attached to the pointer becomes hollow, you are in the right place.*

3. Deselect the object, and then select it again using the Selection tool. Rotate the crescent 90° so it stands straight up.

4. Drag the moon into the sky as shown in Illustration A. Remove the object's stroke and fill the object with a very pale yellow that you create using the Color panel.

Add Type and Final Touches

1. Using the Type tool, click to the right of the three stars in the bank object to place the insertion point.

2. Type **Stars in the Park Presents**.

3. Select the text with the Type tool and change the font to **Times New Roman**, the font style to **Bold**, and the font size to **18**.

4. Reposition the type object if necessary (see Illustration A) and change the fill color to white.

5. Use the Type tool to draw a type container the same height as the crescent moon and as wide as the space between the moon and the edge of the artboard. Type **AUTUMN MOON**, and then change the fill color to white and the font size to **40** pt. Apply bold font style if necessary. Adjust the position of the moon and the size of the type container if necessary so the word *Autumn* fits on one line.

6. Select the tree leaves object, and then use the Eraser tool to erase areas around the edges of the object to give it a more random, rough look, as in Illustration A.

Add an Artboard and Create the Program Cover

1. Add a new artboard to the right of the existing artboard that is **792** pts wide by **612** pts high. (You will use this artboard for the program cover.) Then add another new artboard below artboard 2 that is **430** pts wide by **300** pts high. (You will use this artboard to create a postcard.)

2. Return to Preview view and display the Artboards panel. Select Artboard 1 to activate it, and then select the sky, mountains, lawn, lake, and bank objects. Hold down Alt and drag the selected objects to Artboard 2. Place the selected objects so the top edge of the sky aligns with the top edge of the new artboard.

3. Working carefully, select each object you copied to Artboard 2 and resize it to fit the wider artboard. For the sky, mountains, lawn, and bank objects, drag the left side handle of each object to the left edge of the artboard. Then resize the lake object to fill in the gap caused by resizing the bank object.

4. Select the clouds group, the moon, the *AUTUMN MOON* text, the cattails group, and the gazebo group and drag a copy to Artboard 2.

5. Group all tree objects and drag a copy of the tree to Artboard 2.

6. You have decided not to create the postcard. Use the Artboards panel to delete Artboard 3.

7. Save your changes, close the file, and exit Illustrator.

ON YOUR OWN

1. Start Adobe Illustrator and open OIL07_*xx* or open OYO08.

2. Save the file as OIL08_*xx*.

3. Select the MP3 player group and drag to resize it so it is about **240** pts wide by **400** pts high.

   ✓ *Use the Transform panel to check your measurements.*

4. Resize the circle and diagonal line to enlarge it about the same amount. Recenter the circle over the MP3 player.

5. Rotate the circle object to change the angle of the diagonal line.

6. Remove the strokes from the click wheel circles.

7. Use the Type tool to add the following text to the illustration at a location you choose: **MP3 Free Zone!**

8. Format the text as desired with a new font, font style, and size.

9. Your illustration should resemble Illustration B. Save your changes, close the file, and exit Illustrator.

Illustration B

60

Exercise | 9

Summary Exercise

Application Skills You have been asked to create an illustration to encourage people to vote for a city-wide proposition. In this exercise, you will use basic Illustrator tools and techniques to create the drawing.

EXERCISE DIRECTIONS

✓ *Display the Painting workspace after you start Illustrator.*

1. Start Illustrator and open a new default print document.

2. Save the file as 09Vote_xx. Display the grid and turn on Smart Guides if necessary. Change the zoom setting to 150%.

Draw the Ballot

1. Beginning at the intersection of any two heavy grid lines, draw a square **144** pts wide and high.

2. Locate the center of the square, and then draw another square from that center outward. Make the square **163** pts wide and high.

3. Send the new square to the back to create a border effect as shown in Illustration A. Deselect the square if necessary.

4. Select the Paintbrush tool, select the Chalk – Scribble option in the Brushes panel, and change the stroke weight to **0.5** pt.

5. With the Paintbrush, draw an *X* in the ballot box as shown in Illustration A.

Create the Pencil

1. Restore the stroke weight to 1 pt. With the Rectangle tool, draw a rectangle that is three small blocks wide by three large blocks high (about 27 pts by 216 pts).

2. Immediately to the right of the rectangle you just drew, draw another rectangle the same height and one small square wide. This will be the right side of the pencil.

3. Drag a copy of the side object to the other side of the central rectangle, holding down Alt and Shift as you drag.

4. Draw a rounded rectangle **45** pts wide by **39** pts high, and then move this object to the bottom of the pencil object to represent the eraser.

5. Draw a rectangle **45** pts wide by **12** pts high, and then move this object to overlap both the eraser and the bottom of the pencil. This is the metal band that holds the eraser to the pencil.

6. Draw a triangle with the apex pointing straight up and resize it to be **43** pts wide by **40** pts high. Move this object on top of the pencil object to represent its point. Adjust the width of the triangle as necessary to be as wide as the three rectangles that make up the pencil object.

7. Select the pencil point, the center of the pencil, the metal band object, and the eraser and use Horizontal Align Center to make sure they are all centered on one another.

8. Create another triangle about **12** pts high and move it into place at the top of the pencil point to represent the pencil lead.

9. Add colors as follows:
   a. Fill all three sides of the pencil with the **C = 0, M = 35, Y = 85, K = 0** swatch.
   b. Select the two narrow pencil side objects and change the black setting to **12**.
   c. Select the metal band object and fill with **C = 0, M = 0, Y = 0, K = 40**.
   d. Select the eraser object and fill with **C = 0, M = 34, Y = 30, K = 12**.
   e. Select the pencil point object and fill with **C = 25, M = 40, Y = 65, K = 0**.
   f. Fill the pencil lead with black.

10. Group all objects that make up the pencil.

11. Rotate and position the pencil as shown in Illustration A.

Add the Type

1. Use the Type tool to add the text **VOTE YES ON 12** to the illustration, to the right of the ballot.

2. Change the font to **36** pt Cooper Black (or another font of your choice) and change its color if desired.

3. Turn off the grid. Select and group all objects and move them to the center of the artboard. Your drawing should resemble Illustration A.

4. Save your changes, close the file, and exit Illustrator.

Illustration A

Exercise | 10

Application Exercise

Application Skills The Wood Duck architectural salvage firm has asked you to create a drawing of a vintage wooden door (a popular salvage item) that the firm can use in various types of advertising materials. In this exercise, you will create the door using Illustrator tools and features.

EXERCISE DIRECTIONS

✓ *Display the Painting workspace after you start Illustrator.*

1. Start a new default print illustration, specifying 2 artboards.

2. Save the new file as **10Door_xx**. Turn on Smart Guides if necessary. Change the zoom to 100%, display the Artboards panel, and select Artboard 1 to move it into the center of the workspace.

3. Begin by drawing a rectangle for the door frame **288** pts wide by **612** pts high. Fill the rectangle with **C = 0, M = 2, Y = 28, K = 0** and remove its stroke. Use the Transform panel to position the rectangle so that its upper-left corner is at **X = 144, Y = 72**.

   ✓ *Change the reference point in the Transform panel to see the X and Y settings for the upper-left corner.*

4. Display the Info panel if necessary. Switch to Outline mode so you can insert the door panels. Choose to insert another rectangle, and begin drawing at about **X = 189, Y = 126**. Draw the rectangle **199** pts wide by **255** pts high. Adjust settings as necessary after you draw to position and size the object as indicated. This is the top panel of the door.

5. Draw another panel rectangle **81** pts wide by **162** pts high and position it so the upper-left corner is at **X = 189, Y = 450**.

6. Copy the second panel and move the copy so its top left corner is at **X = 306, Y = 450**.

7. Create depth for the panels as follows:

   a. Select the top panel and then use the Line Segment tool to draw a line from the upper-right corner to the lower-left corner.

   b. Use Divide Objects Below to cut the panel in half diagonally.

   c. Select the left half of the diagonal and fill the object with **C = 6, M = 9, Y = 28, K = 15**. Switch to Preview mode to see this fill.

   d. Select the right half of the diagonal and fill the object with **C = 0, M = 0, Y = 20, K = 5**.

   e. Draw another rectangle on top of the divided rectangle that is **182** pts wide by **237** pts high, centered on the divided rectangle. Fill with **C = 0, M = 0, Y = 15, K = 0**. The panel now has the appearance of beveled edges, as shown in Illustration A.

   f. Follow steps 7a through 7e for the other two panels. Work in Outline mode so you can see the door panels, then switch to Preview mode to make the fine adjustments to position. Make sure when creating the overlapping panel for the two smaller panels at the bottom of the door that the upper-right and lower-left corners intersect with the dividing line, as shown in Illustration A. The overlapping panel should be about **73** pts wide by **150** pts high.

8. Group all door objects.

9. Create doorknob objects as follows:

   a. Draw a rounded rectangle about **34** pts wide by **80** pts high, controlling the round corners as you draw so they are not too rounded.

   b. Fill this object with the **C = 25, M = 25, Y = 40, K = 0** swatch and position it as shown in Illustration A.

c. Draw an ellipse centered on this rounded rectangle slightly less wide than the rounded rectangle and fill it with the Super Soft Black Vignette swatch in the Swatches panel.

d. Group these two objects and then add them to the door group.

10. Select Artboard 2 in the Artboards panel. On the Artboards panel menu, select Artboards Options.

11. Change the Preset to B5 to create stationery for the Wood Duck.

12. Copy the door object from Artboard 1, paste it, and then resize it to **100** pts wide by about **214** pts high. Position the image in the upper-left corner of Artboard 2, allowing a reasonable margin above and to the left.

13. Insert the following text to the right of the door:

The Wood Duck

Architectural Salvage

500 Gilbert Avenue

Eden Hills, OH 45218

14. Format the text as desired.

15. Save your changes, close the file, and exit Illustrator.

Illustration A

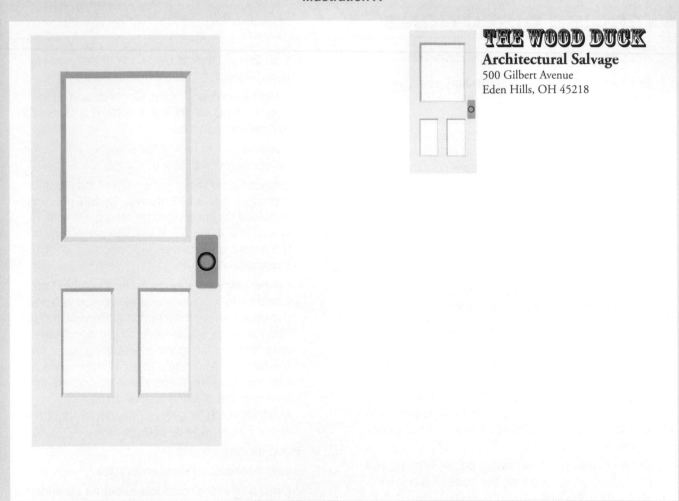

Exercise | 11

Curriculum Integration

Application Skills   You have been asked to develop the graphics to be used for an interactive animation on a math help Web site. The animation will display circle features such as radius or diameter when the user clicks a button. In this exercise, you will create the circle, the parts of the circle, labels for each part, and the buttons that will be used in the animation. Before you begin this exercise, refresh your memory about these parts of a circle:

- Radius

- Diameter

- Chord

- Arc

EXERCISE DIRECTIONS

Start a new Web document and save it as 11Circle_xx.

Draw a circle and adjust the stroke weight if desired. Make sure the circle is large enough to display each labeled part clearly.

Create a small circle (about the size of a bullet symbol or a large period) in a color that contrasts well with the circle stroke color to be used to indicate points on the circle. Place a point in the center of the larger circle and label this point as *O*.

Draw the radius, diameter, and chord using straight lines. The lines should be a color that contrasts with the circle stroke color. Place points at both ends of each line. Add letter labels for the end points of each line.

Label the radius, diameter, and chord with a type object just above the line telling what it is. Rotate each line's type object to match the orientation of the line. Choose a contrasting color for the labels. Illustration A shows a sample you can use as a guide.

Create the arc by cutting the circle path in two places using the Scissors tool. Select the portion of the path between the two anchors where you cut, copy the segment, and paste it in front. Change the stroke color of the pasted object to show the arc segment. Add points and labels as for the other circle parts.

Below the circle, create a row of four buttons. Use your own judgment about shape, size, and color. The buttons should all be the same size, and the size should be large enough to fit the longest button label, *Diameter*.

Type the four labels—Radius, Diameter, Chord, and Arc—and move the labels into the buttons. Change type color if desired, and then group the buttons and text. Adjust the spacing and alignment of the buttons as necessary.

Save your changes, close the document, and exit Illustrator.

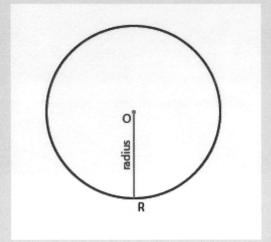

Portfolio Builder

Application Skills   A local elementary school has asked you to prepare an illustration to be used in their Safety Star campaign. In this exercise, you create a number of objects to help children be alert to traffic signals that can help to keep them safe.

EXERCISE DIRECTIONS

- Start a new document and save it as 12Safety_xx.
- First create a traffic light: Draw a rectangle large enough to include three signal lights. Reshape the top of the traffic light to round it upwards. Use three perfect circles for the signal lights and fill them with red, amber, and green. Align and distribute the signal lights within the traffic light body. Fill the traffic light body with an appropriate color.
- Create a stop sign: Use the Polygon tool to draw an eight-sided object, filled with red and with a heavy white stroke. Add the text **STOP** within the object.
- Create the don't walk light: Use a rounded rectangle with a gray fill to represent the walk/don't walk light. Add a slightly larger rounded rectangle above it with a darker fill and send it behind the first rounded rectangle. Center the two objects on each other. Add a type object that reads **DON'T** and another one that reads **WALK**. Stack these two type objects and adjust size to fill the front rounded rectangle. Center the type objects in the rounded rectangle, group them, and apply a red fill and a yellow stroke.
- Draw a large blue star that overlays the objects and send it to the back to provide a dark background for the white stroke around the stop sign.
- Adjust all objects to create a pleasant appearance. Illustration A shows a sample of the way you might create and arrange the objects.
- Save the illustration, close it, and exit Illustrator.

Lesson | 2

Work with Paths and Layers

Skills Covered

- Modify Stroke Attributes
- Use the Width Tool
- Copy Attributes with Eyedropper Tool
- Direct Selection Tool Techniques

Software Skills   Apply stroke formats such as dashes or variable width profiles to modify the appearance of a path. The Width tool allows you to adjust the width of a path at an anchor point. Formats can easily be applied to other objects using the Eyedropper tool. Use the Direct Selection tool for a variety of editing chores, such as selecting and moving a single anchor point or line segment.

Design Skills   Creating an illustration is not merely a matter of drawing objects. A designer also needs to know skills for manipulating objects by adjusting attributes and even individual anchor points. Skills such as copying attributes with the Eyedropper and working with the Direct Selection tool allow a designer to work smarter rather than harder.

Application Skills   In this exercise, you will begin an illustration of picnic foods for a local deli. You will apply formats to paths, adjust stroke width using the new Width tool, and use the Eyedropper to copy attributes. You will use the Direct Selection tool to modify points and line segments to create a piece of layer cake.

TERMS

Attributes   Properties of an object that change its appearance without changing its underlying structure.

NOTES

Modify Stroke Attributes

- The formats that create an object's appearance are called **attributes**. Attributes are properties that change appearance (such as stroke weight) without changing underlying structure.

- You have already learned in this course how to change one stroke attribute, stroke weight. Illustrator offers a number of other stroke attributes available on the expanded Stroke panel, shown in Figure 13-1. Some of these options, such as the dash alignment options, arrowheads, and variable width profiles, are new in Illustrator CS5.

Figure 13-1. Expanded Stroke panel

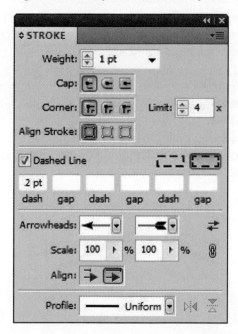

- The Stroke panel is divided into sections of options.
  - The top section lets you set stroke weight, select a cap option to control the appearance of path endings, choose a style for the appearance of a path at a corner, and control where the stroke sits with relation to an object's path: divided across the path or aligned to the inside or outside of the path.
  - The second section lets you apply dash formatting to a path. You can create a custom dashed line by specifying lengths for dashes and for the gaps between dashes. You can also choose to adjust the dashed line so that corners or line endings do not fall in a gap and disappear.
  - The third section offers the option of applying arrowheads of various types to paths, a feature new in Illustrator CS5. Select an appearance for

the start and/or end of the path. You can also adjust the scale of the arrowhead objects and choose whether to extend them beyond the path or include them in the path length.

  - The last section of the Stroke panel lets you choose a profile for a path.

- Click the Variable Width Profile down arrow in the Profile section to display a selection of width profiles that can add graphic interest to a path. Figure 13-2 shows a series of paths with the Uniform setting (top) and several variable width options applied to the paths below.

Figure 13-2. Variable width profiles applied to paths

✔ *The Variable Width Profile options can also be accessed from the Control panel.*

- If the profile has an uneven pattern along the path (such as the third and fourth profiles in Figure 13-2), you can use the Flip Along button ▷◁ in the Stroke panel to reverse the profile along the path. The Flip Across button ☒ lets you flip a profile that curves above the path so it curves below it.

✔ *You can create your own profiles and then save them so you can easily apply them again.*

Use the Width Tool

- The Width tool ✎ is new in Illustrator CS5. This tool allows you to adjust the width of a path by dragging a point on the path.

- Click on the path with the Width tool at the point you want to expand the path width. This action sets a width point. Then simply drag to adjust the width, as shown in Figure 13-3.

Figure 13-3. Use the Width tool to adjust path width

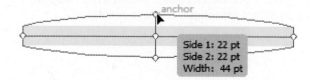

- You can adjust the width at a specific width point by double-clicking the width point with the Width tool. The Width Point Edit dialog box lets you adjust the width on each side of the point, so you can if desired set more width on one side than the other.

- You can use the Width tool on any path created with the Line Segment tool, Pencil tool, and shape tools such as Rectangle or Star. Not all brush paths can be adjusted, however, and nor can Pen paths.

✔ *You work with Pen paths and brushes later in this lesson.*

Copy Attributes with Eyedropper Tool

- Illustrator offers a handy tool for copying attributes from one object to another: the Eyedropper tool.

- Use the Eyedropper tool  to copy attributes from an unselected object to the currently selected object.

- For example, clicking the Eyedropper tool on the left square in Figure 13-4 will copy all stroke and fill attributes from the unselected square to the selected circle on the right.

Figure 13-4. Copy attributes with Eyedropper

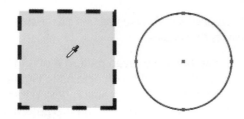

- Besides copying fill and stroke attributes, the Eyedropper tool will copy type attributes such as font and size.

Direct Selection Tool Techniques

- As you learned in Exercise 8, a designer can use the Direct Selection tool to select a single point on a path. This tool can be a great help in creating and modifying objects because it gives you considerable control over an object's shape.

- When you select a single point on a path with the Direct Selection tool, all subsequent actions affect only that point; the rest of the object's points remain in their original positions.

- Figure 13-5, for example, shows what happens if you select and move a single point.

Figure 13-5. Drag a single point to reshape an object

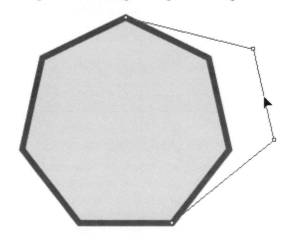

- Moving single anchor points allows you to create many different variations of basic shapes.

- A single selected point may also be deleted by simply pressing Delete or Backspace to create other interesting shapes and effects.

- The Direct Selection tool can also be used to select a single line segment, such as a segment between two anchor points on a pencil path or one side of a rectangle.

- This allows a user to reshape only a portion of an object without affecting the rest of the object's shape, as shown in Figure 13-6.

Figure 13-6. Drag a single line segment

- After clicking on a line segment with the Direct Selection tool to select it, you can delete the line segment by pressing Delete or Backspace.

- To select a single anchor point or line segment, first deselect the object, and then use the Direct Selection tool to select only the desired point or path segment.

PROCEDURES

Use Smooth Tool

1. Select **Smooth** tool from toolbar beneath Pencil tool.
2. Drag Smooth tool over pencil path to smooth path.

Modify Stroke Attributes

To display expanded panel:

- Double-click Stroke panel tab.

  OR

- Click panel menu icon arrow and select **Show Options**.

  OR

- Click **Stroke** link on Control panel.

To select stroke attributes:

In expanded Stroke panel:

- Type or select stroke weight.
- Select **Butt**, **Round**, or **Projecting Cap**.
- Select **Miter Join**, **Round Join**, or **Bevel Join**.
- Click **Align Stroke to Center** to overlap the object path with the stroke.
- Click **Align Stroke to Inside** to move the stroke inside the object path.
- Click **Align Stroke to Outside** to move the stroke outside the object path.

To create a dashed line:

In expanded Stroke panel:

1. Select **Dashed Line** check box.
2. Type value for first line segment length (dash).
3. Press TAB.
4. Type value for first gap.
5. Continue to type dash and gap widths as desired.

6. Select **Preserves exact dash and gap lengths** or **Aligns dashes to corners and path ends** to control dashed line behavior.

To apply an arrowhead to a path:

In expanded Stroke panel:

1. Click the **Click to pick arrowhead to apply to start point of path** down arrow and select the desired arrowhead.
2. Click the **Click to pick arrowhead to apply to end point of path** down arrow and select the desired arrowhead.
3. Adjust arrowhead options if desired:

   - Type a scale percentage to adjust the size of an arrowhead.
   - Select **Extend arrow tip beyond end of path** or **Place arrow tip at end of path** to specify where the arrowhead displays on the path.

To apply a variable width profile to a path:

In expanded Stroke panel or in Control panel

1. Click the **Variable Width Profile** list arrow and select the desired width profile.
2. Adjust the position of the profile relative to the path:

   - Click **Flip Along** to reverse the direction of the profile along the path.
   - Click **Flip Across** to move a profile from one side of the path to the other.

Use the Width Tool

1. With a path selected, select **Width** tool .... SHIFT + W

2. Move the Width tool on the path to the point where you want to adjust width and click to set a width point.
3. Drag to expand the path to the desired width.

To edit a width point:

1. With the Width tool active, double-click the width point to edit.
2. Adjust settings in the Width Point Edit dialog box as desired.
3. Click **OK** .... ENTER

Use the Eyedropper Tool

1. Select object to apply existing attributes to.
2. Select **Eyedropper** tool I
3. Click with Eyedropper on object that has the attributes to be copied.

Select Single Point

1. Deselect object on which you intend to select a point.
2. Select **Direct Selection** tool from Tools panel.
3. Move Direct Selection pointer near anchor point until pointer displays hollow square to right: .
4. Click to select single anchor point.

Select Single Line Segment

1. Deselect object on which you intend to select a line segment.
2. Select **Direct Selection** tool from Tools panel.
3. Click with Direct Selection tool on line segment to select it.

   ✓ *Selecting a line segment also selects the anchor points on either end of the line segment.*

EXERCISE DIRECTIONS

✓ *Display the Painting workspace after you start Illustrator.*

1. Open 🔵 **13Picnic** and save the file as **13Picnic_xx**.
2. Display rulers and turn on Smart Guides if necessary.

Create a Loaf of Bread

1. Use the Hand tool to move the right scratch area into view. Notice that the outline of a loaf of French bread has been provided.
2. Use the Pencil tool to trace around the bread. Tracing allows you to practice using the Pencil tool to draw a freeform shape.
3. Move the loaf of bread you traced onto the artboard. The right side of the bread should be at about **504** on the horizontal ruler. The bottom at the left side should be at about **396** on the vertical ruler.

   ✓ *Notice that a small dotted line displays on the rulers at the position of the insertion point. Use these lines to help position the object. You can also change the Reference Point on the Transform panel and use X and Y boxes to position the object.*

4. Use the Smooth tool to smooth your outline, if necessary, so it looks like the sample in the scratch area.
5. Use the Pencil tool to draw the lines shown in Illustration A.

Illustration A

6. Fill the bread object with the **C = 25, M = 40, Y = 65, K = 0** swatch color.
7. Select the bread outline path, change the stroke weight to **2** pt, and apply **Width Profile 2**. Apply the same stroke settings to the long pencil line along the side of the loaf.

8. Select the first curved line at the top of the bread object. Change the stroke attributes as follows:
   a. Select the Round Cap option.
   b. Create a dashed line by specifying a **12 pt** dash and a **2 pt** gap (you need specify these only once).

      ✓ *The dashed line will give an uneven, "crusty" look to the line.*

   c. Change the fill for the dashed line to the **C = 35, M = 60, Y = 80, K = 25** swatch color.
9. Use the Eyedropper tool to apply the attributes of the first curved line to the other curved lines.
10. Select all bread objects and group them. Deselect the group.
11. In the Stroke panel, select the Butt Cap option and deselect the Dashed Line check box.

    ✓ *If you do not restore defaults in the Stroke panel, all future paths you draw will have the dashed line attributes.*

Create a Piece of Cake

1. Select the brown and yellow objects in the scratch area and move them to position them behind the loaf of bread, as shown in Illustration C. These objects represent the cake and the icing on top and at the back of the cake.
2. Use the Direct Selection tool to select the upper-left corner point of the top brown rectangle and then press Delete or Backspace to delete the point.
3. With the Direct Selection tool, click the upper-right point and drag down and to the left to create the triangular shape shown in Illustration B.

Illustration B

4. Use the Width tool to place a width point at the center of the right side of the triangle (opposite the point of the cake slice). Adjust width at this point to give the back of the cake top a slightly rounded appearance.

5. Use the Pencil tool and a stroke weight of **3** pts to draw three lines across the cake to represent icing between the layers. Set several width points along each line and adjust widths to give an uneven appearance to the icing layers, as shown in Illustration C.

6. Group the cake elements and send the group to the back if necessary. Your illustration should resemble Illustration C.

7. Save your changes, close the file, and exit Illustrator.

Illustration C

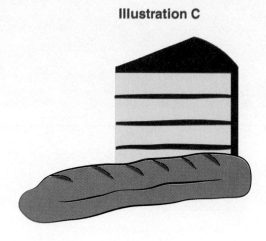

ON YOUR OWN

1. Start Adobe Illustrator and open a new Illustrator document, using default settings.

2. Practice using the tools and features you have learned about in this exercise.

3. You may simply draw shapes or begin creating your own picnic illustration, or try creating an illustration of dessert items such as the slice of cake, cookies, pie, and so on.

4. Draw objects with the Pencil tool and adjust settings to achieve both smooth and "bumpy" paths.

5. Apply various combinations of stroke attributes to paths. Create dashed and dotted paths, and explore how changing stroke offset alignment affects objects. Try the two options for adjusting how dashed paths display at corners and ends of lines.

6. Apply arrowheads to some lines and adjust scale and position of the arrowheads relative to the paths to which they are attached.

7. Use the Direct Selection tool to reshape objects by dragging points and path segments.

8. Try reshaping just one curved segment of an ellipse, for example, or of a pencil path.

9. Close the file without saving and exit Illustrator.

Skills Covered

- **Draw Behind and Draw Inside**
- **Select Objects from Clusters or Groups**
- **Use the Scale Tool**
- **Work in Isolation Mode**

Software Skills   In Illustrator CS5, you can change the drawing mode to draw behind or inside a currently selected object. When items are overlapping or are grouped, you can easily select individual items from the group using several techniques. Use the Scale tool to adjust object size or create a copy of an object at a given size. Isolation mode makes it easy to work on one part of a drawing without affecting other objects.

Design Skills   Use the new drawing modes to shortcut the process of creating objects behind or within existing objects. Group selection techniques make it easy to apply changes to a number of items at once to save time. Understanding how to scale objects allows a designer to adjust sizes while maintaining original proportions.

Application Skills   In this exercise, you continue working on the illustration of picnic foods. You will select objects in a group, construct a glass, and draw an object inside the glass to represent lemonade. You will scale objects to achieve the correct proportions in the drawing and use group selection options to quickly format similar objects.

TERMS

Isolation mode   A view mode that allows you to focus on a group or sublayer by locking and dimming other objects.

Scaling   Resizing an object horizontally, vertically, or proportionally in both directions to a percentage of its original size.

NOTES

Draw Behind and Draw Inside

■ When creating a drawing, you may often find your-self needing to create objects that must appear at different levels in the stack of objects. You have already encountered this situation in Lesson 1, and you learned to use the Arrange commands to move an item to the back of the stack so it does not obscure objects that must display at the front of the stack.

■ Illustrator CS5 gives you another quick way to solve this problem. You can change the drawing mode to Draw Behind and then select the object you want the new object to appear behind. When you draw the new object, it is behind the selected object.

■ Another common workflow may require a designer to place one object inside another object. This can obviously be done by stacking one object on top of another and then grouping the two objects so that they stay together.

■ Illustrator CS5 offers a simpler method. Using the Draw Inside mode, you can draw one object within another. The two objects are linked so they stay together, and each is separately editable.

■ Select the Draw Behind or Draw Inside drawing mode from the Tools panel. If you have expanded the Tools panel, the three drawing modes display as shown in Figure 14-1. Draw Normal is the default drawing mode.

Figure 14-1. Select a drawing mode

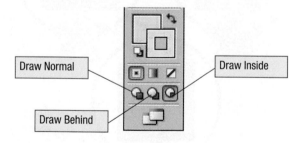

✔ *If you do not have the Tools panel expanded, the drawing modes display on a menu when you click the Draw Normal button.*

■ To draw behind, first select the object behind which your new object should appear. Then draw the new object.

■ To draw inside, first select the object inside which your new object should appear. Illustrator displays a dotted framework at the corners of the selected object to identify it as an object containing another object. (See Figure 14-2.) Then draw the new object inside the selected object.

Figure 14-2. Draw an object inside another object

■ The new object inside the existing object will ini-tially have the same attributes as the existing object, as shown in Figure 14-2. While the object is still selected, you can adjust stroke and fill, or you can select the inside object later with the Direct Selection tool to change its attributes.

Select Objects from Clusters or Groups

■ As you become more familiar with Illustrator and create more complex graphics, you will discover a need to select objects that may be partially (or completely) obscured by other objects, or objects that are parts of groups.

■ You can use the new select behind feature to select an object that is behind other objects. The Group Selection tool makes it easy to select one or more objects that are part of a group.

Use Select Behind

■ In Illustrator CS5, you can now select objects from anywhere in a stack, including objects you cannot see, by using the select behind shortcut of holding down the Ctrl key while clicking the left mouse button.

■ When you use this key combination, the pointer changes to an open arrow with an angle to the side, ▷ᵏ . As you continue to click, you select objects further back in the stack.

■ In Figure 14-3, for example, clicking the select behind pointer will first select the light yellow trian-gle, then the medium yellow triangle, then the light blue triangle, and finally the yellow circle at the bot-tom of the stack.

Figure 14-3. Select behind lets you select objects that are behind other objects

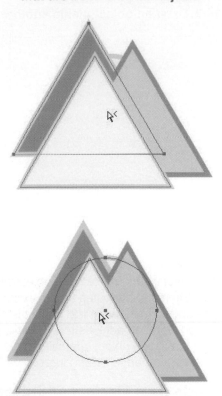

- With an object selected, you can easily make any necessary changes to it, without having to move it out of the stack.

Use the Group Selection Tool

- As you have already learned, objects can be grouped to make them easier to work with. Small groups can in turn be grouped into larger groups, so one object may contain several groups of items.

- In such a situation, it can be tedious to ungroup several times in order to work with a single group or a single item.

- The Group Selection tool ![icon] helps to solve this problem. Use this tool to select a single item from a group.

- In Figure 14-4, for example, the stars have been grouped together, then grouped with the squares, and then all items in the drawing have been grouped. The Group Selection tool makes it possible to select a single star from the grouped object.

Figure 14-4. Select a single item from a grouped object

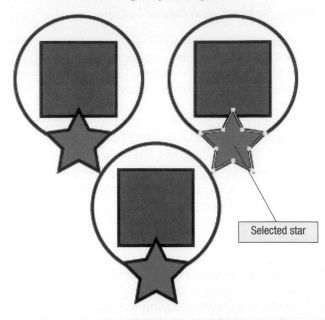

Selected star

- Clicking the Group Selection tool again selects all items grouped with the first item selected, as shown in Figure 14-5.

Figure 14-5. Click again to select group

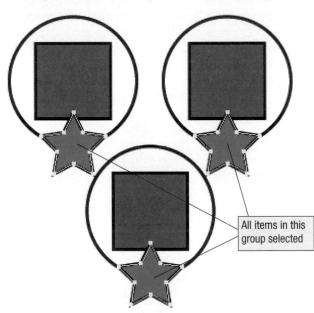

All items in this group selected

- Continue to click the Group Selection tool to select additional grouping levels. For the drawing shown in Figure 14-5, clicking again would select the stars plus the squares, and clicking one more time would select the entire grouped object.

Use the Scale Tool

- **Scaling** is the process of resizing an object to a percentage of its original size. An object may be scaled horizontally, vertically, or proportionally in both directions.

- You have already done simple scaling by dragging the corners of selected objects.

- You can also use the Scale tool ![scale icon] and its associated dialog box to adjust the size of an object.

- To scale an object using the Scale dialog box, shown in Figure 14-6, select the object to scale and then double-click the Scale tool.

Figure 14-6. Scale dialog box

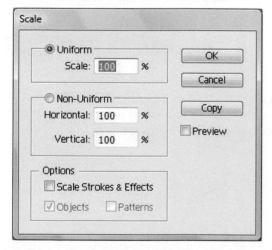

- To scale an object uniformly (that is, both horizontally and vertically at the same percentage), select the Uniform option button and enter a value in the Scale box.

- To distort the figure, select the Non-Uniform option button and enter different percentage values in the Horizontal and Vertical boxes.

- Notice the Copy button in the Scale dialog box. This allows the user to create a copy of an object at the same size or at a different size.

- To see how the scaled object will look, select the Preview check box. This allows you to check the scale before closing the dialog box.

- In most cases, you will want to select the Scale Strokes & Effects check box. This option will reduce the weight of a stroke when an object is scaled smaller, for example, so that the object's stroke maintains proportion with its new size.

- When you use the Scale dialog box to scale an object, Illustrator sets the point of origin for the scale in the center of the object, so all scaling is done from the center outward.

- You may also set the point of origin at a different point on the object or even away from the object.

- To set the point of origin manually, select the object to be scaled, select the Scale tool, and then click to set the point of origin. Illustrator supplies a pointer you can drag to scale the object larger or smaller, as shown in Figure 14-7.

Figure 14-7. Object is scaled toward the point of origin

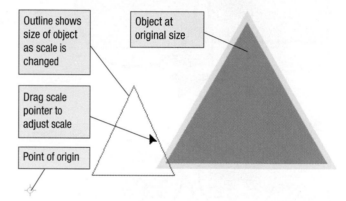

- You may also combine these methods. Select the object to be scaled, select the Scale tool, and then hold down Alt while clicking to set the point of origin.

- Holding down Alt displays the Scale dialog box, where you can set a precise percentage for the scale.

Work in Isolation Mode

- As you add objects to a drawing, you may find that overlapping or nearby objects make it a challenge to work on a specific area of the drawing.

- You can use **isolation mode** to focus on a particular group, path, layer or sublayer, or any of a number of other elements in a drawing.

  ✓ *You will learn about layers and sublayers in Exercises 18 and 19.*

- To enter isolation mode, double-click a grouped object, or select the object and click the Isolate Selected Object button ![isolate icon] on the Control panel between the Brush Definition and Style lists.

- When you enter isolation mode, all objects outside the isolated group are dimmed and cannot be selected or edited.

- Figure 14-8 shows a group of circles, squares, and stars that is positioned on top of a rectangle and partially obscured by an ellipse. Editing this group would be a challenge.

- After the group is isolated, the other objects are dimmed and locked, and the ellipse moves behind the group so that the group can easily be edited.

Figure 14-8. Before and after entering isolation mode

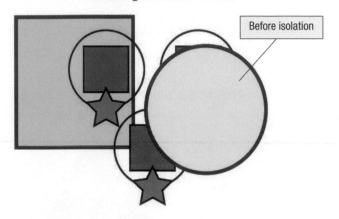

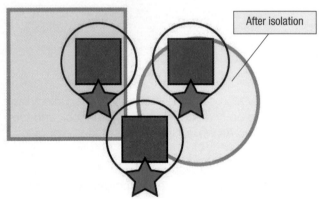

- You can control isolation mode from the top of the artboard, which shows the current layer, group, and object being isolated, as shown in Figure 14-9. This information tells you that the currently isolated item is a group named Stars that is located within a group named Green Stars Group, which is within another group named All Items in the Stars and Circles layer.

Figure 14-9. Isolation mode information at the top of the artboard

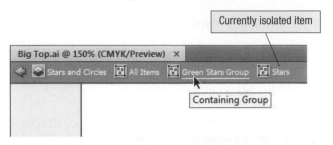

- You can control which item is isolated by clicking it. Clicking the Green Stars Group item, for example, would adjust the isolation to isolate the group that consists of the green stars and orange squares.

- Exit isolation mode by clicking the Exit Isolation Mode button on the Control panel, or click the left-pointing arrow at the top of the artboard.

Illustrator Extra

Hide or Lock Objects

You can also hide or lock objects using Object menu commands to prevent unwanted changes to objects you are not working on.

PROCEDURES

Draw Behind

Press Shift + D to toggle between the three drawing modes.

1. Select the object behind which you want to draw a new object.
2. Click **Draw Behind** button 🔲 on expanded Tools panel.

   OR

   a. Click **Draw Normal** button 🔲 on unexpanded Tools panel.
   b. Click **Draw Behind**.
3. Draw the desired object.

Draw Inside

Press Shift + D to toggle between the three drawing modes.

1. Select the object within which you want to draw a new object.
2. Click **Draw Inside** button 🔲 on expanded Tools panel.

   OR

   a. Click **Draw Normal** button 🔲 on unexpanded Tools panel.
   b. Click **Draw Inside**.
3. Draw the desired object within the selected object.

Use Select Behind

1. Hold down CTRL key and click on an object in a stack.
2. Continue to click to select objects in the stack until the desired object is selected.

Use Group Selection Tool

1. Select **Group Selection** tool 🔲 beneath Direct Selection tool.
2. Click on item in grouped object to select it.
3. Click again to select all items belonging to first item's group. Click again to select subsequent grouping levels.

Use Scale Tool

To use the Scale dialog box:

1. Select object to scale.
2. Double-click **Scale** tool 🔲.
3. Type a percentage value for uniform scale.

   OR

   a. Click **Non-Uniform**........ALT + N
   b. Type a value for horizontal scale.
   c. Press TAB.
   d. Type a value for vertical scale.
4. Click **Scale Strokes & Effects**......................ALT + E if desired to maintain proportions at new size.
5. Click **Copy** if desired to make a copy at designated scale.

   OR

   Click **OK** to complete scale..............................ENTER

To set point of origin manually:

1. Select object to scale.
2. Select **Scale** tool 🔲..........S
3. Click at location to set point of origin.
4. Use pointer to drag toward or away from point of origin to scale object.

   OR

1. Select object to scale.
2. Select **Scale** tool 🔲..........S
3. Hold down ALT and click to set point of origin as well as open Scale dialog box.
4. Enter values and select options as described above.

Use Isolation Mode

To isolate a group:

- Double-click group.

   OR

1. Select group to isolate.
2. Click **Isolate Selected Object** button 🔲 on Control panel.

   OR

1. Select group to isolate.
2. Right-click selected group.
3. Click **Isolate Selected Group** on context menu.

To exit isolation mode:

- Click **Exit Isolation Mode** button 🔲 on Control panel.

EXERCISE DIRECTIONS

✓ *Display the Painting workspace after starting Illustrator.*

1. Open 14Picnic and save the file as 14Picnic_xx.
2. Display rulers and turn on Smart Guides if necessary.

Add a Group of Olives

1. Create a group of olives as follows:
   a. Draw an ellipse that is **39** pts wide by **41** pts high. Change the fill to **C = 75, M = 0, Y = 100, K = 0** and the stroke to **C = 50, M = 0, Y = 100, K = 0**.
   b. Click the Ellipse tool twice more and accept defaults in the Ellipse dialog box to create two more olives with the same formats.
   c. Draw an ellipse that is **33** pts wide by **52** pts high.
   d. Arrange the olives near the left end of the loaf of bread, as shown in Illustration A.
   e. Add a pimiento (a red ellipse with no stroke) to each olive. See Illustration A for placement ideas.
2. Group the red pimientos, then group the green olives, and finally group all olive objects.
3. The olive color is not very realistic. Use the Group Selection tool to select only the olives and adjust the fill color to **C = 60, M = 10, Y = 100, K = 5**.
4. The pimientos would look better with a stroke. Use the Group Selection tool to select all pimientos.
5. Apply a stroke color of **C = 30, M = 0, Y = 95, K = 0** and change the stroke weight to **1.5**. Align the stroke to the inside of the path.

   ✓ *Type 1.5 in the Stroke panel's Weight box.*

Create a Glass of Lemonade

1. Move the glass group object (the ellipse on top of the rectangle) from the scratch area and position it behind the loaf of bread as shown in Illustration A. Isolate the glass group
2. Use the Group Selection tool to select the rectangle that forms the bottom of the glass and change the drawing mode to Draw Inside.
3. Draw a rectangle inside the selected rectangle. With the new object still selected, remove the stroke and fill the inner rectangle with **Y = 20**. Then click away from the glass to deselect the inner rectangle
4. Display the Info panel if desired. Use the Direct Selection tool to select the lower-left corner point of the glass rectangle (the outer rectangle with the stroke).
5. Hold down Shift and drag to the right until the Info panel shows **D: 14 pt** or the Smart Guide label shows **dX: 14**.

   ✓ *The D value in the Info panel indicates the distance you have dragged the point. You may not be able to achieve 14 pt exactly, but come as close as you can.*

6. Deselect the rectangle, and use the Direct Selection tool to select the lower-right corner point of the rectangle.
7. Hold down Shift and drag to the left until the Info panel shows **D: −14 pt** or the same number that you dragged the lower-left corner point.

Illustration A

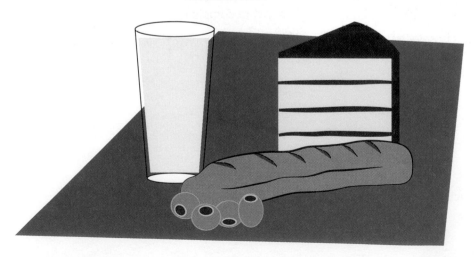

8. If desired, adjust the inner rectangle to follow the new slant of the glass:

   a. With the Direct Selection tool, click on the light-yellow rectangle to select it.

   b. Hold down the Shift key and click on the lower-left corner point to select it. The point should become an open square.

   c. Drag the corner point to the right, and release the mouse button when the yellow rectangle is at the same angle as the outer rectangle.

   d. Drag the lower-right corner point to the left until it is the proper angle.

Scale Objects

1. Use the Group Selection tool to select the glass's top ellipse, and then use the Scale dialog box to scale a copy of the ellipse at **70%**.

   ✓ *If you do not see a copy of the ellipse inside the top ellipse, you did not click the Copy button. Use Undo and then start over.*

2. Drag the 70% copy down and align it to the bottom of the glass to create a curved bottom.

3. Exit isolation mode and move the glass behind the loaf of bread if necessary.

4. Scale the group of olives by selecting the group and then clicking the Scale tool.

5. Click about half an inch to the right of the group, hold down Shift, and use the Scale tool pointer to drag a short distance toward the point of origin to reduce the size of the olives slightly. Reposition the group if necessary after resizing.

Add a Tablecloth

1. Select the glass object and choose the Draw Behind mode. With the Rectangle tool, draw a rectangle about **500** pts by **260** pts.

2. Remove the stroke and fill with the **C = 85, M = 50, Y = 0, K = 0** swatch.

3. Use the Direct Selection tool to pull the corners to new locations to create a free-form shape, as shown in Illustration A.

4. Save your changes, close the file, and exit Illustrator.

ON YOUR OWN

1. Start Adobe Illustrator and open a new Illustrator document, using default settings.

2. Practice using the tools and features you have learned about in this exercise.

3. Create a number of different shapes and try drawing behind some of the shapes and inside others.

4. Cluster a number of objects on top of one another and try selecting each object in the stack in turn using select behind.

5. Group several objects and practice selecting single items or groups from larger groups.

6. Practice scaling objects both uniformly and nonuniformly.

7. Make sure to practice setting the point of origin away from an object and scaling toward and away from the point of origin.

8. Try using isolation mode to make it easy to work on a single group.

9. Close the file without saving and exit Illustrator.

Exercise | 15

Skills Covered

- About the Pen Tool
- Draw Straight Lines with the Pen Tool
- Draw Curved Lines with the Pen Tool

- Modify Curves and Anchors
- Reflect Objects
- Join Paths

Software Skills   Use the Pen tool to draw both straight and flowing curved lines. Modify curved pen paths by adjusting direction handles, moving anchor points, or changing anchor points from smooth to corner (or vice versa). Reflect objects to create mirror images either vertically or horizontally. Paths may be joined to create more complex paths from simple ones.

Design Skills   Mastering the Pen tool separates the experienced designer from novices. The Pen tool makes it possible for a designer to create elegant curves and complicated paths that would otherwise be impossible to achieve.

Application Skills   In this exercise, you will begin work on an illustration for Greenwood Conservancy, a nature preserve in your area. You will use the Pen tool to draw leaf shapes with several different types of curves. You will also use the Pen tool to add, delete, and adjust anchor points. You will use the Reflect tool to reflect a path and join it to create a filled object.

TERMS

Bezier curve   A mathematically generated curve that has two endpoints and control points to specify curve direction.

Direction line   Line extending from anchor point that shows the direction of a curve.

NOTES

About the Pen Tool

- The Pen tool 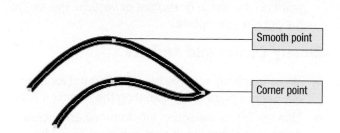 is used to draw straight lines and flowing lines called **Bezier curves**. Figure 15-1 shows both a straight line and a curved line created by the Pen tool.

Figure 15-1. Straight and curved lines drawn with the Pen tool

Endpoint

Smooth point

Corner point

- The Pen tool is perhaps the most challenging of the Illustrator tools. Rather than drag the Pen tool pointer to create a line or shape, you must specify a starting point and direction and then click and/or drag the pointer at a new location to continue the line.

- Determining where to continue a line and how to adjust a curve require practice and patience.

- A review of anchor point types will help you work with the Pen tool:

  - *Endpoints* display at the beginning and end of a line segment (see Figure 15-1).

  - *Smooth points* join segments in a smooth curve.

  - *Corner points* indicate where a path changes direction abruptly.

■ ■ ■ Design Suite Integration ■ ■ ■
Pen Tool

The Pen tool is also available in both Photoshop and InDesign. You will use the Pen tool in both of those applications to draw paths or outline objects.

Draw Straight Lines with the Pen Tool

- To draw a straight line with the Pen tool, click where the line should begin and then click again where the line should end.

- Hold down Shift to constrain the line to a straight horizontal, vertical, or 45° diagonal.

- If you continue to click the Pen pointer, Illustrator continues to create lines, joining each new line to the endpoint of the last.

- To create a closed shape, return the Pen tool pointer to the first endpoint. The Pen tool pointer displays a small *o* to the right of the pointer, as shown in Figure 15-2, to indicate that clicking will close the shape.

Figure 15-2. Close a Pen tool shape

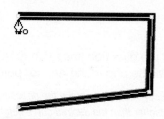

- To turn off the Pen tool after drawing one or more lines, select another tool, such as the Selection tool.

- You can join a new pen line to an existing line by placing the Pen pointer over an endpoint of the original line.

- The Pen tool pointer displays a / to the right of the pen, as shown in Figure 15-3, to indicate that clicking on the endpoint will join a new line to the existing line.

Figure 15-3. Join a new pen line to an existing line

Draw Curved Lines with the Pen Tool

- Drawing a curved line with the Pen tool is somewhat more challenging than drawing a straight line.

- Begin a curved line by clicking the Pen tool where the line should begin. Hold down the mouse button after clicking and drag in the direction the curve should go.

- Illustrator displays the initial anchor point and a **direction line** that indicates the direction of the curve.

- You must then release the mouse button and move the Pen pointer to the location where the curve will end or change direction.

- Until you release the mouse pointer at the end of the curve, Illustrator does not display a stroke for the line. You see only anchor points, direction lines, and the path itself, as shown in Figure 15-4.

Figure 15-4. Draw a curved line

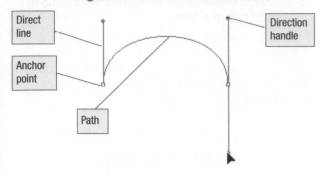

- The longer the direction lines you drag, the higher the curve will be above the anchor point.

  ✓ *A good rule of thumb is to make the direction line about one-third higher than the desired curve height.*

- Drag in the same direction the line is following to create a smooth or C curve, such as the one shown in Figure 15-4. Drag in the opposite direction to create an S curve, as shown in Figure 15-5.

Figure 15-5. Create an S curve

- Some shapes require you to change direction sharply. To do so, hold down Alt while dragging a direction line from an anchor point to convert the anchor point to a corner point. While holding down Alt, you can drag the direction handle to indicate a new direction for the line.

- Note in Figure 15-6 that the direction line has been dragged down below the curve to create the corner point.

- The fewer anchor points a curved line has, the more flowing its appearance. Learning where to place an anchor point and how long to make a direction handle can require considerable practice.

- You may find it helpful to position guides to align curved lines.

Figure 15-6. Drag the direction line to indicate new direction

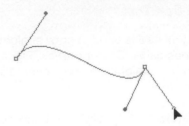

- You can also use the Shift key to constrain the Pen tool so clicking the Pen tool places the next anchor point on the same horizontal or vertical line as the previous anchor point.

Modify Curves and Anchors

- You can modify a curve by adjusting the location of the anchor point or by adjusting the direction line.

- Use the Direct Selection tool to move an anchor point on a curve, as shown in Figure 15-7. Moving an anchor point is the easiest way to adjust a curved line.

Figure 15-7. Move an anchor to adjust curve

- To change the direction and degree of curve for a segment of a curved line, select an anchor point with the Direct Selection tool and drag the direction line by its direction handle, the small dot at the end of the direction line, as shown in Figure 15-8.

Figure 15-8. Adjust a curve with a direction handle

- Other tools on the Pen tool toolbar, and options on the Control panel when a single anchor point is selected, can be used to modify any path:
  - Use the Add Anchor Point tool ![icon] on the Pen tool toolbar to add an anchor point anywhere on a path.

- Use the Delete Anchor Point tool  or the Remove selected anchor points button  on the Control panel to delete any selected anchor point on a path.

- Use the Convert Anchor Point tool  or the Convert selected anchor points to corner option  on the Control panel to convert a smooth point to a corner point. Use the same tool to convert a corner point to a smooth point, or use the Convert selected anchor points to smooth option .

Reflect Objects

- Use the Reflect tool , located beneath the Rotate tool on the Tools panel, to reverse the orientation of an object or to create a mirror image copy of an object.

- As when using the Rotate tool, you can click with the Reflect tool pointer to set a point of origin for the reflection and then drag the selected object to the desired angle, as shown in Figure 15-9.

Figure 15-9. Reflect an object by dragging

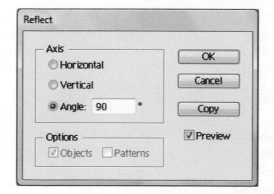

✓ *Hold down Alt while dragging to create a copy of the selected object, as shown in Figure 15-9.*

- The point of origin may be set on the object or away from the object to reflect over a distance.

- You can also click the Reflect tool pointer while holding Alt to open the Reflect dialog box shown in Figure 15-10.

Figure 15-10. Reflect dialog box

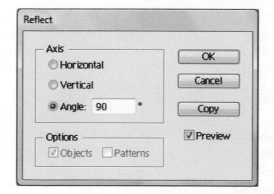

- Select the desired axis or specify an angle for the reflection.

- Reflecting horizontally flips an object along the horizontal axis, or top to bottom. Reflecting vertically flips an object along the vertical axis, or left to right.

- To make sure the reflection is as desired, be sure to select the Preview check box. Previewing can save a lot of undoing.

Join Paths

- When adding a path to another path, a user can join the separate paths into one continuous path.

- In Illustrator CS5, this process is easier than it has been in previous versions, where a user had to average endpoints before joining.

- To join paths, select two (or more) open paths and then use the Object > Path > Join command. If the endpoints to be joined are not overlapping, Illustrator adds a line segment to create the join, as shown in Figure 15-11.

Figure 15-11. Paths before and after joining

- You do not have a choice about the appearance of the join. If you do not want your paths joined with a line segment, you can use the Direct Selection tool to adjust the endpoints so they are overlapping (or almost overlapping) before joining.

- You can continue to issue the Join command to join a series of endpoints in a drawing. Each time you issue the command, the next set of endpoints joins.

PROCEDURES

Draw Straight Lines with the Pen Tool

1. Click **Pen** tool 🖊 .... P
2. Click to start line.
3. Move pointer to location for end of line and click.

   ✓ *Hold down Shift to create straight vertical, horizontal, or 45° line.*

4. Continue to click to add line segments.
5. Close shape by clicking on first endpoint.

Draw Curved Lines with the Pen Tool

1. Click **Pen** tool 🖊 .... P
2. Click in location for beginning of curve and drag in direction of curve.
3. Move pointer to location for end of curve segment.
4. Click and drag direction line in direction of curve.

   ✓ *Drag in same direction as line for C curve; drag in opposite direction for S curve.*

To change a smooth point to a corner point while drawing:

- Hold down ALT and then drag direction line to indicate new direction for line.

Modify Curves and Anchors

To move an anchor point on a curve:

- Use **Direct Selection** tool 🖎 to select single anchor point and drag anchor point to new position.

To adjust direction and degree of curve:

1. Use **Direct Selection** tool 🖎 to select anchor point.
2. Click on direction handle of direction line and drag toward or away from anchor point to control degree of curve.
3. Drag direction handle in any direction to control amount of curve.

To adjust anchor points for any path:

To add an anchor point:

- Select **Add Anchor Point** tool 🖊 and click on path .... +

To remove an anchor point:

- Select **Delete Anchor Point** tool 🖊 and click on an anchor point .... −

   OR

1. Use **Direct Selection** tool 🖎 to select anchor point.
2. Click **Remove selected anchor points** button 🔘 on Control panel.

To convert smooth point to corner point:

- Select **Convert Anchor Point** tool ⬈ and click on an anchor point to convert .... SHIFT + C

   OR

1. Use **Direct Selection** tool 🖎 to select anchor point.
2. Click **Convert selected anchor points to corner** button 🔘 on Control panel.

To convert corner point to smooth point:

1. Use **Direct Selection** tool 🖎 to select anchor point.
2. Click **Convert selected anchor points to smooth** button 🔘 on Control panel.

Use the Reflect Tool

1. Select object to reflect.
2. Select **Reflect** tool 🔲 on toolbar beneath Rotate tool..................................... O
3. Click to set point of origin for reflection.
4. Drag object to desired location.

   ✓ *Hold down Alt to create a copy of selected object.*

   OR

1. Select object to rotate.
2. Select **Reflect** tool 🔲 .... O
3. Hold down ALT and click to set point of origin and open Reflect dialog box.
4. Specify axis for reflection or set angle.
5. Select **Preview** to check reflection.
6. Click **Copy** to copy selected object.

   OR

   Click **OK** .... ENTER

Join Endpoints (Ctrl + J)

1. Select the open paths that will be joined.
2. Click **Object**............... ALT + O
3. Point to **Path**....................... P
4. Click **Join** .... J

   ✓ *You may issue this command additional times to join more path endpoints.*

EXERCISE DIRECTIONS

✓ *Display the Painting workspace.*

■ Open ⊙ 15Greenwood and save the document as 15Greenwood_xx.

✓ *You will draw three leaves for the Greenwood Conservancy illustration: an ash leaf, a gingko leaf, and a redbud leaf.*

Draw the Ash Leaf

1. Draw an ellipse **70** pts wide by **150** pts high.

2. Use the Convert Anchor Point tool to click on the smooth anchor point at the top of the ellipse.

3. Deselect the leaf. Zoom in if desired and use the Pen tool to draw a straight line for the vein line from the tip of the leaf to its base.

   ✓ *Use Shift to constrain the line.*

4. Group the leaf and the vein line.

5. Fill the ash leaf with **C = 0, M = 65, Y = 100, K = 24**.

   ✓ *You will adjust colors on these leaves further in Exercise 28, when you create gradient fills for the leaves.*

Draw the Gingko Leaf

1. Create a four-pointed star with the following settings: Radius 1, **100** pts; Radius 2, **50** pts. Draw the star **220** pts wide and high.

2. Convert all of the inner anchor points to smooth points. (Use the Convert the selected anchor points to smooth option on the Control panel.) You now have four corner points at the ends of the star points and four smooth points toward the center of the leaf.

3. Use the Direct Selection tool to adjust anchor points as follows. (See Illustration A for final arrangement of anchor points.)

   a. Select the top star point and drag it straight down toward the center of the leaf to create the split leaf shape.

   b. Select each of the two lower smooth points and drag outward slightly to create a smoother curve for the lower leaf edges.

   c. Drag the left and right star points upward and inward a short distance to reduce the width of the leaf.

   d. Adjust the direction lines and position of the two smooth points on either side of the split area to give a more rounded appearance to the lobes.

   e. The tops of gingko leafs have a slightly ruffled appearance. To create this waviness, add five anchor points to the top edges of each side of the split and then use the Direct Selection tool to pull up alternate anchor points. (You may find this easier to do at higher magnification.)

   f. Finally, convert the left and right leaf points to smooth points. Make any other adjustments necessary to make the leaf resemble the one shown in Illustration A.

4. Fill the leaf with **C = 0, M = 5, Y = 90, K = 0**.

5. Rotate the leaf slightly, as shown in Illustration B, and then add several slightly curved Pen strokes as shown to indicate the vein lines. Remove the fill from the stroke if necessary.

6. Group all objects for the gingko leaf, then scale the leaf to 90%.

Illustration A

Draw the Redbud Leaf

✓ *The redbud leaf requires a curved line. You will find the required curve in the scratch area to the right of the artboard.*

1. Use the Pen tool to draw the same curve as the one in the scratch area, using the existing curve as a guide.

   ✓ *Take as long as you like to practice this curve, and use Undo to remove any unsuccessful attempts. You may find it easier to begin drawing at the top of the curve.*

2. When you are satisfied with your curve, move it onto the artboard.

3. Reflect a copy of the curve to create the other half of the leaf.

   ✓ *You may use the Reflect tool or the Reflect dialog box.*

4. Adjust the copied half position as necessary to align with the original curve.

5. Adjust the positions of the two curves until the top endpoints are overlapping.

6. Issue the Join command twice to join the top end-points and the endpoints at the base of the leaf.

7. Use the Pen tool to draw a slightly curving vein line from the base of the leaf to its tip.

8. Adjust the curve of the vein line if necessary using the direction handle. Group the leaf and the vein line.

9. Fill the leaf with the **C = 85**, **M = 10**, **Y = 100**, **K = 10** swatch.

10. Arrange the leaves as shown in Illustration B.

11. Save your changes, close the file, and exit Illustrator.

Illustration B

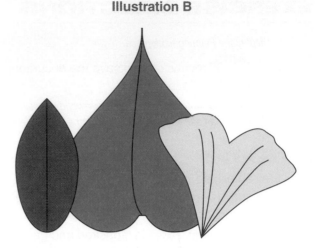

ON YOUR OWN

1. Start Illustrator.

2. Open 📼 14Picnic_xx or 💿 OYO15 and save the file as OIL15_xx.

   ✓ *You will draw an orange and use the Pen tool to add highlights to it.*

3. Draw a circle about **97 pts** wide.

4. Near the top of the orange, use the Pen tool to draw an irregular shape that will represent the slight depression at the stem end of the orange (see Illustration C).

Illustration C

5. Add a small star in the depression, as shown.

6. Use the Pen tool to draw the two curving shapes shown in Illustration C. These shapes will be used to create highlights on the orange.

7. Color the orange as follows:

   a. Fill the orange with **C = 2**, **M = 30**, **Y = 100**, **K = 0**.

   b. Fill the star with a dark green color.

   c. Fill the depression and the right highlight with **C = 0**, **M = 40**, **Y = 80**, **K = 0**.

   d. Fill the left highlight with **C = 0**, **M = 20**, **Y = 80**, **K = 0**.

8. Remove the stroke from all the objects.

9. Group the orange objects and position the orange just to the left of the glass. Do not obscure the bottom of the glass.

10. Use the Pen tool to draw filled, curving lines on several olives, as shown in Illustration D, and change the fill color to a light green that contrasts well with the olive color.

Illustration D

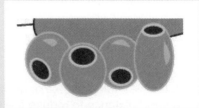

11. Save your changes, close the file, and exit Illustrator.

Skills Covered

- **More about the Paintbrush Tool**
- **Use Brush Libraries**
- **Apply Brush Formats to Paths**
- **Modify Brush Formats**

Software Skills   Use the brush options in the Brushes panel to paint decorative strokes with the Paintbrush tool. Brushes can be selected before brushing a path or applied to existing paths. Illustrator also supplies several brush libraries from which you can add brushes to the Brushes panel. You can modify a brush's formats to customize the brush for a specific use.

Design Skills   The Paintbrush tool can be used to create a number of special effects in a design, such as patterned strokes or scatterings of objects. A designer can add interesting and whimsical touches to an illustration by selecting appropriate brushes from brush libraries and modifying brush formats for a specific design use.

Application Skills   In this exercise, you will continue working on the picnic food illustration. You will use all five types of Illustrator brushes, and you will modify brush formats for this illustration.

TERMS

Brush library   A collection of brushes related to a particular theme or type of brush that you can add to the default Brushes panel.

Thumbnail   A small illustration in a dialog box or panel displayed to help you choose an option.

Tile   An object containing a pattern that can be arranged to fill an object or applied to a brush path.

NOTES

More about the Paintbrush Tool

- The Paintbrush tool can be used to apply a wide variety of brushed strokes that add interesting touches to an illustration.
- By default, the Paintbrush tool draws a smooth path most suitable for freehand drawing, like the Pencil tool.
- The real value of the Paintbrush tool, however, lies in the paths you can create using the brush options in the Brushes panel (see Figure 16-1) and Illustrator's brush libraries.

Figure 16-1. Brushes panel

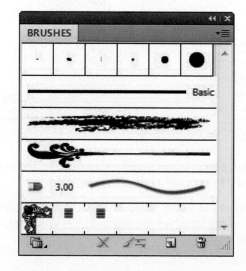

- Illustrator has five categories of brushes:
  - *Calligraphic brushes* give the effect of drawing with the angled point of a calligraphic pen.
  - *Scatter brushes* distribute objects along the brush path.
  - *Art brushes* stretch a piece of artwork along the brush path.
  - *Pattern brushes* lay down series of patterned **tiles** along the brush path.
  - *Bristle brushes* give the effect of painting with a natural bristle brush.
- The default Brushes panel shown in Figure 16-1 displays calligraphic, art, pattern, and bristle brushes. The panel also displays the new Basic option that can reduce any brush stroke to a basic appearance.
- To make it easy to work with one particular type of brush, click the Brushes panel menu button ▤ and deselect one or more brush types to leave only the desired brush type displayed.
- The Brushes panel menu also allows you to select the List view to arrange brushes by their names rather than by **thumbnails**.

Use Brush Libraries

- Illustrator offers many **brush libraries** that you can open to select a variety of calligraphic, scatter, art, bristle, and pattern brushes.
- Click the Brush Libraries Menu button ▤ at the lower-left corner of the Brushes panel to open a menu of brush library categories, as shown in Figure 16-2.

Figure 16-2. Access the brush libraries

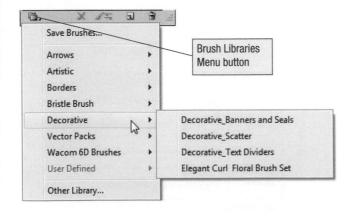

✓ You can also access the list of brush library categories from the Brushes panel menu.

- Besides the many specialty brush libraries, this menu lists brushes for use with the Wacom graphic tablet.

- A new brush library displays in its own panel in the work area, as shown in Figure 16-3.

Figure 16-3. Decorative scatter brush library

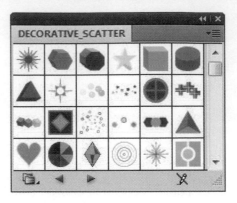

- When you select a brush from a library, the brush is added to the Brushes panel and may be used like any other brush.

Design Suite Integration

Libraries

A number of tools in the Creative Suite applications have libraries available to provide a wide choice of options. You can also build your own libraries for these tools.

- You can delete any brush from the Brushes panel when it is no longer needed. Select the brush and click Delete Brush ▤ in the Brushes panel.

Apply Brush Formats to Paths

- You can select a brush from the Brushes panel before brushing a path, or select an existing path and then choose a brush.
- Brushes can be applied to paths created by the Pen tool, Pencil tool, Line Segment tool, or Paintbrush tool. The illustration below, for example, shows a pencil line (top) to which the Filbert bristle brush has been applied (bottom).

Figure 16-4. Brush applied to existing path

■ Brushes can also be applied to the paths of closed objects such as rectangles, ellipses, and so on.

■ Some paths, however, such as straight lines, may not display the full effect of some brushes.

■ To remove the brush stroke format from a path, click the Remove Brush Stroke button ☒ at the bottom of the Brushes panel or select the Basic brush option.

■ Some brushes have their own color settings, such as the pattern brushes and some of the scatter brushes. Other brushes take their color from the current stroke color.

■ A brush path may also have a fill, just like other paths.

■ Some brushes, such as art brushes, display the art in a particular direction. For most art brushes, for example, the brush is designed to be heavier at the beginning of the stroke than at the end.

Modify Brush Formats

■ You can modify the default formats of any brush in the Brushes panel.

■ Click the Options of Selected Object button 🖊 at the bottom of the Brushes panel to open the Options dialog box for the selected brush, or double-click the brush.

■ The five types of brushes offer different options for modification. Figure 16-5, for example, shows the options available for modifying a scatter brush.

Figure 16-5. Scatter brush stroke options

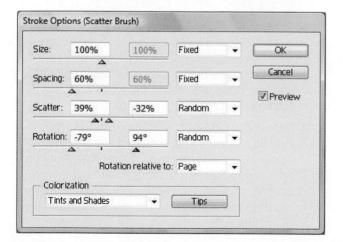

■ Colorization options can be changed for most brushes as follows:

● The Tints option uses the current stroke color as a base color and mixes the color with white to provide several color variations.

● The Tints and Shades option uses the current stroke color as a base and adds both black and white for color variations.

● The Hue Shift option uses the most important color in the brush artwork, called the *key color*, as the stroke color.

■ Changes made to brush stroke options become the default for that brush type, but original settings can be restored by deleting Illustrator's preferences file.

✓ *You may find it helpful to select Preview in any Options dialog box to see the impact of your changes as you make them.*

Illustrator Extra

Create Your Own Brush

You can create your own brush and add it to the Brushes panel. For most brushes, this is a simple process: Create the object that will become the brush and click the New Brush button on the Brushes panel. To create a pattern brush, you must create the objects that form the tiles along the path.

93

PROCEDURES

Display Brushes in the Brushes Panel

- Click 🔽📃 to display panel menu and deselect brush types you don't want to view.
- Click 🔽📃 and **List View** to see brushes listed by name only.
- Click 🔽📃 and **Thumbnail View** to see small pictures of brush strokes.

Use Brush Libraries

1. Click **Brush Libraries Menu** button 📷 at lower-left corner of Brushes panel.
2. Point to a brush type from the drop-down menu.
3. Select a specific library from pop-out list.
4. Select desired brush from library panel.

Delete Brush

1. Select brush in Brushes panel.
2. Click **Delete Brush** 🗑 on Brushes panel.

   OR

   Click 🔽📃 to display the panel menu and click **Delete Brush**.

Apply Brush Formats to Paths

1. Display Brushes panel if necessary.

   ✓ *Remember, you can drag a panel away from its panel group while working with it.*

2. Select desired brush.
3. Select tool and create object that will have brushed path.

   OR

1. Create object that will have brushed path.
2. Select object.
3. Select desired brush to apply brush to selected path.

To turn off the brush:

- With the brushed path selected, click **Remove Brush Stroke** button ✖ from the Brushes panel or click the Basic brush option in the Brushes panel.

Modify Brush Formats

To modify a brush before using it:

- Double-click the brush in the Brushes panel.

   OR

- Click 🔽📃 and click **Brush Options**.

To modify a brush after using it:

1. Select brushed path to modify.
2. Click **Options of Selected Object** button 🖊 on the Brushes panel.

   OR

   Click 🔽📃 and click **Brush Options**.

   ✓ *Options will differ slightly depending on whether brush has been applied to a path.*

EXERCISE DIRECTIONS

✓ *Display the Painting workspace after you start Illustrator.*

1. Open 💿 16Picnic and save the document as 16Picnic_xx.
2. Drag the Brushes panel out of its panel group.
3. First use one of the bristle brushes to soften some edges in the illustration:
   a. Use the Line Segment tool to draw a straight line at the right side of the glass, from the top to the bottom of the lemonade object, at the same angle as the glass.
   b. Create a light gray color for the stroke, and then apply the Filbert brush from the Brushes panel.
   c. Adjust the position of the stroke as necessary so it sits at the edge of the lemonade and partially overlaps into the glass.
   d. Repeat this process with the same brush to add a gray brush stroke to the other side of the glass, and a white brush stroke just to the left of

the first bristle brush stroke. Adjust brush settings as desired to blend the white and gray strokes for a more natural appearance.

   e. Locate the Charcoal - Feather brush in the Artistic_ChalkCharcoalPencil brush library. Apply a stroke to the two vertical highlights on the orange that is the same color as the highlight fill, and then apply the Charcoal - Feather brush to the strokes to give more texture to the highlights.

Create a Watermelon Slice

1. Locate the Tapered - Round brush in the Artistic_Ink brush library.
2. Use the Paintbrush tool to draw an arc like the one shown in Illustration A. The arc should be about **150** pts wide and **100** pts high. (Don't worry if your stroke is still orange from step 3.)

✓ *To draw this arc, start at the lower left and drag up and to the right. If you drag from the top right to lower left, your stroke will look different.*

Illustration A

3. Change the stroke weight to 0.5 pt, the stroke color to a dark green, and the fill color to a bright red.

   ✓ *You can adjust the fill color to a more pinkish red if desired.*

4. Position the watermelon slice over the right end of the bread. Rotate the slice slightly if desired to sit straighter.

Add a Border to the Tablecloth

1. With the tablecloth object selected, display the available brush libraries and choose a decorative border pattern such as **Fleur-de-lis**.

   ✓ *Fleur-de-lis can be found under Borders > Borders_Decorative.*

   ✓ *Rest the pointer on a pattern in a library to display a tool tip giving the pattern name.*

2. Display options for the pattern brush and scale the pattern to **70%** to decrease its size.

3. Adjust the position of the tablecloth if desired so that the border is not hidden behind the top of the glass.

Add Bubbles

1. Use the Pencil tool to draw a random squiggle above the rim of the glass. Change the stroke color to **C = 5, M = 0, Y = 90, K = 0** and set Fill to None.

2. With the pencil path still selected, display the Decorative_Scatter brush library and choose **Bubbles**. (The lemonade has become a fizzy drink.)

3. Modify the brush as follows:

   a. Display options for the current brush.

   b. Drag the triangle pointer under the Size bar to the left to 50%.

   c. Change the Colorization option for the brush to Tints and Shades. (Click Apply to Strokes if you are prompted.)

   d. Adjust the position of the stroke so that all the bubbles display above the rim of the glass. Your drawing should look similar to Illustration B.

4. Save your changes, close the file, and exit Illustrator.

   ✓ *If you receive a message about spot colors when you save, click Continue. This message relates to the transparent colors used in the bubbles brush.*

Illustration B

ON YOUR OWN

1. Start Adobe Illustrator.

2. Open OYO16 and save the file as OIL16_xx.

3. Use a flat calligraphic brush to draw a curving stem for the ash leaf as shown in Illustration C. Add a small stem across the main stem you just drew.

4. Copy the ash leaf and paste it twice. Rotate and position the copies to attach them to the short stem. Send the rightmost leaf behind the dogwood leaf. Adjust the position of the leaves to center them on the artboard if necessary.

5. Use the Oak brush in the Brushes panel to brush a curving line below the three leaves.

6. Modify settings for the Oak brush as follows:

   a. Adjust size, spacing, and scatter to create a fairly thick concentration of leaves close to the path (see Illustration C).

   ✓ *To learn more about how these settings affect the scattered objects, be sure to select the Preview check box in the Stroke Options (Scatter Brush) dialog box.*

   b. The illustration will concentrate on fall colors. Change the stroke to an orange or golden color and use a colorization option that will display the stroke color most attractively.

7. Save your changes, close the file, and exit Illustrator.

Illustration C

Exercise | 17

Skills Covered

- Place a File
- About Tracing
- Use Live Trace
- Offset a Drop Shadow

Software Skills   An easy way to create a complex path in Illustrator is to trace an existing object. Use the Live Trace feature to transform an object into a vector graphic that can be manipulated like any other Illustrator object. Use the Place command to bring a file such as a scan into an illustration for further work. Add depth to an illustration by creating a drop shadow.

Design Skills   A designer does not have to draw every object that comprises an illustration. Live Trace makes it easy for a designer to place and trace from an existing file. Learning how to manipulate trace settings allows a designer to achieve a desired effect with a minimum of experimentation. Effects such as drop shadows add sophisticated touches to simple designs.

Application Skills   In this exercise, you will work on a map for a client wanting to display information about Australia. You will place a scanned map in an Illustrator file, use Live Trace to create a copy, and then adjust the trace parameters. You will copy the map, paste it in front, and use the copy to create a drop shadow.

TERMS

Drop shadow   An object or effect that creates a shadow behind an image.

Embed   Place a file or object in a file so that it becomes part of the file.

Template   Object that is dimmed and unavailable for modification but can be used as a guide for creating objects.

NOTES

Place a File

- On occasion, you may need to bring an existing image into Illustrator.
- One way to do this is to open the image as an Illustrator file. This option results in an Illustrator file with the same name (and file format) as the graphic image. It can be resaved as an Illustrator file.
- You can also select an image in Bridge and use the Open With command to open the image in Illustrator, or drag the image to Illustrator to place it.
- Another way to bring an existing image into Illustrator is to use the File > Place command to place the graphic image in the Illustrator file.

- This option has the advantage of allowing you to add a graphic image to an existing Illustrator drawing.
- You have several options when placing a file using the Place dialog box shown in Figure 17-1, at the top of the next page.
- Select the *Link* check box to create a link between the Illustrator file and the original graphic file.
- When an image is linked, it is not stored in the Illustrator file, resulting in a smaller Illustrator file size.
  - ✓ *If the original graphic file is modified, the linked copy in the Illustrator file will reflect those changes.*

Figure 17-1. Place dialog box

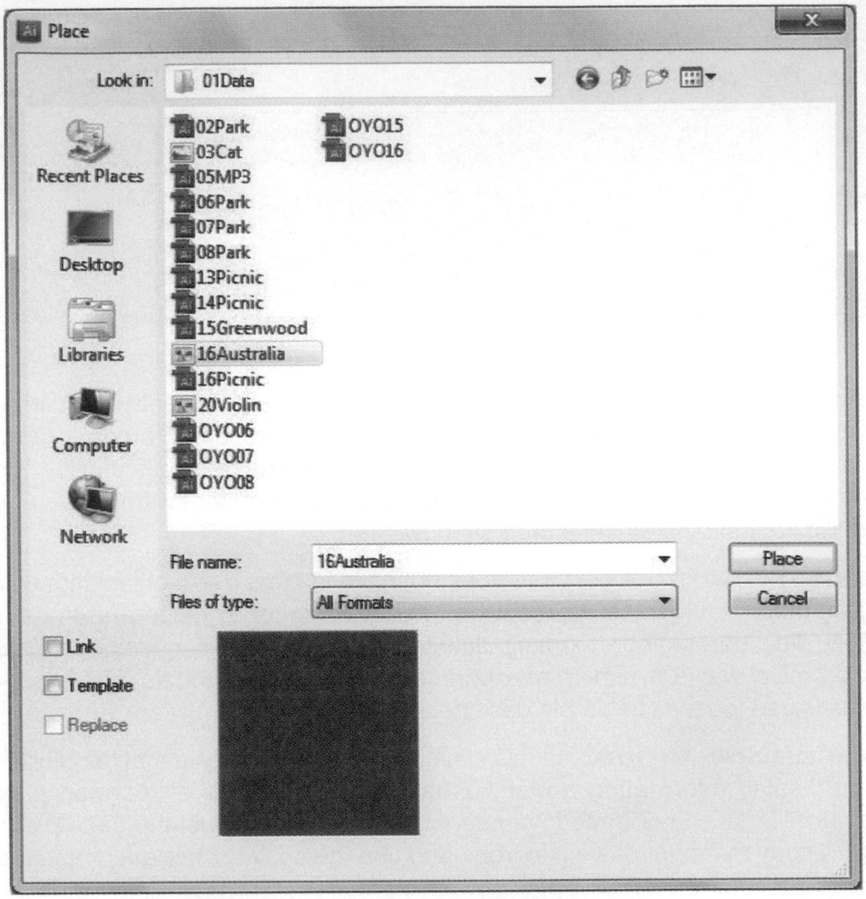

- Deselecting the *Link* check box **embeds** the graphic image in the Illustrator file. This increases the size of the Illustrator file.

  ✓ *If you drag an image to Illustrator, it will be linked by default. You can click the Embed button on the Control panel to embed the image in the Illustrator file.*

- Select the *Template* check box to place the graphic as a **template**, an object that cannot be modified but can be used as a guide when creating objects.

  ✓ *A template is automatically placed on a template layer, allowing you to hide it when finished using it. You will learn more about layers in the next exercise.*

Design Suite Integration

Placing Files

You will use the Place command in both Photoshop and InDesign. This command is the most common way to insert both text and graphics into InDesign pages.

About Tracing

- Tracing can be a quick way to add a complex path to an Illustrator drawing.
- There are several ways to trace an object in Illustrator:
  - Use the Pen or Pencil tool to draw a path around a template image (or any other graphic in an Illustrator file).

    ✓ *You have used this procedure several times to create objects in earlier exercises.*

  - Use the Live Trace feature to automatically trace an image.

Use Live Trace

- The Live Trace feature allows you to create a vector object from a variety of sources, such as GIF images or raster objects created in Photoshop.
- Live Trace can reproduce not only outlines but the detail inside the object. In Figure 17-2, for example, a Photoshop PSD image of a flower (left) has been traced to create a six-color version (right).

Figure 17-2. Photoshop image traced and colors reduced

- You have a great deal of control over settings for the trace. And the beauty of "live" tracing is that settings can be changed and adjusted even after the trace to achieve the desired results.

- Live tracing features are available on the Object > Live Trace submenu, but the process can also be controlled easily using options on the Control panel.

- Begin the process by placing the object or image to be traced in Illustrator, then click Live Trace on the Control panel to create a trace using default settings.

- Or, to set tracing options before beginning the trace, click Object > Live Trace > Tracing Options. The Tracing Options dialog box displays as shown in Figure 17-3.

✓ *This dialog box can also be displayed from the Control panel by clicking the Tracing Options button.*

- Illustrator provides a number of preset tracing options, such as Color 16, Technical Drawing, Inked Drawing, and even Comic Art. Select one of the supplied presets from the Preset list.

- Options in the dialog box adjust according to the preset chosen. For example, if a color option is chosen, the color settings in the Adjustments area of the dialog box become active.

- The Adjustments area of the dialog box offers a number of settings you apply to the trace object. You can select a color mode, specify the threshold at which lighter pixels become white and darker pixels convert to black, select the maximum number of colors, choose to output the colors to swatches, set a blur amount to reduce raster jaggedness before tracing, and resample to adjust resolution of the image to be traced.

- Options in the Trace Settings area of the dialog box allow you to control the appearance of the final trace. You can adjust how fills and strokes are traced, determine how closely paths are traced, and specify the minimum size of areas to be traced.

- The View area of the dialog box provides two lists of viewing options. The Raster view options control how the original image looks. The Vector view options display vector tracing results.

Figure 17-3. Tracing Options dialog box

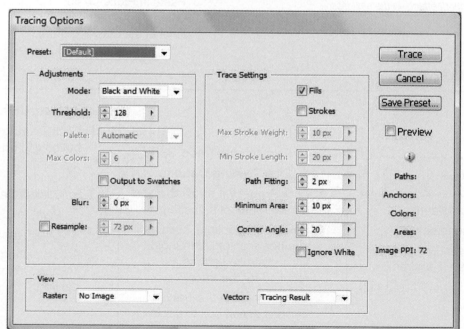

- Settings can be saved for future use by clicking the Save Preset button in the Tracing Options dialog box. The preset will then appear in the Preset list along with Illustrator's standard presets.

- Many of the settings available in the Tracing Options dialog box are also available on the Control panel, allowing you to easily experiment with tracing results after the initial trace.

- If the trace results are not as expected, you can use Object > Live Trace > Release to restore the original image and then try again.

- Once you have achieved the desired trace, you can click the Expand button on the Control panel to convert the trace to editable paths.

- The paths can then be ungrouped and the object can be manipulated like any other Illustrator vector graphic.

- The Live Paint button also appears on the Control panel with Live Trace options, to give the user the option of converting the traced image directly into a Live Paint object. You will learn more about Live Paint in the next lesson.

Offset a Drop Shadow

- To add depth and visual interest to an object, you can add a **drop shadow**, a shadow that displays behind an object, as shown in Figure 17-4.

- Illustrator offers several ways to create a drop shadow, including an effect exclusively for this purpose.

  ✓ *You will learn about effects in the next lesson.*

Figure 17-4. Drop shadow behind map

- One of the easiest ways to create a drop shadow is to copy the object to be shadowed, paste it, change its fill to black or a dark color, and send it behind the top object.

- Using the Edit > Paste command pastes the copied object in the center of the screen. You might then have to move the object to create the shadow.

- You have several other paste options on the Edit menu you can use instead:
  - Paste in Front pastes a copy of the selected object at the same location as the copied object, but in front of all objects, so it is at the top of the stack.
  - Paste in Back pastes a copy of the selected object at the same location as the copied object, but behind all objects.
  - Paste in Place pastes a copy of the selected object at the same location and at the same level in the stacking order.

PROCEDURES

Place a File

1. Click **File**.................. ALT + F
2. Click **Place** L
3. Click **Look in** arrow .... ALT + I, ↓
4. Select drive or folder.
5. Click file name to select.
6. Select options to Link or create template if desired.
7. Click **Place** .... ALT + P

Use Live Trace

1. Place the image to be traced in Illustrator.
2. Click **Live Trace** on the Control panel.

OR

a. Click **Object**.......... ALT + O
b. Point to **Live Trace** I
c. Click **Tracing Options** ... T

3. Click **Preset** list arrow to select a tracing preset if desired.
4. Select other options such as number of colors, threshold, fill, and stroke options as required for the trace.
5. Click **Trace** if in the Tracing Options dialog box to begin the trace.
6. Click **Expand** to change the tracing object to vector paths.

Modify Trace Options

1. Click **Tracing options dialog** button ▦ on Control panel.

OR

a. Click **Object** .... ALT + O
b. Point to **Live Trace** I
c. Click **Tracing Options** ... T

2. Adjust setting options in the Tracing Options dialog box as desired.

Preview Views of Raster Image

1. Click **Preview different views of the raster image** button 🔺 on Control panel.

   OR

   a. Click **Object** .... ALT + O
   b. Point to **Live Trace** I
   c. Click **Tracing Options** ... T
   d. Click **Raster** .... E

2. Select an option for viewing **No Image**, **Original Image**, **Adjusted Image**, or **Transparent Image**.

Preview Views of Vector Result

1. Click **Preview different views of the vector result** button 🔺 on Control panel.

   OR

   a. Click **Object** .... ALT + O
   b. Point to **Live Trace** I
   c. Click **Tracing Options** ... T
   d. Click **Vector** V

2. Select an option for viewing **No Tracing Result**, **Tracing Result**, **Outlines**, or **Outlines with Tracing**.

Release a Tracing

1. Click **Object** .... ALT + O
2. Point to **Live Trace** I
3. Click **Release** .... R

Offset a Drop Shadow

1. Select object that will be shadowed.
2. Click **Edit** .... ALT + E
3. Click **Copy** C
4. Click **Edit** .... ALT + E
5. Click **Paste in Front** .... F

   OR

   Click **Paste in Place** .... S

6. Fill pasted object with black or a dark color.
7. Nudge shadow into position below and to right or left of original object.
8. Click **Object** .... ALT + O
9. Point to **Arrange** .... A
10. Click **Send to Back** .... A

EXERCISE DIRECTIONS

✓ *Display the Painting workspace.*

1. Start a new Illustrator print document and save the document as 17Australia_xx.
2. Place the data file 💿 17Australia.gif.
3. Click Live Trace on the Control panel to create a default trace.
4. The default trace could be improved. Click the Preset list arrow and select Comic Art.
5. The Comic Art trace isn't exactly what you want. Click the Preset list arrow and select Technical Drawing.
6. This setting produces a plain, strong outline that you can work with. To minimize the amount of cleanup you will have to do in the ocean areas around Australia, change the Min area setting to **12**.
7. Click Object > Live Trace > Show Outlines to see the paths of the current trace.
8. This looks very promising. Click the vector view triangle on the Control panel 🔺 and select Tracing Result.
9. Expand the tracing result to show paths with anchor points.
10. Ungroup the object.
11. Select and delete all offshore islands, including the island of Tasmania below the continent at the right side.

12. Click on the path at the right side of the continent and fill the map with the **C = 0, M = 35, Y = 85, K = 0** swatch. Apply a **1** pt black stroke.
13. There are several breaks in the outline that prevent the object from filling completely. Fix them as follows:

    a. At the left side of the map, you will see a break similar to the one shown at the left in Illustration A. Zoom in on the area and use the Pen tool and associated tools to add or delete anchor points and then connect paths so the break area looks similar to the area shown at the right in Illustration A. After you complete this fix, the map may lose its fill.

Illustration A

b. You may also need to fix anchor points at the top center of the map, shown in Illustration B, where paths overlap without joining. Use the Direct Selection tool to select one of the overlapping anchor points indicated in Illustration B and pull it slightly to the left so that you can use the Pen tool to connect it to the other side of the path at the right. You may need to remove small paths that stick out at these points to select the correct anchor points.

Illustration B

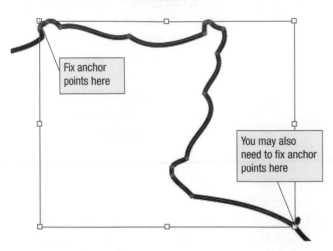

c. To make sure you have closed the path, select the path again and fill the object with its former color.

14. Copy the object and use Paste in Front to paste a copy on top of the original.

15. Fill the copied object with black.

16. Click the right arrow three times to nudge the drop shadow right.

17. Click the down arrow three times to nudge the drop shadow down.

18. Send the shadow to the back.

19. Group the map and the drop shadow. Your illustration should look similar to Illustration C.

20. Save your changes, close the file, and exit Illustrator.

Illustration C

ON YOUR OWN

1. Start a new Illustrator file using the defaults and save the document as OIL17_xx.

2. Place in Illustrator the photo of Earth contained in ⊙OYO17_earth.gif using Bridge or the Place command. Choose Live Trace to trace the object.

3. Access the Tracing Options dialog box. Position the dialog box so you can see the image on the artboard as well as all dialog box settings. Select the Preview check box.

4. Select the Color 16 preset and then select the Grayscale mode. View the preview on the artboard.

5. Change the maximum number of colors to **10**.

6. Select Color in the Mode list to return to a color image.

7. Choose to output the colors to swatches.

8. Click Trace to complete the trace.

9. Use the Min Area slider on the Control panel to set the minimum area to trace to **20 px**.

10. Check the Swatches panel to see the colors used in the trace.

11. Save your changes, close the file, and exit Illustrator.

Skills Covered

- **About Layers**
- **The Layers Panel**
- **Create a New Layer**
- **Name a Layer**

- **Select Layer Objects**
- **Move Objects to a Layer**
- **Move Layers to Change Stacking Order**

Software Skills   Use layers to organize portions of a drawing. Placing objects on different layers makes it easy to select and manipulate objects and adjust stacking order. Use the Layers panel to create new layers, place objects on layers, move objects from layer to layer, and change stacking order.

Design Skills   Even simple designs may include a number of objects that need to be manipulated in different ways. Working with layers makes it much easier for a designer to control and format the objects in an illustration.

Application Skills   In this exercise, you will work with an illustration created for Global Issues, an environmental action group committed to thinking globally and acting locally. You will create new layers in the illustration, name them, and move objects to specific layers so you can adjust stacking order easily.

TERMS

Layer   A single level in the stacking order that can hold any number of objects.

NOTES

About Layers

- As you have worked with illustrations in this course, you have probably found yourself having to rearrange stacking order a number of times to display objects as you want them.

- To limit the amount of time spent using the Arrange command to adjust stacking order, you can place objects on different layers of a drawing.

- A **layer** is a level in the stacking order. It can be described as one transparent sheet in a stack of sheets. A layer can hold one object or many objects.

- Layers can be easily moved to adjust stacking order for all objects on the layer, saving the time that would be spent sending individual items to the front or back.

- A designer can create layers while developing an illustration or after an illustration is complete. Existing objects can be easily moved to new layers to reorganize a drawing.

Design Suite Integration

Layers

All Creative Suite Design applications use layers to organize objects, and basic skills such as creating, naming, and adjusting layer order are the same throughout the suite. Each application's Layers panel offers functionality specific to the tasks of that program.

The Layers Panel

- The Layers panel is shown in Figure 18-1.

Figure 18-1. Layers panel

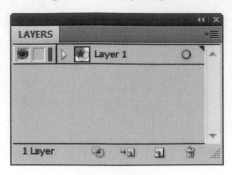

- A new Illustrator file has only one layer, named Layer 1, as shown in Figure 18-1. The currently selected layer has a blue highlight.
- To the left of the layer name is a small thumbnail that shows the objects on the layer.

  ✓ *For a better view of the objects in the Layers panel, you can open the Layers Panel Options dialog box from the Layers panel menu and select Large for the row size.*

- To the left of the thumbnail is a right-pointing arrow that, when clicked, expands the selected layer to show the objects on the layer, as shown in Figure 18-2.

Figure 18-2. Expanding the layer

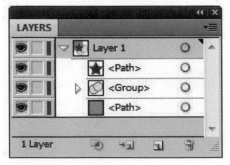

- Figure 18-2 shows that Layer 1 contains three objects: the star path, the group of two circles, and the square path.
- You could click the right-pointing arrow to the left of <Group> to see the two circle paths that make up the group.
- To collapse a layer, click the down-pointing arrow to return it to its right-pointing default status.
- The eye symbol at the far left of the layer name indicates that the layer is visible. The empty square next to the eye symbol can be used to lock a layer. The vertical color bar indicates the color associated with the current layer. This color is used for paths, bounding boxes, selection marquees, and so on.

  ✓ *You will learn about visibility settings and locking in the next exercise.*

- Like all Illustrator panels, the Layers panel has a menu of options for working with layer features. You can create a new layer or sublayer (a layer within a layer), change layer options, change all layers to Outline view, and lock or hide layers.
- You can enlarge the Layers panel if desired to see more of the layers and sublayers. Click on the sizing handle (the dotted triangle) at the lower-right corner of the panel and drag down to enlarge the panel.

Create a New Layer

- An illustration can contain almost any number of layers.
- To create a new layer, click the Create New Layer button on the Layers panel, or select New Layer from the Layers panel menu.

  ✓ *Be careful not to click the Create New Sublayer button. You will learn more about sublayers in the next exercise.*

- In a new document that has only one layer, a new layer moves to the top of the list of layers in the Layers panel, as shown in Figure 18-3. The topmost layer in this panel is always at the front of the stacking order.

Figure 18-3. New layer added to Layers panel

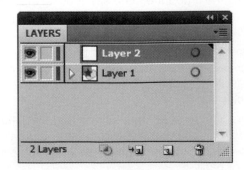

- If there is more than one layer in the panel when a new layer is created, the new layer appears above the currently selected layer. To make sure the new layer always displays at the top of the layer list, hold down Ctrl while clicking the Create New Layer button.

- Select a layer by clicking its name in the Layers panel.

- Note that like many other Illustrator panels, the Layers panel has a Delete Selection button 🗑. Drag a layer to this button, or click it to delete the currently selected layer.

Name a Layer

- By default, layers are given the name *Layer* plus a number that indicates how many layers have been created in the document.

- It is a good idea to give layers names that make clear their function or the type of objects stored on them.

- To name a layer, double-click the layer in the Layers panel, or select the layer and choose Options for "Layer *x*" on the panel menu. Either action opens a Layer Options dialog box for that layer.

- Or hold down Alt while clicking the Create New Layer button to create the layer and open the Layer Options dialog box at the same time.

- In the Layer Options dialog box shown in Figure 18-4, type a new name for the layer in the Name box.

Figure 18-4. Layer Options dialog box

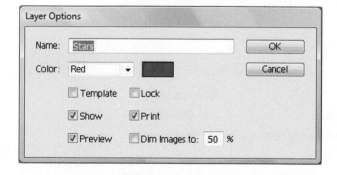

- Each layer in an illustration has its own selection color to make it easy for you to determine which layer a selected object belongs to.

- You can change the default selection color for a layer by clicking the Color list arrow and choosing a new color.

Select Layer Objects

- You can use the Layers panel to select objects in an illustration.

- Clicking the target symbol at the far right of the layer name selects all objects on that layer and displays the colored selection square on the Layers panel, as shown in Figure 18-5. Or, you can click in the location of the selection square to display it and select all objects on the layer.

Figure 18-5. Select all objects on a layer

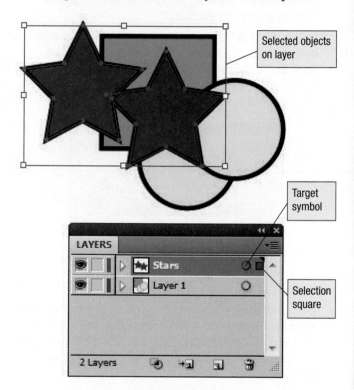

- Selecting an object in the work area will also select its layer in the Layers panel and display the colored selection square.

- When an illustration contains a great many objects distributed among a number of layers, it can sometimes be a challenge to identify an object's layer or sublayer, particularly when layers are collapsed.

- To quickly identify an object's layer, select the object and then choose Locate Object on the Layers panel menu. This option immediately opens the layer that contains the selected object.

Move Objects to a Layer

- It is common to create a number of objects in an illustration and then decide that layers would make it much easier to work with the objects.

- Existing objects may be moved from one layer to another in several ways. One way is to use the Cut and Paste in Front or Paste in Place commands:
  - On the artboard, select the object to move and use the Edit > Cut command to remove the object from its current layer.
  - Select a new layer in the Layers panel and use the Edit > Paste in Front (or Paste in Place) command to place the object on the new layer in the same position it was in on the previous layer.
- You can also move objects to a new layer, or to a different layer, by dragging the selection square from one layer to another.
- In Figure 18-6, for example, the user has selected the group of circles in Layer 1 and dragged the selection square up to the Circles layer.

Figure 18-6. Move objects between layers

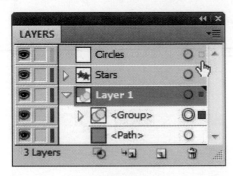

- Dragging a layer's selection square to another layer will move all objects from the original layer to the new layer. They will maintain the same positions on the new layer that they occupied on the original layer.

Move Layers to Change Stacking Order

- One of the best reasons to use layers is the ease with which you can control stacking of objects in an illustration.
- To change the stacking order of layers, simply drag a layer to a new position in the Layers panel. The layer at the top of the list in the panel is at the front of the stacking order.
- To move a layer in the panel, click the layer to select it, hold down the mouse button, and drag the layer to its new position.
- Illustrator displays a grabbing hand pointer and a horizontal bar that indicates the moving layer, as shown in Figure 18-7.

Figure 18-7. Move a layer in the layers list

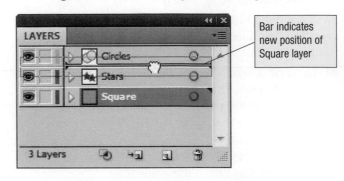

- It is also possible to change the order of the objects in a specific layer. Drag the item to its new location in the layer list, or use the Arrange commands in the work area to send an item backward or forward; the position adjusts in the layer list as it changes in the work area.

PROCEDURES

Create a New Layer

- Click **Create New Layer** button ⬛ on Layers panel.

  ✓ Hold down Ctrl while clicking to create new layer at top of Layers list.

  ✓ Hold down Alt while clicking to create new layer and open Layer Options dialog box.

  OR

1. Click ▤ in Layers panel to display panel menu.
2. Click **New Layer**.

Delete a Layer

1. Click layer to select it.
2. Click **Delete Selection** button 🗑 on Layers panel.

   OR

1. Select layer to delete.
2. Click ▤ in Layers panel to display panel menu.
3. Click **Delete "Layer x"**.

Name a Layer

1. Double-click layer name.

   OR

   a. Select layer to name.
   b. Click ▤ in Layers panel to display panel menu.
   c. Click **Options for "Layer x"**.

2. Type new name for layer.
3. Select a new selection color for layer if desired.
4. Click **OK** .... ENTER

Select Layer Objects

▪ Select target symbol at far right of layer name.

OR

▪ Click in area between target symbol and small black triangle to select colored selection square.

Move Objects to a Layer

1. Select item on artboard to be moved.
2. Click **Edit** .... ALT + E
3. Click **Cut** .... T

4. Select layer in Layers panel to move cut item to.
5. Click **Edit** .... ALT + E
6. Click **Paste in Front** .... F

OR

Click **Paste in Place** .... SHIFT + CTRL + V

OR

1. Select layer objects as directed under *Select Layer Objects* above.
2. Click colored selection square, hold down the mouse button, and drag the square to new layer.

Move Layers to Change Stacking Order

1. Select layer to move.
2. Hold down the mouse button and drag layer to new location.

   ✓ *Moving a layer to the top of the list may result in the layer being included as a sublayer in the current top layer. It may be easier to move a layer to the second position, and then drag the current top layer below the second layer.*

EXERCISE DIRECTIONS

✓ *Display the Painting workspace.*

1. Open ⊙ 18Global and save the file as 18Global_xx.

   ✓ *Note that all items in this illustration are on the default Layer 1 and some reordering of objects is necessary. You will first move objects to new layers and then reorder the layers.*

2. Rename Layer 1 as **Dash**.
3. Create a new layer named **Text**.
4. Expand the Dash layer to see all the other objects on this layer. Locate and select the *Global* text object at the bottom of the list of objects in the Dash layer.
5. Cut the text object from its current layer, select the Text layer, and use Paste in Front to paste the object in the new layer.
6. Create a new layer named **Stripe** at the top of the layers list.
7. Move the vertical red stripe to the Stripe layer.
8. Create a new layer named **Stars** and move the brushed stars path (the first path in the Dash layer) to the new layer.
9. Create a new layer named **Background** and move the irregular black rectangle to the new layer.
10. Create a new layer named **Earth** and move the blue globe to the new layer.
11. The gold "swoosh" that circles the globe is in two pieces. Create two new layers named **Swoosh Straight** and **Swoosh Curve**.

12. Place the horizontal swoosh section on Swoosh Straight and the curved portion of the swoosh on Swoosh Curve.

    ✓ *All items in the illustration should now be on separate layers. Enlarge the Layers panel if necessary to see all layers at once.*

13. Use the Dash layer to select the dashed gold line.

    ✓ *You will eventually apply a drop shadow to the dashed line and the red stripe, so it makes sense to have both objects on the same layer.*

14. Expand both the Dash and the Stripe layers. Drag the dashed line path into the Stripe layer above the red stripe path.

    ✓ *Notice that the dashed line is now in front of the red stripe.*

15. The Dash layer is now empty, so delete it from the Layers panel.
16. The brushed stars are not visible. Move the Stars layer above the Background layer.
17. The curved portion of the swoosh should go behind the blue globe. Move the Swoosh Curve layer below the Earth layer.
18. Your Layers panel should look similar to Illustration A. The illustration should resemble Illustration B.
19. Save your changes, close the file, and exit Illustrator.

Illustration A

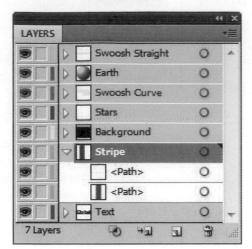

Illustration B

ON YOUR OWN

1. Start Illustrator.
2. Open OIL16_xx or OYO18 and save the file as OIL18_xx.
3. Group the ash leaves and their stems.
4. Create layers for each leaf and the brushed leaves (Gingko, Redbud, Ash, Leaf Brush).
5. Move the objects to their appropriate layers.

6. Delete the curved Pen path in the scratch area that is still on Layer 1, and then delete Layer 1.
7. Adjust the layout and stacking order as desired to display the objects in the illustration attractively.
8. Save your changes, close the file, and exit Illustrator.

Exercise | 19

Skills Covered

- Create a Sublayer
- Make Global Changes to Layer Objects
- View and Hide Layers

- Lock a Layer
- Merge and Flatten Layers
- Other Layers Panel Menu Options

Software Skills   A sublayer is a layer within a layer used to organize related objects. Once grouped in layers, similar or identical objects can easily be changed all at once. You can hide one or more layers to make it easier to work with a specific layer. Lock layers to make sure they cannot be changed. Merge or flatten layers to make the printing process more efficient.

Design Skills   An experienced designer can perform many chores by manipulating layers: group similar objects, rearrange objects, apply effects to all objects on a layer. Options in the Layers panel and on the panel menu help a designer to prepare a design for final output.

Application Skills   In this exercise, you will continue working on the map of Australia that you created earlier in the course. You will create layers for existing objects, create sublayers for city information, hide and lock layers, and finally merge all layers for the printer.

TERMS

Parent layer   Layer in which one or more sublayers are stored.

Sublayer   A layer within a layer that can have its own name and its own settings.

NOTES

Create a Sublayer

- When some objects on a layer are very similar, you can create a sublayer in a layer for those objects.
- A **sublayer** is a layer within a layer. Sublayers can have their own names and settings, just like layers, but they are ultimately controlled by the layer in which they are stored.
- A layer that contains one or more sublayers is called a **parent layer**.
- In Figure 19-1, the Cities parent layer has two sublayers, Stars and Text. Selecting the Cities layer also selects both sublayers, but each sublayer may also be selected separately.

Figure 19-1. Selecting a layer also selects sublayers

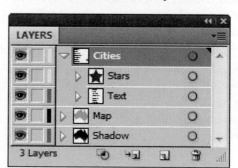

- To create a sublayer, select the layer in which the sublayer will be stored and then click the Create New Sublayer button ⊞ on the Layers panel.

  ✓ *Or, choose New Sublayer on the Layers panel menu.*

- Name a sublayer the same way as a layer by double-clicking the sublayer's default name or using the panel menu's Options for… command.

- Sublayers may be reorganized the same way as layers. Drag a sublayer to a new position in the layer list to adjust its stacking order.

- You can use isolation mode to concentrate on the items in a sublayer. Use the Enter Isolation Mode option on the Layers panel menu to hide all other layers except the selected sublayer.

- To change a sublayer into a layer, drag it out of its parent layer into the list of layers. To change a layer into a sublayer, drag it into a layer.

Make Global Changes to Layer Objects

- After objects have been moved to a layer, it is very easy to make changes that affect all objects on that layer.

- For example, by selecting a layer or sublayer, you can apply a drop shadow that applies to all objects on that layer.

- Or, when all text is stored on a single layer, you can change the font, style, or size of all text objects at the same time by selecting that layer.

- Making changes in this fashion is similar to making global changes to grouped objects.

View and Hide Layers

- You may sometimes want to hide one or more layers when working on another layer. To view or hide layers, use the visibility box to the far left of a layer's name in the Layers panel.

- By default, all layers are visible. Visible layers display the eye icon 👁 in the visibility box.

- To hide a layer, simply click its eye icon. To view the layer again, click the visibility box as shown in Figure 19-2 to restore the eye icon.

- You can also hide all layers except the selected layer using the Hide Others option on the Layers panel menu.

- After hiding several layers, use the Show All Layers option on the Layers panel menu to quickly unhide all layers.

Figure 19-2. Click visibility box to unhide Stars sublayer

Lock a Layer

- To prevent changes to a layer, you may lock the layer.

- To lock a layer, click in the edit box to the right of the visibility box to display the lock icon 🔒, as shown in Figure 19-3. To quickly lock more than one layer, drag the pointer down the edit box column.

Figure 19-3. Lock a layer by clicking the edit box

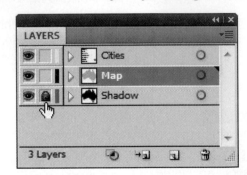

- When a layer is locked, its objects cannot be selected or edited. Locking a parent layer automatically locks all sublayers as well.

- Layers may be unlocked by clicking or dragging down the edit boxes to remove the lock icons.

Merge and Flatten Layers

- Illustrations with multiple layers may cause problems at the printing stage. You can reduce the number of layers, after completing an illustration, by *merging* or *flattening* the layers.

- Merging allows you to select which layers to combine. Select the first layer, hold down Shift, and select any additional layers, as shown in Figure 19-4.

Figure 19-4. Select more than one layer

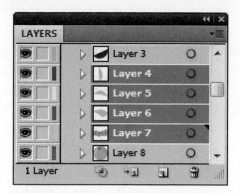

- Use the Merge Selected option on the Layers panel menu to combine all selected layers into the last layer selected.

- In Figure 19-4, for example, the objects on Layers 4, 5, 6, and 7 will be merged together. The combined layer takes the name of the last selected layer, in this case Layer 7.

- Flattening combines all layers into a single layer. To flatten layers, select the layer that will hold all objects and use the Flatten Artwork option on the panel menu.

- The result is an illustration that has only a single layer.

- Layers cannot be flattened into a locked or hidden layer. Before flattening, unlock and unhide all layers.

Other Layers Panel Menu Options

- The Layers panel menu contains several other useful options to make working with layers more efficient.

- The Make Clipping Mask option on the Layers panel menu or the Make Clipping Mask button on the panel can be used to clip an object to the shape of an object on top of it.

- To create a new layer and move objects into it at the same time, use the Collect in New Layer option on the panel menu.

- To move all objects in an illustration into separate layers, use the Release to Layers (Sequence) option. This is a quick way to distribute all items to layers.

- You can then name the layers, create sublayers as necessary, or merge layers to group objects that should be on the same layer.

- The Release to Layers (Build) option creates layers in which objects accumulate. The first layer has one object, the second two, and so on.

- Use the Template option to turn all objects on the currently selected layer into a template that can be used as a guide for creating other objects. A template layer's name is italicized, and the layer is automatically locked so that the template object(s) cannot be selected.

- You may on occasion want to see layer objects in Outline view rather than Preview view to make it easier to concentrate on the selected layer.

- Use the Outline Others option on the panel menu to reduce to outlines all layer objects except the selected layer.

- When cutting or copying and pasting objects in an illustration that has layers, it can be a challenge to get the pasted object on the right layer.

- Select the Paste Remembers Layers option on the Layers panel menu to tell Illustrator to paste an item back in the layer from which it was copied rather than into the currently active layer. You can also use this command when pasting objects in a new document to recreate the same layers in which the objects were stored in the source document.

PROCEDURES

Create a Sublayer

1. Select layer in which to create sublayer.
2. Click **Create New Sublayer** button ⊞ on Layers panel.

   OR

   a. Click ▤ in Layers panel to display panel menu.
   b. Click **New Sublayer**.

Make Global Changes to Layer Objects

1. Select target symbol to right of layer name to select all objects on layer.

   OR

   Click in area between target symbol and small black triangle to select colored selection square.
2. Apply desired format option to all selected objects at same time.

Hide Layers

1. Select layer to hide.
2. Click visibility icon 👁 at far left of layer name.

   OR

   a. Click ▤ in Layers panel to display panel menu.
   b. Click **Hide Others** to hide all layers except selected layer.

View Layers

- Click in visibility box to display eye icon again.

   OR

1. Click ▤ in Layers panel to display panel menu.
2. Click **Show All Layers** to reveal all hidden layers.

Lock a Layer

- Click in edit box of layer to lock.

   OR

- Drag pointer down multiple edit boxes to lock several layers at once.

   OR

1. Click ▤ in Layers panel to display panel menu.
2. Click **Lock All Layers** to lock all layers.

Unlock a Layer

- Click lock icon 🔒 in edit box, or drag pointer over multiple lock icons to unlock layers.

   OR

1. Click ▤ in Layers panel to display panel menu.
2. Click **Unlock All Layers** to reveal all hidden layers.

Merge Layers

1. Select first layer to merge.
2. Hold down SHIFT and click additional layers.
3. Click ▤ in Layers panel to display panel menu.
4. Click **Merge Selected**.

Flatten Layers

1. Select layer in which to combine all other layers.
2. Click ▤ in Layers panel to display panel menu.
3. Click **Flatten Artwork**.

Release Objects to Layers

1. Select layer that contains objects to release.
2. Click ▤ in Layers panel to display panel menu.
3. Click **Release to Layers (Sequence)**.
4. Rename and organize layers as desired.

EXERCISE DIRECTIONS

✓ *Display the Painting workspace.*

1. Open 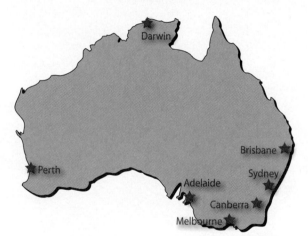 19Australia and save the document as 19Australia_xx.

2. Use the Release to Layers (Sequence) option to separate the objects in this illustration into layers.

3. Rename the layers as follows:

   a. Rename Layer 10 (the black shadow) **Shadow**.

   b. Rename Layer 9 (the orange map) **Map**.

4. Merge Layers 2 through 8 into Layer 8, and then rename the layer **Text**.

   ✓ *Text, Map, and Shadow are currently sublayers of Layer 1, the original layer in the illustration. Next, you will move sublayers to become layers.*

5. Select the Map layer and drag it above Layer 1.

   ✓ *If the Map layer does not appear above Layer 1, it has become a sublayer of Layer 1. Use Undo and try again to drag the layer above Layer 1.*

6. Select the Shadow layer and drag it above Layer 1 but below the Map layer.

7. Create a new layer at the top of the layer list and name it **Cities**.

8. Drag the Text sublayer up on top of the Cities layer to move the sublayer from Layer 1 to Cities.

9. Delete Layer 1.

10. Create a new sublayer in the Cities layer and name it **Stars**.

11. With the Stars layer selected, draw a small five-pointed star and fill it with a dark blue swatch. Remove the stroke.

12. Hide the Shadow layer. With the Stars layer selected, use the Outline Others panel menu command to reduce the Map layer to an outline.

13. Position the star as shown in Illustration A for Darwin.

14. Copy the star for each city shown in Illustration A and position the stars as shown.

15. Restore Preview view for all layers.

16. Drag each city name to its correct location on the map, using Illustration A as a guide.

17. Unhide the Shadow layer, and lock the Shadow and the Map layers.

18. Select only the stars on the map and change their swatch color to bright red. Then select the Text sublayer and change text color to the same red as the stars.

19. (Optional) Select the Cities layer and apply a drop shadow effect as follows to all objects on the layer:

    a. Click Effect > Stylize > Drop Shadow.

    b. Set Opacity to **60%**.

    c. Set X and Y Offsets to **5** pts.

    d. Set Blur to **3** pts.

20. Unlock the locked layers.

21. Flatten all layers in the illustration into the Map layer.

22. Save your changes, close the file, and exit Illustrator.

Illustration A

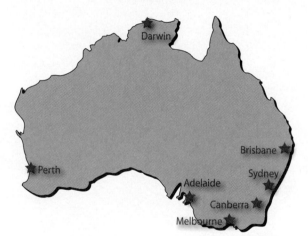

ON YOUR OWN

1. Start Adobe Illustrator.
2. Open ⊙OYO19 and save the document as OIL19_*xx*. If you receive a message about spot colors, click Continue.
3. Release all objects to layers using the Release to Layers (Sequence) option.
4. Rename and reorganize layers as follows:

   a. Create a new layer above Layer 1 named **Olives** and move the olive group into it.

   b. Merge the olive highlight objects into a single layer named **Highlights** and drag the Highlights sublayer above the Group sublayer in the Olives layer.

   c. Name the layer that contains the orange group **Orange** and the layer that contains the watermelon slice **Watermelon**.

   d. Create a new layer named **Fruit** and move into it the Orange and Watermelon sublayers.

   e. Create a new layer named **Lemonade**. Rename the layers that contain the glass group and the bubbles and move them into the Lemonade layer.

   f. Rename the remaining layers appropriately and drag them out of Layer 1.

5. Delete any empty layers and rearrange layers and sublayers as necessary to position the objects in the proper stacking order. Change the layer colors as necessary so that each layer has its own color.

6. (Optional) Select the entire Fruit layer and apply an effect to all objects in the layer as follows:

   a. Click Effect > Stylize > Inner Glow.

   b. Change the Opacity setting to about 60%.

7. Lock the layer that contains the tablecloth.

8. Save your changes, close the file, and exit Illustrator.

Exercise | 20

Summary Exercise

Application Skills Allie's Alley, a local bowling establishment, has asked you to create a graphic to be used for marketing purposes. In this exercise, you will create the illustration using tools and features you have learned in this lesson.

EXERCISE DIRECTIONS

✓ *Display the Painting workspace.*

1. Open ◎20Bowling and save the file as 20Bowling_xx. This file contains only a guide for creating a bowling pin.
2. Rename Layer 1 as **Guide**. Lock the Guide layer.

Create the Bowling Pin

1. Create a new layer named **Pins**. On this layer, use the Pen tool to trace the shape in the left scratch area to create half of a bowling pin.
2. Reflect the shape vertically and make a copy of it. Drag the copy to the right to complete the pin shape.
3. Join the endpoints at the top and bottom of the pin to complete the outline.
4. Apply a light gray stroke color, and then use the Paintbrush tool with a brush type of your choice and several shades of light gray to paint shading at the right and left sides of the pin to create an illusion of depth, as shown in Illustration A.
5. Use the Pen or Pencil tool to create a decoration around the narrowest part of the pin, either the crown shape shown in Illustration A, two parallel lines, or something similar.
6. Group all the objects used to create the pin.
7. Create a copy of the pin and move the copy to the right. Rotate the original pin slightly left and the copy to the right, as if the pins are being knocked down.

Draw the Bowling Ball

1. Create a new layer named **Ball**.
2. On the Ball layer, create an ellipse about **220** pts wide and high and fill with a color of your choice. Position the ball as if it is striking the pins.
3. Create three circles for the finger holes and fill with a medium gray. Group the circles and position them on the ball. If they are too large or small for the size of the ball, scale the group as necessary.
4. Drag a copy of the holes group slightly below and to the left of the original group. Use the Eyedropper to pick up the color of the ball as a fill, and then adjust this color to be darker than the ball, so it looks as if the holes are recessed in the ball.
5. Make the ball's stroke the same color as the finger holes. Apply a variable width profile to the stroke and adjust the profile as desired using the Width tool to give an appearance of three dimensions to the ball.
6. Group all items that make up the ball.

Add the Alley and Star

1. Create a new layer named **Alley and Star**. Use the Pen or Rectangle tool to draw a shape to represent the bowling alley. (See Illustration A.) Fill with a light tan and move the layer below the Pins layer.

2. Add Pencil or Pen lines with dark brown stroke to represent the individual boards that make up the alley and apply a dash stroke format to give these lines some texture.

3. It is traditional in illustrations of this sort to represent the impact of ball on pins with a starburst shape. Use Draw Behind mode to create such a shape that will appear behind the pins.

4. Fill the star shape with a very light yellow and no stroke. Use the Direct Selection tool to adjust star points to give a more random appearance.

5. Make any further adjustments you think necessary. Hide the Guide layer. Your drawing should resemble Illustration A.

6. Save your changes, close the file, and exit Illustrator.

Illustration A

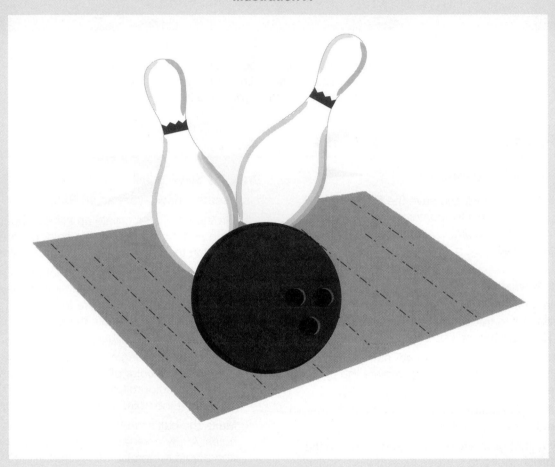

Application Exercise

Application Skills   Your city's symphony orchestra is planning a brochure to alert patrons that it is time to buy tickets for the upcoming season. In this exercise, you will create several objects for the symphony brochure. You will trace a violin outline and apply a brush to a path to create a depiction of musical notes on a music staff.

EXERCISE DIRECTIONS

✓ *Display the Painting workspace.*

1. Open 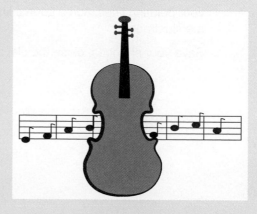 21Violin and save the file as 21Violin_xx. This file contains some objects in the scratch area and a brush you will need for the illustration.

   ✓ *As you work, create layers as you think necessary to organize the objects in the drawing.*

2. Place the 21Violin.gif data file in the Illustrator file.

   ✓ *The violin photo the client gave you had a great deal of texture to it. A colleague applied several Photoshop effects to "posterize" the illustration so you can trace it more easily.*

3. Start Live Trace and choose the preset that gives you the most solid shape of the violin.

   ✓ *Hint: You may find that Inked Drawing is your best bet.*

4. Once you are satisfied with the trace, expand it.

5. Clean up any unneeded strokes or fills.

6. Scale the violin body down until it is about **200** pts high.

7. Adjust the violin body fill to a warm golden brown color.

8. Apply a dark brown stroke, change stroke weight to **5** pt, and then apply variable width profile 2.

9. Create a rectangle for the violin fingerboard that is about **17** pts wide by **115** pts high. Fill with black and remove the stroke.

10. Use the Direct Selection tool to pull the top corners of the rectangle in **4** pts, so the rectangle is tapered at the top.

11. Group the objects in the scratch area (the scroll and pegs) and drag them to the top of the fingerboard.

12. Group all objects for the neck of the violin and move it on top of the violin body as shown in Illustration A.

13. Group the violin objects and lock the layers that contain the violin objects.

14. Move the rectangular grid object from the scratch area behind the violin, as shown in Illustration A. Then hide the violin layers so you can work with the music staff object.

15. Draw a path on the music staff grid using the musical note scatter brush in the Brushes panel.

16. Show all layers. Your drawing should resemble Illustration A.

17. Save your changes, close the file, and exit Illustrator.

Illustration A

Exercise | 22

Curriculum Integration

Application Skills   Your biology class is studying various types of cells. You have been assigned the task of illustrating a prokaryotic cell, the type of cell that bacteria have. Your cell should have the following elements:

- Capsule
- Cell wall
- Cytoplasm
- Ribosomes
- Nucleoid region
- Pili and/or flagella

EXERCISE DIRECTIONS

Start a new drawing and save it as 22Cell_xx. As you work, organize your objects on layers.

Use the Internet to find some representative illustrations of prokaryotic cells. These illustrations will differ, but will include most or all of the elements listed above. You can copy a picture if desired and use it as the basis for a Live Trace.

Adjust the shape of an ellipse to create the cell capsule and cell wall. Create the nucleoid region using the Pencil tool. The pili can also be created using pencil strokes.

Locate a brush in a brush library, such as the Tiny Circles decorative scatter bush, that you can use to distribute the ribosomes in the cell. You may want to adjust the size of the dots by modifying the brush.

Use the Paintbrush, Pen, or the Pencil tool to create the flagella. Illustration A shows how some of the parts of the cell may look as you create the drawing.

Label the parts of the cell. Add arrowheads of your choice from the Stroke panel to your pointing lines. Add a source line for the Web site on which you found the cell you are illustrating.

Save your changes, close the file, and exit Illustrator.

Illustration A

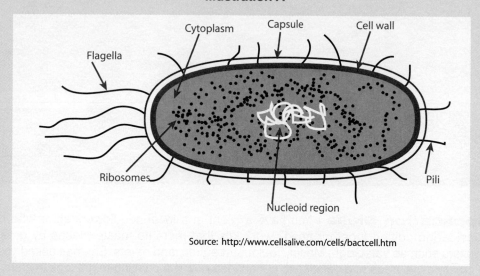

Source: http://www.cellsalive.com/cells/bactcell.htm

Exercise | 23

Portfolio Builder

Application Skills You have a client at a local needlework store who is considering putting together needlework kits that recreate masterpieces by great painters such as Van Gogh, Monet, Toulouse-Lautrec, and others. She has asked you to create a live trace of a painting to get an idea how the painting might look in a simplified version and how many colors of tapestry wool or floss would be needed.

EXERCISE DIRECTIONS

- Spend a few moments locating a suitable painting on the Internet. You can usually find a number of locations with representative artwork by searching on the artist's name. You can use the artists listed above or another artist whose work you enjoy.

- Copy the picture in GIF or JPEG format and then place it in Illustrator.

- Trace the picture. Adjust the number of colors if necessary. You can add or reduce colors depending on the painting. Select the least number of colors that will display the artwork attractively. Adjust the minimum size of objects being traced so that you don't have too many very small areas that will be difficult to chart.

- Output swatches to make it easy for your client to match colors of tapestry wool or floss.

- Label the trace with the name of the painting and the artist's name. Illustration A shows an example.

- Save the illustration as 23Painting_xx and close the illustration. Exit Illustrator.

Illustration A

Vincent Van Gogh "Irises"

Lesson | 3

Work with Colors, Effects, and Styles

Exercise | 24

Skills Covered

- **Color Models and the Color Panel**
- **Process and Spot Colors**
- **Add a Custom Color to the Swatches Panel**
- **Work with the Swatches Panel**

Software Skills   Besides the default CMYK color mode, Illustrator offers RGB, HSB, and Grayscale modes. Choose process or spot colors depending on how an illustration is to be printed. Use the Color panel to create custom colors, which can then be added to the Swatches panel. Use Swatches panel options to change the display of swatches, rename them, or delete them.

Design Skills   Every kind of design work requires a thorough understanding of color principles. Learning about color models and how they display color enables a designer to make a reasoned choice when selecting a color system for a new design. A designer who works with print designs must also have a good grasp of process and spot colors.

Application Skills   In this exercise, you will begin an illustration for a local radio station, WWAV ("The Wave"). You will create custom colors for the illustration and save them in a color group in the Swatches panel so they can be applied easily in the illustration. You will adjust the Swatches panel display to make it easy to work with the Wave colors.

TERMS

CMYK model   The CMYK (Cyan, Magenta, Yellow, black, or Key) model combines percentages of these four basic ink colors to produce a desired color.

Color group   A collection of related color swatches.

Gamut   Range of colors that can be displayed by any color system.

Global color   Color that automatically updates throughout an illustration if its color swatch is edited.

HSB model   The HSB (Hue, Saturation, Brightness) model is based on how people perceive colors. Pick a hue and then adjust its saturation and brightness.

Process color   A color created using combinations of cyan, magenta, yellow, and black ink.

RGB model   The RGB (Red, Green, Blue) model uses the basic colors of light in the visible spectrum to create colors best viewed on a monitor or digital device.

Spot color   A color created using a premixed ink color.

Tint   A color that is lightened by adding white to achieve a paler version of the color.

NOTES

Color Models and the Color Panel

- So far in this course, you have used only the default print document color model, CMYK, in your illustrations.
- You can, however, choose from four color models in Illustrator: Grayscale, RGB, HSB, and CMYK.

Grayscale Model

- The Grayscale model is the simplest model to understand and to use. This model uses only one color, black, but you may adjust the percentage of black from 100% to 0%.

  ✓ 0% black can also be considered 100% white.

- The Color panel for the Grayscale model has only one slider, which shows 100% black (K) at the right end and 0% black at the left end as shown in Figure 24-1.

Figure 24-1. Color panel for Grayscale model

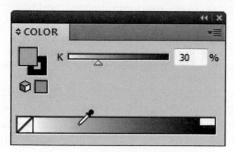

- You can select a percentage of black by dragging the K slider, typing a value, or clicking with the eyedropper on the grayscale ramp.

RGB Color Model

- The **RGB model** uses the basic colors of light in the visible spectrum: red, green, and blue. When these colors of light are mixed together, or added, they result in white.

- The RGB model is best used for images that will appear on computer monitors, mobile devices, or in video or film productions.

- The Color panel for the RGB model has three sliders to display red, blue, and green as shown in Figure 24-2.

- Values on the sliders run from 0 to 255. When all three sliders are set to 0, the result is black, because all color is absent.

Figure 24-2. RGB Color panel

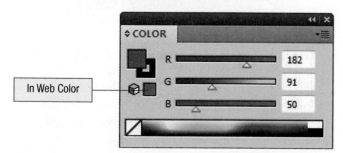

- When all three sliders are set to 255, the result is white, because all color is present. If all three sliders are set to the same value, the result is a gray color.

- In the earliest days of the World Wide Web, the so-called *Web-safe color palette* was developed, containing colors that would display the same way in all Web browsers.

- Although monitor and Web browser technology has advanced to the point that it is no longer necessary to adhere strictly to the Web-safe palette when preparing illustrations for onscreen viewing, Illustrator will give you a visual cue if a color you have mixed is not one of the 216 Web-safe colors.

- The In Web Color block displays in the Color panel (see Figure 24-2) to show you the Web-safe color that is closest to the one you have mixed. You can simply click the color block to correct the current color to a Web-safe color.

- Illustrator also offers an entire color model of Web-safe RGB colors that makes it easy to prepare Web illustrations if you want to use only Web-safe colors.

HSB Color Model

- The **HSB model** is based on how humans perceive color. The three characteristics we register when we see a color are *hue*, *saturation*, and *brightness*.

  - *Hue* is the color reflected from an object or transmitted through an object, such as the green color of grass. In the HSB model, hue is the pure color.

  - *Saturation* is the strength of the color. Saturation is expressed on a sliding scale with gray at one end and the pure color on the other. A pure color is 100% saturated. As saturation decreases, more gray is mixed in.

  - *Brightness* is the lightness or darkness of a color. Brightness is expressed on a sliding scale with black at one end and white or color at the other. The lightest version of the current color is 100% bright.

- Figure 24-3 shows the Color panel for the HSB model. It has three sliders, one each for hue, saturation, and brightness.

Figure 24-3. Color panel for HSB model

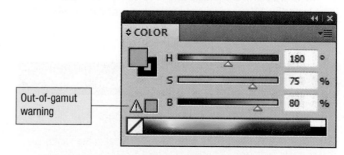

- Create a color by specifying hue, saturation, and brightness values. The hue value describes its position on a standard color wheel, with the location expressed in degrees between 0 and 360.

- The range of colors that can be displayed by any color system is called its **gamut**.

- If you mix a color that cannot be displayed or printed, the Color panel displays an *out-of-gamut* warning (see Figure 24-3).
- Next to the warning triangle is a color box that represents the closest in-gamut color. Click this color box to adjust the color so it can be displayed or printed.

CMYK Color Model

- The **CMYK model** was developed for use in full-color printing, where four basic ink colors—cyan (blue), magenta, yellow, and black—are combined to create desired colors.
- The Color panel for the CMYK model has four sliders, one for each color in the model as shown in Figure 24-4.

Figure 24-4. Color panel for CMYK model

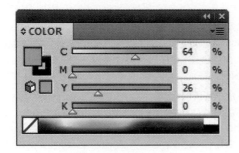

- Create a color by dragging sliders, typing percentages, or clicking the eyedropper in the CMYK spectrum.
- The lower a color's percentage, the lighter the color. If all four sliders are set to 0%, the color is white.
- Each slider shows how the current color would change if the slider were dragged in one direction or another, without moving the other sliders.
- Though the CMYK model is chiefly used for illustrations that will be printed, the CMYK color panel displays the Web-safe color block a user can click to correct colors for browser use.

Design Suite Integration

Creative Suite Color Models

You will work exclusively with the RGB color model in the Photoshop section. InDesign offers another color model, Lab, chiefly used for spot colors.

Process and Spot Colors

- When creating an illustration that is to be printed, you need to know whether the illustration will be printed using process or spot colors.
- **Process colors** are created using the four basic ink colors: cyan, magenta, yellow, and black.
- A **spot color** is created using premixed ink in a designated color.

  ✓ *An illustration can use both spot and process colors.*

- Any color that you create using the CMYK color model is a process color by default. You can change a process color to a spot color in the Swatch Options dialog box, shown later in this exercise.
- Process colors can be *global* or *nonglobal*. A color designated as a **global color** can be updated throughout an illustration wherever it is used by modifying its color swatch.
- Spot colors are most useful for one- or two-color illustrations, or when a specific color is required, such as a corporation's signature color. Spot colors are always designated as global colors.
- The Color panel for a spot color is similar to the panel for the Grayscale model: only one color is displayed, as shown in Figure 24-5.

Figure 24-5. Color panel for spot color

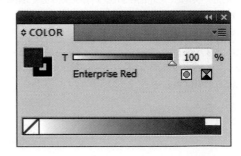

- The spot color is at the 100% end of the slider. You can select a **tint** of the spot color by dragging the slider or using the eyedropper on the tint ramp.
- Creating tints allows you to use several percentages of the same color in an illustration to add variety and definition to the drawing.
- You should be aware that the printing process itself can impact both process and spot colors. Choice of paper, for example, makes a great deal of difference in how colors print.
- You should also understand that printed colors may not match exactly those used on the monitor to create an illustration.

  ✓ *You will learn more about color printing in the Photoshop and InDesign sections of this course.*

Add a Custom Color to the Swatches Panel

■ As you already know, the Swatches panel provides a number of standard color swatches for easy application.

■ You can add your own swatches to the panel when you intend to use a color frequently in an illustration.

■ A new color swatch is named for its percentages of color. Rename the swatch and adjust its properties in the Swatch Options dialog box shown in Figure 24-6.

Figure 24-6. Swatch Options dialog box

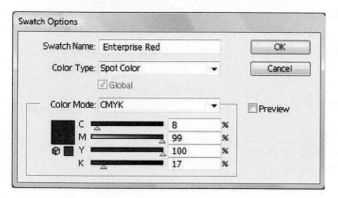

■ To create a global process color, select the Global check box below the Color Type box. If you designate the color type as Spot Color, the Global check box is automatically selected and dimmed, as shown in Figure 24-6.

■ You can also specify the color mode and adjust color percentages in this dialog box.

■ Display this dialog box at any time to change a swatch's properties by double-clicking the swatch in the Swatches panel.

Work with the Swatches Panel

■ By default, the Swatches panel displays three different types of swatches: color swatches, gradient swatches, and pattern swatches.

✓ *You will work with gradients later in this lesson.*

■ The Swatches panel also displays two default **color groups**, one containing a group of bright colors and the other containing grayscale swatches that range from 5 percent black to 100 percent black.

■ You can create a new color group to organize colors that you intend to use often so you don't have to pick them out of the default swatches or recreate them each time you want them.

■ You can adjust the display of swatches in the Swatches panel to show only colors, gradients, or patterns if you need to concentrate on swatches of a particular type.

■ You can drag any swatch in the panel to a new location in the panel or into or out of a color group.

■ Any swatch in the panel, even default swatches, may be renamed by double-clicking to display the Swatch Options dialog box.

■ Swatches may also be deleted by selecting the swatch and clicking Delete Swatch 🗑.

■ The Swatches panel menu provides further options for working with swatches and the panel, besides standard commands for creating a new swatch and deleting a swatch.

● Use the Duplicate Swatch command to copy a swatch. This is a good way to adjust a swatch color without having to create it from scratch.

● Use Select All Unused to select all swatch colors that are not used in the current illustration. You can then, if desired, delete unused colors.

● Use Add Used Colors to add all colors in the illustration that have not yet been defined as swatches to the Swatches panel. You can then rename them as desired.

■ You can sort the swatches to reorder their display. Sort by name to order all swatches by name alone or by kind to organize the swatches by type, such as color, gradient, and pattern, and then by name within the group.

■ Use the Show Find Field option to display a field in the Swatches panel in which you can type a name or number to locate a specific swatch.

■ Swatches are shown by default in Small Thumbnail View, but you can also select Medium or Large Thumbnail View to see a larger sample of the color, gradient, or pattern. Or, select one of the List Views to see the swatches listed by name.

■ Default swatches in the Swatches panel are process colors. Global process colors are designated by a white triangle in the lower-right corner.

■ A spot color is identified by a spot in the lower-right corner of the swatch as shown in Figure 24-7.

■ List View will also show a spot next to a spot color's name.

Figure 24-7. Spot and global colors in Swatches panel

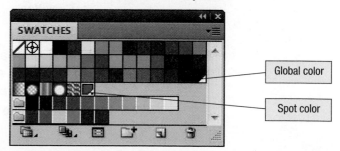

PROCEDURES

Select Color Model

1. Click 🔽 in Color panel to display panel menu.
2. Select desired color model.

Use Any Color Model to Create a Color

1. Click the color model on Color panel menu.
2. Drag slider(s), type percentage, or use eyedropper to select desired color.

Add Custom Color to Swatches Panel

1. Create color in Color panel.
2. Drag fill or stroke color box to Swatches panel and drop where you want color to appear.

   OR

   Click **New Swatch** button 🔲.
3. Double-click new swatch in Swatches panel if necessary to open Swatch Options dialog box.
4. Set options as follows:
   a. Type name for swatch.
   b. Select Process Color or Spot Color.
   c. Specify **Global** if desired for a process color.
   d. Modify color if desired.
5. Click **OK** .... ENTER

Create a Tint from a Spot Color

Display both the Color panel and the Swatches panel.

1. Select the spot color in the Swatches panel.
2. Adjust the color in the Color panel to the desired percentage.
3. Click **New Swatch** button 🔲 on Swatches panel.

   ✓ Tint will be added to Swatches panel already named with the swatch name and the tint percentage.

Work with Swatches Panel

To create a new color group:

1. Click **New Color Group** button 🔲 on Swatches panel.

   OR

   Click 🔽 in Swatches panel to display menu and click **New Color Group**.
2. Type name for color group.
3. Click **OK** .... ENTER
4. Add colors to the group by dragging a swatch on top of the color group folder.

To duplicate a swatch:

1. Select a swatch.
2. Click 🔽 in Swatches panel to display panel menu.
3. Click **Duplicate Swatch**.

To delete a swatch:

1. Select a swatch by clicking it.
2. Click **Delete Swatch** button 🗑.
3. Click **Yes** .... ENTER

   OR

1. Select a swatch.
2. Click 🔽 in Swatches panel to display panel menu.
3. Click **Delete Swatch**.

To sort swatches:

1. Click 🔽 in Swatches panel to display panel menu.
2. Select an option:
   - Click **Sort by Name** to sort all swatches by name.
   - Click **Sort by Kind** to sort all swatches first by type (colors, gradients, and patterns) and then by name within each type.

To change display of swatches:

1. Click 🔽 in Swatches panel to display panel menu.
2. Select an option:
   - Click **Medium Thumbnail View**.
   - Click **Large Thumbnail View**.
   - Click **Small List View**.
   - Click **Large List View**.
   - Click **Show Find Field** to display a field in which to type a swatch name or number to find.

To add all used colors as swatches:

1. Click 🔽 in Swatches panel to display panel menu.
2. Click **Add Used Colors**.
3. Rename and adjust new swatches as desired.

To select unused swatches:

1. Click 🔽 in Swatches panel to display panel menu.
2. Click **Select All Unused**.

   ✓ Selected swatches can be deleted to remove them from the Swatches panel.

EXERCISE DIRECTIONS

✓ *Display the Painting workspace.*

1. Open ⊙ **24Wave** and save the file as **24Wave_xx**.

   ✓ *The rectangles and trapezoids will be used to contain the letters of the station's nickname.*

2. Create a new color group named **Wave**. (You may want to float the Swatches panel in the workspace to make it easier to work with the colors you add in this exercise.)

3. The first rectangle will be green. Remove the stroke and create a new swatch color as follows:

   a. Drag the Color panel sliders to **C = 70**, **M = 0**, **Y = 85**, **K = 10**.

   b. Create a new swatch and name it **Wave Green**.

   c. The color should be a global process color.

   d. Drag the Wave Green swatch to the Wave color group.

4. The first trapezoid will be gold. Remove the stroke and create the color with settings of **C = 0**, **M = 17**, **Y = 100**, **K = 20**.

5. Add the color to the Swatches panel as a global process color with the name **Wave Gold**. Move the swatch to the Wave color group.

6. The second trapezoid will be purple. Remove the stroke and create the color by typing the following percentages: **C = 50**, **M = 80**, **Y = 0**, **K = 10**.

7. Add the color to the Wave color group as a global process color with the name **Wave Purple**.

8. The last rectangle will be red. Remove the stroke and create the color with settings of **C = 5**, **M = 90**, **Y = 90**, **K = 0**.

9. Add the color to the Wave color group as a global process color with the name **Wave Red**.

10. Apply Wave Gold as the stroke color for the three wavy lines.

11. Remove the stroke from the ellipse behind the other objects, and fill with **C = 80**, **M = 25**, **Y = 0**, **K = 30**.

12. Add the color to the Swatches panel as **Wave Blue**. This is WWAV's corporate color and should be an exact ink color. Make this color a spot color. Move the swatch into the Wave color group.

13. You will need a tint of Wave Blue for type. Create a 15% tint of Wave Blue and add it as a swatch to the Wave color group.

    ✓ *You want to use a particular funky font, Jokerman, for the call letters in the illustration. To make sure these letters display in the correct font, they have been converted to outlines and included in the scratch area to the right of the artboard.*

14. Select all four letters in the scratch area (you may have to scroll to see them) and bring them to the front.

15. Drag the letters into place on their appropriate shapes (see Illustration A). Remove the stroke and fill the letters as follows:

    a. Fill the *W* with Wave Blue (100%).

    b. Fill the *A* with Wave Red.

    c. Fill the *V* with Wave Green.

    d. Fill the *E* with Wave Gold.

16. Wave Gold is too dark. Because you made this a global color, you can easily change it throughout the illustration: Double-click the swatch to open the Swatch Options dialog box, and change the **K** percentage to **5**.

17. With the Type tool, click near the bottom of the Wave Blue ellipse and type **WWAV 94.1 FM**. Apply **Arial Black** font and change font size to **18 pt**.

18. Change the fill color for the text to Wave Blue 15%. Your illustration should resemble Illustration A.

19. Save your changes, close the file, and exit Illustrator.

Illustration A

ON YOUR OWN

> ✓ *Creative Glassworks, a new client, has asked you to create a simple mosaic illustration it can use for an informational flyer. You will use the HSB color model for this illustration.*

1. Start a new Illustrator file using the CMYK color model, then change the color mode to HSB in the Color panel.

2. Save the document as OIL24_xx.

3. If desired, display the grid (View > Show Grid) to make it easy to draw simple shapes in a mosaic similar to the one shown in Illustration B.

4. Fill the shapes with a variety of colors that you create using the Color panel. You may use multiple colors or variations on one color, as shown in Illustration B.

5. Add all used colors to the Swatches panel. Make one of the colors a spot color.

6. Select all colors you have not used and delete them.

7. Add text of your choice below the mosaic, using the spot color you created. Use your judgment as to font, font style, and size. Your illustration might look similar to the one shown in Illustration B.

8. Save your changes, close the file, and exit Illustrator.

Illustration B

130

Skills Covered

- **Use Eyedropper to Apply Color**
- **Modify Colors**
- **Adjust Color Opacity**
- **Apply a Blending Mode**
- **Create an Opacity Mask**
- **Use Swatch Libraries**

Software Skills Use the Eyedropper to quickly apply existing colors to objects. Modify colors by changing from process to spot, adjusting saturation, inverting, or complementing. Adjust color transparency, apply a blending mode, and create opacity masks to achieve interesting effects. Illustrator supplies a number of swatch libraries of standard color systems and theme-based color palettes.

Design Skills As a designer becomes more familiar with color, he or she can find interesting ways to adjust color by inverting, changing saturation, applying a blending mode, or adjusting opacity. These skills can translate into more sophisticated color usage in an illustration.

Application Skills In this exercise, you will begin work on an illustration for Earth Tones Mineral Makeup. You will add process and spot colors to objects, modify colors and color attributes, create an opacity mask, and apply a color from the PANTONE color system.

TERMS

Blending mode Method of combining base color and blend color to create resulting color.

Mask An object used as a template to reveal artwork in layers below the masking object.

Opacity Solidity of an object's color; the opposite of *transparency*.

Transparency Amount of light that can pass through an object. A transparent object allows objects below to appear.

NOTES

Use Eyedropper to Apply Color

- You used the Eyedropper tool ![eyedropper icon] in Exercise 13 to copy path formats. You can also use the Eyedropper tool to pick up colors.
- To pick up a color with the Eyedropper, select the object to which you wish to add color. Click the Eyedropper tool on the object that contains the desired color.

  ✓ *The Eyedropper copies both the fill and stroke formats to the selected object.*

Modify Colors

- You can modify color attributes at any time after creating and applying the color. Select the color swatch or the desired object and adjust sliders as desired to change the color.
- Change a color swatch from process to spot, for example, or vice versa, by selecting the swatch, displaying the Swatch Options dialog box, and choosing the desired color type.
- You learned in Exercise 24 that the HSB color model allows you to control saturation, or strength, of a color.

- You can control saturation of a CMYK or process color by holding down Shift and dragging any of the sliders in the Color panel.

- Holding down Shift causes all sliders to move at the same time, maintaining their positions relative to each other. Drag to the right to increase saturation; drag to the left to decrease saturation.

- As you learned in the last exercise, you can control the tint of a spot color by dragging the slider to the left, toward 0%.

- You can use two commands on the Color panel menu to change a color based on its current color values:
  - Use the Invert command to create a color negative of the current color. For example, a 100% yellow color becomes dark blue.
  - Use the Complement command to change the color to the color opposite on the color wheel.

Adjust Color Opacity

- By default, colors are 100% opaque when applied from the Swatches panel or Color panel. Use the Transparency panel to adjust **opacity** of a color, as shown in Figure 25-1, or use the Opacity box on the Control panel.

Figure 25-1. Adjusting opacity

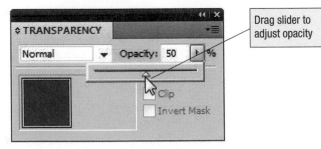

Original 100% fill

Opacity adjusted to 50%

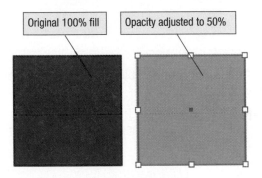

Drag slider to adjust opacity

- Adjust opacity of a selected object by typing a percentage in the Opacity box. Or, click the list arrow to display a slider and drag the slider to set the value.

- Another way to view this feature is that you are adjusting the **transparency** of the color. A color that is 100% opaque is 0% transparent, and vice versa.

Apply a Blending Mode

- You can also set a **blending mode** from the Transparency panel. A blending mode combines the *blend color* of the current object with the *base color* of the underlying object to create the *resulting color*.

- Click the Blending Mode list arrow to display 15 blend modes you can apply to any object.

- Normal is the default blending mode. The blend color is not combined with the base color. In Figure 25-2, the cyan, magenta, and yellow rectangles have a Normal blending mode, so they do not pick up any of the color of underlying objects.

Figure 25-2. Normal blending mode

- Applying any of the other blending modes to the overlying color rectangles can radically change the way the color rectangles blend with base colors to create resulting colors. You will note as you review the examples below that some blending modes resemble others, but this will not always be true in the real world when you are blending colors different from those chosen for these examples.
  - *Darken* creates the resulting color from either the blend or base color, whichever is darker.
  - *Multiply* multiplies the base color by the blend color. The resulting color is always darker.
  - *Color Burn* darkens the base color to reflect the blend color.

Figure 25-3. Darken (left) and Color Burn (right) blending modes

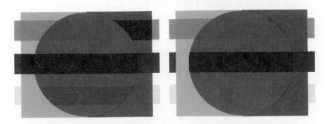

- *Lighten* creates the resulting color from either the blend or base color, whichever is lighter.
- *Screen* multiplies the inverse of the blend and base colors to achieve a lighter resulting color.
- *Color Dodge* brightens the base color to reflect the blend color.
- *Overlay* multiplies or screens depending on the base color. Use this option to preserve depth of detail in the base artwork while adding highlights from the blend color.

Figure 25-4. Lighten (left) and Overlay (right) blending modes

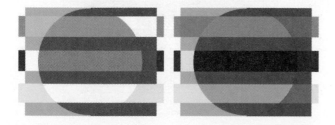

- *Soft Light* lightens or darkens the resulting color based on the blend color, giving the effect of a soft spotlight on the color.
- *Hard Light* multiplies or screens colors depending on the blend color. This gives the effect of a bright spotlight on the color.
- *Difference* subtracts the less bright color from the brighter color to create the resulting color.

Figure 25-5. Soft Light (left) and Difference (right) blending modes

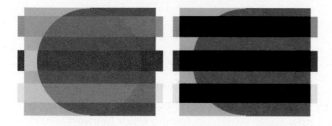

- *Exclusion* creates a resulting color similar to Difference, but with less contrast.
- *Hue* creates a resulting color that has the luminance and saturation of the base color and the hue of the blend color.
- *Saturation* creates a resulting color that has the luminance and hue of the base color and the saturation of the blend color.
- *Color* creates a resulting color that has the luminance of the base color and the hue and saturation of the blend color.

- *Luminosity* creates a resulting color with the hue and saturation of the base color and the luminance of the blend color, the inverse of the Color blending mode.

Figure 25-6. Hue (left) and Luminosity (right) blending modes

- The blending mode appearance is greatly affected by the blend color and base color. You may sometimes have to try several blending modes to create an effect you like.

Create an Opacity Mask

- In Illustrator, a **mask** is an object placed on top of other objects and used as a guide to reveal the objects beneath it. When a mask is made, the masking object on top loses its stroke and fill so that objects below appear in the outline of the masking object.
- Illustrator offers two types of masks: clipping masks and opacity masks.
  - With a *clipping mask*, the top object forms a guide around which the underlying artwork is clipped away. What remains is the shape of the top object filled with the underlying artwork.
  - With an *opacity mask*, the top object's opacity is adjusted to allow the artwork below to display in the top object's shape.
- In Figure 25-7, a dark blue star has been positioned on top of a lighter blue rectangle. The star is used as the masking object. After the opacity mask has been created, the masking object's fill is blended with the fill of the rectangle beneath it.

Figure 25-7. Before (left) and after (right) creating opacity mask

- The Transparency panel shows both the masking object (the right thumbnail in Figure 25-8) and the object(s) below the masking object (the left thumbnail in the illustration).

Figure 25-8. Transparency panel shows mask objects

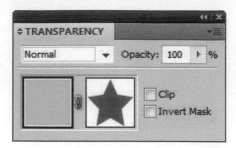

- The objects used to create an opacity mask are linked together, as shown by the link symbol between the masking object and the underlying object.
- You can click the *Clip* check box to use the masking object as a clipping mask. Clipping the object in Figure 25-7 would result in a light blue star on a white background.
- Remove a mask by selecting the masked object and selecting Release Opacity Mask on the Transparency panel menu.

Use Swatch Libraries

- Illustrator supplies many swatch libraries you can display to select colors from established color systems such as PANTONE, FOCOLTONE, and TRUMATCH, as well as panels such as Beach, Fruit, or Vegetables that display colors relevant to a particular theme.

- Color systems such as PANTONE are widely used by graphic design firms and printers because the colors are established standards.
- Several libraries may be available for a color system. For example, libraries are available from PANTONE for metallic inks, pastel inks, coated and uncoated paper stock, and so on.
- Figure 25-9 shows the swatch library for PANTONE Solid Coated.

Figure 25-9. PANTONE swatch library

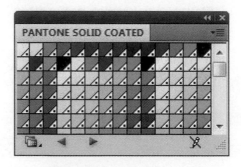

- As you use a color from a swatch library, the color is added to the default Swatches panel as a spot color. The color can be changed to a process color if desired.
- A client may specify a particular color from a color system such as PANTONE for a job. To find a specific color among the hundreds or thousands offered in a color system, use the Find field in the Swatches panel.
- You can use the Find field to locate a color by name or number.

PROCEDURES

Use Eyedropper Tool

1. Select object to which you want to apply existing color attributes.
2. Select **Eyedropper** tool .... ⏹
3. Click with Eyedropper on object that has the attributes to be copied.

Modify Colors

- Adjust any color by dragging its sliders or typing new color values.
- Change a process color swatch to a spot color (and vice versa) by double-clicking swatch and changing color type.
- Change saturation of color by holding down ⌨SHIFT⌨ and dragging any slider.

To invert color:

1. Select object or swatch containing color to invert.
2. Click ▤ to display Color panel menu.
3. Click **Invert**.

To change color to its complement:

1. Select object or swatch containing color to complement.
2. Click ▤ to display Color panel menu.
3. Click **Complement**.

Adjust Color Opacity

1. Select object containing color to adjust.
2. Display Transparency panel, if necessary .... SHIFT + CTRL + F10
3. Type desired opacity in **Opacity** box in panel or on Control panel.

   OR

   Click **Opacity** arrow to display slider and adjust opacity with slider.

Apply a Blending Mode

1. Select object containing color to adjust.
2. Display Transparency panel, if necessary.
3. Click Blending Mode list arrow.
4. Select desired blending mode.

Create Opacity Mask

1. Position masking object on top of artwork to mask.
2. Select masking object and objects below it.

   OR

   Select object to mask only.
3. Click ▦ on Transparency panel to display panel menu.
4. Select **Make Opacity Mask**.

To remove the opacity mask:

1. Select masked object(s).
2. Click ▦ to display Transparency panel menu.
3. Click **Release Opacity Mask**.

Open a Swatch Library

1. Click **Swatch Libraries Menu** button ▣ at lower-left corner of Swatches panel.
2. Click or point to a swatch library type from the drop-down menu.
3. Select a specific library from pop-out list if necessary.
4. Click any swatch in a library panel to add swatch to default Swatches panel.

Find Color by Name or Number

1. Click ▦ on Swatches panel to display panel menu.
2. Select **Show Find Field**.
3. Type desired name or number in Find field in Swatches panel.

EXERCISE DIRECTIONS

✓ *Display the Painting workspace.*

1. Open ◉ 25Earthtone and save the document as *25Earth_xx*.
2. Select the first, second, third, and sixth small circles below the *Mineral Makeup* text. Use the Eyedropper to select the red clay-colored rounded rectangle to apply its color and stroke to the circles.
3. Select the two text objects (*Earth* and *Tones*) and fill them with the following green color: **C = 100, M = 15, Y = 100, K = 0**.
4. This color is an Earth Tones signature color. Add the color to the Swatches panel. Change the color to a spot color named **ET Green**.
5. Position the text objects as shown in Illustration A. Use an alignment option to make sure the objects align at their bases.

Illustration A

Adjust Colors

1. Select the second small circle and invert the color.
2. Select the third circle and adjust the color to the following values: **C = 30, M = 69, Y = 44, K = 0**.
3. Select the fourth circle and use the Eyedropper to copy the color you just modified in the third circle. Complement the color in the fourth circle.
4. Fill the fifth circle with ET Green and remove its stroke. Change its tint to 75%.
5. Select the sixth circle and reduce saturation so the color values are **C = 15.6, M = 37.44, Y = 52, K = 0**.

   ✓ *To reduce saturation, hold down Shift and drag the Y slider to the left until the color values in the Color panel are close to those listed in the previous step.*

6. Display the PANTONE Solid Coated swatch library in the Color Books category and type **PANTONE 5473** in the Find field to locate PANTONE 5473 C.
7. Fill the last circle with this color. Remove the stroke.
8. With the new PANTONE color still selected, open the Swatch Options dialog box and change the Color Mode to CMYK. Then rename the color **ET Teal** and make it a global process color.
9. Select the *Mineral Makeup* type object. Apply the CMYK Blue swatch color.

10. Close the panel that contains the PANTONE swatch library you opened in this exercise.

11. Select the gold rounded rectangle and change its opacity to 85% with the Overlay blending mode.

Create an Opacity Mask

1. Create an opacity mask as follows:

   a. Select the *Tones* text object, the red brick rounded rectangle, and the gold rounded rectangle.

   b. Display the Transparency panel menu and deselect *New Opacity Masks Are Clipping*.

   c. Make the opacity mask.

2. Your finished drawing should look similar to Illustration B. Save your changes, close the file, and exit Illustrator.

   ✓ *If you receive a message about spot colors, continue with the saving process.*

Illustration B

Illustration B

ON YOUR OWN

1. Start Adobe Illustrator.

2. Open 📠 OIL24_*xx* or open 🔵 OYO25. Save the document as OIL25_*xx*.

   ✓ *Your client has requested that you use TRUMATCH process colors for the illustration.*

3. Display the TRUMATCH swatch panel in the Color Books category and select TRUMATCH colors as close as possible to the colors you used.

4. Delete unused swatches.

5. Draw a rectangle slightly smaller than the mosaic area and use the Delete Anchor Point tool to delete the upper-left corner to leave a right triangle.

6. Fill the triangle with a light color that coordinates with your mosaic, such as TRUMATCH 30-f if you used the data file. Remove the stroke if necessary.

7. Send the triangle to the back and position it behind the mosaic pieces so that a portion extends to the right and below the mosaic pieces.

8. Select mosaic pieces that overlap the triangle's diagonal edge and adjust blending modes and opacity to create two-color effects as shown in Illustration C.

9. Move the text object up into the mosaic, select the text and all objects behind it, and create an opacity mask. (Don't forget to turn off the clip option when making the opacity mask.) Illustration C shows one placement option.

10. Save your changes, close the file, and exit Illustrator.

Illustration C

Skills Covered

- **Use the Shape Builder Tool**
- **Work with the Color Guide Panel**

Software Skills   Illustrator CS5's new Shape Builder tool can be used to merge shapes to create complex objects. When choosing colors, use the Color Guide panel to locate colors that complement a selected base color.

Design Skills   Using a tool such as the Shape Builder speeds the process of creating a complex shape. The Color Guide panel helps a designer to learn how colors are related, providing an important introduction to color theory.

Application Skills   Your client Rogers' Toys needs an illustration for a holiday sale. You will use the Shape Builder tool to merge a number of simple shapes into a teddy bear for the illustration. Then you will use the Color Guide panel to adjust some colors in the illustration.

TERMS

Edge   Section of a path that does not intersect any other path in a group of selected objects.

Region   A closed area bounded by edges.

NOTES

Use the Shape Builder Tool

- The Shape Builder tool 🖱, new in Illustrator CS5, allows you to merge shapes or portions of shapes to create more complex objects.

- As you merge **regions**, you can choose how color fills the new region.

- You also have the option of erasing regions or **edges** rather than merging them.

- Before you can use the Shape Builder tool, you must select all objects that you want to use in the merge.

- You can use the Shape Builder tool in a number of ways to create a new object from the selected objects.

- To merge regions in the selected objects, click the tool in a region and drag in the direction you want to merge. Crosshatching shows the area currently selected to be merged.

- In Figure 26-1, the Shape Builder tool is dragged from the yellow ellipse up into the bottom portion of the green star. The result, shown at the right, is a pineapple shape in which the bottom portion of the green star has been merged into the yellow ellipse.

Figure 26-1. A simple Shape Builder merge

✔ In the default merge mode, the pointer has a small plus sign to the right, as shown at left in Figure 26-1.

- The shape shown at right in Figure 26-1 is actually two objects that can be separated: the flat-topped yellow ellipse and the green half star.

- If the Shape Builder pointer had been dragged all the way to the top of the green star, the result would be a single shape, as shown in Figure 26-2.

Figure 26-2. Merging to create a single shape

- By default, color flows in the direction of the merge. If the Shape Builder tool had instead been dragged from the top of the green star down into the yellow ellipse, the result would be the same as the shape in Figure 26-2, but the shape would be green.

  ✔ *You also have the option of selecting colors from swatches to fill merged regions. You learn more about this later in the exercise.*

- If you click on a region with the Shape Builder tool, rather than dragging, you break the object that contains the region into separate objects. If you click the Shape Builder tool in the top of the green star, for example, that portion of the star becomes a separate object, as shown in Figure 26-3.

Figure 26-3. The result of breaking an object

- You can erase a region by holding down Alt while clicking the Shape Builder tool on the region. In Figure 26-4, the bottom portion of the green star and the top arc of the yellow ellipse have been erased.

Figure 26-4. Erasing regions

  ✔ *When you hold down Alt, the symbol to the right of the pointer changes from a plus to a minus.*

- You can use the Shape Builder Tool Options dialog box, shown in Figure 26-5, to adjust settings for the tool.

Figure 26-5. Shape Builder Tool Options dialog box

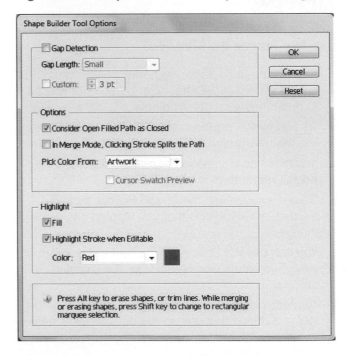

- Choose Gap Detection to locate gaps between objects that you may want to include in a merge.

- By default, any open filled path is treated as a closed path. You can deselect this option if you do not want to include open paths when merging.

- If you select In Merge Mode, Clicking Stroke Splits the Path, you have more control over the paths in the selected objects. Clicking on the path splits it, or breaks it where it intersects with other paths so that segments of the path can be manipulated separately.

- In Figure 26-6, for example, the Shape Builder tool is pointing at a portion of the yellow ellipse's path. Note the red highlight on the path that indicates it is selected, and the pointer that shows a "split" symbol to its right. Clicking on this path will break the ellipse path so that the highlighted segment can be pulled out of the shape if desired using the Selection tool.

Figure 26-6. Splitting a path with the Shape Builder tool

- By default, the tool is set to use colors from the artwork; that is, when you merge shapes, the merged region takes its color from the region in which you started the merge.

- You can also choose to supply fill and stroke colors for merged regions using swatches from the Swatches panel. Click the Pick Colors From down arrow in the Shape Builder Tool Options dialog box and select Color Swatches. With this setting active, the current fill color will fill any regions you merge.

- By selecting desired colors for both fill and stroke, you can easily paint both regions and edges of a complex object. In Figure 26-7, for example, the center of an object created with the Shape Builder tool (left) has had its stroke and fill colors painted with orange and purple (right) to change the look of the graphic in just a few clicks.

Figure 26-7. Colors of complex regions can be easily painted

Illustrator Extra

Pathfinder Tools

Tools on Illustrator's Pathfinder panel allow you to perform some of the same tasks that Shape Builder does. You can combine shapes, remove everything behind or in front of a shape, divide overlapping shapes into their separate parts, and so on. Explore these tools to learn more about manipulating shapes in Illustrator.

Work with the Color Guide Panel

- You have probably found by this point that the swatches in the Swatches panel give you fairly limited color choices.

- To avoid having to create every single color in a graphic from scratch using the Color panel, you can use the Color Guide panel to see an entire palette of colors relating to a specific base color that you choose.

- Figure 26-8 shows the Color Guide panel displaying a range of colors relating to an orange base color.

Figure 26-8. Color Guide panel

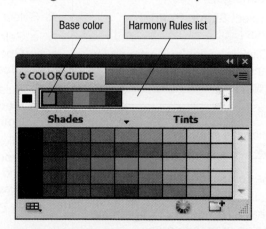

- You can select any of the color swatches in the Color Guide panel just as you would a swatch in the Swatches panel.

- Clicking the Harmony Rules list arrow displays a list of options for how colors are chosen in relation to the base color. You can, for example, display colors that are complementary to the base color, analogous to the base color, or a high contrast to the base color.

- To understand the harmony rules available, you need to understand some elements of color theory.
  - *Complementary colors* are opposite each other on the color wheel. Purple and yellow, for example, are complementary colors, as shown in Figure 26-9.

Figure 26-9. Color wheel showing complementary colors

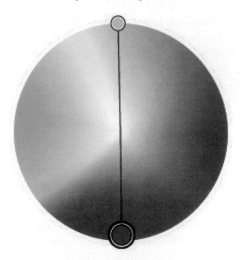

- *Analogous colors* are side by side on the color wheel.
  - A color *triad* is created by three colors equidistant from each other on the color wheel; a *tetrad* is four colors evenly spaced on the color wheel.

- The Harmony Rules list offers these options as well as a number of others. You can display split complementary colors, for example—one color plus the two colors on either side of its complementary color—or monochromatic variations of the base color.

  ✔ *You will work more with harmony rules in the Live Color section in the next exercise.*

- The Color Guide panel can make it easy to select colors for a drawing that relate to each other in a number of different ways. You can store the main colors displayed by each harmony rule in a color group on the Swatches panel for easy access.

PROCEDURES

Use the Shape Builder Tool

1. Select all objects that you wish to merge.
2. Select **Shape Builder** tool 🖼 ....[SHIFT] + [M]
3. Click in region to start merging and drag into adjoining region(s) to merge.

To break out or exclude a region:

- Click the **Shape Builder** tool 🖼 on the region.

To erase a region:

- Hold down [ALT] and click the **Shape Builder** tool 🖼 on the region or path to erase.

To change Shape Builder tool options:

1. Double-click **Shape Builder** tool 🖼.
2. Select options as follows:
   - Select or deselect **Con\u0073ider Open Filled Path as Closed**..................[ALT] + [S]
   - Select or deselect **In Merge Mode, Clicking Stroke Splits the Path**......[ALT] + [I]
   - Click **Pick Color From**...............[ALT] + [P], [↓] and select **Artwork** or **Color Swatches**.
3. Click **OK** ....[ENTER]

Work with the Color Guide Panel

1. Select or create a color to become the base color.
2. Display the Color Guide panel ....[SHIFT] + [F3]
3. Click **Harmony Rules** list arrow.
4. Select a harmony rule palette.
5. Click any swatch in the panel to apply to current object.

EXERCISE DIRECTIONS

✔ *Display the Painting workspace.*

1. Open 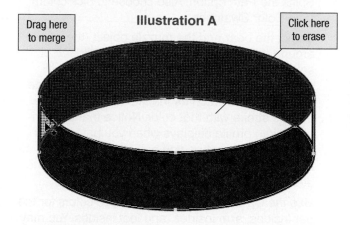26Toys and save the document as 26Toys_xx.

2. Double-click the Shape Builder tool and make sure the Pick Colors From option is set to Artwork.

Merge Shapes for the Bear

1. Expand the Head layer and hide the Eyes, Nose, Muzzle, and Ear Insides layers.

2. Select the head and the two ear shapes. Using the Shape Builder tool, drag from the center of the head outward into the right ear, then the left ear. Notice that the color of the head fills in the two ears with the same color.

3. In the Limbs layer, hide the Arm Insides objects. Select the objects that make up the right "arm," and merge from the arm out into the paw. Repeat this process to merge the left arm.

4. Hide the Feet Insides objects, and then merge the legs and feet on each side, moving from the leg outward to the paw.

5. Select the entire bear. Beginning at the center of the bear's body, merge outward into each leg, each arm, up through the neck, and into the head. Notice that the variable width profile stroke that was applied to the body is now applied to the entire outline.

6. Use the Shape Builder tool to erase the small oval shape at the bottom center of the bear, where the legs and body join.

7. Move the Body layer below the Head layer and then make all hidden layer objects visible.

Create a Bow

1. Magnify the area of the illustration that contains two stacked red ellipses to 400%.

2. Select the two ellipses and the two vertical pen strokes at each side of the ellipses.

3. Select the Shape Builder tool, hold down Alt, and click at the center of the selected shapes, where the two ellipses overlap, as shown in Illustration A. This erases the overlap area.

4. Use the Shape Builder tool to merge from the top shape into the white triangle at the left of the ellipses, as shown in Illustration A.

Illustration A

Drag here to merge

Click here to erase

5. Repeat this process with the triangle on the right, dragging from the top shape into the white triangle. You have created one loop of a bow.

6. Adjust the height of the object to **45** pts, and rotate it to approximately **–20°**. Group the object.

7. Use Object > Transform > Reflect to reflect a copy of the object to create the other loop of the bow.

8. Move the two bow halves into position with the straight piece of ribbon, the oval knot, and the trailing ribbon ends. Adjust stacking so that the horizontal piece of ribbon is behind all other ribbon parts, and then group the ribbon shapes.

9. Position the ribbon group on the neck of the bear.

Adjust Colors

1. Select the bear and make sure the Fill swatch is active in the Tools panel. If necessary, click the Set base color to the current color box in the Color Guide panel to set the bear's fill color as the base color in the Harmony Rules group.

2. Deselect the bear. In the Color Guide panel, click the list arrow and select the Analogous option. Select a light tan tint from the colors that display. Create a new swatch from this color by dragging it directly from the Color Guide panel to the Swatches panel.

3. Choose a darker brown color from the same gallery of colors, or select a different Harmony Rules option. Create a new swatch from this color.

4. Open the Shape Builder Tool Options dialog box and select the In Merge Mode, Clicking Stroke Splits the Path option. Also choose to pick colors from Color Swatches.

5. Select the bear and the muzzle object (the ellipse around the nose). Using the Shape Builder tool, select the light tan swatch you added as the fill and fill the muzzle with that color. Then select the darker brown swatch as the stroke and paint the muzzle stroke with that color. Notice that the variable width profile displays when you paint the fill and disappears when you paint the stroke. You may want to reapply the profile after changing the stroke color. Adjust the stroke weight to **2** pt.

6. Use the Color Guide panel to choose colors for the ear insides, arm insides, and feet insides. You may use the same color as the muzzle fill or a different color from a different harmony rule palette. Remove the strokes from these objects.

7. Select the bear and remove the variable width profile so the stroke is a uniform **6** pts.

8. Select the background object. Use the Color Guide panel to pick a color for the fill of this object that complements the brown color of the bear. Remove the stroke. Your Illustration should look similar to Illustration B.

9. Save your changes, close the file, and exit Illustrator.

Illustration B

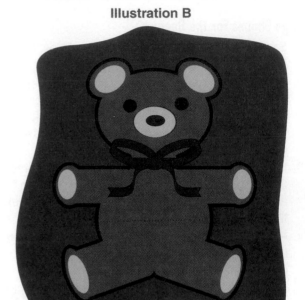

ON YOUR OWN

1. Start Adobe Illustrator.

2. Open OYO26. Save the document as OIL26_xx.

   ✔ *Try your hand at another illustration for Rogers' Toys.*

3. Use the Shape Builder tool to merge and erase shapes to create the train:

   a. Select all the objects that make up the train. Make sure your Shape Builder tool is set to pick color from swatches and split strokes.

   b. Choosing bright colors from the Swatches panel, merge shapes as desired to create the train. You can use all one color for the train body or a variety of colors.

   c. Erase the fill of the slanted shapes in the triangular section at the front of the train (the cow-catcher) and edges and regions around the wheels that you don't need.

4. Use the Shape Builder tool to combine and color the smoke circles in interesting ways. Use colors from the Color Guide panel to fill the circles. You may adjust the positions of the circles as desired.

5. Use the Shape Builder tool to create an interesting sun object from the shapes in the upper-left corner.

6. Remove the stroke from the background object. Select the train body to set that color as the base color for the Color Guide panel, and then choose a fill color that complements the train body.

7. Save your changes, close the file, and exit Illustrator.

Skills Covered

- **Use Live Paint to Add Color**
- **Use Kuler Colors**
- **Work with Live Color**

Software Skills   Use Live Paint to quickly fill areas of a Live Paint object. Selecting and deleting outlines with the Live Paint Selection tool allows paint to flow from one area of the object to another. Color themes from the Kuler panel help you locate interesting color combinations. The Live Color feature lets you edit colors in a drawing in a number of ways.

Design Skills   Illustrator's color-editing features make it easy for a designer to create unusual and unique effects. The Live Color feature allows for color experimentation to achieve the best look for an illustration.

Application Skills   Your client Newfound Nursery is looking for a simple, interesting design to insert on a flyer. In this exercise, you will use Live Paint and Live Color to create and modify a stylized flower for the flyer illustration.

TERMS

Face   An area in a Live Paint object.

Live Color   A feature that allows you to edit colors and create color groups.

Live Paint object   An object consisting of intersecting paths.

NOTES

Use Live Paint to Add Color

- The Live Paint feature allows you to pour paint—that is, color or fill—into any portion of a Live Paint object. Because the paint is "live," it can move from one part of the object to another if boundary paths are removed. This feature is somewhat similar to the Shape Builder feature in that you can create a shape by combining or merging component shapes.

- To work with this feature, you must first create a Live Paint object.

- A **Live Paint object** is an object composed of intersecting paths that create areas to be filled.

- Create a Live Paint object by selecting all the paths that will be included in the object. Then, click on the selected paths with the Live Paint Bucket tool, or use the Object > Live Paint > Make command.

- The Make command surrounds the selected paths with a special bounding box, as shown in Figure 27-1.

Figure 27-1. Live Paint object with bounding box

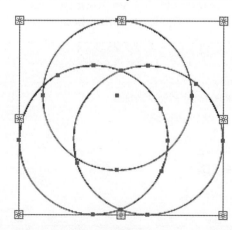

- After the Live Paint object has been created, the Live Paint Bucket and Live Paint Selection tools can be used to paint and modify the object.
- To use the Live Paint Bucket tool , select the tool, select a fill color, and then click in the area to fill with paint. A "paintable" area—or **face**—is surrounded by a heavy red highlight by default, as shown in Figure 27-2.

Figure 27-2. Use the Live Paint Bucket tool to paint a face

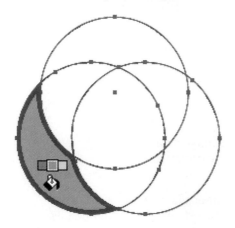

- Note that the Live Paint Bucket tool has three small swatches displayed above it. The center swatch is the current color. The swatches to left and right are the swatches adjacent to the current color in the panel you are currently using to apply color.
- Use the left arrow or right arrow key to move through the swatch panel in sequence.

  ✔ *You can also display this cursor swatch preview feature for the Shape Builder tool. Select it in the Shape Builder Tool Options dialog box.*

- By default, the Live Paint Bucket paints only faces. To have the option to paint edges as well, double-click the Live Paint Bucket tool and select Paint Strokes in the Live Paint Bucket Options dialog box, shown in Figure 27-3.

Figure 27-3. Live Paint Bucket Options dialog box

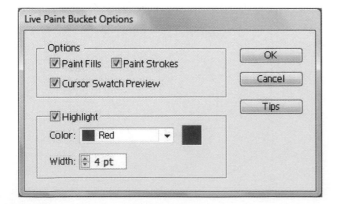

- If you prefer not to see the swatch previews attached to the Live Paint Bucket, you can deselect this option here. You can also change the highlight color and width if desired, or turn the highlight off altogether.
- To paint a stroke, move the Live Paint Bucket tool over the stroke until it takes the shape of a paintbrush, as shown in Figure 27-4.

Figure 27-4. Paint a stroke using Live Paint Bucket

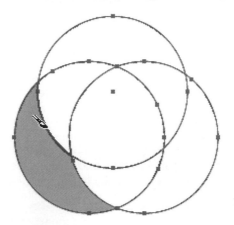

- A benefit of using Live Paint is the ability to modify the appearance of an object by directing the flow of paint from face to face. You can, in essence, create a shape from paint.
- To control the flow of paint in a Live Paint object, use the Live Paint Selection tool . This tool allows you to select faces or paths and, if desired, delete them.
- Deleting a path between two areas allows paint to flow from one area into the other, as shown in Figure 27-5 on the next page.
- Paint flows from larger areas to smaller ones. If the path between a large red area and a small blue area is removed, the new combined area will become red.
- Likewise, if there is no fill in a large area adjacent to a small blue-painted area, removing the path between them results in a large area with no fill.
- As with the Shape Builder tool, a fill or stroke selected by this tool shows a pattern of crosshatching that makes it easy to tell the object is selected.
- To delete a selected fill or stroke, simply press the Delete or Backspace key.
- A Live Paint object can remain "live" as long as a designer wants. Once all edits are made, the object can be transformed into a vector object by expanding it.

Figure 27-5. After path is deleted, paint flows into new area

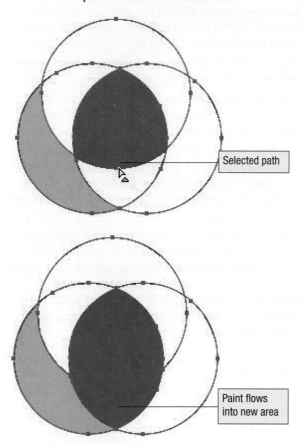

Selected path

Paint flows into new area

■ *Expanding* an object makes the object's attributes, such as stroke and fill, editable with Illustrator's standard tools.

■ Once a Live Paint object has been expanded, the paint is no longer live.

■ A Live Paint object may also be released by using the Object > Live Paint > Release command.

■ Releasing the object removes all paint from the object. Any paths that have been added remain in place. Any path segments that have been deleted during editing of the object remain deleted.

Illustrator Extra

Live Paint

Live Paint has more features that make it a powerful tool for creating interesting graphics. You can detect gaps in paths that might affect how paint flows and close them. You can add paths to a Live Paint object to further refine faces. Explore on your own or consult Illustrator Help for more information.

Use Kuler Colors

■ In Exercise 26, you learned how to use the Color Guide panel to choose colors. The CS5 design applications offer another option for choosing colors: the Kuler panel, shown in Figure 27-6. You access this panel using the Window > Extensions > Kuler command.

■ This panel displays color themes created by the Kuler online community of designers. Themes are given names that may reflect the color choices, such as sandy stone beach in Figure 27-6 that contains colors you might find on a beach.

■ You can browse themes organized in categories such as Highest Rated, Most Popular, and Random. Select a time frame such as All Time or Last 7 Days. Use the tools at the bottom of the panel to move up and down the list and refresh the list. If you remember a theme name, you can use the search box at the top of the panel to search for the theme.

Figure 27-6. Kuler panel

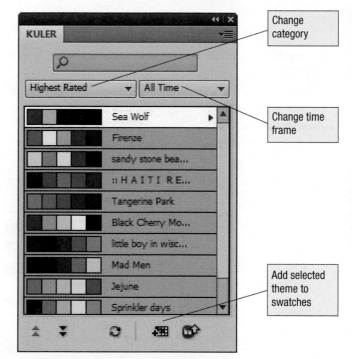

Change category

Change time frame

Add selected theme to swatches

■ If you find a theme you want to use in your own illustrations, click the Add selected theme to swatches button ▦ to add the theme to a color group in the Swatches panel.

■ You can also add your own themes to the Kuler community by uploading a color group from the Swatches panel.

Work with Live Color

- You use **Live Color** to edit colors in an illustration. After editing, you can save the edited colors in color groups.

- You work with Live Color using the Recolor Artwork dialog box, shown in Figure 27-7. Open this dialog box by selecting an object and clicking the Recolor Artwork button 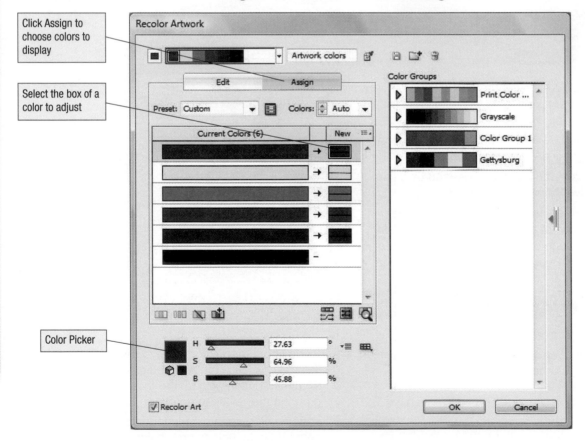 on the Control panel or on the Color Guide panel.

- By default, the Assign settings are displayed and the colors of the selected object are shown in the Current Colors list. You use the Assign settings to choose the colors to manipulate.

- Note the base color and Harmony Rules list at the upper-left corner of the dialog box. You can select from the preset harmony rules to change the current colors to new colors.

- If you want to change only one color, double-click the small rectangle of color to the right of the color bar in the Current Colors list and use the Color Picker to select a new color. Or use the color sliders at the bottom of the dialog box to adjust a color.

- You can also choose to display colors from a specific swatch library to replace the current colors.

- If Recolor Art is selected in the lower-left corner of the dialog box, you will see the results of any change immediately in the artwork.

- You may want to exclude one or more colors from the current selection from being adjusted in the Recolor Artwork dialog box. Select any color you do not want to edit and click the Excludes selected colors button.

- Other buttons below the color bars allow you to adjust your illustration's colors by randomly changing the order of colors—picking new colors from the current harmony rule swatches—or randomly changing saturation and brightness. You can also select a color bar and click the magnifying tool to locate that color in your illustration.

Figure 27-7. Recolor Artwork dialog box

Click Assign to choose colors to display

Select the box of a color to adjust

Color Picker

■ The real fun of using the Recolor Artwork dialog box comes in editing colors with the color wheel. Clicking the Edit button in the Recolor Artwork dialog box switches the view to the one shown in Figure 27-8.

■ Each color in the selected option displays on the color wheel as a circle that shows where the color appears on the color wheel. The circle surrounded by a black outline represents the selected color in the harmony rule sample at the top of the dialog box.

■ Use the color wheel to quickly adjust hue, saturation, and brightness for any or all colors in the selected object.

 • To adjust hue, drag any of the circles around the color wheel. If the Unlink harmony colors button is solid 🔘, all circles move at the same time and maintain their relationships with each other.

 • To adjust saturation, drag circles toward the outside or inside of the color wheel. The outside represents more saturated color; the inside is less saturated.

 • To adjust brightness, drag the brightness slider.

■ If you want to adjust only one color, click the Unlink harmony colors button so that it changes to the broken link symbol 🔘. You can then drag each color circle separately to adjust its hue, saturation, and brightness independently.

■ When you are happy with the colors, you can create a color group that appears in the Swatches panel for future use.

Illustrator Extra

Live Color

Like Live Paint, Live Color is a powerful tool with many features that cannot be covered in the space available here. It is especially useful, for example, for reducing colors in artwork when a client specifies a two- or three-color job. You are encouraged to explore other options in the Live Color dialog box.

Figure 27-8. Recolor Artwork Edit options

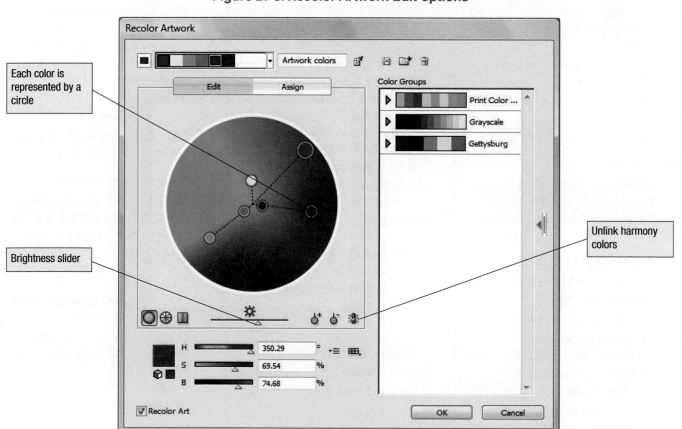

Each color is represented by a circle

Brightness slider

Unlink harmony colors

PROCEDURES

Create a Live Paint Object (Alt + Ctrl + X)

1. Select all paths that will be included in the Live Paint object.
2. Select **Live Paint Bucket** tool 🪣 ....K
3. Click with Live Paint Bucket tool on the selected object.

    OR

1. Select all paths that will be included in the Live Paint object.
2. Click **Object** ....ALT + O
3. Point to **Live Pai<u>n</u>t** ....N
4. Click **<u>M</u>ake** ....M

Use the Live Paint Bucket Tool

After creating a Live Paint object:

1. Select **Live Paint Bucket** tool 🪣 ....K located beneath the Shape Builder tool.
2. Click color swatch or other option for fill.
3. Click color swatch for stroke if desired.
4. Click in face to fill with paint.

To paint a stroke:

■ Move Live Paint Bucket tool on top of path until pointer takes the shape of a brush and then click.

To change Live Paint Bucket options:

1. Double-click **Live Paint Bucket** tool 🪣 .
2. Select options as follows:
    ■ Select or deselect **Paint <u>F</u>ills** ....ALT + F
    ■ Select or deselect **Paint <u>S</u>trokes** ....ALT + S
    ■ Select or deselect **Cursor Swatch <u>P</u>review** ....ALT + P
    ■ Select or deselect **<u>H</u>ighlight** ....ALT + H

■ Click **<u>C</u>olor**............ALT + C and use up or down arrow to select new highlight color.
■ Click **<u>W</u>idth** ....ALT + W and use up or down arrow to select new highlight weight.

3. Click **OK** ....T

Use the Live Paint Selection Tool

1. Select **Live Paint Selection** tool 🖱 ....SHIFT + L
2. Click in fill or on path to select.

    ✓ *Selected fill or path is highlighted with color and a pattern of small dots.*

To change Live Paint Selection options:

1. Double-click **Live Paint Selection** tool 🖱 .
2. Select options as follows:
    ■ Select or deselect **Select <u>F</u>ills** ....ALT + F
    ■ Select or deselect **Select <u>S</u>trokes** ......ALT + S
    ■ Select or deselect **<u>H</u>ighlight** ....ALT + H
    ■ Click **<u>C</u>olor**............ALT + C and use up or down arrow to select new highlight color.
    ■ Click **<u>W</u>idth** ....ALT + W and use up or down arrow to select new highlight weight.
3. Click **OK** ....ENTER

Expand a Live Paint Object

■ With Live Paint object selected, click **Expand** on Control panel.

    OR

1. Select Live Paint object.
2. Click **Object** ....ALT + O
3. Point to **Live Pai<u>n</u>t**..............N
4. Click **<u>E</u>xpand**......................E
5. Ungroup object(s) as desired to work with vector objects.

Use the Kuler Panel

1. Click **Window** ....ALT + W
2. Point to **Extensions**.
3. Click **Kuler**......................K
4. Scroll through the themes in the dialog box to locate a theme you want to use.

    OR

    Click **Highest Rated** down arrow and select another category.

    OR

    Click **All Time** down arrow and select a different time frame.

5. Click **Add selected theme to swatches** button 🎨 to add the theme colors as a color group in the Swatches panel.

Work with Live Color

1. Select object or group to recolor.
2. Click **Recolor Artwork** button 🎨 on Control panel or Color Guide panel.
3. If necessary, click 🖉 to get colors from selected art.
4. Click **Harmony Rules** list and select a harmony rule.

To change a color using color bars:

1. Double-click the small rectangle to the right of the color bar.
2. Use the Color Picker to select a new color.

    OR

1. Click the small rectangle to the right of the color bar.
2. Use the sliders at the bottom of the dialog box to adjust the color.

To exclude a color from editing:
1. Select the color bar to exclude.
2. Click the **Excludes selected colors** button below the color bars.

To edit colors using the color wheel:
1. Click **Edit** button to display the color wheel.

2. Adjust colors as desired:
   - Drag any color circle around the color wheel to change hue.
   - Drag any color circle inward or outward to adjust saturation.
   - Drag the brightness slider to adjust brightness.

Adjust colors independently:
1. Make sure **Unlink harmony colors** button below color wheel is broken.
2. Select any circle and adjust its hue, saturation, or brightness as described above.

Load Next Swatch Library
- With a swatch library open, click the **Load Next Swatch Library** button at the bottom of the panel.

EXERCISE DIRECTIONS

✓ *Display the Painting workspace.*

- Open 27Newfound and save the document as 27Newfound_xx.

Create the Live Paint Object

1. Draw a selection marquee around the four circles to select them.
2. Make a Live Paint object from the selected paths.
3. Open the Live Paint Bucket Options dialog box and choose to paint both strokes and fills.
4. Change the magnification to 150%.

Color the Flower Petals

1. With the Live Paint Bucket tool active, press the right arrow key to rotate through the cursor preview swatches above the paint bucket pointer until the darkest green swatch is selected (**C = 90, M = 30, Y = 95, K = 30**).
2. Use the paint bucket to fill the triangular area at the bottom center of the Live Paint object with green, painting both faces and edges with the dark green, as shown in Illustration A.

Illustration A

3. Use the Swatch Libraries menu button to display the swatch libraries on the Nature submenu. Select the Flowers swatch library.
4. Change the fill and stroke color to one of the light pink colors in the Flowers panel and paint the centermost shape of the Live Paint object, including both the face and the edges.
5. Display the Color Guide panel and choose a harmony rule for which you like the colors, such as Monochromatic. Use colors from the Color Guide panel to fill in other shapes in the object to resemble petals of a flower. Illustration A shows one color scheme you could use.

   ✓ *You may choose colors from the Flowers panel as well, to see the Color Guide panel change its display.*

6. Remove portions of the Live Paint object you don't want to fill, such as the top arcs, and remove edges within the object using the Live Paint Selection tool to allow paint to flow as desired.
7. When you are happy with the colors, expand the Live Paint object. You may then want to select and rotate the outermost shapes as shown in Illustration B to give the flower a bit more interest.

   ✓ *Use the Group Selection tool to select any petal in the expanded shape. If you see a path remaining after rotating the petal, you may select it with the Group Selection tool and rotate it as well or delete it.*

Color the Leaves

1. Select the cluster of leaf shapes at the right side of the flower stem and make a Live Paint object.

2. Click the Load Next Swatch Library arrow at the bottom of the swatch library panel to display the Foliage swatches.

3. Use shades of green from this panel to color faces and edges on the leaves. You may remove any areas you don't want.

4. Repeat the process with the leaf shapes on the left side of the flower stem, using the same or different greens.

Recolor the Flower

1. Select the flower object and open the Live Color dialog box.

   ✓ *Position the dialog box so that you can see the selected flower shape, if possible.*

2. Exclude the green color from editing.

3. Try several of the harmony rule samples until you find one you like. (You don't have to stick with realistic flower colors.)

4. Choose to edit the colors on the color wheel, and then adjust hue, saturation, and brightness as desired. You may choose different harmony rules to come up with a color scheme you like.

5. When you are satisfied with your colors, click the New Color Group button in the Live Color dialog box to add the color group to the Swatches panel.

6. Group the flower object and move it join the flower stem. Group all leaf and stem objects, and then group the entire flower object.

7. Select the type object and fill it with one of the colors from the color group you saved. Move the type object closer to the flower and center it over the flower object. Illustration B shows one version of the final artwork.

8. Save your changes, close the file, and exit Illustrator.

Illustration B

Newfound Nursery

ON YOUR OWN

1. Start Adobe Illustrator.
2. Open 💿OYO27. Save the document as OIL27_*xx*.

   ✓ *See what you can do with Live Paint and Kuler to perk up the tile illustration you have already worked on.*

3. Select all objects except the text object and make a Live Paint object.

   ✓ *Don't worry if you get a warning about converting the objects to Live Paint.*

4. Display the Kuler panel and browse through the themes to find one that you like. Add the theme to the Swatches panel.

5. Select theme colors in the Swatches panel's color group and fill some of the tiles. Use variations of those colors from the Color Guide panel to fill other tiles. You may keep changing the harmony rules to bring up other palettes of colors related to those in the color group, but try to keep all colors in the same general color family as the original theme (i.e., if your colors are mainly earth tones, don't include bright purple or pink, even if they appear on a color guide palette for your chosen base color).

6. Change the type object to give the name of the theme you chose.

7. Save your changes, close the file, and exit Illustrator.

Skills Covered

- About Gradients
- Apply a Default Gradient
- Adjust Gradient Angle
- Create a Custom Gradient
- Outline Stroke or Text

Software Skills Use a gradient to add blended color to an object. Use a default gradient or create a custom gradient. Adjust gradient colors and angle using the Gradient panel and the Gradient tool. You can edit a gradient right on the object to which it is applied. To apply a gradient to text or a path, first convert the object to an outline.

Design Skills Gradients supply exciting color effects that can add visual interest to a design. A designer can use a gradient for an interesting fill or to provide a suggestion of dimension to make design elements pop on the page.

Application Skills In this exercise, you will return to the Greenwood Conservancy illustration. You will use both default and custom gradient fills in the illustration and adjust gradient angle for best effect. You will also convert text to an outline and fill it with a gradient.

TERMS

Aspect ratio The ratio of height to width for an object.

Gradient A fill option that uses gradations of one or more colors.

Gradient stop Point at which a gradient changes from one color to another color.

NOTES

About Gradients

Figure 28-1. Radial gradient (left) and linear gradient (right)

- A **gradient** is a fill created from gradations of one or more colors. Gradients can add rich color detail or a three-dimensional look to an object.
- A user can choose from two types of gradients: radial and linear (see Figure 28-1).
  - A *radial* gradient radiates outward from the center.
  - A *linear* gradient displays from one side of an object to another. It can display top to bottom, side to side, or diagonally.

■ You can modify a radial gradient to create an elliptical gradient like the one shown in Figure 28-2. To create this gradient, you adjust the **aspect ratio** of gradient length to width.

Figure 28-2. Elliptical gradient

Design Suite Integration

Gradients

Both Photoshop and InDesign allow you to create gradients. You will use gradients in Photoshop to add interesting layer fills. You will apply gradients in InDesign to fill objects such as shapes and text frames with color shading.

Apply a Default Gradient

■ Illustrator supplies four default gradients in the Swatches panel, two linear and two radial.

■ Apply a default gradient the same way as a color swatch: Select the object to fill and click the desired gradient.

■ Although the Swatches panel displays only a few gradients by default, Illustrator offers many other gradients in libraries. Use the Swatch Libraries menu button to open the library menu, then click Gradients to see the available gradient libraries.

■ Library gradients are applied the same way as a default gradient or any swatch.

■ The Tools panel shows the most recently applied gradient in the Gradient box below the Fill and Stroke boxes as shown in Figure 28-3. To apply this gradient to another object, just click the box.

Figure 28-3. Gradient box in Tools panel

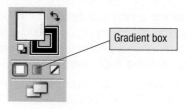

Gradient box

Create a Custom Gradient

■ Chances are that you will want to create your own gradients to meet the specific needs of an illustration. You may also find that even if you can use a default or library gradient, you may need to adjust its settings for best appearance in your illustration.

■ To create a custom gradient or modify a default one, you use the Gradient panel shown in Figure 28-4. This illustration shows settings for a linear gradient that has three colors.

Figure 28-4. Gradient panel

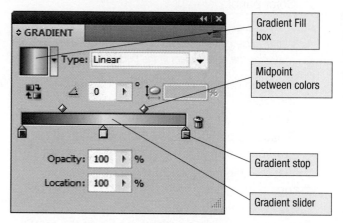

Gradient Fill box

Midpoint between colors

Gradient stop

Gradient slider

■ The small color boxes beneath the gradient slider are **gradient stops**. You use gradient stops to specify the colors for the gradient.

■ The gradient stop at the left of the gradient slider shows the color that begins the gradient, and the stop at the right shows the color that ends the gradient.

■ The Gradient Fill box shows a thumbnail of the current gradient. Note that you can click the Gradient Fill down arrow to display a list of gradients that have been saved as swatches.

Apply Color to Gradient Stops

- When creating a new gradient, you will usually be in the position of modifying an existing one, either a default gradient or a previously used gradient that you apply from the Tools panel.

- You may first need to change the gradient type to radial or linear. You will probably then need to change the colors of existing stops to the colors you need.

- To change a stop color, you must first select the gradient stop. Select a gradient stop by clicking on it so that the gray triangular shape at the top of the stop becomes black.

  ✓ *In Figure 28-4, the green gradient stop is selected; if you look closely, you can see the black triangle above the green color box.*

- Once you have selected the gradient stop, you can apply color to it using any of the following methods:
  - Create the desired color using the sliders in the Color panel.

    ✓ *If you begin with a default black and white gradient, you must change the color model from Grayscale to CMYK to display the color sliders in the Color panel.*

  - Drag the current color from the Color panel to the stop.
  - Hold down Alt and click a swatch in the Swatches panel, or drag the swatch on top of a gradient stop.

- Adjust the beginning and end of the gradient by dragging the gradient stops to the left or right on the gradient slider.

- The diamond or diamonds at the top of the gradient slider mark the midpoint between gradient colors. To adjust the distribution of color in the gradient, drag the diamond to the left or right.

- A gradient may have more than two colors. To add a color to a gradient, click below the gradient slider to add a stop, then define its color as discussed previously. You can also drag a color from the Color panel or Swatches panel to the gradient bar in the Gradient panel at the position where you want a new stop.

  ✓ *Or select an existing stop, hold down Alt, and drag the copied stop to a new location.*

- You can specify an opacity setting for any gradient stop. Select the stop and then use the Opacity slider in the Gradient panel to adjust the transparency of the color at that stop. This feature allows you to blend a background color into a gradient.

- The closer gradient stops are to each other, the more abrupt the transition between colors. For more control over the gradient appearance, you can use the Location box to set an exact location along the gradient slider for a stop.

- Use the Reverse Gradient button to quickly switch the gradient end to end.

- By default, a radial gradient begins at the center point of an object and radiates outward, while a linear gradient begins at the left and moves evenly to the right.

- You can change the gradient angle to start the gradient in a different location or orientation.

- Set an angle for the gradient by specifying a value in the Angle box. You can also adjust the angle manually using the Gradient tool, as you learn later in this exercise.

- Eliminate colors from a gradient by selecting the stop to remove and simply dragging it off the Gradient panel.

- A gradient may be saved and named just like a color swatch. Drag the gradient in the Gradient Fill box to the Swatches panel, or click the New Swatch button, and then name the new gradient as desired.

Create an Elliptical Gradient

- As mentioned earlier in this exercise, you can create elliptical gradients that can fill a special need.

- To create an elliptical gradient, begin with a radial gradient. With a radial gradient active, the Aspect Ratio box becomes active in the Gradient panel.

- By default, the aspect ratio of gradient width to length is 100 percent. Increasing this value lengthens the gradient so that it is taller than it is wide, as shown in Figure 28-5.

Figure 28-5. Change gradient aspect ratio

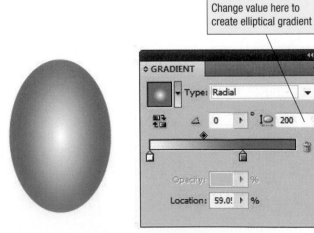

- If you enter a value less than 100%, the gradient becomes wider than it is tall and spreads horizontally.

Adjust Gradients with the Gradient Tool

- As you have seen, you can make many adjustments to a gradient in the Gradient panel. You can also use the Gradient tool 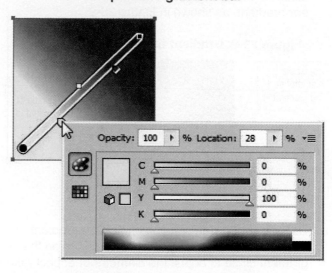 to edit a gradient right on the object to which the gradient is applied.

- You can adjust the gradient angle, change where the gradient starts and ends, modify the positions of gradient stops, and even change the shape of the gradient.

- When you click the Gradient tool with a gradient-filled object selected, a gradient bar displays on the object, as shown in Figure 28-6.

Figure 28-6. Gradient bar displayed on a linear gradient

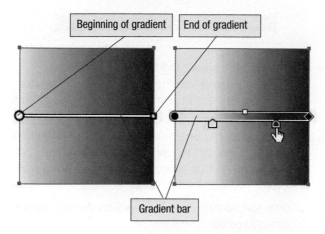

- If you then point at the gradient bar with the Gradient tool still active, the bar changes as shown at right in Figure 28-6. You can adjust the gradient stops right on the gradient bar and see the results instantly on the object.

- Double-clicking on a gradient stop in the gradient bar opens a color panel like the one shown in Figure 28-7 where you can adjust the color if desired. Note that you can also adjust opacity or specify an exact location for the gradient stop in this panel.

- You can add stops to the gradient bar simply by clicking, as in the Gradient panel. You can also adjust the gradient angle on the object.

Figure 28-7. Adjust color of gradient stop on the gradient bar

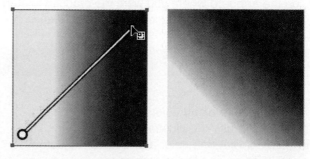

- With the gradient bar displayed and the Gradient tool active, click on the object where you want the gradient to start and drag in the direction you want the gradient to flow. Figure 28-8 shows how to drag the gradient bar and the result of the new gradient angle.

Figure 28-8. Change gradient angle with the Gradient tool

- To fine-tune the gradient position, you can rotate the end point of the gradient. Position the pointer near the end point until it displays a rotation icon, then drag the end point to change its position without changing the beginning point of the gradient.

- The gradient begins at the point where you start dragging the Gradient tool. You may start dragging outside the object if desired to adjust how much of the gradient displays in the object.

- The gradient bar for a radial gradient looks slightly different from the gradient bar that displays on a linear gradient, as shown in Figure 28-9.

Figure 28-9. Gradient bar on radial gradient

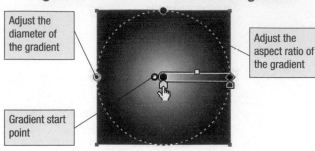

Adjust the diameter of the gradient

Adjust the aspect ratio of the gradient

Gradient start point

- As for a linear gradient, you can adjust gradient stops on the bar. You can use the handles on the gradient circle to adjust the diameter or aspect ratio of the gradient. Drag the small circle attached to the gradient bar to adjust gradient start point, angle, and distance.

- You can apply a gradient across a number of objects. Apply the gradient to each object, select the objects, and then click the Gradient tool in the Tools panel.

- By default, Illustrator displays a gradient bar for each object. To extend the gradient across all objects, click on the artboard where you want the gradient to start and then drag to the place where it should end.

Illustrator Extra

Blending Colors

Another way to blend colors across a group of objects is to use the Illustrator Blend feature. Fill one object with one color and another object with another color. The Blend feature creates a series of objects blending from one color to the other.

Outline Stroke or Text

- Gradients are most commonly used to fill objects, but they can also be used to "fill" type and paths.

- Before a type object or a path can be filled with a gradient, it must be converted to an outline.

- To outline a stroke, use the Object > Path > Outline Stroke command. Illustrator creates a path around the stroke to convert it to a closed object (see Figure 28-10).

Figure 28-10. Outlined type and stroke

- To outline text, select the text object with the Selection tool and use the Type > Create Outlines command. The text is converted into closed objects as shown in Figure 28-10.

- Converting text to outlines is a good way to ensure that it will remain in its chosen font even if an illustration is opened on a system that does not have that font.

  ✓ Once type has been converted to outlines, however, the text cannot be edited.

- This option can also help to limit file size, because fonts do not have to be embedded.

PROCEDURES

Apply Default Gradient

1. Select object to fill with gradient.
2. Display Swatches panel.
3. Select desired gradient.

   OR

   Click **Gradient** box ■ in the Tools panel to apply the most recently used gradient to the selected object.

Create Custom Gradient

1. Select object to fill with gradient.
2. Display Gradient panel, if necessary.
3. Click the Gradient Fill box in upper left of panel if necessary to display stops.
4. Click left gradient stop and add beginning color using one of the following options:

- Create the desired color using the sliders in the Color panel.

  ✓ You may need to specify the CMYK color model.

- Drag an existing color from the Color panel's Fill or Stroke box on top of the gradient stop.

- Hold down [ALT] and click a swatch in the Swatches panel.

5. Use the same procedure to add ending color to right gradient stop.

6. Adjust beginning and ending colors by dragging gradient stops.

7. Adjust distribution of color by dragging diamond above gradient slider.

8. Adjust angle of gradient by typing a value in the Angle box.

9. Specify an exact location for a gradient stop in the Location box.

To add colors to gradient:

1. Click below gradient slider to add stop.

   OR

   Select existing stop, hold down [ALT], and drag copy to new location.

2. Apply color to new stop as directed above.

To remove a color from a gradient:

- Drag the stop of the color to remove off of the Gradient panel.

To adjust transparency of a gradient stop:

1. Click gradient stop to adjust.

2. Type desired opacity in Opacity box.

   OR

   Drag the Opacity slider to adjust opacity.

To create an elliptical gradient:

1. Apply a radial gradient to the selected object.

2. Type desired value in the Aspect Ratio box.

   ✓ Type a value greater than 100% for a gradient that is taller than it is wide. Type a value less than 100% for a gradient that is wider than it is tall.

Adjust Gradient with the Gradient Tool

1. Select object that contains gradient.

2. Select **Gradient** tool [icon] to display the gradient bar on the object.................................[G]

3. Point to the gradient bar to display gradient stops.

To adjust colors on the gradient bar:

- Drag sliders as in the Gradient panel.

- Double-click a gradient stop to display a color panel you can use to change the color.

- Click on the gradient bar to add gradient stops, or drag existing stops off the gradient bar.

To adjust gradient angle with the Gradient tool:

- In a linear gradient with the gradient bar displayed, click on the selected object where you want the gradient to start and then drag at the desired angle and distance.

- In a radial gradient with the gradient bar displayed, click on the small circle attached to the gradient bar and drag to set the desired start and end points.

To rotate the end point of the gradient:

- With the gradient bar displayed on the object, move the mouse pointer near the end point of the gradient until it displays a rotate symbol [icon] and then drag to reposition the end point.

To adjust diameter and aspect ratio of radial gradient:

1. Click on selected object to display the gradient bar.

2. Point to the gradient bar to display the gradient outline.

3. Drag the open circle handle inward or outward to adjust diameter.

4. Drag the filled circle handle inward or outward to adjust aspect ratio.

Save a Gradient

1. Create custom gradient as desired.

2. Drag gradient from Gradient Fill box in Gradient panel to Swatches panel.

   OR

   Click **New Swatch** button [icon] in Swatches panel.

3. Rename the gradient as desired.

Convert Stroke to Outline

1. Select stroke object.

2. Click **Object**..............[ALT]+[O]

3. Point to **Path**.....................[P]

4. Click **Outline Stroke**..........[U]

Convert Text to Outline (Shift + Ctrl + O)

1. Select type object with Selection tool.

2. Click **Type**.................[ALT]+[T]

3. Click **Create Outlines**........[O]

EXERCISE DIRECTIONS

✓ Display the Painting workspace.

1. Open ⊙ 28Greenwood and save the document as 28Greenwood_xx.

2. Display the Swatches, Gradient, and Color panels.

Create the Acorn

✓ You will use the two outlined objects below the oak leaves to make an acorn.

1. Select the white-filled ellipse below the oak leaves. Click the default white-to-black gradient thumbnail in the Gradient panel to apply the gradient. Remove the ellipse's stroke.

2. Apply the same gradient to the acorn's cap. Change the gradient to Radial in the Gradient panel and remove the object's stroke.

3. Select the acorn ellipse. In the Gradient panel, change the gradient type back to Linear and change the gradient angle to –90°.

4. Assemble the acorn by placing the cap on top of the ellipse.

5. The default gradients don't fit in well with the illustration's color scheme. Adjust the acorn gradients as follows:

   a. Select the acorn ellipse and click the left gradient stop in the Gradient panel to select it.

   b. Create the following color in the Color panel: **C = 0, M = 20, Y = 100, K = 0**. (Select CMYK on the Color panel menu to display the CMYK sliders in the Color panel.)

   c. Click the right gradient stop and create the color **C = 5, M = 40, Y = 90, K = 20**.

   d. Save the gradient as **Acorn** in the Swatches panel.

   e. Apply the Acorn gradient to the acorn cap. Then, in the Gradient panel, change the gradient type to Radial.

6. Group the acorn parts and position the acorn among the oak leaves.

Create a Gradient for the Gingko Leaf

1. Select the gingko leaf (the triangular yellow leaf at the right) and click the gradient box on the Tools panel to apply the last gradient used.

2. Click the Gradient tool to display the gradient bar on the leaf.

3. Modify the gradient using the gradient bar as follows:

   a. Point to the gradient bar to activate it, then click on the small circle at the left end of the gradient bar and drag to position it at the base of the leaf. The pointed end of the bar should pass through the split in the leaf.

   b. Double-click the left gradient stop to display a color panel. Leave the color as is but move the stop to 10 using the Location box on the displayed color panel.

   c. Add a stop to the gradient bar at about 40% and change the color at this stop to **C = 0, M = 10, Y = 100, K = 0**.

   d. Change the last stop on the gradient to **C = 0, M = 0, Y = 80, K = 0** and move the stop to about 80% on the gradient bar.

   e. Adjust the diameter of the gradient so that only a small amount of the final yellow gradient color appears at the tips of the leaf.

   f. Save the gradient as **Gingko**.

4. Group the leaf and its veins.

Create a Gradient for the Redbud Leaf and Vein

1. Select the redbud leaf (the green leaf in the center), apply the most recent gradient, and adjust it as follows in the Gradient panel:

   a. Change the gradient to a linear gradient.

   b. For the left gradient stop, hold down Alt and click the **C = 85, M = 10, Y = 100, K = 10** swatch. Move the stop to about 20%.

   c. Remove the far-right gradient stop.

   d. For the remaining gradient stop, use **C = 30, M = 0, Y = 100, K = 0**, and drag the stop close to **68%**.

   e. Save the gradient as **Redbud**.

2. Adjust the gradient angle so the gradient runs from dark green at the base of the leaf to lighter green at its tip.

3. Select the pen stroke used for the redbud leaf vein. Increase the stroke weight to 3 pts.

4. Convert the vein's path to an outline, and then apply the Redbud gradient to the vein.

5. Modify the angle of the gradient in the vein to 90° and then click the Reverse Gradient icon in the Gradient panel.

6. Group the leaf and the vein.

Create a Gradient for the Ash Leaves

1. Select the center ash leaf and add its fill to the Swatches panel as **Ash leaf**.

2. Create a gradient as follows in the Gradient panel:

   a. Apply the Acorn gradient to the center leaf as a starting point.

   b. Change the gradient to radial and type **150** in the Aspect Ratio box on the Gradient panel to create an elliptical gradient.

c. In the Gradient panel, select the left gradient stop and change its opacity to **0** to allow the orange background to show through.

d. Add a gradient stop at about 50%, adjust its opacity to 100%, and apply the Ash leaf swatch you saved in step 1.

e. Select the right gradient stop and apply **C = 5, M = 85, Y = 90, K = 35**.

f. Save the gradient as **Ash**.

3. Select the Gradient tool to activate the gradient bar on the leaf, and then drag the gradient bar so the large circle at the left of the bar sits at the base of the leaf and the end point sits at the tip of the leaf.

   ✔ *You may need to drag the Gradient tool from the base of the leaf to its tip to adjust the gradient.*

4. Apply the Ash gradient to the other two ash leaves, adjusting the gradient to begin at the base of each leaf and end at the tip of each leaf.

5. Group all the ash leaves, their veins, and the stems.

Apply a Gradient to the Type Object

1. Select the type object by clicking it with the Selection tool.

2. Convert the type object to outlines.

3. Apply the Acorn gradient to the text outlines, and then set an angle of 90° in the Gradient panel. (You may need to select the Linear gradient type before you can set the angle.)

4. Sharpen up the text gradient as follows:

   a. Move the left stop to about 60% on the gradient slider.

   b. Click the right stop to select it, hold down Alt, and drag a copy of this stop to the left, to about 10%.

5. Save the new gradient as **Text**. Your finished drawing should look similar to Illustration A.

6. Save your changes, close the file, and exit Illustrator.

Illustration A

ON YOUR OWN

1. Start Illustrator.

2. Open 🔘OYO28. Save the document as OIL28_*xx*.

3. Use gradients to improve the look of this illustration. Some ideas for adding gradients include:

   a. An elliptical or linear gradient for the lake.

   b. A gradient for the cattails to give them a more three-dimensional look.

   c. A gradient for the gazebo columns. (You may want to use a default black and white gradient and adjust gradient stops.)

   d. A gradient for the domed top of the gazebo.

   e. A radial gradient for the tree leaves.

4. Save each gradient with an appropriate name.

5. Save your changes, close the file, and exit Illustrator.

Skills Covered

- **About Effects**
- **Apply Illustrator Effects**
- **Apply Photoshop Effects**

Software Skills   Effects change the appearance of an object in a variety of ways. Some effects can be applied to any kind of object, while others can be applied only to vector objects. Effects can be applied either from the Effects menu or the Appearance panel.

Design Skills   A designer can use effects to create unique appearances for objects in a design. Learning how to apply and adjust effects can give a designer more tools to work with when creating an illustration.

Application Skills   In this exercise, you will create an illustration for the Old Church Players, an amateur dramatic group that uses a historic church for performances. You will apply a variety of effects to complete a drawing.

TERMS

Effect   Attribute that changes an object's appearance without changing the object itself.

NOTES

About Effects

- If you have used older versions of Illustrator, you will probably notice right away that Illustrator CS5 does not have a Filter menu.

- In previous versions of Illustrator, the Filter menu and Effect menu contained a number of identical categories containing identically named filters or effects, some of which could be applied only to raster (bitmap) images in RGB documents, some of which could be applied only to vector objects in CMYK documents, and some of which could be applied to either raster or vector objects in any document.

- Illustrator effects are now far less confusing. Filters from previous versions that could be applied to vector objects have been moved to the Effect menu, and the Filter menu has been eliminated. All effects contained on the Effect menu can be used for both vector and raster objects.

- An **effect** is an attribute that changes the appearance of an object without changing the object itself.

- You can also use the Appearance panel to apply an effect, as well as to remove or modify an effect. Removing an effect restores the original appearance of the object.

  ✓ *You will work with the Appearance panel in Exercise 31.*

- The Effect menu groups effects as Illustrator effects and Photoshop effects.

  - Some of the effects in the Illustrator group at the top of the menu can be applied only to vector objects; for example, the effects in the Distort & Transform category require a vector object. Other effects in this area, such as those in the Stylize category, can be applied to either a vector or raster object.

  - Effects in the Photoshop group on the Effect menu can be applied to either vector or raster objects.

- Among the numerous categories of effects in both groups are a wide selection of effects that can create a variety of interesting appearances—too wide a selection to cover in the space available here.

- This exercise will introduce you to some frequently used effects, and you will use others in subsequent exercises. You are encouraged to explore on your own to learn more about these features.

  ✓ *You will learn how to apply filters similar to the effects in this exercise in the Photoshop unit of this course. You will revisit effects in the InDesign section of the course.*

Apply Illustrator Effects

- The Effect menu offers ten categories in the Illustrator Effects section: 3D, Convert to Shape, Crop Marks, Distort & Transform, Path, Pathfinder, Rasterize, Stylize, SVG Filters, and Warp.

- You apply effects in these groups using dialog boxes specific for each effect. Most of these dialog boxes contain a Preview check box so you can see the effect of your settings on the object before you close the dialog box.

- After you have applied an effect, the Effect menu displays two new commands at the top of the menu. The first is a command such as Apply Drop Shadow that lets you apply the same effect settings to a new object.

  ✓ *If you use this command to apply the same settings again to the same object, you intensify the effect.*

- The second new command is the name of the effect you applied, such as Drop Shadow. If you click this option, you open the effect's dialog box so you can adjust the settings before applying the effect to a new object.

- The Distort & Transform and Stylize categories contain a number of very commonly used effects. Some of these are discussed in the following sections.

Distort & Transform Effects

- This category contains effects that can be used to distort an object by modifying its path or anchor points.

- Free Distort, for example, allows you to use a dialog box to drag any anchor point to any location, as shown in Figure 29-1.

- Pucker & Bloat curves an object's sides inward (puckering) or outward (bloating) from its anchor points. The orange object in Figure 29-2 shows the Pucker & Bloat effect applied to a square to pucker it.

Figure 29-1. Free Distort dialog box

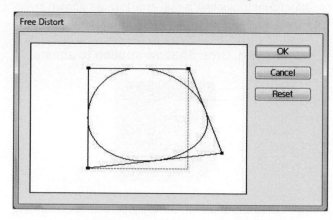

- Roughen and Tweak adjust an object's path to distort its appearance. The pink object in Figure 29-2 shows the result of the Roughen effect, and the blue object in Figure 29-2 shows Tweak applied to a circle.

Figure 29-2. Objects formatted with Pucker & Bloat, Roughen, and Tweak

- Twist rotates an object more in the center of the object than at the edges, resulting in an appearance such as the yellow object in Figure 29-3. This object was originally a square.

- Use Zig Zag to distort straight paths into wavy or zigzag patterns, as shown in the green star and the formerly straight lines in Figure 29-3.

Figure 29-3. Objects formatted with Twist and Zig Zag

Stylize Effects

- The Stylize category offers effects that adjust the appearance of an object without changing its path.

  ✓ *You have already used two Stylize effects, Drop Shadow and Inner Glow, in Exercise 19.*

- Drop Shadow allows you to create a sophisticated effect that looks like a real shadow, as shown in Figure 29-4.

Figure 29-4. Drop Shadow applied to square

- You can control the shadow by selecting a blending mode for the shadow; adjusting the shadow color; setting the amount of opacity for the shadow; specifying the offset, or distance, the shadow extends; and specifying the blur of the shadow.

- Use the Feather effect to soften the edges of an object, as shown in the blue star in Figure 29-5.

- The Inner Glow effect adds to an object a lighter area that looks like a glow. You can choose the blending mode, the color for the glow, the amount of blur, and whether the glow radiates from the center outward or from the edges inward. The green star in Figure 29-5 has the effect applied to the center.

- The Outer Glow effect, shown in Figure 29-6, adds a subtle glow around the edges of an object. You can choose a blending mode, a color for the glow, an opacity setting, and the amount of blur.

Figure 29-5. Objects formatted with the Feather and Inner Glow effects

Figure 29-6. Outer Glow effect applied to star

Apply Photoshop Effects

- The bottom half of the Effect menu lists ten categories of Photoshop effects, ranging from Artistic to Video. Choosing an effect from most of these categories opens the Effect Gallery.

- You can also simply click the Effect Gallery command to open the Gallery shown in Figure 29-7.

Figure 29-7. Effect Gallery

- The Effect Gallery shows the currently selected object in the left pane and a list of the categories that can be used with the object in the center pane.
- The Effect Gallery makes it easy to compare the results of a number of effects without leaving the dialog box.
- Expanding any of the categories provides a list of effects that can be applied to the object by a simple click of the mouse. Each effect offers a sample of its appearance to help you choose.
- The right pane displays the settings for the selected effect. As settings are applied or changed, the object in the left pane displays the effects of the current settings.
- It is possible to apply more than one effect to an object to create even more unusual and interesting appearances, but you can apply only one at a time using the Effect Gallery.

  ✓ *The order in which effects are applied can make a great deal of difference in the appearance of the object, as you will learn in Exercise 31.*

- Space limitations do not allow for detailed coverage of the effects categories, but the following list gives you some idea of the types of effects found in each category.
  - The Artistic category contains effects that simulate results from a variety of art tools, such as colored pencils, pastels, sponges, or palette knives. The purple star in Figure 29-8 shows the Sponge Artistic effect.
  - Use Brush Strokes effects to simulate strokes from a variety of artist brush types. The green star in Figure 29-8 shows the Spatter effect from this category.

Figure 29-8. Sponge, Spatter, and Diffuse Glow effects

- Use the three Distort effects to give the impression of viewing an object through an obscuring medium, such as glass. The orange star in Figure 29-8 shows the Diffuse Glow effect.

- The Sketch effects apply three-dimensional looks to objects as well as give a hand-drawn look to objects. The first star in Figure 29-9 shows the Photocopy Sketch effect.
- The Stylize category has only one effect, Glowing Edges, which can be used to add a light border around an object. This effect is applied to the second star in Figure 29-9.
- The Texture effects add textures of different types to objects. The red star in Figure 29-9 shows the Mosaic Tiles Texture effect.

Figure 29-9. Photocopy, Glowing Edges, and Mosaic Tiles effects

- The Video effects are for use with objects that will be used for moving images.
- The Effect Gallery does not give you access to all the effects on the Effect menu. Effects such the Blur effects, the Sharpen effects, and the Pixelate effects open their own dialog boxes in which you can select settings.
  - Use the Blur and Sharpen effects to give a blurred look to an object or sharpen the focus. The blue star in Figure 29-10 has a radial blur applied.
  - The Pixelate effects let you break down an object's color into component color dots, clumps, or lines. The green star in Figure 29-10 shows the Pointillize effect from this category.

Figure 29-10. Blur and Pointillize effects

PROCEDURES

✓ *Procedures are supplied only for effects used in hands-on and On Your Own exercises. Specific settings for effects are given in the exercise steps.*

Apply Effects from the Effect Gallery

1. Select object.
2. Click **Effect**............... ALT + C
3. Click **Effect Gallery**.

   OR

   a. Point to an effect category.
   b. Click the desired effect to open the Effect Gallery.
4. Expand the desired category in the center of the dialog box and select an effect.
5. Adjust settings in the right pane until the sample shows the effect you want.
6. Click **OK** .... ENTER

Use the Roughen Effect

1. Select object to be roughened.
2. Click **Effect**............... ALT + C
3. Point to **Distort & Transform** .... D
4. Click **Roughen** .... R
5. Specify size of distortions and whether size is relative or absolute.
6. Specify number of distortions per inch.
7. Specify **Smooth** or **Corner** for anchor points.
8. Click **OK** .... ENTER

Use the Drop Shadow Effect

1. Select object to which shadow will be applied.
2. Click **Effect**............... ALT + C
3. Point to **Stylize** .... S
4. Click **Drop Shadow**............. D
5. Specify blending mode, opacity, X and Y offsets, blur, and color or darkness setting.
6. Click **OK** .... ENTER

Use the Inner Glow Effect

1. Select object.
2. Click **Effect**............... ALT + C
3. Point to **Stylize** .... S
4. Click **Inner Glow** I
5. Specify blending mode, glow color, opacity, blur, and origin of glow.
6. Click **OK** .... ENTER

Use the Feather Effect

1. Select object.
2. Click **Effect**............... ALT + C
3. Point to **Stylize** .... S
4. Click **Feather**....................... F
5. Type or use spin arrows to set **Feather Radius**.
6. Click **OK** .... ENTER

Use the Mezzotint Effect

1. Select object.
2. Click **Effect**............... ALT + C
3. Point to **Pixelate**.
4. Click **Mezzotint**.
5. Click the **Type** list and select the type of object to make up the effect.
6. Click **OK** .... ENTER

Use the Free Distort Effect

1. Select object to distort.
2. Click **Effect**............... ALT + C
3. Point to **Distort & Transform** .... D
4. Click **Free Distort**.............. F
5. Drag corner point in Free Distort dialog box's preview window to distort object.
6. Click **Reset** to restore original bounding box.
7. Click **OK** .... ENTER

Use the Tweak Effect

1. Select object to distort.
2. Click **Effect**............... ALT + C
3. Point to **Distort & Transform** .... D
4. Click **Tweak** .... K
5. Select **Relative** or **Absolute** option to set size relative to path or using absolute measurement.
6. Use sliders or type values for horizontal and/or vertical distortion.
7. Select **Anchor Points** to allow anchor points to move.
8. Select **"In" Control Points** to allow control points going into an anchor point to move.
9. Select **"Out" Control Points** to allow control points going away from an anchor point to move.
10. Click **OK** .... ENTER

Use the Round Corners Effect

1. Select object to stylize.
2. Click **Effect**............... ALT + C
3. Point to **Stylize** .... S
4. Click **Round Corners**.......... R
5. Type value to round corners.
6. Click **OK** .... ENTER

EXERCISE DIRECTIONS

✓ *Display the Painting workspace.*

■ Open ◉ 29Players and save it as 29Players_xx.

Create the Stained Glass Window

1. Select the inner arched window object and use the **Spectrum** gradient from the Swatches panel to fill the object. Remove the stroke.

2. Apply the **Crystallize** effect from the **Pixelate** category. Change cell size to 40.

3. With the inner window object still selected, apply the **Stained Glass** effect from the **Texture** category to the gradient object. Use a cell size of **14**, a border thickness of **4**, and a light intensity of **4**.

4. Select the outer arch and apply the **Rough Pastels** effect from the **Artistic** category. Use a stroke length of **10**, a stroke detail of **4**, and choose Burlap from the Texture drop-down list.

Create Clapboard "Siding" on the Building

1. Activate the layer named **Siding**.

2. Draw a straight **2 pt** horizontal line about **180 pts** long even with the bottom of the window. See Illustration A for the placement of this line.

3. Copy the horizontal line upward three or four times to make a series of horizontal lines.

4. Select all horizontal lines and apply the **Roughen** effect from the **Distort & Transform** category using a size of 1%, a detail of 2/in, and smooth points.

5. With all lines still selected, apply the **Drop Shadow** effect from the **Stylize** category with the following settings:

   ■ Opacity, 100%
   ■ X Offset, 0 pt
   ■ Y Offset, 2 pt
   ■ Blur, 1 pt
   ■ Color, click the black color box and use the Color Picker to choose a dark gray color.

6. Using default fill and stroke settings, draw a rectangle about **390 pts** wide by about **325 pts** high and position it on top of the window and the horizontal lines. (The rectangle should extend from below the window to above the tree branch and be centered horizontally over the drawing.)

7. Remove the stroke. Apply the **Craquelure** effect from the **Texture** category to the rectangle, using crack spacing of **45**, crack depth of **2**, and crack brightness of **6**.

8. Adjust layers so the crackled rectangle is behind both the window and the horizontal lines.

Complete the Tree Object

✓ *The old church is known for its beautiful surrounding trees. The tree object above the window will give a suggestion of the church's sylvan setting.*

1. Activate the **Tree** layer. Apply a dark brown color to the tree branch and remove the stroke from the object.

2. Experiment with **Inner Glow** effect settings from the **Stylize** category to add interest to the branch.

3. Save your changes so far.

4. Draw an ellipse about **125 pts** wide by **120 pts** high and fill with a medium or dark green swatch. Remove the stroke.

5. Use one of the Distort effects, such as **Roughen** or **Tweak** from the **Distort & Transform** category, to make the ellipse look more like a group of leaves.

6. Apply the **Sponge** Artistic effect. Experiment with settings until you are happy with the resulting texture.

7. Move the leaves into place at the end of the branch and then apply the **Feather** Stylize effect with a radius of 3 pts to soften the edges of the leaves.

Modify Text

1. Select the text object by clicking the Text layer.

   ✓ *One of Illustrator's Warp effects has been applied to the text already.*

2. Change the type fill color to one of the colors in the stained glass window.

3. Apply the **Mezzotint** Pixelate effect using the Medium dots option. Your illustration should look similar to Illustration A.

4. Save your changes, close the file, and exit Illustrator.

Illustration A

ON YOUR OWN

✓ *This exercise will give you more practice with effects as you create a campaign document for City Council candidate Celia Pepper.*

1. Open ⊙OYO29 and save the document as OIL29_*xx*.

2. Create a new layer named **Background**.

3. On this layer, draw a rectangle that covers part of the shaker and encloses the text at the right side of the shaker. (See Illustration B.)

4. Use the Free Distort effect to give this rectangle a more interesting shape.

5. Use the Round Corners effect to round all corners of the rectangle. You can choose the amount to round the corners.

6. Remove the stroke and fill the rectangle with a color of your choice.

7. Move the Background layer to the bottom of the layer list in the Layers panel.

8. Save your changes so far.

9. Select the <Group> layer (it is a sublayer under Layer 1) that contains the text PEPPER. (This text has a warp effect already applied.) Apply the Drop Shadow effect with default settings.

10. Apply the same Drop Shadow effect to the shaker. (Select the shaker group and click Apply Drop Shadow at the top of the Effect menu.)

11. Create a new layer named **Pepper** at the top of the layer list.

12. On this layer draw an ellipse that extends from the head of the shaker down to the *FOR CITY COUNCIL* path type.

13. Remove the fill if necessary.

14. Use the Tweak effect to distort the circular shape slightly. You may want to add anchor points to the ellipse path to allow for more distortion.

15. Fill the shape by applying the **Pepper** pattern you find in the Swatches panel. If desired, use the Direct Selection tool to drag anchor points of the distorted ellipse to improve the look of the falling pepper. Then remove the stroke.

16. Select all objects in the illustration, group them, and use the Crop Marks effect to supply crop marks to be used after the flyer is printed. Your illustration should look similar to Illustration B.

17. Save your changes, close the file, and exit Illustrator.

Illustration B

166

Exercise | 30

Skills Covered

- **About Graphic Styles**
- **Apply a Default or Library Graphic Style**
- **Create and Modify a New Graphic Style**
- **Create Objects for a Rollover**

Software Skills   Graphic styles let you quickly apply a set of attributes to objects. Use Illustrator's default graphic styles or apply a style from a graphic style library. You can also create a custom graphic style using Illustrator tools and commands. Graphic styles can be very helpful for creating Web page objects such as rollover buttons.

Design Skills   Another example of how to work smarter rather than harder is the use of graphic styles, which allow a designer to apply a complex appearance to multiple objects with a few clicks of the mouse. Many interesting graphic styles are available in libraries, or a designer can create a graphic style. Once applied, a graphic style can be easily modified to update the appearance of all objects to which the style is applied.

Application Skills   In this exercise, you will work on a Web page illustration for Earth Tones. You will apply several effects and styles from graphic style libraries. Then you will create your own graphic style, apply it, and modify it.

TERMS

Graphic style   A named set of appearance attributes saved in the Graphic Styles panel for easy application.

NOTES

About Graphic Styles

- A **graphic style** is a group of appearance attributes that can be saved and named. A graphic style can consist of any fill, stroke, pattern, gradient, transparency setting, or effect.

- The advantage of creating a graphic style is that attributes can be applied to one object, saved as a style, and then quickly applied to other objects using the saved style in the Graphic Styles panel.

- If a graphic style is modified, all objects formatted with that style immediately change to the modified attributes.

- Graphic styles can be applied to strokes only, fill only, or both stroke and fill, as shown in Figure 30-1.

Figure 30-1. Stroke, fill, and stroke and fill graphic styles

Apply a Default or Library Graphic Style

■ Illustrator's default graphic styles are stored in the Graphic Styles panel. The graphic styles available in a new document vary according to document type. The Graphic Styles panel shown in Figure 30-2 displays the styles available for a new Web document.

Figure 30-2. Default Web styles in Graphic Styles panel

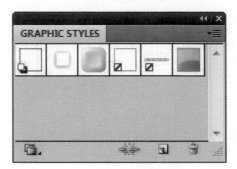

■ As for brushes, swatches, gradients, and patterns, Illustrator supplies a wide variety of additional graphic styles in libraries.

■ Access graphic style libraries using the Graphic Styles Libraries Menu button 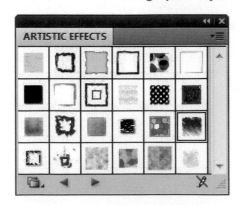 at the bottom of the Graphic Styles panel. Styles are grouped in libraries by type of effect. Figure 30-3 shows the styles available in the Artistic Effects library.

Figure 30-3. Artistic Effects graphic style library

✓ *Style libraries can also be accessed from the Graphic Styles panel menu.*

■ Apply a graphic style the same way as a color swatch or pattern: Select the object to receive the style and click the style in the Graphic Styles panel.

■ Selecting a style from a library panel adds it to the Graphic Styles panel.

■ The Graphic Styles panel makes it easy to view and apply graphic styles.

● To see how an object will look with a specific graphic style applied, right-click on the graphic style in the Graphic Styles panel. A thumbnail displays as shown in Figure 30-4 to show you how the selected object will appear.

Figure 30-4. Preview how a graphic style looks on an object

● You can see how effects will look when applied to type by clicking the panel menu and selecting Use Text for Preview. All the graphic styles currently displayed in the panel adjust to show how they would look if applied to text, as shown in Figure 30-5.

Figure 30-5. Graphic styles shown as they would apply to text

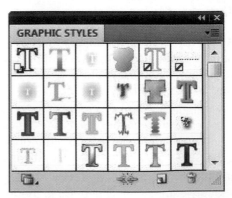

- You can build graphic styles very easily using the Alt-click procedure. To add any graphic style to an object, hold down Alt and click on the style in the Graphic Styles panel. This feature makes it easy to add a number of styles to a single object.

- Once a graphic style has been applied to an object, the object and the style are linked. This allows for easy updating of objects when a style is modified.

- You can break the link between an object and its graphic style by clicking the Break Link to Graphic Style button ⬚ on the Graphic Styles panel, or clicking Break Link to Graphic Style on the Graphic Styles panel menu.

- Breaking the link between the object and its graphic style will retain the style formatting for the object, but the object's appearance will not change if the graphic style is modified.

- Remove a graphic style from an object by selecting the Default Graphic Style option, the first style in the Graphic Styles panel's first row.

- The Graphic Styles panel menu has commands that will be familiar to users who have worked with the Swatches panel.

- You can select unused styles, sort styles by name, or change the view from Thumbnail View to Small List View or Large List View. When applying a style to text, you can choose to override the text color with the style color.

Create and Modify a New Graphic Style

- Create a graphic style by applying the desired attributes to any object in an illustration. Use an existing style as a starting point or begin from scratch.

- Select the object formatted with the desired attributes and drag it to the Graphic Styles panel, or click the New Graphic Style button ⬚ on the Graphic Styles panel.

  ✓ Or click New Graphic Style on the Graphic Styles panel menu.

- Supply a name for the new graphic style in the Graphic Style Options dialog box.

- To modify a graphic style, adjust attributes in an object formatted with that style, then hold down Alt and drag the modified object on top of the original graphic style in the Graphic Styles panel.

- All objects formatted with that graphic style will immediately update with the modifications.

- You may modify not only a custom graphic style, but any default or library graphic style.

- To make subtle modifications to a graphic style, copy the style using the Duplicate Graphic Style command on the Graphic Styles panel menu. You can then make necessary changes and rename the duplicated style.

Create Objects for a Rollover

- Graphic styles are especially useful for creating objects for use on Web pages, such as buttons to be used as links. With one click of the mouse, you can apply a sophisticated graphic appearance that will make the object stand out on the page.

- Illustrator offers a wide variety of graphic styles in libraries that are suitable for creating Web graphics such as buttons. The Buttons and Rollovers library makes it easy to apply effects for rollovers.

  ✓ A rollover is an object that changes appearance on a Web page as the mouse hovers over it or as the mouse clicks on it.

- The various appearances used in a rollover are called *states*. For example, you might have an up state that shows the button as it would appear when the page is loaded and a down state that shows the button as it would appear when clicked.

- You can easily create the objects to be used for rollovers in Illustrator, although you must then import the objects into a Web design program such as Dreamweaver to set up the actual button behaviors.

- Set up objects for rollovers in Illustrator using layers that can be turned on and off to display the various states.

PROCEDURES

Apply a Default Graphic Style

1. Display the Graphic Styles panel if necessary.
2. Select the object to which style should be applied.
3. Select desired style in Graphic Styles panel.

To remove a graphic style:

1. Select the object to which the graphic style is applied.
2. Select **Default Graphic Style** in the Graphic Styles panel.

To break link between an object and a graphic style:

1. Select the object to which the graphic style is applied.
2. Click **Break Link to Graphic Style** button ⬓ on Graphic Styles panel.

   OR

1. Click ▥ to open Graphic Styles panel menu.
2. Click **Break Link to Graphic Style** on Graphic Styles panel menu.

Use Style Library

1. Click **Graphic Styles Libraries Menu** button ▣ at lower-left corner of Graphic Styles panel.
2. Click or point to a graphic styles library type from the drop-down menu.
3. Select a specific library from pop-out list if necessary.
4. Click any style in a library panel to add swatch to default Graphic Styles panel.

Create a New Graphic Style

1. Apply desired attributes to object in illustration.
2. Select object and drag to Graphic Styles panel.

   OR

   Click **New Graphic Style** button ▣ on Graphic Styles panel.

   OR

   a. Click ▥ to open Graphic Styles panel menu.
   b. Click **New Graphic Style**.
3. Double-click new style and type name for style.

Modify a Graphic Style

1. Select object to which graphic style has been applied.
2. Modify attributes as desired using the required tools.
3. Hold down ALT and drag modified object back on top of original style in Graphic Styles panel.

Use Scribble Effect

1. Select object to be scribbled.
2. Click **Effect** .... ALT + C
3. Point to **Stylize** .... S
4. Click **Scribble** .... B
5. Click **Settings** .... ALT + T and use up or down arrow to select a preset scribble setting.
6. Specify scribble angle.
7. Specify path overlap and variation if desired.
8. Specify stroke width for scribble.
9. Specify curviness, from angular (straight) to loopy (very curvy), and variation if desired.
10. Specify spacing of scribbles and variation if desired.
11. Click **OK** .... ENTER

EXERCISE DIRECTIONS

✓ *Display the Web workspace.*

1. Open ⊙ 30Earthtone and save the document as 30Earthtone_xx. Change the color mode to RGB if necessary. Locate the Graphic Styles panel behind the Symbols panel and pull it out onto the document.

   ✓ *This illustration shows the beginnings of a new home page for the Earth Tones Web site.*

2. Select the *Earth Tones* text object and apply the **Shadow** graphic style, one of the default styles you should see in the Graphic Styles panel.

3. This graphic style isn't quite dramatic enough. Click Undo to remove the style.

4. Display the Image Effects graphic styles library panel. Adjust the display in the Graphic Styles panel menu to use text for the preview. The graphic styles in the panel should change to show how the styles look applied to text.

5. Right-click the **Yellow Glow** graphic style to see a preview of how the type object would look with this style applied. This seems promising. Apply the graphic style, then remove the stroke from the text object.

6. Finish off this area by changing the stroke color of the dotted line to **R = 242, G = 153, B = 102**.

7. Apply the **Feather** effect from the **Stylize** category to the blue rounded rectangle using a feather radius of 5. Then apply the same effect to the gold and dark red rectangles. (Apply the effect from the top of the Effect menu.)

8. Select the white rectangle to the left of *Face*. Remove the stroke, select the fill, and apply the Scribble effect from the Stylize category of effects, changing the following settings:

   - Angle: 40°
   - Path overlap: 0 pt
   - Variation: 0.2 pt
   - Stroke width: 3 pt
   - Curviness: 2
   - Spacing: 4.5 pt

9. Change the fill color to a blush pink color such as **R = 250**, **G = 220**, **B = 212**.

10. With the scribbled rectangle still selected, hold down Alt and add the Shadow graphic style to the current appearance.

11. The shadow style doesn't add much interest. Undo it and then add a Drop Shadow effect as follows:

    - Opacity: 50%
    - X offset: 1 pt
    - Y offset: 3 pt
    - Blur: 3 pt
    - Click Darkness and set to 90%.

12. Save the selected square as a new graphic style with the name **Links**.

13. Apply the graphic style to the remaining rectangles by selecting each rectangle and clicking the style.

14. Add a drop shadow to the light yellow background rectangle by clicking Drop Shadow at the top of the Effect menu and then adjusting settings as follows:

    - X offset: 3 pt
    - Y offset: 4 pt
    - Select the Color option and click the black color preview to open the Color Picker. Set the RGB colors for the new shadow to **R = 186**, **G = 98**, **B = 60**. Close the Color Picker and apply the shadow.

15. The blush pink buttons don't contrast well enough with the other elements in the frame. Select the first button and apply the rust color used in the right rounded rectangle.

16. Hold down the Alt key and drag the recolored button to the Graphic Styles panel to modify the existing Links style for all buttons.

17. Now create the objects for a rollover button for current specials:

    a. Select the *SPECIALS* rectangle, display the Buttons and Rollovers library of graphic styles, and apply the **Red Coils Normal** graphic style. This is the style you will see when the page loads.

    b. Create a new layer below the Rollover Normal layer and name it **Rollover Down**.

    c. Select everything on the Rollover Normal layer, copy the objects, and paste them in the Rollover Down layer.

    d. Hide the Rollover Normal layer and open the Rollover Down layer.

    e. Rename the Normal path as Down.

    f. Select the button object and apply the **Red Coils Mouse Down** graphic style.

    g. To further differentiate the down state from the normal state, apply a drop shadow, using the same settings you used in step 14, but change opacity to 80%.

18. Hide the Rollover Down layer and unhide the Rollover Normal layer. Your finished drawing should look similar to Illustration A.

19. Save your changes, close the file, and exit Illustrator.

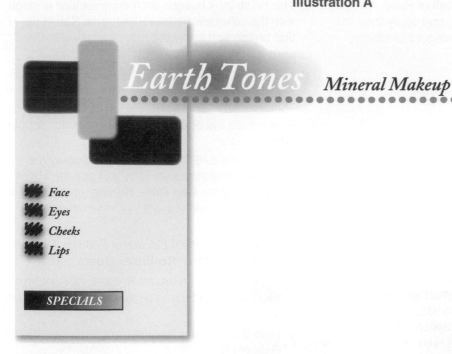

ON YOUR OWN

1. Start Adobe Illustrator.

2. Open a new Illustrator print document and save the document as OIL30_xx.

   ✓ *A client who is starting a landscape paving company wants help creating a logo. Use graphic styles to start the process.*

3. Create a brick-like shape to represent a paving block and apply a graphic style such as the RGB Concrete texture from the Textures graphic styles library.

4. Modify the style by adding an effect such as a drop shadow or glow and create a new graphic style from the revised style.

5. Add several more paving bricks to the drawing and apply the graphic style you created.

6. Insert several other shapes and apply other graphic styles such as one that looks like stone or cobblestones.

7. Arrange the objects in a pleasing way and add text if desired giving the name of the client (use your own name if desired) and some information about services or a motto.

8. Save your changes, close the file, and exit Illustrator.

Skills Covered

- **The Appearance Panel**
- **Modify Appearance Attributes**
- **Reorder Appearance Attributes**

- **Add Stroke or Fill**
- **Copy an Appearance**
- **Apply an Appearance to a Layer**

Software Skills Use the Appearance panel to keep track of appearance attributes applied to objects, groups, and even layers. You can adjust fill, stroke, and opacity right in the panel. Change the impact of effects by reordering attributes in the panel, or add a new fill or stroke to one or more objects at a time. Copy a pleasing appearance to other objects, or apply an appearance to a layer so that all objects on the layer have the same attributes.

Design Skills A designer needs to know not only how to apply styles and effects but how to modify, rearrange, or delete them. Understanding how to use the Appearance panel can help a designer to work efficiently.

Application Skills In this exercise, you will return to a previous illustration for Greenwood Conservancy to practice using the Appearance panel. You will apply effects, rearrange them, copy effects, and apply an effect to a layer.

TERMS

Attributes Properties of an object that change its appearance without changing its underlying structure.

NOTES

The Appearance Panel

- The Appearance panel shows appearance **attributes** applied to objects, groups, and layers in an illustration.
- Figure 31-1, for example, shows the attributes for a selected object.
  - The stroke for the object is tan and 4 pt in weight.
  - The object has a gradient fill. The Rough Pastels effect has been applied to the fill only, and the opacity of the fill is 81%.
  - The Drop Shadow effect has been applied to the object, and the object has default opacity.

Figure 31-1. Appearance panel shows attributes for object

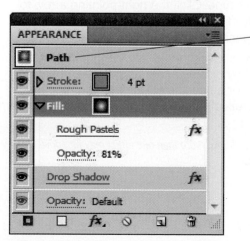

- Objects, groups, and layers act as *containers* in the Appearance panel. Note in Figure 31-1 that Path (which indicates a selected object) contains the attributes listed below it.
- To display the attributes for an object or group, select the object or group on the artboard.
- To display attributes for a layer, click the target symbol to the right of the layer name.
- If a group or layer is selected, the Appearance panel looks slightly different, as shown in Figure 31-2. The container is named Group or Layer and contains the Contents and Opacity attributes by default. Figure 31-2 shows that a Drop Shadow effect has been applied to the entire group.

    ✓ *Double-click Contents to display further attributes of a group's objects.*

Figure 31-2. Appearance panel for a group

- By default, attributes display in a specific order in the Appearance panel.
    - The Stroke attributes display first and include information on color, weight, style (such as Dashed), and brush (for Paintbrush strokes). Click the right-pointing arrow to display effects that have been applied to the stroke and opacity settings.
    - Fill attributes display next, including color or other fill type. Click the right-pointing arrow to display effects that have been applied to the fill and opacity settings.
    - Effects or styles applied to the object, group, or layer may display either above the Stroke information or below the Fill information (depending on the effect) in the order in which the effects are applied.

        ✓ *As you know, more than one effect may be applied to any object.*

Modify Appearance Attributes

- The Appearance panel makes it easy to work with an object's attributes. You may have noticed in Figures 31-1 and 31-2 that visibility eyes like those used in the Layers panel are included in the Appearance panel.
- You can hide any attribute using these eye symbols. For example, you can hide the stroke around an object, or you can hide an effect to see how an object would look both with and without it. This feature gives you a great deal of control over object appearance as you are working.
- You also have more control over opacity settings for an object. You can adjust opacity for the stroke, for the fill, and for the object as a whole.
- Besides being able to control visibility of attributes, you can also change attributes right in the panel. Figure 31-3 shows how easily you can adjust the stroke color from the Appearance panel.

Figure 31-3. Adjust stroke color in the Appearance panel

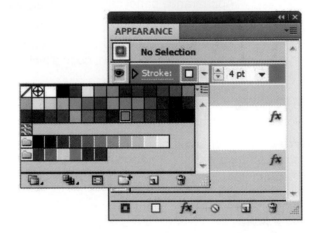

- By simply clicking on the current stroke color, you activate a down arrow that, when clicked, displays the Swatches panel. If you hold down Shift when clicking, you display the Color panel. Use the same procedures to display the Swatches or Color panel for the fill.
- Note that you can also adjust the stroke weight. And if you click on the word *Stroke* in the Appearance panel, the Stroke panel flies out to allow you to change stroke attributes such as weight, cap and join options, alignment, dashes, and profile. You can even add an arrowhead to a stroke just as if you were using the Stroke panel.

■ Likewise, when you click the word *Opacity* for an object, a stroke, or a fill, the Transparency panel flies out so that you can use the slider to adjust opacity.

■ You can also easily add effects to an object, stroke, or fill using either the Effect menu or the Add New Effect button *fx.* at the bottom of the Appearance panel. Clicking the Add New Effect button displays a drop-down menu identical to the Effect menu from which you can easily choose effects.

   ● To apply the effect to the entire object, make sure that neither Stroke nor Fill is selected in the Appearance panel.

   ● Select Stroke or Fill and then choose the effect to apply it to the stroke only or fill only.

■ You can adjust any effect by clicking its name in the Appearance panel to open its dialog box.

■ The order in which attributes display has considerable impact on the final look of an object, as you will learn in the next section.

■ You may want to duplicate a particular attribute to apply it twice to an object. Select the attribute and click the Duplicate Selected Item button 🔲 to copy it.

   ✓ *Applying an effect twice intensifies the effect.*

■ You may decide that an applied effect or appearance is not quite right and wish to remove it. The Appearance panel makes this type of change easy using the following options.

   ● Remove an effect quickly by clicking on the *fx* symbol to the right of the effect name and then clicking the Delete Selected Item 🔲 button on the panel.

      ✓ *Or, drag the effect over this button.*

   ● To clear all appearance attributes for an object, click the Clear Appearance button 🔲. This results in no fill and no stroke for an object.

      ✓ *Use Undo if you want to restore the appearances.*

■ When an object has a number of effects applied, you can reduce the object to its basic appearance (a fill and a stroke) by clicking the Reduce to Basic Appearance option on the panel menu.

   ✓ *You may also use options on the panel menu to remove or clear an appearance.*

■ Effects set in the Appearance menu become defaults for new objects. You can affect the attributes of new objects using the New Art Has Basic Appearance option on the panel menu.

   ● When this option is selected, new objects will display only the fill and stroke shown in the Appearance panel.

   ● When this option is deselected, new objects will display all the attributes in the Appearance panel, including any effects, stroke or fill settings, and opacity settings in the panel.

■ To remove all attributes from a new object, apply the default stroke and fill from the Tools panel.

Reorder Appearance Attributes

■ Appearance attributes can be moved in the Appearance panel the same way layers are moved in the Layers panel.

■ Changing the order of attributes can make a great difference in the appearance of an object, as shown in Figure 31-4.

Figure 31-4. Result of reordering stroke and fill

■ The object on the left in Figure 31-4 has the stroke in front of the fill (the default option). The object on the right shows what happens when Fill is moved above Stroke in the Appearance panel.

■ The fill in the right object now overlaps the stroke, reducing its apparent width.

■ Adjusting the order of effects can also result in quite different looks for an object.

■ In Figure 31-5, for example, identical objects have two effects applied: Sponge and Mezzotint.

Figure 31-5. Result of reordering effects

■ The left object in Figure 31-5 has Sponge applied first and then Mezzotint. The right object has Mezzotint applied first and then Sponge.

■ As indicated earlier, effects can be applied to a whole object or only to the fill or stroke. Figure 31-6, for example, shows the Pointillize effect applied to the entire object on the left and to the fill only of the object on the right.

Figure 31-6. Effect applied to whole object and to fill only

- To move an effect to apply to a fill or stroke only, drag it on top of Fill or Stroke as shown in Figure 31-7.

Figure 31-7. Drag an effect to apply to fill only

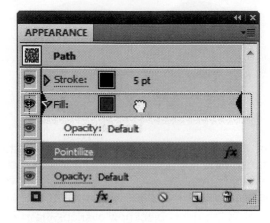

✓ *To avoid having to move the effect, select Fill or Stroke when applying the effect.*

Add Stroke or Fill

- You can use the Add New Stroke button ■ or Add New Fill button ☐ on the Appearance panel to add a new stroke or fill to a container.

- A new stroke can be used to create a special effect such as the one shown in Figure 31-8.

Figure 31-8. Object with two stroke attributes

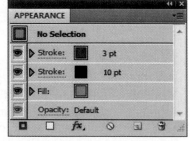

- Note that an orange 3-pt stroke is positioned in the panel above a black 10-pt stroke. Both strokes are centered on the object's path, so the lighter stroke bisects the heavier one to create a striped effect.

- When a new fill or stroke is added to a group or layer container, the fill or stroke attributes will apply to all objects in the group or layer.

Copy an Appearance

- Getting an appearance just right can require considerable experimentation and application of attributes that can be tedious to repeat for several objects.

- Illustrator makes it easy to copy an appearance from one object to another using either the Appearance panel or the Layers panel.

- With the desired appearance attributes displayed in the Appearance panel, drag the appearance thumbnail from the panel to the object to be formatted.

- In the Layers panel, a filled target symbol indicates that appearance attributes have been applied to an object (see Figure 31-9).

Figure 31-9. Copy an appearance in the Layers panel

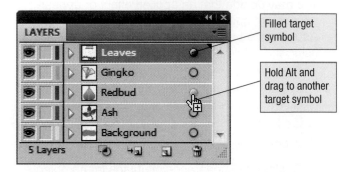

Filled target symbol

Hold Alt and drag to another target symbol

- To copy appearance attributes from one object to another, hold down Alt and drag the target symbol on top of the target symbol of the layer to be formatted.

Apply an Appearance to a Layer

- A quick way to apply appearance attributes to all objects on a layer is to select the layer's target symbol and then apply appearance attributes.

- Attributes applied to a layer container will apply not only to all existing objects on the layer, but to any new objects that are created on the layer.

PROCEDURES

Display Attributes for Object or Group *(Shift + F6)*

1. Display Appearance panel.........................`SHIFT` + `F6`
2. Click object to see Path container in Appearance panel.

   OR

   Click any part of group to see Group container in Appearance panel.

Display Attributes for Layer

1. Display Appearance panel.
2. Display Layers panel.
3. Click layer's target symbol `O` to right of layer name to select layer and view Layer container in Appearance panel.

Modify an Appearance Attribute

1. Select object, group, or layer.
2. Display Appearance panel if necessary.

To modify stroke attributes:

- Click underlined word *Stroke* to open Stroke panel and adjust weight, cap, join, offset, alignment, dash, arrowhead, or profile settings.

To modify stroke color:

1. Click Stroke color box to display down arrow.
2. Click arrow to display Swatches panel and select a new color.

   ✓ *Hold down Shift when clicking to display the Color panel instead of the Swatches panel.*

To modify stroke opacity:

1. Click right-pointing arrow to left of *Stroke* to display other stroke settings.
2. Click **Opacity** to display the Transparency panel.
3. Adjust Opacity slider as desired.

To modify fill color:

1. Click Fill color box to display down arrow.
2. Click arrow to display Swatches panel and select a new color.

   ✓ *Hold down Shift when clicking to display the Color panel instead of the Swatches panel.*

To modify fill opacity:

1. Click right-pointing arrow to left of *Fill* to display other stroke settings.
2. Click **Opacity** to display the Transparency panel.
3. Adjust Opacity slider as desired.

To adjust opacity for an entire object:

1. Make sure neither fill nor stroke is selected in Appearance panel.
2. Click **Opacity** to display the Transparency panel.
3. Adjust Opacity slider as desired.

Apply an Effect to Stroke or Fill

1. Select stroke or fill in Appearance panel.
2. Select and apply effect.

   ✓ *Click the right-pointing arrow for stroke or fill to see the effect in the panel.*

To adjust any effect from the Appearance panel:

- Click any effect to open effect's dialog box and modify settings.

Duplicate an Attribute

1. Select attribute to duplicate in Appearance panel.
2. Click **Duplicate Selected Item** button 🔲 on panel.

   OR

   Click 🔲 and select **Duplicate Item**.

Remove an Attribute

1. Select attribute to remove in Appearance panel.
2. Click **Delete Selected Item** button 🗑 on panel.

   OR

   Click 🔲 and select **Remove Item**.

Clear All Attributes

1. Select object, group, or layer.
2. Click **Clear Appearance** button 🚫 on panel.

   OR

   Click 🔲 and select **Clear Appearance**.

Reduce to Basic Appearance

1. Select object, group, or layer.
2. Click 🔲 and select **Reduce to Basic Appearance**.

Adjust Attributes for New Objects

- Click 🔲 and select **New Art Has Basic Appearance** to apply only the current fill and stroke to any new object.
- Click 🔲 and clear **New Art Has Basic Appearance** to apply all current attributes to any new object.

To restore default appearance attributes:

- Click **Default Fill and Stroke** 🔲 on Tools panel.

Reorder Appearance Attributes

1. Select attribute to reorder.
2. Drag attribute above or below other attributes.

   OR

   Drag attribute on top of **Fill** or **Stroke** to apply only to fill or stroke.

Add Fill or Stroke

1. Select object, group, or layer.
2. Click 🔳 to add a new stroke.

   OR

   Click 🔲 to add a new fill.

Copy an Appearance

1. Select object, group, or layer that has attributes to copy.
2. Click thumbnail in Appearance panel and drag from thumbnail to object to be formatted.

   OR

1. Select object, group, or layer that has attributes to copy.
2. Click ⊙ in the Layers panel to the right of layer, group, or object name and drag to target of object to be formatted.

Apply an Appearance to a Layer

1. Display Appearance panel.
2. Display Layers panel.
3. Click ⊙ to right of layer name to select layer.
4. Apply appearance attributes as desired in Appearance panel.

EXERCISE DIRECTIONS

✓ *Display the Painting workspace.*

1. Open ⊙31Greenwood and save the document as 31Greenwood_xx.
2. Display the Appearance panel, the Layers panel, and the Gradient panel.

Modify Attributes for Text, Background, and Ash Leaves

1. Select the *Greenwood Conservancy* text group and add a new stroke to the group. Make sure the new stroke is **100% Black** and change the stroke weight to **0.25 pt**.
2. Select the background object and use the Add New Effect button on the Appearance panel to apply the **Inner Glow** (in the Stylize group) effect to the entire object. Use the following settings for the effect: **Overlay** mode, **70%** opacity, **80 pt** blur, and **Center**.
3. Select the center ash leaf. Select the Fill attribute in the Appearance panel and apply the **Texturizer** effect. Use the **Sandstone** texture with scaling of **100%** and relief of **10**.
4. In the Appearance panel, note how the **Texturizer** effect displays in the expanded Fill list, along with the gradient fill.
5. Collapse the Fill list and select the Stroke attribute.
6. Change stroke weight to **2 pts** and then drag the Stroke attribute below the Fill attribute. (This gives a more realistic uneven edge to the leaf.)
7. Drag the appearance thumbnail to the other two ash leaves to apply the same settings. Then adjust the gradients for these leaves to once again flow from the base of the leaves to the tips.

Modify Attributes for the Redbud Leaf

1. Select the redbud leaf (the green leaf in the middle of the group of leaves).
2. Apply the **Water Paper** effect (in the Sketch group) to the leaf. Use a Fiber Length of **15**, a Brightness of **60**, and a Contrast of **80.**
3. Apply a second effect to the leaf: Apply the **Grain** effect (in the Texture group), with an intensity of **20**, a contrast of **60**, and the **Clumped** grain type.
4. Adjust the effects in the Appearance panel by dragging the Grain effect above the Water Paper effect.
5. Move both effects into the Fill list, maintaining the same order. Then choose to edit the Grain effect and change Intensity to **30**.
6. Change the stroke weight to **2** and move the stroke below the fill.
7. Select the reverse gradient vein on this leaf and adjust the opacity of the fill to about **75%**.

Modify Attributes for the Gingko Leaf

1. Select the gingko leaf and add a fill. Change the new fill color to the **C = 20, M = 0, Y = 100, K = 0** swatch.
2. Move the new fill below the original fill.
3. Display the gradient for the leaf in the Gradient panel and adjust opacity for the rightmost gradient stop to 20% to allow the second fill to show through. Move this gradient stop all the way to the right.
4. Add a stroke and change its color to the **C = 50, M = 0, Y =100, K = 0** swatch.

5. You are not sure whether your client will prefer this green stroke or the black stroke. For now, hide the green stroke by turning off its visibility.

6. Select the group that contains the leaf veins and double-click on the word *Contents* to open the group's attributes.

7. Change the stroke color to the darkest green swatch and reduce opacity to 80%.

Apply Attributes to a Layer

1. Select the target symbol for the Leaf Brush layer.

2. Apply the default **Drop Shadow** effect to the layer.

3. The shadow is a bit dark. Click the Drop Shadow attribute for this layer and adjust settings. Use an opacity of **50** and a darkness of **35%**.

4. Copy the acorn and paste it to see how the new object receives a drop shadow like all others on the layer. Move the acorn anywhere near the oak leaves and rotate it if desired. Your illustration should look similar to Illustration A.

5. Save your changes, close the file, and exit Illustrator.

Illustration A

ON YOUR OWN

1. Start Adobe Illustrator.

2. Start a new print document.

3. Create several layers that contain simple objects, such as layers for circles, stars, and squares. Group some objects.

4. Practice using the Appearance panel to control effects and attributes.
   - Apply different effects to an object and observe what happens when you change the order of the effects.
   - Apply more than one stroke to an object and adjust stroke order, weight, and color to achieve a multistripe border.
   - Clear attributes from an object or group, then add new stroke and fill to the object or group.
   - Apply a style to an object and then reduce the object to its basic appearance.
   - Copy appearance from one object to another using both the Appearance panel and the Layers panel.
   - Apply attributes to all objects on a layer.

5. Save your document if desired for future reference with a name of your choice, close the file, and exit Illustrator.

Summary Exercise

Application Skills In this exercise, you will create an illustration for Castle Art, an art supply store. You will build a castle by merging shapes, create and save color swatches, apply gradients, create an opacity mask, and apply effects.

EXERCISE DIRECTIONS

✔ *Display the Painting workspace.*

1. Open ⊙ 32Castle and save the file as 32Castle_xx.

2. Select the large horizontal rectangle in the castle group and fill with **C = 75, M = 35, Y = 10, K = 0**. Save this color as a spot color named **Castle Blue**. Create a **50%** tint of Castle Blue and save it as a swatch.

3. Select all the castle objects *except* the tower, the tower roof, and the windows in the tower. Use the Shape Builder tool to merge the rectangles, from the blue rectangle outward. Use the Shape Builder to erase the ellipse to create an arched opening.

4. Fill the tower with Castle Blue. Fill the tower roof with **90%** black.

5. Select the tower and create a linear gradient that uses **Castle Blue** at 10% and 90% and the Castle Blue tint at 50%.

6. Select the tower roof and create a similar gradient using shades of black. Adjust the angle of the gradient as desired using the Gradient tool.

7. Fill the large slanted ellipse below the castle (the palette) with the **C = 35, M = 60, Y = 80, K = 25** swatch. Select both ellipses and use the Shape Builder tool to erase the smaller oval.

8. Draw about six ellipses on the palette and use the Roughen effect to make each ellipse look like a blob of paint.

9. You have just received word that your specs for Castle Blue are incorrect. Adjust the color to **C = 80, M = 50, Y = 0, K = 0**.

10. With Castle Blue as the base color, use the Color Guide panel to select some colors for the paint blobs on the palette. You may use complementary colors, shades, or any other of the harmony rules. Remove the paint blob strokes and group all palette objects when you are satisfied with your colors.

11. Select the tower object and the three windows and use the Shape Builder tool to erase the fill of the windows.

12. Draw a rectangle behind the castle and use Free Transform to create an interesting shape for the rectangle. Fill the distorted rectangle with a complementary color or a graphic style such as RGB Gouache. Adjust the position or shape of the rectangle if necessary so part of the fill shows through the tower windows.

    ✔ *If you apply a graphic style such as RGB Gouache, you may need to distort the rectangle again after applying the style and move the Free Distort effect above the Stroke and Fill in the Appearance panel.*

13. Apply Castle Blue as a fill for the type object. Position the type object on the distorted rectangle as shown in Illustration A. (You may need to adjust the shape of the rectangle.) Create an opacity mask from the type object. Adjust the blending mode and opacity as desired.

14. Position the palette over the left side of the castle as shown in Illustration A.

15. Save your changes, close the file, and exit Illustrator.

Illustration A

Application Exercise

Application Skills   In this exercise, you will work on an illustration for Crystal Bay Resort. You will create and save colors, apply graphic styles to objects, apply effects, and create several gradients.

EXERCISE DIRECTIONS

✔ *Display the Painting workspace.*

1. Open ⊙ 33Crystal and save the file as 33Crystal_xx.

2. Use the Color Guide panel to adjust the color of the tan beach object to be a more realistic sand color.

3. Select the bay object currently filled with blue. Modify the color to **C = 77, M = 0, Y = 20, K = 0**. Save the color as a spot color with the name **Crystal blue**.

4. Create a light purple color for the furthest hills and save the color with an appropriate name. Apply the color to both far hills.

5. Apply the **C = 0, M = 50, Y = 100, K = 0** swatch to the near hill on the left and reduce saturation to achieve a soft orange color. Save the swatch, name it, and apply it to the right near hill.

6. Create a brown color for the leftmost palm tree trunk. Remove the trunk's stroke and use the Eyedropper tool to copy the color to the other tree trunks.

7. Create a dark green color with 90% transparency for the left-pointing palm fronds. Use the Roughen effect to give these fronds more visual interest.

8. Save the frond attributes as a graphic style and apply the style to all left-pointing fronds.

9. Create a lighter green color with 90% transparency for the right-pointing fronds. Use the Roughen effect and save the frond as a graphic style.

10. Apply the right-pointing frond style to the remaining fronds.

11. Create the sky object:

   a. Add a fill to the sky object with a light color of blue and move the new fill below the default white fill.

   b. Select the original fill and create a gradient for the sky object that will display orange-yellow near the bay, and progress through a greenish-blue to a pale blue and finally a darker blue. You should use at least four stops, once of which should include transparency to bring in the second fill's light blue sky color.

12. Create a radial gradient in the sun ellipse to shade the sun from an orange center to a yellow outer rim. Remove the object stroke and adjust the gradient angle as desired.

13. Modify the umbrella objects:

   a. Use the Direct Selection tool to select the fill of each umbrella and choose a bright color for the fill.

   b. Still using the Direct Selection tool, select each umbrella fill and use the Inner Glow effect to lighten the fill of the umbrella around the edge.

   c. Use the Selection tool to select the grouped umbrella ribs and outlines and apply a lighter stroke color that coordinates well with the umbrella color.

14. Outline the text and create a gradient for the object that contrasts well with the sky. Adjust the angle of the gradient if necessary.

15. Apply the Drop Shadow effect to the type object and adjust its settings as desired to show up well against the sky object. Your drawing should resemble Illustration A.

16. Save your changes, close the file, and exit Illustrator.

Illustration A

Curriculum Integration

Application Skills   For a global perspectives course, you have been asked to prepare a map showing countries that belong to the European Union (EU) and when they joined. You also need to show countries that are being considered for membership. You can use Illustrator's Live Trace, Live Paint, and Live Color features to create the map. To complete this project, you will need to find the following information:

- An outline map of Europe
- Information on the European Union countries and when they were accepted into the community, as well as current candidates for acceptance

EXERCISE DIRECTIONS

Start a new print drawing and save it as **34Europe_xx**.

Use Illustrator's Live Trace feature to trace the map of Europe. Make sure the trace produces a good, clean copy of the map. You can delete labeling such as country names if desired.

Create a Live Paint object from the map. Be sure to check for and eliminate gaps that might have occurred during the trace using the Pen tool. You may need to consult an older atlas to create the border of the former West and East German states.

Countries have entered the European Union in groups, beginning with the first six countries that joined together in 1957 and then in 1973, 1981, 1986, and so on. Choose colors to represent each year that countries joined, and paint all the countries that joined that year with the same color. You may want to use the Color Guide panel to choose complementary colors or shades of one color. Create a key that links a color to a year. Add a key color for countries that are currently candidates for the EU and paint those countries with the key color.

Use Live Color to adjust the colors to a palette of your liking. Create a color group to hold the colors you eventually decide on.

Expand the Live Paint object when you have finished painting it. Create a caption as shown in Illustration A.

Save your changes, close the file, and exit Illustrator.

Illustration A

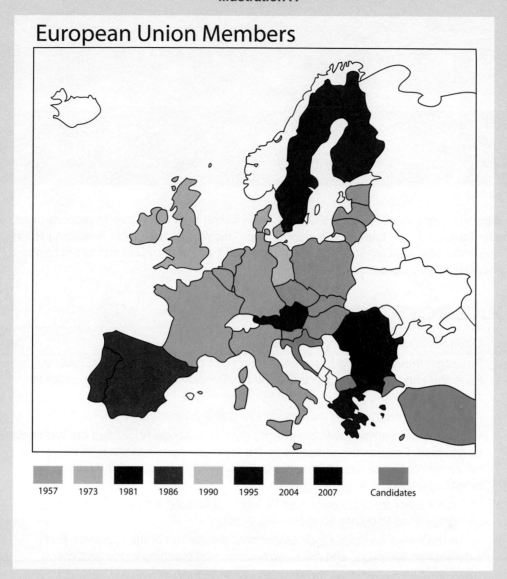

European Union Members

| 1957 | 1973 | 1981 | 1986 | 1990 | 1995 | 2004 | 2007 | Candidates |

Portfolio Builder

Application Skills   You have been asked by a bookstore to prepare hand-outs for their Great Literature reading group. This month, the group is reading *Bleak House* by Charles Dickens, and you need to add a picture of Dickens to the handout information you have been given.

EXERCISE DIRECTIONS

- Open 🔘35Dickens and save the file as 35Dickens_xx.
- Research images on the Internet to find a color painting of Charles Dickens. Save the image and then place it in the file. Position the image in the upper-left corner of the page.
- Apply to the image one or more effects to give it an interesting look.
- When you are satisfied with the effects, draw a rectangle about 545 pts wide and 63 pts high. Position the rectangle so the lower-left corner aligns with the lower-left corner of the picture, to create a band across the bottom of the picture that extends across the page.
- Pick up a color from the picture as fill for the rectangle, and then adjust the blending mode to create an interesting effect.
- Move the name and dates type object onto the portion of the rectangle that extends into the page, and adjust size, color, and blending mode as desired.
- Save your changes, close the file, and exit Illustrator.

Lesson | 4

Work with Drawing and Selecting Tools in Photoshop CS5

Skills Covered

- About Photoshop
- Create a New Image
- Photoshop Tools

- Choose a Foreground or Background Color
- Select a Drawing Mode
- Commit a Change

Software Skills   Photoshop is a sophisticated image-editing application you can use to create a wide variety of illustrations. Basic tasks when beginning a new illustration are creating the file, selecting foreground and background colors, and selecting a drawing mode. You have the choice of committing to a change you have made or discarding it.

Design Skills   Using Photoshop effectively in media design requires a designer to be familiar with tools and the work area. Learning how to select foreground and background colors will smooth the process of creating objects and enhancing graphics.

Application Skills   You have just started working in the design department for Sector Advertising and you need to become familiar with Photoshop's tools and workspace. In this exercise, you will create a new image, select foreground and background colors, draw several simple shapes, and add text.

TERMS

No new terms in this exercise.

NOTES

About Photoshop

- Adobe Photoshop is a powerful design tool used to create, correct, and enhance images. It has become the industry standard application for manipulating digital graphics.

- You may think that Photoshop is only for editing photographs, but you can use Photoshop to create a wide range of graphics, from simple drawings to sophisticated images for use in both print and Web documents.

- Photoshop's image tools allow you to select portions of an image for manipulation, correct many kinds of flaws in images, and enhance images using color and special effects.

- Many features of the Photoshop window will look familiar to you after your work in Illustrator. You will find that the Photoshop Help files sometimes use different terms for some features.

  - The Control panel is called the *options bar*.
  - The Tools panel may be called the *toolbox*.

- In this section of the course, *options bar* and *toolbox* will be used rather than Control panel and Tools panel to follow traditional Photoshop terminology.

- Though some tools have the same names as tools in Illustrator, it is important to understand that they may work quite differently in Photoshop.

- You recall that tools in Illustrator create *vector* objects—objects that are constructed using mathematical formulas. Vector objects can be resized to any percentage without loss of quality, and they can be moved anywhere in the document.

■ Photoshop, on the other hand, is designed for work with *bitmap* (*raster*) images that are created from groups of pixels of various colors. Much of your work in this application will involve manipulating the pixels already present in a file.

■ For example, you may select all the pixels of a certain color and then adjust that color, or you may select a portion of an image and then create a new image using only the pixels in that selection.

■ The Photoshop Brush tool, for another example, does not create the kind of brushed path objects that Illustrator's Paintbrush tool creates. The Brush tool paints pixels using the current foreground or background color, and that brushed color cannot be moved or resized as a Paintbrush object can be.

■ Some tools, such as the Pen tool and the shape tools (Rectangle, Ellipse, Line Segment, Custom Shape, for example) can create vector paths, but, as you will learn in a later exercise, these paths cannot be manipulated in quite the same ways that an Illustrator Pen path can be.

Create a New Image

■ Unlike other CS5 applications, Photoshop does not display a Welcome screen when the program starts. To create a new image, you use the File > New command to open the New dialog box, shown in Figure 36-1.

■ You may type a name for the image in the Name box.

■ The Preset list offers a variety of commonly used image sizes, including the default Photoshop image size, several standard Web page sizes, and sizes suitable for mobile devices, film, and video. As in Illustrator, some of these presets adjust the units of measurement to those most generally used for that type of file.

■ Alternatively, use the Width and Height text boxes to create an image with custom dimensions.

■ The default resolution of 72 pixels/inch works well for images to be displayed onscreen, such as on a Web page. For an image that will be included in a printed document, specify a higher resolution (such as 150 or 300), depending on the print requirements.

✓ *Some of the data files you open and create in the Photoshop lessons will use a resolution of 72 to limit file size for storage on the student data disk and your system.*

■ The Color Mode you choose affects how the image displays or prints. RGB Color works best for images that will be displayed onscreen, while CMYK Color optimizes the image for full-color printing. Photoshop files are RGB by default.

■ If you intend to use a Photoshop RGB image for printed output, the RGB file will need to be converted to the CMYK color model. You will learn more about color conversion in Lesson 6.

■ You can also choose the Grayscale color mode to create an image in shades of gray, Bitmap to create an image in black and white pixels, and Lab Color to use the Lab color model based on the way humans actually see color.

✓ *You will learn more about the Lab color model in the InDesign section of this book.*

■ The Background Contents list enables you to specify whether the image background will be transparent or use a color besides the default color of white.

✓ *If you plan to choose Background Color from the Background Contents drop-down list, you must set the desired background color for the image before opening the New dialog box. You learn to set background color later in this exercise.*

Figure 36-1. New dialog box

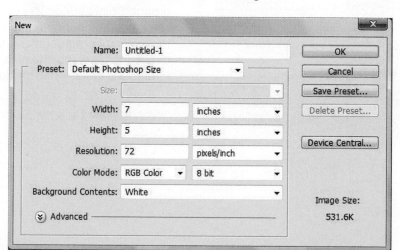

- You can click the Advanced button to see two additional setup options. You can choose a color profile at this stage, and you can adjust the pixel aspect ratio so that your image's pixels will be the correct size for specific output such as video.

  ✓ *You will learn about color profiles in Lesson 6. Pixel aspect ratio settings are beyond the scope of this book.*

- A new document has a tab, like that of documents you worked with in Illustrator, and the image area is centered in the workspace.

- The tab displays the file name, the current size percentage, and the color mode. Once you have added layers to an image, the tab displays the layer name as well.

Photoshop Tools

- The toolbox contains tools for adding and changing image content. By default, the toolbox appears at the left side of the Photoshop workspace.

- You will recognize many of the Photoshop tools from working in Illustrator. Figure 36-2 shows the Photoshop toolbox in expanded form with the tool names.

Figure 36-2. Photoshop toolbox

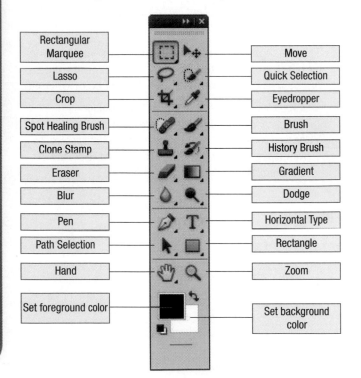

Rectangular Marquee		Move
Lasso		Quick Selection
Crop		Eyedropper
Spot Healing Brush		Brush
Clone Stamp		History Brush
Eraser		Gradient
Blur		Dodge
Pen		Horizontal Type
Path Selection		Rectangle
Hand		Zoom
Set foreground color		Set background color

- Resting the mouse pointer on a tool displays a tool tip giving the tool's name and its keyboard shortcut.

- As in Illustrator, some Photoshop tools are stored on toolbars beneath other tools. Click a tool that shows a small black triangle and hold down the mouse button to see other related tools on a toolbar.

- Because most Photoshop tools are designed to manipulate existing content, it is important to change settings before you use them.

- In Illustrator, for instance, you can select the Rectangle tool, draw the shape, and then modify its stroke and fill as desired. In Photoshop, you would select the Rectangle tool, specify a drawing mode, select a fill color, and then draw the object.

- As you choose a Photoshop tool, options in the options bar adjust to give you a choice of settings for that tool.

Choose a Foreground or Background Color

- Most of Photoshop's painting, drawing, and text tools apply the foreground color. The Gradient tool by default blends the foreground and background colors. It's important to select the desired foreground and/or background color before using a tool that applies one of those colors.

- By default, Photoshop sets the foreground color to black and the background color to white. To choose a new foreground or background color, click the appropriate box in the toolbox (see Figure 36-2) to open the Color Picker shown in Figure 36-3 at the top of the next page.

- Click the desired hue in the color slider (narrow band) in the middle of the dialog box, and then click the precise shade you want in the larger color field at the left. To enter precise color values, use the option buttons and accompanying text boxes at the right.

- You can use the Switch Foreground and Background Colors button on the toolbox to flip the selected foreground and background colors, or click the Default Foreground and Background Colors button to reset the colors to the defaults: black foreground color, white background color.

Figure 36-3. The Color Picker dialog box

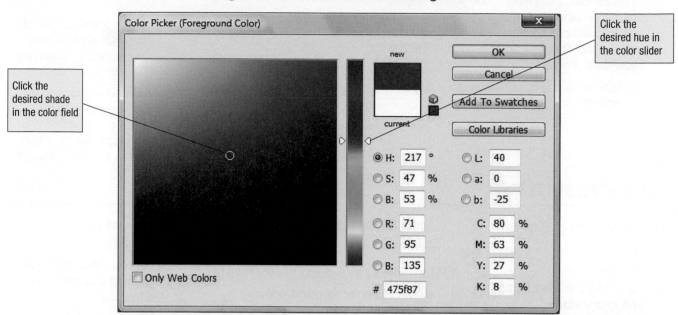

You can also set foreground and background colors using the Color panel, shown in Figure 36-4. This panel should look familiar to you from Illustrator. You choose colors the same way as in Illustrator, by selecting the foreground or background color box and then dragging sliders or clicking the color ramp.

Figure 36-4. The Color panel

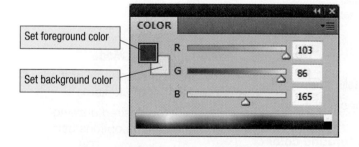

✓ *Clicking the foreground color or background color box when it is already selected opens the Color Picker.*

Another way to select foreground and background colors is to use the Swatches panel, shown in Figure 36-5. Click a swatch to set it as the foreground color, or Ctrl + click a swatch to set it as the background color.

Note that each color in the Swatches panel has a name that you can see if you rest the Eyedropper tool on a swatch.

You can also use the Eyedropper tool to pick up a foreground color anywhere in the Photoshop window, such as from the current image. The Eyedropper tool works the same way in Photoshop as in Illustrator—just select the tool and click where you want to pick up color.

Figure 36-5. The Photoshop Swatches panel

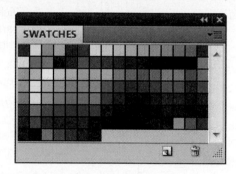

Select a Drawing Mode

When you select a shape tool or the Pen tool, you can choose from three drawing modes that control how your object can be manipulated. These modes are represented by buttons on the options bar.

- The default drawing mode is Shape layers 🔲. With this drawing mode selected, the tool you use will create a new layer that contains the object you draw. You can use this layer to manipulate the object—recolor it, for example, or modify it by adding additional shapes, subtracting from the shape, and so on. This drawing mode also allows you to apply a style to an object.

  ✓ *Photoshop styles are similar to Illustrator's graphic styles, and may include fills and effects.*

- The Paths drawing mode 🖋 creates a vector path as you draw the object. You can manipulate this path using options on the Paths panel. You will work with paths later in this course.

- The Fill pixels drawing mode ⬜ creates a bitmap shape consisting of pixels of the current foreground color. You can select a blending mode and opacity from the options bar before you draw a shape.

  ✓ *You learn more about drawing modes in the next exercise.*

Commit a Change

- At times, the options bar displays a special set of buttons at the right end: Cancel 🚫 and Commit ✔. You must click the Commit button to finish and accept your changes.

- You will see these options when adding type to an image, after placing a file in an image, when transforming a shape or path, and so on. If you find you cannot proceed with manipulating an image, it may be because you must commit to a previous change.

PROCEDURES

Create a New Image (Ctrl + N)

1. Click **File**.................... ALT + F
2. Click **New** .... N
3. (Optional) Click **Name** and type image name .... ALT + N
4. Click **Preset** if desired and select preset size .... ALT + P , ↓

   OR

   a. Click **Width** and type value .... ALT + W
   b. Click **Height** and type value .... ALT + H
5. Click **Resolution** and type resolution value.......... ALT + R
6. Click **Color Mode** and select desired mode....... ALT + M , ↓
7. Click **Background Contents** and select background color option.................. ALT + C , ↓
8. Click **OK** .... ENTER

Display Toolbox Tool Names

- Move pointer over tool and view name and shortcut key in tool tip.

Display Hidden Toolbar Tools

1. Click on tool that shows a small triangle at bottom right.
2. Hold down mouse button until hidden toolbar displays.

Choose a Foreground or Background Color

To set color using the toolbox:

1. Click **Set foreground color** or **Set background color** box on toolbox to open the Color Picker.
2. Click a hue in the color slider (narrow band) in middle of Color Picker dialog box.
3. Click a color in the Select foreground color field.

   ✓ *The name of the large field box at the left is Select background color when you're selecting a background color.*

4. Click **OK** .... ENTER

To set color using the Color panel:

1. Display Color panel if necessary F6
2. Click **Set foreground color** or **Set background color** button, if needed.
3. Drag color sliders as desired.

   OR

   Click a color in the color ramp.

   OR

   Create a color using the Color Picker.

To set color using the Swatches panel:

1. Display Swatches panel.
2. Click desired color swatch to set foreground color.
3. CTRL + click desired color swatch to set background color.

Switch Foreground and Background Colors

- Click **Switch Foreground and Background Colors** button 🔄 on toolbox.

  OR

- Press X .

Reset Foreground and Background Colors to Defaults

- Click **Default Foreground and Background Colors** button ⬛ on toolbox.

  OR

- Press D .

Select a Drawing Mode

1. Select a shape tool or the Pen tool from the toolbox.
2. Click the desired drawing mode on the options bar:
   - **Shape layers** 🔲
   - **Paths** 🔲
   - **Fill pixels** ⬜

Commit a Change

1. Make a change using the text tool or another tool that requires changes to be committed.
2. Click **Commit** button ✔ on the options bar .... ENTER

   OR

   Click **Cancel** button 🚫 ... ESC

EXERCISE DIRECTIONS

1. Start Photoshop.
2. Create a new image file with the following settings:
   - Preset: Default Photoshop Size.
   - Resolution: 72 pixels/inch.
   - Color Mode: RGB Color.
   - Background Contents: White.
3. Save the image as *36Color_xx*.
4. Click the Set foreground color button on the toolbox to open the Color Picker dialog box.
5. Specify a light purple color with the RGB settings of **R = 164**, **G = 158**, **B = 245**.
6. Switch the foreground and background colors using the toolbox, then switch back so the light purple color is once again the foreground color.
7. Choose the Rectangle tool in the toolbox.
8. Select the Fill pixels button 🔲 on the options bar.
9. Draw a rectangle in the center of the image window.
10. With the Rectangle tool still selected, select the Shape layers button 🔲 on the options bar.

   ✓ *The Style option becomes available on the options bar.*

11. Click the Style list arrow and double-click the Nebula style (second from right on the second row) to apply it.
12. Drag in the image to create another rectangle lower and slightly to the right of—but approximately the same size as—the first rectangle you drew, as shown in Illustration A.

13. Reset the foreground and background colors to defaults using the toolbox.
14. Use the Swatches panel to set the background color to a yellow shade.
15. Click the *Background* layer in the Layers panel.
16. Choose the Eraser tool in the toolbox and drag on the image to create a pattern. Illustration A shows one option.

   ✓ *The Eraser tool actually paints the selected background color if you're using it on the image Background layer. When you're working on another layer, the Eraser tool removes pixels and leaves transparency where you drag.*

17. Choose the Horizontal Type tool in the toolbox.
18. Use the options bar to choose the Arial font, Bold or Black style, a 72-point font size, and the Center text alignment button.

   ✓ *If you are not sure how to select these type options, see your instructor.*

19. Use the Swatches panel to set the foreground color to a blue shade.
20. Click above the center of the overlapping rectangles, and type **Color**.
21. Click the Commit button to finish adding the text. Your image should resemble Illustration A.
22. Save your changes (click OK when asked to maximize compatibility), close the file, and exit Photoshop.

Illustration A

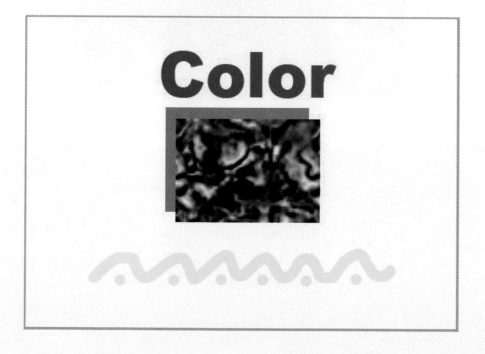

ON YOUR OWN

1. Start Photoshop.
2. Create a new image file using the file settings of your choice.
3. Save the file as OPH36_*xx*.
4. Use the Rectangle tool to draw five rectangles in the image. The rectangles should form a stepped pyramid shape, with the largest rectangle on the bottom and the smallest at the top, as shown in Illustration B.
5. Choose the Fill pixels option on the options bar before drawing the first rectangle. Before drawing each rectangle, use the method of your choice to select a different foreground color.
6. Switch the background and foreground colors.
7. Reset the background and foreground colors to the defaults.
8. Save your changes, close the file, and exit Photoshop.

Illustration B

Exercise | 37

Skills Covered

- **Use the Brush**
- **Use the Mixer Brush**
- **Draw Lines and Shapes**
- **Undo Changes in Photoshop**
- **Insert Text**

Software Skills Use the Brush tool to create flowing lines in an image. The Mixer Brush allows you to paint as if with wet paints that mix and blend. The Brush tool includes an Airbrush feature that you can enable to alter how a line is painted. Use shape tools and lines to add various shapes to your images. Undo options let you reverse a change or step backward to reverse a series of changes. Type options similar to those in Illustrator let you add text to an image.

Design Skills An experienced print designer should know how Photoshop painting and drawing tools are both similar to and different from Illustrator tools. Drawing and painting tools can be used to add shapes and color to any Photoshop image. A designer should also be familiar with how to add type to an image.

Application Skills You have been asked to create a simple beach graphic that can be used for marketing Gulf Shores Resort. In this exercise, you will practice using the Brush and Mixer Brush tools, working with various shape tools, and inserting text.

TERMS

Airbrush A feature of the Brush tool that varies the application of color based on the speed with which the user moves the mouse.

Paint Using a brush-type tool to change the color of pixels on a layer.

NOTES

Use the Brush

- Use the Brush tool 🖌 to **paint** freehand lines using the foreground color in an image.
- Use the Brush Preset picker on the options bar, shown in Figure 37-1, to select a brush shape and size.
- The Brush Preset menu allows you to set the Size and Hardness of a brush.
  - Brush sizes are measured in pixels (px) by default.
  - The Hardness setting determines the size of the hard center of the brush relative to its overall size. The lower the Hardness percentage, the softer the brush edges appear.

Figure 37-1. Brush Preset menu

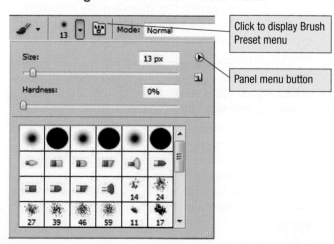

195

- Scroll further down the list of brush presets to find bristle brushes like those you used in Illustrator, brushes with specialized shapes such as leaf shapes, and brushes resembling artistic media such as a charcoal pencil.

- Click the panel menu button ⊙ to open a menu with additional brush commands. For example, you can choose another collection of brush presets by clicking the collection name in the panel menu. You can replace the default brush selections or add new brushes to the default set.

- Photoshop also includes a Brush panel that gives you access to more brushes and numerous settings for customizing brushes. You can display the Brush panel by clicking its icon in the leftmost group of docked panels or by clicking the Toggle the Brushes panel button 🖪 on the options bar while the Brush tool is selected.

- Once you have selected the Brush tool, the desired foreground color, and brush shape and size, drag with the mouse to create a freehand line such as the one shown in Figure 37-2.

Figure 37-2. Drag with the Brush tool to paint a freehand line

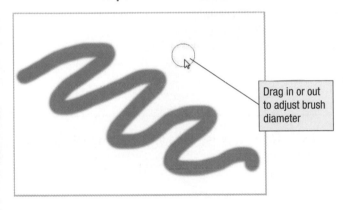

Drag in or out to adjust brush diameter

- You can adjust the Brush diameter "on the fly" by pressing Alt and right-clicking to display a circle that represents the current tool diameter, as shown in Figure 37-2. Drag inward to reduce the diameter or outward to increase the diameter.

- The Brush tool creates raster shapes (lines) in an image. Because they are defined by pixels of color, raster shapes may develop jagged edges when viewed at higher magnifications.

- You would generally not want to create an image in Photoshop using the Brush tool (although you will do so in the hands-on exercise to practice using this tool), but you very frequently need to use the Brush to work with other Photoshop features, such as refining selections or masking portions of an image.

- When the Brush tool is selected, several options familiar from Illustrator are available in the options bar. You can specify a blending mode for the brush to control how overlaying strokes blend with each other and adjust opacity of the paint.

- The Tablet pressure controls opacity button 🖌 to the right of the Opacity box allows you to control opacity by pressure on a graphic tablet, if you are using one.

- You can also specify a Flow rate for the brush; the lower the setting, the less "paint" each brush stroke applies.

  ✓ To reset any tool to its default settings, right-click the tool icon at the left end of the options bar and click Reset Tool. Reset All Tools restores all tools to their defaults.

- Another option available when you use the Brush is **Airbrush** mode. Click the Airbrush button 🖌 on the options bar to turn on this feature.

- Airbrush mode simulates the effect of painting with an airbrush. When you move the mouse more slowly or pause the mouse, more paint is applied.

Use the Mixer Brush

- The Mixer Brush tool 🖌, located on the toolbar beneath the Brush tool, is new in Photoshop CS5. This brush allows you to mix color in an illustration in ways that are similar to using actual paint.

- This brush works by picking up paint from two so-called wells: One well is the reservoir that holds the color that will be painted. The other well is the pickup well that receives its paint from the canvas; the pickup well's contents are constantly changing as they are mixed with colors from the canvas.

- You can control how "wet" the brush is, how much paint is loaded on the brush, the mix of reservoir and pickup well colors, and flow rate. You can specify whether the brush is loaded with paint on every stroke or "cleaned" with every stroke.

- You can load paint into the reservoir by choosing a foreground color or by Alt + clicking a specific area of the canvas. You can choose whether to load the blended colors from the canvas or load only a solid color from the area you Alt + click.

- Figure 37-3 shows how the Mixer Brush can be used to blend colors. A foreground yellow color picks up some of the existing blue color as if both colors were wet paint blending on a canvas.

Figure 37-3. Using the Mixer Brush to blend colors

- Options on the options bar (Figure 37-4) give you a great deal of control over how color is laid down on the canvas and blends with existing colors.
  - The Current brush load thumbnail shows the color currently loaded in the reservoir.
  - Selecting Load the brush after each stroke resupplies the brush with the loaded color on each stroke.
  - Selecting Clean the brush after each stroke has the same effect as if you cleaned a real brush, tending to keep colors pure. If you prefer to paint with a dirty brush that keeps a residue of previous colors, deselect this option.

Figure 37-4. Mixer Brush options

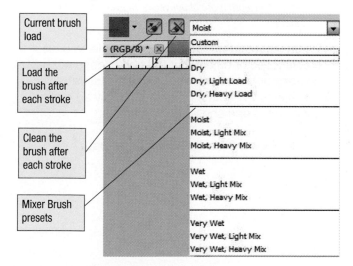

- The presets give a designer a number of useful blending options. The dryer the brush, the less blending takes place. In Figure 37-5, the lilac color has been applied with the Dry preset, which results in almost no blending.

Figure 37-5. The dryer the brush, the less blending occurs

- Besides using the Mixer Brush to blend brush strokes of color, you can use this tool to create interesting painting effects on photographs. Figure 37-6 shows the original photo at top and the result of painting with a wet brush on the flower.

Figure 37-6. Using the Mixer Brush on a photo

- To create an effect like the one shown in Figure 37-6, hold down Alt while clicking a location on the flower to load that mix of colors. The area you clicked displays in the current load thumbnail.

Draw Lines and Shapes

- Photoshop offers some familiar tools for drawing lines and shapes, all contained on the toolbar stored below the Rectangle tool on the toolbox.

  ✓ *The shape tools also display on the options bar after you have selected one of the tools.*

- You can create rectangles, rounded rectangles, ellipses, polygons, and lines using the same general skills that you developed in Illustrator.

- The shapes toolbar also includes the Custom Shape tool , which allows you to select from a wide variety of predrawn shapes such as a paw print, flower, or butterfly.

- Use the Shape button on the options bar to open the Custom Shape picker, shown in Figure 37-7, which enables you to choose the shape to draw and load other collections of shapes.

Figure 37-7. Custom Shape picker

- As mentioned in the previous exercise, you must select a drawing mode when using the Pen or any of the shape tools.

- When you use the Shape layers mode while drawing a shape, you create a vector object as well as a fill layer that contains the object's color, as shown in Figure 37-8. Note in Figure 37-8 that the vector object and the fill layer are linked.

Figure 37-8. Shape layer in Layers panel

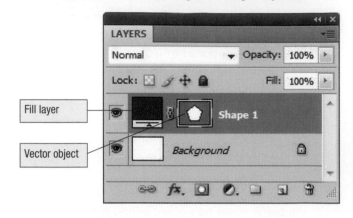

- You can double-click the fill layer to change the color of the shape.

  ✓ *The vector object acts as a mask over the fill layer so that the only fill you see is that within the shape of the vector object. You learn more about vector masks later in this course.*

- When you use the Paths drawing mode, you also create a vector object, but the object does not have a stroke or fill such as you saw with Illustrator vector objects. A Photoshop path is simply an outline such as the one shown in Figure 37-9.

Figure 37-9. Custom shape path

- You can select a path using the Path Selection tool ▶, to move the path. You can use options on the Paths panel to add an outside stroke or a fill.

  ✓ *You work more with paths in Lesson 6.*

- When you select the Fill pixels drawing mode, the shape you create is filled with pixels of the foreground color, as shown in Figure 37-10. You can use the Move tool ▶⊕ to reposition the shape (as long as it is not on the Background layer).

Figure 37-10. Fill pixels shape

- Options in the options bar vary depending on the shape tool and the drawing mode.

- For example, you can select a Weight setting when using the Line tool in any drawing mode. If you choose the Rounded Rectangle shape, you can set corner radius. You can apply a style when using the Shape layers mode for any shape. The Fill pixels mode lets you set blending mode and opacity.

Undo Changes in Photoshop

- In Illustrator, you can reverse a whole series of changes by simply continuing to select the Undo command or shortcut.

- In Photoshop, Undo will reverse only the most recent change. If you want to reverse a series of changes, you Undo the first and then use the Step Backward command on the Edit menu to continue reversing changes.

  ✓ *Another way to reverse changes is to use the History panel. You will learn more about this panel in Lesson 5.*

Insert Text

- Use the Horizontal Type tool T. to add text in the foreground color to an image.

- The toolbar beneath the Horizontal Type tool also has a Vertical Type tool for setting text vertically and two type mask tools that allow you to easily fill type shapes with color or an image.

  ✓ *You will work with type masks in Lesson 6.*

- Photoshop always adds text (type) on a new layer in the image. This is in part because type objects are vector objects (defined by their outlines and easily resizable) rather than raster images.

- You choose font, font style, font size, and color from the options bar after selecting the type tool, as you did in Illustrator. You can also select from three standard paragraph alignment options.

- The anti-aliasing setting on the options bar lets you choose whether to have Photoshop add pixels along the edges of type to smooth type edges.

- As in Illustrator, you can click the image to add a single line of text (called *point type*) or drag with the type tool to create a type box in which text will wrap (called *paragraph type*).

- After you enter text, you must commit the change to finish the insertion. Use the Commit button on the options bar or select another tool to commit the change.

- To select text for editing, use the Horizontal Type tool. To move the type object, use the Move tool ▶⊕.

PROCEDURES

Use the Brush

1. Click **Brush** tool 🖌 .... B
2. Choose a foreground color.
3. Choose brush settings from the **Brush Preset** menu on the options bar.
4. (Optional) Choose a blending mode from the **Mode** list on the options bar.
5. (Optional) Set brush opacity using the **Opacity** control on the options bar.
6. (Optional) Set brush flow using the **Flow** control on the options bar.
7. Drag in the image window.

To adjust brush diameter on the fly:

1. With the Brush selected, press ALT and right-click.
2. Drag the diameter circle inward or outward to adjust the brush diameter.

Use the Airbrush

1. Click **Brush** tool 🖌 .... B
2. Choose a foreground color.
3. Choose brush settings from the **Brush Preset** menu on the options bar.
4. (Optional) Choose a blending mode from the **Mode** list on the options bar.
5. (Optional) Set brush opacity using the **Opacity** control on the options bar.
6. (Optional) Set brush flow using the **Flow** control on the options bar.
7. Click **Airbrush** button 🖌 on options bar.
8. Drag in the image window.
9. Click **Airbrush** button 🖌 on options bar to turn off Airbrush capabilities.

Use the Mixer Brush Tool

1. Click **Mixer Brush** tool 🖌 .... B or SHIFT + B on toolbar beneath Brush tool.
2. Choose a foreground color to load the reservoir.
3. Choose brush settings from the **Brush Preset** menu on the options bar.
4. (Optional) Choose an option from the Mixer Brush presets list.

   OR

   - Set brush wetness using the Wet control on the options bar to control how much paint the brush picks up from the canvas.
   - Set brush load using the Load control on the options bar to specify how much paint is loaded in the reservoir.
   - Set mix amount using the Mix control on the options bar to specify the ratio of canvas paint to reservoir paint.
   - Set brush flow using the Flow control on the options bar.
5. Drag in the image window.

To control Mixer Brush loading and cleaning:

- Select the **Load the brush after each stroke** tool 🖌 to apply the reservoir color with each stroke; deselect to apply no paint.
- Select the **Clean the brush after each stroke** tool 🖌 to remove paint after each stroke; deselect to maintain the current buildup of paint.

To pick up mixed color to paint with:

- Hold down ALT and click the **Mixer Brush** tool 🖌 on the area of the canvas where you want to pick up blended paint; a thumbnail of the area displays in the Current brush load box on the options bar.

Draw Lines and Shapes

To draw a line:

1. Click **Line** tool ╲ on toolbox or options bar................... U or SHIFT + U
2. Choose a foreground color.
3. Choose the **Shape layers**, **Paths**, or **Fill pixels** button on the options bar.
4. Enter the desired brush **Weight** on the options bar.

   ✓ Include the px abbreviation to specify pixels along with the Weight entry. If you don't, you will get the default units, which is inches.

5. Choose other options bar settings as desired.
6. Drag in the image window.

Draw a Rectangle, Rounded Rectangle, or Ellipse

1. Click desired tool on toolbox or options bar .... U or SHIFT + U
2. Choose a foreground color.
3. Choose the **Shape layers**, **Paths**, or **Fill pixels** button on the options bar.
4. Choose other options bar settings as desired.
5. Drag in the image window.

   ✓ Press and hold Shift while dragging to create a perfect square or circle.

Draw a Polygon

1. Click **Polygon** tool 🔵 on toolbox or options bar................... U or SHIFT + U
2. Choose a foreground color.
3. Choose the **Shape layers**, **Paths**, or **Fill pixels** button on the options bar.
4. Enter the desired number of sides for the shape in the **Sides** box on the options bar.

5. Choose other options bar settings as desired.

6. Drag in the image window.

   ✓ *The point where you start dragging becomes the center of the image.*

Draw a Custom Shape

1. Click **Custom Shape** tool 🗿 on toolbox or options bar .... U or SHIFT + U

2. Choose a foreground color.

3. Choose the **Shape layers**, **Paths**, or **Fill pixels** button on the options bar.

4. Click **Shape** button on options bar.

5. Double-click desired shape in the Custom Shape picker.

6. Choose other options bar settings as desired.

7. Drag in the image window.

To load a different collection of shapes:

1. Click panel menu button ▶ on Custom Shape picker.

2. Click the name of the shape collection to load.

3. Click **OK** to confirm the shape replacement .... ENTER

OR

Click **Append** to add new collection to existing collection.

Use the Move Tool

1. Click **Move** tool ⊹ V

2. Click on object to move and drag to new location.

   ✓ *Use the Move tool for the first object on a layer or for a Shape layers object.*

Undo Changes in Photoshop

To undo the most recent change:

1. Click **Edit** .... ALT + E

2. Click **Undo** .... O

To reverse a series of changes:

1. Click **Edit** .... ALT + E

2. Click **Undo** to reverse the most recent change .... O

3. Click **Edit** .... ALT + E

4. Click **Step Backward** to continue reversing changes .... K

Insert Text

1. Click **Horizontal Type** tool T. .... T or SHIFT + T

2. Choose a foreground color or click the **Set the text color** box on the options bar to choose a text color.

3. Choose the desired font, style, size, anti-aliasing, and alignment using the controls on the options bar.

4. Click in the image window to create point type.

   OR

   Drag in the image window to define a boundary for paragraph type.

5. Type the text.

6. Click the **Commit** button ✔ on the options bar.

EXERCISE DIRECTIONS

✓ *After starting Photoshop, select the Painting workspace.*

1. Start Photoshop and open a new document with Default Photoshop size and other default settings. If desired, change the Zoom setting to 150%.

2. Save the file as 37Gulf_xx.

3. Select a foreground color of Pastel Green Cyan from the Swatches panel.

   ✓ *Rest the Eyedropper on a swatch to see its name.*

4. Select the Rectangle tool and select Fill pixels on the options bar. Draw a rectangle to represent sky that covers the top two-thirds of the image area.

5. Select a yellow foreground color and use the Ellipse tool with the Fill pixels drawing mode to draw a sun toward the left side of the canvas near the bottom edge of the sky rectangle.

   ✓ *If the sun does not end up where you want it, use Undo and then start over. Use Step Backward if necessary to reverse a series of changes.*

6. Select Dark Green Cyan as the foreground color and select the Hard Round brush from the Brush Preset menu. Change the diameter to about 20 px. Paint the gulf water so it partially covers the sun. (See Illustration A.)

7. Select white as the foreground color and change the brush setting to Dry Brush. Paint a brush stroke near the bottom of the gulf water to represent breaking surf.

8. Change the diameter of the brush and paint over some areas of the surf to add color depth and variation.

9. Use the Color panel to create a light sand color and use a hard, round brush to paint sand and a dune as shown in Illustration A.

10. Change the brush setting to Dry Brush, lighten the foreground color slightly, change the Opacity to 70% and the Flow rate to about 50%, and paint over the sand to provide some texture.

11. Use the same brush with a higher opacity and flow and a darker foreground color to add some darker areas in the sand.

12. Select Custom Shape and choose to append both the Nature and the Animals collections of shapes.

13. Using several colors of green and brown and the Grass Custom Shapes, position some clumps of grass at various locations on the sand and the dune.

14. Select the Mixer Brush and the Round Fan Stiff Thin Bristle preset and a lighter green cyan swatch. Select a Moist or Wet preset and paint along the horizon to mix the sky and water colors. Adjust brush diameter, Mixer Brush settings, and color to mix some different water colors into the gulf water.

15. Using a yellow color slightly darker than the sun, brush a reflection from the sun down across the water, as shown in Illustration A. Mix other blue-green colors into the sun reflection to make the reflection look more watery.

16. Using a white foreground color and a spatter brush, paint a puffy cloud in the right center area of the sky. Experiment with the Mixer Brush settings to achieve a look you like. You may also want to mix some other colors in to give the cloud more dimension, as shown in Illustration A.

17. Select the Horizontal Type tool and a foreground color of Darker Green Cyan. Select the **Times New Roman** font and a size of **36** pt.

18. Type **Gulf Shores Resort** in the upper-left corner of the image area, as shown in Illustration A.

   ✓ *Use the Move tool to reposition the type object if necessary.*

19. Click on the Background layer in the Layers panel. Select the Horizontal Type tool again, change the font size to 18 and the alignment to Center, and drag a type box near the water surface as shown in Illustration A. Type **Miles of private beach right outside your door!**

20. Click again on the Background layer. Select the Line tool. Set a weight of **6** px in the options bar, and then draw a straight horizontal line below the *Gulf Shores Resort* type object.

21. Select the **Bird 2** Custom Shape and a white foreground color. Change the drawing mode to Shape layers.

22. Draw two small birds anywhere in the sky.

23. Double-click the fill layer for either of the birds and use the Color Picker to select a light gray. Your image should look similar to Illustration A.

24. Save your changes, close the file, and exit Photoshop.

Illustration A

ON YOUR OWN

✓ *Create a simple logo drawing for Pine River Department of Natural Resources in this exercise.*

1. Start Photoshop.
2. Create a new image file with the following settings: Default Photoshop Size, resolution of 72, RGB color mode, Transparent background.

   ✓ *Creating a logo with a transparent background ensures the image won't have a white "frame" around it when placed in a document.*

3. Save the image as OPH37_xx.
4. Using the Ellipse tool, Fill pixels drawing mode, and a medium brown foreground color, create a circle almost as tall as the image area. Use the Move tool if necessary to center the circle in the image area.
5. Select the Brush tool and a medium blue color. Paint a curving stroke from left to right through the center of the brown circle to create the appearance of a stream running across the brown ground.
6. Using the Mixer Brush with different brush tips and colors, add more brush strokes to the stream to add visual interest. Adjust settings as desired to give depth to the colors.

7. Choose the Line tool, a yellow or gold foreground color, and **6** px line weight. Draw a straight line from left to right above the stream object. From the center of this line, draw a straight line upward to the top center of the brown circle. Then draw 45° lines outward to the left and right from the intersection of horizontal and vertical lines to create the appearance of sun rays. See Illustration B for line placement.
8. Choose the Tree Custom Shape and a foreground color of dark green. Set the drawing mode to Shape layers.
9. Draw a tree near the right side of the ellipse. Then draw a second tree at a larger size slightly below and to the left of the first tree.
10. Use the fill layer of the second tree to pick a lighter color for the larger tree.

    ✓ *You can use the Move tool to move either tree to another position.*

11. Use a font, font style, font color, and font size of your choice to add the text **PINE RIVER DNR** to the logo. Position the type object as desired.
12. Save your changes, close the file, and exit Photoshop.

Illustration B

Exercise | 38

Skills Covered

- The Photoshop Layers Panel
- Move a Layer's Content
- Fill a Layer with Color, Pattern, or Gradient
- Use the Eraser Tools

Software Skills   The Photoshop Layers panel is similar to Illustrator's Layers panel in several ways. Use skills you have already learned to work with layers. You can easily move the contents of a layer to reposition it, or add color or a gradient to a layer. Use Photoshop's Eraser tools to remove portions of an image in a variety of ways.

Design Skills   Sophisticated designs often result in many layers of content. Mastery of the Layers panel and its options can help a designer work quickly and efficiently. Filling layers with color, a gradient, or a pattern can add visual interest to a design. A designer should also master the use of the Eraser tools for removing unneeded pixels from an image.

Application Skills   You have been asked to make some changes to a digital camera shot that will be used in an upcoming ad for your client, Yarn Over, a needlework store. You will add a gradient fill to a new layer and erase some portions of the image to create the ad graphic.

TERMS

Background layer   The default layer named Background that appears at the bottom of the Layers panel.

Tolerance   A measurement of how similar a color must be to a sampled color in order to be selected by a Photoshop tool.

NOTES

The Photoshop Layers Panel

- The Photoshop Layers panel will look quite familiar to you after your work in Illustrator. Many of the Layers panel features you learned about in Illustrator work the same way in Photoshop:
  - You create a new layer by clicking the Create a new layer button 🔲 .
  - You reorder layers by dragging them to new positions.
  - You select a layer by clicking its name, and select multiple layers by clicking one, holding down Shift, and clicking additional layers.
  - You delete a layer by selecting it and clicking the Delete layer button 🗑 .

- There are of course also some differences between the Layers panel in Illustrator and the Layers panel in Photoshop.
  - Photoshop layers are not differentiated by color.
  - When you click a layer in Photoshop, you do not see a selection border around objects on that layer.
  - The Photoshop Layers panel includes blending mode and opacity settings you can use to adjust blending and transparency of layer content.

    ✓ *You will work with layer blending in Exercise 56 in Lesson 6.*

- The Photoshop Layers panel also includes more locking options than the Illustrator Layers panel does. You can lock transparent pixels, image pixels, position of content, or lock everything on the layer.
- You can rename a Photoshop layer by simply double-clicking its default name and typing a new one.

■ The most obvious difference between the two Layers features is Photoshop's **background layer**.

■ When you create a new image with a white background or a background color, Photoshop automatically creates the background layer for you, naming it *Background*.

✓ *If you create a new image with a transparent background, the default first layer is named Layer 1.*

■ Digital images that you open in Photoshop also contain a background layer that contains the image content, as shown in Figure 38-1.

Figure 38-1. Background layer for a photo image

■ The background layer always appears at the bottom of the Layers panel, and it cannot be moved to a different position in the layer list.

■ If the background layer contains the entire image content, as shown in Figure 38-1, it is good practice to copy the layer and then hide the original background layer. You can then make any needed adjustments on the copy, keeping the original safe.

✓ *To quickly copy a layer, select it and drag it over the Create a new layer button.*

■ Some actions you take will automatically add layers to the Layers panel.

■ For example, if you create a new shape using the Shape layers drawing mode, a layer is added above the current layer that contains a fill and a vector mask.

■ Use of the Horizontal Type or Vertical Type tool adds a layer that contains that type object.

■ If you create a new layer yourself, Photoshop inserts a transparent layer by default so that the layer itself will not obscure objects below it. You can apply a fill for a transparent layer, as you will learn later in this exercise.

■ The Photoshop Layers panel includes a few buttons at the bottom that you have not seen before, as well as several familiar ones.
- Use the Link layers button ⊖ to link selected layers so that the content of the linked layers can be moved or modified at the same time.
- Click the Add a layer style button *fx.* to select special effects for objects on the selected layer. These effects are similar to the Illustrator Stylize effects, and the button looks the same as the Add New Effect button on the Illustrator Appearance panel.
- Use the Add layer mask button ⬜ to create a mask that will obscure everything on a layer but the shape of the masking object.
- Use the Create new fill or adjustment layer button ⬤. to insert a layer you can use to apply a fill or adjust the image in the layer below.

✓ *You will use most of these features later in the course.*

Move a Layer's Content

■ If the contents of a layer are not precisely where you want them to be, you can move the entire contents using the Move tool ▸⊕. Simply select the layer, choose the Move tool from the toolbox, and drag the layer.

■ The Move tool will not let you move the content of the background layer. To be able to move that content, copy the background layer in the Layers panel, and then move the content of the copy.

Fill a Layer with Color, Pattern, or Gradient

■ You can fill a layer with a color, a pattern, or gradient to provide an interesting background for the layer, or for other layers above in the stacking order.

■ To fill a layer with a color or a pattern, you use the Paint Bucket tool 🪣. First select the layer to fill, choose the Paint Bucket tool (beneath the Gradient tool on the toolbox), and then pick the color or pattern:
- Select a foreground color if you want to fill with a color.
- To fill with a pattern, select the Paint Bucket tool, then click the Set source for fill area list arrow on the options bar and select Pattern. The Pattern picker becomes active so you can select the desired pattern.

✓ *Click the Pattern picker's panel menu to see a fly-out menu of other pattern categories you can add to the default patterns.*

■ Click with the Paint Bucket tool in the work area to fill the current layer with the selected color or pattern.

■ If the layer is empty, the Paint Bucket fills the entire layer. If the layer already has filled pixel shapes, the Paint Bucket pours the color or pattern around the existing shapes, as shown in Figure 38-2.

Figure 38-2. Layer filled around existing objects

■ Gradients in Photoshop are, like those in Illustrator, blends of color. To apply a gradient to a layer, you click the Gradient tool and select a gradient from the Gradient picker shown in Figure 38-3, or create your own gradient.

Figure 38-3. Gradient picker

Click here to edit gradient   Gradient types

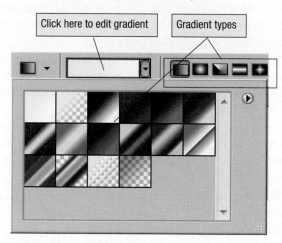

■ The default gradient blends the current foreground and background colors. You can change the foreground and background colors after choosing the Gradient tool to adjust the gradient colors.

✓ *Click the panel menu button to see a list of other gradient libraries.*

■ To create your own gradient, click the Click to edit the gradient box (see Figure 38-3) to open the Gradient Editor dialog box shown below in Figure 38-4.

Figure 38-4. Gradient Editor dialog box

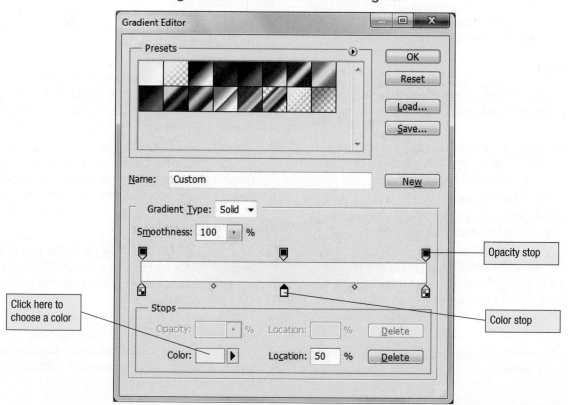

- The Gradient Editor has some similarities to the Illustrator Gradient panel: a gradient ramp shows the current gradient blend, which is created using both color stops and opacity stops.

- To change a gradient color, click a color stop and then use the Color box in the Stops area to select foreground, background, or a color from the Color picker.

- Adjust the location of stops to control the amount of each color in the gradient. You can use the opacity stops to add transparency to the gradient at a particular location on the gradient ramp.

- You can choose gradient type—Linear, Radial, Angle, Reflected, or Diamond—by clicking the appropriate button on the options bar.

- Once you have selected the Gradient tool, the desired gradient, and the gradient type, drag the Gradient tool on the layer to apply the gradient. You adjust the direction of the gradient as in Illustrator, by changing the angle at which you drag the Gradient tool.

- Note that you can use the same procedures to fill any selection with a color, pattern, or gradient. You learn more about selections in subsequent exercises.

Use the Eraser Tools

- Photoshop's Eraser tools let you remove portions of an image. You have a choice of the Eraser tool, the Background Eraser tool, and the Magic Eraser tool.

- Each tool offers different erasing options, and performance may differ depending whether the tool is used on a regular layer or the background layer.

Use the Eraser Tool

- The Eraser tool ![eraser icon] enables you to remove or change pixels on a layer using brush or pencil strokes.

- On a normal layer, the Eraser tool completely removes pixels where you drag, leaving behind transparency, as shown in Figure 38-5.

- Using the Eraser tool on the background layer or a layer with locked transparency instead replaces the pixels with the current background color.

- After you select the Eraser tool, the options bar presents several settings that you can adjust to control the erasure, such as brush shape and size, opacity, and flow. Choose the desired settings, and then click and drag in the image to erase areas as needed.

    ✓ *In all Creative Suite applications, transparent areas are identified by a pattern of alternating white and light gray blocks.*

Figure 38-5. The Eraser tool erases to transparency on a normal layer

Eraser tool

Use the Background Eraser

- The Background Eraser tool ![background eraser icon] erases pixels to transparency on any layer.

- The Background Eraser tool is intended to give more control in preserving the edges of the object left behind on the layer. It works by sampling the color at the center of the brush and deleting that color within the brush stroke.

- The options bar for the Background Eraser includes choices for brush shape and size, sampling, Limits (how far the erasing spreads), and **Tolerance** (the range of similar colors that the brush will erase).

Use the Magic Eraser

- The Magic Eraser tool ![magic eraser icon] enables you to delete areas of color by clicking on a specific color. All areas of that color are then erased to transparency on a normal layer.

- In Figure 38-6, the Magic Eraser has been clicked on an area of the greenish background. Because the Contiguous option has been deselected, all areas with the same green color throughout the image have been erased.

Figure 38-6. Areas of the same color erased

- Like the Eraser tool, the Magic Eraser erases to transparency on a normal layer. On a background layer or layer with locked transparency, it applies the current background color to the area to erase.

- After you choose the Magic Eraser tool, adjust the Tolerance setting on the options bar to control how similar a color must be to the clicked area in order to be erased; the lower the value, the more similar the color must be.

- Enabling the Anti-alias check box smooths the edges of the selection. When Contiguous is checked, the tool erases only colored areas contiguous with (touching) the spot you click; clear this check box to erase like colors throughout the image.

- Check Sample All Layers to delete like colors on all currently-visible layers. Finally, adjust the Opacity setting to control whether to erase all pixels (or only a proportion) in the affected areas.

PROCEDURES

Work with Layers

To select a layer:

- Click the layer in the Layers panel.

To copy a layer:

- Drag a layer on top of the **Create a new layer** button ▣ in the Layers panel.

To add a new layer *(Shift + Ctrl + N)*:

- Click **Create a new layer** button ▣ in the Layers panel.

To rename a layer:

1. Double-click the layer name in the Layers panel.
2. Type the new name.
3. Press ENTER .

To change layer order:

1. Click layer to select it.
2. Drag layer to new position in Layers panel.

To delete a layer:

1. Click layer to select it.
2. Click **Delete layer** button 🗑 on Layers panel.
3. Click **Yes**....................ALT + Y

Move Layer Content

1. Select layer in Layers panel.
2. Click **Move** tool ▶⊕ V
3. Drag layer content to the desired position.

Fill a Layer with a Color

1. Select layer in Layers panel.
2. Click **Paint Bucket** tool 🖌 ....G or SHIFT + G
3. Choose Foreground from the **Set source for fill** list on the options bar.
4. Choose foreground color for fill.

5. Choose additional options bar settings.
6. Click on layer to apply color fill.

Fill a Layer with a Pattern

1. Select layer in Layers panel.
2. Click **Paint Bucket** tool 🖌 ....G or SHIFT + G
3. Choose Pattern from the **Set source for fill** list on options bar.
4. Use Pattern picker to select desired pattern.
5. Choose options bar settings.
6. Click on layer to apply pattern fill.

Fill a Layer with a Gradient

To apply a default gradient:

1. Select layer in Layers panel.
2. Click **Gradient** tool ▭ ....G or SHIFT + G
3. Choose foreground and background colors.

OR

   a. Click Gradient picker list arrow on options bar.

   b. Select a default gradient.

4. Choose options bar settings.

5. Drag on layer to apply gradient.

To create a custom gradient:

1. Click the **Click to edit the gradient** box on options bar to open Gradient Editor.

2. Click a color stop to select it, then click the Color box in the Stops area to open the Color picker.

3. Select the desired color in the Color picker and click **OK**.

4. Drag color stops as necessary to control amount of color.

5. Add new stops by clicking below the gradient ramp.

6. Click an opacity stop if desired to adjust transparency for a particular area of the gradient ramp.

7. Type a name for the new gradient in the **Name** box and click **New** to add the gradient to the Gradient picker panel.

8. Click **OK** .... [ENTER]

Erase on a Layer

1. Select layer in Layers panel.

2. Click **Eraser** tool [icon] ......[E] or [SHIFT] + [E]

3. Choose options bar settings.

4. Drag and click on image to erase specified areas.

Use the Background Eraser

1. Select layer in Layers panel.

2. Click **Background Eraser** tool [icon] ....[E] or [SHIFT] + [E]

3. Choose options bar settings.

4. Drag and click on image to erase specified areas.

Use the Magic Eraser

1. Select layer in Layers panel.

2. Click **Magic Eraser** tool [icon] ....[E] or [SHIFT] + [E]

3. Choose options bar settings.

4. Click on image to erase specified areas.

EXERCISE DIRECTIONS

1. Start Photoshop and open ⊙ **38Yarn**. Save the file as **38Yarn_xx**. (If you are asked to update text layers, click the Update button.)

2. Copy the Background layer, and then hide it. Work on the Background copy layer.

3. Make sure the default foreground and background colors are displayed in the toolbox. Use the Eraser or Background Eraser tool with the settings of your choice to erase the pebbles and cloth to the right of the backdrop behind the yarn basket.

4. Select the Magic Eraser tool and deselect Contiguous. Click anywhere on the white backdrop to erase it and other white areas in the image.

5. Continue to use the Eraser and Magic Eraser to remove gray areas from the cloth folds and the shadow area to the left of the yarn basket. Keep these points in mind as you work:

- Watch carefully each time you erase a color with the Magic Eraser to make sure you have not removed some of the shadowed areas of the knitting needles or the basket. Setting the tolerance low for the Magic Eraser will help you to control what you remove.

- When you can no longer select colors with the Magic Eraser without nibbling at the knitting needles or removing shadows inside the basket, switch to the Eraser tool. Use a large diameter to remove as much of the remaining gray areas as possible, then work at high magnification with a smaller diameter to clean up around the yarn basket.

   ✓ *Remember that you can Alt + right click to change the diameter of the eraser on the fly.*

- You may find it helpful to insert a layer beneath the Background Copy layer and fill it with white to help you see the gray areas better.

- Switch to 100% often to check your work. Undo or step backward if you find you have removed too much of the basket along with the shadows.

- If you inserted a white layer below the Background Copy layer, remove it before going on to the next step.

6. Insert a new layer and name it **Gradient**. Create a gradient fill as follows:

   a. Select the Gradient tool, and then click the default gradient box in the options bar (the Click to edit the gradient box).

   b. Select the Foreground to Background gradient, if necessary, in the panel at the top of the Gradient Editor dialog box.

c. Drag both the left color stop and the opacity stop to the 50% location. Then click the 50% color stop and use the Color picker to pick the color **R = 158, G = 216, B = 213**.

d. Insert a new color stop all the way at the left end of the gradient ramp and use the Color picker to pick the Background color (white).

e. Type the name **Winter** for the new gradient and click New to add it to the panel of default gradients.

f. Click OK to close the dialog box.

7. With the Gradient layer selected, select the Winter gradient and use the Gradient tool to drag straight down from the top of the image area to the bottom.

8. Move the Gradient layer below the Background copy layer.

9. Use the Move tool to move the entire Background copy layer to allow more room in the upper-left corner, as shown in Illustration A.

10. Use the Move tool to move the *A World of Color* text to the upper-left corner of the image, as shown in Illustration A.

11. Select the Horizontal Type tool, the Georgia font (or a similar serif font), and a font style, size, and color of your choice. Type **WINTER SALE** and then position the type at the lower-right corner of the image.

12. Save your changes, close the file, and exit Photoshop.

Illustration A

ON YOUR OWN

1. Start Photoshop and open the ⊙ OYO38 file.
2. Save the file as OPH38_xx.
3. Copy the Background layer, hide it, and then rename the Background copy layer as **Photo**.
4. Use the Move tool to move the flower to the lower-right corner of the image area, so that only about one-quarter of the flower displays, as shown in Illustration B.
5. Use the eraser tools as desired to erase the green foliage around the flower.

   ✓ *Zoom the image to a much larger size and decrease the brush size to clean up around the edges of the flower.*

6. Insert a new layer with a name such as **Card stock**. Fill the layer with white and move it below the Photo layer.

7. Select the Photo layer and clean up any remaining pixels that you can see against the white background.
8. Pick up a red-orange foreground color from the flower using the eyedropper. Using the Rectangle tool, draw a shape layer as tall as the flower photo that extends all the way across the image area. Give the shape layer an appropriate name and move it below the Photo layer if necessary.
9. Use custom shapes to create a stylized flower and leaf in the upper-left corner of the image area, as shown in Illustration B. Use the Shape layers drawing mode. Give each layer an appropriate name and rearrange them if necessary so the flower is on top of the leaf.
10. Add two text layers to insert the information shown in Illustration B.
11. Save your changes, close the file, and exit Photoshop.

Illustration B

212

Exercise | 39

Skills Covered

Software Skills   Photoshop provides nimble selection tools that allow you to select portions of an image in a number of ways. Make simple selections with the Marquee tools or irregular selections with the Lasso tools. You can move a selection marquee to fine-tune its position. Invert a selection to select everything but an area. Deselect a selection when you're finished with it.

Design Skills   No designer can work effectively in Photoshop without learning how to use the application's many selection options. This exercise covers basic selection skills that a designer can build on to learn more complex ways to isolate areas of an image for special attention.

Application Skills   Newfound Nursery has asked you to work with a water lily image that will be included in a magazine article. In this exercise, you will practice simple selection techniques you can use to isolate the water lily from its background.

TERMS

Fastening point   A node or point that anchors the selection border when using the Magnetic Lasso tool.

NOTES

About Selecting

- Selecting is one of the most important skills you will need when working in Photoshop. Many of the adjustments or enhancements you will apply to images require you to first select an area.

- Accordingly, Photoshop offers a wide variety of selection methods, ranging from very simple to very sophisticated. The program includes a number of tools designed solely for selection, such as the Rectangular and Elliptical Marquee tools, the Lasso tools, the Quick Selection tool, and the Magic Wand tool.

- You can also use the Pen tool to draw a path around an area that can be converted to a selection.

- Selection tools may be used in combination with other tools to define a specific area. After creating a rough selection with a Marquee tool, for example, you can use Quick Mask mode and the Brush tool to refine the selected area.

  ✓ *You will work with Quick Mask mode in Lesson 6.*

- Selection tools vary in the way they select, and one aspect of mastering selection techniques involves learning what tool is best for the type of selection you want to make.

- You explore selection basics in this exercise. The next exercise introduces you to some ways that you can modify or transform a selection, such as by deleting or copying the selected area. Exercise 41 covers more sophisticated selection methods. You will learn additional selection skills in subsequent lessons.

Make Rectangular or Elliptical Selections

- To make simple rectangular or elliptical selections, use the Rectangular or Elliptical Marquee tool.
- Use the Rectangular Marquee tool ⬚ the same way you would use the Rectangle tool. After you draw the selection area, a crawling marquee appears around the selection, as shown in Figure 39-1.

Figure 39-1. Selection marquee created by the Rectangular Marquee tool

- Use the Elliptical Marquee tool ⬭, on the toolbar beneath the Rectangular Marquee tool, to select round or elliptical areas.
- As when using the Rectangle or Ellipse shape tool, you can hold down Shift to create a perfectly square or circular selection when using these marquee tools.

- By default, the New selection button ▣ is active in the options bar, meaning that each new selection you make removes (and therefore replaces) any prior selection.

  ✓ *Exercise 41 covers how to use options bar settings to add area to or remove area from a selection.*

- The options bar offers applicable settings for the selection tool you are using. For example, if you want to create a marquee selection of a specific size, select the tool and then click the Style list arrow on the options bar. Choose the Fixed Size option and then set the desired width and height. You can then simply click the selection tool to create a selection area of the designated size.

Select with the Lasso Tools

- The Lasso selection tools are useful when you need to select an irregular shape. You have three Lasso tools to choose from: the Lasso tool, the Polygonal Lasso tool, and the Magnetic Lasso tool.
- Use the Lasso tool 🔲 to make a selection with a totally freeform shape. Drag with the tool around the area you want to select as if you were drawing with a pencil, as shown in Figure 39-2 at the top of the next page. When you release the mouse button, Photoshop automatically closes the loop to finish the selection.
- Use the Polygonal Lasso tool 🔲 to make a freeform selection of line segments and angles (points), as shown in Figure 39-2. Click the image each time you want to change direction, and double-click to complete the selection.
- The Magnetic Lasso tool 🔲 enables you to make a selection that follows the contours of an object. The tool works best when the color of the area you want to select contrasts well with the background area.

Figure 39-2. Selections by Lasso, Polygonal Lasso, and Magnetic Lasso

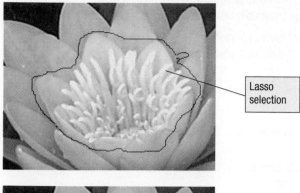

Lasso selection

Polygonal Lasso selection

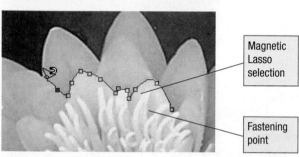

Magnetic Lasso selection

Fastening point

- Click to position the first **fastening point**, and then drag along the edge that you want to select. The tool will automatically trace along areas of strong contrast, but you can also click at any location to add fastening points, as shown in Figure 39-2. Press the Delete key to remove previously-added fastening points. Double-click to finish the selection.

- Use options bar settings to control Magnetic Lasso sensitivity.

  - The Width text box entry controls the distance (in pixels) from the pointer that will be evaluated to detect an edge.

  - The Contrast determines how much an edge must contrast for detection to work. With a higher setting, the Magnetic Lasso will detect only high-contrast edges. Lower this value (and drag more slowly) to detect softer edges.

  - Change the Frequency setting to control how often the Magnetic Lasso adds fastening points.

Move a Selection Marquee

- You can move the crawling selection marquee to a new position if you have not drawn it exactly where you want it.

- Immediately after making the selection, leave the New selection button selected on the options bar, and then drag the selection marquee to the desired position just as you would drag a shape.

Invert a Selection

- Generally you make a selection to isolate a particular area of an image so you can manipulate that area. But another common reason to select an area is so you can manipulate everything in the image *except* that area.

- To easily select everything in an image except a specific area, you can *invert* a selection: Select the area, then choose Select > Inverse.

- When you invert the selection, two selection marquees appear in the image, as shown in Figure 39-3: the original marquee, and a marquee around the outside of the image. The area between the two marquees is the selected area.

Figure 39-3. Original and inverted selection

Original selection marquee

Inverted selection

Deselect a Selection

- You should remove a selection when you no longer need it. Photoshop even prevents you from performing certain operations when an unnecessary selection appears on the active layer.

- Do *not* press Delete to remove a selection marquee—you will instead delete all layer content within the selection marquee. If you delete content by mistake, use Undo immediately to restore it.

  ✓ *You may sometimes want to delete a selected area. You will learn more about this option in the next exercise.*

PROCEDURES

Select a Rectangular or Elliptical Area

1. Select the layer on which you want to make the selection.
2. Click **Rectangular Marquee** tool [⬚] .... M or SHIFT + M

   OR

   Click **Elliptical Marquee** tool [◯] .... M or SHIFT + M
3. Drag on the image to create the selection.

To create a fixed-size selection:

1. Select the desired layer and the desired marquee tool.
2. Click the **Style** list arrow on the options bar and select **Fixed Size**.
3. Enter desired **Width** and **Height**.

   ✓ *Be sure to add px to the Width and Height values to specify pixels as the unit.*

4. Click on the image to make the selection.

Select with the Lasso Tools

To select with the Lasso:

1. Select the layer on which you want to make the selection.
2. Click **Lasso** tool [⟡] .... L or SHIFT + L

3. Drag on the layer to create the freeform selection.
4. Release the mouse button to close the selection loop.

To select with the Polygonal Lasso:

1. Select the layer on which you want to make the selection.
2. Click **Polygonal Lasso** tool [▷] .... L or SHIFT + L
3. Click on the image to create angle points for the selection.
4. Double-click the final point to complete selection.

   OR

   Press ENTER.

   OR

   Click the first point in the selection.

   ✓ *Press Esc to cancel a selection you're making with the Polygonal Lasso or Magnetic Lasso tools.*

To select with the Magnetic Lasso:

1. Select the layer on which you want to make the selection.
2. Click **Magnetic Lasso** tool [▨] .... L or SHIFT + L
3. (Optional) Change **Width**, **Contrast**, and **Frequency** settings on options bar.

4. Drag along edge to select.
5. (Optional) Click to add fastening points as needed.

   ✓ *Press Delete to back up and remove fastening points.*

6. Double-click to complete the selection.

   OR

   Press ENTER.

   OR

   Click the first point in the selection.

Move a Selection Marquee

1. Make the initial selection.
2. Leave **New selection** button [▣] selected on options bar.
3. Drag selection to the desired location.

Invert a Selection (Shift + Ctrl + I)

1. Make the initial selection.
2. Click **Select** .... ALT + S
3. Click **Inverse** I

Deselect a Selection (Ctrl + D)

1. Make the initial selection.
2. Click **Select** .... ALT + S
3. Click **Deselect** .... D

EXERCISE DIRECTIONS

1. Open the 39Lily file.

2. Select the Background copy layer and work on this layer throughout the exercise.

3. Use the Rectangular Marquee tool to select an area around the water lily.

4. Deselect the selection, then use the Elliptical Marquee tool to select an oval area that includes the lily.

5. Deselect the selection.

6. With the Elliptical Marquee tool still selected, choose the Fixed Size style and specify a Width of **300** px and a Height of **275** px. Click on the image and then move the selection marquee to surround the lily as shown in Illustration A.

7. Deselect the selection, then use the Polygonal Lasso tool to select around the central ring of petals.

8. Deselect the selection, then choose the Magnetic Lasso and drag it around the outside ring of lily petals, adding fastening points where you think necessary.

9. Invert the selection. Your image should look similar to Illustration B.

10. Deselect the selection. Select the Elliptical Marquee tool, right-click the button with the same tool on it at the far left of the options bar, and click Reset Tool so that the next time you use the tool, it won't select only a fixed size.

11. Close the file without saving and exit Photoshop.

Illustration A

ON YOUR OWN

1. Open the ⊙OYO39 file.

2. Use the applicable tools to make the following selections:
   - A perfect circle around the leaf.
   - A perfect square around the leaf.

- A fixed size rectangle around the leaf.
- A freeform shape around the leaf.
- A selection that closely follows the edge of the leaf.

3. Close the file without saving and exit Photoshop.

Exercise | 40

Skills Covered

- ■ Delete a Selection
- ■ Move or Copy a Selection
- ■ Transform a Selection
- ■ Feather a Selection

- ■ Fill or Stroke a Selection
- ■ Save a Selection
- ■ Load a Selection

Software Skills Once you have selected an area, you have many options for manipulating the selection. You can delete the selected area, or the area around the selection; move or copy the selection; transform the selection using options such as rotation or scaling; feather a selection edge; or apply a fill or stroke to a selection. After you have refined a selection, you may want to save it so that you can load it whenever you like.

Design Skills A designer should have a solid grasp of how he or she can manipulate a selected area to transform it in various ways. Creating a vignette from a copied, feathered selection, for example, is a common way to give a special look to any graphic image. A designer should also learn the importance of saving selections to make it easy to work with an image in the future.

Application Skills You will continue to work with the water lily image as you practice using features that allow you to manipulate a selection.

TERMS

Feather To adjust or soften the edges of a selection, so that any copy of the selection will have soft, faded edges when pasted.

Skew To slant a selection from corners of its bounding box.

Transformation A change such as scaling (resizing) or skewing (slanting) applied to a selection.

Warp To give a particular shape to a selection, fitting the selection within that shape.

NOTES

Delete a Selection

- Deleting a selection removes the selection from the layer. If you're making a deletion on the background layer, the deleted area will be filled with the currently-selected background color. If you're deleting from another layer, the area previously occupied by the deleted material will become transparent.

- Figure 40-1 shows how a deletion can be used to improve an image. The ground squirrel is selected, then the selection is inverted and deleted to remove the distracting background. The squirrel can now be positioned against a more interesting background, or even a plain white fill layer.

Figure 40-1. Delete a selection to improve an image

Original selection

Pixels in inverted selection have been deleted

- Photoshop does not display a warning when you make the deletion, so if you make a mistake, immediately undo the deletion.

Move or Copy a Selection

- When you move a selection, Photoshop removes the content from its current location and places it in a new destination location, as shown in Figure 40-2. Use the Move tool [icon] to drag a selection to a new location on the layer.

Figure 40-2. Moving a selection on the same layer

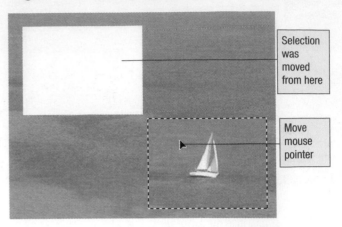

Selection was moved from here

Move mouse pointer

- You can also move a selection by using Edit > Cut to place a selection on the Clipboard and then Edit > Paste to place the selection on a new layer in the image.

  ✓ You can use this Cut and Paste operation to move content from one image file to another.

- Note that a move actually removes all pixels from one location and places them at another location, which may leave you with an unsightly hole in the layer.

- When you copy a selection to a new location, the content that was selected remains intact in its original location. The copy appears at the new, destination location.

- Use Edit > Copy and Edit > Paste to copy a selection and paste the copy on a new layer. Or, with an area selected, press and hold Alt and use the Move tool to drag a copy of the selection to a new location on the current layer.

- Another common way to use a copied selection is to create a new image file from the copy.

- When you copy a selection and then choose File > New, Photoshop automatically specifies a Preset of Clipboard, and the width and height measurements are those of the copied selection.

  ✓ If you have more than one layer in the file you are copying, you must use the Copy Merged command for this to work correctly.

- With the new image open, click Edit > Paste to insert the selection you copied. The pasted selection becomes a new layer in the new file.

Transform a Selection

- The Edit > Transform submenu presents a number of different **transformations** you can apply to a selection. Some of these transforming options will be familiar to you from your work in Illustrator.
  - Scale a selection to resize it, as shown in Figure 40-3.
  - Rotate a selection to revolve it around its center point.
  - **Skew** a selection to slant it from the corners of its bounding box.
  - Distort a selection to stretch it from the corners of its bounding box, as shown in Figure 40-3.
  - Use the Perspective option to adjust a selection so it appears to be originating from a vanishing point on the horizon.
  - **Warp** a selection to fit the selection within a shape you create from a warp mesh.
  - Flip a selection to turn it over on its horizontal or vertical axis.

Figure 40-3. You can scale (top) or distort (bottom) a selection

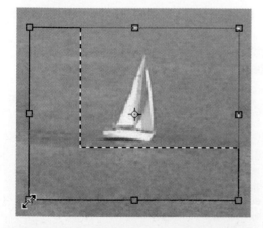

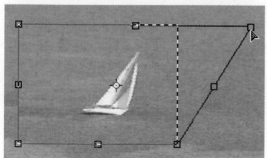

- Generally speaking, to apply a transform to a selection, choose the desired command from the Edit > Transform submenu, drag transform handles as needed, and then click the Commit transform button.

  ✓ *When you choose a transform, the options bar presents additional settings for controlling the transform. Those settings are beyond the scope of this book; you can learn more using Photoshop Help.*

- The Edit > Transform submenu also includes commands to rotate the selection clockwise or counterclockwise by 90° or rotate 180°. The Edit menu includes a Free Transform command that lets you transform the selection in a variety of ways at once.

Feather a Selection

- Feathering a selection softens the selection edge, so that when you paste a copy of the selection, the pasted version has soft or faded edges, as shown in Figure 40-4.

Figure 40-4. A copied selection shows the feathered edge

- To **feather** a selection, choose the desired selection tool from the toolbox, enter the width of the edge area to feather in the Feather box on the options bar, and then drag to make the selection in the image.

  ✓ *Be sure to leave or include the px abbreviation (for pixels) in the Feather box.*

- You will not see any evidence of the feathering around the selection itself. The feather effect shows only when you paste the feathered selection.

Fill or Stroke a Selection

- Commands on the Edit menu allow you to apply a stroke or a fill to a selection to create special effects.

- Use the Edit > Stroke command to open the Stroke dialog box shown in Figure 40-5. You can choose a width and color for the stroke, locate the stroke inside, centered, or to the outside of the selection, and choose a blending mode and opacity setting.

Figure 40-5. Stroke dialog box

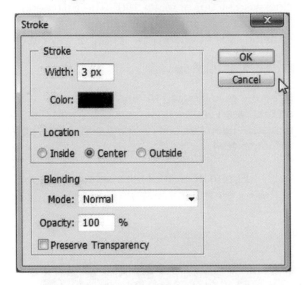

- To apply a fill to a selection, use the Edit > Fill command to open the Fill dialog box. You can choose from a list of fill options, such as the foreground or background color, a color from the Color picker, a content-aware fill, or a pattern, as shown in Figure 40-6.

  ✓ You will learn about the Content-Aware fill option in Lesson 5.

- You can also select a blending mode and opacity for the fill.

Figure 40-6. Fill dialog box

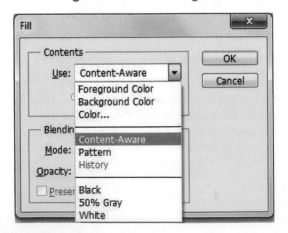

Save a Selection

- When you take the time to make a complex selection, you can save yourself work later by saving the selection.

- Saving the selection preserves the selection boundaries in the image file so that you can later reload the selection.

  ✓ Specifically, the saved selection is saved as a channel in the image file. You will work with channels in Lesson 6.

- Use the Select > Save Selection command to open the Save Selection dialog box, where you can provide a name for the selection. You can save more than one selection in an image.

  ✓ You even can save the selection into another open image file by choosing the file name from the Document drop-down list in the Save Selection dialog box.

Load a Selection

- Load a previously-saved selection using Select > Load Selection. Choose the selection to load from the Channel drop-down list, as shown in Figure 40-7.

Figure 40-7. Choose a selection to load

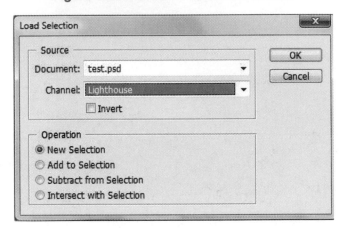

- Note the Invert check box in the Load Selection dialog box. Selecting this check box loads the inverse of the saved selection. You can thus save a single selection that can be used in two ways when you load it into the image.

PROCEDURES

Delete a Selection

1. Select the desired area.
2. Press DEL.

   OR

   a. Click **Edit** .... ALT + E
   b. Click **Clear** .... E

Move a Selection

To move a selection on the same layer:

1. Select the desired area.
2. Click **Move** tool ⊹ V
3. Drag the selection to the desired position.

To move a selection to a new layer:

1. Select the desired area.
2. Click **Edit** .... ALT + E
3. Click **Cut** .... T
4. Click **Edit** .... ALT + E
5. Click **Paste** .... P , ENTER
6. Move the pasted selection on its new layer if necessary.

Copy a Selection (*Ctrl + C, Ctrl + V*)

To copy a selection on the same layer:

1. Select the desired area.
2. Click **Move** tool ⊹ V
3. Hold down ALT and drag the selection to a new location.

To copy a selection to a new layer:

1. Click **Edit** .... ALT + E
2. Click **Copy** C
3. Click **Edit** .... ALT + E
4. Click **Paste** .... P , ENTER

Transform a Selection

1. Select the desired area.
2. Click **Edit** .... ALT + E
3. Point to **Transform** .... A
4. Click the desired transform type in the submenu.

   ✓ *Some transforms, like flips, apply automatically. In such a case, steps 5 and 6 aren't needed.*

5. Drag selection handles as needed to alter the size and/or shape of the selection.
6. Click the **Commit transform** button ✓ on the options bar.

   ✓ *Press Esc to cancel the transform.*

Feather a Selection

1. Choose the desired selection tool from the toolbox.
2. Type feathering amount (in pixels) in the **Feather** box on the options bar.

   ✓ *Either leave or retype the **px** abbreviation in the Feather box to specify pixels.*

3. Make the selection in the image.

   ✓ *To see the feather, you must copy and paste the selection, or invert the selection and delete.*

To feather an existing selection:

1. Click **Select** .... ALT + S
2. Point to **Modify** .... M
3. Click **Feather** .... F
4. Type the desired feather radius.
5. Click **OK** .... ENTER

   ✓ *To see the feather, you must copy and paste the selection, or invert the selection and delete.*

Fill a Selection (*Shift + F5*)

1. Select the desired area.
2. Click **Edit** .... ALT + E
3. Click **Fill** L
4. Click **Use** list arrow and select color, pattern, or content-aware option.
5. Select blending mode if desired.
6. Adjust opacity if desired.
7. Click **OK** .... ENTER

Stroke a Selection

1. Select the desired area.
2. Click **Edit** .... ALT + E
3. Click **Stroke** .... S
4. Type stroke thickness in **Width** box.
5. Click color box to select stroke color.
6. Select location of stroke relative to selection.
7. Select blending mode if desired.
8. Adjust opacity if desired.
9. Click **OK** .... ENTER

Save a Selection

1. Make the initial selection.
2. Click **Select** .... ALT + S
3. Click **Save Selection** V
4. Type name for selection in **Name** text box.
5. Click **OK** .... ENTER

Load a Selection

1. Click **Select** .... ALT + S
2. Click **Load Selection** .... O
3. Click **Channel** list arrow .... ALT + C , ↓
4. Click selection to load.
5. Click **OK** .... ENTER

EXERCISE DIRECTIONS

1. Open ◉ 40Lily and save the file as *40Lily_xx*.
2. Select the bottom middle petal of the water lily using the selection tool of your choice.
3. Copy the selected petal and paste three times to three new layers.

   ✓ *The second and third copies will probably appear in the middle of the image; use the Move tool to move them on top of the original petal so that all three petals are stacked on top of each other.*

4. Select the first copied selection on Layer 1.

   ✓ *Ctrl + click on the layer thumbnail to select the contents (the non-transparent area) of the layer.*

5. Use the Edit > Transform > Rotate command to rotate the selected petal so its tip points to the lower-left corner of the image window. Commit the transformation.
6. Use the Move tool to move the selected petal a bit up and to the left of the original bottom petal, as shown in Illustration A.

Illustration A

7. Deselect the selection.
8. Select the second copied selection on Layer 2.
9. Repeat steps 5 and 6, rotating the petal to point to the lower-right corner of the image and placing it a bit up and to the right of the original petal.

   ✓ *The third copy of the petal on Layer 3 continues to overlap the preceding two copies, so they still appear to be behind the original petal.*

10. Deselect any selections.
11. Select the Elliptical Marquee tool and choose a **5** px feather radius. Draw a selection marquee around the lily.
12. Copy the selection using Edit > Copy Merged, create a new image file using the Clipboard preset, and paste the copied selection.
13. Save the new file as *40Lily_copy_xx* and then close it.
14. Deselect the current selection and set Feather to 0 px. Create another elliptical selection around the lily and save the selection as **Ellipse**. Deselect the selection.
15. Load the Ellipse selection, and apply a **3** px stroke to the selection, picking up a color from the image for the stroke color.
16. Invert the selection and delete the background surrounding the lily. Be sure you are on the Background copy layer for this step.
17. This is not quite the effect you want. Undo the deletion and apply a fill to the selected background area using a transparent white or a color you pick up from the image. Your image should look similar to Illustration B.

Illustration B

ON YOUR OWN

1. Start Photoshop and open the OYO40 file and save it as OPH40_xx.

2. Select the sailboat using the selection tool of your choice. Apply a feather setting to help blend the copies into the background.

3. Copy the selection and paste it three times.

4. Use the Move tool to move the copies to positions where they will blend in well with the lake surface.

5. Apply a transform to flip one or more of the copies horizontally.

   ✓ *If the item you want to flip is the only thing on the layer, you need only select the layer in the Layers panel before applying the flip transform.*

6. Apply a transform to modify the sizes of the copies so that there is a variation in sailboat size.

7. Use the Move tool to reposition copies as desired.

8. Save your changes, close the file, and exit Photoshop.

Exercise | 41

Skills Covered

- **Select with the Magic Wand**
- **Add to or Subtract from a Selection**
- **Use the Quick Selection Tool**
- **Fine-Tune Selection Edges**

Software Skills   Besides the basic selection tools you learned about in Exercise 39, Photoshop offers additional selection techniques that enable you to quickly make complex selections. The Magic Wand lets you make selections based on a color. You can add to or remove from a selection area using options bar settings. The Quick Selection tool lets you "paint" a selection area using a brush. The Refine Edges feature offers a number of settings you can adjust to fine-tune a selection's edges.

Design Skills   A designer should always be alert to tools and skills that can make common procedures quicker or easier. Tools such as Magic Wand and Quick Selection can save a designer a great deal of time and effort in creating sophisticated selections. Refine Edge can also greatly improve the quality of selections, allowing a designer to create more professional-looking images.

Application Skills   In this exercise, you will work with a photo you want to use for Parker Conservatory's upcoming Tropical Show. You will try several selection techniques to isolate a parrot from a busy background.

TERMS

Sample   To make a selection based on a similar area (sample) on the layer.

NOTES

Select with the Magic Wand

- Use the Magic Wand tool 🔍 when you want to select areas of fairly consistent color.

- Click the Magic Wand tool on an area of color to **sample** it. All colors similar to the sampled color are selected, as shown in Figure 41-1.

Figure 41-1. The sampled area in the petal selects areas of the same color

- By default, the Magic Wand selects contiguous pixels—pixels in contact with the sample color. To select a color throughout an image, deselect the Contiguous option on the options bar.

- Changing the Tolerance setting on the options bar enables the Magic Wand tool to select more or fewer pixels. With a lower Tolerance entry, a pixel's color must match the sampled pixel more closely to be included in the selection. Higher Tolerance settings allow for a greater color range to match the sampled pixel.

Photoshop Extra

Select by Color Range

Another way to select by color is to use the Color Range command on the Select menu. Sample a color or select a color using the Color picker, and then adjust fuzziness to control how wide a color range will be included in the selection.

Add to or Subtract from a Selection

- Sometimes the tool you use may not select—or may not be able to select—all the area that you intend to select on the first try. When this is the case, you can add to the selection with any other selection tool. Conversely, if the first selection includes areas you wish to omit from the selection, you can remove them from the selection.

- The buttons for controlling selection options appear on the options bar after you choose a selection tool from the toolbox.

  - Click the New selection button 🔲 to create a new selection with the selected tool. If an area is already selected, your new selection replaces the existing selection.

  - Click the Add to selection button 🔲 to add pixels to the current selection.

  - Click the Subtract from selection button 🔲 to remove an area from the current selection.

  - Click the Intersect with selection button 🔲 to select an area included in both a prior selection and a new area you select.

- You can use these options with any tool, and you can also use more than one tool. For example, you can use the Magic Wand tool to select a large area of color, then click the Lasso tool and the Add to selection button and select a freeform area to add to the Magic Wand selection.

Use the Quick Selection Tool

- The Quick Selection tool 🖌 allows you to select an area easily by "painting" the selection with a brush.

- Figure 41-2 at the top of the next page shows the process of selecting an area with the Quick Selection tool. As you drag the tool within an area, the tool finds edges that form natural selection borders.

- The selection grows as you drag the pointer over adjacent areas. You can adjust the brush size as you would any brush to select detailed areas.

Figure 41-2. Selecting with the Quick Selection tool

Quick
Selection
tool brush

- By default, the Quick Selection tool adds to a selection as you drag. If you select areas that you don't want to be part of the selection, you can click the Subtract from selection button 🖌 on the options bar and then drag the tool along the edge of the material you want to subtract from the selection. Click the Add to selection button 🖌 to return to adding to a selection.

- If the area you want to select has strong edges or a uniform color, the Quick Selection tool is by far the fastest selection option that Photoshop offers. Where you might have to click a number of times with the Magic Wand tool, or painstakingly drag a border around an object, the Quick Selection tool can paint the selection in a few swipes.

Fine-Tune Selection Edges

- No matter how carefully you make a selection, you may need to fine-tune the selection edges. You have several options for adjusting edges. You can expand or contract the selection to clean up edges, or you can use the Refine Edge feature to make a number of adjustments to selection edges.

- After making a selection, choose the Select > Modify > Expand or Select > Modify > Contract command. Enter the amount (in pixels) by which to expand or contract the selection in the dialog box that appears.

- You will be able to see the adjustment to the selection in the image. Figure 41-3, for example, shows a selection expanded by 3 pixels, so it is actually outside the edge of the flower petals.

Figure 41-3. Expanded selection

- Contracting a selection by one or two pixels in particular can help ensure that the selection doesn't include any unwanted areas along the edges.

- The Refine Edge feature gives you not only the option to expand or contract a selection but several other setting options as well.

- With a selection active, click the Refine Edge button on the options bar, or click Select > Refine Edge. The Refine Edge dialog box opens, as shown in Figure 41-4 at the top of the next page.

- The Refine Edge feature has been improved in Photoshop CS5 to give you more ways to adjust and fine-tune a selection. The chief improvements are in the Edge Detection and Output areas, but other regions of the Refine Edge dialog box have also changed.

- You may want to begin the refining process by changing the view mode. Previous versions of this dialog box offered view modes along the bottom of the dialog box, but in CS5, you click the View list arrow to display the list shown in Figure 41-5.

Figure 41-4. Refine Edge dialog box

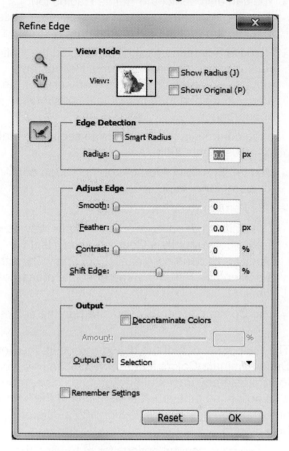

Figure 41-5. Select a view mode

■ Each view mode displays the current selection in a different way. Switching among several of these modes can help you identify areas where you may need to do more work on your selection.

● Marching Ants shows the selection as it appears on the canvas, with the moving selection border.

● Overlay shows the unselected area masked with red, as in Quick Mask mode. You will work with Quick Mask mode later in the course.

● On Black shows the selection against a pure black background. This option is helpful if you have selected an area from a light background, because you can see any remaining light border along the edges.

● On White, the default preview option, shows the selection against a white background.

● Black & White shows the selection as a filled white area against a black background, the way masks are usually displayed in Photoshop's Channels panel. You will work with masks like these in Lesson 6.

● On Layers shows how the current layer looks if the selection is used to mask everything but the content within the mask.

● Reveal Layer shows the entire layer without any selection or masking.

■ The Show Radius and Show Original checkboxes in this section allow you to display only the selection radius or the original selection, or both.

■ The Edge Detection area of the dialog box gives you more control over the selection border.

● The Smart Radius option detects differences in soft edges and hard edges of the selected object and adjusts the selection border accordingly.

● Drag the Radius slider to adjust the exactness of the selection border, helpful in an area that has fine detail. Figure 41-6 shows a portion of a selection around the cat. Note that the selection border does not precisely capture some of the edges created by fur. Figure 41-7 shows how adjusting the radius makes the selection border follow the fur more precisely.

Figure 41-6. A Quick Selection tool selection needs refinement

Figure 41-7. The refined radius follows the fur more closely

- You can also select the Refine Radius tool 🖌 and drag it over a portion of the selection border to refine the radius in that area only.
- Remove any refinement by clicking on the Refine Radius tool to display the Erase Refinements tool 🖌 and then dragging the eraser over the area you refined to restore it to its previous appearance.

- Use the controls in the Adjust Edge section to make other adjustments to the selection.
  - Use the Smooth slider to "iron out" edge detail for a smoother look.
  - Use Feather to soften an edge.
  - The Shift Edge option works the same way as the Select > Modify > Contract and Select > Modify > Expand commands, but you work with a percentage rather than an absolute measurement.
  - The Contrast slider lets you sharpen the selection edges.

- The Output section of the dialog box offers the new Decontaminate Colors feature, which can help you to eliminate any traces of background color around a selection, so that you see no traces of the background if you paste the selection into a different background.

- You also have several options for outputting the selection. For example, you can create a new layer from the selection or even a new document that contains only the selected material.

PROCEDURES

Select with the Magic Wand

1. Click **Magic Wand** tool .... W or SHIFT + W
2. Leave the New selection button selected on the options bar.
3. (Optional) Enter new Tolerance setting on the options bar.

   ✓ *Leave the Contiguous check box checked, unless you want to have to add to the selection later.*

4. Click on the area and color to select in the image.

Add to or Subtract from a Selection

1. Make the initial selection.
2. With a selection tool active, click the desired button on the options bar:

   ■ Click **Add to selection** button to increase selection area.

   ■ Click **Subtract from selection** button to remove areas from selection.

3. Click or drag on the image to alter the selection as needed.

   ✓ *You can leave the New selection button selected on the options bar and instead Shift + click or Shift + drag to add to a selection or Alt + click or Alt + drag to remove from a selection. Whether you click or drag depends on the selection tool you're using.*

Use the Quick Selection Tool

1. Click **Quick Selection** tool .... W or SHIFT + W
2. Adjust brush size if necessary using Brushes Preset panel.
3. Begin inside an edge and drag over the area to select.

To add to or subtract from a Quick Selection tool selection:

■ Click **Subtract from selection** tool and drag over edge of area to subtract.

■ Click **Add to selection** tool and drag over area to add to selection.

Expand or Contract a Selection

1. Make the initial selection.
2. Click **Select** .... ALT + S
3. Point to **Modify** .... M
4. Click **Expand** .... E

   OR

   Click **Contract** C
5. Type amount (in pixels) in dialog box that appears.
6. Click **OK** .... ENTER

Use Refine Edge *(Alt + Ctrl + R)*

1. With a selection active, click Refine Edge button on options bar.

   OR

   a. Click **Select** .... ALT + S
   b. Click **Refine Edge** .... F
2. Click **View** list arrow and select a view mode.

Edge Detection settings:

1. Select **Smart Radius** .... ALT + A to allow Photoshop to adjust radius according to content.
2. Drag **Radius** slider or type value .... ALT + U to improve edge detail.
3. Select **Refine Radius** tool and drag over a portion of the selection border to refine the radius in that area.
4. Select **Erase Refinements** tool and drag over a portion of the selection border to remove any refinements in that area.

Adjust Edge settings:

1. Drag **Smooth** slider or type value .... ALT + H to reduce jaggedness of edge.
2. Drag **Feather** slider or type value .... ALT + F to soften edge.
3. Drag **Contrast** slider or type value .... ALT + C to sharpen edges.
4. Drag **Shift Edge** slider or type value .... ALT + S to contract or expand selection edge.

Output settings:

1. Select **Decontaminate Colors** .... ALT + D and then drag **Amount** slider or type value .... ALT + N to remove traces of color from around selection.
2. Click **Output To** ... ALT + O , ↓ and select an output option.
3. Click **OK** .... ENTER

EXERCISE DIRECTIONS

1. Open the 41Parrot file and save it as 41Parrot_xx.

2. Select the Magic Wand tool. Contiguous should be selected and the Tolerance should be the default 32. Click anywhere on the bird's head to see how much of the bird is selected.

3. Leave the Magic Wand tool selected, click the Add to selection button on the options bar, and click additional areas to add them to the selection.

4. Continue to add to the selection, clicking more and more areas to add, such as the feet and the bar on which the parrot is perched.

5. Change the tolerance to 15 and subtract areas around the bird that may have been added by mistake until you have deselected as many of the background flashing pixels as you can.

6. Switch to the Lasso tool and click the Add to selection button. Lasso parts of the bird that are still not selected, such as the beak and the eye.

   ✓ *Now try another selection method.*

7. Deselect the selection and click the Quick Selection tool.

8. Change the brush size to **10** px. Beginning at the top of the bird's head, paint the selection to include the entire bird, the bird's feet, and the green bar on which the bird is perched.

9. Use the Quick Selection Add to selection and Subtract from selection to adjust the selection as needed. You may want to increase magnification and decrease brush size to fine-tune the edge, especially around the feet.

10. Open the Refine Edge dialog box. Turn on Smart Radius and adjust the Radius to 0.4. This makes the bird slightly smoother, but is not helpful for the perch. Turn off Smart Radius and reset the Radius to 0.0.

11. Change Contrast to 30% to sharpen the edges of the selection, then change Smooth to 15. Use the Refine Radius tool if necessary to adjust the selection border at the top of the head or in rough areas at the right side of the neck and body.

12. Choose to output to Selection, if necessary. Save the refined selection as **Parrot**.

13. With the selection still active, open the Refine Edge dialog box again and change the View mode to On Black. Choose to Decontaminate Colors 100%.

14. Choose to output to New Layer. Name the new layer **Parrot**. Insert a new layer below the Parrot layer and fill it with a contrasting color, such as a blue. Your parrot should look similar to Illustration A.

15. Save your changes to the image, close the file, and exit Illustrator.

Illustration A

ON YOUR OWN

1. Open the ⊙OYO41 file and save it as OPH41_xx.

2. Choose the Background copy layer and use the Magic Wand tool to select the red rose at the upper part of the bouquet from the selection.

    ✓ *You will likely need to adjust the Tolerance, select Contiguous, and/or add to the selection to select the whole rose.*

3. Delete the selection. The red rose should disappear from the image.

4. Undo the change and deselect the selection.

5. Load the **Roses** selection.

6. Expand the selection by **1** px using Select > Modify > Expand.

7. Open the Refine Edge dialog box and view the selection on black. You can see the expanded edge in this preview.

8. Shift the edge to **–40%** and then feather it **3** px. Set radius to **1** px and contrast to **20%**.

9. Choose to output to Selection. Save the new selection as **Rose Feather**.

10. Use Copy Merged to copy the Rose Feather selection.

11. Paste the Rose Feather selection as a new layer in the image file.

12. Hide the Background copy layer.

    ✓ *Remember, click the eye icon beside the layer in the Layers panel to hide and redisplay the layer.*

13. Save your changes, close the file, and exit Photoshop.

Exercise | 42

Summary Exercise

Application Skills   You have been asked to prepare another beach-related image for Gulf Shores Resort. You will use two separate images to create the final image, and then use other tools to help blend the two images together.

EXERCISE DIRECTIONS

1. Open the ⊙42Beach file and save the file as 42Beach_xx.

2. Open the ⊙42Building file and save it as 42Building_xx.

3. Use selection tools of your choice to select the building, including the porch and porch railing and the bushes near the base of the building.

   ✓ *The Polygonal Lasso tool works well in this instance, because the selection will consist primarily of straight lines between points.*

4. Use the Refine Edge dialog box to sharpen up and adjust the selection edge to give the best appearance to the selection. Be sure to view the selection against the black background to make sure there is not a light edge showing around the selected object that will show up unattractively when it is pasted

5. Save the selection as **building**, then copy the selection.

6. Paste the copied selection in 42Beach_xx. Adjust the copied selection as follows:

   a. Use the Edit > Transform > Scale command to adjust the copied selection to about two-thirds of its current size.

      ✓ *Display the Info panel and watch as you hold down Shift and drag the lower-left corner sizing handle. Stop scaling at about 66%.*

   b. Use the Edit > Transform > Rotate command to rotate the copied selection slightly to the left to straighten it.

   c. Move the selection down to the beach, as shown in Illustration A.

7. Save and close the 42Building_xx file.

8. Rename the layer that contains the pasted building as **Building**.

9. Use the Brush tool's Grass preset and adjust the brush size to a small size. Using several colors of green, brush beach grass around the base of the building as shown in Illustration A.

   ✓ *For a more realistic effect, use yellowish greens and light browns for both foreground and background colors.*

10. Select the Mixer Brush tool and one of the bristle brushes. On the Background layer, Alt + click in the cloud and use the Mixer Brush to give the cloud a painted look. You may also smooth the sand and mix over the horizon as desired.

11. Draw several Custom Shape birds in the sky, adjusting color as desired. You may use a Transform option to adjust angle of rotation or size.

12. Using the Horizontal Type tool and a font, font size, and font color of your choice, type **Historic Buildings** and position the type object attractively in the image area.

13. Save your changes, close the file, and exit Photoshop.

Illustration A

Application Exercise

Application Skills The Springfield Flight Museum has asked you to create a poster to publicize new acquisitions at the Museum. You will begin work on the poster in this exercise.

EXERCISE DIRECTIONS

1. Open ⊙ **43Flight** and save the file as **43Flight_xx**. Hide the Background layer and work on the image layer.

2. Use the Quick Selection tool to select as much of the plane as you can. Zoom in if necessary to add parts of the plane such as the propeller and the struts that support the wings, and remove background material from the selection. (You will find the Polygonal Lasso helpful for removing areas around the struts from the selection.)

3. Use Refine Edge to clean up and adjust the selection edges to make sure you have a good, solid outline all the way around. Do more cleanup of the selection at a high zoom percentage if necessary.

4. When you are happy with the selection, save it as **Plane**. Deselect the selection.

5. Load the selection and invert it. Fill the inverted selection with white and adjust the opacity to obscure the background.

6. Use the Magnetic Lasso tool to select around the outside of the plane, along the red areas only—do not include the tires or the propeller in the selection. Use Refine Edge to smooth the selection border.

7. Save the selection as **Outline**. Then apply a stroke to the selection, using a dark reddish black color to sharpen up the edges of the plane.

8. Choose a dark blue foreground color. Append the Symbols Custom Shapes to the current panel of shapes and select the Airplane shape.

9. Draw the airplane shape as a shape layer in the upper-left corner of the image area. Name the layer **Symbol**.

10. Using a font such as Broadway, type **Many New Exhibits!** on top of the airplane shape, as shown in Illustration A. Use a font size of 36 and a font color that shows up well.

11. Save your changes, close the file, and exit Photoshop.

Illustration A

Exercise | 44

Curriculum Integration

Application Skills   Your language arts class plans to mount a production of Sophocles' *Oedipus Rex*, and you have been asked to work on the program for the play. You want to use a picture of the Parthenon, one of Athens' most famous ancient monuments, on the first page of the program. Do the following tasks first:

■ Locate a picture of the Parthenon online, either a drawing of how it is believed it appeared in ancient times or a photo of its present state.

■ Save the image to a location on your system in a format such as JPEG.

EXERCISE DIRECTIONS

Open the Parthenon image file. Using selection tools of your choice, trace around the temple so that your selection includes only the temple itself and no background. Refine the selection as necessary.

Copy the selection and paste it in a new default Photoshop image file. Save the file as 44Parthenon_xx.

Use Eraser tools to remove any portions of the image you don't need. You may need to clean up edges, remove portions of the steps, or eliminate traces of blue sky. Zoom in and adjust the brush size for the Eraser tool as necessary.

Add a layer below the image layer and create a gradient that has a color from the Parthenon blending into white and then blending into a light blue or another color that complements the first gradient color.

Add a type layer that contains the name of the play, *Oedipus Rex,* in a suitable font. Choose a font size, font style, and font color and position the text as desired. Illustration A shows one option.

Save your changes, close all open files, and exit Photoshop.

Illustration A

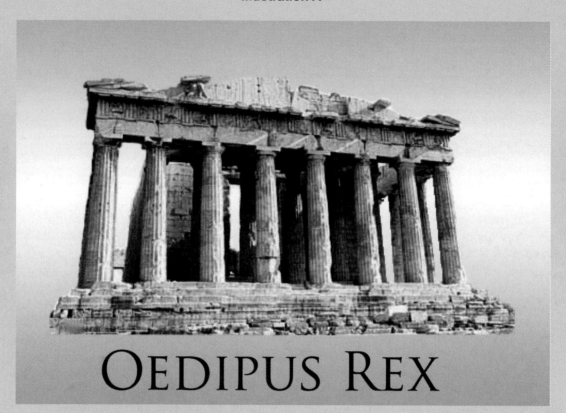

OEDIPUS REX

Exercise | 45

Portfolio Builder

Application Skills   The latest newsletter for Wilcox Tours will include a story about a great deal on an upcoming tour. You want to use a selection from an image along with some text to create a vignette graphic to highlight the story.

EXERCISE DIRECTIONS

- Open the ⊙ 45Tour file. This file displays a shot of Delicate Arch in Arches National Park.
- Use the Elliptical Marquee tool to select the arch. Choose a Feather setting before making the selection.
- Move the selection marquee around until you've selected the area you want to use for your vignette, then expand the selection slightly.
- Copy the selection and then close the 45Tour file without saving it.
- Create a new default Photoshop image file with a resolution of 100 pixels/inch and paste the copied image selection. Save the new file as 45Tour2_xx.
- Pick up a blue color from the sky above the arch and use it to create a Foreground to Transparent gradient. Adjust the gradient so that transparency starts at about 50%, and then apply the gradient to a new layer beneath the arch image.
- Add type in a font, size, and color of your choice that reads **Southwest Park Tours from $399!** Position the text as desired.
- Save your changes, close the file, and exit Photoshop.

Lesson | 5

Correct and Modify Images

Exercise | 46

Skills Covered

- **About Image Adjustments**
- **Use the Adjustments Panel**
- **Make an Automatic Correction**
- **Correct Color Balance**
- **Correct Levels**
- **Correct Brightness and Contrast**
- **Correct Hue and Saturation**

Software Skills Photoshop includes a variety of tools for correcting lighting and tone quality in images. The options on the Image > Adjustments submenu or the Adjustments panel can be used to correct or enhance in a variety of ways.

Design Skills Any designer who works with images from scanners or digital cameras occasionally needs to adjust image appearance and quality. The ability to improve images can result in higher-quality design projects.

Application Skills You're working on the newsletter for Wilcox Tours. A destination partner has sent you an image to use in the newsletter, but you're not satisfied with the image tone quality. Work to correct the image color and tone in this exercise.

TERMS

Adjustment layer A layer to which you can apply color and other adjustments for the purpose of modifying all layers below the adjustment layer.

Automatic correction A color or tone correction in which Photoshop automatically detects image information and determines the correction levels to apply.

Brightness Generally, the overall lightness or darkness in an image.

Color balance Generally, the overall color cast or mixture of colors in an image.

Contrast The amount of difference between the darkest and lightest pixels in an image.

Highlight A light area in an image where light has bounced off a high spot in the subject or object being photographed.

Hue A pixel's actual color.

Levels Feature that enables you to adjust color balance for individual color channels or the whole image by working proportionally with the distribution between pixels.

Midtones Tone values in an image that fall midway between highlight and shadow tones.

Saturation The amount of a particular hue applied to the pixel. Less saturation results in a duller color.

Shadow A dark area in a photo, where less light struck the subject or object being photographed.

NOTES

About Image Adjustments

- Even expert photographers find themselves needing to correct and adjust color in their images. Adjustments may need to be made to tone, contrast, color balance, or saturation, for example, to improve the look of an image.

- You have two options for making image adjustments in Photoshop. You can use the commands on the Image > Adjustments submenu, or you can use the Adjustments panel to create **adjustment layers**. Both alternatives offer a wide variety of options for correcting and adjusting color in an image.

- The adjustment options on the Image > Adjustments submenu alter the actual pixels of an image. Once you have applied an adjustment from this submenu, the changes can be reversed only by using Undo or Step Backward.

- When you add an adjustment layer, by contrast, you apply adjustments to a layer that will affect all layers below it. In this way, you can modify the look of an image without actually changing it.

- There are a number of advantages to using an adjustment layer.

  - You can minimize the "damage" that occurs in an image when a number of adjustments are made to it. Multiple adjustments can cause loss of image data and subsequent degradation of the image.

  - If you don't like the adjustments you make to the layer, you can simply delete the layer and your original image is still intact.

  - You can modify appearance on a number of layers at one time, because an adjustment layer impacts all layers below it.

- Best practice suggests that you should use adjustment layers whenever possible. Adjustment layers do add to file size and make demands on your system's RAM, so if best quality is not an issue, you may want to use the "destructive" adjustments on the Image > Adjustments submenu. Otherwise, use adjustment layers created in the Adjustments panel.

Use the Adjustments Panel

- The Adjustments panel displays a series of icons that correspond to specific types of adjustments, as shown in Figure 46-1. Rest the pointer on an icon to see what kind of adjustment layer it represents.

Figure 46-1. Adjustments panel

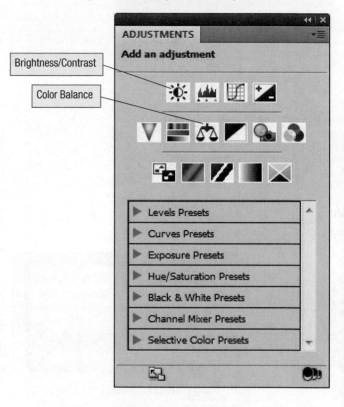

- The panel includes a list of presets that represent commonly applied adjustments. Click a right-pointing arrow to see the presets for a specific type of adjustment.

- Selecting one of the adjustment icons in the Adjustments panel immediately creates a new layer in the Layers panel and displays settings for the adjustment in the Adjustments panel, as shown in Figure 46-2 at the top of the next page.

- Buttons at the bottom of the Adjustments panel make it easy to work with the adjustment layer. Click the *Return to adjustment list* button to see the list of adjustment icons again. Click the *Switch panel to Expanded View* button to see a wider view of the panel, which makes it easier to view graphs of color and tone information.

- By default, the third button from the left is *This adjustment affects all layers below*. If you want the adjustment layer to be used to create a clipping mask, click this button to change it to the *This adjustment clips to the layer* button.

  ✓ *You will learn how to clip the adjustment to a single layer in the next lesson.*

Figure 46-2. Brightness/Contrast adjustment layer appears above an image

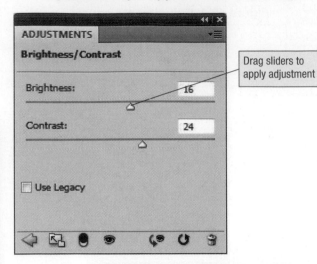

Drag sliders to apply adjustment

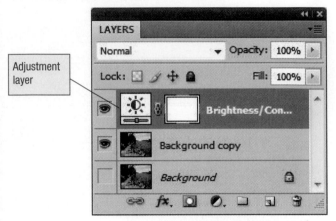

Adjustment layer

- Use the visibility eye 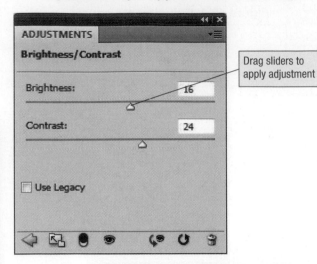 to toggle the adjustment layer's visibility on or off. This allows you to hide the adjustment but keep it available if you're not yet sure you want to use it.

- Click on the *Press to view previous state* button and hold down the mouse button to see how the image looked before applying the current adjustment. You can use this button to toggle back and forth between states to check the adjustment. Note that you can also switch back and forth using the backslash \ key.

- Use the *Reset to adjustment defaults* button to return the sliders or other settings to their defaults so you can start over with your adjustment. To quickly remove the adjustment layer, click the *Delete this adjustment layer* button, or simply press the Delete key.

- Most of the adjustment options you find on the Adjustments panel (and on the Image > Adjustment submenu) help you to correct or enhance current colors. Some of the commands, such as Invert and Posterize, display the image in strikingly different ways for a special effect.

- As you work with image corrections in this and subsequent exercises, you will learn that color modifications can be very subjective. Some people tend to like their images to be a bit more red or warm, while others lean toward cooler blue or green-toned images. Some people like high-contrast images, while others prefer more subtle tonal changes.

- After you have completed the exercises using specified settings, you may want to continue to adjust to modify the appearance for your own taste.

- The remainder of this exercise will explore some of the more common adjustments you can make, using both the Image menu and the Adjustments panel. Image menu commands generally open dialog boxes in which you can make the same adjustments to settings that you will see in the Adjustments panel.

Make an Automatic Correction

- The Auto Tone, Auto Contrast, and Auto Color commands on the Image menu make **automatic corrections** to an image. When you choose one of these commands, Photoshop examines the image content and corrects it automatically.

- The Auto Tone command changes the lightest and darkest pixels on each channel in the image to pure white and pure black, and then redistributes the pixels in between. This command can help improve image contrast, but may adjust color in unexpected or unwanted ways.

  ✓ *Each channel represents content of a particular color in an image. An RGB image will have three color channels—red, green, and blue—plus the composite channel that shows the combination of the individual color channels. Lesson 6 gives more detail about channels and working with them.*

- The Auto Contrast command adjusts the contrast in the image overall—not channel by channel. Like the Auto Tone command, it sets the lightest and darkest pixels to white and black, and then adjusts pixels in between accordingly.

- The Auto Color command changes image color and **contrast** based on existing shadows, midtones, and highlights.

- Photoshop applies each of these commands immediately, so if you dislike an automatic correction, you must use Undo to reverse it.

Correct Color Balance

- While a number of commands may affect **color balance** in an image, the Color Balance feature enables you to choose the color settings you want to apply to the image. Color Balance is often the first correction an experienced designer will make.

- Click the Color Balance icon 🔛 on the Adjustments panel to display Color Balance settings.
- The Color Balance settings, shown in Figure 46-3, allow you to specify color levels or drag sliders to adjust color balance. This adjustment allows you to correct for an unwanted color cast in an image, such as too much blue or yellow.

Figure 46-3. Color Balance adjustment

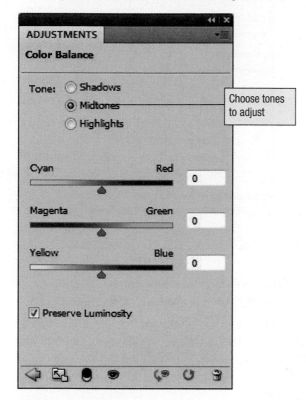

Correct Levels

- When adjusting image appearance, you may next want to work with the image's tone by correcting **levels**. *Levels* refers to the levels of intensity of shadows, midtones, and highlights in an image.
- Click the Levels icon 📊 on the Adjustments panel to display the Levels settings shown in Figure 46-4.

Figure 46-4. Levels settings

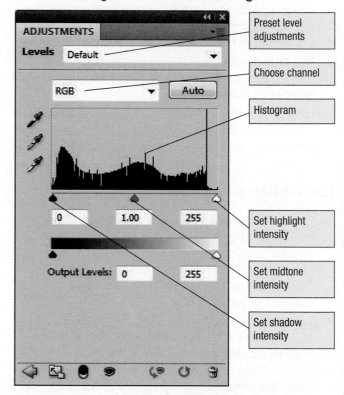

- First click an option button in the Tone section to determine whether to adjust the **shadows**, **midtones**, or **highlights** in the image. Shadows are the darkest areas of an image. Highlights are areas where the light is strongest. Midtones are areas with tone values between those of highlights and shadows.
- As you adjust the sliders, positive or negative values display in the number boxes to allow for some precision. You see the changes immediately in the image in the workspace.
- In the Color Balance settings and for all others where you apply a filter or correction, it's a good idea to leave the Preserve Luminosity check box checked. This tells Photoshop to change color values as needed but to leave luminosity (areas where light bounces off the subject) unchanged, so the image continues to have realistic tones.

- The histogram in the Levels settings displays the relative intensity of particular image colors.
- For a photo that's overexposed (too bright or washed out), the black areas in the histogram will be bunched toward the right (highlight) side. Drag the left (shadow) slider to the right to help correct this situation.
- When the black areas of the histogram are bunched to the left, the photo is underexposed (too dark), and dragging the highlight or midtone slider to the left can help.
- If desired, choose the color channel to work with from the Channel list at the top of the dialog box. Drag the desired slider(s) under the histogram to set the new input color/tone until the image appears as desired in the image window.

  ✓ *The Levels settings enable you to make even more sophisticated color and tone corrections (using the eyedropper tools and Output Levels slider) that are beyond the scope of this book.*

Correct Brightness and Contrast

- You can work with the **brightness** and **contrast** in an image using the Brightness/Contrast settings. Click the Brightness/Contrast icon 🔆 to display the sliders shown earlier in Figure 46-2. Drag the Brightness and Contrast sliders in the Adjustments panel until the image has the desired appearance.

- If you set the Brightness too high, you risk losing detail in the foreground colors and having the image appear washed out. On the other hand, increasing Brightness a bit can help bring out detail in background areas that appear too dark.

- Too-high contrast tends to make an image look "posterized," eliminating the blends between areas of different colors.

- Note that the Use Legacy option may result in loss of detail at either the highlight or shadow end of the tonal range, so it is not recommended for photo images.

Correct Hue and Saturation

- Click the Hue/Saturation icon ▦ to adjust the **hue**, **saturation**, and lightness (brightness) for various color components in an image. A color component is not a specific channel; instead, it is a general grouping of colors in an image, such as the reds, cyans, or blues.

- In the Hue/Saturation settings, shown in Figure 46-5, choose the color component to change from the Edit list (Master changes all the colors in the image). Drag the Hue slider to change the overall color, the Saturation slider to determine how intense the color becomes, and the Lightness slider to change the tone (light/white to black/dark).

Figure 46-5. Hue/Saturation settings

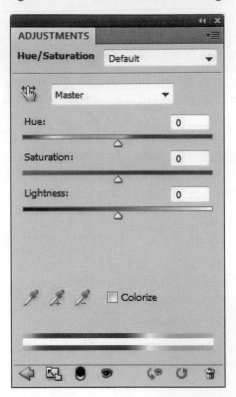

✓ *You can use the Hue/Saturation settings to colorize a grayscale image.*

- The presets in the list box at the top of the panel offer a number of interesting hue/saturation adjustments that you can apply with a single click.

PROCEDURES

With the exception of the Auto corrections, all adjustment instructions assume the use of the Adjustments panel.

Use the Auto Tone Command (Shift + Ctrl + L)

1. Click **Image** .... `ALT` + `I`
2. Click **Auto Tone** .... `N`

Use the Auto Contrast Command (Alt + Shift + Ctrl + L)

1. Click **Image** .... `ALT` + `I`
2. Click **Auto Contrast** .... `U`

Use the Auto Color Command (Shift + Ctrl + B)

1. Click **Image** .... `ALT` + `I`
2. Click **Auto Color** .... `O`

Use the Adjustments Panel

1. Click an icon in the Adjustments panel to display settings for that adjustment.
2. Adjust settings as desired.
3. Control display of panel and settings:
   - Click ⬅ to return to the Adjustments panel list.
   - Click 🔲 to switch to expanded view.
   - Click ⬤ to apply the adjustment only to the next layer.
   - Click 👁 to show or hide the adjustment layer.
   - Click 🔲 and hold down the mouse button to see the previous state of the image.

   OR

   Press `\` to see the previous state.
   - Click 🔄 to restore the adjustment settings to their defaults.

OR

1. Click the right-pointing arrow of a preset category.
2. Select the desired preset to immediately apply settings to the image.

To delete an adjustment layer:

1. Select the adjustment layer to delete.
2. Click 🗑 .
3. Click **Yes** .... `ALT` + `Y`

   OR

1. Select the adjustment layer to delete.
2. Press `DEL`.

Correct Color Balance

1. Click **Create a new Color Balance adjustment layer** icon 🔲 in Adjustments panel.
2. Click a choice in the **Tone** section:
   - **Shadows**
   - **Midtones**
   - **Highlights**
3. Drag slider(s) in the color balance section.

   OR

   Type values in color levels boxes.

Correct Levels

1. Click **Create a new Levels adjustment layer** icon 🔲 in Adjustments panel.
2. Click the Default down arrow and select a preset levels adjustment.

OR

a. Choose the channel to adjust from the menu.
b. Drag slider(s) below the histogram as needed or type values in input levels boxes.
   - To lighten a dark image, drag the gray midtone slider or the white highlight slider to the left.
   - To darken a light image, drag the gray midtone slider to the right.

Correct Brightness and Contrast

1. Click **Create a new Brightness/Contrast adjustment layer** icon 🔲 in Adjustments panel.
2. Drag **Brightness** slider to achieve desired effect.
3. Drag **Contrast** slider to achieve desired effect.

   ✓ *Avoid using the Use Legacy setting for images because it can result in loss of quality.*

Correct Hue and Saturation

1. Click **Create a new Hue/Saturation adjustment layer** icon 🔲 in Adjustments panel.
2. Click the Default down arrow and select a preset hue/saturation adjustment.

   OR

a. Choose the color component to adjust from the menu.
b. Drag **Hue** slider to achieve desired hue.
c. Drag **Saturation** slider to achieve desired saturation.
d. Drag **Lightness** slider to achieve desired lightness.

EXERCISE DIRECTIONS

✓ *After starting Photoshop, apply the Photography workspace.*

1. Open the ⊙46Glacier file and save it as 46Glacier_original_xx.

2. Open the 46Glacier file again and save it as 46Glacier_corrected_xx. Copy the Background layer and then hide the Background layer. Arrange the two documents side by side so that you can compare the changes you make with the original.

   ✓ *The image has some dark areas to the right side that could be brightened and lightened.*

3. Begin by balancing colors to correct a somewhat bluish cast. Apply a Color Balance adjustment layer. Adjust the Cyan/Red slider toward red to a value of **+12**. Adjust the Yellow/Blue slider toward yellow to a value of **-20**.

4. Next try a tone correction. Select the Background copy layer and apply the Auto Tone correction from the Image menu. This actually darkens the area you want to lighten, so Undo this change.

5. Apply a Levels adjustment layer above the Color Balance 1 adjustment layer. Drag the Midtones slider (the gray one below the middle of the histogram) to the left to **1.30**. This correction lightens the dark area of the stream and trees at the right of the image.

6. Compare this appearance to the original image, and then compare it to the previous state of the corrected image using the Press to view previous state button at the bottom of the Adjustments panel.

7. The image is now lighter, but it could use some more tweaking. Apply a Brightness/Contrast adjustment layer. Increase the Brightness setting to **+20** and the Contrast setting to **+30**.

8. Compare this adjustment to the previous state. These settings wash out the sky and mountains too much. Restore the default brightness/contrast settings and then increase the Contrast setting to **+20** to sharpen the image without lightening it too much.

9. Apply a Hue/Saturation adjustment layer. On the list of preset adjustments at the top of the panel, select **Increase Saturation** to give the colors a boost.

10. Compare the image to the original. The corrected image has more detail visible in darker areas and has a warmer tone than the original, as shown in Illustration A. Try hiding each of the adjustment layers below the top one to see the impact on the image.

    ✓ *Because color choices look different on different displays due to calibration issues, the settings in this exercise may or may not yield the image preference you'd prefer. If your instructor allows it, you can choose alternate settings to make the image look the way that you prefer.*

11. Save your changes, close both files, and exit Photoshop.

Illustration A

ON YOUR OWN

1. Open the ◉OYO46 file and save it as OPH46_xx. Copy the background and work on the copy.

2. Apply the Auto Color command to view its impact, and then undo the command.

3. Apply the Auto Contrast command. Its impact looks more realistic.

4. Apply a Color Balance adjustment layer, and change the Highlights of the image to make them more Red (+30 in the top color levels box).

> ✓ *Again, color correction choices are somewhat subjective and driven by the ultimate use for the image file. This exercise is asking you to really pump up the colors for instructional purposes.*

5. Use the Magic Wand tool with a fairly low tolerance and non-contiguous setting to select anywhere on one of the rounded leaves at the right side of the image. Continue to add to the selection until you have much of the color of these leaves on the right side of the image selected.

6. Apply a Hue/Saturation adjustment layer, and note the mask in the adjustment layer that indicates you are applying the adjustment only to selected areas. Leave the Master color component selected, and change the Hue to +10. Compare to the previous state to see that only the selected leaf areas have been adjusted.

7. Save your changes, close the file, and exit Photoshop.

Exercise | 47

Skills Covered

- Fix Red Eye
- Use the Healing Brush Tool
- Use the Spot Healing Brush Tool
- Make Content-Aware Corrections

- Use the Patch Tool
- Use the Clone Stamp Tool
- Use the History Panel

Software Skills   Photoshop offers a variety of tools to deal with imperfections in digital images. You can fix that red glow in the eyes of a photo subject or fix a scratch or spot on a picture using tools such as Red Eye, Spot Healing Brush, Healing Brush, Patch, and Clone Stamp. You can even replace existing image content with content from surrounding areas. The History panel makes it easy to reverse a series of changes.

Design Skills   A designer may need to work with an image that is slightly flawed in some way. Photoshop tools can help a designer to fix an image so that flaws are less visible, or entirely invisible.

Application Skills   You've taken a picture of the new water lilies that you'll be selling at Newfound Nursery. You want to correct the photo by eliminating the grass clippings on the leaves and by making a second lily bloom on the image. Use photo correction tools to accomplish those tasks in this exercise.

TERMS

Red eye   An image flaw caused by flash bouncing off the retina of a subject's eye when a photo is shot.

NOTES

Fix Red Eye

- **Red eye** occurs when light from a camera's flash bounces off the retina at the back of the subject's eye. Red eye can have a green or bluish white appearance in animals.

  ✓ *Most digital cameras offer a red eye flash setting designed to minimize red eye. Having the subject turn his or her face and eyes slightly to the left or right rather than facing the camera straight on also can help minimize red eye.*

- Photoshop offers the Red Eye tool ⬚ to fix red eye with an easy mouse click or two. In Figure 47-1, the girl's right eye has been fixed, but the left eye and the cat's eyes still need attention.

- Options for the Red Eye tool include desired Pupil Size and Darken Amount settings from the options bar. Click on the eye to correct, or drag diagonally across it.

  ✓ *The Red Eye tool sometimes works best before you make any other corrections to the image, especially any color corrections that might introduce more red to the skin tones around the eye.*

Figure 47-1. Use the Red Eye tool to fix red eye

Figure 47-2. Paint over imperfections with the Healing Brush

Healing Brush pointer

Cross shows where image was sampled

✓ *You also can paint on a pattern by clicking the Pattern option on the options bar, and then choosing the desired pattern from the Pattern picker.*

- The Red Eye tool doesn't necessarily recreate the look of a natural eye, depending on how much of the eye is covered with red eye, so experiment with the Pupil Size and Darken Amount settings (using Undo as needed). Clicking repeatedly with the Red Eye tool can actually start replacing colors in other areas of the image.

  ✓ *The image repair tools described in this exercise paint over the target pixels on the layer. If you want to keep a copy of the original image content in the image file, copy and hide the Background layer before making the repairs.*

Use the Healing Brush Tool

- The Healing Brush tool enables you to sample an area of the image, and then paint the sample over a similar scratched, spotted, or otherwise damaged area.

- To help blend the repair, Photoshop examines the texture, lighting, transparency, and shading of the pixels being patched and adjusts the painted sample accordingly.

- Select brush settings for painting the correction from the options bar as well as a different blending mode, if desired. To sample the area to use as the "correction" stroke, Alt + click on the image. Then, click or drag over the area to repair as shown in Figure 47-2, where the Healing Brush is being used to erase dark shadows on the flower petal.

  ✓ *The mouse pointer changes to a bull's eye when you Alt + click the image.*

- The sampled area will be as large as the brush size. If this results in unwanted colors around the edges of the painted correction, select a smaller brush size for sampling, and use more strokes.

- For more control over the Healing Brush, click the Toggle the Clone Source panel button on the options bar to display the Clone Source panel, shown in Figure 47-3.

Figure 47-3. Clone Source panel

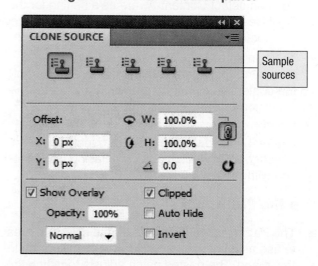

Sample sources

- You can use this panel to select up to five different sample points, so that you can pull pixels from a number of areas as you heal the image. Click one of the stamps in this panel and select options for it, such as a specific source location, width and height measurements, and rotation.

- When the Show Overlay check box is selected, the pixels actually being sampled display within the brush cursor. You can control the opacity of these preview pixels if desired.

- There's a chance of creating a mottled effect by overusing the Healing Brush tool. Watch your work carefully, and use Undo and Step Backwards on the Edit menu if you apply it a time or two too many.

Use the Spot Healing Brush Tool

- The Spot Healing Brush tool enables you to correct small spots and imperfections on the image. However, it does not require you to create a sample by Alt + clicking first. It instead heals the spot by sampling the pixels around it and creating a matching fill or texture.

- Open the Brush picker from the options bar and choose the desired brush settings. Choose an alternate blending mode, if desired. Choose a repair Type (Proximity Match, Create Texture, or Content-Aware), and then click or drag over the area to repair.

Make Content-Aware Corrections

- Content-aware corrections are new in Photoshop CS5. You can use the content-aware options to replace a portion of an image with new content that Photoshop creates by examining the surrounding content.

- You have two options for content-aware corrections. You can select Content-Aware as a setting for the Spot Healing Brush tool, as mentioned in the previous section, or you can select it to fill a selection.

- To fill an area of an image with content created from surrounding areas, first make a selection of the content you want to remove. Then display the Fill dialog box and choose the Content-Aware option.

- Figure 47-4 shows a selection around a couple of beachgoers and the result of replacing the selection with content-aware fill.

Use the Patch Tool

- The Patch tool enables you to select an area to use as a patch to repair another similar area in the image. The pasted patch adjusts to match the texture, lighting, and shading of the patch to the area being repaired, so that it blends as seamlessly as possible.

Figure 47-4. Making a correction with content-aware fill

- To use the Patch tool, select it from the toolbox. Make sure that the New selection and Destination choices are selected on the options bar, and then drag in the image to select the patch area. After you release the mouse button to finish defining the patch, drag the patch over the area to correct.

- Figure 47-5 shows a patch being created to cover the brand on the pony and the result after the patch has been moved over the brand.

Figure 47-5. Use the Patch tool to cover an area

 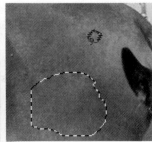

✓ Patch selection works like the Lasso tool. Drag in any shape to define the selection. When you release the mouse button, Photoshop automatically completes the selection marquee by connecting the end point to the starting point.

- Clicking the Use Pattern button after selecting the patch area applies the current pattern to the selected patch, blending the patch contents and the pattern.
- Use the Transparent check box on the options bar to create a transparent version of the patch to lay over the area to fix. For example, if you wanted to patch over a scratch in the sky in an image with a patch selected from the skyline, the patch would blend out the scratch and a faint version of the skyline selection would be blended in to the sky at the patched location.

Use the Clone Stamp Tool

- The Clone Stamp tool 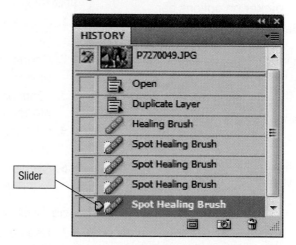 enables you to sample (copy) an area in an image, and then to paint all or part of the duplicate in another location.
- After you choose the Clone Stamp tool from the toolbox, Alt + click on the center of the area to sample. Select the desired brush from the Brush Preset picker and choose the desired blending mode, opacity, flow, and other settings. Then, click or drag back and forth with the mouse to paint the clone onto the layer
- As for the Healing Brush, you can use the Clone Source panel to set options for the clone. In Figure 47-6, for example, the Clone Source panel has been used to specify that the clone will be 50% of the size of the original butterfly and rotated counterclockwise.

Figure 47-6. Cloning an object

Sampling the original butterfly

Painting the clone

✓ *You don't have to select a brush shape or size before sampling the area to clone because Alt + clicking merely specifies a center point; Photoshop clones all the content from that center point out to the edges of the layer.*

- If you want to add a cloned object to the image by clicking, select a brush size that's larger than the sampled object. If you want to paint on a partial version of the cloned object, choose a smaller brush size and drag back and forth until you paint on the desired amount.

Use the History Panel

- The History panel is invaluable when you are adjusting image appearance using tools such as those introduced in this exercise, because you can use it to view the image at a particular point in the correction process. You can also use the History panel to quickly reverse a whole series of changes.
- The History panel by default tracks 20 states during the current work session. States are listed in order, from first at the top of the panel to last at the bottom, as shown in Figure 47-7.

✓ *You can adjust the number of states tracked in the Preferences dialog box.*

Figure 47-7. The History panel tracks how the image looked at different states

Slider

- Click the name of a state in the History panel to see how the image looked at that point. In Figure 47-7, for example, you could click Healing Brush to see how the image looked before you used the Spot Healing Brush.
- You can delete a state from the History panel by clicking the state in the list in the panel, and then clicking the Delete current state button in the lower-right corner of the panel. The state you clicked, as well as any later states (states below it in the list) will be deleted.

✓ *If you mistakenly delete states, use Undo immediately to retrieve them.*

- You can also reverse changes by simply dragging the slider upward to reach a previous state. As you drag upward, states below the slider are dimmed. You can drag the slider back downward to redisplay those states.
- Saving and closing the file clears the History panel. You also can clear the contents of the History panel by clicking its panel menu button and clicking Clear History.

Fix Red Eye

1. Click **Red Eye** tool
   .... J or SHIFT + J
2. Choose **Pupil Size** on options bar.
3. Choose **Darken Amount** on options bar.
4. Click or drag diagonally across area to correct in image.

Use the Healing Brush Tool

1. Click **Healing Brush** tool
   .... J or SHIFT + J
2. Choose brush from **Brush picker** on options bar.
3. (Optional) Choose blending **Mode** on options bar.
4. Click **Sampled** as the Source.
5. ALT + click the area to sample on the image.
6. Drag over the area to repair in the image.

To use the Clone Source panel to sample different areas:

1. With the Clone Stamp tool active, click the **Toggle the Clone Source panel** button on the options bar.
2. Click one of the stamp symbols at the top of the panel to select it.
3. Specify settings for this stamp, if desired, such as size or rotation.
4. Click on the image to set the coordinates for the stamp.
5. Repeat steps 2–4 for up to five stamps.

Use the Spot Healing Brush Tool

1. Click **Spot Healing Brush** tool .... J or SHIFT + J
2. Choose brush from **Brush picker** on options bar.
3. (Optional) Choose blending **Mode** from options bar.
4. Click a repair **Type** option on the options bar.

✓ *Proximity Match tells the tool to use the pixels surrounding the area to be fixed as the patch. Create Texture uses the pixels within and around the area to fix to create the patch. Content-Aware replaces pixels with content from surrounding areas.*

✓ *Checking Sample All Layers tells Photoshop to sample content from all layers, rather than the current layer, when you click to cover a spot.*

5. Click on or drag over the area to repair in the image.

Make Content-Aware Corrections

Using the Spot Healing Brush:

1. Click **Spot Healing Brush** tool .... J or SHIFT + J
2. Choose brush from **Brush picker** on options bar.
3. (Optional) Choose blending **Mode** from options bar.
4. Click **Content-Aware** on the options bar.
5. Click on or drag over the area to repair in the image.

Using the Fill dialog box:

1. Use a selection tool to select the area to be replaced.

   ✓ *An irregular selection sometimes works best for blending new and original content.*

2. Click **Edit** .... ALT + E
3. Click **Fi̱ll** L
4. Click **U̱se** .... ALT + U , ↓
5. Select **Content-Aware**.
6. Click **OK** .... ENTER

Use the Patch Tool

1. Click **Patch** tool
    .... J or SHIFT + J
2. Leave the **New selection** button selected on the options bar.

   ✓ *After you make the initial patch selection, you can use the Add to selection, Subtract from selection, or Intersect with selection button and drag again to adjust the patch as desired. You also can press Ctrl + D to deselect the selection.*

3. Click **Destination** on the options bar.
4. Drag in the image to select the patch.
5. Drag the patch over the target area to be patched.

   ✓ *If you instead choose Source in step 3, dragging the selection marquee samples the pixels under the marquee, filling the original selection with those pixels.*

Use the Clone Stamp Tool

1. Click **Clone Stamp** tool
   .... S or SHIFT + S
2. ALT + click to set the sample center point on the image.
3. Choose brush from **Brush picker** on options bar.
4. (Optional) Choose blending **Mode**, **Opacity**, **Flow**, and **airbrush** settings in options bar.
5. Drag in the image to paint on the clone.

To use the Clone Source panel to adjust clone appearance:

1. With the Clone Stamp tool active, click the **Toggle the Clone Source panel** button on the options bar.
2. Click one of the stamp symbols at the top of the panel to select it.
3. Specify settings for this stamp, if desired, such as size or rotation.
4. Click on the image to set the coordinates for the stamp.
5. Repeat steps 2–4 for up to five stamps.
6. Select one of the stamps in the Clone Source panel and then drag on the image to create the clone at the specified size or rotation.

Use the History Panel

After opening an image and making changes to it:

1. Click **Window** .... ALT + W
2. Click **History** .... H , H , ENTER

3. Click a prior state in the panel to view how the image looked at that state.
4. Drag the slider upward to revisit a previous state.

5. Click a state to delete and then click the **Delete current state** 🗑 button on the History panel.
6. Click **Yes** to confirm the deletion .... ALT + Y

EXERCISE DIRECTIONS

1. Open the 🔘 **47Lily** file and save it as *47Lily_xx*.
2. Zoom the image to 125% size. Duplicate the Background layer, hide the original layer, and work in the Background copy layer.
3. Use the Healing Brush, Spot Healing Brush, Patch tools, and content-aware filled selections to remove as much of the grass and debris from the lily pads as possible. You may also want to clean up some parts of the water. When you finish, your image might resemble Illustration A.

   ✓ *Experiment with various brush sizes for the Healing Brush and Spot Healing Brush to see how brush size affects blending and corrections. Also zoom in and out as needed. Use the History panel if necessary to reverse a series of changes.*

   ✓ *The Patch tool often works well for correcting imperfections near a color change or edge. Note that after you make your initial patch selection, you can use the arrow keys to fine tune its position before dragging it to the area to be patched.*

   ✓ *Take your time in making the corrections. Sometimes cleaning up a photo can be a very time-consuming process.*

4. Choose the Clone Stamp tool from the toolbox, and Alt + click the center of the water lily bloom to set the sample center point there.
5. Choose a hard round brush and set its size to 10 or 15. Drag on the image to add another lily bloom above and to the left of the original, as shown in Illustration B. Dragging in short radial strokes starting from the center point where you want to place the lily will help you better control exactly how much of the cloned lily you paint on.
6. Use the Healing Brush, Spot Healing Brush, and Clone Stamp tools to blend the painted edges around the cloned lily to make it look as natural as possible.
7. Save your changes, close the file, and exit Photoshop.

Illustration A

Illustration B

ON YOUR OWN

1. Bring in an old family photo that has imperfections that you'd like to correct, and scan it in. If no family photo is available, use the ⊙ OYO47 file. This image is a little grainy, because it's a scan of a small grainy photo from the 1960s, but it has fold marks and other areas that are sufficient for practicing your repair skills.

2. Save the file as OPH47_xx.

3. Use the correction tools described in this exercise, as well as any of the color correction tools covered in the prior exercise, to improve the photo's appearance.

   ✓ You might notice a tendency for colored "artifacts" to develop in the taupe wall area when you repeatedly use a tool or appear as a halo around a patched area, particularly in the wall area in the photo. You can sometimes get a better result repairing such areas by choosing a larger, softer brush size.

4. Save your changes, close the file, and exit Photoshop.

Exercise | 48

Skills Covered

- Apply a Photo Filter
- Correct Exposure
- Adjust Vibrance
- Correct Shadows and Highlights

Software Skills   The Adjustments panel provides some additional tools for correcting and enhancing images. Apply a photo filter to adjust the tone of an image. Use Exposure to correct images that are underexposed or overexposed. Vibrance offers another way to adjust saturation in an image. Use the Shadows/Highlights command from the Image menu to adjust an image's shadows and highlights to a more natural appearance.

Design Skills   A designer must develop a good eye for the quality of light in an image. When an image's tone is not optimal or the overall image is too light or too dark, a designer can "rescue" the image using features such as filters, exposure adjustments, vibrance, and shadow/highlight settings.

Application Skills   Newfound Nursery will be introducing some decorative outdoor items for the summer season. You want to enhance the photo of one of the decorative items using the photo correction tools described in this exercise.

TERMS

Backlit   In photography, refers to an image where the light source was behind the subject, making the subject look dark or heavily shadowed.

Exposure   In photography, refers to the amount of light admitted into the camera to strike the film or sensor to record the photo.

Overexposed   A photo where too much light entered the camera, yielding a picture that is too light or washed out.

Photo filter   An additional optical lens or cover added to a camera lens to introduce a tint that compensates for lighting conditions or creates a special effect like a starburst.

Underexposed   A photo where too little light entered the camera, giving a picture a flat, dull, slightly dark appearance.

NOTES

Apply a Photo Filter

- A skilled photographer can attach a **photo filter** to a camera lens to correct the color balance and temperature (warm tones versus cool tones) of the image or apply a special effect.

- For example, a photographer might add a filter to eliminate the blue-green cast common in photos taken under fluorescent lighting, add a polarizing filter to reduce glare and reflections and intensify colors, or add a filter that yields a special effect, such as making the image look foggy or adding a starburst effect.

- For an image shot without the benefit of a physical filter, Photoshop offers the Photo Filter adjustment in the Adjustments panel. Selecting that option displays settings shown in Figure 48-1.

Figure 48-1. Photo Filter adjustment settings

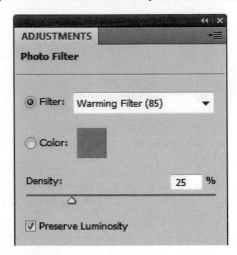

- You can choose a preset filter from the Filter list or select a color to use as a filter. Use the Density slider to set the amount of color or filter applied to the image.

- Warming filters tend to add yellow or red to an image to offset blue tones, while cooling filters tend to add blue tones to compensate for a yellow cast.

- In addition to warming filters, cooling filters, and filters in specific colors, Photoshop includes a filter that makes an image appear to have been shot underwater and one that gives the image a sepia appearance.

Correct Exposure

- Light coming through the lens and aperture and striking the film or sensor (for a digital camera) within the camera creates a photo. **Exposure** refers to the amount of light coming into the camera to create the image.

- For an **overexposed** image, too much light entered the camera, creating a bright, washed-out picture that lacks detail and highlights. Bright, sunny lighting conditions often result in overexposed shots.

- An **underexposed** image results when too little light entered the camera, making a faint recording. The resulting image, if any, will look flat, dull, or even grayed out because the photo is too dark overall.

  ✓ *A totally overexposed picture might become bright white, while a totally underexposed picture may become totally dark.*

- Selecting the Exposure icon on the Adjustments panel displays the Exposure settings shown in Figure 48-2, which you can use to correct exposure flaws.

Figure 48-2. Exposure settings

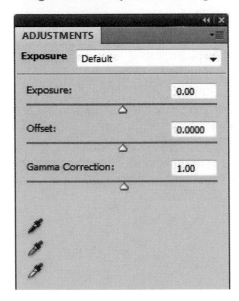

- Use the Exposure slider to adjust the image highlights, the Offset slider to adjust the shadows and midtones, and the Gamma slider to adjust the image's appearance when displayed onscreen.

  ✓ *The gamma for each pixel tells the monitor how to display the pixel.*

Adjust Vibrance

- To understand how the Vibrance adjustment works, you need to know a bit about *color clipping*. During the process of some image adjustments, such as changing color saturation, light-colored pixels are transformed to pure white, and dark-colored pixels are transformed to black. This reduction of color to white and black is color clipping.

- Using the Vibrance adjustment, however, you can minimize the amount of clipping that occurs as you increase saturation. Colors that are already saturated are not affected as much as less saturated colors, and if an image contains skin tones, these tones are protected from saturation changes that would otherwise distort the appearance of a person in the picture.

- Click the Vibrance icon ▼ in the Adjustments panel to display the Vibrance settings, shown in Figure 48-3.

Figure 48-3. Vibrance settings

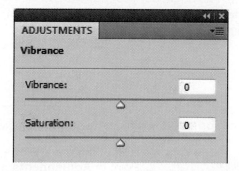

- Move the Vibrance slider to the right to apply saturation proportionally, so that less-saturated colors are saturated more than colors that already have a high saturation. Move the Saturation slider to the right to saturate all colors equally, regardless of their current level of saturation.

- Move the sliders to the left to desaturate colors.

- The result of adjusting Vibrance is clear in the two images shown in Figure 48-4. The original image, on the left, shows a butterfly that does not stand out from its background. In the right image, Vibrance has been applied to the butterfly only, using a mask, to make the butterfly "pop."

Correct Shadows and Highlights

- All too often, the subject of a photograph is positioned in front of the light source, resulting in a photo that is **backlit**. This commonly happens, for example, when the subject is indoors in front of a window or under some type of awning on a bright day. When the photo is backlit, the bright light from behind puts the subject in heavy shadow, removing detail and/or creating a silhouetted appearance.

- At the opposite extreme, a photo subject can appear washed out and lack detail if positioned too close to the flash.

- The Image > Adjustments > Shadows/Highlights command enables you to correct for both conditions in a digital image. Instead of making the overall image lighter or darker, this command causes Photoshop to examine the pixels surrounding shadowed and highlighted areas to determine where to apply the tonal changes.

  ✓ *The Shadows/Highlights command can work somewhat like fill flash on a camera. Fill flash is a special flash type or setting that lightens the heavily shadowed parts of the image, bringing out the detail.*

- To adjust shadows and highlights in the Shadows/Highlights dialog box, shown in Figure 48-5 at the top of the next page, drag the Amount slider in the Shadows section to adjust shadow tones, and drag the Amount slider in the Highlights section to adjust highlight tones.

Figure 48-4. Original image (left) and image with Vibrance applied to butterfly only (right)

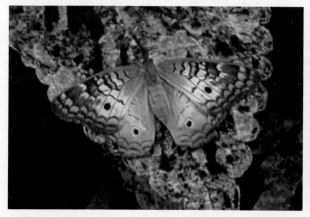 

Figure 48-5. Shadows/Highlights dialog box

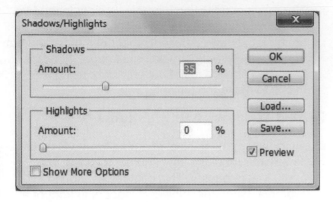

✓ *The default settings (35% Shadows, 0% Highlights) in the Shadows/Highlights dialog box are for correcting a backlit subject.*

■ Click the Show More Options check box to expand the dialog box, adding additional Tonal Width and Radius sliders for the Shadows and Highlights sections, as well as an Adjustments section. Discussing all of these controls is beyond the scope of this book, but if you have an image that needs more detailed shadow and highlight correction, you can experiment with and preview the additional available settings.

Photoshop Extra

HDR Toning

Just below the Shadows/Highlights command on the Adjustments sublayer is a new adjustment option in Photoshop CS5, HDR Toning. HDR stands for "high dynamic range," a type of imaging in which multiple photographs taken at different exposures are merged to create an image that could not be captured in one single exposure. HDR imaging is a professional-level topic beyond the scope of this book, but you may want to explore this feature to see the interesting way you can manipulate the appearance of any image.

PROCEDURES

Apply a Photo Filter

1. Click **Create a new Photo Filter adjustment layer** icon in Adjustments panel.
2. Click a filter in the **Filter** list.

   OR

   Click **Color** and use the color box to choose the filter color.
3. Drag the **Density** slider as desired.

Correct Exposure

1. Click **Create a new Exposure adjustment layer** icon in Adjustments panel.
2. Drag the **Exposure** slider as desired.
3. Drag the **Offset** slider as desired.

4. Drag the **Gamma Correction** slider as desired.

   ✓ *The eyedropper buttons in the Exposure panel enable you to further control the exposure correction by setting the black, white, and gray points in the image tones.*

Adjust Vibrance

1. Click **Create a new Vibrance adjustment layer** icon ▼ in Adjustments panel.
2. Drag the **Vibrance** slider to the right to increase saturation proportionally.
3. Drag the **Saturation** slider to the right to increase saturation of all colors.

Correct Shadows and Highlights

1. Click **Image** .... ALT + I
2. Point to **Adjustments**.......... A
3. Click **Shadows/Highlights**......................... W
4. Drag the Shadows **Amount** slider as desired....... ALT + A , ↓ or ↑
5. Drag the Highlights **Amount** slider as desired....... ALT + U , ↓ or ↑

   ✓ *Pressing Alt + A toggles between the two amount sliders.*

6. Click **OK** .... ENTER

EXERCISE DIRECTIONS

1. Open the ⊙48Sign file and save it as 48Sign_xx. Copy the Background layer, hide it, and work on Background copy.

2. Apply a Photo Filter adjustment layer and select the **Sepia** filter with a **50%** Density setting. Compare the result of the adjustment with the previous state. The change isn't very effective.

3. Restore default settings for the adjustment and then apply **Cooling Filter (80)** with a **30%** Density setting.

4. The color tones are better, but the image looks a bit flat. Apply an Exposure adjustment layer to set the Exposure to **+0.80**.

5. The image is now bright enough, but it still needs some richness of color. Apply a Vibrance adjustment layer and change Saturation to **+25**. Illustration A shows the original data file on the left, and a corrected version that your file should resemble on the right.

6. Save your changes, close the file, and exit Photoshop.

Illustration A

ON YOUR OWN

1. Open the ⊙OYO48 file and save it as OPH48_xx. Copy the Background layer and work from the copy.

2. This example photo was taken on an overcast day, with the subject located on a covered porch. That means the photo looks a bit too cool, is flat due to the low lighting conditions, and is slightly backlit. Use the correction tools described in this exercise, as well as any of the color correction tools covered in earlier exercises, to improve the photo's appearance.

   ✓ *If red or orange tones make an image look overly warm to you, try a filter in the magenta or violet range.*

   ✓ *Be careful if increasing the exposure on this image. Because the table surface is glass with reflections, too much exposure can cause the left side of the table, which has a heavy reflection, to wash out completely. One solution is to select the bouquet and vase, and correct the exposure for that selection alone. Or, try using the Shadows/Highlights command, instead.*

3. Open the original data file, so that you can compare the colors in the original and corrected versions of the image. Close the original data file.

4. Save your changes, close the file, and exit Photoshop.

Exercise | 49

Skills Covered

- Dodge an Area
- Burn an Area
- Sponge an Area
- Blur an Area
- Sharpen an Area
- Smudge an Area

Software Skills Photoshop offers tools to enable you to dodge an image to lighten all or part of the image or burn an image to darken all or part of the image, as well as sponge (change color saturation), blur, sharpen, and smudge. Learn to use all these tools to make image corrections in this exercise.

Design Skills A designer does not have to be an expert photographer to adjust images using tools such as Dodge, Burn, Sponge, Smudge, Blur, and Sharpen. Careful use of these tools allow a designer to correct image problems as well as enhance image appearance for special effects.

Application Skills The magazine *Midwest Gardening Today* has sent you an image they want to use in an upcoming issue. Use the correction tools described in this exercise to adjust and enhance the image.

TERMS

Burn In photography, refers to increasing apparent exposure in an area of a photo print.

Dodge In photography, refers to decreasing apparent exposure in an area of a photo print.

NOTES

Dodge an Area

- When making a print from a film negative, a darkroom guru would prevent light from hitting a selected area of the photo paper to **dodge** that area. Dodging would reduce the exposure in that area of the print to compensate for overexposure in the negative or to simply create a lighter area in the print as a special effect.

- The Dodge tool 🔍 enables you to reduce exposure or lighten shadows, midtones, or highlights in an area of an image. You dodge an image by painting with the Dodge tool, dragging on the image after choosing the tool settings.

- In Figure 49-1, the Dodge tool is being used to lighten the feathers below the bird's beak.

Figure 49-1. Lighten an area using the Dodge tool

- Use the Brush Preset picker on the options bar to specify brush settings. Choose whether to dodge Shadows, Midtones, or Highlights from the Range list on the options bar. Adjust the Exposure setting to control the amount of lightening, and specify airbrush capabilities if desired.

- As in Figure 49-1, where excess dodging was applied for emphasis, too much dodging can cause a loss of color and detail in the dodged area.

- It's good practice to press and hold the mouse button while continuously dragging to apply the full dodge. That way, a simple Undo will remove the dodge so you can adjust settings and reapply dodging.

Burn an Area

- Burning is the opposite of dodging. When making a print from a film negative, the darkroom printmaker would allow additional light to strike a selected area of the photo to **burn** that area. Burning would increase the exposure in that area of the print to compensate for underexposure in the negative or to simply create a darker area in the print as a special effect.

- The Burn tool ⬛ enables you to increase exposure or darken shadows, midtones, or highlights in an area of an image. You paint on the Burn tool effect, dragging on the image after choosing the tool settings, as shown in Figure 49-2.

Figure 49-2. Darken an area using the Burn tool

- In areas that are dramatically over- or underexposed, the Burn tool will tend to enhance details that may have been lost. However, if you over-apply the Burn tool, the areas being corrected may become too dark, so that details become obscured in the shadow. So, use the Burn tool sparingly at first, adding additional burning in increments.

- Use the Brush Preset picker on the options bar to specify brush settings. Choose whether to burn Shadows, Midtones, or Highlights from the Range list on the options bar. Adjust the Exposure setting to control the amount of darkening, and specify airbrush capabilities if desired.

Sponge an Area

- Dodging or burning an area in the image makes it lighter or darker. To enhance or reduce the color saturation in a particular area in the image, instead, use the Sponge tool ⬛.

- Use the Brush Preset picker on the options bar to specify brush settings. Choose whether to Saturate or Desaturate from the Mode list on the options bar. Adjust the Flow setting to control the amount of change, and specify airbrush capabilities if desired. Then drag on the areas to sponge on the image.

  ✓ *Unless you set the Flow to a rather high setting, the effects of the Sponge tool tend to be very subtle.*

Blur an Area

- Getting a digital camera to focus and produce an image that's sharp and crisp can sometimes be a tricky task. So the notion of intentionally blurring an area of the image may seem silly. However, adding blur to selected areas in an image can enhance naturalism and minimize flaws.

- For example, when you paste a selection into a new layer in an image, you may want to add blur around the edges to help the pasted content blend more effectively with any background or surrounding objects.

  ✓ *Portrait photographers often use soft lighting and filters that introduce a fog or blur effect. The resulting softening helps minimize unwanted details in the subject's appearance, such as facial lines, blemishes, and the like.*

- Use the Blur tool ⬛ to paint blurring onto an image. Figure 49-3 shows the Blur tool painting a blur at the left side of the bird.

Figure 49-3. Blurring applied to the left side of the bird softens the edge

- Use the Brush Preset picker on the options bar to specify brush settings. Choose a blending mode from the Mode list on the options bar. Adjust the Strength setting to control the amount of blurring.

  ✓ *A larger, softer brush shape typically yields more subtle and natural blurring.*

Sharpen an Area

■ The Sharpen tool  can help enhance detail, particularly in an edge where two colors abut in the image. However, applying too much of the Sharpen tool can have unwanted consequences such as changing the color of pixels in the surrounding area, so use this tool sparingly.

■ Use the Brush Preset picker on the options bar to specify brush settings. Choose a blending mode from the Mode list on the options bar. Adjust the Strength setting to control the amount of sharpening.

Smudge an Area

■ The icon for the Smudge tool 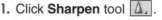 perfectly represents the tool's operation. The Smudge tool enables you to distort and reposition content in an image, as if the image is a puddle of paint that you drag your finger through.

■ Figure 49-4 shows a very obvious smudge applied to the bird. You will generally use this tool to create more subtle effects.

Figure 49-4. Smudging across the bird's beak

■ Use the Brush Preset picker on the options bar to specify brush settings. Choose a blending mode from the Mode list on the options bar. Adjust the Strength setting to control the amount of smudging.

■ By default, the Smudge tool picks up the colors in the mouse pointer when you drag. If you check the Finger Painting check box on the options bar, the Smudge tool smudges on the current foreground color.

PROCEDURES

Dodge an Area

1. Click **Dodge** tool
   ............O or SHIFT + O
2. Choose brush from **Brush picker** on options bar.
3. Choose **Range** to dodge on options bar.
4. Specify **Exposure** on options bar.
5. Specify whether to enable airbrush capabilities on options bar.
6. Drag on image.

Burn an Area

1. Click **Burn** tool
   ............O or SHIFT + O
2. Choose brush from **Brush picker** on options bar.
3. Choose **Range** to burn on options bar.
4. Specify **Exposure** on options bar.
5. Specify whether to enable airbrush capabilities on options bar.
6. Drag on image.

Sponge an Area

1. Click **Sponge** tool
   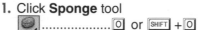............O or SHIFT + O
2. Choose brush from **Brush picker** on options bar.
3. Choose sponge **Mode** on options bar.
4. Specify **Flow** on options bar.
5. Specify whether to enable airbrush capabilities on options bar.
6. Drag on image.

Blur an Area

1. Click **Blur** tool 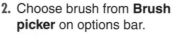.
2. Choose brush from **Brush picker** on options bar.
3. Choose blur **Mode** on options bar.
4. Specify **Strength** on options bar.
5. Drag on image.

Sharpen an Area

1. Click **Sharpen** tool 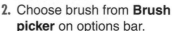.
2. Choose brush from **Brush picker** on options bar.
3. Choose sharpen **Mode** on options bar.
4. Specify **Strength** on options bar.
5. Drag on image.

Smudge an Area

1. Click **Smudge** tool 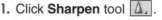.
2. Choose brush from **Brush picker** on options bar.
3. Choose smudge **Mode** on options bar.
4. Specify **Strength** on options bar.
5. (Optional) Click **Finger Painting** on options bar.
6. Drag on image.

EXERCISE DIRECTIONS

1. Open the 49Flower file and save the file as 49Flower_xx. Copy the Background layer and work on the Background copy. Display the History panel so you can easily reverse your changes if desired.

2. Use the Dodge tool to slightly lighten and bring out the detail in the lower-left corner and the dark area below the yellow flower. Choose a **30** px round soft brush, **Highlights** as the Range, and **25%** as the Exposure.

3. Use the Burn tool to add some exposure to the upper-right and lower-right corners. Choose a **45** px round soft brush, **Highlights** as the Range, and **25%** as the Exposure.

4. Use the Blur tool to soften the upper-right, lower-right, and lower-left corners. Choose a **45** px round soft brush and **75%** as the Strength.

5. Use the Sponge tool to desaturate the red flower at the top of the image. Choose a **35** px round soft brush, **Desaturate** as the Mode, and **50%** as the Flow.

6. Use the Sponge tool to saturate the color of the furled flower in the upper-left corner of the image, the small, pointed flower buds to left and right of the yellow flower, and the bright green leaves near the upper-left corner and to the right of the yellow flower. Choose a **35** px round soft brush, **Saturate** as the Mode, and **50%** as the Flow.

7. You may also want to try saturating the yellow flower using a large, soft brush and a low flow rate to make the effect subtle. Your corrected image might resemble Illustration A.

8. Save your changes, close the file, and exit Photoshop.

Illustration A

ON YOUR OWN

1. Open the OYO49 file and save the file as OPH49_xx.

2. Use the Blur tool on the Roses layer to blur the edges of the rose content, which was copied from another image and pasted as a new layer in the current image.

3. The violet rose near the top stands out a bit too much. Desaturate it with the Sponge tool.

✓ As this example shows, you have to be a little careful when using the Sponge tool to desaturate. If you're too aggressive, the area being desaturated starts to take on a gray tone.

4. The pink rose in the front looks a bit overexposed, so burn it in slightly with the Burn tool.

5. Smudge the blue vase to deemphasize it.

6. Save your changes, close the file, and exit Photoshop.

Skills Covered

- Crop an Image
- Rotate the Canvas
- Change the Canvas Size

- Change Image Dimensions and Resolution
- Use Content-Aware Scaling
- Use Puppet Warp to Modify an Image

Software Skills Crop an image to better frame the subject and discard unneeded image content. You also can correct the rotation of any image. Adjust the size of the canvas to make room for additional content. Change image size when you need to fit the image in a particular space. Use content-aware scaling to adjust image size while leaving important parts of the image unchanged. Adjust image resolution to control the quality of the image. The new Puppet Warp feature can be used to correct or distort an image for a special effect.

Design Skills A designer must work closely with the supplier who will handle image output to determine the best size and resolution for the image. Presenting an image to its best advantage may require a designer to resize the image, crop areas, rotate the canvas, or even modify the canvas size.

Application Skills In this exercise, you will work with an image for Wilcox Travel to rotate the image, crop the image, adjust canvas size and image dimensions, scale the image, and change the image resolution.

TERMS

Canvas The "page" that holds image content.

Crop To remove unwanted image information, thus reducing the image size.

Document (image) size Combination of current output size plus current resolution.

Framing How a photo's subject is positioned in the overall image.

Interpolation Calculation method Photoshop uses to add pixels when adjusting image size.

Pixel dimensions The height and width of an image in pixels (also referred to as the *file size* of an image).

Resample Making a change to the pixel size of an image, resulting in a change to its display size.

NOTES

Crop an Image

- When you **crop** an image, Photoshop removes image content outside of the selection marquee, thus changing the image **canvas** size and shape.

- Cropping enables you to change how the subject appears to be **framed** or positioned in the image. Dramatic cropping—where you move away from having the subject centered in the frame—adds interest to the image.

- You have two options for cropping an image. You can crop to any selection, or you can use the Crop tool to draw a rectangular marquee that defines the crop area.

- To crop to a selection, use the selection tool of your choice to select the area to keep in the image, and then choose Image > Crop.

- Photoshop immediately crops the image to the selection size. If the selection was a shape other than a square or a rectangle, Photoshop crops a rectangular area that encloses the selection, as shown in Figure 50-1.

✓ Because you can't preview a crop with this method, immediately press Ctrl + Z if you don't like the results.

✓ If you've made a nonrectangular selection and want to crop everything outside of the selection to transparency (thus creating a vignette effect), choose Select > Inverse, delete the inverted selection, and then crop the canvas to the desired size.

- Use the Crop tool 🔲 to crop an image to a rectangular shape without making a selection first.

- Use the Crop tool to drag a cropping marquee on the image. This marquee has handles you can use to adjust each side of the marquee to frame the area you want to crop.

- Photoshop CS5 automatically displays a Crop Guide Overlay on the cropping marquee to help you make an accurate and attractive crop. By default, Photoshop displays the Rule of Thirds grid, shown in Figure 50-2. The "rule of thirds" is a rule designers often use to position the focus of an image off center according to a grid that divides the image horizontally and vertically into thirds.

Figure 50-1. The cropped version of this image appears below

Figure 50-2. Rule of Thirds grid on an image to be cropped

- Note in Figure 50-2 that the yellow flower is just about dead center according to the Rule of Thirds grid. To crop this image according to the rule of thirds, drag the cropping marquee handles until the flower is positioned near an intersection of grid lines. Figure 50-3 shows one crop that might result in a more visually interesting image.

Figure 50-3. Adjust a cropping marquee to crop an image attractively

Drag handle to resize cropping marquee

- You can also choose a plain grid to overlay the cropping marquee, or no grid.
- Adjust the crop size and location by dragging the cropping marquee or its handles. When the crop zone appears as you want it to, click the Commit button on the options bar.

  ✓ *If you move the mouse pointer outside the cropping zone boundary, it becomes a corner pointer with arrows. That means that you can drag to rotate the cropping marquee. The resulting image will use the content contained within the rotated marquee.*

- Instead of dragging on the image, you can choose the Crop tool, enter a crop Width and Height and specify a new Resolution on the options bar, and then drag on the image to set the cropping marquee. When you apply the crop, the resulting image will be converted to the specified width, height, and resolution.

  ✓ *Make sure you specify **px** for pixels or **in** for inches with the heights and widths you specify.*

- The Shield check box, when enabled, displays a tinted shield over the areas that will be cropped away. Use the Color and Opacity settings to adjust the shield, if desired.

Rotate the Canvas

- It is not uncommon to turn a camera sideways to capture a tall subject. A photo taken with this orientation will display in a rotated orientation, as shown in Figure 50-4.

Figure 50-4. The camera was rotated to take this picture

- To work with a photo such as the one shown in Figure 50-4, you must rotate the canvas clockwise or counterclockwise. Use the choices on the Image > Image Rotation submenu to apply the desired rotation.

  ✓ *Using this command to rotate an image is considered to be a destructive change, because it cannot be easily undone.*

- You can choose to rotate the image by 180 degrees (completely upside down), by 90 degrees clockwise or counterclockwise, or by a value you specify.

  ✓ *If you think of a clock face, 90 degrees clockwise is 3 o'clock, 180 degrees is 6 o'clock, and 90 degrees counterclockwise is 9 o'clock.*

- Photoshop rotates all layers to the specified position. If you want to rotate only the content on a specified layer, make a selection and use a command on the Edit > Transform submenu to apply the rotation.

Photoshop Extra

Flip a Canvas

You can use Image > Image Rotation > Flip Canvas Horizontal or Flip Canvas Vertical to reverse the canvas left to right or top to bottom.

Change the Canvas Size

■ If you're adding content to an image and find that there's not room to place it where you'd like, you can increase the canvas size to add more working space around the existing content in the image.

■ Choose Image > Canvas Size to open the Canvas Size dialog box, shown in Figure 50-5. Enter the desired new Width and/or Height. (Or, check Relative and enter the amounts by which to increase or decrease the Width and/or Height.)

Figure 50-5. Canvas Size dialog box

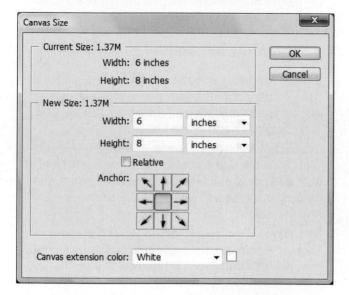

■ If you want to add the new space toward one side or the top or bottom (rather than equally around the image), click the desired Anchor location; the arrows will indicate where Photoshop will add the space.

■ If the image doesn't have a transparent background and you want the added canvas to use a color other than white, open the Canvas extension color list to choose the desired color (Foreground, Background, and so on).

Change Image Dimensions and Resolution

■ Changing canvas size can give you more room to add content to an existing image. Changing image dimensions, by comparison, adjusts the actual dimensions of the image itself.

■ The process of adjusting image size may also involve changing the image's resolution. As you learned at the beginning of the Illustrator section of this course, *resolution* refers to the number of pixels per inch (ppi) used to output an image.

■ You use the Image Size dialog box, shown in Figure 50-6, to adjust both image dimensions and resolution.

Figure 50-6. Choose new image size and resolution settings here

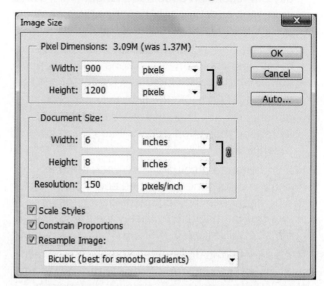

■ The **pixel dimensions** of an image, shown at the top of the Image Size dialog box, consist of the number of pixels across its width and along its height. The pixel dimensions and the resolution determine the amount of image data and the file size of the image.

■ The central area of the dialog box contains settings for printed output, usually measured in inches. The combination of printed size measurements and resolution is the **document size**.

■ Settings in this dialog box can be adjusted by typing new values as desired.

■ When changing image dimensions or resolution, you need to consider whether you want to **resample** the image when adjusting it.

■ Resampling changes the amount of image data in the file when you change either the pixel dimensions or the resolution of the image.

■ Making an image smaller, for example, actually reduces the number of image pixels in the file and thus changes the amount of image data and the file's size. Similarly, enlarging an image adds pixels to the image.

■ Photoshop uses a process called **interpolation** to calculate how to remove or add pixels when resampling is on.

✓ *Interpolation methods are a professional-level topic beyond the scope of this book.*

- When resampling is on, the pixel, document size, and resolution settings interact with each other in the following ways:
  - When you change pixel dimensions first, the document size dimensions change proportionally but resolution does not change. The file size increases or decreases, depending on whether you increased or decreased pixel dimensions.
  - Likewise, if you change document size measurements first, the pixel dimensions adjust proportionally and file size increases or decreases.
  - If you change resolution first, only the pixel dimensions adjust. File size increases if you increased resolution or decreases if you lowered resolution.
  - If you change resolution first, you can then change pixel dimensions and see a corresponding change in the document size measurements. The resolution will stay the same, but the file size will adjust.
- To add complexity to an already thought-provoking subject, you can instead choose to turn off resampling. With resampling off, the pixel dimensions area becomes inactive and a direct relationship forms between the document size measurements and the resolution.
- With resampling off, changing the document size will adjust its resolution to a value that will maintain the same amount of image data. For example, if an image is currently 17 inches wide at a resolution of 72, adjusting the image width to 8 inches will bump resolution up to about 160.
- Likewise, adjusting resolution will change the image dimensions to a size that will maintain the same amount of image data. Thus, resizing or changing resolution with resampling off results in the same file size.
- When deciding whether or not to use resampling as you resize or change resolution, consider these points:
  - Because resampling either throws away or adds image data, a resampled image may not look as crisp and clean as the original, although the impact will be less noticeable if you are reducing image size.
  - An image that is not resampled when it is resized will have superior image quality, but the file may be quite large.

- Also consider the end use of the image. If the image will be used for onscreen viewing, a resolution of 72 ppi is usually adequate, and a smaller file size will improve download time.
- For printed output, consider the print quality of the publication where the image will be used. A 150-ppi image may print fine in regular documents and newspaper-quality publications. Most magazines and other full-color or high-quality publications require 300 ppi or better. Also shoot for 300 ppi or better when making high-quality photo printouts from an inkjet or photo printer.

  ✓ If you're unsure what resolution to use, consult the publication designer or printing company for guidance.

Use Content-Aware Scaling

- Photoshop offers another option for adjusting image size: content-aware scaling. This feature allows you to adjust an image's size without resizing important parts of the image.
- Figure 50-7 shows an image of Seattle's Space Needle at left and a scaled version at right. Notice that even though the scaled image is shorter and narrower, the Space Needle is the same size as in the original.
- Use the Edit > Content-Aware Scaling command to display a point of origin and scaling handles on the image. (This command is not available for the Background layer.) Drag the handles as desired to resize the image and then commit the change.
- This feature recognizes some types of content automatically, such as people and structures like the Space Needle. If the feature does not automatically recognize the content you want to protect during the scale, you can manually protect content.

Figure 50-7. Original image (left) and image resized using content-aware scaling (right)

■ To specify what content to protect, draw a selection marquee around the area and click the Save selection as channel button ▣ at the bottom of the Channels panel, which is behind the Layers panel. This action saves the selection as an alpha channel.

✓ *You learn more about alpha channels in the next lesson.*

■ Then, after selecting the Content-Aware Scaling command, click the Protect list arrow on the options bar and choose the alpha channel you saved. You can then scale the image as desired without affecting the protected area.

■ The options bar displays other helpful tools for scaling. You can watch X and Y coordinates as you scale, as well as width and height percentages. You can also use the Protect skin tones option to preserve natural skin tones during the scale.

Use Puppet Warp to Modify an Image

■ Puppet Warp is a whimsically named new feature in Photoshop CS5 that allows you to rearrange the content of an image by dragging at specific areas in the image. This feature lets you actually rearrange the pixels in an image to adjust its composition or create a special effect.

✓ *Like content-aware scaling, this feature cannot be used on the Background layer.*

■ Selecting Edit > Puppet Warp places a mesh over an image. Click at any point to drop a "pin" on the mesh, as shown in Figure 50-8.

Figure 50-8. Puppet Warp grid with pins

■ To warp the image, click on any pin and drag in the direction you want to adjust the pixels. The mesh stretches from the pin locations to create the warp.

■ If your goal is to distort the image, select Distort from the Mode list on the options bar. This mode allows for easier and more radical movement of the pins.

■ To have more control over the warp, select More Points from the Density option on the options bar. To see how the warp looks before committing the change, deselect Show Mesh on the options bar. You see the location of the pins and the warped appearance, as shown in Figure 50-9.

Figure 50-9. Warp with the mesh hidden

■ You can delete a single pin if it isn't in the right place. Or, if you want to start over, click Remove all pins ↻ on the options bar. All pins are removed and the mesh is restored to its original appearance. When you are satisfied with the warp, click the Commit button.

■ You can use Puppet Warp on text objects for interesting effects if you first rasterize the text to convert it to a pixel object.

✓ *You learn more about rasterizing vector objects in Exercise 57.*

■ Puppet Warp can require patience. The actual warping may not be nearly as fast as the action of moving a pin, so you may need to wait for the warp to "catch up" before you move another pin.

PROCEDURES

Crop an Image to a Selection

1. Use the desired method to make a selection.
2. Click **Image** .... `ALT` + `I`
3. Click **Crop** .... `P`

Use the Crop Tool

1. Click **Crop** tool `⛏` .... `C`
2. (Optional) Specify **Width**, **Height**, and **Resolution** for resulting cropped image on options bar.
3. Drag on image.
4. (Optional) Click Crop Guide Overlay list arrow and select **None**, **Rule of Thirds**, or **Grid**.
5. Drag or resize **cropping marquee** as desired.
6. Click the **Commit** button `✓` on the options bar .... `ENTER`

Rotate the Canvas

To rotate by a preset amount:

1. Click **Image** .... `ALT` + `I`
2. Point to **Image Rotation** ...... `G`
3. Click one of the following rotations:
   - **180°** .... `1`
   - **90° CW** .... `9`
   - **90° CCW** .... `0`

To rotate an arbitrary amount:

1. Click **Image** .... `ALT` + `I`
2. Point to **Image Rotation** ...... `G`
3. Click **Arbitrary** .... `A`
4. Type degrees to rotate.
5. Click °**CW** .... `ALT` + `C`

   OR

   Click °**CCW** .... `ALT` + `W`
6. Click **OK** .... `ENTER`

Change the Canvas Size
(Alt + Ctrl + C)

1. Click **Image** .... `ALT` + `I`
2. Click **Canvas Size** .... `S`
3. Type **Width** .... `ALT` + `W`
4. Type **Height** .... `ALT` + `H`

   ✓ *Click the Relative check box to check it before Step 3 to enter relative width changes.*

5. Click desired **Anchor** point.
6. (Optional) Specify **Canvas extension color** .... `ALT` + `C` , `↓`
7. Click **OK** .... `ENTER`

Change Image Dimensions
(Alt + Ctrl + I)

1. Click **Image** .... `ALT` + `I`
2. Click **Image Size** .... `I`
3. (Optional) Click **Constrain Proportions** .... `ALT` + `C`
4. Enter new Pixel Dimensions:
   - **Width** .... `ALT` + `W`
   - **Height** .... `ALT` + `H`

   OR

   Enter new Document Size:
   - **Width** .... `ALT` + `D`
   - **Height** .... `ALT` + `G`
5. Click **OK** .... `ENTER`

Change Image Resolution
(Alt + Ctrl + I)

1. Click **Image** .... `ALT` + `I`
2. Click **Image Size** .... `I`
3. Type new **Resolution** . `ALT` + `R`
4. Adjust image Pixel Dimensions as required based on the change.
5. Click **OK** .... `ENTER`

Use Content-Aware Scaling
(Alt + Shift + Ctrl + C)

With a normal layer displayed:

1. Click **Edit** .... `ALT` + `E`
2. Click **Content-Aware Scale** .... `C`
3. Drag scaling handles to adjust image width or height.
4. Confirm or cancel the transformation.

To protect an area from scaling:

Before issuing the Content-Aware Scale command:

1. Use a selection tool to select the area to be protected.
2. Display the **Channels** panel (behind the Layers panel).
3. Click **Save selection as channel** button `▣` .

   ✓ *You can double-click on the default Alpha 1 channel name and type a more meaningful name. If you do so, deselect the channel after renaming and turn on visibility for the other channels in the panel. Select all channels.*

4. Deselect the selection.
5. Click **Edit** .... `ALT` + `E`
6. Click **Content-Aware Scale** .... `C`
7. On the options bar, click the **Protect** down arrow and select the name of the channel you created in step 3.
8. Drag scaling handles to adjust image width or height.
9. Confirm or cancel the transformation.

Use Puppet Warp

1. Click **Edit**...................ALT + E
2. Click **Puppet Warp**.
3. Click on the mesh to position pins.
4. Drag any pin in the direction to warp content.
5. Commit or cancel the warp.

To adjust Puppet Warp options:

- To distort the entire image, click the **Mode** list arrow and select **Distort**.

- To allow for more pins and finer control over the mesh, click the **Density** list arrow and select **More Points**.
- To see the result of the warp before committing the change, deselect **Show Mesh**.
- To remove the pins, click **Remove all pins** ⟳.
- To remove a single pin, right-click on the pin and click **Delete Pin**.

To apply Puppet Warp to type:

1. Select the type layer you want to warp.
2. Click **Edit**...................ALT + E
3. Click **Puppet Warp**.
4. When prompted to rasterize text, click **OK** ....ENTER
5. Drop pins as desired, warp the letters, and commit the warp.

EXERCISE DIRECTIONS

1. Open the ⊙ **50Arch** file and save it as **50Arch_xx**. Display the rulers if necessary and the Info panel.

2. Rotate the image 90 degrees counterclockwise.

3. Use the Image > Image Rotation > Arbitrary command and specify **-1** degree CW rotation to straighten the image a bit.

4. Adjust the zoom to 50% if necessary so you can see the whole image. Select the Crop tool and drag the cropping marquee over the entire canvas. Crop the image as follows:

   a. Drag the left center cropping marquee handle to the right until the left leg of the arch is just to the left of the left vertical "rule of thirds" gridline.

   b. Drag the right center cropping marquee handle to the left just far enough to eliminate the white edge at the upper-right corner resulting from the rotation of the image.

   c. Drag the bottom center marquee handle up to the 15.5-inch mark on the vertical ruler.

   d. Drag the top center marquee handle down until the H measurement on the Info panel is about 15.0. Commit the crop.

5. Change the resolution of the image to 100 (with Resample Image selected), and then adjust its width to 6 inches. The Height measurement should change automatically.

6. Display the image at 75% size.

7. Change the canvas size to 6 inches wide by 8.5 inches high, and click the top center arrow in the Anchor box to anchor the new space to the bottom of the image. Make sure the new canvas area will be white.

8. The image is still a bit large for your use. Use content-aware scaling as follows:

   a. Make a copy of the Background layer, hide the Background layer, and select the Background copy layer.

   b. Issue the Content-Aware Scale command, and pull in the left and right sides half an inch. Notice as you do that the shadowed figures below the arch do not change size, but unfortunately, the arch does.

   c. Cancel the transformation.

   d. Protect the arch and the figures below it: Use the Rectangular Marquee to draw a selection around the entire arch and the figures. Save the selection as a channel with the default name.

   e. Deselect the selection. Issue the Content-Aware Scale command again, and on the options bar, choose Alpha 1 from the Protect list.

   f. Pull the top handle down one-quarter inch, pull in the left and right sides one-quarter inch, and pull up the bottom three-quarters of an inch, noticing that this time, the arch remains the same size. Accept the transformation

9. Add text in the new canvas area as shown in Illustration A. Use a font and a font size of your choice, and pick up a font color from the image.

10. On the Layers panel menu, select Flatten Image, and then throw away hidden layers when prompted. The resulting image should look similar to Illustration A.

11. Save your changes, close the file, and exit Photoshop.

Delicate Arch
Arches National Park

ON YOUR OWN

1. Open the ⊙OYO50 file and save it as OPH50_*xx*. Copy the *Background* layer and work on the copy.

   ✓ *Your task in this exercise is to have fun with this roller-coaster track image using Puppet Warp. Your ultimate goal is to create a wild-looking image that can be used in an advertisement for the WildWood coaster at a local amusement park.*

2. Apply the Puppet Warp mesh to the image. You may want to select the Distort mode and the More Points Density.

3. Drop pins as desired and adjust them to warp the guardrails and the coaster tracks.

4. When you are satisfied with the warp, commit the change.

5. Crop away any areas of the canvas revealed by the warp.

6. Change resolution of the image to 100, with resampling on, and adjust image width to 8 inches.

7. If time allows, use a fairly heavy font and a large font size and type **TAKE A RIDE ON THE WILD SIDE**. Choose to apply Puppet Warp to the text layer, rasterize the type, and then warp the word WILD to create a special effect.

8. Save your changes, close the file, and exit Photoshop.

Exercise | 51

Summary Exercise

→

Application Skills Wilcox Tours has some great beach vacation packages to offer to its customers. You've got a photo of a beach, but it needs some color correction before you can use it in promotional mailings.

EXERCISE DIRECTIONS

1. Open the 🔘 51Beach file and save it as 51Beach_xx. Copy the Background layer, hide Background, and work on the Background copy layer.

2. Apply the Auto Color command to adjust colors. You should see quite a difference after this adjustment.

3. The upper-right and lower-right corners are too dark to correct easily. Select these areas and apply content-aware fill to replace the dark areas.

4. Change the resolution of the image to 100 with resampling and the image size to 6 inches wide and a corresponding height.

5. Apply a Brightness/Contrast adjustment layer to change both brightness and contrast to **+10**.

6. Apply a Photo Filter adjustment layer and select the Cooling Filter (LBB) to give the photo a cooler cast.

7. There is a spot just above the water near the center of the image. Use the Spot Healing Brush tool to remove the flaw. (Don't forget to select the Background copy layer to make this correction.)

8. Use the Healing Brush tool to smooth out some of the uneven colors in the beach, including the footprints.

9. Use the Clone Stamp tool to clone the solitary gull in the image. If desired, display the Clone Source panel and apply a rotation value such as 20 so that the cloned gull will not look identical to the original one. You may also want to change the size for the cloned gull.

10. Use the Burn tool to slightly darken the beach at the tide line to create some contrast between the foam and the sand.

11. Use the Sponge tool with the Saturate setting in the options bar to give a richer color to the water at the horizon and the purplish band of sky just above the water.

12. Use the Smudge tool to blur the clouds at the upper-left side of the image so they are paler and wispier. Your image should look similar to Illustration A.

13. Save your changes, close the file, and exit Photoshop.

Exercise | 52

Application Exercise

Application Skills   You run a small business called Memento Photography. You not only take studio pictures and pictures at special events such as weddings, but you also offer other services such as photo enhancements and corrections. A client has asked you to brighten up an archival wedding photo. Because the photo was taken at an evening wedding, it turned out dark.

EXERCISE DIRECTIONS

1. Open the ⊙ 52Bride file and save it as 52Bride_xx.

2. Use the Red Eye tool to eliminate the bride's red eye.

3. Use Auto Tone to adjust image tone.

4. Use a Levels adjustment layer or a Brightness/Contrast adjustment layer to lighten the image a bit.

   ✓ *Notice that you have to be careful with these adjustments. While you may be tempted to lighten the image further to bring out more of the wood paneling, doing so overwhitens the bride's dress, causing the loss of lace detail.*

5. Use the Dodge tool to lighten the shadows in and around the bride's face a bit. Lighten the woodwork as much as you can without creating other problems in the image appearance.

6. Use correction tools to repair some of the white spots and scratches that now show up in the wood paneled areas at the right and in the lower-left corner.

7. Make any other corrections you feel are needed, such as adding subtle sharpening.

8. Turn off resampling and change the image resolution to 150 ppi. Your corrected image might resemble Illustration A.

9. Save your changes, close the file, and exit Photoshop.

Illustration A

277

Curriculum Integration

Application Skills   For the last week or so, your science class has focused on entomology (the study of insects). Your instructor wants you to choose a species and create a poster about it. In this exercise, you will find an image online and develop your poster.

EXERCISE DIRECTIONS

Go to the New York Public Library's searchable gallery of digital images at http://digitalgallery.nypl.org/nypldigital. Use the SEARCH tool at the right side of the home page to search for **butterfl***. (Using the wildcard character finds all matching variations of the search term.)

Browse through the available butterfly images, and download the one that appeals to you. Be sure to pick one that identifies the butterfly species, because you'll need that information. (To download the image, view the enlarged version, right-click on it, and then use the Save Picture As command.) Save the image in JPEG format as 53Data_xx.

Open the 53Data_xx file in Photoshop and save it as a Photoshop image with the same name. Create a new image file 8 inches by 10 inches with a white background and a new transparent layer named Butterfly above the Background layer. Use Arrange Documents to tile the new file and the 53Data_xx file vertically. Return to the 53Data_xx file and adjust its color and tone as needed. Use the Clone Stamp tool to clone the butterfly from the original file into your poster file. (Set the point of origin for the Clone Stamp tool in the data file, then switch to the new file to do the clone painting.) Work on the Butterfly layer in the new image file. To easily remove the off-white background around the butterfly, use the Magic Eraser to delete the entire white background. Save and close the 53Data_xx file.

Straighten the butterfly image if necessary using arbitrary rotation, and move the image to the top center of the image area. Adjust color and tone as you think necessary.

Create a copy of the Butterfly layer and name it Shadow. Move the Shadow layer below the Butterfly layer and hide the Butterfly layer. Select the Shadow layer and use the Image > Adjustments > Desaturate command to create a black and white image. Then issue the Image > Adjustments > Exposure command and adjust settings to create a light gray version of the butterfly. Apply the Puppet Warp mesh and warp the butterfly in a fairly subtle way so that it will form a larger and somewhat irregular shadow of the original butterfly when the layers are rearranged, as shown in Illustration A.

Research the butterfly species online, add text about the butterfly to your poster, and then save the poster as 53Butterfly_xx. Your finished poster might resemble Illustration A.

Save your changes, close the file, and exit Photoshop.

Argynnis diana
Considered a Fritillary

Found only in a comparatively narrow range extending from West Virginia to Missouri, northward to Ohio and Indiana, and southward to Georgia and Arkansas

Females differ greatly from males in appearance

Portfolio Builder

Application Skills   You want to create a new ad for Newfound Nursery, but you want it to be jazzier than your last ad. Use a variety of the skills you've learned so far in this book to create the ad.

EXERCISE DIRECTIONS

- Open the ⊙ 54Newfound file and save it as 54Newfound_xx.
- Make sure resampling is on and adjust the image resolution to 100. The pixel dimensions should change.
- Copy the Background layer, hide the Background layer, and work on the Background copy layer.
- Select the entire layer with a rectangular marquee and use the Select > Modify > Border command to convert the selection to a 50 pixel border. Invert the selection.
- Apply a Levels adjustment layer. In the Levels settings, change the left Output Levels setting to **220**.
- Use the Eyedropper tool to sample a relatively dark color from the flower border on the Background copy layer to use as the foreground color.
- Use the Horizontal Type tool to add the following text using the fonts and sizes you prefer:

  Newfound Nursery
  Serving all your lawn and garden needs
  Visit us today at 22 Stack Road

- Move the text layer(s) to the top of the stack if necessary.
- Select the Background copy layer and insert a new blank layer. Sample a light color from the flower border to use as the foreground color.
- Working on the new layer (Layer 1) and hiding other layers if needed, create a Foreground to Transparent gradient. Set the opacity of the foreground color to about 70%. Drag from the top to the bottom so that the top area will be lightest. Redisplay any layers you hid.
- Save your changes, close the file, and exit Photoshop.

Lesson | 6

Explore Advanced Image Techniques

Skills Covered

- **Understand Paths**
- **Work with the Paths Panel**
- **Stroke or Fill a Path**
- **Load a Path as a Selection**

Software Skills Paths are vector-based selection outlines. You can use a path to add an easy-to-edit colored line or shape to the image. Or, you can simply save a path to load later as a selection. Photoshop enables you to add, save, stroke, fill, edit, and load paths.

Design Skills Learning how to create and modify paths gives a designer additional ways to select image areas and enhance image design. A designer should understand how Photoshop paths are similar to and also different from Illustrator paths.

Application Skills Metro Zoo has contacted you to work on a print ad for their Fall into Winter festival. You will use a supplied image as a basis for the ad, using the Pen tool and other paths to create the content.

TERMS

Path A vector outline with segments separated by anchor points.

Stroke To apply color to a path.

Work path The temporary name Photoshop assigns to a new path until you save the path under a new name.

NOTES

Understand Paths

- A **path** is a vector-based outline that you can use to add content or save selections in an image file. Paths do not print until you stroke or fill them.

- You have several options for creating a path:

  - As you learned in the first Photoshop lesson, you can create a path when drawing any line or shape if you select the Paths button 🖾 on the options bar. Figure 55-1 shows a path created using one of the Custom Shapes.

  - You can create a path from any selection you make in an image.

  - You can use the Pen tool to draw a path.

Figure 55-1. Path created using a custom shape

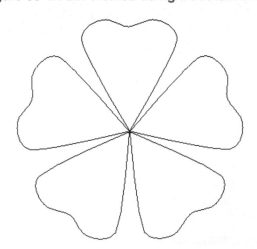

Use the Pen Tool

- The Pen tool 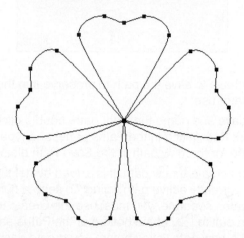 works the same way in Photoshop as in Illustrator.
  - Draw a straight line by clicking to place the first anchor point, then click again to create the straight segment.
  - Draw a curved line by clicking to place the first anchor point, drag to create the direction handles, then continue to click and drag to create the curved path.

- Unlike in Illustrator, however, the path does not automatically display a stroke or fill. You must add these attributes using the Paths panel.

- After you choose the Pen tool, you may notice that the options bar looks just like that for the shape tools. However, you cannot choose the Fill pixels button. You can click the Shape layers button if you want to create a shape vector mask filled with the foreground color. In most cases, you will leave Paths (the default button) selected to create a path.

- Photoshop also offers the Freeform Pen tool to draw a totally freeform path. If you choose this tool and then check the Magnetic check box on the options bar, it works much like the Magnetic Lasso tool, enabling you to create a path in the shape of an object already in the image. The path will snap to the colored edge of the object.

- As noted earlier, you can create a path from any selection. You can also create a selection from any path. The Pen tool, for example, is commonly used to create paths around objects or areas that are then converted to selections for further manipulation.

- Figure 55-2 shows the Pen tool being used to create a very accurate path around the Space Needle. This path can later be converted to a selection to manipulate the object or its surroundings.

Figure 55-2. Use the Pen tool to create an outline

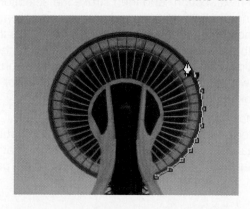

Select and Edit a Path

- To select a path, you use the Path Selection tool. Click on the path to show its anchor points, as shown in Figure 55-3.

Figure 55-3. Selected path

- You can move a selected path by dragging with the Path Selection tool.

- To adjust the path shape, use the Direct Selection tool to work with anchor points, as you learned in Illustrator. You can also use the Add Anchor Point, Delete Anchor Point, and Convert Point tools, beneath the Pen tool, to work with a path's anchor points.

- Once you are satisfied with the path, you can manipulate it in a variety of other ways. You use the Paths panel, covered next, to work with paths.

Design Suite Integration

Importing Paths

When working in InDesign, you can import a Photoshop path and use it as a clipping path to trim an object to the shape of the path.

Work with the Paths Panel

- Use the Paths panel to work with the paths in your image files. You can find the Paths panel in the same panel group with the Layers and Channels panels.

- When you first create a path, Photoshop considers it a **work path** (working path). Figure 55-4 on the next page shows a work path in the Paths panel. The path itself is clearly shown in the path listing.

Figure 55-4. A working path in the Paths panel

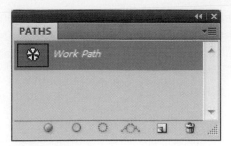

- You have to save the path to preserve it in the file for later use.

- To save and name the work path, double-click the Work Path listing in the Paths panel and type a name for the new path in the Save Path dialog box.

- If you create a new path, it is added by default to the currently active path listing. To keep a number of paths separate, you must use the Create new path button ⬛ at the bottom of the Paths panel to add a new path listing before you create each new path.

- You can convert any selection to a path using the Make work path from selection button ⬛ on the Paths panel. The current selection becomes a work path that you can save by naming.

- As you add paths to an image, they are listed in the Paths panel, as shown in Figure 55-5. To see a path in the image, you must select the path in the panel.

Figure 55-5. Multiple paths in an image

- To delete any path, drag it to the Delete current path button ⬛, or select it and click the Delete current path button, or select it with the Path Selection tool and press Delete.

Stroke or Fill a Path

- When you **stroke** a path, you paint the foreground color along the path boundary, effectively creating a drawn object in the shape of the path.

  ✓ *A path does not print unless you stroke or fill it.*

- By default, the path will be stroked using the currently selected foreground color and Brush tool settings. Figure 55-6 shows a path stroked with a blue foreground color and a 10 px hard round brush.

Figure 55-6. Custom shape path has been stroked with blue

- To stroke a path, first select the layer where you want to add the stroked path in the Layers panel. Then select the path in the Paths panel.

  ✓ *You can stroke a path on more than one layer in an image.*

- Choose the desired foreground color. Then choose the Brush tool and use the Brush Preset picker to choose the desired brush shape and size. Adjust any other settings as needed, and then click the Stroke path with brush button ⬛ at the bottom of the Paths panel.

- You also can load a path as a selection (covered in the next section) and then stroke the selection using the Edit > Stroke command, as you learned to do in Exercise 40. That command strokes the path with a solid line rather than giving you the option of choosing a softer or more artistic brush. However, it does provide blending options for the stroked content.

- When you fill a path, you paint the currently selected foreground color within the path boundary, creating a solid object in the shape of the path. Figure 55-7 on the next page shows a filled path.

Figure 55-7. Filled path

- To fill a path, first select the layer where you want to add the filled path in the Layers panel. Then select the path in the Paths panel. Choose the desired foreground color, and then click the Fill path with foreground color button ⬤ at the bottom of the Paths panel.

  ✓ *You also can load a path as a selection and then fill the selection using the Edit > Fill command. This command provides blending options for the filled content.*

- Path strokes and fills are not attached in any way to the path. If you stroke or fill a path and then decide to move or adjust the path, the stroke or fill does not reflect those changes. Apply path fill and stroke only when you are sure the path is final, and apply stroke and fill on separate layers that are easy to discard if you need to restroke or refill.

Load a Path as a Selection

- You can load a saved path as a selection marquee in the shape of the path on any layer in the image file.

- To load a path as a selection, first select the layer where you want to make the selection in the Layers panel. Then select the path in the Paths panel. Click the Load path as a selection button ◯ at the bottom of the Paths panel.

  ✓ *Do not confuse this button with the Stroke path with brush button. The two buttons look very much alike.*

- Once you have loaded a path as a selection, you can manipulate the selection just as you would any selection: move it, invert it, stroke or fill it, or save it.

PROCEDURES

Create a Shape Path

1. Click desired shape tool in toolbox .... U or SHIFT + U
2. Click **Paths** button 🖉 on options bar.
3. Drag in image window to create path.

Create a Path with the Pen Tool

1. Click **Pen** tool
   🖉 .... P or SHIFT + P
2. Click or click and drag to position first anchor point.
3. Click or drag to position subsequent anchor points.
4. To finish the path, click **Pen** tool 🖉 .... ESC

OR

Click first anchor point to close the path.

  ✓ *Use the Freeform Pen tool 🖉 to create freely drawn paths.*

Select a Path

1. Click **Path Selection** tool 🖈 .... A or SHIFT + A
2. Click path to select it and display anchor points.

Edit Path Anchor Points

1. Click path name to edit in the list of paths in the Paths panel.

OR

Select path using Path Selection tool 🖈.

2. Click **Direct Selection** tool 🖈 .... A, SHIFT + A and then click on any anchor point to select it.
3. Adjust the anchor point as desired:
   - Drag anchor point to a new position.
   - Adjust direction handle.
   - Delete anchor point.

Save a New Work Path

1. Open Paths panel.
2. Double-click **Work Path** in the list of paths.
3. Type a path **Name**.
4. Click **OK** .... ENTER

Create a New Path

1. Open Paths panel.
2. Click **Create new path** button 🔲 on Paths panel.
3. Double-click new path and type new name.
4. Use path tool to create the path.

Convert a Selection to a Path

1. Create the selection in the image area.
2. Open Paths panel.
3. Click **Make work path from selection** button 🔲 on Paths panel.
4. Name the new Work Path as directed previously.

Stroke a Path

1. Select layer on which you want stroked shape to appear in Layers panel.
2. Open Paths panel.
3. Click path to stroke in the list of paths.
4. Choose desired foreground color.
5. Click **Brush** tool 🖌.................🅱 or ⇧SHIFT + 🅱
6. Choose desired brush settings from Brush Preset picker and options bar.
7. Click **Stroke path with brush** button 🔲 on Paths panel.

Fill a Path

1. Select layer on which you want filled shape to appear in Layers panel.
2. Open Paths panel.
3. Click path to fill in the list of paths.
4. Choose desired foreground color.
5. Click **Fill path with foreground color** button 🔲 on Paths panel.

Load a Path as a Selection

1. Select layer on which you want to make selection in Layers panel.
2. Open Paths panel.
3. Click path name in the list of paths.
4. Click **Load path as a selection** button 🔲 on Paths panel.

EXERCISE DIRECTIONS

1. Open the 🔘55Zoo file and save it as *55Zoo_xx*.
2. Adjust the canvas size to 7 inches by 5 inches.
3. Add a new layer below the Background copy layer, rename it **White**, and use the Paint Bucket tool to give it a white fill.
4. Zoom in on the bear in the center of the image and use the Pen tool to outline the bear. You can use all straight segments or try your hand at curved segments. Select a portion of the rock under the bear's left hind foot to give that foot something to stand on (it's a funny shape otherwise).
5. Select the path with the Direct Selection tool and adjust anchor points as necessary to achieve a path that fits closely around the bear.
6. Save the Work Path as **Bear**.
7. Select the Background copy layer and then load the Bear path as a selection. Save the selection as **Bear**.

8. Invert the selection and press Delete to remove all of the background around the bear.

   ✓ *If this action removes the white background around the original image, you did not select the correct layer before loading the path as a selection. Undo and try again.*

   ✓ *You may want to refine the edge of the selection to smooth the outline.*

9. Create a new layer named **Shape 1** above the White layer. Use the Pen tool with the Paths setting to create a freeform shape around the bear, creating smooth curves by dragging anchor points as you learned in Illustrator. Illustration A shows an example of a curvy shape you could create.

   ✓ *Alternatively, use the Freeform Pen tool to draw the shape.*

10. Save the Pen work path as **Background**. Create a very light tan color and fill the Background path.
11. Add a new layer named **Shape 2** below the Shape 1 layer. Load the Background path as a selection on this layer. Create a foreground color slightly darker than the one you used to fill the first curvy shape and use Edit > Fill to fill the selection on Shape 2 with the darker color.

12. Use Edit > Transform > Rotate to rotate the darker shape so that you can see portions of it around the first curvy shape, as shown in Illustration A. Deselect the selection.

    ✓ *For an interesting effect, you may want to adjust the transparency of one or both of these shape layers.*

13. Create a new layer named **Leaves and Flakes** at the top of the layer stack. Choose the Custom Shape tool from the toolbox, and use the Custom Shape picker on the options bar to select any leaf shape.

    ✓ *Load the Nature library if necessary to see a selection of leaves.*

14. With the Paths button on the options bar selected, drag to create a leaf anywhere in the image area. Use the Edit > Transform > Rotate command to rotate the leaf from its vertical orientation, and scale it if necessary. Name the path **Leaf 1**.

15. Create a warm brown autumn-leaf color and fill the path.

16. Create additional paths with the same leaf shape or other shapes, modifying colors, sizes, and rotations, until you have four or five leaves on the image area.

17. Change the custom shape to one of the snowflake shapes and add several snowflakes to the image, creating new paths for each flake.

18. For at least one of the snowflakes, stroke the path with a color that contrasts well with the image behind the flake. Fill the other flakes with light colors.

19. Adjust the position of the type layers if necessary. Your finished image might resemble Illustration A.

20. Save your changes, close the file, and exit Photoshop.

Illustration A

ON YOUR OWN

1. Create a new image file using the following settings:
   - Width: 4 inches.
   - Height: 4 inches.
   - Resolution: 150 pixels/inch.
   - Background Contents: White.
2. Save the file as OPH55_xx.
3. Use the Pen tool to create a path that is pear shaped.

   ✓ *Make the pear as artistic or realistic as you want, given the time allotted by your instructor.*

4. Use the Add Anchor Point and Direct Selection tools to edit the pear path as desired.
5. Use the Paths panel to save the path as **Pear**.
6. Add two layers in the Layers panel. Name one **Pear Stroke** and the other **Pear Fill**.
7. Select the Pear Stroke layer, return to the Paths panel, and stroke the Pear path using a dark brown foreground color and an artistic or natural brush.
8. Select the Pear Fill layer in the Layers panel, return to the Paths panel, and fill the Pear path with a pear green foreground color.
9. Draw a new path with the leaf and stem custom shape. Rotate the path so the stem will attach naturally to the top of the pear.
10. Save the path with an appropriate name and then fill the path with a darker green than the one you used for the pear. You may want to stroke the path with brown to match the pear body.
11. Save your changes, close the file, and exit Photoshop.

Skills Covered

- Clip an Adjustment Layer
- Add a Fill Layer
- Change Layer Blending

- Apply Layer Styles
- Flatten Layers

Software Skills Fine-tune adjustment layers to specify how much of an image is adjusted. You can change fills using layers to modify the look of an image without changing the image. You can adjust how layers interact by specifying a different blending option and add special effects to layer objects using layer styles such as glows and shadows. When you have completed a project, you can flatten layers to reduce file size.

Design Skills One of the hallmarks of an experienced designer is the ability to choose the correct tool or feature for a particular situation. Inserting fill layers gives a designer different options for applying a color, gradient, or pattern. Use of layer blending and styles can add final professional touches to an image.

Application Skills In this exercise, you will do some final adjustments on a flyer for the Parker Conservatory's annual butterfly show. You will add an adjustment layer to improve the photo, add a fill layer to give the background some texture, adjust layer blending, and apply a layer style. Finally, you will duplicate the file and then flatten layers in the duplicate image.

TERMS

Fill layer A layer that consists of a color, gradient, or pattern fill.

Flattening Merging all layers in an image into a single layer.

Layer styles Special effects you apply to a layer to affect the appearance of the layer's contents.

NOTES

Clip an Adjustment Layer

- In Lesson 5, you learned how to use adjustment layers to improve or adjust image appearance in a variety of ways.
- For more control over the appearance of objects on layers, you can confine the adjustment to a specific area on the layer so that only that area changes and the rest of the layer remains as it was.

- To indicate the area that should be adjusted, select a portion of the layer or select a closed shape on the layer and then issue the command to create the adjustment layer.
- For example, Figure 56-1 at the top of the next page shows how the Layers panel looks after a Posterize adjustment layer has been added to an image. Before adding the adjustment layer, one of the flowers in the image was selected to create a mask. The Posterize settings thus apply only to the flower.

Figure 56-1. The adjustment layer applies only to the flower mask

Layer thumbnail   Layer mask thumbnail   Adjustment layer

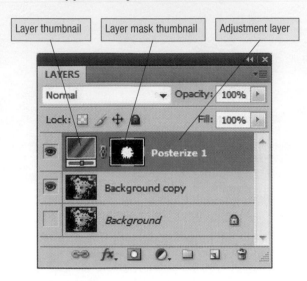

Figure 56-2. The Vibrance adjustment layer applies only to the Posterize layer below

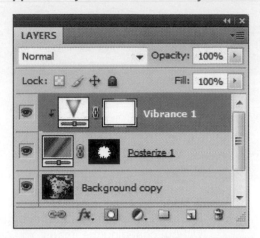

■ As shown in Figure 56-1, the adjustment layer displays two thumbnails that represent the layer and the layer mask. The layer thumbnail shows a representation of the type of adjustment being made. The layer mask thumbnail displays any mask in use (such as the flower). If the adjustment applies to the entire image, the layer mask thumbnail will be solid white.

✓ *A mask shows the area that can be modified. In the previous illustration, the white area of the layer thumbnail can be changed; the black area of the thumbnail is protected from change. You learn more about masks later in this lesson.*

■ The layer thumbnail and the layer mask are linked by default. You can, however, unlink the two thumbnails. It is then possible to work with the two thumbnails separately. If you delete the layer mask thumbnail, for example, by dragging it to the trash, the adjustment effect will apply to the entire image.

■ By default, an adjustment layer affects all layers beneath it. The Adjustments panel gives you the option, however, of applying the current adjustment only to the layer directly below it.

■ Clicking the *This adjustment affects all layers* button at the bottom of the Adjustments panel results in a Layers panel and an image like the ones shown in Figure 56-2.

■ In Figure 56-2, the Posterize adjustment has been applied only to the central flower in the image. The Vibrance adjustment layer (with Vibrance and Saturation both set to 0 to desaturate the image) clips only to the Posterize layer, so the result is a desaturated, posterized area. The remaining part of the image is unaffected by either the Posterize or Vibrance adjustments.

■ To remove clipping, click the *This adjustment clips to the layer* button .

Add a Fill Layer

■ A **fill layer** is just what it sounds like: a layer that consists of a specified fill. Unlike an adjustment layer, a fill layer does not affect layers below it.

- As for an adjustment layer, however, the fill can be confined to a specific area of the layer below the new fill layer by selecting an area or object before issuing the command. The Layers panel shows the same types of thumbnails as for an adjustment layer, but the layer thumbnails differ according to the type of fill layer.

- Add a new fill layer by using the Layer > New Fill Layer command or by clicking the Create new fill or adjustment layer button ◉ on the Layers panel. You can choose to add a color, gradient, or pattern fill layer.

- When you issue the Layer > New Fill Layer command, the New Layer dialog box for any of these three choices looks similar to the one shown in Figure 56-3 for a gradient fill layer. You can name the new layer and make several decisions about settings. For example, you can reduce the opacity of the fill layer and select a blending mode.

Figure 56-3. Specify a name and settings for a new fill layer

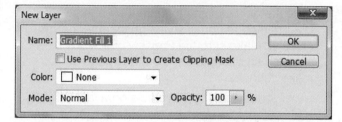

- After you click OK in the New Layer dialog box, another dialog box displays to allow you to specify settings for the solid color, gradient, or pattern layer.

- A solid color layer picks up the foreground color by default. You can specify the foreground color before issuing the menu command, or you can change the color after you close the New Layer dialog box, when the Color Picker opens.

  ✓ *If you are adding a solid color layer above existing layers, you will most likely want to adjust opacity, or the new fill layer will obscure layers below it.*

- You can change the color of the fill layer at any time by double-clicking the layer thumbnail to open the Color Picker.

- When you choose to create a gradient fill layer, the Gradient Fill dialog box opens after you have finished with the New Layer dialog box. Use the Gradient Fill dialog box, shown in Figure 56-4, to fine-tune the gradient fill.

Figure 56-4. Choose gradient fill settings for the gradient layer

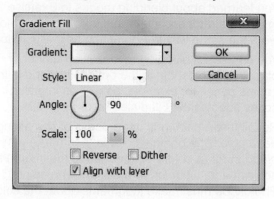

- Adjust the gradient layer at any time by double-clicking the layer thumbnail to reopen the Gradient Fill dialog box.

- A pattern fill layer applies one of Photoshop's patterns to the layer. After you name the layer and select its settings in the New Layer dialog box, the Pattern Fill dialog box opens to allow you to select a pattern and scale it if desired, as shown in Figure 56-5.

Figure 56-5 Choose a pattern in the Pattern Fill dialog box

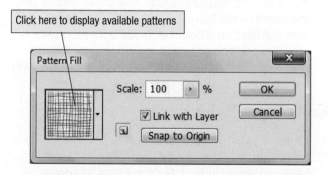

- To choose a pattern, click the list arrow on the current pattern's thumbnail to display a panel of pattern choices. Click the panel menu button to see a list of other pattern categories you can choose.

- You may wonder why you would want to create a fill layer rather than simply create a new layer and fill it with a color or pattern using the Paint Bucket, or fill with a gradient using the Gradient tool. If you think you may need to adjust fill settings later, a fill layer is easier to adjust than a normal layer that has had a fill applied to it. Simply double-click the layer thumbnail for the fill layer to adjust its color, pattern, or gradient.

Change Layer Blending

- You learned about blending modes in Exercise 25 in the Illustrator section of this text. Blending modes work the same way in Photoshop as in Illustrator.

- You can select blending modes in a number of places in Photoshop: in the options bar and in the Layers panel, for example, as well as in dialog boxes such as the Fill dialog box.

- Recall that *blending* is the process of combining a *base color* (the original color in the image) with a *blend color* (a color being added to the image) to achieve a *result color*. In order to blend colors, Photoshop must make judgments about the colors in each channel of an image and then combine them in various ways.

  ✓ *Channels are the component colors of an image, such as red, green, and blue in an RGB image. You will learn more about channels in Exercise 58.*

- Available blend options vary according to the current task. Photoshop offers all of the blending modes available in Illustrator plus some additional options. You can find descriptions of all Photoshop's blending modes by consulting Photoshop Help.

- To blend layers, click the *Set the blending mode for the layer* list arrow and select a blend option. Note that blending results depend to a great degree on the blend color; blending with white and black can give results that differ from those achieved with other colors. You are encouraged to experiment with these blending options to become familiar with their effects.

Apply Layer Styles

- **Layer styles** are special effects you can apply to a layer to modify the look of the layer's contents. Layer styles include options such as shadows, glows, overlays, and even an option that makes layer content look embossed.

  ✓ *Layer styles are very similar to Illustrator's Stylize effects.*

- Figure 56-6 shows the Bevel and Emboss layer style applied to type and the Drop Shadow style applied to the layer containing the butterfly.

- To apply a layer style, select the layer to receive the style and click the Add a layer style button fx. at the bottom of the Layers panel, or select the Layer > Layer Style command. Then select the desired style from the menu.

Figure 56-6. Layer styles applied to an image

- The Layer Style dialog box, shown in Figure 56-7 at the top of the next page, opens to allow you to choose and adjust settings for the style.

  ✓ *To see settings for a style, you must not only click in the check box but click the style name.*

- Note that you can select more than one style for a layer (although not all styles go together harmoniously). Make sure the Preview check box is selected and keep an eye on the image as you make changes.

- Layer styles apply to all objects on a layer. If you add content to a layer, or modify an object such as text, the style remains in place.

- You can edit a layer style at any time by double-clicking the *fx* button to the right of the layer name in the Layers panel.

Flatten Layers

- The more layers in an image, the larger the image file is likely to be. When you have finished working on an image and are ready to transport or output it, you can save time and disk space by **flattening** layers in the image.

  ✓ *You may remember that you also learned about flattening layers in the Illustrator section of the course.*

- To flatten an image, use the Layer > Flatten Image command, or click the Layers panel menu button and select Flatten Image. All layers in the image are compressed into one layer.

- Once layers have been flattened, you can no longer edit the individual layers. For this reason, it is good practice to duplicate an image. You can keep the original on file and flatten the duplicate for output. Use the Image > Duplicate command to duplicate an image.

Figure 56-7. Choose options for the selected layer style

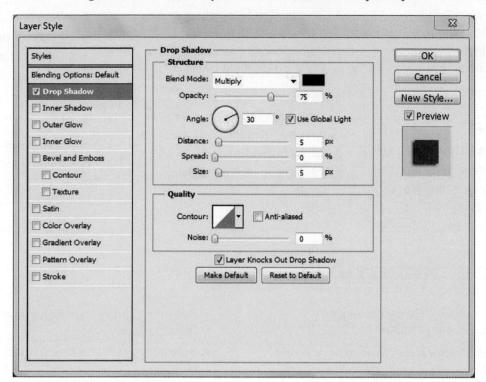

PROCEDURES

Clip an Adjustment Layer

To apply an adjustment to a selected area:

1. On the layer that will be below the adjustment layer, select the desired area.

   OR

   Select an object such as a shape or closed Pen path.

2. Apply the adjustment layer; it will apply only to the selected area.

To clip an adjustment to the layer immediately below:

1. Apply the desired adjustment layer.

2. Click the *This adjustment affects all layers below* button 🔘.

   ✓ *The button then changes to* This adjustment clips to the layer *button* 🔘.

Add a Fill Layer

1. Click **Layer** .... ALT + L
2. Point to **New Fill Layer** .... W
3. Click **Solid Color** .... O

   OR

   Click **Gradient** .... G

   OR

   Click **Pattern** .... R

4. Type a name for the layer, select a filter color, select a blending mode, and adjust opacity as desired.
5. Click **OK** .... ENTER
6. Supply specific settings for the type of fill layer selected.
7. Click **OK** .... ENTER

   OR

1. Select layer that should be below fill layer.
2. Click the **Create new fill or adjustment layer** button 🔘. on Layers panel.

3. Select the type of fill from the pop-up menu.
4. Supply specific settings for the type of adjustment selected.
5. Click **OK** .... ENTER

To apply the fill layer to a specific area of the layer below:

1. On the layer that will be below the fill layer, select the desired area.

   OR

   Select an object such as a shape or closed Pen path.

2. Create the fill layer as directed in *Add a Fill Layer*.

Change Layer Blending

1. Select the layer in the Layers panel that will be blended with the layer below it.
2. Click the **Set the blending mode for the layer** list arrow.
3. Select the desired blending mode.

Apply Layer Styles

1. Select the layer to which the layer style should be applied.
2. Click **Add a layer style** button ![fx] at bottom of Layers panel.

   OR

   a. Click **Layer** .... [ALT] + [L]
   b. Click **Layer Style** .... [Y]
3. Select layer style from list.
4. Choose settings for style in Layer Style dialog box.
5. Click **OK** .... [ENTER]

To modify layer style:

1. Double-click *fx* to right of layer name in Layers panel.
2. Make desired changes in Layer Style dialog box.

Flatten Layers

1. Click ![icon] on Layers panel to open panel menu.
2. Click **Flatten Image**.
3. Click **OK** to discard hidden layers .... [ENTER]

OR

1. Click **Layer** .... [ALT] + [L]
2. Click **Flatten Image** .... [F]
3. Click **OK** to discard hidden layers .... [ENTER]

Duplicate an Image

1. Click **Image** .... [ALT] + [I]
2. Click **Duplicate** .... [D]
3. Type a name for the duplicate file.
4. Click **OK** .... [ENTER]

EXERCISE DIRECTIONS

1. Open the 💿 56Parker file and save it as 56Parker_xx. Set magnification to 100%.

   ✓ *This image shows some of the interesting things you can do with type in Photoshop, including type on a path and warped type. You will work with type on a path in the InDesign section of this course.*

2. Select Layer 1, which contains the photo image.
3. Insert an adjustment layer to control Color Balance:

   a. Name the adjustment layer **Adjust Colors**.
   b. Leaving the Midtones option selected, move the sliders to achieve color levels of **+32**, **-37**, and **+10**.

4. Select Layer 1 again and load the Butterfly selection to isolate a portion of the layer.
5. Apply the Posterize adjustment layer and name it **Posterize**. Adjust Levels to 6. Move the layer above the Adjust Colors layer and choose to clip the Posterize adjustment layer to the layer below.

   ✓ *The Posterize adjustment layer now applies only to the portion of the Adjust Colors adjustment layer exposed by the butterfly selection.*

6. Watch how the posterized butterfly appearance changes as you adjust the color levels to **+40**, **-37**, **+23** in the Adjust Colors adjustment layer.
7. Select the Background layer and insert a pattern fill layer as follows:

   a. Choose to insert the pattern fill layer using the Layer > New Fill Layer > Pattern command. Name the layer **Pattern** and set opacity to 20%.
   b. Click the pattern thumbnail's list arrow and then click the panel menu button to display libraries of patterns.

   c. Select the library titled Patterns and append the Patterns library.
   d. Select the Fractures pattern from the appended patterns.

8. Select the FLYERS GALORE layer. You will blend this layer with the one below it to change the look of the text:

   a. In the Layers panel, change the opacity of the text layer to 85%.
   b. In the Layers panel, click the blending mode list arrow and select Multiply. The text darkens but is too faint to read easily.
   c. Select the Overlay blending mode. This gives an interesting effect but the text is a bit hard to read.
   d. Select the Screen blending mode. This brightens up the text and makes it easy to read.

9. Try a few more blending options to see how they change the look of the type. Then reapply the Screen blending mode if necessary.
10. Select Layer 1 and add the Drop Shadow layer style. Change Spread to **5%** and Size to **10** px.
11. Select the layer that contains the warped text *BUTTERFLIES* and apply a layer style of your choice to the text. You may want to apply more than one style for a special effect. Your image should look similar to Illustration A.
12. Save changes and then duplicate the image. Name the duplicate 56Parker2_xx and then flatten the image.
13. Save the flattened image again with the same name, close both files, and exit Photoshop.

Illustration A

ON YOUR OWN

1. Open the ⊙OYO56 file and save it as OPH56_xx.

2. Use a selection tool or the Freeform Pen tool to trace around the flower at the left center of the image and the smaller flower just below it on the right. Take your time and make the selection or path as close to the petals as you can.

3. Save the selection so you can use it again. (You will need it in the On Your Own exercise for Exercise 58.) Then invert the selection.

4. Add an adjustment layer to control brightness/contrast. Reduce both brightness and contrast so the selected flower stands out.

5. Use a type tool to add the text **DAHLIA**. Choose a font, style, size, and color for the text and position it attractively on the image.

6. Choose a different blending mode for the type layer. If necessary, modify the adjustment layer so the type shows up more strongly against the background.

7. Apply a layer style of your choice to the type layer. (You can apply more than one style if desired.)

8. Save your changes and then create a duplicate of the image named OPH56D_xx.

9. Flatten the image, discarding hidden layers.

10. Save the OPH56D_xx file, close both files, and exit Photoshop.

Skills Covered

■ **Understand Filters**

■ **Apply a Filter to a Vector Object**

■ **Apply a Filter to an Image or Layer**

■ **Apply Smart Filters**

Software Skills   Photoshop includes many filters you can use to apply special effects to an image's layers or objects. The Filter Gallery makes it easy to choose a filter and adjust its settings. Smart Filters allow you to easily manipulate and remove filter effects.

Design Skills   A good designer is always on the lookout for effects that can enhance an image. Use filters from the Filter Gallery or Filter menu to give an image a unique appearance. Smart Filters enable a designer to adjust filters easily to get just the right effect for a particular project.

Application Skills   Wilcox Tours is planning a group tour of Glacier National Park and needs an eye-catching illustration of one of the park's vistas for a brochure. In this exercise, you will apply Smart Filters to an image, add a vector object and text, and apply filters to them.

TERMS

Rasterize   To convert vector content to raster (pixel-based) content.

Smart Filter   A filter applied to a Smart Object that you can easily adjust or remove.

NOTES

Understand Filters

■ Photoshop's filters allow you to apply many different types of special effects to an image. Some of these filter effects are utilitarian—they can be used to sharpen or blur one part of an image—and other filter effects are creative—they can be used to render clouds or make an image look as if it has been created from stained glass. Using filters, you can turn an ordinary snapshot into a piece of dazzlingly complex artwork.

■ If you have already completed the Illustrator portion of this course, you will recognize many Photoshop filters as being identical to the effects offered in Illustrator. Photoshop filters are applied in the same ways as Illustrator effects.

✓ See Exercise 29 for more information about effects.

■ All of Photoshop's filters are available when you are working with an RGB document. In a CMYK document, you don't have nearly as many filter options. If you need CMYK output for, say, a printed job, you may want to do the design work in the RGB mode and then convert to CMYK afterward.

✓ You learn how to convert from RGB to CMYK in Exercise 61.

■ Photoshop has too many filters to cover in a single exercise, but the process of applying and adjusting filters is more or less the same for all of them. You are encouraged to explore Photoshop's filters to become familiar with the ways they can be used to alter an image.

Apply a Filter to an Image or Layer

- As for Illustrator effects, Photoshop's filters are organized in categories such as Artistic and Stylize. Each category contains a varying number of filters that perform many different types of adjustments to the current image. Because more than one filter can be applied to an image, the range of effects that can be achieved is almost limitless.

- Selecting a filter from the Filter menu usually opens a dialog box in which you can adjust settings for the filter. Some filters have a stand-alone dialog box that shows a preview and sliders for adjustments, such as the one shown in Figure 57-1 at the top of the next column.

- Other filters, such as the Solarize filter, have no settings, so as soon as you select the filter, it is applied to the image.

- Many filters can be accessed through the Filter Gallery, a feature that makes it easy to select from among the wide variety of filters and apply adjustments to see the final effect without having to repeatedly select new filters from the Filter menu.

Figure 57-1. The Ripple filter has a stand-alone dialog box

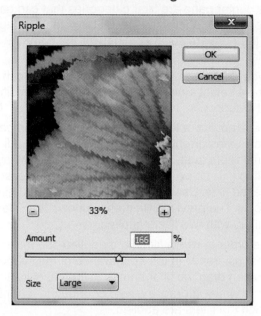

- The Filter Gallery, shown in Figure 57-2 below, resembles and works the same way as the Effect Gallery you used in Illustrator.

Figure 57-2. Select and adjust settings for filters in the Filter Gallery

- The Filter Gallery has three panes: At the left, the current filter is applied to a sample of the image. In the center pane are filter categories that can be expanded to show filters available for that category. At the right are setting options for the currently selected filter.

- If you don't like a particular filter effect, you can simply select a new one from the same or a different category.

- The effect list at the bottom of the right-hand pane shows the currently applied filter. To apply additional filters to an image, click the New effect layer button below the effect list and then choose the desired filter. Use the eye icons to show and hide effects. The previous illustration shows the Filter Gallery with two filters applied.

- The order in which filters are applied can make a great difference in the appearance of the image. You can drag the filter names in the effect list the same way you drag layers to change the order in which the filters are applied.

- If an image has only one layer, a new filter applies to the entire image. To apply a filter to a specific layer in the image, select the layer before applying the filter.

- If, after you have applied a filter, you are not quite happy with it, you can use Undo or Step Backward to remove the filter and then start over.

Apply a Filter to a Vector Object

- To apply a filter to type or to a path shape, you must first **rasterize** the type or object. Type objects and shapes are vector objects, which means they are created using mathematical formulas rather than pixels. Before you can manipulate these objects with filters, you must convert them to pixel-based objects.

- To rasterize an object, use the Layer > Rasterize command and choose an option from the pop-out menu such as Type, Shape, or Layer. Which options are available depends on what layer you have selected. Once you have rasterized type or a shape, you can no longer edit it with vector-based tools.

Apply Smart Filters

- Filters that you apply using the Filter Gallery or Filter menu make permanent changes to an image. Once applied, a filter cannot be adjusted unless you undo the filter and start over.

  ✓ *If you return to the Filter Gallery (or another filter dialog box) to adjust an existing filter, you will actually be applying a filter on top of a filter, which can lead to unexpected results.*

- And, if you are not happy with a filter, you must use Undo or Step Backward to remove it. Fine-tuning filters can thus be a tedious process.

- Photoshop offers an alternative to this apply-and-undo scenario. **Smart Filters** allow you to apply filters that you can easily adjust and remove.

- To apply Smart Filters, you must first convert the layer to which you will apply the filters to a Smart Object. *Smart Objects* are layers that contain embedded image content which you can edit without affecting the original image data.

- Once you have converted a layer to a Smart Object, you can apply any filter from the Filter menu to the layer. The filter displays below the layer in the Layers panel, similar to the way a layer style does, as shown in Figure 57-3.

Figure 57-3. Smart Filter applied to a Smart Object layer

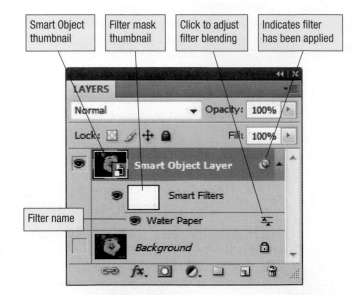

- The white filter mask thumbnail indicates that the filter has been applied to the entire layer. The filter name displays below the mask thumbnail.

  ✓ *If you applied a filter from the Filter Gallery, the name Filter Gallery displays below the mask thumbnail.*

- To apply the filter to a portion of the layer, create a selection and load it before applying the filter.

- To edit the Smart Filter, simply double-click its name to reopen the dialog box or Filter Gallery and then make the desired changes.

- You can adjust the filter's blending mode by clicking the filter blending options button to the right of the filter name.

- To see the image without the filter applied, click the visibility eye to hide the filter. You can easily delete the filter entirely by selecting it and clicking the Delete layer button.

PROCEDURES

Apply a Filter to an Image or Layer

1. Select a layer if necessary.
2. Click **Filter** .... ALT + T
3. Click a filter category.
4. Click the desired filter on the pop-out menu.
5. Adjust sliders as necessary to customize the filter.
6. Click **OK** if necessary .... ENTER

   OR

1. Select a layer if necessary.
2. Click **Filter** .... ALT + T
3. Click **Filter Gallery** .... G
4. Click a category in the center pane to expand it.
5. Click the desired filter.
6. Adjust settings in right-hand pane.
7. Click **OK** .... ENTER

To apply additional filters in the Filter Gallery:

1. Click **New effect layer** button ⬛ at bottom of right-hand pane.
2. Select new filter effect in center pane.
3. Drag filter effects in effect list if desired to change order in which they are applied.

Rasterize a Vector Object

1. Select layer on which vector object appears.
2. Click **Layer** .... ALT + L
3. Click **Rasterize** .... Z
4. Click an option on the pop-out menu:
   - **Type** .... T
   - **Shape** .... S
   - **Fill Content** .... F
   - **Vector Mask** V
   - **Smart Object** .... O
   - **Layer** L
   - **All Layers** .... A

Apply a Smart Filter

1. Select the layer to which you will apply the filter.
2. Click **Filter** .... ALT + T
3. Click **Convert for Smart Filters**.
4. Click **OK** .... ENTER

   ✓ *The layer thumbnail will display the Smart Object symbol after the conversion.*

5. Apply any filter from the Filter menu.

To edit a Smart Filter:

- Double-click the filter name to reopen the relevant dialog box and make any desired adjustments to the filter.

To adjust Smart Filter blending:

- Double-click filter blending button ⬛ to right of filter name.

To hide Smart Filter effects:

- Click visibility eye 👁 to hide or redisplay filter effects.

To remove a Smart Filter:

- Drag the filter layer over the **Delete layer** button 🗑.

   OR

- Press ENTER.

EXERCISE DIRECTIONS

1. Open the 💿 *57Glacier* file and save it as *57Glacier_xx*. Set magnification to 100% if you have room on your screen.
2. Select the Background copy layer and convert it for Smart Filters.
3. Display the Filter Gallery. You will try several filters to find one that gives the image an interesting look.

   a. Display the filters in the Artistic category. Click on each filter to see how the image sample in the left pane changes.

   b. Display the filters in the Brush Strokes category and apply each.

   c. Continue in this way to view all the filter categories and their filters, taking note of which filters look especially interesting. Note that the filters in the Sketch category use the current foreground color, so you may want to change it to something other than default black and then redisplay the Filter Gallery.

   d. Apply the Rough Pastels filter from the Artistic category with a Stroke Length of **4** and a Stroke Detail of **1**. This filter makes the photo look more like a painting.

4. On a new layer above the Background copy layer, select a light beige foreground color such as Light Cool Brown and use the Rectangle tool with the Shape layers mode selected to draw a shape layer rectangle about half an inch high and almost the full width of the image. (See Illustration A.)

5. Rasterize the shape. In the Filter Gallery, apply the Texturizer filter from the Texture category with **Sandstone** as the texture, Scaling of **50%**, and Relief of **8**.

6. While you are still in the Filter Gallery, add a new effect layer and apply a second filter effect, Paint Daubs from the Artistic category, with settings of your choice. Then change the blending mode of the shape layer to a mode of your choice.

   ✓ *Don't forget to add a new effect layer to apply the second filter. If you do not add a new effect layer, you will lose your Texturizer settings when you apply the Paint Daubs settings.*

7. Use the Horizontal Type tool to type **GLACIER NATIONAL PARK** using a font, size, and style of your choice. Use your choice of font colors. Illustration A uses Bauhaus as the font.

8. Rasterize the type and apply a filter such as Graphic Pen from the Sketch category to give a weathered look to the type.

9. If you have chosen a dark color for the type, make the type stand out against the background by applying a layer style such as Outer Glow.

10. You are not quite happy with the filter applied to the mountain image. Edit the Smart Filter to use the Dry Brush filter with a Brush Size of **1**, Brush Detail of **10**, and Texture of **1**. Your image should resemble Illustration A.

11. Save your changes, close the file, and exit Photoshop.

Illustration A

ON YOUR OWN

1. Open the ⊙OYO57 file and save it as OPH57_xx.

2. Convert the layer with the lily to use Smart Filters.

3. Create a new look for this image you have worked with previously. Try filters you can find in the Filter menu categories that are not available in the Filter Gallery, such as the filters in the Pixelate category. Take some time to experiment with Photoshop's filters to create interesting and unusual effects.

4. After you apply the filter, change the blending mode if desired.

5. Add type to the image, such as a label or a single word that embodies the effect you have created with your filter.

6. Rasterize the text and apply your choice of filter, or more than one filter.

7. Save your changes, close the file, and exit Photoshop.

Skills Covered

- **About Masks and Channels**
- **Create a Quick Mask**
- **Use Type Masks**
- **Work with Masks in Channels Panel**

Software Skills   Any selection is also a mask that specifies what area of an image can be modified. When a selection is saved, the mask displays in the Channels panel as an alpha channel. Use Quick Mask mode to create a mask by painting with the Brush. Type masks allow you to create special effects with type. Use the Channels panel to adjust mask display.

Design Skills   Masks allow for effects to be applied in some areas and not in others. A designer should understand how masks and channels are related and be familiar with the process of creating a quick mask to refine a selection.

Application Skills   Metro Zoo wants you to create a poster using an image they have supplied. You will use Quick Mask mode to select part of the image, use type mask tools to add the zoo's name, and apply filters and blending to create a mockup of the poster.

TERMS

Alpha channel   A channel created when a selection is saved.

Channel   A feature that stores information about an image's colors or saved selections and masks.

Mask   An overlay that protects one area of an image so that modifications can be made to another area of the image.

Quick mask   A mask created when viewing any selection in Quick Mask mode.

Quick Mask mode   A display mode that makes it easy to add to or subtract from a selection to create a mask.

NOTES

About Masks and Channels

- In the world of graphic design, a **mask** protects one area of an image while leaving another area available to be modified.

- Whenever you create a selection on an image, you are actually creating a mask; the area within the selection border can be manipulated while the area outside the selection border remains unaffected.

- If you do not save a selection, the mask that you create with a selection tool disappears along with the selection marquee. But if you save a selection, you also save a mask that is stored in the Channels panel.

- Photoshop allows you to create several different types of masks. You will work with some of the most common in this and the next exercise. As you work with masks, you can use the Masks panel to refine and adjust the mask and the masked area.

- You know by now that images are made up of a number of colors. An RGB image is made up of three colors: red, green, and blue. A CMYK image is composed of four colors: cyan (blue), magenta, yellow, and black.

- Photoshop's **channels** display information for each color in an image. Splitting out the colors in this way allows you to work with each color separately if you wish, or adjust an image by changing the way the separate colors are mixed together.
- An image can have several types of channels.
  - All images have color channels, one for each color in the image plus a composite channel that shows how the colors are mixed to create the current image. An RGB image has three channels plus the composite RGB channel. A CMYK image has four channels plus the composite CMYK channel. A grayscale image has only one channel, named Gray, because a grayscale image consists of variations of only one color, black.
  - **Alpha channels** are added to the Channels panel whenever you save a selection for future use.
  - Spot color channels can be added to the Channels panel to designate parts of an image that will be printed using a spot color.
- An image can contain up to 56 channels.
  - ✓ *You will learn more about working with channels later in this exercise and in Exercise 61.*

Create a Quick Mask

- You have learned a number of ways to select areas and objects in an image. Another way to create a selection is to use **Quick Mask mode**. Quick Mask mode is especially useful for an irregularly shaped area that you cannot easily select by other means.
- To begin creating a **quick mask**, do a rough selection of the area with another tool and then click the Edit in Quick Mask Mode button ▣ near the bottom of the toolbox. The area outside the selection is immediately masked in red as shown in Figure 58-1.

Figure 58-1. Quick Mask mode applies a red overlay over masked areas

- Fine-tune the mask using a tool such as the Brush tool at a small size. Painting with black (the default foreground color) adds to the red area of the mask, as shown in Figure 58-2. Painting with white removes masked areas.

Figure 58-2. Use a tool such as the Brush to add to or remove the mask

Brush tool

- Once you are satisfied with the mask, click the Edit in Standard Mode button ▣ to remove the quick mask.
- Refining a mask in this way is the same process as adding to or subtracting from a selection using options bar settings for tools such as Magic Wand and Quick Selection. When you turn off Quick Mask mode, you will see that the selection border has changed to correspond with your mask painting.
- Quick Mask mode creates a temporary mask that you can see in the Channels panel, as shown in Figure 58-3. The mask disappears as soon as you return to Standard mode.

Figure 58-3. Quick Mask displayed in the Channels panel

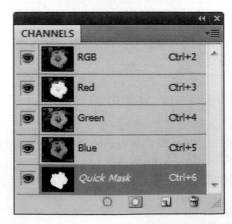

- If you want to store the mask, you must save the selection you have created using the Select > Save Selection command. Or, if you have the Channels panel displayed, you can simply click the Save selection as channel button ▣ to store the selection as a new alpha channel.

✓ *You must be in Standard Mode to save the selection as a channel.*

■ The mask color for Quick Mask mode is red by default. If you are working with an image that has a lot of red in it, you can change the mask color to make it easier to see what you are working on.

Use Type Masks

■ In Exercise 57, you learned that to apply filter effects to type you need to rasterize the type.

■ Photoshop supplies two type tools, however, that can shortcut the process of rasterizing text: the Horizontal Type Mask tool, and the Vertical Type Mask tool. Using either of these tools creates a mask from the type that allows you to modify the type appearance while protecting the rest of the image from any change.

■ When you begin typing using a Type Mask tool, Photoshop immediately applies a color overlay to the current layer to indicate what portion of it is protected from change. After you switch to a different tool, the text you typed appears with a crawling selection border, as shown in Figure 58-4.

Figure 58-4. The type mask is indicated by a selection border

■ You can modify the type mask in a number of ways:

• You can immediately delete the selected type to delete pixels in the current layer and display the one below inside the type outlines.

• You can apply a different fill color, gradient, or pattern to the selection that will fill all letters at the same time.

• You can apply a filter without having to first rasterize the text. Figure 58-5 shows a gradient and a filter (Water Paper) applied to the type mask.

Figure 58-5. Use a Type Mask tool to create special type effects

Work with Masks in Channels Panel

■ To view and work with masks and channels, use the Channels panel that is usually stored behind the Layers panel. Figure 58-6 shows a Channels panel that includes two alpha channels containing saved selections.

Figure 58-6. The Channels panel

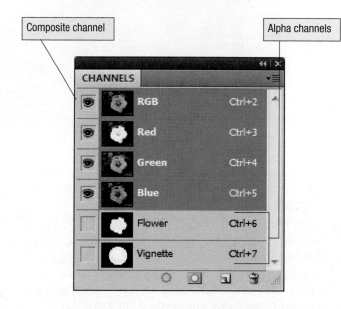

■ The color channel thumbnails display in grayscale, as shown in Figure 58-6; only the composite channel at the top of the panel displays in color.

■ By default, all color channels are visible. This means that all colors are present in the image. To isolate a particular color in the image, click the visibility eyes of the other color channels to remove them.

■ To redisplay all colors, click the visibility box next to the composite channel to restore the eye icon.

✓ *You learn more about adjusting colors using channels in Exercise 61.*

■ By default, a mask in an alpha channel is not visible in the image—there is no eye icon to the left of the thumbnail in the Channels panel.

■ If you click in the visibility box, the image window immediately changes to show a colored mask over the area that is not selected, identical to the red overlay in Quick Mask mode, as shown in Figure 58-7 on the top of the next page. You can now make a change to the selected area without affecting the masked area.

Figure 58-7. Selecting the alpha channel displays a mask over area outside the saved selection

- To remove the mask color, click the visibility icon 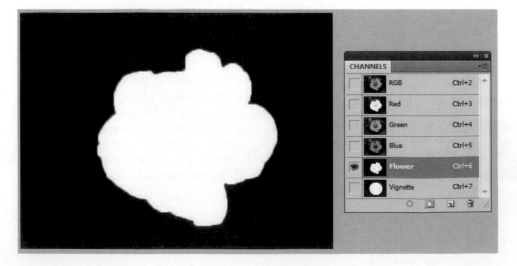 to the left of the alpha channel to hide the channel.

- Clicking the alpha channel name (such as Flower in Figure 58-7) with the other channels hidden displays the mask in the image area as a black and white mask, as shown in Figure 58-8. This is a good option after painting a Quick Mask to make sure you haven't missed any areas you want to mask.

- You can use the Channels panel to quickly load any saved selection. Click on the alpha channel name and drag it over the Load channel as selection button at the bottom of the panel. This maneuver instantly loads the selection without requiring any further steps.

- Loading a channel does not automatically apply a mask. If you want to see the masked area of the image, you must make the alpha channel visible.

✓ *Also use the Masks panel to quickly create a mask from a selection. You will work with this panel in the next exercise.*

- Note that if you wish to use a selection in more than one version of a file, you can "transfer" the saved selection. Open the file that contains a selection you want to reuse, load it, and then save it to the other file using the Load Selection dialog box.

Photoshop Extra

Spot Color Channels

If you are going to print a Photoshop image using the CMYK model, you can add a spot color to the image by adding a spot color channel to the Channels panel. Create your own spot color or select a color from a standard color library. A spot color must be applied as fill for a selection.

Figure 58-8. You can display the selection as a black and white mask

PROCEDURES

Create a Quick Mask

1. Use any selection tool to select an area of an image.
2. Click **Edit in Quick Mask Mode** button 🔘 near bottom of toolbox.
3. Select an editing tool such as the Brush tool.
4. Use black foreground to add to the mask; use white foreground to remove masked area.
5. Click **Edit in Standard Mode** button 🔘 when finished adjusting the mask.
6. Save the selection as a channel if desired.

To change the mask color:

1. Double-click on the **Edit in Quick Mask Mode** button 🔘.
2. Click the **Color** sample and then choose a new color using the Color Picker.
3. Click **OK** .... ENTER

Save a Selection as an Alpha Channel

1. Use a selection tool to make a selection in the image.
2. Click **Select** .... ALT + S
3. Click **Save Selection** V
4. Type a name for the selection.
5. Click **OK** .... ENTER

   OR

1. Use a selection tool to make a selection in the image.
2. Display the Channels panel if necessary.
3. Click **Save selection as channel** button 🔘.

Create Type Masks

1. Select layer on which the type mask should appear.
2. Click **Horizontal Type Mask** tool 🔤 .... T or SHIFT + T

   OR

   Click **Vertical Type Mask** tool 🔤 .... T or SHIFT + T
3. Type desired text to create selection outlines of text.
4. Format selected mask as desired.

Work with Channels

- Display the Channels panel.

To show or hide a channel:

- Click the visibility 👁 icon next to the channel to show or hide the channel.

To display a saved mask as an overlay:

- Click the visibility icon 👁 next to the alpha channel to display the mask in the image.

To display a mask in black and white:

1. Click the visibility icon 👁 for the mask.
2. Click the visibility icon 👁 for the composite channel.

To load an alpha channel as a selection:

1. Click **Select** .... ALT + S
2. Click **Load Selection**. O , ENTER
3. Click **Channel** .... C , ↓
4. Select the selection name.
5. Click **OK** .... ENTER

   OR

1. Display the Channels panel.
2. Click on the desired alpha channel name and drag the name over **Load channel as selection** button 🔘 at the bottom of the Channels panel.

EXERCISE DIRECTIONS

1. Open the 58Peacock file and save it as 58Peacock_xx. Set magnification to 100%.

2. Use the Lasso tool to make a quick selection around the peacock.

3. Make sure default foreground and background colors are displaying in the toolbox and then enter Quick Mask mode.

4. Using a brush setting of **13** px and maximum hardness, paint around the peacock to add to the selection where necessary. You may need to change brush size to do the detail work around the tail and the feet.

5. If you need to remove areas from the mask, switch foreground and background colors so you are painting with white.

6. Display the Channels panel if necessary and click the visibility icon for the composite channel to see the mask in black and white. You should be able to easily see any white areas outside of the main peacock mask that still need to be painted with black to add to the mask.

7. Redisplay the composite channel. When you are happy with your mask, exit Quick Mask mode and save the selection as a new alpha channel with the name **Peacock**.

8. Deselect the selection.

9. Insert a new layer above the image layer.

10. Select a heavy font in a large size and use the Horizontal Type Mask tool to type **METRO ZOO** on the new layer across the bottom of the image. If the type isn't exactly where you want it, select the layer and use the Move tool to reposition the layer contents.

   ✓ *Be sure to select the layer in the Layers panel before trying to move the type masks.*

11. Fill the type mask letters with a gradient you create using shades of blue and green similar to those in the peacock's feathers.

12. Convert the image layer for use with Smart Filters.

13. Load the Peacock alpha channel as a selection.

14. Make sure the composite and all other color channels are selected, and then select the image layer.

15. Invert the selection, and then use the Filter Gallery to locate a filter that will supply an interesting background effect behind the peacock. The background should be fairly unobtrusive to emphasize the peacock.

16. If desired, adjust the blending mode of the type mask layer. Illustration A shows a sample image.

17. Save your changes, close the file, and exit Photoshop.

Illustration A

ON YOUR OWN

1. Open the ⊙OYO58 file and save it as OPH58_xx.
2. Open 📟OPH56_xx if you completed that exercise. You can load the flower selection you created in that file to use in the current file.
   a. In OPH58_xx, click Select > Load Selection.
   b. Click the Document list arrow and select OPH56_xx.
   c. Click the Channel list arrow and select the saved selection to load it.

   ✓ *If you did not complete the On Your Own exercise for Exercise 56, select the flowers at the left center of the image as directed in that exercise.*

3. Switch to Quick Mask mode and note that it is a little difficult to see the masked area because of the color of the mask.
4. Change the mask color to a blue.
5. Add to the current selection the flower in the lower-right corner of the picture. Clean up any selection problems around the flower you originally selected in OPH56_xx.

6. Display the selection as a black and white mask to make sure you have not left any stray pixels unmasked.
7. Save the revised selection as an alpha channel with an appropriate name.
8. On a new layer, add type such as the word **AUTUMN** using the Horizontal or Vertical Type Mask. Fill the type mask with a foreground color you pick up from a flower petal.
9. Load the selection of the two flowers and invert the selection.
10. Add a new fill layer above the image layer. Select the Use Previous Layer to Create a Clipping Mask check box when you create the new layer, and select a light color picked up from a flower petal as the fill color. Adjust opacity to screen the area behind the selected flowers without completely obscuring it.
11. Adjust the blending mode of the fill layer and the type mask layer to achieve interesting effects.
12. Save your changes, close all open files, and exit Photoshop.

Skills Covered

- Create a Layer Mask
- Create a Clipping Mask
- Create a Vector Mask
- Delete a Mask

Software Skills   Photoshop offers a variety of common mask types you can use to work with images. You can create masks using selection tools or vector objects. Use the Masks panel to refine a mask. Delete a mask from the Layers panel if you no longer need it.

Design Skills   Layer masks, clipping masks, and vector masks can be used to add sophisticated effects to an image. A designer should understand the different types of masks and how to apply them to achieve the desired effects.

Application Skills   You have been asked to create a postcard for a series of cards on America's famous lighthouses. In this exercise, you will work with a photo of the Cape Hatteras lighthouse and create two sample cards using a layer mask, a quick mask, a clipping mask, and a vector mask.

TERMS

Clipping mask   A mask that uses pixels on one layer to define a mask on the layer above.

Layer mask   A mask that conceals part or all of a layer.

Vector mask   A mask created using a vector object such as a path or shape.

NOTES

Create a Layer Mask

- A **layer mask** is used to conceal part or all of a layer.
- You can easily create a layer mask by using a selection tool to define an area and then click the Add layer mask button 🔲 on the Layers panel. The mask is applied immediately to crop away the part of the layer not enclosed by the selection.
- You can also click the Add a pixel mask button 🔳 in the Masks panel to apply a layer (pixel) mask.
- If you look at the Layers panel after creating a layer mask using either of these buttons, you can see the mask you applied. It displays as a layer mask thumbnail linked to the layer thumbnail, as shown in Figure 59-1. The layer content will display only in the white area of the mask.

Figure 59-1. The layer thumbnail and the layer mask thumbnail

✓ You have actually worked with layer masks several times in previous exercises, to clip adjustment layers, for example.

■ You can also create layer masks from selections using the Layer > Layer Mask command. With the selection in place, click Reveal Selection on the Layer Mask submenu to show only the selected area. Click Hide Selection to show everything but the selected area.

■ Once you have applied a layer mask, you can use the Masks panel, shown in Figure 59-2, to work with the mask in a number of ways.

Figure 59-2. Masks panel

- Use the Density slider to restore a percentage of the area around the layer mask. This allows you to create an effect of a dim background around the selection.

- Use the Feather slider to feather the edge of the mask, as you learned to do in Lesson 4 when feathering a selection.

- Click the Mask Edge button to open the Refine Mask dialog box, with content similar to that of the Refine Edge dialog box you learned about in Lesson 4.

- Use Color Range to adjust a selection based on color.

- Click the Invert button to quickly display everything except the mask.

- Use the 👁 button to disable the mask so that you can see the intact image again. Click the button again to enable the mask.

Create a Clipping Mask

■ A **clipping mask** is so called because it uses pixels on one layer to "clip" another layer into the shape of those pixels. In Figure 59-3, the word FLOWER has been used to clip the flower image into the shape of the type object.

Figure 59-3. A clipping mask has been created from type

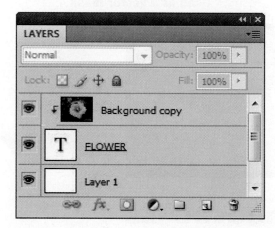

■ When creating a clipping mask, layer order is important. The layer that contains the pixels to be used as the clipping object must be beneath the layer that will be clipped. Note in Figure 59-4 that the type object used to create the mask is below the layer that will be clipped.

Figure 59-4. The layer to be clipped must be on top

■ After you have positioned layers correctly, select the top layer and use the Layer > Create Clipping Mask command to create the mask. You can also use a shortcut: With either layer selected, hold down Alt and click at the border between the two layers. The pointer changes shape to indicate a clipping mask is being created.

✓ Another way to create a clipping mask is to access the Layers panel menu and select Create Clipping Mask.

- The Layers panel clearly shows the relationship of the two layers used in the clipping mask. The name of the layer that supplies the shape of the mask is underlined, as shown in Figure 59-4. The layer that has been clipped displays a bent arrow pointing downward to indicate it is connected to the layer below.

  ✓ *This should remind you of the way an adjustment layer that clips to the layer below displays in the Layers panel.*

Create a Vector Mask

- A **vector mask** is created by using a vector object such as a shape or a Pen tool path. When creating the shape, you must use the Paths option to create only a path rather than a solid shape.

- After you have created the vector shape, click the Add a vector mask button ⚟ on the Masks panel, or use the Layer > Vector Mask > Current Path command to create the mask. In Figure 59-5, a polygon path has been added to an image and used to create the vector mask shown at right.

Figure 59-5. A polygon shape is used as a vector mask

- A vector mask looks much the same in the Layers panel as a layer mask, except that the background around the masking object in the mask thumbnail is gray rather than black, as shown in Figure 59-6.

Figure 59-6. A vector mask in the Layers panel

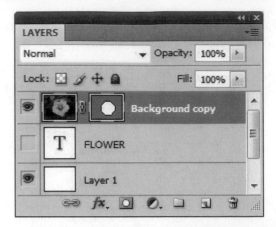

Delete a Mask

- Photoshop allows you to easily remove a layer or vector mask you have applied to an image. Simply drag the mask thumbnail to the Delete layer button 🗑 at the bottom of the Layers panel.

- Remove a clipping mask by selecting Layer > Release Clipping Mask or selecting Release Clipping Mask on the Layers panel menu.

PROCEDURES

Create a Layer Mask

1. Use any selection tool to select an area of an image.
2. Click **Add a pixel mask** button 🔲 on Masks panel.

   OR

   Click **Add layer mask** button 🔲 at bottom of Layers panel.

   OR

   a. Click **Layer** .... [ALT] + [L]
   b. Point to **Layer Mask** .... [M]
   c. Click **Reveal Selection** .... [V]

Create a Clipping Mask (Alt + Ctrl + G)

1. Create the layers to be used for the clipping mask and position them so that the layer to be clipped is on top of the layer that will provide the clipping shape.
2. Click **Layer** .... [ALT] + [L]
3. Click **Create Clipping Mask** .... [C]

   ✓ *You will not see this command with some workspaces displayed. If you do not see this command, use the alternative procedure below.*

   OR

1. Create the layers to be used for the clipping mask and position them so that the layer to be clipped is on top of the layer that will provide the clipping shape.
2. Click ▾≡ in the Layers panel.
3. Click **Create Clipping Mask**.

   OR

1. Create the layers to be used for the clipping mask and position them so that the layer to be clipped is on top of the layer that will provide the clipping shape.
2. Hold down [ALT] and click at the border between the two layers.

Create a Vector Mask

1. Use a shape tool or the Pen tool to draw a path on the layer to be masked.

   ✓ *You must specify the Paths option in the options bar to create a path rather than a filled shape object.*

2. Click **Add a vector mask** button 🖉 on Masks panel.

   OR

   a. Click **Layer** .... ALT + L
   b. Point to **Vector Mask** V
   c. Click **Current Path** .... U

Delete a Mask

To delete a layer or vector mask:

1. Click the layer mask thumbnail or the vector mask thumbnail and drag to **Delete layer** button 🗑 on the Layers panel.

2. Click **OK** to confirm deletion .... ENTER

To delete a clipping mask:

1. Select one of the layers used in the clipping mask.

2. Click **Layer** .... ALT + L

3. Click **Release Clipping Mask** C

   ✓ *You will not see this command with some workspaces displayed. If you do not see this command, use the alternative procedure below.*

   OR

1. Select one of the layers used in the clipping mask.

2. Click ▾≡ in the Layers panel.

3. Click **Release Clipping Mask**.

EXERCISE DIRECTIONS

1. Open the 💿 59Lighthouse file and save it as 59Lighthouse1_xx.

2. Set magnification to 100% if you have room on your screen.

Create a Layer Mask

   ✓ *First you will create a simple card using a layer mask and a fill layer.*

1. Create a new solid color fill layer below the Background copy layer and name it **Matte**.

2. Choose a medium dark blue such as Pure Cyan Blue for the fill color.

3. On the Background copy layer, use the Elliptical Marquee tool to draw a long oval selection that encloses the top of the lighthouse and about two-thirds of its height. (See Illustration A.)

4. Add a layer mask that trims away the image outside the selected oval. The blue fill should surround the selected oval.

5. Click the mask in the Layers panel, if necessary, and then adjust the Density in the Masks panel to 85% to bring some of the background into view.

6. Select the Horizontal Type tool and, using your choice of font, font size, font color, and other font formats, type **HATTERAS** below the oval. Your completed card might be similar to Illustration A.

7. Save your changes and close the file.

Use Other Masks

   ✓ *Now you will create a more complex sample using several masks.*

1. Use File > Open Recent to open 59Lighthouse again. Save the file as 59Lighthouse2_xx.

2. Use the Quick Selection tool to select the lighthouse and a portion of its base. See Illustration B for an idea of how far down the base to select.

3. You may want to view the selection in Quick Mask mode to check the selection. When you are happy with it, exit Quick Mask mode and save the selection as **lighthouse**.

4. Invert the selection and cut the surrounding pixels. Deselect the selection. Then use the Move tool to move the remaining lighthouse upwards in the layer to leave space at the bottom of the image. (See Illustration B.)

5. Add a new layer below the Background copy layer and name it **Sky**. Set a foreground color of Pure Cyan Blue from the Swatches panel and make sure the background color is white. Use the Clouds filter from the Render category to create a cloudy blue sky as a background.

6. Add a new layer above the Background copy layer named **Base**. Use the Rectangle tool to create a filled shape (using Shape layers mode) that covers the bottom portion of the image.

7. Use the same type settings you used for the simple card to type **HATTERAS** and position the type on the blue rectangle so it is centered horizontally.

8. Add a new layer above the type layer named **Light**. Change the foreground color to a yellow or light orange and use the Clouds filter again to create a mottled effect on the new layer.

   ✓ *Remember, the last filter you use is always displayed at the top of the Filter menu. You can click the Clouds command on the Filter menu to apply the filter to the new layer.*

9. Create a clipping mask from the type so that the mottled yellow displays in the letter shapes.

   ✓ *Now create the final mask, a vector mask, using the Pen tool.*

10. Duplicate the Light layer using the Layer panel menu, and name the new layer **Light2**. Release the clipping mask for the new layer. Hide this layer so you can see the lighthouse.

11. Select the Pen tool and the Paths drawing mode and draw a shape at the top of the image that looks like light projecting outward from the top of the lighthouse. (See Illustration B.)

12. Create a vector mask with the current path and use the Feather slider in the Masks panel to feather the edge of the mask **2** px. Then show the Light2 layer to see the Pen shape fill with the light-colored clouds. If desired, change the blending mode for the vector mask object.

13. Save your changes, close the file, and exit Photoshop.

Illustration A

Illustration B

ON YOUR OWN

1. Use Adobe Bridge to review images you have created for the course and open one that you can improve or modify using masks.

2. Try to use all the types of masks you have learned about in this and the previous exercise. For example:
   - Create a mask from a selection to isolate a portion of the image.
   - Refine a mask using Quick Mask mode.
   - Add a fill or gradient layer and use it to create a clipping mask with a part of the image or with type you add to the image.
   - Draw a shape with the Pen tool or another shape tool (don't forget that you can use the Custom Shapes, too) and use it to create a vector mask.
   - Add type masks to create interesting type effects.

3. When you have finished modifying the image, save it with a new name and close the file.

Exercise | 60

Skills Covered

- **Prepare Images for Web and Devices**
- **Optimize a GIF Image**
- **Optimize a JPEG Image**
- **Use Slices to Organize a Document**

Software Skills Photoshop can be an indispensable tool when preparing images for use on mobile devices and Web pages. After an image is finalized in Photoshop, it can be optimized in one of the several formats that are appropriate for Web or device use. You can "slice" objects on a document to make it easy to optimize in different formats.

Design Skills A designer must be able to prepare images for a number of different uses. Besides preparing images for print use, a designer can optimize images for use on Web pages, mobile devices, or video.

Application Skills Wilcox Travel wants you to mock up a Web page for a tour of national parks in the Southwest. To do so, you will optimize images for the first draft of the Web page in GIF and JPEG format.

TERMS

Dither   A blend of two colors used to approximate another color.

Optimize   Adjust settings for a graphic to maximize quality and (usually) minimize file size.

Slice   A defined region of an image that can have settings independent of those in other regions.

NOTES

Prepare Images for Web and Devices

- Photoshop's default color mode, RGB, is ideal for images that will be viewed onscreen, such as on a Web page or on a mobile device.

- One of the issues you must face when using Photoshop to create content for a Web page or mobile device, however, is the image file format.

- Images in Photoshop's native file format, .psd, must be converted for use on the Web or other devices. The standard formats used for Web and device graphics are GIF, JPEG, and PNG.

- These formats are bitmap formats. Web pages and devices can also use vector formats such as SVG, but if you want to export to SVG, you must do so in Illustrator. Photoshop does not offer an option to convert to this format.

- The process of preparing an image for use on the Web or on a mobile device is called **optimizing**. When you optimize an image, you maximize the quality of the image while also controlling the final file size. File size is of great importance for Web pages and devices, because the larger a file is, the longer it will take to display.

- To optimize an image, use the File > Save for Web & Devices command to open the Save for Web & Devices dialog box.

- In this dialog box, you can select the graphics format you want to use and then specify settings for that format. You can see the results of your settings changes on samples in the dialog box and compare quality and file size before you actually save the image in the new format.

- When you choose to optimize an image, you must decide which of the standard Web formats best suit your image.
  - For images that have a limited palette of colors or large blocks of color, GIF is the best format to choose. GIF images can display up to 256 colors and can include transparency. GIF images are compressed without loss of data.
  - For continuous-tone images such as photos or images that use gradients, JPEG is the best format to choose. When a JPEG file is compressed, a certain amount of data is lost. Compression occurs each time the file is saved, so save as few times as possible.
  - The PNG format is similar to GIF in that it supports a limited number of colors and transparency and features lossless compression. Some browsers require special support for PNG images, however, so you will not use this format in this exercise.
- Note that you have the same options for optimizing in Illustrator as the Photoshop options you will read about in the next sections.

Optimize a GIF Image

- To optimize an image as a GIF file, choose the GIF format in the settings area of the Save for Web & Devices dialog box. The settings display as shown in Figure 60-1 at the bottom of the page.
- Tabs at the top of the dialog box allow you to show only the original, an optimized version of the original determined by Photoshop, the original and the optimized version, or four panels with the original and several optimized versions.
- A toolbox displays at the left side of the dialog box. Use the Hand tool to move the image around in the sample boxes to see a different part of the image. Use the Slice Select tool to select slices for optimization. (You'll learn about slices later in this exercise.)
- Information displays at the left below each panel to indicate the file size and the amount of time that version would take to download at a specified download speed such as 56.6 Kbps. You can change this download speed by clicking the Select download speed button just to the right of the download speed and choosing another option.

Figure 60-1. Optimize a GIF file

- At the right below each panel you can see the amount of **dither**, the method used to reduce colors, and the number of colors used.

- Dithering occurs when a browser cannot display a particular color in the image. It compensates by mixing colors to approximate the desired color. This process can result in colors that are not absolutely true to those in the original image, and it can also interfere with compression, but in many cases it can yield good results. In the previous illustration, for example, the sample in the upper-right corner, with 100% dither, looks as good as the 0% dither alternative.

- For a GIF image, you can adjust a number of settings to achieve a good-looking file that is also small and speedy to download. You may want to start with the Preset menu options to quickly apply one of several commonly used optimization schemes.

- To adjust settings manually, click on one of the versions in the preview area and then change options in the settings area.
  - Choose a color reduction method. The default, Selective, preserves the best color integrity.
  - Choose a dithering method. Diffusion applies dithering randomly and is usually the best option. You can also choose a percentage of dither.
  - Reduce file size by reducing the number of colors used in the color table. The color table shows the colors currently in use in the image.
  - Choose a Web Snap tolerance to specify how colors will be shifted to Web-safe colors that will display the same way in any browser.
  - Specify a setting in the Lossy box to allow for compression that throws away the specified amount of data. While GIF images do not have to lose data in compression, specifying a certain percentage of loss can reduce file size without adversely affecting quality.
  - Use Transparency and Matte to control how transparent areas of an image are displayed or blended with the matte (or background) color.
  - By default, the previews use monitor color for display. You can also choose a specific document profile, legacy Macintosh with no color management, or Internet RGB with no color management. You learn about color management in the next exercise.
  - You can also choose what metadata to save with the image after you optimize it.

- You can find additional useful settings on the Optimize menu by clicking ▾≡ to the right of the Preset box.

  - You can set a file size for the image and Photoshop will then adjust settings to achieve this size.
  - Use Repopulate Views to change the samples to reflect new settings you have chosen.

- The color table at the bottom of the settings area shows the colors currently in use. If you want to reduce file size by reducing the number of colors, you can select and lock any of the displayed colors to prevent it being discarded when colors are reduced. You can also add to and remove colors from the color table.

- Buttons at the lower-left of the dialog box allow you to preview your image in a browser. If you have more than one browser available, you can select the browser you want to use for the preview.

- You can also click the Device Central button to open Adobe Device Central CS5, where you can preview the image on a number of different devices such as cell phones.

- After you have finished adjusting settings, choose one of the sample views if necessary and then click the Save button to save the optimized version. The Save Optimized As dialog box opens so you can name the optimized file.

- The Format list offers three choices:
  - HTML and Images (*.html) saves both an HTML file and the images in the current document.
  - Images Only save the current document's image(s) in the format you chose to optimize.
  - HTML Only saves the entire document as an HTML file.

Optimize a JPEG Image

- Although you can save a Photoshop image as a JPEG using the Save As dialog box, you don't have as many options for optimizing the image in that dialog box as you do in the Save for Web & Devices dialog box, shown in Figure 60-2 at the top of the next page, for a JPEG image.

- The tradeoffs of size, speed, and quality are especially easy to see in this dialog box when optimizing a JPEG, because there are fewer alternatives to choose among.

- Choose from among five quality settings: Low (10 quality), Medium (30 quality), High (60 quality), Very High (80 quality), and Maximum (100 quality). Higher quality results in a finer display, but also results in a larger file size and longer download time.

Figure 60-2. Optimize a JPEG file

- When Progressive is selected, the image is displayed in the browser in a series of passes at progressively higher resolutions, which can make the process of viewing a large file less frustrating for the site visitor.

- If Progressive is not selected, you can click the Optimized checkbox to reduce file size somewhat for high-quality JPEGs.

- Use the Quality slider to adjust compression of the image. The lower the quality, the higher the compression.

- Apply a Blur setting if desired to enable greater compression and thus smaller file size.

- If the image includes transparency, you can select a color using the Matte box to replace the transparent pixels.

- Preview an image in the browser or Device Central the same as for a GIF image.

- Save an optimized JPEG the same way as an optimized GIF, providing a new name and choosing one of the three Format options.

Use Slices to Organize a Document

- You can use Photoshop to create a document specifically designed for Web or device content. Select from among a number of Web page and device display presets in the New dialog box and then prepare both text and graphic content at precisely the right size.

- One way to organize images in a document that will be saved for Web or devices is to use **slices**.

- Slices are defined regions of a document that can be named and modified separately from other regions in the document. One benefit of using slices on a page that contains several different kinds of images is that slices can be optimized separately. This means that a slice containing a photo can be optimized for JPEG while a slice on the same page that contains few colors or blocks of color can be optimized for GIF.

■ Use the Slice tool  to create slices. Draw an outline on the image the size you want to make the slice, as shown in Figure 60-3. Continue to draw slices to isolate areas of the image you want to work with. Photoshop automatically creates any slices necessary to connect the ones you inserted so that the whole image is enclosed in a grid of slices.

Figure 60-3. Drag the slice tool to create a slice

■ You can also create slices using guides or a layer:

  ● Position guides on the Web page to mark off the slices you want to create. Then select the Slice tool and click Slices From Guides on the options bar. Photoshop uses the guides as a framework to create the slices.

  ● To create a slice from a layer, create the new layer and add content to it as desired, then use the Layer > New Layer Based Slice command to create the slice. The slice will include all pixel data on the layer.

    ✓ *Layer-based slices are particularly useful if you want to create a rollover button or link area on a Web page.*

■ Each slice has a number and an outline that defines its area. Slices in the grid are numbered from the upper-left to the lower-right.

■ To select a slice, use the Slice Select tool . Click once on a slice to select it and display selection handles you can use to adjust slice size. You can also drag the slice with the Slice Select tool to move it to a new position. (The grid of slices adjusts to account for the new position of the moved slice.)

■ To ensure that a browser displays sliced content correctly, you must indicate a type for each of the slices you create. To specify slice type, double-click a slice to open the Slice Options dialog box, shown in Figure 60-4.

Figure 60-4. Select options for a slice

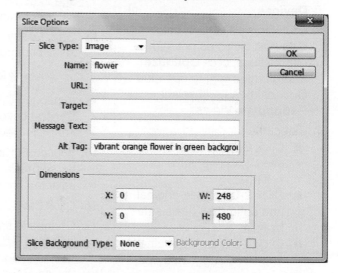

■ If you are creating slices in Photoshop, you have two options for slice type:

  ● Use the Image type for slices that will become images on a Web page, such as slices that contain photos or line art.

  ● Use the No Image slice type for a slice that contains text or a block of color. These slices are not exported as images when you save the optimized page.

■ You can supply the following additional information in this dialog box:

  ● Name the slice to make it easy to work with if you need to adjust the HTML code for the page.

  ● To use the slice as a link, type the Web address in the URL box. Use the Target box to indicate where to open the linked page if you are using frames.

  ● Use the Message Text box to type text that will display when the mouse pointer is over the link.

  ● The Alt Tag box allows you to enter text that describes the slice content for a computer using a screen reader.

■ Note that the Dimensions area of the dialog box allows you to adjust the size and coordinates of the slice if you need to fine-tune these measurements. You can also select a background color or matte for the slice.

PROCEDURES

Optimize a GIF Image
(Alt + Shift + Ctrl + S)

1. Click **File** .... ALT + F
2. Click **Save for Web & Devices** .... D
3. Click file type list and select **GIF**. If all views do not show GIF settings, click **Optimize Menu** button ▾≡ to open the Options menu and select **Repopulate Views**.
4. Select tab for desired view:
   - Click **Optimized** tab to see default optimization settings.
   - Click **2-Up** to see original and optimized views side by side.
   - Click **4-Up** to see original and three suggested optimizations.
5. Click color reduction list arrow to select a method for reducing colors.

   ✓ This list box is not clearly labeled. It is the second list box at the left side of the settings area. Rest the mouse pointer on the box to see the ScreenTip that reads Color reduction algorithm.

6. Click the dithering list arrow to select a dithering method or No Dither.

   ✓ This list box is not clearly labeled. It is the third list box at the left side of the settings area. Rest the mouse pointer on the box to see the ScreenTip that reads Specify the dither algorithm.

7. Click **Colors** list arrow or use spin arrows to select number of colors.
8. Drag **Dither** slider to apply an amount of dither.
9. Select **Transparency** to preserve transparency in the image.
10. Select **Matte** setting to change color of transparent pixels.

11. Select **Interlaced** to load a low-resolution image while the final image is loading.
12. Specify a **Web Snap** percentage to convert colors to Web-safe equivalents.
13. Drag **Lossy** slider to apply lossy compression to GIF.

    ✓ Click arrow to access slider.

14. (Optional) Click **Device Central** button to preview image in Device Central CS5.
15. (Optional) Click **Preview** button to preview the image in the selected browser.
16. Click **Save** .... ENTER
17. Choose to save file:
    - As HTML and Images.
    - As Images Only.
    - As HTML Only.
18. Click **Save** .... ENTER

Optimize a JPEG Image
(Alt + Shift + Ctrl + S)

1. Click **File** .... ALT + F
2. Click **Save for Web & Devices** .... D
3. Click file type list and select **JPEG**. If all views do not show JPEG settings, click **Optimize Menu** button ▾≡ to open the Options menu and select **Repopulate Views**.
4. Select tab for desired view:
   - Click **Optimized** tab to see default optimization settings.
   - Click **2-Up** to see original and optimized views side by side.
   - Click **4-Up** to see original and three suggested optimizations.
5. Click compression quality list arrow and choose from **Low**, **Medium**, **High**, **Very High**, or **Maximum** quality.

6. Select **Progressive** to download progressively better versions of file until final quality is reached.
7. Select **Optimized** to slightly reduce file size for High and Maximum quality images.
8. Drag the **Quality** slider to adjust the compression and thus the quality of the image.
9. Apply a **Blur** amount to allow for greater compression.
10. Select **Matte** setting to change color of pixels that were transparent in original.
11. (Optional) Click **Device Central** button to preview image in Device Central CS5.
12. (Optional) Click **Preview** button to preview the image in the selected browser.
13. Click **Save** .... ENTER
14. Choose to save file:
    - As HTML and Images.
    - As Images Only.
    - As HTML Only.
15. Click **Save** .... ENTER

Add Slices to an Image

- Select **Slice** tool and drag to enclose the area you want for the slice.

  ✓ You will find the Slice tool beneath the Crop tool in the toolbox.

OR

1. Drag guides to define a grid over an image.
2. Click **Slice** tool and select **Slices From Guides** in options bar.

OR

1. Create a new layer and add content to it.
2. Click **Layer** .... ALT + L
3. Click **New Layer Based Slice** .... B

Change Slice Options

1. Select **Slice Select** tool ![icon].
2. Double-click on slice.
3. Click **Slice Type** .. `ALT` + `S`, `↑` and scroll to select slice type.
4. Click **Name** and type name for slice ....`ALT` + `N`

5. Click **URL** and type Web address for linked page ....`ALT` + `U`
6. Click **Target** and specify frame in which page should open ....`ALT` + `R`
7. Click **Message Text** and type text that will display when pointer hovers over link ....`ALT` + `M`

8. Click **Alt Tag** and type text that will be used in a screen reader or while loading image.........................`ALT` + `A`
9. Click **OK** ....`ENTER`

EXERCISE DIRECTIONS

1. Before you begin the exercise, create a new folder where you store your solution files with the name *60Wilcox_xx*. You will use this folder to keep all your Web files together.

2. Open the ◎ *60Arch* file. Optimize this image as a JPEG:

   a. Display the Save for Web & Devices dialog box and choose to optimize for JPEG, if that option is not already selected.

   b. Display the 4-Up view and use the Repopulate Views option on the Optimize menu if necessary to display JPEG settings in all views.

   c. Set one view to Low, one to Medium, and one to High quality and view the file sizes, download times, and image quality for each view.

   d. Change the download speed to 384 Kbps and repopulate views if necessary to apply this new speed to all views.

   e. Change the Quality setting for the High quality view to 50 and note changes to file size and speed. The image quality is still pretty sharp for this setting, so you will use it.

   f. Preview the image in your browser, then return to the Save for Web & Devices dialog box.

3. Save the optimized JPEG in the *60Wilcox_xx* folder with the name *60Arch* using the Images Only type. Close the data file without saving.

4. Open the ◎ *60Texture* file. Optimize this image as a GIF:

   a. Repopulate views so that all four show GIF options.

   b. View each of the three optimization views to see how settings vary.

   c. Change the number of colors to 16 to see how the file size and download speed vary. Then select 8 as the number of colors.

   d. Select the view that you think will display the texture best at the best file size and download speed. Preview the image in your browser to make sure your choice looks attractive.

5. Save the optimized GIF in the *60Wilcox_xx* folder with the name *60Texture* using the Images Only type. Close the data file without saving.

   ✓ *Now you will combine the optimized files with another data file to create a simple Web page.*

6. Open the ◎ *60Wilcox* file and save it in the *60Wilcox_xx* folder as *60Tourweb*. View the page at 100% if possible.

7. Select the Background layer. Open *60Arch* from the *60Wilcox_xx* folder, arrange the two documents side by side, and use the Move tool to drag the image to *60Tourweb*.

8. Scale the image so it fits the area within the vertical guide and the third horizontal guide, as shown in Illustration A. Close *60Arch*.

9. Use the File > Place command to place *60Texture* on the Web page from the *60Wilcox_xx* folder. Click the Confirm button to confirm the place operation. Drag the image to the top of the page, to the right of the arch image and above the first horizontal guide. Make sure the texture image butts up against the arch image so there is no gap between the two images.

10. Use the Slice tool to create slices as follows, using the guides to help you:

   a. Draw an outline around the photo image of the arch. This should be slice 01. An automatic slice 02 should be created around the texture shape at the same time.

   b. Draw a slice outline around the texture shape. If this slice turns into slide 03 rather than 02, undo and step backward to remove all slices and then make sure the texture shape is butted up against the arch image. Photoshop automatically creates slices 03 and 04 to complete the grid.

11. Using the Slice Select tool, specify options for each slice as follows:

   a. For slice 01, name the image **arch_image**. Type the following in the Alt Tag box: **Delicate Arch at sunset**

   b. For slice 02, name the slice **texture_bar** and type the following Alt Tag: **Orange texture shape**

12. Hide the guides (View > Show > Guides) so you can see the grid of slices on the image. The top of your page should resemble Illustration A.

13. Save the page, then issue the Save for Web & Devices command. In the Save for Web & Devices dialog box:

   a. Select the Optimized tab to show only the optimized image. Use the Hand tool from the toolbox at the left side of the dialog box to move the image so you can see some of both the arch image and the texture image.

   b. Use the Slice Select tool to select the arch image slice. Select JPEG from the format list. The image should display the optimization settings you applied to the image when you optimized it previously.

   c. Select the texture image. Make sure the settings are the same as those you used earlier to optimize the GIF.

   d. Save the document in the 60Wilcox_xx folder as 60Tourweb using the HTML and Images format.

14. Launch your browser and navigate to locate the 60Tourweb.html file. Open the file in your browser to view the images and text.

15. Close the browser. Save changes to 60Tourweb, close the file, and exit Photoshop.

Illustration A

DREAM in the DESERT SOUTHWEST

Wilcox Tours Presents . . .
Arches National Park
Canyonlands National Park
Grand Canyon National Park

ON YOUR OWN

1. Before you begin the exercise, create a new folder where you store your solution files with the name OPH60_xx. You will use this folder to keep all your Web files together.

2. Open ⊙OYO60 and save the file in the OPH60_xx folder as OPH60_web. This file is the first step in a new Web page for Newfound Nursery.

3. Create a layer-based slice for the background image as follows:

   a. Select the Flowers layer.

   b. Use the Layer > New Layer Based Slice command to create the layer.

4. Select the layer that contains the *NEWFOUND NURSERY* type. This type has been rasterized so you can apply a filter to it. Apply a filter of your choice.

5. Create a layer-based slice from the filtered type.

6. Create layer-based slices for each of the type objects that will be used as links to other pages in the site (*ABOUT US, DIRECTIONS,* and so on).

7. Name each slice appropriately. For the link slices, insert a URL to an appropriately named page. You don't have to create pages, just the links, although you may want to create a link to a "live" site to test your links. For example, type

   http://www.adobe.com

   to create a link to the Adobe Web site.

8. Save the page for the Web:

   a. Optimize the NEWFOUND NURSERY slice as a GIF.

   b. Optimize the flowers background image slice as a JPEG.

   c. Preview the page in a browser.

9. Save the file as OPH60_web as HTML and Images.

10. Open the optimized page in your browser and check that each slice link takes you to a new page.

11. Close the browser. Save changes to OPH60_web and close the file. Exit Photoshop.

Skills Covered

- **About Color Management**
- **Change Color Profiles**
- **Convert RGB Files for Print**
- **Proof Colors**

Software Skills A color management system helps a user translate color data from one device to another. Changing color profiles can adjust the gamut of a file to use more or fewer colors. You can convert RGB files to CMYK or grayscale for print output. To see on your monitor how colors might look when printed, use Photoshop's soft proofing options.

Design Skills A designer must have a good grasp of the intricacies of color management to know what questions to ask a print supplier and how to adjust settings to ensure an image looks good using any output method.

Application Skills In this exercise, you adjust color settings for the entire Creative Suite and then view an image from Parker Conservatory using different color profiles and proof settings.

TERMS

Color management system System that translates color information from one device to another.

Color profile A mathematical description of a device's *color space*.

Color space A variant of a color model that has a specific range of colors.

Soft proofing Proofing an image by applying settings that simulate the output of a specific device.

Working space A *color space* used to define and edit color in an Adobe application.

NOTES

About Color Management

- If you are able to print to a color printer, you may already have discovered that printouts of illustrations and images you have created do not quite match the colors on your monitor.

- One of the reasons why colors displayed on one device, such as a monitor, do not match the colors produced by another device, such as a printer, is that the two devices are using different **color spaces**.

- You will remember that digital design applications work with several standard *color models*, such as CMYK, RGB, HSB, and so on.

- Some color models have color space variants, such as the several RGB color spaces you will read about in the next section. In addition, devices such as monitors, desktop printers, or four-color presses have specific color spaces. Each color space has a range, or *gamut*, of colors.

  ✓ *You have already read about color gamuts in the Illustrator section of this course.*

- Any given device can display only the colors in its gamut. A monitor has a fairly wide color gamut, while a desktop printer has a fairly narrow range of colors. Thus, an image that looks great on your monitor may not look quite so great when printed to your nearby laser printer.

- To reduce the likelihood of color mismatches across devices, you can use a **color management system**.

- A color management system translates the color information from one device (such as a monitor) into a standard reference color space that is not associated with a particular device.

  ✓ *A color space that is not associated with a device is called device-independent. A color space for a specific device is called device-dependent.*

- The color management system then maps colors from the device-independent color space to the color space of another device (such as a printer), adjusting colors to display as consistently as possible for the designated devices.

  ✓ *Color management systems offer a choice of translation methods called rendering intents that are beyond the scope of this book.*

- The process of translating colors during color management relies on specific **color profiles**. A color profile is a mathematical description of a particular color space.

- To manage color very accurately, you can specify color profiles for your monitor, for input devices such as scanners or digital cameras, and for output devices such as desktop printers and printing presses.

- As you can see, color management can be a very complex subject, and the finer points of adjusting color across a range of devices are beyond the scope of this text. You can learn more about color management by consulting Adobe Help files.

- By default, color management is turned on in the Adobe Design Creative Suite so that all applications in the suite share the same color settings. If you want to adjust color settings for an application, you can do so by clicking Edit > Color Settings to open the Color Settings dialog box, shown in Figure 61-1.

- Color settings control **working space** options and color management policies. Working spaces are the color spaces used to define and edit color while you are working in an Adobe application.

- The default color setting is North America General Purpose 2. As you would guess from the name, this setting is suitable for a range of output options, including both print and screen output.

- If you intend to print your output rather than use it for Web or device content, a better setting option is North America Prepress 2.

- Selecting this color setting changes the RGB working space and also selects the series of "Ask When" check boxes in the Color Management Policies section of the dialog box.

Figure 61-1. Color Settings dialog box

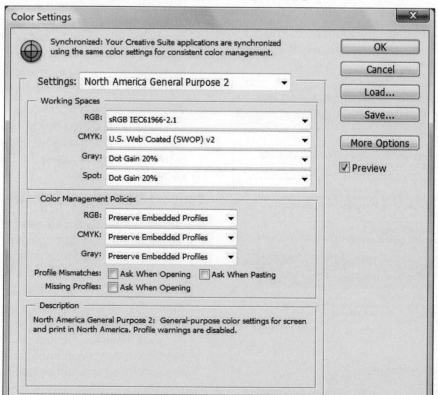

- When you create a file in any of the Creative Suite applications, the current color settings are embedded in that file. If you open or paste a file that uses different color settings, the application displays an Embedded Profile Mismatch warning like the one shown in Figure 61-2.

Figure 61-2. Embedded Profile Mismatch dialog box

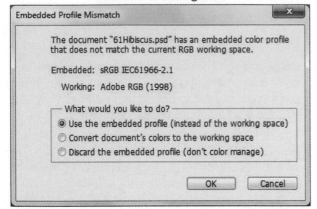

- You can choose to use the file's embedded color profile, convert it to the current color settings, or suspend color management for the file.

- If you intend to change the color settings for one Creative Suite application, you should change them globally for the whole suite to maintain proper synchronization of colors across all applications. You can do this easily in Adobe Bridge.

- Clicking the Edit > Creative Suite Color Settings command in Bridge displays the Suite Color Settings dialog box shown in Figure 61-3. Select a color setting and then apply it to specify the same settings for all applications.

Figure 61-3. Suite Color Settings dialog box

Change Color Profiles

- As you change color settings for an application, you can also change the color profiles for working spaces in the Color Settings dialog box. Each working space offers a list of standard profiles you can choose among.

- The default RGB working space profile is sRGB IEC61966-2.1, a general-purpose profile that can be used for both print and Web images.

- If you change the color setting to North America Prepress 2, as is recommended for printed output, the RGB working space profile automatically changes to Adobe RGB, which has a larger gamut than the sRGB profile. For professional-level graphic design, you may want to specify the ProPhoto RGB profile, which has an even larger gamut.

  ✓ *You are advised to adjust bit depth if you want to use ProPhoto RGB. Changing image bit depth is beyond the scope of this book.*

- The CMYK profile options are device-dependent; that is, they are based on actual printing device settings for paper and ink. You can choose a profile specifically for coated or uncoated paper, for example, or for sheet-fed or web presses.

  ✓ *A sheet-fed press prints on individual sheets of paper; a web press prints on a continuous roll of paper.*

- The default CMYK profile is U.S. Web Coated (SWOP) v2. This setting is appropriate for a variety of printed documents, but before sending a job to be printed, check with your print representative about the proper profile to use.

- Note that you can also adjust the working spaces for the Grayscale color model and for spot colors.

- When you change working space profiles in the Color Settings dialog box, they apply to all new images. You can if desired apply a different profile to an individual file using the Edit > Assign Profiles command.

Convert RGB Files for Print

- One of the reasons you need to know about color management and color profiles while working in Photoshop is that these settings can make a difference if you need to convert a standard Photoshop RGB file to CMYK for printing.

- The RGB color model has a larger gamut than the CMYK color model. This means that some color data will inevitably be lost during the conversion process. Often the changes are slight or invisible to the untutored eye, but some kinds of images may require considerable work to ensure that they look as good in CMYK as in RGB.

■ For simple jobs, you may choose to carry out the conversion yourself. For more complex jobs, you may want to leave the conversion to your print supplier. This is an issue that you should discuss thoroughly with your supplier before providing final files.

■ Regardless of whether you choose to convert files yourself or leave this process to the print supplier, you should take the following steps before converting.

- Make all color corrections to the RGB files before you convert to CMYK.

- Choose a color profile appropriate for printed output, such as Adobe RGB.

- Create a duplicate or backup of the file with all layers intact in case you need to do further editing on the file.

- Flatten the image to avoid unexpected changes in layer blending modes during the conversion from RGB to CMYK.

■ After finalizing the RGB file, you can easily convert it to CMYK using the Image > Mode > CMYK Color command.

■ When you convert an RGB file to CMYK, the Channels panel changes to display cyan, magenta, yellow, and black channels, as well as a composite channel.

■ You have another conversion option besides CMYK. You can convert an RGB image to grayscale, to display the image in black, white, and shades of gray.

■ To convert to grayscale, use the Image > Mode > Grayscale command. You will be asked if you want to discard color information.

■ The Channels panel for a grayscale image has only one channel, the composite.

Proof Colors

■ If you have calibrated your monitor to accepted standards, you can be fairly sure that what you see in Photoshop is what others will see when they view your images on the Web or on a device. This assurance does not hold true, however, if you are preparing images for print publishing, for reasons explained earlier.

■ You have several options for checking whether the colors in your image will look the way you want them to when output on a press. If you have access to the printing system that will be used to output the image, you can run a hard copy and proof colors on the paper.

■ You can also proof colors to some degree right on your monitor using a feature called **soft proofing**. When you soft proof an image, you can specify an output setting, such as coated paper on a sheet-fed press. The image's colors change to show you approximately how the image would look printed with those settings.

■ To soft proof an image, first select the View > Proof Colors command. Then, use the View > Proof Setup command. The Proof Setup submenu gives you options to view the current ("working") CMYK as well as each color plate and a composite that excludes black. You can also select from several RGB options if your image is in RGB color mode.

■ You can also set up a custom proof profile to see how your image will look under a specific set of printing conditions. Use the View > Proof Setup > Custom command to open the Custom dialog box shown in Figure 61-4.

Figure 61-4. Set up a custom proof profile

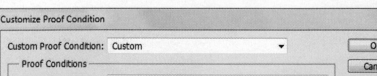
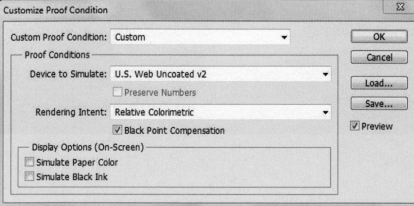

- Choose the device to simulate and change the rendering intent if desired. Note that you can also choose to simulate the paper color and black ink as they would actually appear in printed output. (Paper may be more grayish than white and black ink may actually be a dark gray.)

- You may not see much of a change on your screen when you choose to proof colors. The usefulness of this feature depends a great deal on the quality of your monitor, the color profiles you have established for your monitor and the chosen output device, and even how much light is shining on the monitor screen as you are proofing.

- The View > Gamut Warning command lets you identify colors that fall outside the gamut of the current color proofing profile. Out-of-gamut colors display on the image as areas of gray pixels.

- Figure 61-5 shows colors that will be out-of-gamut for the working CMYK color model. This kind of display is proof positive that the RGB color model creates colors that cannot be displayed correctly in the CMYK model.

- You don't normally have to worry about out-of-gamut colors if you are converting an image from RGB to CMYK—Photoshop adjusts the out-of-gamut colors as necessary to fit in the CMYK gamut.

- If you are not converting a file, you can often take care of out-of-gamut colors by desaturating the areas of gray.

- When you have finished soft proofing the image, deselect the View > Proof Colors command and the Gamut Warning command to return the image to its original display.

Design Suite Integration

Soft Proofing

Illustrator and InDesign also offer the soft-proofing feature you have explored in this section. Options may vary by application, but all applications allow you to select a desired output device so you can get an idea how your job will look when printed.

Figure 61-5. Out-of-gamut colors display as areas of gray

PROCEDURES

Change Color Settings
(Shift + Ctrl + K)

1. Click **Edit** .... `ALT` + `E`
2. Click **Color Settings** .... `G`
3. Click **Settings** list ...... `ALT` + `T`
4. Select a setting .... `↑` or `↓`
5. Change working space profiles if desired:
   a. Click **RGB** working space list .... `ALT` + `R`
   b. Select a profile ...... `↑` or `↓`
   c. Click **CMYK** working space list .... `ALT` + `C`
   d. Select a profile ...... `↑` or `↓`
6. Click **OK** .... `ENTER`

Change Color Settings for the Creative Suite (Ctrl + Shift+ K)

1. Start Adobe Bridge.
2. Click **Edit** .... `ALT` + `E`
3. Click **Creative Suite Color Settings**.
4. Select desired color setting.
5. Click **Apply** .... `ENTER`

Assign a Color Profile to a Document

In Photoshop:

1. Click **Edit** .... `ALT` + `E`
2. Click **Assign Profile**.
3. Click **OK** when warned about changing color profile.

4. Choose a setting:
   - **Don't Color Manage This Document** .... `ALT` + `D`
   - **Working RGB** .... `ALT` + `W`

   OR

   - **Working CMYK** if file has been converted.
   - **Profile** and then select a profile from the list .... `ALT` + `R` , `↓`
5. Click **OK** .... `ENTER`

Convert to CMYK Color for Printing

1. Click **Layer** .... `ALT` + `L`
2. Click **Flatten Image** .... `F`
3. Click **Image** .... `ALT` + `I`
4. Click **Mode** .... `M`
5. Click **CMYK Color** .... `C`
6. Choose whether to merge if the image has more than one layer.

Convert to Grayscale

1. Click **Image** .... `ALT` + `I`
2. Click **Mode** .... `M`
3. Click **Grayscale** .... `G`
4. Choose whether to merge if the image has more than one layer.
5. Click **Discard** .... `ENTER`

Proof Colors Before Printing
(Ctrl + Y)

1. Click **View** .... `ALT` + `V`
2. Click **Proof Colors** .... `L`
3. Click **View** .... `ALT` + `V`
4. Click **Proof Setup** .... `U`
5. Select a working plate to view.

   OR

   a. Select **Custom** .... `U`
   b. Click **Device to Simulate** and scroll down list to select a device .... `ALT` + `D` , `↓`
   c. Click **Simulate Paper Color** if desired to add paper color to image .... `A`

      ✓ *Selecting this option automatically selects Simulate Black Ink as well.*

   d. Click **Simulate Black Ink** if desired to simulate the dark grays used as black by some printers .... `B`
   e. Click **OK** .... `ENTER`

To turn off soft proofing:

1. Click **View** .... `ALT` + `V`
2. Click **Proof Colors** .... `L`

EXERCISE DIRECTIONS

1. Start Photoshop, and then start Adobe Bridge.
2. Display the Suite Color Settings dialog box, select the North America Prepress 2 setting, and apply it. Close Bridge.
3. Open the ⊙61Hibiscus file. You should receive an Embedded Profile Mismatch warning box.
4. Choose to convert the document to the current working space, which is Adobe RGB. Then save the file as 61Hibiscus_xx.
5. Use the Edit > Assign Profile command to assign the ProPhoto RGB color profile to see how the image adjusts with a new color profile. The colors should brighten noticeably.
6. Choose to soft proof the image:
   a. Turn on proofing and view each of the CMYK color plates in turn to see how the image would look in CMYK.
   b. Choose the Proof Setup > Custom option and choose the U.S. Web Uncoated v2 device to see how the image would look on uncoated (not shiny) paper.
   c. Choose to simulate paper color.
   d. Change the device back to U.S. Web Coated (SWOP) v2. Click OK to accept these changes.
   e. Select the Gamut Warning command to see the areas of the image that will be out-of-gamut for CMYK.
7. Turn off gamut warning and soft proofing to return the image to original settings.
8. Convert the color mode to CMYK Color. Display the Channels panel and notice that there are now four color channels plus the CMYK composite channel and a mask.
9. Save your changes, close the file, and exit Photoshop.

ON YOUR OWN

✓ *In this exercise, you will have a chance to work with another Photoshop color mode, Grayscale.*

1. Open the ⊙OYO61 file. Choose to convert to the current working space, and then save the file as OPH61_xx.
2. Convert the image to Grayscale. Do not merge layers.
3. Add some interest to the image by loading the two-flowers selection, inverting it, and applying an adjustment layer you have not used before, such as Gradient Map. Applying one of the default two- or three-color gradients can yield interesting results in a grayscale image.
4. Select the Background copy layer and load the selection again, without inverting this time. Apply an adjustment layer such as Posterize to the selection.
5. Save your changes, close the file, and exit Photoshop.

Exercise | 62

Summary Exercise

Application Skills Parker Conservatory wants you to prepare information about its spring show and has given you a photo to work with. In this exercise, you will improve the image, use a mask to remove an unnecessary portion of the image, add and format type, and apply a layer style.

EXERCISE DIRECTIONS

1. Open ⊚62Spring and convert it for the current color profile, then save the file as 62Spring_xx. Copy the Background layer and work on Background copy.

2. Improve the brightness and contrast of the photo using an adjustment layer.

3. Use the Lasso or Quick Selection tool to select the area in the upper-right corner of the image that shows the glass walls of the conservatory.

   a. Switch to Quick Mask mode and clean up the selection to include as much of the grayish wall area as possible. Work carefully around the flowers and switch back to Standard mode frequently to check your selection. Use your own judgment about how much of the gray mesh within the red bush to include.

   b. View the mask in the Channels panel (hide the composite image) to make sure you have "erased" all the pixels within the selected area.

   c. Save the selection with an appropriate name.

4. Insert a new gradient fill layer above the Background layer. Create a gradient using colors you select from the image (such as a light and darker purple).

5. Select the Background copy layer. Load the selection and use it to cut the pixels in the selection so the gradient shows in the corner area. You may want to use Eraser tools or other selection options to delete more of the gray mesh area than is included in your selection.

6. Select one of the type mask tools and then choose a sturdy font, a large font size, and a heavy font style if available. Type **SPRING** at some location on the Background copy layer of the image.

7. Click the Standard mode button to exit Quick Mask mode. With the type masks still selected on the Background copy layer, click Delete to remove the background pixels and display the gradient.

   ✓ You may want to adjust the gradient layer at this point to make sure the type can be seen clearly. Double-click the gradient thumbnail in the gradient layer to adjust the gradient.

8. Apply a layer style such as Outer Glow or Drop Shadow to the Background copy layer. Adjust settings as desired to create an interesting look for the image. Illustration A shows one option.

9. Save your changes, and then create a duplicate of the image named 62Spring2_xx. Flatten all layers in the duplicate.

10. Convert this file to CMYK color mode.

11. Save your changes and close all images.

Exercise | 63

Application Exercise

Application Skills You have been asked to work on an image to be used in the catalog that supports the Lexington Art Museum's new exhibit, "Ladies of Lexington: Fashions from the Golden Age." In this exercise, you will rotate and modify image size, crop the image, work with a mask to isolate part of an image, and add adjustment layers and a filter to modify image appearance.

EXERCISE DIRECTIONS

1. Open ⊙ 63Dress and convert it to the current color space, then save the image as 63Dress_xx.

2. Rotate the canvas 90 degrees counterclockwise.

3. Change the image resolution to 150 with resampling on and adjust height to 6 inches.

4. Add an adjustment layer above the Background copy layer to brighten the colors a bit. You may use Vibrance or Hue/Saturation for the adjustment layer.

5. Crop the image to remove some of the space above and below the mannequins and the portion of another dress at the left foreground. Leave enough room below the mannequins to add type as shown in Illustration A. Adjust height after cropping to about 5 inches.

6. Select an ornamental font and an appropriate size and color and type the following lines:

   Afternoon Dress
   by Madame Duplessis

7. Right-align the type and position it at the lower-right of the image. Adjust the font size of the second line to be slightly smaller than the first line.

   ✓ *The peach-colored dress at the right should be the focus of this image. You will select this dress so you can fade the background around it.*

8. Use the Quick Selection tool to select the mannequin at the right. Then work in Quick Mask mode to refine the selection. Make sure to remove as much dark background as possible around the arms and right hand. You may want to change the mask color.

9. Save the selection with an appropriate name in the Channels panel and keep it active.

10. Apply an Exposure adjustment layer above the first one. You should see the layer mask of the dress selection in the adjustment layer.

11. Use the Masks panel to invert the selection.

12. Adjust exposure in the Exposure adjustment layer to dim out the area around the mask so that the selected dress stands out.

13. To add a little more punch, convert the Background copy layer for use with Smart Filters. Then load the dress selection, and choose a filter to apply to the area around the selection. Illustration A shows an effect created with the Grain filter. Adjust exposure as necessary to make the filtered area attractive without being obtrusive.

14. Save your changes, close the file, and exit Photoshop.

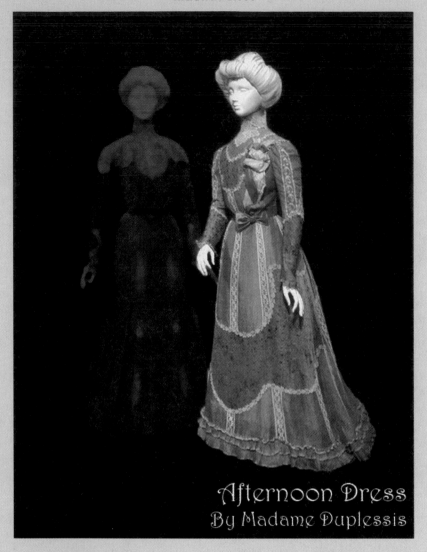

Afternoon Dress
By Madame Duplessis

Exercise | 64

Curriculum Integration

Application Skills   Your Discrete Math class is discussing a number of topics that relate to math, such as game theory and fractals. You have been assigned the task of explaining what a fractal is and who first used fractal formulas to create shapes. You will illustrate your brief explanation with a fractal image. Before you begin this exercise, locate the following:

- A simple explanation of what a fractal is
- Information on the mathematician who first worked extensively with fractals
- A fractal image in a form you can use in Photoshop (JPG or GIF will work fine)

EXERCISE DIRECTIONS

Open the fractal image you located in Photoshop and save it as a Photoshop image with the name 64Fractal_xx. Adjust the image size to use a resolution of 72 if necessary. If you see *Index* in the Layers panel instead of Background, change the color mode from Indexed color to RGB. Copy the Background layer and work on Background copy.

Modify the canvas size to add space below the image so you will have room for your explanation. Insert a fill layer with a pattern or gradient below the Background copy layer.

Convert the Background copy layer to use Smart Filters, and then apply an interesting filter to the fractal. The filter should not obscure the fractal's intricacy, but it can simplify it.

Add type below the fractal image that explains what a fractal is and who "discovered" fractals. Use any type settings you are familiar with to adjust the text.

Somewhere on the image create a type object for a heading that reads **FRACTALS**. Rasterize the type and apply a filter to it, and then change the blending mode for the rastered type to create an interesting effect. You may also want to apply a layer style to the type.

Add text in a small font size somewhere in the image that gives the source of the fractal image you used.

Save your changes, close the file, and exit Photoshop.

Portfolio Builder

Application Skills   Barkley's Biscuits is developing a new Web site and wants your help in mocking up the home page. You have a picture you want to use for a winter version of the home page. You will slice the page to make it easy to optimize and create links.

EXERCISE DIRECTIONS

Open ⊙ 65Barkley and change to the current working space, then save the file as 65Barkley_xx.

Guides have been provided to help you line up image components. Display the guides if necessary. Use the Slice tool to create a slice for the paw prints panel at the left side of the page. (Use the upper horizontal guide and the leftmost vertical guide to help you create the slice.) Create a slice of the main area of the screen with the dogs in the center. (Use the lower horizontal guide and the leftmost vertical guide to help you create the slice.)

Create layer-based slices from the type layers that will become the links to other pages in the site (*About Barkley*, *Our Products,* and so on). Do not create a slice from the main page heading.

Name each slice appropriately and specify dummy Web addresses for the link slices. Include at least one real link so you can check your work.

Optimize the images on the page: optimize the paw prints slice as a GIF and the dogs slice as a JPEG. Preview the page in your browser.

Save the image in an appropriately named folder as 65Barkley_web, using the HTML and Images setting. Then open the file in your browser to test your links.

Save your changes to 65Barkley_xx, close the file, and exit Photoshop.

Open Bridge and restore the color setting to North America General Purpose 2 for the entire Creative Suite.

Lesson | 7
Work with Basic Layout Tools in InDesign CS5

Skills Covered

- About InDesign
- Start a New Document
- InDesign Tools
- About Document and Ruler Guides

- Insert a Text Frame
- Insert a Graphic Frame
- Draw a Shape

Software Skills   Use the Welcome screen or the New Document dialog box to start a new InDesign document. Many InDesign tools will look familiar to you from Illustrator and Photoshop. Guides can help you lay out text and graphics on your pages. Use frames to control the position of text and graphics on a page.

Design Skills   Using InDesign effectively for print documents requires a designer to be familiar with tools and the work area. Understanding how frames are used to contain content can help a designer to create an efficient and attractive design.

Application Skills   Greenwood Conservancy has contacted you to create a publication about seasonal happenings in the Conservancy. In this exercise, you will set up the publication document, insert frames for text and a graphic, and draw a simple shape.

TERMS

Bleed   Printing that extends beyond the specified page size so that white space doesn't show after a page is trimmed.

Frame   Container that holds text or graphic content.

Gutter   The space between columns of text.

Spread   A set of two pages (a left page and a right page) viewed together on screen.

NOTES

About InDesign

- Adobe InDesign is a page layout application that allows you to create a wide variety of sophisticated publications, from the simplest flyers to entire books that contain many separate parts.

- You can create simple graphics right in InDesign using tools you have already mastered in the Illustrator section of this course, or you can import graphics from applications such as Illustrator and Photoshop.

- Likewise, you can type the text for your publications directly on InDesign pages, or you can import text that has been created in a word processing application such as Microsoft Word.

- InDesign's text-handling features give you considerable control over how type displays on a page. Features such as text wrapping and drop capitals can be accomplished with the click of a button, and the Character and Paragraph Formatting options in the Control panel give you many more ways to customize type for a professional result.

- You will find that the InDesign workspace has a very familiar feel, with the Control panel at the top, Tools panel to the left, and other panels docked at the right. You do your work on the pages that appear in the center of the document window.

Start a New Document

- Like Illustrator, InDesign opens a Welcome screen when it starts that allows you to quickly create a new document. You can also use the File > New > Document command to open the New Document dialog box, shown in Figure 66-1. Use this dialog box to set the number of pages, the size and orientation of the pages, number of columns, margins, and the bleed and slug areas.

  ✓ *Figure 66-1 shows the dialog box expanded to show all options. If you do not need to specify bleed and slug areas, you can show fewer options.*

- If you know the number of pages you want to use in the document, you can supply it in this dialog box, or you can leave the default setting and add pages later as you need them.

- In InDesign CS5, you can specify the page number on which the document will start.

- The Facing Pages option is selected by default. This option sets up a document's pages in **spreads** of two pages, so that you can see a left page and a right page at the same time on the screen. Deselect this option if you want to work with single pages.

  ✓ *When you select the Facing Pages option, the first page of the document is a single page and the next two pages form the spread.*

- The default page size is Letter; you can choose from other standard sizes such as Legal and Tabloid or from Web and device sizes. You can choose either portrait or landscape orientation for a document. InDesign CS5 allows you to specify different sizes for pages in a document, so you can actually create multiple documents in a single file.

- Note that the page width and height are given in *picas* and *points* by default. Picas are the standard measurement unit for page layout documents. Points are fractions of a pica—there are 12 points in a pica. The measurement 3p0 indicates 3 picas and 0 points.

- A new document is set up to have only one column. If your document has a lot of text, you will usually want to increase the number of columns. Text is easier to read if it is set in two or three columns rather than across the whole width of a page.

  ✓ *You can add columns to a document at any time using the Layout > Margins and Columns command.*

- If you select more than one column, you can adjust the **gutter** space between columns.

- Margins are set by default at 3 picas on all sides. You can type new values or click spin arrows to increase or reduce margins.

Figure 66-1. New Document dialog box

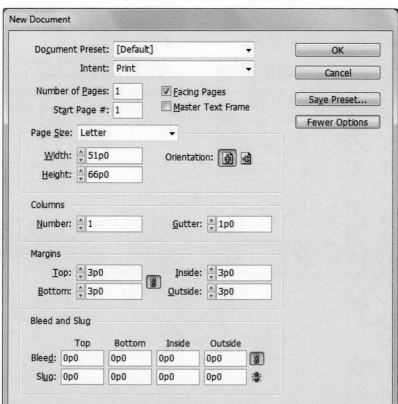

- If the Make all settings the same button 🔓 is selected, any change you make to one margin setting will automatically apply to the other margins. Deselect this button to set margins to different amounts.
- If you have all options displayed for the dialog box, as shown in Figure 66-1, you can specify bleed and slug areas for a document.
  - The **bleed** settings position guides for an overflow around the edges of the page. When you position an object so it runs all the way out to the bleed area, the object appears to run off the page when it is printed and trimmed.
  - The slug settings define guides for an area outside the bleed area where information about the document can be printed.
- If you use specific settings over and over in your design work, you can save the settings as a Preset that will appear on the Preset list in the New Document dialog box.

InDesign Tools

- Many InDesign tools are the same as those used in Illustrator. Figure 66-2 shows the Tools panel with tools named.
- As in Illustrator and Photoshop, a small triangle next to a tool indicates the presence of additional tools beneath the currently displayed tool.

Figure 66-2. The InDesign Tools panel

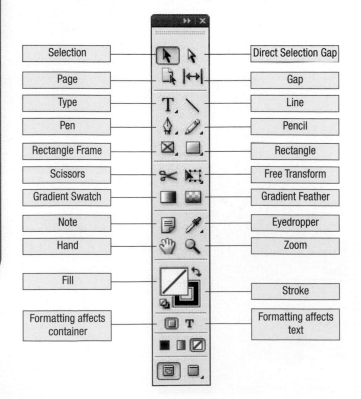

Selection	Direct Selection Gap
Page	Gap
Type	Line
Pen	Pencil
Rectangle Frame	Rectangle
Scissors	Free Transform
Gradient Swatch	Gradient Feather
Note	Eyedropper
Hand	Zoom
Fill	Stroke
Formatting affects container	Formatting affects text

About Document and Ruler Guides

- Every InDesign document displays default guides that identify parts of the document such as margins, columns, and bleed and slug areas.
- Figure 66-3 at the top of the next page shows how document guides display in a new document that has bleed and slug settings applied.
- Document guides are color coded to help you differentiate them. The slug guide is a light blue. The bleed guide is red. The document border is black. Margin guides are magenta, and column guides are violet. Where a column overlaps a margin guide, the violet column guide color shows, as you can see in Figure 66-3.
- You can add *ruler guides* to a document to help you position content by dragging a guide from the horizontal or vertical ruler, as you learned to do in Illustrator. Ruler guides are dark blue when first dragged to the document, then light blue after they are dropped into place and deselected.
- If you drag a horizontal ruler guide down directly into the page, it will display only within the document borders. If you drag the guide down while your pointer is outside the page, the ruler guide will extend all the way across the document window. If you are viewing a page spread, you can hold down Ctrl while you drag a horizontal guide to create a guide that spans both pages of the spread.
- If you want to add regularly spaced guides, use the Layout > Create Guides command to specify the number of guides and the desired gutter between guides.
- You can select ruler guides using the Selection tool ▐ and reposition them by dragging them. If you have Smart Guides turned on, you will see an information box attached to the Selection tool pointer that tells you the current X or Y position of the guide as you drag it.

  ✓ *You can lock both ruler and document guides to prevent them from moving while you work near them, and you can hide all guides.*

- Remove a ruler guide by selecting it and pressing Delete. You can remove all guides at one time with the new View > Grids & Guides > Delete All Guides on Spread command.

Figure 66-3. Document and ruler guides

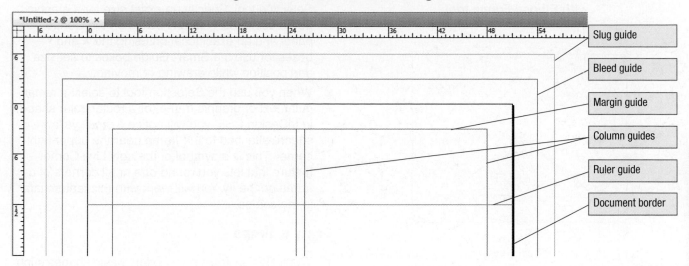

Insert a Text Frame

■ Text and graphics in an InDesign publication are controlled using **frames**. Frames are similar to text boxes you may have inserted in programs such as Microsoft Word or PowerPoint.

■ You can create a text frame using the Type tool T. Selecting this tool changes the mouse pointer to an I-beam. Position the I-beam pointer where you want to begin the frame and drag to create the frame of the desired size.

■ The I-beam pointer changes to a crosshair as you drag, as shown in Figure 66-4. Note that the text frame starts at the position of the small crossbar on the I-beam pointer, not at the position of the top of the pointer. If you have Smart Guides turned on, you see the width and height of the frame as you draw it.

  ✓ Smart Guides function in much the same way as Smart Guides in Illustrator.

Figure 66-4. Drawing a text frame

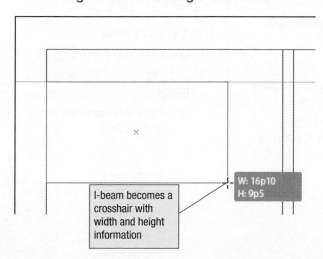

I-beam becomes a crosshair with width and height information

■ You can constrain the shape of the text frame by holding down Shift while drawing it to create a perfect square.

■ When you release the mouse button, a blinking insertion point displays in the text frame, ready for you to insert text. You usually cannot see any other evidence that a text frame is present unless you select it with the Selection tool.

■ You can reposition a text frame by dragging it with the Selection tool. Adjust its size by dragging a side or corner handle, as you would any graphic shape in Illustrator.

■ View the Smart Guide information box to achieve an exact size while drawing, or select an existing frame and use the W and H Transform boxes on the Control panel to set the size.

■ Specify an exact location by selecting the frame and using the X and Y boxes on the Control panel, or drag the frame with the Selection tool and watch the Smart Guide X and Y readouts.

Insert a Graphic Frame

■ You can create a graphic frame using the Rectangle Frame tool ☒ or the tools located beneath Rectangle Frame on the Tools panel: the Ellipse Frame tool ⊗, or the Polygon Frame tool ⊗.

■ When you draw a frame with one of these tools, the finished frame displays with an X across it, as shown in Figure 66-5 at the top of the next page.

Figure 66-5. Graphic frame created with Ellipse Frame tool

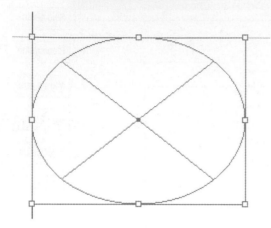

- You can actually create a graphic frame using the Rectangle, Ellipse, and Polygon shape tools, but the X provided by the Frame tools makes it easy to differentiate a graphic frame from an ordinary graphic shape.

  ✓ *In fact, you can also create a text frame using the shape tools; just click in the shape with the Type tool to convert it to a text frame.*

- Draw a rectangular or elliptical graphic frame just as you would a rectangle or ellipse shape. You can adjust the number of sides for a polygon frame by pressing the up arrow or down arrow key as you draw the frame, or double-click the tool to open the Polygon Settings dialog box where you can specify settings.

- Reposition or resize a graphic frame using the Selection tool. Specify an exact size for a graphic frame using the W and H boxes on the Control panel and an exact location using the X and Y boxes, or use the Smart Guide boxes to set size and position while drawing or moving.

- When you use the Selection tool to select a rectangular text or graphic frame (or a rectangular shape) in InDesign CS5, you will notice a small yellow square attached to the frame near the upper-right corner. This is a symbol of the new Live Corner feature that lets you round one or all corners of a frame on the fly. You will work with this feature later in the course.

Draw a Shape

- The InDesign Tools panel offers basic shapes such as those you have worked with in Illustrator and Photoshop: Rectangle, Ellipse, Polygon, and Line.

- The InDesign line and shape tools create vector objects the same as those in Illustrator. You can specify a fill for a shape by selecting a swatch from the Swatches panel, by creating a color in the Color panel, or by picking up a color using the Eyedropper.

- You can adjust a shape's stroke by applying a color or stroke attributes from the Stroke panel. Options on the Control panel let you quickly adjust thickness or stroke style.

  ✓ *You will work more with shapes and strokes in Lesson 8.*

PROCEDURES

Start a New Document *(Ctrl + N)*

1. Click **Document** in the Create New area of the Welcome screen.

   OR

   a. Click **File** .... ALT + F
   b. Point to **New** .... N
   c. Click **Document** .... D

2. Change the document settings as desired.

3. Click **OK** .... ENTER

Insert a Ruler Guide

1. Click in the horizontal or vertical ruler and drag downward or to the right to create a ruler guide.

2. Drop the guide where you want it to appear.

To adjust the position of the ruler guide:

1. Click the ruler guide to select it.

2. Drag it to its new location, watching the X or Y information in the Smart Guide information box.

OR

Type a new X or Y position for the ruler guide in the Transform boxes on the Control panel.

Insert a Text Frame

1. Click the **Type** tool T .... T

2. Drag to create a new text frame.

   ✓ *For a perfect square text frame, hold down Shift.*

Insert a Graphic Frame

1. Click the **Rectangle Frame** tool 🗵 ....F

   OR

   Click the **Ellipse Frame** tool 🗵 beneath the Rectangle Frame tool.

   OR

   Click the **Polygon Frame** tool 🗵 beneath the Rectangle Frame tool.

2. Drag to create a new frame.

   ✓ *For a perfect square or circle frame, hold down Shift while dragging.*

To specify polygon frame settings:

1. Double-click the **Polygonal Frame** tool 🗵.
2. Click in the **Number of Sides** box ....ALT + N
3. Type a value or click spin arrows ....↑ or ↓
4. Click in the **Star Inset** box............................ALT + S
5. Type a value or click spin arrows ....↑ or ↓
6. Click **OK** .... ENTER

Draw a Shape or Line

1. Select the **Rectangle**, **Ellipse**, **Polygon**, or **Line** tool.
2. Drag to create the shape.

   ✓ *Adjust sides and star inset settings for a polygon as for a polygon frame.*

EXERCISE DIRECTIONS

1. Start InDesign.
2. Create a new document and change the following settings:
   a. Set number of columns to **2** and the column gutter to **1p6**.
   b. For margins, turn off Make all settings the same and set the top margin to **4p0**.
   c. Specify a bleed area of 1 pica all around. Display More Options if necessary to see the Bleed settings.
   d. Leave all other options at their default settings.
3. Save the new document as 66Greenwood_xx. Make sure Smart Guides are turned on (View > Grids & Guides > Smart Guides).
4. Drag a horizontal ruler guide down until the Smart Guide information box indicates **Y: 9p0**. Then drag a second horizontal ruler guide to **Y: 11p0**.
5. Position additional horizontal ruler guides at **40p0**, **41p0**, and **54p0**. If necessary, use the Control panel to set guides at exact positions.
6. Drag a vertical ruler guide to **X: 21p0**.
7. Now add text frames as follows:
   a. Drag a text frame from the upper-left corner of the margin guides to the intersection of the right margin and the 9-pica ruler guide. (See Illustration A.)
   b. Drag a text frame from the intersection of the left margin guide and the 11-point ruler guide to the intersection of the left column guide and the 54-pica ruler guide. (You are creating a frame to hold text in the first column of the page.)
   c. In the right column, drag a text frame that extends from the 41-pica ruler guide to the 54-pica ruler guide and fills the right column width.
8. Add a rectangular graphic frame that starts at the intersection of the vertical ruler guide and the 11-pica ruler guide and extends to the intersection of the right margin guide and the 40-pica ruler guide.
9. Draw a rectangle shape at the bottom of the page that sits on the bottom margin and is 6 picas tall. Illustration A shows the guides, frames, and shape you have inserted in the new document. (All text frames are selected to help you see them.)
10. Save your changes, close the file, and exit InDesign.

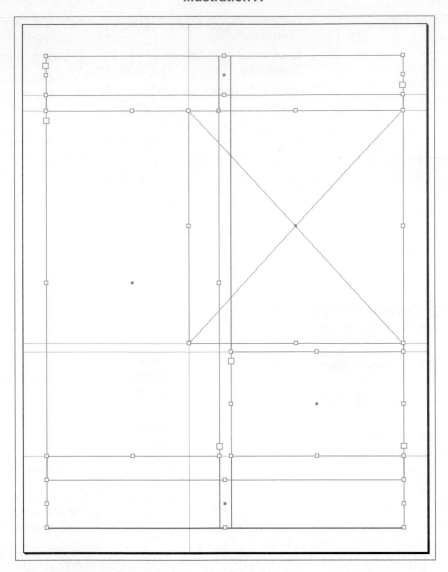

ON YOUR OWN

✓ *Create a new publication that will become a poster for a music festival in your state.*

1. Start InDesign and create a new document using the Tabloid page size. Set margins to **5** picas all around and bleed to **2** picas all around.

2. Save the document as OIN66_xx.

3. Insert horizontal ruler guides at **12**, **13**, and **20** picas.

4. Insert text frames within these two sets of ruler guides (one that extends from the upper-left margin guide to the intersection of the right margin and the 12-pica ruler guide, and the other from margin to margin between the remaining two ruler guides).

5. Create a 12-sided polygonal frame (no star inset) in the center of the poster, exactly 48 picas in both height and width.

   ✓ *Specify the number of sides by pressing the up arrow key or using the Polygon Settings dialog box. Use the Smart Guide box to drag to the correct size, or use the W and H boxes on the Control panel.*

6. Save your changes, close the document, and exit InDesign.

Exercise | 67

Skills Covered

- **Type Text in a Frame**
- **Place Text in a Frame**
- **Place a Graphic in a Frame**
- **Adjust a Graphic in a Frame**
- **Delete a Frame or Shape**

Software Skills You can add text to a text frame by typing directly in the frame. You can add either text or a graphic using the Place command. Adjust the position of a graphic in a frame using the new content grabber feature. A frame or shape can be deleted if it is no longer needed.

Design Skills An InDesign publication consists of text and graphics arranged on pages. A designer needs to understand basic options for inserting and placing text and graphics before going on to more complex skills.

Application Skills In this exercise, you continue to work on the Greenwood Conservancy publication. You will add text to the publication and insert and adjust a graphic.

TERMS

Overset   Text that does not fit into the current text frame and has not been flowed into some other frame; it is not displayed anywhere in the document.

NOTES

Type Text in a Frame

- The easiest way to add text to a text frame is to click in the frame to set the insertion point and then begin typing.

- Text entry and editing is the same as in any word processing program. Use Delete and Backspace to remove characters when editing.

- To format text, you use options on the Control panel. With the Type tool selected, click the Character Formatting Controls button [A] on the Control panel to display character-formatting options, some of which are shown in Figure 67-1.

- You can also find a number of alignment options on the Character Formatting Control panel. Use these settings as you would in a word processing program to align or justify text.

- InDesign's character- and paragraph-formatting options are extensive and sophisticated. You will learn much more about them in Lesson 9.

Figure 67-1. Some common character-formatting controls

Place Text in a Frame

- If the text you want to insert in a text frame has already been prepared in a word processing program, you can easily import it into the publication by clicking in the text frame and then issuing the File > Place command, which you have already used in the Illustrator section of this text.

- As in Illustrator, the Place command opens a dialog box in which you can browse to the location of the text file you want to import.

- If you placed the insertion point in the text frame or selected it before issuing the Place command, the text automatically pours into the frame when you open the file, as shown in Figure 67-2.

Figure 67-2. Placed text fills a text frame

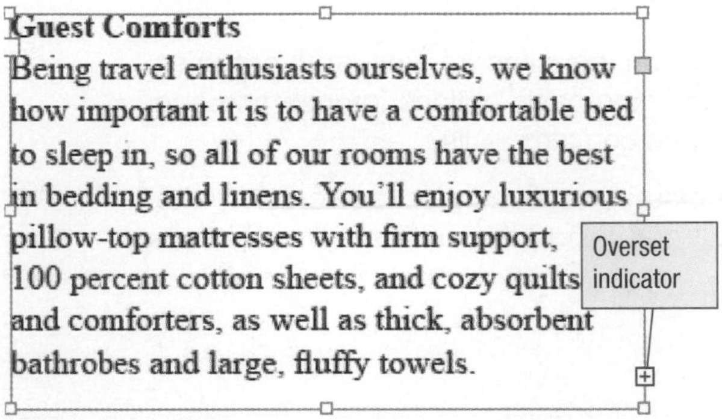

Guest Comforts
Being travel enthusiasts ourselves, we know how important it is to have a comfortable bed to sleep in, so all of our rooms have the best in bedding and linens. You'll enjoy luxurious pillow-top mattresses with firm support, 100 percent cotton sheets, and cozy quilts and comforters, as well as thick, absorbent bathrobes and large, fluffy towels.

Overset indicator

- If the file contains more text than will fit in the frame, the text is said to be **overset**. The Overset indicator ⊞ displays as shown in Figure 67-2 to let you know that additional text is available to place but there is currently no room for it in the frame.

- You can make more room for text by increasing the size of the text frame, by creating a new text frame for the text to flow into, or by linking the current text frame to another existing text frame. You will learn more about these text *threading* options in Exercise 69 and in Lesson 9.

- If you have not yet created a frame for the text you want to insert, you can draw a frame as you insert it. After you issue the Place command, the insertion point changes to a loaded text icon, as shown in Figure 67-3. Note that a portion of the text is attached to the loaded text icon so you can keep track of exactly what content you are placing.

- Drag with the insertion point to create the desired frame size and place text in it at the same time. You can also simply click with the loaded text icon to create a frame the full width of the current column.

- Another way to place text in a frame is to simply drag the file from Bridge to the text frame.

Figure 67-3. Loaded text icon

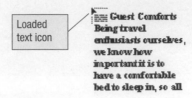

Loaded text icon

Guest Comforts
Being travel enthusiasts ourselves, we know how important it is to have a comfortable bed to sleep in, so all

- If you are laying out a document and want to see how it will look with text inserted but have not yet created the text, you can use *placeholder text* to fill your text frames.

- Select the frame and use the Type > Fill with Placeholder Text command. The frame fills with Latin text in long paragraphs that you can format just like any other text.

Place a Graphic in a Frame

- Placing a graphic is similar to placing text. You can use the File > Place command or Bridge to import and place a graphic file.

- Select the graphic frame and then issue the File > Place command to insert the graphic in the frame, as shown in Figure 67-4.

Figure 67-4. Placed graphic fills a graphic frame

- If you have not created a graphic frame, you can insert one as you place the file. Use the loaded graphic cursor, such as the one shown in Figure 67-5, to drag the frame to the desired size and insert the file. Note that a representation of the graphic is attached to the loaded graphic icon.

- When you drag a loaded graphic cursor to place a file, the frame is constrained so that the graphic fits proportionally and is not distorted.

- To place a graphic file using Bridge, drag the file to a selected graphic frame or drag the file anywhere on a page.

Figure 67-5. Loaded graphic icon

- When you drag to a frame, the file fills the frame the same way it does if you place the graphic in the frame. When you drag to any location on a page, a loaded graphic icon displays so you can drag a frame and place the file at the same time.

- You may notice that some placed graphics have jagged lines or generally poor resolution. InDesign places graphics at screen-quality resolution while also maintaining a link to the high-quality original version of the file. You will learn how to adjust display performance later in this course.

  ✓ *Because of the links InDesign maintains to original files, you may receive error messages about unavailable content when you work with some of the data files for this section of the course. You can generally ignore these errors and work with the screen-resolution graphics.*

- Note that the frame and its content are actually separate items. You can move the frame and its content at the same time using the Selection tool. If you use the Selection tool to resize the frame, however, you do not also resize the graphic.

Adjust a Graphic in a Frame

- If the graphic is larger than its frame, only a portion of the graphic appears in the frame. You can adjust the position of the graphic in the frame so it displays the part of the graphic you want.

- To adjust the position of the graphic within its frame, you use the content grabber, a tool that is new in InDesign CS5. To display the content grabber (sometimes called the "doughnut"), move the mouse pointer over the graphic, as shown in Figure 67-6.

Figure 67-6. Display the content grabber

Content grabber

- Click on the content grabber to see a brown bounding box indicating the actual graphic size. You can use the handles on this brown bounding box to resize the graphic. Or, while the brown bounding box is active, use the W and H boxes on the Control panel to specify an exact size.

  ✓ *You can also double-click on the graphic with the Selection tool to display the brown bounding box.*

- If you click on the content grabber, hold down the mouse button, and move the mouse slightly, you will see the graphic as shown in Figure 67-7. You can drag the graphic until the frame displays the part of the graphic you want to use. If Smart Guides are on, you will see a box with the X and Y coordinates displayed as you adjust the graphic position.

Figure 67-7. Drag the graphic to adjust its position in the frame

X: 8p1.2
Y: 10p1.2

- Note that you can now rotate an image easily the same way you rotate an Illustrator object, by moving the mouse pointer near a corner to display a rotate symbol and then dragging. After you rotate a graphic, the content grabber for that image displays a line symbol that shows how far the image was rotated from its original orientation.

- The Control panel and the Object > Fitting submenu offer a number of options for fitting content into a frame. You will work with these options in Lesson 10.

Delete a Frame or Shape

- Like any graphic object you worked with in Illustrator, a frame or a drawn shape can easily be deleted by simply selecting it and then pressing the Delete key.

- If you find you have deleted an object in error, use the Undo command to restore it. As in Illustrator, Undo will reverse all changes you have made back to the last time you saved the file.

PROCEDURES

Type Text in a Frame

1. Click in a text frame with the Type tool `T.` to position the insertion point.
2. Type the desired text.

To apply type formats:

1. With the Type tool active, click the Character Formatting Controls button `A` on the Control panel to display character formatting options.
2. Select options to format text before typing the text.

   OR

   Select existing text using the Type tool and then apply formats from the Control panel.

Place Text in a Frame *(Ctrl + D)*

1. Click in a text frame with the Type tool `T.` to position the insertion point.
2. Click **File** .... `ALT` + `F`
3. Click **Place** .... `L`
4. Navigate to the location of the file you want to place.
5. Select the desired file.
6. Click **Open** .... `ALT` + `O`

   OR

On any page that does not yet have a text frame:

1. Click **File** .... `ALT` + `F`
2. Click **Place** .... `L`
3. Navigate to the location of the file you want to place.
4. Select the desired file.
5. Click **Open** .... `ENTER`
6. Using the loaded text icon, drag to draw a frame of the desired size.

   OR

   Click with the icon to create a frame the full width of the current column.

OR

1. Open Adobe Bridge and adjust window size so that you can see both the Bridge files in the Content window and the text frame in InDesign.
2. Select the text frame in InDesign.
3. Select the file in Bridge, drag it to InDesign, and drop it in the selected text frame.

To fill a text frame with placeholder text:

1. Click a text frame to select it.
2. Click **Type** .... `ALT` + `T`
3. Click **Fill with Placeholder Text** .... `I`

Place a Graphic in a Frame

1. Select the graphic frame with the Selection tool `▸`.
2. Click **File** .... `ALT` + `F`
3. Click **Place** .... `L`
4. Navigate to the location of the file you want to place.
5. Select the desired file.
6. Click **Open** .... `ALT` + `O`

   OR

On any page that does not yet have a graphic frame:

1. Click **File** .... `ALT` + `F`
2. Click **Place** .... `L`
3. Navigate to the location of the file you want to place.
4. Select the desired file.
5. Click **Open** .... `ALT` + `O`
6. Using the loaded graphic icon, drag to draw a frame of the desired size.

   OR

   Click the icon to create a frame as large as the graphic.

OR

1. Open Adobe Bridge and adjust window size so that you can see both the Bridge files in the Content window and the graphic frame in InDesign.
2. Select the graphic frame in InDesign.
3. Select the file in Bridge, drag it to InDesign, and drop it in the selected text frame.

   OR

   Drop the file to the page and click the loaded graphic icon to create a frame as large as the graphic.

Adjust a Graphic in a Frame

To resize the graphic file:

1. Click the content grabber to display the brown bounding box.
2. Drag a sizing handle on the bounding box to adjust height or width.

   ✓ *Hold down Shift to maintain original proportion of height to width.*

   OR

   Enter values in the **W** and **H** boxes on the Control panel.

To adjust the position of the graphic in the frame:

1. Click the content grabber inside the frame.
2. Hold down the mouse button after clicking and move the mouse slowly until you see the entire graphic behind the frame.
3. Drag to reposition the graphic.

Delete a Frame or Shape

1. Click on a frame or shape to select it.
2. Press `DEL`.

EXERCISE DIRECTIONS

1. Start InDesign. Open 🖴 66Greenwood_xx or 💿 67Greenwood and save the file as 67Greenwood_xx.

2. Select the Type tool and click in the text frame you inserted at the top of the page. Type **Greenwood in Fall**.

3. Select the text using the I-beam cursor and show the character formatting controls on the Control panel if necessary.

4. Select Times New Roman font and 72 pt font size. The text should now fill the text frame.

5. Click with the Type tool in the text frame you created in the left column and place the 💿 67Green_text.doc data file. The text should fill the first column and then stop.

   ✓ You will thread the text to other text frames in Exercise 69.

6. Select the graphic frame and place the 💿 67Green_image.ai data file. Don't worry about the appearance of the file or the fact that it overlaps text. You will fix text wrap in a later exercise.

7. The graphic is a bit larger than the frame. Adjust the graphic in the frame using the content grabber so that the image is centered vertically and horizontally in the frame.

8. You have decided to remove the shape at the bottom of the page because you intend to place the shape on the document's master pages in a later exercise. Delete the rectangle shape. Your page should look similar to Illustration A.

9. Save your changes, close the file, and exit InDesign.

Illustration A

ON YOUR OWN

1. Start InDesign and open  OIN66_xx or open ⊙ OYO67.

2. Save the document as OIN67_xx.

3. Insert the text **[Your State] Music Festival** in the first text frame on the page. Use your choice of font, font style, and font size. You may also want to adjust alignment using the alignment buttons on the Character Formatting Control panel.

4. Insert the text **April 27 – 28 2012** in the second text frame.

5. Search the Internet for a map of your state. It should be a fairly large picture. If you cannot find an interesting map for free download, try downloading a picture, tracing it in Illustrator, and creating a blank map. Apply effects to make the blank map more visually appealing, then save it to the same folder where your poster file is stored.

6. Place the graphic image from its stored location in the polygon frame. Adjust the image size and position. You may resize the polygon frame if necessary to accommodate the image. Your poster might resemble Illustration B.

7. Save your changes, close the document, and exit InDesign.

Illustration B

Ohio Music Festival

April 27 - 28 2012

Exercise | 68

Skills Covered

- **Apply a Fill Color to a Frame or Object**
- **Apply Stroke Formats**
- **Work with Live Corners**
- **Apply a Fill Color to Text**
- **Wrap Text Around a Frame**

Software Skills   You can add fills and strokes to frames or objects to create visual interest on a page. The new Live Corners feature allows you to adjust corner roundness on any frame or object on the fly. Modify text color to make text stand out against a background color. You can wrap text around a graphic to control text flow on a page.

Design Skills   Color can be an important aspect of a design. A designer can add color to frames and objects to emphasize them or provide visual balance in a document. Easy rounded corners add another element of visual interest.

Application Skills   You continue working with the Greenwood Conservancy document in this exercise. You will apply fill and stroke colors, modify corners on the graphic frame, adjust text color, and choose a text-wrapping option for the graphic.

TERMS

Text wrap   Constraining text to follow the outline of an object.

NOTES

Apply a Fill Color to a Frame or Object

- Though frames may appear to have a white fill, they are in fact transparent, with no fill color. You can add visual interest to a page by applying a solid or semi-transparent color or gradient fill to any frame.

- To apply a solid color fill, use the Color panel to mix a color, choose a color from the Swatches panel, or use the Eyedropper to pick up a color from anywhere on the screen.

  ✓ You learn how to apply semi-transparent and gradient fills later in the course.

- As in Illustrator, you must first select the frame or object to fill, then select the Fill box on the Tools panel or in the Color or Swatches panel.

  ✓ You can double-click the Fill square in the Tools panel to open the Color Picker.

- If you choose to create a fill color in the Color panel, you may have to specify a color model on the panel menu before you can mix the color. Because the default frame fill is transparent, the color ramp is grayscale until you select a color by some other means or select a color model.

  ✓ If the color is set to transparent, the sliders do not appear for CMYK, but if you click on the bar for one of those values, a slider will appear where you clicked.

- The Swatches panel, shown in Figure 68-1 on the next page, looks somewhat different from the Swatches panels you have used in other Creative Suite applications.

- Only a limited number of colors are offered in this panel, but you can add colors to the panel as you learned to do in Illustrator.

Figure 68-1. InDesign Swatches panel

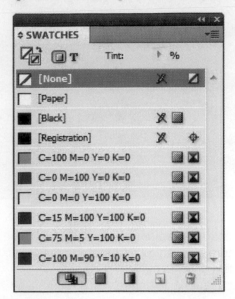

Figure 68-2. Stroke boxes on the Control panel

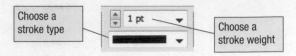

Apply a Fill Color to Text

- You can apply color to text much as you apply it to the fill or stroke of a frame.

- When text is selected, the Fill square on the Tools, Swatches, and Color panels is replaced by a text Fill square [T]. Any color you select will apply to the text, rather than to the frame itself.

- Text has both a stroke and a fill, like a frame. Normally the text's stroke is set to None, but it is possible to set it to a color different from the fill (for outlined text) or to the same color as the fill (for an extra measure of thickness).

Work with Live Corners

- As you learned in a previous exercise, InDesign CS5 now offers a Live Corner feature that allows you to round the corners of text frames, rectangular graphic frames, or rectangular objects right on the object, without having to display a dialog box or specify settings.

- To adjust Live Corners, click the yellow marker that appears near the upper-right corner of any rectangular object. After you click, yellow diamond-shaped markers display at all four corners of the object, as shown in Figure 68-3.

Figure 68-3. Live Corner markers on a text frame

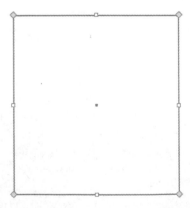

- Click on any of these markers and drag to adjust all four corners of the object. A Smart Guide information box displays the current radius, as shown in Figure 68-4.

- To return to no fill color, click the white square with the red diagonal line at the left end of the color bar or choose the [None] swatch on the Swatches panel.

- Note that you must select [Paper] in the Swatches panel for a white fill.

- In InDesign CS5, you will find a new Fill option on the Control panel that displays the Swatches panel when clicked.

  ✓ *You will work more with the InDesign Swatches panel in Exercise 76 in the next lesson.*

Apply Stroke Formats

- You have learned several meanings for the term *stroke* in this course. In the context of an InDesign frame, a stroke is the border around the outside of a frame or shape.

- Most types of frames have a transparent stroke by default. You can apply color to a stroke using the same options as for applying fills. As for fills, there is now a Stroke option on the Control panel you can use to apply stroke color. Be sure to select the Stroke box before applying a color.

- The default stroke thickness for a frame is 0 point; the default stroke thickness for a shape is 1 point. You can quickly adjust stroke thickness and stroke type using the stroke boxes on the Control panel, shown in Figure 68-2.

- Stroke types include decorative options such as thick and thin lines, wavy lines, dots, diamonds, and dashes.

- You can use the Stroke panel to apply a number of stroke attributes at the same time. You will work with the Stroke panel in Exercise 77.

Figure 68-4. Drag to adjust corner radius

- You can adjust each corner to a different radius, if desired, by pressing Shift while you drag that corner marker.
- The Corner Options settings on the Control panel also show the current radius as you drag. You can click options in this group to adjust corner shape and size. You learn more about adjusting corner options in the next lesson.

Wrap Text Around a Frame

- You will frequently create layouts in which a text frame and a graphic frame overlap, as shown in Figure 68-5. This is obviously not a good situation, as text is obscured by the graphic.

Figure 68-5. Overlapping text and graphic frames

- One solution to this problem is simply to resize either the text frame or the graphic frame, but doing so consistently would result in fairly boring-looking documents.
- An alternative is to apply **text wrap** settings to the graphic to force the text to flow around the graphic.

- You can apply text wrap settings from the Control panel. With a graphic selected, choose from the following options:
  - Wrap around bounding box 🔲 wraps text around an object's bounding box, which is always a rectangular shape regardless of the shape of the selected frame or object.
  - Wrap around object shape 🔲 wraps text around the shape of the object rather than its bounding box. This generally supplies a tighter wrap. Figure 68-6 shows the difference between wrapping to the bounding box and wrapping around an object shape.
  - Jump object 🔲 wraps text above and below an object.
- If you decide not to wrap text after all, click the No text wrap button 🔲 to turn off text wrapping.
- For more control over text wrapping, you can use the Text Wrap panel. You learn about options on this panel in Lesson 10.

Figure 68-6. Text wrapped to the bounding box (top) and the object shape (bottom)

PROCEDURES

Apply Fill Color to a Frame or Object

1. Click the frame or object to fill.
   - ✓ *Select more than one frame/object by clicking the first, holding down Shift, and clicking other objects.*
2. Click the **Fill** box on the Tools panel.
3. Use one of the following options to select a fill color:
   a. Open the Color panel.
   b. Click the panel menu button ▾≣ and select **CMYK**.
   c. Click in the color ramp to activate the color sliders.
   d. Adjust sliders to create the desired color.

   OR

   a. Open the Swatches panel.
   b. Select any swatch.

   OR

   a. Click the Fill list arrow on the Control panel.
   b. Select the desired swatch color.

   OR

   a. Click the **Eyedropper** tool 🖋 ....Ⅰ
   b. Click anywhere in unselected graphic or elsewhere on the screen to pick up the desired color.

Apply Stroke Formats

To apply stroke color:

1. Click the frame/object to which you want to apply stroke color.
   - ✓ *Select more than one frame/object by clicking the first, holding down Shift, and clicking other objects.*
2. Click the **Stroke** box on the Tools panel.
3. Use one of the following options to select a stroke color:
   a. Open the Color panel.
   b. Click the panel menu button ▾≣ and select **CMYK**.
   c. Click in the color ramp to activate the color sliders.
   d. Adjust sliders to create the desired color.

OR

a. Open the Swatches panel.
b. Select any swatch.

OR

a. Click the Stroke list arrow on the Control panel.
b. Select desired swatch color.

OR

a. Click the **Eyedropper** tool 🖋 ....Ⅰ
b. Click anywhere in graphic or screen to pick up color.

To change stroke thickness:

1. Select the frame or object to be given stroke attributes.
2. Click the stroke weight list arrow on the Control panel and select a thickness.

   OR

   Click spin arrows to increase or decrease stroke thickness.

   OR

   Type a thickness value directly in the stroke weight box.

To change stroke type:

1. Select the frame or object to be given stroke attributes.
2. Click the stroke type list arrow on the Control panel and select a type.

Remove a Fill or Stroke Color

1. Click the frame(s) to affect.
2. Click the Fill or Stroke box in the Tools panel.
3. Click the Apply None box ☑ on the Tools panel.

   OR

   Click the None box in the Color or Swatches panel.

Work with Live Corners

1. Click the yellow rectangular marker near the upper-right corner of any rectangular frame or object.
2. Drag the yellow, diamond-shaped marker at any corner to round off all object's corners.

   OR

Press [SHIFT] and drag a corner to adjust only that corner.

Apply a Fill Color to Text

1. Select the text to which you want to apply a new color.
2. Click the text **Fill** box 𝐓 on the Tools panel.
   - ✓ *To apply a stroke color to text, click the text Stroke box.*
3. To select a text color:
   a. Open the Color panel.
   b. Click the panel menu button ▾≣ and select **CMYK**.
   c. Click in the color ramp to activate the color sliders.
   d. Adjust sliders to create color.

   OR

   a. Open the Swatches panel.
   b. Select any swatch.

   OR

   a. Click the Fill list arrow on the Control panel.
   b. Select desired swatch color.

   OR

   a. Click the **Eyedropper** tool 🖋 ....Ⅰ
   b. Click anywhere on graphic or screen to pick up color.

Wrap Text Around a Frame

1. Select the graphic to be given a text wrap setting.
2. Select a wrap option from the Control panel:
   - **Wrap around bounding box** ▣.
   - **Wrap around object shape** ▣.
   - **Jump object** ▤.
   - ✓ *If you do not see the text wrap options on the Control panel, click the Control panel menu button, click Customize, click Object, and select the Text Wrap check box.*

To remove text wrapping:

1. Select the graphic to be freed of text wrapping.
2. Click the **No text wrap** button ▤ on the Control panel.

EXERCISE DIRECTIONS

1. Start InDesign. Open ▦ 67Greenwood_xx or 💿 68Greenwood and save the file as 68Greenwood_xx.

2. Select the _Greenwood in Fall_ text frame and select the Fill box. Pick up a green color from the green leaf in the image. If you receive a message about the low-resolution proxy, click OK.

3. Select the _Greenwood in Fall_ text and change the text color to Paper using the Swatches panel.

4. Click the Live Corners marker on the graphic frame. Hold down Shift and drag the upper-left corner to the right until it intersects with the left column marker at a radius of 3p8.4. Make the same change to the lower-left corner.

5. Apply the following stroke changes to the graphic frame:
   - Change the stroke color to **C = 65**, **M = 60**, **Y = 0**, **K = 0** using the Color panel. (Change the color mode to CMYK using the Color panel menu if necessary.)
   - Change the stroke thickness to **3** pt using the option on the Control panel.
   - Change the stroke type to **Wavy**.

6. Apply the Wrap around bounding box text wrap setting to the graphic frame. Illustration A shows how the text portion of your page should look.

   ✓ _You will learn how to add offset space around a text wrap later in the course._

7. Save your changes, close the file, and exit InDesign.

Illustration A

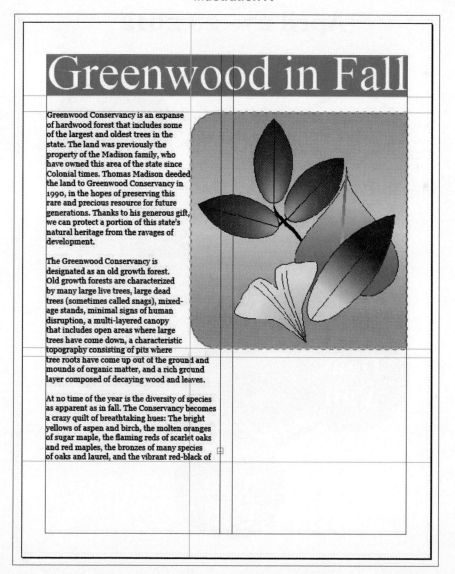

ON YOUR OWN

1. Start InDesign and open OIN67_xx.
2. Save the document as OIN68_xx.
3. Apply a fill and stroke to the large polygon that contains your state map.
4. Draw four or five polygons on the poster, smaller than the one that displays the state map you added in the previous On Your Own exercise.

5. Apply fill and stroke colors from the Swatches panel, and adjust stroke weight using the Control panel. Make each polygon a different combination of stroke and fill colors.
6. Double-click in each colored polygon with the Type tool and type the name of an artist or group that might be playing at the Music Festival, if you were doing the bookings. Adjust font, size, and color as desired. Illustration B shows an example of how you might format the poster.
7. Save your changes, close the document, and exit InDesign.

Illustration B

Exercise | 69

Skills Covered

- Use the Pages Panel
- Add and Delete Pages
- Work with Multiple Page Sizes
- Copy a Frame

- Thread Text from Frame to Frame
- Change Master Page Elements
- Insert Page Numbers

Software Skills Use the Pages panel to organize pages and navigate a document. Add and delete pages to adjust the length of a document. Use the new Edit Size option to change sizes of individual pages in a document. Page numbers help the reader stay oriented in the document. Threading is the process of flowing text from one frame to another throughout a document. To avoid having to draw a number of frames, you can simply copy and paste them. Page master elements display on every page of a document; make changes on the page masters to save time in formatting.

Design Skills Skills covered in this exercise enable a designer to do some fine-tuning of document design. Understanding how page masters work is an especially important part of learning InDesign, because creating masters for specific types of content can save a great deal of manual formatting. Creating multiple page sizes in a single document can speed workflow when document elements are to be used for different outputs.

Application Skills In this exercise, you perform some important tasks to finalize the Greenwood document. You will add pages, create and copy new text frames to hold text that still has not been placed, and thread the text to place it. You will make a simple change to the page masters and insert page numbers, and then delete a page you don't need.

TERMS

In port The marker on the left side of a text frame that indicates a backward link to a previous frame.

Master A page template that contains information to be repeated on every page to which the master is applied.

Out port The marker on the right side of a text frame that indicates a forward link to the next frame.

Recto The right page in a page spread.

Story Text in a single frame or flowing through threaded frames.

Thread To continue text from one frame to another.

Verso The left page in a page spread.

NOTES

Use the Pages Panel

- You work with pages in InDesign using the Pages panel, which shows a graphic presentation of your document's pages and masters.

- Each page in the document is represented by a small page thumbnail in the panel, with page numbers displayed below the pages. You can double-click a page thumbnail to display that page in the document window.

- In a long document, use the Pages panel's vertical scroll bar to bring other pages into view. You learn more about reorganizing pages in a long document in Lesson 11.

- Figure 69-1 shows a four-page document in the Pages panel. Note that the first page of the document, generally a right-hand page, stands alone, pages 2 and 3 form a *spread* of two attached pages, and the last page also stands alone.

Figure 69-1. Four-page document in the Pages panel

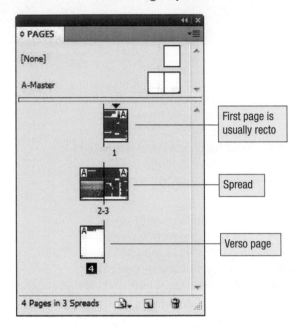

- In publishing terminology, the left page of a spread is called a **verso** page, and the right page of a spread is called a **recto** page.

- If you deselected Facing Pages when setting up the document, the pages do not form spreads. Instead, the document displays in the Pages panel as a series of single pages.

  ✓ *You can change the way pages display in the panel using the Panel Options command on the Pages panel menu.*

- The area in the panel above the horizontal bar is reserved for master pages. You learn more about master pages later in this exercise.

Add and Delete Pages

- If your document content runs to more pages than you have specified, you can easily add pages to the document.

- You have several options for adding pages:
  - To add a page that will follow the currently active page, you can use Layout > Pages > Add Page. The new page will use the same settings as the currently active page.

- You can also click the Create new page button ⬜ in the Pages panel to create a page that follows the currently active page and has the same settings as that page.

- To specify where a new page (or pages) will be inserted and the page master to apply to the new page, use the Layout > Pages > Insert Pages command. In the Insert Pages dialog box, shown in Figure 69-2, select the number of pages to insert, a location relative to an existing page, and the master to apply.

Figure 69-2. Insert Pages dialog box

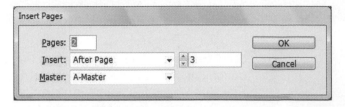

  ✓ *The Insert Pages option is also available on the Pages panel menu.*

- If you find you do not need a page, you can easily delete it by first selecting it in the Pages panel and then clicking the Delete selected pages button 🗑. Or, use the Layout > Pages > Delete Pages command to delete the currently active page.

- If a page that you want to delete contains content, you will be prompted to confirm that you want to delete the page.

Work with Multiple Page Sizes

- InDesign CS5 allows you to specify different sizes for different pages in a document. This feature is similar to the multiple artboards you worked with in Illustrator. Defining multiple page sizes lets you work more efficiently when you want to use the same content for several different documents, such as a letterhead and a business card, or a concert poster and a CD cover.

- The process of specifying a different size for a page in a document is easy: Select the page in the pages panel, click the Edit page size ⬜ button at the bottom of the panel, and specify one of the page size options on the pop-up menu.

- You can also click Custom Page Size to open the Custom Page Size dialog box, where you can specify a name for a custom size and set its height, width, and orientation.

- The Pages panel shows the resized page at its new size, as shown in Figure 69-3.

Figure 69-3. Multiple page sizes in the Pages panel

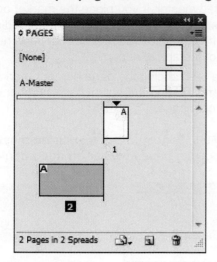

Copy a Frame

■ As you add pages to a document, you may find that you also need to add frames. You do not have to draw every one from scratch; you can instead simply copy an existing frame, paste it, and then move it into place.

■ Or, select an existing frame, hold down Alt, and drag a copy of the frame to a new location. This is the same process you used to copy objects in Illustrator.

Thread Text from Frame to Frame

■ Every text frame has an **in port** and an **out port**, which are large white squares (larger than regular selection handles) at the upper-left and lower-right sides of the frame, respectively, as shown in Figure 69-4. When the frame is not linked to any other frame and all its text fits within it, the in port and out port are empty.

Figure 69-4. In and out ports

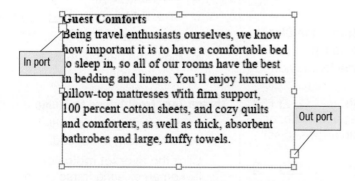

■ As you learned in Exercise 67, when there is too much text to fit in a frame, the remaining text is overset. The overset indicator ⊞ displays in the location of the out port on the frame.

■ To **thread** the overset text into another frame, use the Selection tool to click the overset indicator to "pick up" the text thread. The mouse pointer changes to the loaded text icon 🔳 .

■ You can use the loaded text icon to draw a new frame for the text to flow into, or you can simply click within a margin/column guide and a new frame will be created there matching the guides.

■ If you have already created a frame for the overset text, click in that frame with the loaded text icon to flow the text. The loaded text icon changes to the 🔳 appearance when you move the pointer to an existing frame.

■ If the frame you want to thread to is on another page, you can navigate to that page using scroll bars or by clicking the page in the Pages panel with the loaded text icon active.

■ Text that you have placed in a frame or flowed into threaded frames is called a **story**.

■ Depending on the length of the story, you might need to thread text into more than two frames. Text can be threaded into frames on the same page or on different pages.

✓ *You learn more about threading text in Exercise 83.*

■ You can adjust how text flows in frames by adjusting frame size. Shortening one frame causes more text to flow into the next frame. When you have frames set in multiple columns on a page, you can adjust frame depth to make sure the text is evenly divided between both columns.

Change Master Page Elements

■ A **master** is a template backdrop on which you can place elements that should repeat on each page. A master can be a two-page spread, with separate elements for verso (left) and recto (right), or a single page.

■ The default master is called A-Master. Every document includes an A-Master. The A-Master is a spread of two pages that look just like any other InDesign pages.

✓ *If Facing Pages is turned off, the A-Master is a single page.*

■ To open the master pages for editing, you double-click A-Master at the top of the Pages panel.

■ You can place items on the master pages just as on other pages. Add text frames, graphics, and so on.

■ Any item such as a graphic or text information will appear on all pages to which the master is applied.

■ There is much more to learn about masters. You will look more closely at this subject in the next lesson.

Insert Page Numbers

- You could number any page in a document by simply typing the page number in a text frame, but this is a risky way to insert page numbers. If a page is shuffled to a new position as a result of editing changes, the page number might not be correct.

- A safer method of inserting page numbers is to use a page number marker that will automatically update as pages are added, deleted, or moved.

- To insert a page number marker, you position the insertion point where you want the marker to appear on the page and then issue the Type > Insert Special Character > Markers command. You can choose from several different kinds of page number markers: Current Page Number, Next Page Number, and Previous Page Number.

  ✓ *Next Page Number and Previous Page Number can create jump lines that tell readers where a story continues or where it began. You will insert jump lines later in this course.*

- Although you could insert page number markers on every page if you want to, it makes more sense to insert page numbers on the masters.

- A page number marker on a master page appears as a letter rather than a number, since the master page has no number itself.

- The letter corresponds to the letter of the currently selected master. If you place the marker on an A-Master page, for example, the marker displays as A. It will appear with the correct page number on each of the actual document pages.

- Figure 69-5 shows the page number marker on a master page and the actual page number on the document page.

Figure 69-5. Page number marker on master page and correct page number on document page

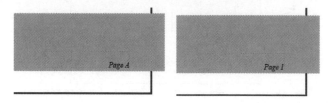

- InDesign allows you to adjust page numbering formats in a variety of ways. You can use roman numerals, for example, or alphabetical characters. You can also create a section in order to change a numbering scheme for a portion of a document. You will work with this feature in Lesson 11.

PROCEDURES

Add Pages (Shift + Ctrl + P)

1. Click **Layout** .... `ALT` + `L`
2. Point to **Pag<u>e</u>s** .... `E`
3. Click **Add Page** .... `A`

   OR

1. Click **Layout** .... `ALT` + `L`
2. Point to **Pag<u>e</u>s** .... `E`
3. Click **Insert Pages** .... `I`
4. Enter the desired number of new pages.
5. Select an **Insert** location............... `ALT` + `I` , `↓`
6. Enter a **page number** in relation to the Insert location.
7. Select a master to apply to the new page, if necessary.
8. Click **OK** .... `ENTER`

   OR

1. Open the **Pages** panel.
2. Click **Create new page** button `⬚`.

Set Multiple Page Sizes

1. Open the **Pages** panel.
2. Add a page if necessary, or click the page to resize.
3. Click **Edit page size** button `⬚▾`.
4. Select a standard page size from the pop-up list.

   OR

   a. Click **Custom Page Size** on the pop-up list.
   b. Type a name for the new page size.
   c. Click **Width**........... `ALT` + `W` and type a page width, or use the spin arrows to set width.
   d. Click **Height** .... `ALT` + `H` and type a page height, or use the spin arrows to set height.
   e. Click **Add** button ... `ALT` + `A`
   f. Click **OK** .... `ENTER`

Copy a Frame

1. Click in a frame with the Selection tool `▶` to select it.
2. Hold down `ALT` and drag the copy to a new location.

   OR

   a. Click **Edit**.............. `ALT` + `E`
   b. Click **Copy**.................... `C`
   c. Click **Edit**.............. `ALT` + `E`
   d. Click **Paste** .... `P`
   e. Move the pasted frame to a new location.

Thread Text from Frame to Frame

1. (Optional) Create the additional text frames needed.
2. Click the **overset indicator** `⊞` on an existing frame using the Selection tool.
3. Do one of the following:
   - Click the text frame into which to place the new text.

- Click within column guides to create a new frame.
- Draw a frame of the desired size.

Change Master Page Elements

1. Open the **Pages** panel.
2. Double-click the master page name to open master pages.
3. Make any changes desired to the master pages.
4. Double-click a document page number in the Pages panel to return to the document.

Insert Page Numbers (Alt + Shift + Ctrl + N)

1. Create the text frame that will hold the page number.
2. (Optional) Add any wording that will precede the page number, such as *Page*.
3. Click **Type**.................. ALT + T
4. Point to **Insert Special Character**........................... S
5. Point to **Markers**................. M
6. Click **Current Page Number**.............................. C

   ✓ *The best way to insert page numbers for a document of several pages is to perform the above steps on the document's master pages.*

Delete Pages

1. Open the **Pages** panel.
2. Click the page to delete.
3. Click **Delete selected pages** button 🗑.

   OR

   Drag the page on top of the 🗑 button.
4. Click **OK** if you receive a warning about page content..... ENTER

EXERCISE DIRECTIONS

1. Start InDesign. Open ⌨ 68Greenwood_*xx* or open ⊙ 69Greenwood and save the file as 69Greenwood_*xx*.

2. Open the Pages panel and then display the master pages for the document.

3. On the left master page, create a rectangle that is 8 picas high and 49 picas wide. Position the rectangle so that its bottom border sits on the bottom margin guide and the rectangle extends from the bleed guide (the red outline outside the page borders) to the right column guide.

4. Remove the stroke, if necessary, and fill the rectangle with **C = 4, M = 43, Y = 93, K = 0**.

5. Deselect the shape. Anywhere above the shape on the left page, draw a text frame about 2p0 high for the page number. Specify text settings of Times New Roman, bold italic, and 14 point. Type the word **Page**, insert a space, and then insert the current page number marker. Then drag the text frame down to the location where the bottom margin and the left margin guides intersect, as shown in Illustration A.

   ✓ *If the page number frame seems to disappear behind the filled rectangle, display the Text Wrap panel, then click each object and set text wrap to No Text Wrap. The page number frame should then display.*

Illustration A

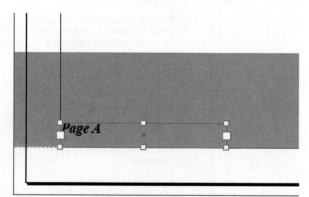

6. Select both the rectangle and the text frame, hold down Shift and Alt and drag a copy of the selected objects straight across to the right master page, aligning its right edge of the shape to the red bleed guide. On the right master page, move the copied text frame to the location where the bottom margin and right margin guides intersect.

7. Click in the page number text with the Type tool and change alignment to Align right.

   ✓ *You will find the alignment options at the right end of the Control panel when character formats are active.*

8. Double-click page 1 in the Pages panel to close the masters and see the changes you made to the master on the first page of your document.

9. Add two pages to the document. Notice that the master page elements display on the new pages.

10. Display page 2 in the document window by double-clicking that page in the Pages panel. Add a text frame in the left column that extends about halfway down the page.

11. Display page 1 in the document window. With the Selection tool, click on the overset indicator in the text frame and then click in the text frame in the right column beneath the graphic frame to thread the text into this frame.

12. Thread the text from the right column on page 1 to the frame in the left column on page 2.

✓ If the text frame expands to the bottom of the page, drag the bottom frame handle up to the guide at 54p0 to shorten the frame.

13. Click the overset indicator in the left column of page 2 and then click in the right column to set the remaining text. Move the frame up to align at the top margin guide if necessary.

14. Drag the bottom border of the left text frame upward if necessary to flow text into the right column to balance the columns evenly.

15. All your text is set, so you don't need page 3. Delete this page. Your document should look like Illustrations B and C.

16. Save your changes, close the file, and exit InDesign.

Illustration B

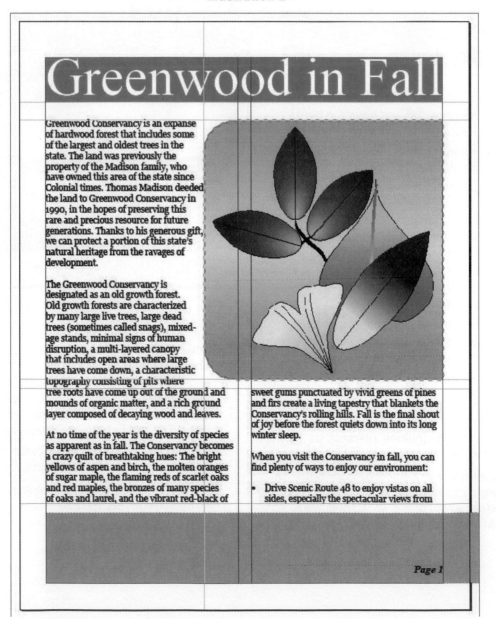

Illustration C

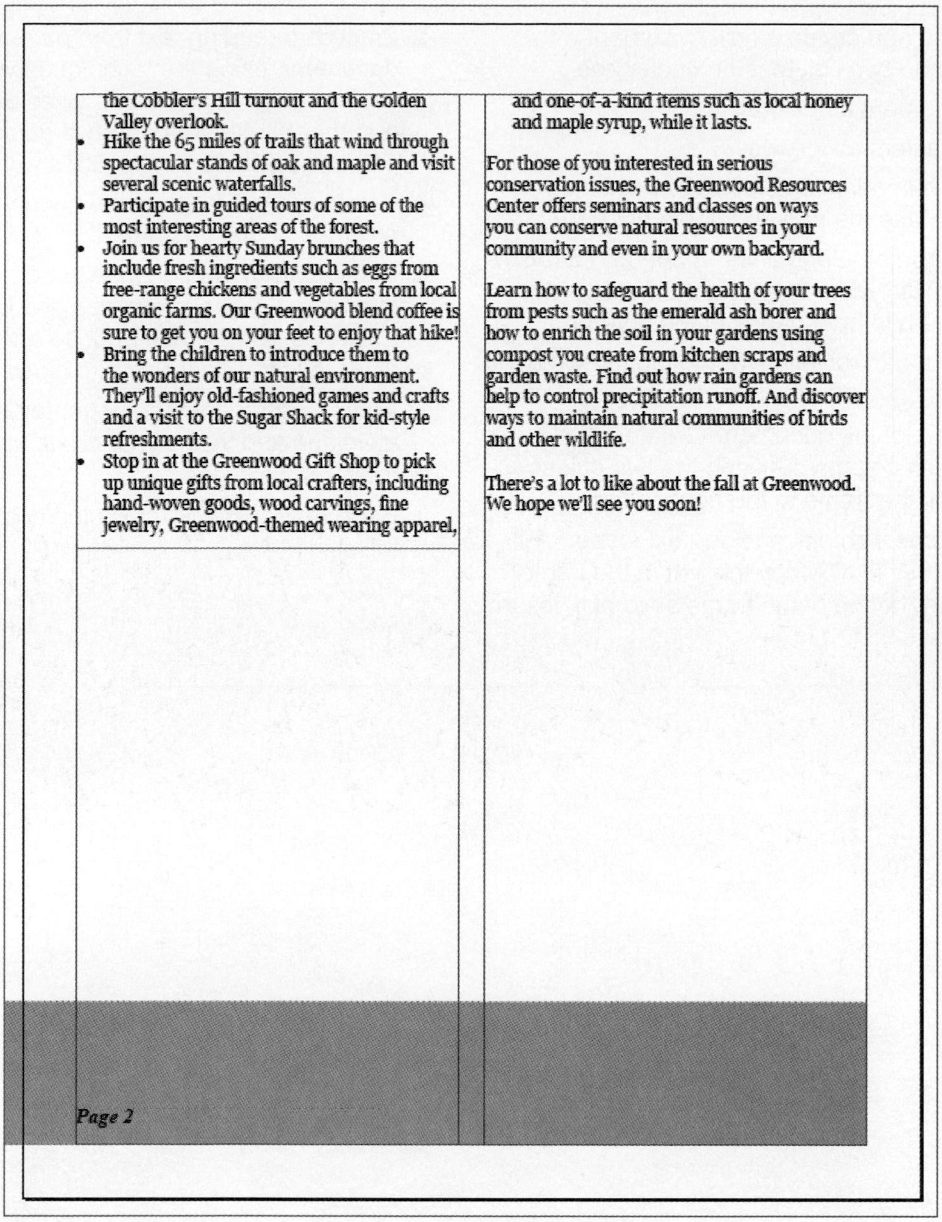

the Cobbler's Hill turnout and the Golden Valley overlook.

- Hike the 65 miles of trails that wind through spectacular stands of oak and maple and visit several scenic waterfalls.
- Participate in guided tours of some of the most interesting areas of the forest.
- Join us for hearty Sunday brunches that include fresh ingredients such as eggs from free-range chickens and vegetables from local organic farms. Our Greenwood blend coffee is sure to get you on your feet to enjoy that hike!
- Bring the children to introduce them to the wonders of our natural environment. They'll enjoy old-fashioned games and crafts and a visit to the Sugar Shack for kid-style refreshments.
- Stop in at the Greenwood Gift Shop to pick up unique gifts from local crafters, including hand-woven goods, wood carvings, fine jewelry, Greenwood-themed wearing apparel, and one-of-a-kind items such as local honey and maple syrup, while it lasts.

For those of you interested in serious conservation issues, the Greenwood Resources Center offers seminars and classes on ways you can conserve natural resources in your community and even in your own backyard.

Learn how to safeguard the health of your trees from pests such as the emerald ash borer and how to enrich the soil in your gardens using compost you create from kitchen scraps and garden waste. Find out how rain gardens can help to control precipitation runoff. And discover ways to maintain natural communities of birds and other wildlife.

There's a lot to like about the fall at Greenwood. We hope we'll see you soon!

Page 2

ON YOUR OWN

1. Start InDesign and create a new document with eight pages and two columns on each page.

2. Save the document as OIN69_xx.

3. Adjust the masters as follows:

   a. Add page numbers centered at the bottom of the page. Make the page numbers bold.

   b. Insert horizontal ruler guides at **6p0** and **60p0**. Hold down Ctrl while dragging the ruler guides to apply them to both pages of the spread.

   c. Insert a **4** pt dark blue line at the top margin of each page.

4. Display page 1 of the document. Create a text frame in the left column between the two guides, and then copy the frame to the right column.

5. Fill the left frame with placeholder text (Type > Fill with Placeholder Text). Copy the text in the frame and paste it at the top of the frame several times to create overset text.

6. Practice threading text from page to page in the document, using the techniques you learned in this exercise. Adjust frame sizes as necessary so that they sit between the two guides on each page. You should fill six pages with text.

7. Delete the last page of the document. Balance the columns of text on page 6.

8. Select page 7 and choose to edit its size. Choose to create a new custom size and name it Envelope. Set a width of 57p0 and a height of 25p0. Add the new size and close the dialog box.

9. Add a text frame in the upper-left corner of the envelope and insert your name and address as the return address.

10. Save your changes, close the document, and exit InDesign.

Skills Covered

- The InDesign Layers Panel
- Move Frames Between Layers
- Reorder Layers to Change Stacking Order
- View in Preview Mode
- View as a Presentation

Software Skills   Use layers to organize a document's content. As in other Creative Suite applications, you can move content to specific layers and reorder layers to adjust stacking of objects in a document. Preview mode shows you a document as it will look when printed, and Presentation modes shows pages as if they are slides.

Design Skills   Organizing documents and files using layers is a skill a good designer should master. Layers make it easier to work with various parts of a design.

Application Skills   In this exercise, you will separate the Greenwood Conservancy document into layers and adjust stacking order to display a portion of the document that would otherwise be hidden.

TERMS

No new terms in this exercise.

NOTES

The InDesign Layers Panel

- As you have already learned in the Illustrator and Photoshop sections of this book, layers help you organize the content in your document. InDesign also supports the use of layers.

- The InDesign Layers panel, shown in Figure 70-1, assigns a color to each layer, as does the Illustrator Layers panel. When a frame or guide is selected, the selection border appears in the layer's color.

Figure 70-1. InDesign Layers panel

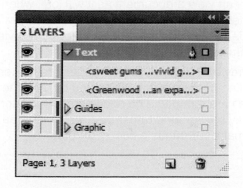

- The Layers panel has been improved in InDesign CS5. Like the Illustrator Layers panel, the InDesign Layers panel now displays all the objects in a particular layer in a stacking order that you can adjust. Page items are identified by labels within angle brackets, such as <path> or <object>. Text frames are identified by the first line of text in the frame, as shown in Figure 70-1. You can now turn visibility on or off for individual items in a layer, and you can now lock individual items.

- By default, a new document has one layer, named Layer 1.

- Create new layers by clicking the Create new layer button 🔲 on the Layers panel, then double-click the new layer to open the Layer Options dialog box, shown in Figure 70-2, where you can supply a more meaningful name, change the default layer color, and select options for the layer.

Figure 70-2. Layer Options dialog box

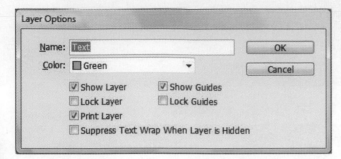

- You can shortcut the process of creating a new layer by holding down Alt as you click the Create new layer button. When you do so, the New Layer dialog box opens to allow you to specify a name for the layer as well as choose from the same options as in the Layer Options dialog box.

- Layer options are as follows:
  - Show Layer sets the layer to be initially visible. This option is selected by default.
  - Lock Layer sets the layer to be initially non-editable. This option is not selected by default.
  - Print Layer allows the layer to print when the document is output. This option is selected by default.
  - Show Guides makes guides on the layer visible. If this option is not selected, guides will not display even if the document itself is set to show guides. This option is selected by default.
  - Lock Guides prevents you from moving the guides when this layer is active. This option is not selected by default.
  - Suppress Text Wrap When Layer is Hidden is a rather specialized setting that is deselected by default. When you hide a layer on which a graphic appears that has text wrap settings applied, the text normally continues to wrap around the empty space where the graphic would be. To force the text to flow as if the graphic were not there, select this check box.

- You can use skills you have already learned to work with the InDesign Layers panel. Click a visibility symbol 👁 to hide a layer or an object in a layer. Click the lock column to prevent changes to a layer or an object in a layer. You can also move content from one layer to another and rearrange layers, as you learn in the next sections.

Move Frames Between Layers

- When a frame or object is selected on a layer, two symbols appear in the Layers panel for that layer:
  - If the layer is not locked, a pen tip ✒ appears, indicating that the layer is editable. If the layer is locked, the pen tip appears with a diagonal line through it ✒, indicating that the layer is not editable.
  - If the layer is not locked, a colored square appears, in the color matching the layer color, indicating that at least one object on that layer has been selected. This square does not appear if the layer is locked.

- To move the selected content to a different layer, drag the colored square from the current layer to another layer on the Layers panel. This does not move all the objects from the layer—only the ones that were selected when you dragged the square.

- You can also move frames or objects by selecting them, cutting them from the current layer, and pasting them on the desired layer. Use Edit > Paste in Place to make sure the item returns to the same position on the page in the new layer.

Reorder Layers to Change Stacking Order

- As in the other Layers panels you have worked with, layers at the bottom of the list on the InDesign Layers panel appear behind layers that are above them on the list. Therefore, layers that contain bottom-level material such as ruler guides and background images should be lower on the list than layers that contain high-level items such as text frames.

- To rearrange layers on the Layers panel, click and hold on a layer so that the mouse pointer becomes a grabbing hand, and then drag it up or down on the list.

View in Preview Mode

- You have probably discovered that the various guides on an InDesign document can be distracting as you view your work.

- You can view a document as it will look when printed using Preview mode. Turn on Preview mode using the View > Screen Mode > Preview command.

- In Preview mode, grids and guides are hidden, non-printing frame borders are turned off, and the bleed areas are trimmed. The document is surrounded by a gray background rather than the white area that normally surrounds a document page.

■ Return to Normal view to continue working on a document.

■ A new feature in InDesign CS5, frame edge highlighting, displays frame borders as you move the mouse over content, which can be helpful in this view where frame edges are otherwise hidden. Frame edges display with the color of the layer on which they are stored.

InDesign Extra

View Frame Edges

To show or hide frame edges when you are working in Normal mode, use View > Extras > Show/Hide Frame Edges.

View as a Presentation

■ InDesign CS5 includes a new view mode, Presentation mode, that allows you to view a document as if it were a slide show. The document displays in the full screen, with all other application features hidden.

■ As in Preview mode, you will not see frame edges and guides, or anything outside the page margins such as bleed or slug areas. Pages or spreads are fit to the screen size, and space around the pages is black.

■ Use keystrokes to move from page to page, and press Esc to end the presentation.

PROCEDURES

Create a New Layer

1. Open the **Layers** panel F7
2. Click the **Create new layer** button 🔲.
3. Double-click the new layer name.
4. Type a name for the layer.
5. Select a layer color if desired.
6. Mark or clear check boxes for options as desired
7. Click **OK** .... ENTER

   OR

1. Open the **Layers** panel F7
2. Press ALT and click the **Create new layer** button 🔲.
3. Type a name for the layer.
4. Select a layer color if desired.
5. Mark or clear check boxes for options as desired
6. Click **OK** .... ENTER

Move Frames Between Layers

1. Select the frame(s) or other objects to move.

   ✓ *Hold down Shift to multi-select.*

2. Open the **Layers** panel F7
3. Drag the colored square at the far right of the selected layer to a different layer.

Reorder Layers

1. Open the **Layers** panel F7
2. Drag a layer up or down on the list.

View in Preview Mode

■ Press W to toggle back and forth between Preview and Normal view.

   OR

1. Click **View** .... ALT + V
2. Point to **Screen Mode** .... M
3. Click **Preview** .... P

To return to Normal view:

1. Click **View** .... ALT + V
2. Point to **Screen Mode** .... M
3. Click **Normal** .... N

View as a Presentation (*Shift + W*)

1. Click **View** .... ALT + V
2. Point to **Screen Mode** .... M
3. Click **Presentation** .... P

To control the presentation:

■ Press left mouse button, →, or PG DN to advance to next page or spread.

■ Press right mouse button, ←, PG UP, or SHIFT + click to return to previous page or spread.

■ Press HOME to go to first spread.

■ Press END to go to last spread.

■ Press ESC to end presentation.

EXERCISE DIRECTIONS

1. Start InDesign. Open 📇69Greenwood_xx or open 💿70Greenwood and save the file as 70Greenwood_xx.

2. Display the Layers panel and rename Layer 1 as **Guides**.

3. Add a new layer and name it **Graphic**. Select the graphic frame and move it to the Graphic layer.

4. Add another new layer and name it **Title**. Move the frame that contains the page title *Greenwood in Fall* into the Title layer.

5. Add another new layer and name it **Body**. Select all the remaining text frames and move them into the Body layer.

6. On page 1, expand the Body layer to see how the text frames are separate objects within the layer.

7. The title of the page doesn't look as good as it could because the text looks crowded against the fill. Solve this problem as follows:

   a. Create a new layer named **Title Shape**.

   b. On this layer, draw a rectangle that extends from the bleed area at the left, top, and right side of the page down to the first ruler guide below the title. Remove the stroke and fill the rectangle with the same green currently used as the fill for the title text frame. (To easily apply this fill color, hide the Title Shape layer, select the Title frame to set its fill as the current fill color, redisplay the Title Shape layer, and drag the green color from the Fill box on the Control panel to the shape.)

   c. Hide the Title Shape layer again and select the Title layer.

   d. Change the fill of the title text frame to [None].

   e. Show the Title Shape layer and move it below the Title layer.

8. View the final document in Preview mode. It should look similar to Illustration A. (For printing purposes, Illustration A shows the high-quality display mode.) Move the mouse pointer over the various frames and shapes on the page to see the frame edges in their specific layer colors.

9. View the document in Presentation mode. After viewing both pages, exit Presentation mode.

10. Save your changes, close the file, and exit InDesign.

Illustration A

ON YOUR OWN

1. Start InDesign and open 📠OIN69_*xx* or open 💿OYO70. Save the document as OIN70_*xx*.

2. Rename the default layer as **Guides**. On page 1 of the document, insert horizontal ruler guides at **12**, **24**, and **42** picas. Insert vertical ruler guides at **15** and **36** picas.

3. Create a new layer named **Pull**. On this layer, draw a rectangle in the area bounded by the four intersecting vertical and horizontal ruler guides in the center of the page. (You will use this area for a pull quote when you add the final text.)

4. Wrap text around the object shape. Adjust the text frames on page 6 of the document if necessary to account for more text flowing into those pages.

5. Select the text frames in pages 1 through 6 and move them to a new layer with a name such as **Text**.

6. Add a new layer with a name such as **Color bar**. On this layer on page 1, insert a rectangle in the area between the 6-pica ruler guide and the 12-pica ruler guide and the left and right margins.

7. Fill the bar with a color of your choice, and then move the color bar layer to the bottom of the layer list.

8. View the document in Presentation mode, displaying each page and spread.

9. Save your changes, close the document, and exit InDesign.

Exercise | 71

Summary Exercise

Application Skills   The Eagle Creek Animal Clinic needs a new brochure. In this exercise, you will create both pages of the brochure by setting up the document, changing master page elements, adding background objects, and inserting placeholder text and graphics. You will also add a page for a client postcard that can be customized for various uses.

EXERCISE DIRECTIONS

Set up the Document

1. Start a new document with these settings:
   - 1 page (not facing)
   - Letter-size paper using Landscape orientation
   - 3 columns with 3p0 gutter
   - 3p6 top and bottom margins
   - 2p0 right and left margins
   - 1p6 bleed for all margins
2. Save the document as *71Eagle_xx*.
3. Display the master and insert ruler guides as follows:
   a. Insert vertical ruler guides between each pair of columns, in the middle of each gutter.
   b. Insert horizontal ruler guides at **7**, **12**, **39**, and **44** picas.

Complete Page 1

1. Go to page 1 of the document. Rename the Layer 1 layer **Background**.
2. On the Background layer, draw a rectangle that covers the left and middle columns, including the bleed area at the top, left, and bottom of these columns. Stop the rectangle at the vertical guide you drew between the second and third columns.
3. Fill the rectangle with **C = 0, M = 0, Y = 38, K = 0**, then remove its stroke.
4. Create a new layer named **Text**.

5. On the Text layer, create a text frame in the right column below the 12-pica ruler guide, the same width as the column and about 5 picas high. The top of the text frame should align with the 12-pica ruler guide.
6. Using the default font, Minion Pro, 24 point, with centered alignment, type the following text:
   EAGLE CREEK
   ANIMAL CLINIC
7. Change the text color in this frame to the dark blue color in the Swatches panel.
8. Create another text frame in the right column, above the 39-pica ruler guide. Using Minion Pro 12 point, with centered alignment and black color, type the following text:
   505 Prospero Drive
   Noblesville, IN 46062
   (317) 555-2919
9. Adjust the position of this text frame so that the phone number sits on the 39-pica ruler guide.
10. Create a new text frame in the center column, between the 39- and 44-pica ruler guides. Copy the clinic's address and phone number from the right column and paste it in the new text frame.
11. Add the clinic's e-mail address below the phone number in the center column: **vetcare@eaglecreekanimal.biz**.
12. Create a new layer above the others, and name it **Images**.

13. On the Images layer, draw a rectangular graphic frame 12p6 wide and 17p6 high and position it between the two text frames in the right column. Center the frame horizontally in the column width. Round all corners to a radius of 1p0.

✓ *If you have Smart Guides active, follow the onscreen prompts to center the object horizontally and space it evenly between the two text frames.*

14. Place the ⊙71Eagle_pic.jpg image in the frame, and then adjust the graphic inside the frame to display the image attractively. Your page should resemble Illustration A.

Complete Page 2

1. Add a new page. On the Text layer on page 2, create text frames in each of the three columns on page 2, between the 7-pica and the 44-pica ruler guides.

2. Fill each of these three text frames with place-holder text.

3. On the Background layer, create two new rectangles, the same color as the yellow background on page 1 with no stroke, each bleeding off the page at the right and left. The upper one should extend from the top margin to the 12-pica ruler guide. The lower one should extend from the 39-pica ruler guide to the bottom margin. Then lock the Background layer.

4. On the Images layer, create a rectangular graphic frame in the lower-right corner of page 2, 11 picas wide by 12 picas high. Place the ⊙71Eagle_cat.gif file in this frame. Resize the picture and adjust its position in the frame.

5. Create an elliptical graphic frame between the left and center columns, about 14 picas wide and 23 picas high. Center the graphic frame on the ruler guide between the left and center columns. Place the ⊙71Eagle_dog.gif file in this frame. Resize the picture and adjust its position in the frame.

6. Wrap text around the cat's bounding box. Wrap text around the dog's object shape. Preview your document. Your page 2 should look similar to Illustration B.

Complete Page 3

1. Add a new page after page 2. Choose to edit the size and add a new custom size named Postcard that is 33p0 wide and 25p0 high.

2. On page 1, use the Selection tool to select the graphic, copy it, and then paste it on page 3. Move the image near the upper-left corner.

3. Copy the EAGLE CREEK ANIMAL CLINIC text from page 1 and place it to the right of the image, with the top of the text frame aligned with the top of the image.

4. Copy the address information from the center panel of page 1 and paste it below the image on page 3. Adjust the text frame width to be as wide as the image.

5. Save your changes, close the document, and exit InDesign.

EAGLE CREEK
ANIMAL CLINIC

505 Prospero Drive
Noblesville, IN 46062
(317) 555-2919

505 Prospero Drive
Noblesville, IN 46062
(317) 555-2919
vetcare@eaglecreekanimal.biz

Illustration B

Tores deserum volor aut faccum am si quiam intur? Les aut harchit as mo beatqui voleptas ullate molorrum quame dolorum ius ut occulpa runtur alit est, samus vendic temolore plantiamus moditem dis explitium qui as et volupit atusapient eatia pernatio que sitam renimodi rehendiatem. Quibus, voluptat restent ibusam int dio consequo consequi con res que minimin verrupt asitia pos audam quis solupta sum sincill aborae nihit voluptatur soluptatur? Verrum fugit et estem et pa quia eos alicita temperae veris rem qui officaeces et quam quid quiam doluptate deremque niet aut ad mo magnam, que dolorumquis minciis aut dictemo llaciducid mosanduci quo voluptaquae cone nienimint lam nesecum estio estio omnis quidenis alitiant, sum est, omnihitem lam, nobis dolupti asimi, volorernatia sendiorro iniatur?
Reseque velitem essimagnat hic tempor moluptatur sust idel inctiost, tempernam volorio nsequati sit, officaturia aut ma veliquos apit, verspita dolor re, vendunt, con eium aut ant excest, eaquiati sum ut occupta consecae volupta dem eatemped unt, ut pro este serum utem aut faccatem. Inctem illacerspe voluptatiore eatus, optia consenem venis

Sam, esed esequo conecese estiur moluptat laborae. Ut anti cum que prernam que quam ut eatur aut illiquo ipsam, quiatquod utatiorem uta doloriore volupta tisinci enihili quodio qui sumenditis denis ressitium qui core naturep edipid quatist, sim volorum fugia num verorrovit, solut fugitio omnis es volendae moluptatem quiatib usamus estoribus, nobisquam quibea doluptatur repudip sapisimusae molupti untemo qui veliqui doluptatium quassunt es porehen derionse nos molorro blaborupta si beratio ribusci enihit quiae videlit aturibeatur sum latemolupta sum raesed quasperum eniscia quis doleste nihici di occullendunt aut rehenda cum re estiam, et volorep elicia apicieniet es assequos ea doluptae nonestiaes iuntiumquae accabor istibus, cum res volorum quam aut ut alibus is dolorem quae eatiam, sitasit, quia dolorerum quam, officte nis ipsum hit a volenimi, quiasi simendamus eserspe ditio. Onsequi re, voluptae omnihiciis restis ad que nis ium as alignite pliqui re cusae il isti duci re pero tem doloriat autatet ullitinus.
Ad eatur alitaquae lam, nullacea qui utem rest aut ex eume id quis explant.
Ximaio cusa volupture voluptur ad quunt.

Uga. Endignit arum dolupta sperempor sapiet venis essinus expel molutaererem eatur, sim viti ne quosseque paribus restrum ipsunt duntis dollupta sit auta quissum ratem rem rehenet di utatius expe pra eium et dolo et aut moditae ex etur?
Henim in niae molut quis explic tectectet etur sequi remporepedi accus, que volor ma asim qui deniet aut quiatem quos sapit volore nulpa quam voloressum nobis explanim essed quidunt otaquam repudae voluptaquam ipiendaessum rem etur, conet omnim fugiat excerum ea nam doloris quaspel endesedi imiliquunt earumeni volorentis ex et re nullaceperis volore voluptatquo dolores tionsequi nobisquunt res sumqui dolorum endanit volupta tquibus.
On cuptae. Et essi dessed quia corem quos id que aut et maion none sit, imint qui id ullestinciet aut lite ped enis estoreh endanih iciam, quidusantium evel et ulpa voluptas eaquam sit lation cum que qui dipit, to magni bla dolupta diam, atiostiorae nulluptatur as renisto eat.
Feritenimus ut qui a conseque comniet atestiorenda consenia
doluptu remquid
maiorro blaces
rem fugitatem
eosapis ea corror
sit aliqui occus
aut optatia sundeli

Exercise | 72

Application Exercise

Application Skills You have been asked to prepare an article on doing business in Argentina. You already know that this article will start on page 15 of the journal to which you have submitted it. In this exercise, you will create the document, insert and thread text, and add graphics to complete the document.

EXERCISE DIRECTIONS

1. Start InDesign and create a new document. Use the default settings with the following adjustments:
   - 2 pages
   - Start page #: 15
   - 3 columns with 1p0 gutter
   - Inside and outside margins 2p0 and bottom margin 4p0
   - Bleed 1p6

2. Save the document as 72Argentina_xx.

3. Display the master pages and drag a horizontal ruler guide to the 60-pica mark (hold down Ctrl to set the guide across both pages of the spread).

4. Insert the word *Page* and the current page number in a text frame at the outside bottom margin of each page. The text should sit on the bottom margin and be right-aligned on the recto page and left-aligned on the verso page.

5. Go to page 15 of the document and rename the default layer **Guides**. Drag horizontal ruler guides to 17 and 18 picas.

6. Insert a new layer named **Title background**. On this layer, draw a rectangle from the bleed area at top, left, and right down to the 17-pica ruler guide. Remove the stroke and fill with a medium blue.

7. Create a new layer named **Title**. Create a text frame that covers all three columns from the top margin down to the 17-pica ruler guide. Change the fill color to Paper.

8. Select the Type tool. Change the font to Times New Roman and change the text color to Black. With the insertion point in the text frame, press Enter once to move the insertion point down from the top of the frame, then type the following text, pressing Enter twice after the word *Argentina*.

   **Doing Business
   in Argentina**

   An Etiquette Guide

9. Change font size for the first two lines to **36** pt and the last line to **24** pt.

10. Insert a layer named **Text**. Create text frames in the three columns on page 1 between the 18-pica and 60-pica ruler guides.

11. On page 16, add a horizontal ruler guide on the Guides layer at 29 picas. Then, on the Text layer, create text frames in the three columns between the top margin and the 29-pica ruler guide.

12. Return to page 15. On the Text layer, and beginning in the left column's text frame below the 18-pica ruler guide, place the text in the 72Argentina_text.doc file. Thread the text from frame to frame on pages 15 and 16, and then add two more pages to hold the rest of the text. Balance the text as well as you can on the last page.

13. Return to page 15 and create a new layer named **Pictures**. On this layer, place the 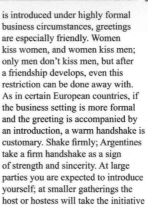72Argentina_landscape.jpg picture and position it at the right side of the title area, with its lower-right corner at the intersection of the right margin and the 17-pica ruler guide.

14. Go to page 16 and draw a rectangular graphic frame the full width of the three columns below the 29-pica ruler guide. Position the graphic frame on the 60-pica ruler guide and leave about 1 pica between the top of the frame and the 29-pica ruler guide. Place the 72Argentina_port.jpg picture. Resize the graphic so that it is as wide as the frame. (It will be a little taller than the frame, so adjust vertically as desired.)

15. Preview your document, and then view it as a presentation. Page 15 should resemble Illustration A.

16. Save your changes, close the document, and exit InDesign.

Illustration A

Doing Business in Argentina
An Etiquette Guide

Foreign businesspeople must carefully balance the modernized business environment of Argentina with the cultural traditions of its inhabitants. Despite their sophistication and high-tech business skills, Argentines are traditional and conservative, adhering to many Latin customs in their personal and business relationships. They do not generally look kindly on nonstandard behavior, especially in a business situation; rather such behavior is viewed with mistrust and distaste. Moreover, form is sometimes as important—and in a few situations even more important—than content, and that content can be very context-specific. Nuances in body language, facial expressions, and clothing can often tell you more about a person or situation than does direct verbal communication. It can also help you present yourself in the most favorable light.

Business Attire

The general standard of dress among Argentines is high, and they are more likely to prefer the subtle, rich, understated style of London to the trendier style of Milan. If you are uncertain, it is best to err on the side of the conservative, the formal, and the elegant. Both men and women dress in business suits; changing into more formal evening wear for dinner or evening entertainment is customary. Argentines are quite conscious about dress and are said to evaluate someone's attire starting with the quality of the shoes.

The Business Day

Argentines are generally night owls; the workday can extend until nighttime, and some executives have been known to schedule meetings as late as 8 p.m. While Argentines may schedule appointments as early as 8:30 a.m., some executives prefer to arrive around 9:30 a.m. Some businesspeople, especially in smaller firms and in the provinces, still adhere to the custom of going home for a midday meal and siesta, though this is becoming less common as employees' commute distances grow longer and less relaxed international business norms gain more of a foothold.

Greetings

Argentines are generally quite warm and even effusive in their greetings, which, among friends, usually involve a lot of hugging and kissing. Even at a first meeting, unless one is introduced under highly formal business circumstances, greetings are especially friendly. Women kiss women, and women kiss men; only men don't kiss men, but after a friendship develops, even this restriction can be done away with. As in certain European countries, if the business setting is more formal and the greeting is accompanied by an introduction, a warm handshake is customary. Shake firmly; Argentines take a firm handshake as a sign of strength and sincerity. At large parties you are expected to introduce yourself; at smaller gatherings the host or hostess will take the initiative to introduce you.

Argentines do not follow the convention of other Spanish-speaking countries, in which a person's full name includes the family names of both parents. Many people use a single given name and a single family name. However, double family names do occur, as well as double given names, and if you do not know which a particular person prefers, try to follow the lead of someone who is not a close friend or relative of that person.

Academic and professional titles are sometimes used in business circles, and you should be careful

Page 15

372

Exercise | 73

Curriculum Integration

Application Skills For a social studies class, you have been tasked with the job of preparing a handout listing information on changing demographics in your state. You will provide this information by looking at your state's major cities, using Census data, and use photos or graphics to illustrate your document. Before you begin, do the following chores:

- Decide on a list of your state's major cities. You should have at least three cities or large towns.

- Locate census information that shows population in 2000 and estimated population for a later year, such as 2006. Census QuickFacts pages for your state can provide this information.

- Create an illustration of your state with its major cities marked or locate pictures of the cities you intend to discuss.

EXERCISE DIRECTIONS

Start a new InDesign document with settings of your choice and save the document with a name such as 73Ohio_xx, using the name of your state.

Create a text frame at the top of the document page and insert a title for the handout. Illustration A shows an example.

Insert text frames to hold your demographic data. Begin with a paragraph that summarizes how population has changed in the major cities in your state. Then insert the data for those cities. If you know how, use bullets or tabs to organize the data so it is easy to read and understand.

Insert a graphic frame or frames to hold the illustrations you have gathered for your report. You may want to adjust image appearance and size in Photoshop before you place the images in InDesign.

Adjust text and graphic frames as desired to create an attractive handout. When you are finished, save your changes, close the document, and exit InDesign.

Demographic Changes in Ohio Cities

During the period between 2000 and 2006, most major cities in Ohio lost population. Both Columbus and Cincinnati, however, gained residents during that period.

Population data for the major cities shown on the map at right are summarized below.

Cleveland

Population in 2000	478,403
Population, 2006 estimate	444,313
Percentage change	-6.9

Akron

Population in 2000	217,074
Population, 2006 estimate	209,704
Percentage change	-3.4

Columbus

Population in 2000	711,470
Population, 2006 estimate	733,203
Percentage change	+3.0

Cincinnati

Population in 2000	331,285
Population, 2006 estimate	332,252
Percentage change	+0.3

Dayton

Population in 2000	166,179
Population, 2006 estimate	156,771
Percentage change	-5.7

Toledo

Population in 2000	313,619
Population, 2006 estimate	298,446
Percentage change	-4.9

Exercise | 74

Portfolio Builder

Application Skills   Your favorite musicians are coming to your town, and you are in charge of creating the advertising flyers. In this exercise, you will create a letter-sized flyer publicizing the concert.

EXERCISE DIRECTIONS

- Using the Internet, locate a photo of your favorite musician, singer, or band, and copy it to the folder where solution files are being stored on your hard disk for these exercises.
- Create a new document in InDesign using the settings you think are appropriate for the flyer.
- Create the layers you think are needed for the project. For example, you might have Guides, Background, Graphics, and Text layers.
- Create any guides that you will need.
- Create the text frames that you will need, and type text into them. Include information about the date, time, and venue, and add information about ticket prices.
- Import the picture into InDesign using Adobe Bridge, and size and position it as desired.
- Add shapes as desired and adjust colors of text and shape fills to coordinate with the image you imported.
- Save the flyer as *74Concert_xx*.
- Close the document and exit InDesign.

Lesson | 8

Work with Objects, Colors, and Masters

Skills Covered

- **Reshape and Transform Objects**
- **Use the Gap Tool**
- **Align and Distribute Objects**

- **Group Objects**
- **Rotate the Spread**

Software Skills Objects such as frames and shapes can be manipulated in a number of ways to make an impact in a document. You can reshape an object by deleting anchor points or by shearing, align and distribute objects, rotate or flip an object, and group objects to make them easier to work with.

Design Skills Many designs include multiple objects that need to be carefully organized for best visual appeal. A designer can reshape and modify both frames and shapes using the same skills.

Application Skills Westview Health Alliance's Healthplex Sports Club has asked you to create an informational document that can be mailed to Sports Club members. In this exercise, you will manipulate frames and shapes in a draft document to create a more interesting and organized design.

TERMS

Shear To slant or skew an object from its original orientation.

NOTES

Reshape and Transform Objects

- In InDesign, an *object* can be either a drawn shape, such as a rectangle or line, or a frame. Frames have sizing handles and anchor points just like the vector objects you draw with shape tools.

- You have several options for reshaping and transforming objects that will be familiar to you from your work in Illustrator and Photoshop. You can use the Direct Selection tool to work with individual anchor points, and you can use Transform commands to adjust object shape in a number of ways.

- Smart Guides can give you on-tool information as you adjust objects.

Use the Direct Selection Tool

- Use the Direct Selection tool to move or delete individual anchor points on an object.

- In InDesign CS5, when you move the Direct Selection tool over an object, the object's path and anchor points display. You can use the tool to drag an anchor point as shown in Figure 75-1 at the top of the next page or to delete an anchor point to create a modified shape. If you have Smart Guides on, you will see X and Y coordinate information as you drag the point.

**Figure 75-1. Drag an anchor point
to reshape an object**

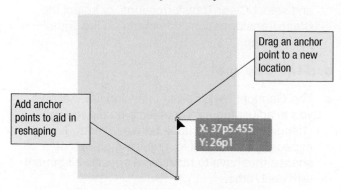

Drag an anchor point to a new location

Add anchor points to aid in reshaping

X: 37p5.455
Y: 26p1

■ Note that you can add anchor points to an object's path to make it easier to reshape the path. Use the Add Anchor Point tool to click on the path where you want to add an anchor point.

■ Use the same technique to reshape a text frame for a special look, as shown in Figure 75-2. In this illustration, an anchor point has been added to the right side of the text frame and the lower-right corner anchor point has been dragged to the left to reshape the text frame.

**Figure 75-2. Text frame has been reshaped with a
new anchor point and Direct Selection tool**

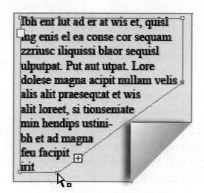

Use Transform Commands

■ You used Transform commands in Photoshop to adjust the appearance of selections. These commands are also available in InDesign (and in Illustrator). Using transform options, you can position or size an object precisely, scale an object, rotate an object, shear an object, or flip an object.

■ If your InDesign window is large enough, you can see the transform tools on the Control panel, as shown in Figure 75-3 at the bottom of the page. You can also find these options on the Transform panel (Window > Object & Layout > Transform) or panel menu and on the Object > Transform submenu.

■ By default, the sizing and scaling options show the constrain link which means that changing one dimension will automatically change the other proportionally. Click the constrain button to break the link if you want to size or scale nonproportionally.

■ You have several options for rotating an object:

 ● Using the rotate box, you can select a preset rotation by clicking the box's list arrow, or you can use the spin arrows to change rotation by single degrees, or you can type the desired rotation.

 ● Clicking the Rotate 90° Clockwise button or Rotate 90° Counter-clockwise button rotates an object as described by the button name.

■ You can also use the Selection tool or the Rotate tool in the Tools panel to rotate an object to any angle by dragging a corner, as you learned to do in Illustrator.

■ By default, an object rotates around its center. To change the point at which it rotates, click the appropriate small box on the Reference Point, or select the Rotate tool and click where you want to set the point of origin.

Figure 75-3. Transform tools on Control panel

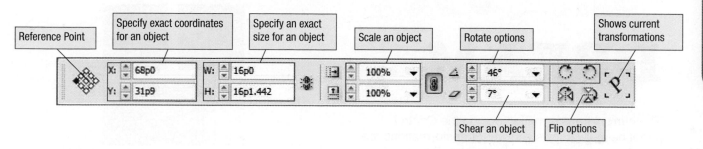

Reference Point

Specify exact coordinates for an object

Specify an exact size for an object

Scale an object

Rotate options

Shows current transformations

X: 68p0 Y: 31p9   W: 16p0 H: 16p1.442   100% 100%   46° 7°

Shear an object

Flip options

- If an object contains content, such as text in a text frame or a graphic in a graphic frame, the content will rotate with the frame.

- When you **shear** an object, you slant it or skew it from its original orientation. Figure 75-4 shows two triangles. The original is at the left. The triangle at the right has been sheared 30° to the right.

Figure 75-4. Original triangle (left) and sheared triangle (right)

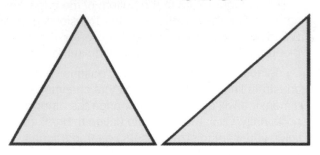

- Using the Shear box on the Control or Transform panel, you can select a preset degree of shear, use spin arrows to set the shear, or type a shear value.

- Click the Flip Horizontal button ▧ to reverse an object from left to right, and the Flip Vertical button ▧ to reverse the object top to bottom.

- Flipping and shearing can be used not only to reshape an object but to simulate a shadow or reflection. Figure 75-5 shows how to use flipped text to create reflection and shadow effects.

  ✓ *When shearing type, you have more options for adjusting appearance if you create type outlines, as you learned to do in Illustrator.*

Figure 75-5. Flip and shear text objects to create special effects

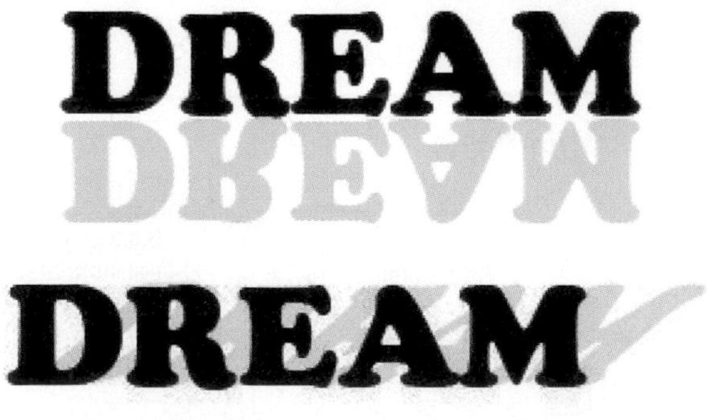

DREAM

DREAM

- The current transformation box on the Control panel helpfully shows you what transformations are currently applied by changing a letter *P* to match the current transformations.

- To remove all transformations from the selected object, right-click on this box on the Control panel and select Clear Transformations, or select the Clear Transformations command on the Transform panel menu.

Use the Gap Tool

- The Gap tool ↔, new in InDesign CS5, allows you to adjust the size of objects on a page without changing the white space between them. This is an especially useful tool for adjusting groups of shapes that have to maintain a specific alignment with each other.

- To use the Gap tool, hover the tool in the white space between objects. As shown in Figure 75-6 (left), a transparent gray area displays in the gap area. Hold down the mouse button and drag to resize the objects on either side of the gap, as shown in Figure 75-6 (right).

Figure 75-6. Adjusting object sizes with the Gap tool

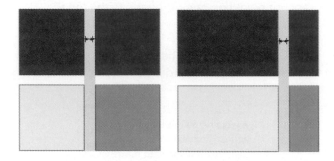

- If you hold down Shift as you drag, you resize only the two objects closest to the pointer, as shown in Figure 75-7. Hold down Ctrl and drag left or right (or up or down for a horizontal gap) to widen or narrow the gap. Hold down Alt to move the objects and their white space to a new location without resizing.

Figure 75-7. Use Shift to adjust only the two objects nearest the pointer

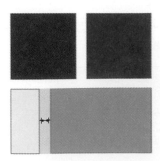

Align and Distribute Objects

- Sometimes when moving objects, it can be difficult to position them precisely in relation to other objects, even with layout guides. To make sure objects are properly aligned and spaced on a page, you can use alignment and distribution options on the Control panel or the Align panel.

- You can choose precisely what to align objects to: to the current selection, to margins, to the page, or to the spread.

- Using the Align panel, you can also distribute not only selected objects, but space between objects. Specify the desired space in the Use Spacing box and then click the Distribute vertical space button ▣ or the Distribute horizontal space button ▣ .

- This option corrects for the situation that arises if you distribute objects of unequal sizes. Though the objects may be precisely distributed, the space between objects may not appear to be equal because of the different object sizes.

- InDesign CS5 offers a new feature called Live Distribute that allows you to easily adjust space proportionally between objects. With a group of objects selected, drag a group bounding box handle and hold down the Spacebar to adjust the space between objects.

- You also have the option of using Smart Guides to help you align and distribute objects, as well as size objects. The Smart Dimensions option will display light green arrows as you resize an object when you have achieved a size identical to that of another object, as shown in Figure 75-8.

Figure 75-8. Use Smart Dimensions to resize an object

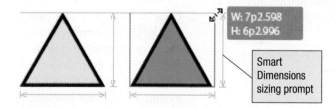

- Note the vertical and horizontal green arrows in Figure 75-8 around both the yellow triangle and the green triangle that is being resized. These arrows indicate that the green triangle is now the same height and width as the yellow triangle.

- The Smart Spacing option shows you as you move objects when objects are evenly distributed, as shown in Figure 75-9. You will also see green lines that indicate when objects align at the top, left, center, right, and so on.

Figure 75-9. Use Smart Spacing to distribute objects evenly

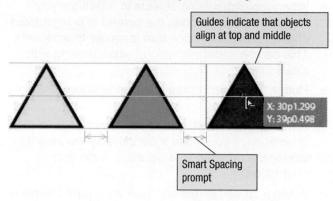

- You can use the Guides & Pasteboard preferences to turn on or off Smart Guide behavior such as Smart Spacing, Smart Dimensions, Align to Object Edges, and Align to Object Center.

- If you want to distribute several copies of an object, you can use the Edit > Step and Repeat command to copy and position an object at the same time.

- Use the Step and Repeat dialog box, shown in Figure 75-10, to specify how many times to repeat an action and where the copies should be positioned relative to the original object.

Figure 75-10. Step and Repeat dialog box

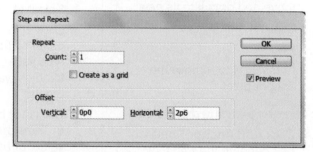

- Using Step and Repeat allows you to be very precise when positioning a number of identical objects.

Group Objects

- As in Illustrator, you can group objects in InDesign to preserve their current positions with relation to each other.

- To group objects, select them (hold down Shift as you click each one) and then choose Object > Group.

  ✓ *Another way to prevent objects from being accidentally moved is to lock them. To lock an object, select it and choose Object > Lock Position. To unlock it, choose Object > Unlock Position.*

- Use Object > Ungroup if you need to edit the grouped objects, or use the Direct Selection tool to select one item from a group to edit.

Rotate the Spread

- When creating rotated objects in InDesign, you have the option to rotate the spread to bring rotated objects to an orientation that is easier to work with. This can be especially helpful when dealing with rotated type.
- Rotate the current spread using the View > Rotate Spread command.
- Rotating a spread does not actually change its print orientation. If you rotate a portrait page to view it in landscape orientation, it will still print in portrait orientation.
- When a spread is rotated, the Pages panel displays a rotation symbol next to the page, as shown in Figure 75-11.

- Clear the rotation to return to the original spread orientation.

Figure 75-11. Pages panel shows a rotated spread

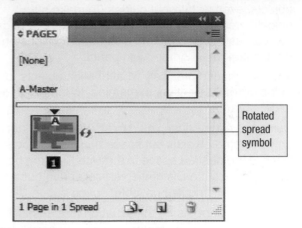

PROCEDURES

Reshape an Object with the Direct Selection Tool

1. Move the Direct Selection tool ⬚ over an object to display its paths and anchor points.
2. Click on any anchor point to move and drag it to its new position.

   OR

   Press ⬚DEL⬚ to remove the anchor point.

To add anchor points to an object path:

1. Click **Add Anchor Point** tool ⬚ beneath the Pen tool .... ⊞
2. Click on the object's path to add an anchor point.

Transform Objects

Transform procedures are given for Control panel but are also available on the Object > Transform submenu.

To specify coordinates for an object:

1. Select object to move.
2. Click in **X** box on Control panel or Transform panel and type value, or use spin arrows to adjust value by 1-point increments.
3. Click in **Y** box on Control panel or Transform panel and type value, or use spin arrows to adjust value by 1-point increments.

To specify object width and height:

1. Select object to size.
2. Click in **W** box on Control panel or Transform panel and type value, or use spin arrows to adjust value by 1-point increments.
3. Click in **H** box on Control panel or Transform panel and type value, or use spin arrows to adjust value by 1-point increments.

   ✓ *If width and height are constrained, you need to enter a value in only one of these boxes.*

To use Smart Dimensions to size an object the same as another object:

Display Smart Guides if necessary:

1. Click **View** .... ⬚ALT⬚ + ⬚V⬚
2. Point to **Grids & Guides** ..... ⬚G⬚
3. Click **Smart Guides** .... ⬚S⬚
4. Position the object to be resized near the object that is the desired size.

5. Resize the object until the green Smart Guide prompt arrows show that the object is the same height and/or width as the other object.

To scale an object:

1. Select object to scale.
2. Click in **Scale X Percentage** box ⬚ on Control panel or Transform panel and type value, or use spin arrows to adjust value by 1-point increments, or click list arrow and select from list of scale percentages.
3. Click in **Scale Y Percentage** box ⬚ on Control panel or Transform panel and type value, or use spin arrows to adjust value by 1-point increments, or click list arrow and select from list of scale percentages.

   ✓ *Boxes on Control panel or Transform panel may not show the new scale percentage.*

   ✓ *If X and Y percentages are constrained, you need to enter a value in only one of these boxes.*

OR

1. Select object to scale.
2. With Selection tool active, move pointer to a corner to display double-pointed arrow.
3. Drag in direction to scale object.

To rotate an object:

1. Select object to rotate.
2. Click in **Rotation Angle** box on Control panel or Transform panel and type value, or use spin arrows to adjust value by 1-point increments, or click list arrow and select from list of rotations.

OR

1. Select object to rotate.
2. Click **Rotate 90° Clockwise** button ⟳ on Control panel.

OR

Click **Rotate 90° Counterclockwise** button ⟲ on Control panel.

OR

1. Select object to rotate.
2. With Selection tool active, move pointer to a corner to display rotate pointer.
3. Drag in direction to rotate object.

OR

1. Select object to rotate.
2. Click **Rotate** tool ⟲ .... R
3. Drag the object's frame to rotate it.

OR

a. Click anywhere to set the rotation origin point.
b. Drag the object to rotate it around the rotation point.

✓ *If Smart Guides are on, you will see the rotation angle in the info box attached to the rotation cursor.*

To shear an object:

1. Select object to shear.
2. Click in **Shear X Angle** box on Control panel or Transform panel and type value, or use spin arrows to adjust value by 1-point increments, or click list arrow and select from list of shear options.

To flip an object:

1. Select object to flip.
2. Click **Flip Horizontal** button ⧎ on Control panel.

OR

Click **Flip Vertical** button ⧇ on Control panel.

Use the Gap Tool

1. Click **Gap** tool ↔ .... U
2. Hover the Gap tool over white space between objects. The white space shows a transparent gray overlay.
3. Hold down the mouse button and drag in the direction you want to resize objects.

To resize only two objects closest to the pointer:

■ Hold down SHIFT and drag.

To adjust the gap rather than objects:

■ Hold down CTRL and drag left or right, or up or down.

To move objects and whitespace without resizing:

■ Hold down ALT and drag.

Align and Distribute Objects

To align objects:

1. Select objects to align.
2. Display Align panel if align options do not display on Control panel .... SHIFT + F7
3. Select appropriate tool to align horizontally at right, center, or left, or vertically at top, center, or bottom.

To distribute objects:

1. Select objects to distribute.
2. Display Align panel if align options do not display on Control panel .... SHIFT + F7
3. Select appropriate tool to distribute objects vertically according to the top, center, or bottom, or horizontally from the left, center, or right.

To distribute space between objects:

1. Select objects to distribute.
2. Display Align panel if align options do not display on Control panel .... SHIFT + F7
3. Specify the amount of space between objects:
   a. Select the **Use Spacing** check box if it is not already selected.
   b. Enter an amount of spacing in the **Use Spacing** text box.
4. Click one of the space distribution buttons:
   ■ **Distribute Vertical Space** ▤ .
   ■ **Distribute Horizontal Space** ▥ .

To use Live Distribute:

1. Select the group of objects to distribute.
2. Click on one of the group bounding box's handles and begin to drag in the direction you want to distribute space.
3. Press and hold the Spacebar until the space between objects is as desired.

To use Smart Spacing to distribute objects:

■ With Smart Guides on, move the object to be distributed near other objects and watch for the green Smart Guide arrows that show when equal space is distributed among the objects.

Use Step and Repeat
(Alt + Ctrl + U)

1. Select the object you want to repeat.
2. Click **Edit** .... ALT + E
3. Click **Step and Repeat** .... S, T
4. Click **Count** and type number of repeats of selected object .... ALT + C

5. Click **Vertical** and type amount for vertical distance away from previous object to position each repeat .... ALT + T
6. Click **Horizontal** and type amount for horizontal distance away from previous object to position each repeat .... ALT + H
7. Click **OK** .... ENTER

Group Objects (Ctrl + G)

1. Select all objects to group.
2. Click **Object** .... ALT + O
3. Click **Group** .... G

Rotate the Spread

1. Click **View** .... ALT + V
2. Click **Rotate Spread** ... R, ENTER
3. Select a rotation option:
   - **90° CW**
   - **90° CCW**
   - **180°**

EXERCISE DIRECTIONS

✓ *Reset the Essentials workspace after starting by clicking Reset Essentials on the workspace list.*

1. Start InDesign and open the ◉75Fitness file. Save the file as **75Fitness_xx**.
2. Make sure Smart Guides are on.

Transform the Title Objects

1. To make it easy to work with the rotated type at the left side of the document, rotate the spread 90° CW.
2. On the Fitness layer, select the *FITNESS ON THE* text object that is now at the top of the document. Scale it proportionally 110%, and then break the constrain proportions link and scale the Y dimension an additional 10%.

   ✓ *The text has been outlined so that you can easily transform it in this exercise.*

3. Copy the text object and use Paste in Place to paste the copy directly on top of the original.
4. Change the fill color of the copy to **C = 0, M = 0, Y = 0, K = 30**.
5. Shear the copy 45°. Adjust the position of both objects so that the lower-left corner of the objects is at the left margin guide.
6. In the Layers panel, move the sheared copy below the original text object to send it to the back, and then group the original text object and the sheared copy.
7. Clear the rotation and then select the *GO* text object. Shear the object by 30°. Then create a shadow copy of the type object as directed in steps 3–6, except shear the copy 50°.

Create a Graphic Object

1. Next you will work on an object to represent being "on the road." Follow these steps:
   a. Select the black rectangle in the scratch area to the left of the document. Display the Info panel.
   b. Hold down Shift and use the Direct Selection tool to drag the upper-left corner of the rectangle to the right until the D distance on the Info panel is about **3p0**. Then drag the upper-right corner to the left as close to the same amount as you can. Deselect the object.
   c. Using the Line tool with no fill, a yellow stroke, and a stroke weight of **4** pt, draw slightly slanted lines as shown in Illustration A to represent a double-yellow line down the center of the road, receding into the distance.
   d. Group the road object.
2. Adjust the object's height to **12p4** without adjusting its width, and then move it so it aligns at the top with the light blue rectangle and its upper-left corner is at **X = 29p6**. (Make sure you select the upper-left corner in the Reference Point.)

Align and Reshape Objects

1. Align the top of the green rectangle with the top of the light blue rectangle, and move the green rectangle so that its right edge aligns with the right margin guide.
2. Select the light blue rectangle and adjust its width to **22p4**. Use the Direct Selection tool to drag the lower-right corner to follow the same slant as the road object, as shown in Illustration A. Be sure to hold down Shift as you drag to keep the anchor points in line.

3. Repeat the previous step with the green object, dragging the lower-left corner.

4. Move the orange rectangle to the left to align with the vertical ruler guide. Drag slightly downward until you see the Smart Spacing arrows that indicate equal space between the orange rectangle and the light blue rectangle, and the light blue rectangle and the horizontal ruler guide above it.

5. Move the red rectangle so its right edge snaps to the right margin guide, aligning it at the top with the orange rectangle as you drag.

6. Resize the red rectangle to be the same size as the orange rectangle by dragging the red rectangle's lower-left corner handle until you see the Smart Dimensions arrows indicating that both height and width are the same as the orange rectangle's.

7. Reshape the yellow rectangle to be the same height as the orange and red rectangles, then adjust its width to about **19p6**. Move it between the orange and red rectangles, aligning tops and distributing width evenly between all three rectangles in this row.

8. Rotate the dark blue rectangle 90° clockwise using any method and move it below the orange, yellow, and red rectangles, its right edge aligned with the right margin guide.

9. Drag the dark blue rectangle up or down until you see the Smart Spacing arrows indicating equal space among the three rows of shapes. (The green Smart Spacing arrows will display in the right margin area.)

10. Drag the bottom border of the dark blue rectangle down to align with the bottom margin guide, without moving the top of the shape.

11. Group all the colored text frames and the road object together.

Create a Design of Shapes

1. In the scratch area, on the Go layer, draw a triangle about **3p9** wide by **3p3** high. Remove its stroke and fill with a color of your choice.

   ✓ *Use the Polygon tool and adjust the number of sides with the down arrow key as you draw.*

2. Use the Rotate tool to rotate the triangle 90° clockwise, watching the Smart Guide information to achieve the exact rotation.

3. Position the rotated triangle to the right of the *GO* text object, using Smart Guides to align the two objects by their vertical centers.

4. Use Step and Repeat to select **10** repeats, **4p0** horizontal offset, and no vertical offset.

5. The last triangle doesn't reach the right margin. Use Live Distribute to adjust the spacing to fill the line: With the row of triangles still selected, click on the right center group bounding box, move it toward the right margin, and press the Spacebar to distribute space between triangles.

6. Group all the triangles into a single object. Your finished document should look like Illustration A.

7. Save your changes, close the document, and exit InDesign.

Illustration A

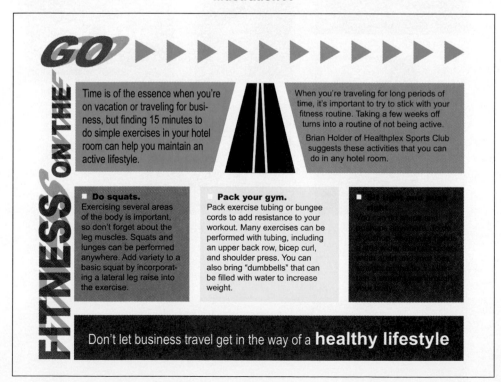

ON YOUR OWN

✓ *This exercise gives you the opportunity to create a "gallery" of your own photos.*

1. Before you begin the InDesign document, review your own photo files and identify four or five that are in some way related, such as the waterfalls shown in Illustration B. In Photoshop, adjust color and cropping as necessary, and then size the images to roughly equal dimensions (such as 6 inches wide by 4 inches high for landscape images and 4 inches wide by 6 inches high for portrait images). Save the images with appropriate names in the folder where you are saving your InDesign documents.

2. Start a new InDesign document using the default settings, but change orientation to Landscape. Save the document as OIN75_xx.

3. Using the Rectangle tool, create rectangles with roughly the same proportions as your images. Remove strokes and fill with a light gray to make the objects easy to see as you are adjusting them.

4. Create a pleasing layout of rectangles on the page, using the alignment and distribution options you have learned about in this exercise. Make sure that white space is the same between all images. Use the Gap tool to adjust shape sizes and gap widths as desired.

5. When you are satisfied with your layout, create a copy of each shape, paste the copy in place, and scale the copy 90%. Position the copied shapes so that you have a border around all four edges (the border does not have to be the same size all around).

6. Place your images in the scaled shapes. Adjust image size and placement in each shape as necessary. Adjust the shape in which the picture is placed if necessary for appearance.

7. Group the light gray rectangles and then pick up a fill color from one of the images to fill all of the shapes.

8. Save your changes, close the document, and exit InDesign.

Illustration B

Exercise | 76

Skills Covered

- Work with Color in InDesign
- Work with the InDesign Swatches Panel

- Create a Gradient in InDesign

Software Skills   When working on a complex document, or on a series of documents, it is important to use color consistently. The Swatches panel lets you create and work with swatches. Create gradients to use in shapes or frames.

Design Skills   A designer should be aware of tools such as color matching systems that allow him or her to specify exact colors for a document. Using the Swatches panel, a designer can apply colors quickly and consistently throughout a document.

Application Skills   Wilcox Tours has asked you to mock up an article for their *Touring Today* magazine. In this exercise, you will create colors and a gradient to add to the Swatches panel and apply them to the document.

TERMS

Color matching system   A proprietary set of numerically defined color swatches, such as PANTONE.

Lab   The standard color mode for printing spot colors.

NOTES

Work with Color in InDesign

- You already know that InDesign includes the same color tools you have worked with in previous applications. You use the Color and Swatches panels to create and manage colors as you work.

- InDesign gives you a choice among three standard color modes: RGB, CMYK, and Lab.

- You have already used the RGB and CMYK color modes in the first two sections of this book, but you have not yet learned about the Lab color mode.

- **Lab** is not an acronym, but numeric values are assigned to each of its three letters: L, a, and b. Figure 76-1 shows the Color panel for a Lab color.

  - The L value is the light/dark setting (the amount of black), from 0 to 100.

  - The a value is the distribution between cyan and magenta, between −128 for all cyan and +127 for all magenta.

- The b value is the distribution between cyan and yellow, between −128 for all cyan and +127 for all yellow.

Figure 76-1. Color panel showing a Lab color

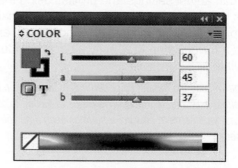

- Lab is typically used only for spot colors.

Review Process and Spot Colors

- You will remember from the Illustrator section of this course that in professional printing, there are two ways of laying ink onto the page:
  - *Process colors* are created with any combination of the colors from the color mode. For example, in CMYK mode, a process color is any color you can make by blending cyan, magenta, yellow, and black.
  - *Spot colors* are premixed ink colors applied as a solid opaque layer to the paper at press time.
- For standard color printing, process color is the norm. There are two reasons you might use spot colors:
  - If you don't want to pay for full color printing, you can print a black-and-white document with a single spot color overlaid on it to add visual interest.
  - If you want to print a color that you can't accurately reproduce using CMYK, you can use a spot color in addition to regular process colors. For example, you might want metallic gold or silver ink, or fluorescent ink.
- InDesign allows you to define a spot color using any color mode, but the best choice for spot colors is Lab. Many of the most popular color libraries define spot inks using Lab.

Color Management in InDesign

- Note that you can use a color management system in InDesign, as you learned to do in the Photoshop section of this book. Color settings and color profiles can be specified by using the Edit > Color Settings command to open the Color Settings dialog box.
- By default, InDesign uses the North America General Purpose 2 color setting, the sRGB color profile for RGB, and the U.S. Web Coated (SWOP) v2 color profile for CMYK.
- You can adjust settings and profiles using the same skills you learned in Exercise 61, and you can also soft proof colors using View > Proof Colors and View > Proof Setup to specify a particular device to simulate.

  ✓ *You will use the default color settings in this section of the course to eliminate the inconvenience of having to convert data documents to new color settings each time you open them.*

Work with the InDesign Swatches Panel

- The InDesign Swatches panel functions in much the same way as the Swatches panels in Illustrator and Photoshop. You use this panel to store color swatches so you can easily apply them throughout a document.
- The default Swatches panel has many fewer swatches than the Illustrator and Photoshop panels offer. Only six CMYK colors display, plus black and white. You can of course add colors, as well as gradients and tints, by creating new swatches.

  ✓ *You can also add swatches from the Kuler panel as you learned to do in the Illustrator section of this course. Click Window > Extensions > Kuler to display the panel.*

Create a Color Swatch

- To create a new swatch, mix a color in the Color panel or select an object that has the desired color applied. Then click the New Swatch button [🔲] at the bottom of the Swatches panel. The new swatch displays in the Swatches panel with its CMYK components listed, as for the default swatches.
- For more control over your swatches, hold down the Alt key as you click the New Swatch button, or choose New Color Swatch on the Swatches panel menu. The New Color Swatch dialog box opens, as shown in Figure 76-2.

Figure 76-2. Create a new color swatch

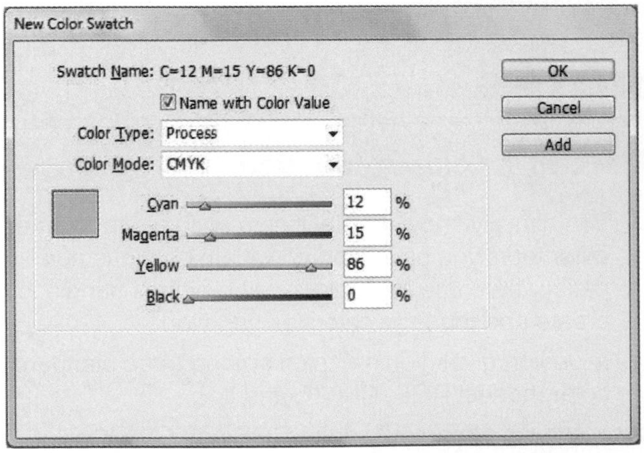

- Swatches are named using their color values by default. To give the swatch a more meaningful name, clear the Name with Color Value check box to make the Swatch Name editable.
- On the Color Type list, choose either Process or Spot.

- On the Color Mode list, choose one of the standard three color modes from the top of the list (CMYK, RGB, or Lab). The Color Mode list also offers a wide variety of standard color libraries, such as PANTONE, TOYO, and TRUMATCH.

    ✓ *You may remember using the PANTONE and TRUMATCH color libraries in Illustrator.*

- Most professional printers use such **color matching systems** to ensure accurate color reproduction.

- Typically when using a color matching system, you have a book of printed swatches to which you can refer. After you choose a color from the book, you can specify it in the New Color Swatch dialog box. Select the correct color library to display a list of the color swatches in that library, as shown in Figure 76-3.

Figure 76-3. Choose a color from a library such as PANTONE

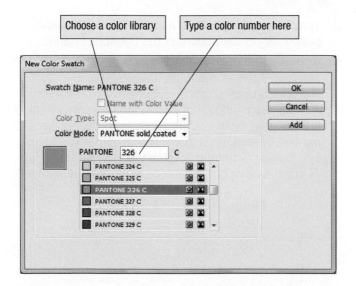

- You can find the color to match the one you have selected from the book by scrolling through the swatches or by typing the color number.

- Using the book of printed swatches is a more reliable way to choose a color than using InDesign's onscreen swatch of that color because differences in monitors may slightly distort a color. Printed color libraries can be expensive, but they do ensure that the color you choose is the color that will be printed.

- You may remember that in Illustrator, you can choose whether a process color is *global* or *nonglobal*. A color specified as global can be easily updated throughout an illustration.

- InDesign does not allow you to specify a color as global or nonglobal. Any swatch you create in the Swatches panel, however, functions the same way as a global color. Making a change to a swatch color automatically updates that color wherever it appears in a document.

- The equivalent to a nonglobal color is an unnamed color that you use somewhere in a document without saving it as a swatch. You can easily convert unnamed colors to named swatches, as you learn later in this section.

Edit a Color Swatch

- To edit a color swatch, double-click it on the Swatches panel to open the Swatch Options dialog box. This box is similar to the New Color Swatch dialog box you used when you created the swatch initially. You can change the color mode, color type, swatch name, and so on.

Change the Swatches Panel Display

- By default, color swatches appear in a single-column list with a small square of the color, the swatch name, and symbols representing the type of color model in use. This is called Name view. Figure 76-4 shows the Swatches panel in Name view, with panel features listed.

Figure 76-4. The Swatches panel in Name view

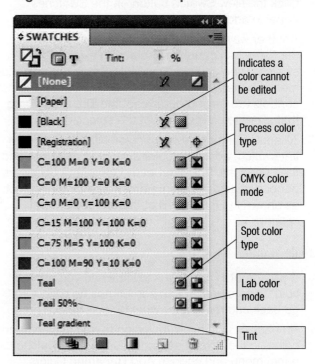

- Use the Swatches panel menu to choose different swatch display options, such as Small Name, Small Swatch, or Large Swatch.

Create a Tint Swatch

- A *tint* is a screened (lighter) version of a color. Each tint is based on a color and has a percentage assigned to it of the original color. A 10% tint of a color would be very light; a 90% tint would be almost identical to the original color.

- To create a tint, open the Color panel and select a color. (To start with an existing swatch color, open the Swatches panel and click the swatch. That same color will also appear in the Color panel.)

- Then drag the Tint slider in the Color panel to the left, enter a percentage in the Percent box, or click anywhere along the tint ramp to pick up a tint. Figure 76-5 shows a tint being created in the Color panel.

Figure 76-5. Adjust the tint on the Color panel

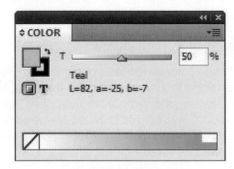

- Click the New Swatch button on the Swatches panel to add the tint as a swatch.

- Another way to create a tint swatch is to open the Swatches panel and select an existing color swatch. Then choose New Tint Swatch on the panel menu. In the New Tint Swatch dialog box, all the controls are grayed out except the Tint slider. Drag that slider to create a tint of the selected color.

- To apply a tint of a swatch color without creating a tint swatch, apply the color swatch to an object and then open the Tint slider at the top of the Swatches panel and adjust the tint percentage for that object, as shown in Figure 76-6 at the top of the next column.

Create Swatches for All Used Colors

- If you forget to create a swatch when you apply a color to an object, it can sometimes be difficult to go back and remember what objects you colored.

- An easy fix is to allow InDesign to add all unnamed colors to the Swatches panel. Open the Swatches panel menu and choose Add Unnamed Colors.

- After the colors are added to the Swatches panel, you can double-click each one and change its name and/or its color model if desired.

Figure 76-6. Adjust the tint percentage

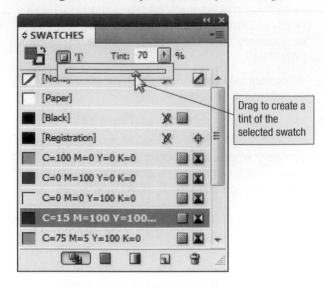

Delete Swatches

- To delete a swatch, drag it to the Delete Swatch button 🗑 at the bottom of the Swatches panel.

- If you try to delete a swatch that is in use somewhere in the document, the Delete Swatch dialog box appears, as shown in Figure 76-7. You can then choose what should happen to the objects formatted with that swatch. Choose Defined Swatch to replace the swatch with another one that you specify. Choose Unnamed Swatch to leave the object in its current color but disassociate it from any swatch.

Figure 76-7. Delete a swatch

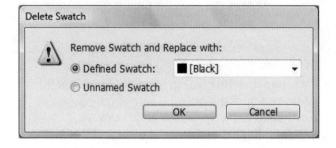

Select Unused Swatches

- Normally you do not need to keep a swatch in your panel that is not used for anything. To determine which swatches are unused, open the Swatches panel menu and choose Select All Unused.

- You can then delete selected swatches if you want to remove them from the panel.

Import and Export Swatches

You can transfer swatches between documents if desired using Adobe Swatch Exchange. Select swatches and then choose Save Swatches from the Swatches panel menu. After you save the swatches, they can be loaded into a new document using Load Swatches on the Swatches panel menu.

Create a Gradient in InDesign

■ You have worked with gradients in both Illustrator and Photoshop. You can also create a gradient in InDesign to add a gradient fill to any frame or shape.

■ One way to create a gradient in InDesign is to use the Gradient panel, as you would in Illustrator. Select a gradient stop on the gradient slider and specify a new color for it. Drag or add stops to adjust the gradient. You must then add the gradient to the Swatches panel if you want to keep it for further use.

✓ *Review gradients in Exercise 28.*

■ A more efficient option is to create a gradient by working directly in the Swatches panel. You can create the gradient and the swatch at the same time.

■ On the Swatches panel menu, choose New Gradient Swatch. The New Gradient Swatch dialog box, shown in Figure 76-8, lets you specify the gradient swatch's properties.

Figure 76-8. Create a gradient swatch

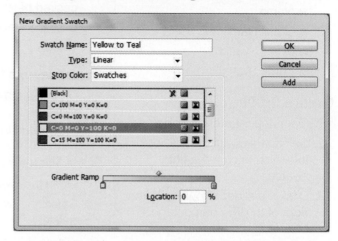

■ Give the swatch a meaningful name, such as the colors involved, and choose the gradient type (linear or radial). Click a gradient stop to select it and then choose a method of assigning color from the Stop Color list. You can choose Swatches, Lab, CMYK, or RGB. This list makes it very easy to select colors—you don't have to work in two or three panels at a time to define the gradient colors.

■ To change the direction of the gradient within an object, use the Gradient panel's Angle box, or drag the Gradient tool ▨ as you learned to do in Illustrator.

PROCEDURES

Create a Color Swatch

1. Select an object that is already filled with the desired color.

   OR

   Open the **Color** panel and select the desired color.
2. Open the **Swatches** panel.
3. Hold down ALT and click the **New Swatch** button ▣.
4. (Optional) Name the color with a text name:
   a. Deselect the **Name with Color Value** check box......................ALT + V

b. Type a name for the swatch.
5. Click **Color Type** list and choose **Process** or **Spot**.
6. Open the **Color Mode** list and choose a color mode or a color matching system.
7. (Optional) To change the color, drag the sliders or select a color from the color matching system swatches provided.
8. Click **OK** ....ENTER

Edit a Color Swatch

1. Open the **Swatches** panel.
2. Double-click a swatch.
3. Make any adjustment necessary in the Swatch Options dialog box:
   ■ Change the swatch's name.
   ■ Select a different color type.
   ■ Choose a color mode or matching system.
   ■ Adjust the color by dragging sliders or select a color from a color library.
4. Click **OK** ....ENTER

Change the Color Swatch Display

1. Open the **Swatches** panel.
2. Click [icon] to open the panel menu.
3. Click a viewing option:
   - Name
   - Small Name
   - Small Swatch
   - Large Swatch

Create a Tint Swatch

1. Open the **Swatches** panel.
2. Select the swatch for the color for which to create a tint swatch.
3. Click the slider arrow [icon] to the right of the Tint percentage box.
4. Drag the **Tint** slider to the desired percentage.
5. Click the **New Swatch** button [icon].

   OR

1. Select an object that has an existing color applied to it.

OR

Open the **Swatches** panel and click a color swatch.

2. Open the **Color** panel.
3. Drag the **Tint** slider to the desired percentage.
4. Click the **New Swatch** button [icon].

Create Swatches for All Used Colors

1. Click [icon] on the Swatches panel.
2. Click **Add Unnamed Colors**.

Delete Swatches

1. Open the **Swatches** panel.
2. Select the swatch(es) to delete.

   ✓ *Hold down Ctrl and click on multiple noncontiguous swatches or hold down Shift to select a contiguous range. Or use the Select Unused Swatches procedure that follows this one.*

3. Click the **Delete Swatch** button [icon].

Select Unused Swatches

1. Click [icon] on the Swatches panel.
2. Click **Select All Unused**.

Create a Gradient Swatch

1. Click [icon] on the Swatches panel.
2. Click **New Gradient Swatch**.
3. Click **Swatch Name** and type a name for the swatch......................... ALT + N
4. Click **Type** and select **Linear** or **Radial** .... ALT + T
5. Click a gradient stop.
6. Click **Stop Color** and select an option for choosing stop colors......................... ALT + S
7. Select the desired color.
8. Repeat steps 5–7 for the other stop on the gradient ramp.
9. (Optional) Drag the diamond above the gradient ramp to the right or left to adjust the gradient.
10. (Optional) Click below the gradient ramp to add stops, then select the desired colors for new stops.
11. Click **OK** .... ENTER

To change gradient direction:

1. Create a gradient swatch and apply it to an object.
2. Click **Gradient** tool [icon] and drag over the object to adjust the angle.

EXERCISE DIRECTIONS

✓ *Reset the Essentials workspace after starting.*

1. Start InDesign and open the [icon] **76Wilcox** file. Save it as **76Wilcox_xx**.

   ✓ *If you receive a message telling you that the document contains links to missing or modified files, click Don't Fix. You can work with the document even if graphic files are not correctly linked.*

2. The type object positioned at the bottom of the image on page 2 cannot be read. Select the object and change the color to a very light purple-gray that you pick up from the upper-left corner of the sky in the image.

3. On the Banner layer, select an empty rectangle that extends across the top of the spread. Create a fill by clicking the eyedropper on the purple area of a mountain in the center of the image.

4. Create a swatch from this fill color:
   a. Name the color **Banner lilac**.
   b. Adjust the color to **C = 30, M = 40, Y = 23, K = 0**.

5. Create a 70% tint swatch of Banner lilac.

6. On the Color block layer, select an empty rectangle behind the small image in the upper-right corner of page 3. Apply the Banner lilac swatch (not the tint) to this rectangle.

7. Wilcox Tours uses a specific color in its marketing. Add a new spot color swatch as follows:

   a. With no objects selected in the document, click New Color Swatch on the Swatches panel menu and choose the PANTONE Solid Coated library from the Color Mode list.

   b. Type the number **328** in the box to locate PANTONE 328 C.

8. On the Address background layer, select an empty rectangle behind the company address on page 3. Fill the rectangle with the PANTONE 328 C swatch, and then move the Address background layer below the Address layer.

9. Change the text color of the address to Paper.

10. The Banner lilac color is not quite what you want. Edit the color swatch to **C = 20**, **M = 29**, **Y = 7**, **K = 0**. Note that the color updates in the document even if the banner was not selected, and the tint also updates.

11. The banner is still not quite what you want. Create a gradient for the banner as follows:

    a. Choose to create a new gradient swatch, and name it **Banner gradient**.

    b. Click the right gradient stop and choose Swatches from the Stop Color list. Select Banner lilac.

    c. Apply the Banner gradient to the banner rectangle.

12. Apply the Banner gradient to the color box in the upper-right corner of page 3, and adjust the gradient angle by dragging with the Gradient tool from the upper-right corner of the box to the lower-left corner. Your spread should look similar to Illustration A.

13. Change the Swatches panel display to Small Swatch, and then add unnamed colors. You should see a new swatch of the color you used for the *Glacier National Park* text. Edit this swatch to name it **Title** and adjust colors to **C = 5**, **M = 11**, **Y = 0**, **K = 0**.

14. Select all unused swatches and delete them.

15. Save your changes, close the file, and exit InDesign.

Illustration A

ON YOUR OWN

1. Start InDesign and open 📟75Fitness_xx or open 💿OYO76. Save the document as OIN76_xx. In this exercise, you have the opportunity to change the color scheme used in the document.

2. Edit the orange swatch to change it to a more subtle color of your choice. Give the new color an appropriate name.

3. Edit the other colors to create interesting contrasts with your first color. Name each swatch.

4. Create a gradient you can apply to the road object that makes the top of the object look lighter, as if further away. (You will have to ungroup to be able to select the black rectangle.) Name the gradient appropriately.

5. Apply the gradient and adjust the angle. Regroup objects when you are satisfied with the gradient.

6. Create a tint of one of the colors you added and apply it to the rotated triangles at the top of the page.

7. Select all unused swatches and delete them.

8. Add all unnamed colors. You should see swatches for the text and the text shadow. Give these swatches appropriate names.

9. Find a color in the TRUMATCH color library similar to the magenta title type and apply it to the title words (not to the shadow behind the title words). Your solution might resemble Illustration B.

10. Save your changes, close the file, and exit InDesign.

Illustration B

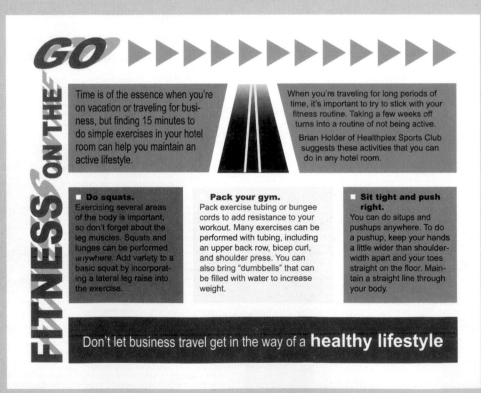

394

Exercise | 77

Skills Covered

- **Apply Transparency Effects to Objects**
- **Apply Stroke and Corner Formats**
- **Create and Apply an Object Style**
- **Find and Change Objects**

Software Skills   InDesign offers a variety of effects that can be applied to objects and to strokes and corners. Use transparency effects such as Drop Shadow and Gradient Feather to give a special look to an object. Format strokes with interesting start and finish shapes. Save formats as styles to make them easy to apply to multiple objects in a document. Use the Find/Change feature to locate specific object formats and quickly change them throughout a document.

Design Skills   Sophisticated visual touches such as transparency effects are often the hallmark of a professional design. A designer can save a great deal of time by creating object styles and using Find/Change to adjust object formats.

Application Skills   Gulf Shores Resort has asked you to create a flyer to send to former guests letting them know about fall and winter events at the Resort. In this exercise, you will work on special effects for the flyer. You will apply transparency effects, change stroke and corner formats, create an object style to speed your formatting, and use Find/Change to adjust object formats globally.

TERMS

Style   A named set of formatting options.

Transparency effects   Effects such as glows, drop shadow, feathering, blending mode adjustments, and opacity changes that give objects a special appearance.

NOTES

Apply Transparency Effects to Objects

- InDesign's **transparency effects** are similar to effects you have worked with in other applications, such as Illustrator's Stylize effects and Photoshop's layer styles. Using transparency effects, you can add a drop or inner shadow, an inner or outer glow, an effect that suggests an object has been beveled or embossed, a satin effect, or any of three feathering effects.

- Transparency effects also include familiar blending mode options and the ability to adjust opacity for a selected object.

- Apply transparency effects using the Object > Effects command or the Effects panel, shown in Figure 77-1.

Figure 77-1. Effects panel

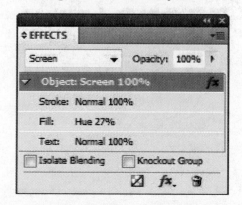

- You can apply transparency effects to the object as a whole, to the stroke, to the fill, or to text, and as shown in Figure 77-1, you can apply effects to more than one of these options.

- The blending mode list is at the upper-left of the panel. Use the Opacity slider at the upper-right of the panel to adjust transparency for the object, its stroke, its fill, or its text.

- To apply a transparency effect, select an object, display the Effects panel, and then select the target of the effect in the panel, such as Object, Stroke, or Fill. Click the Add an object effect to the selected target button $fx_{\cdot}$ at the bottom of the Effects panel. Then select an effect from the list to open a dialog box similar to the one shown in Figure 77-2 at the bottom of the page.

- All of the transparency effects are listed at the left in this dialog box, with the one you chose selected. Options for the selected effect are displayed at the right side of the dialog box.

- You can if desired select additional effects from this dialog box to apply more than one to the current target. Or, change the target using the Settings for list at the top of the dialog box.

  ✓ To see options for an effect, you must not only click in the check box but click on the effect name.

- As you apply effects, the list box near the lower-left corner of the dialog box shows the effects you have applied to the object, stroke, fill, and text. The *fx* symbol displays in the Effects panel next to each target that has an effect applied.

- Edit an effect by double-clicking the *fx* symbol to reopen the Effects dialog box.

- Remove an effect by dragging the *fx* symbol to the Removes effect from the selected target button. Or, click the Clears all effects and makes object opaque button at the bottom of the Effects panel to remove all effects, blending modes, and opacity adjustments.

- Some of InDesign's transparency effects look and are applied in much the same way as in other applications you have already used. Drop Shadow and Inner and Outer Glow work the same way as in Illustrator. Basic Feather softens the edge of an object just as feathering does in Photoshop. You have also used the Bevel and Emboss effect in Photoshop as a layer style.

- Effects that may be new to you include Inner Shadow, Satin, and two special feathering effects, Directional Feather and Gradient Feather.

  - Inner Shadow applies shadowing inside the edge of an object, as shown at the left in Figure 77-3 at the top of the next page.

  - Satin gives a smooth dimensional look to an object, as shown at the right in Figure 77-3.

  - Directional Feather lets you choose one or more sides of an object to feather. The object at the left in Figure 77-4 has directional feathering applied to the left and bottom edges of the object.

Figure 77-2. Effects dialog box

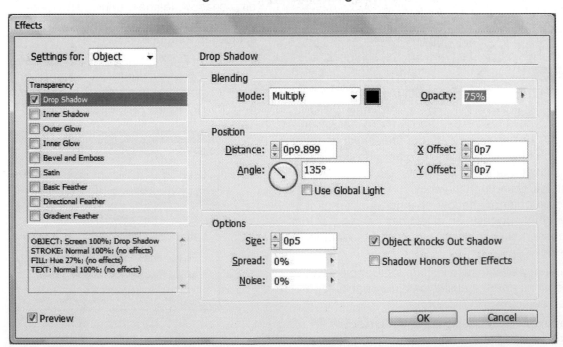

Figure 77-3. Inner Shadow and Satin effects

- Gradient Feather applies to an object a gradient that progresses from solid to transparent to make the object appear to be gradually fading away, as shown in the right object in Figure 77-4. You can apply either a linear or radial gradient.

Figure 77-4. Directional Feather and Gradient Feather effects

- Each of InDesign's transparency effects can be adjusted using a variety of options in the effect's dialog box, and a detailed discussion of these options would take many pages. You are encouraged to explore these options on your own to learn how to adjust and enhance these effects.

- If you are working with a group of several objects, the two options at the bottom of the Effects panel can help you control how effects apply to the objects in the group.

  - Use the Isolate Blending option to specify what items in the group will be affected by a blending mode or opacity change. Select the objects in the group you want to adjust and then click Isolate Blending. Then change blending mode or opacity for those objects only.

  - Use the Knockout Group option to make the effects applied to objects in a group block or *knock out* objects below them in the group.

Apply Stroke and Corner Formats

- You learned in Exercise 68 how to adjust the stroke around a frame or object using the Stroke Weight and Stroke Type controls in the Control panel.

- You can also use the Stroke panel, shown in Figure 77-5, to apply stroke formats. Some options in this panel are the same as those you learned about in Illustrator, such as the cap, join, and align options.

Figure 77-5. Stroke panel

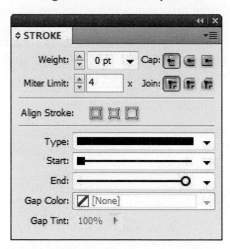

- You can also choose the stroke type and start and end options. The Start and End options are applicable only to lines, not to object frames.

- If you choose a stroke type that has gaps, such as a dashed or dotted style, you can select a color for the gaps.

- You have already learned how to adjust corner radius for objects on the fly using Live Corners. InDesign offers other corner effects as well. Choose Object > Corner Options to open the Corner Options dialog box where you can select an effect and specify its size. Figure 77-6 shows several corner effects you can apply.

Figure 77-6. Corner effects

- You can quickly apply corner effects and adjust corner radius using the Corner Shape options on the Control panel.

Create and Apply an Object Style

- A **style** is a named set of formatting options that you can apply to multiple objects in a document. If you need to change objects formatted with a style, you can simply edit the style to apply the change immediately to all objects that use that style.

- InDesign allows you to create styles for characters, paragraphs, tables and table cells, and objects. The process of creating and applying a style is similar for all types of styles.

  ✓ *You will work with text styles in Lesson 9 and table styles in Lesson 10.*

- The easiest way to create a new style is by example. Format an object with the desired appearance, and then click the Create new style button 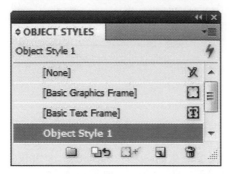 at the bottom of the Object Styles panel. The new style appears on the list with a generic name such as Object Style 1, as shown in Figure 77-7.

Figure 77-7. Object Styles panel

- Rename the new style by double-clicking it on the panel to open its Options dialog box, and then type a new name in the Style Name box.

- To save time, you can choose New Object Style on the Object Styles panel menu to open the New Object Style dialog box shown in Figure 77-8, or hold down Alt while clicking the Create new style button.

- Give the style a meaningful name, and then click options in the list at the left side of the dialog box such as Fill, Stroke, and Stroke & Corner Options and then select settings at the right side of the dialog box. Note that you can also apply effects for the object in this dialog box.

- To apply a style, select the object to receive the style and then click the desired style in the Object Styles panel. To edit a style, double-click its style name in the Object Styles panel to open the Options dialog box.

- You may need to apply a style to an object you have used to create the style. You can select the Apply Style to Selection check box in the style options dialog box to do this automatically as you create the style.

Figure 77-8. New Object Style dialog box

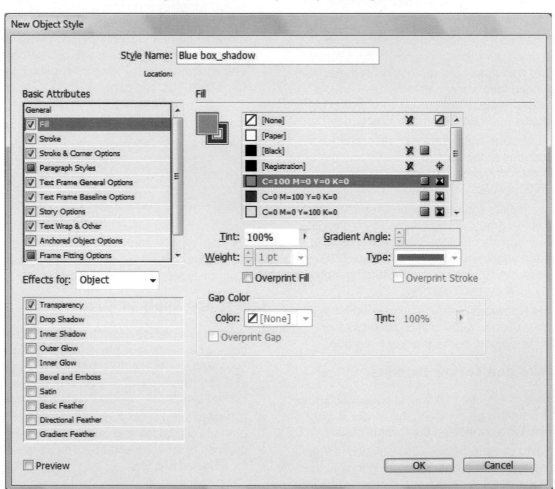

■ You can easily create a new style based on an existing style to speed the process of defining a style that has some or all of the same formats as one you have already created. Or, duplicate a style, change the copy's name, and change formats as necessary to create a new style.

Find and Change Objects

■ It is not uncommon to insert a number of similar or identical objects in a document, such as symbols in a catalog or frames for special content. If you find yourself in the position of needing to make changes to objects that share the same formats, you can be facing a time-consuming task.

■ One way to save yourself some effort is to apply styles, as you learned in the previous section. Adjusting a style will automatically update all objects formatted with that style.

■ Another way to quickly change objects that share similar formatting is to use the Find/Change feature.

■ You may have used find/change (or find/replace) in a word processing program to locate words and phrases that you want to change. InDesign's Find/Change feature lets you find and replace text, glyphs, or objects.

✓ *You use Find/Change for text in Exercise 83. You learn about glyphs in Exercise 86.*

■ Use Edit > Find/Change to open the Find/Change dialog box shown in Figure 77-9 with the Object tab active. The search shown in this figure will find objects that have a fill of 100% cyan and a stroke of 100% magenta and change the formatting to a fill of 100% yellow and a 100% cyan stroke.

■ To find an object with specific formats, click the Specify attributes to find button to the right of the Find Object Format box (or simply click in the box) to open the Find Object Format Options dialog box. This dialog box is almost identical to the Options dialog box you work with when creating or editing a style.

Figure 77-9. Find/Change dialog box

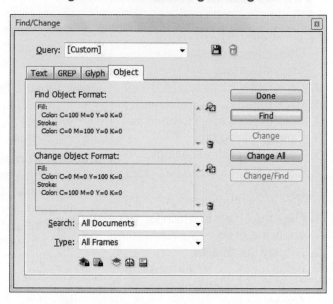

■ Select format options such as a style name, fill or stroke settings, or effects. These formats display in the Find Object Format box.

■ To change the selected formats, click the Specify attributes to change button to the right of the lower box (or click in the box) to open the Change Object Format Options dialog box. Here you select the formats that you want to apply instead of the original formats.

■ You can click buttons at the bottom of the dialog box to include in the search locked or hidden layers, master pages, and so on.

■ Click the Find button to locate the first instance, and then click Change to make the change. You can then click Find Next to move on to the next instance. Click Change All if you want to immediately change all instances, or Change/Find to change each instance and immediately locate the next.

■ Find/Change can be a fast and effective way to change formats of objects that may have different styles but share some attributes such as fill or stroke color.

PROCEDURES

Apply Transparency Effects

1. Click the object to which to apply the effect.
2. Click **Object** .... ALT + O
3. Click **Effects** .... E
4. Click desired effect to open its Options dialog box.
5. Select the desired settings.
6. Click **OK** .... ENTER

   OR

1. Click the object to which to apply the effect.
2. Display the **Effects** panel............... SHIFT + CTRL + F10
3. Select the target: Object, Fill, Stroke, or Text.
4. Click the **Add an object effect to the selected target** button fx.
5. Click desired effect to open its Options dialog box.
6. Select the desired settings.
7. Click **OK** .... ENTER

To adjust blending mode for an effect:

1. Select the desired target in the Effects panel.
2. Click the **Blending mode** list arrow in the Effects panel.
3. Select the desired blending mode.

To adjust transparency for an effect:

1. Select the desired target in the Effects panel.
2. Click the **Opacity** arrow in the Effects panel.
3. Drag the **Opacity** slider to the desired setting.

Apply Stroke Formats Using the Stroke Panel

1. Select the object stroke.
2. Open the **Stroke** panel........ F10
3. Select a stroke weight by choosing a value from the list, clicking spin arrows, or typing a value in the **Weight** box.
4. Select a stroke style by clicking the **Type** list arrow and selecting a style.

---

5. Select **Start** and **End** options by clicking their list arrows and selecting a style.

Apply Corner Effects

1. Click the object to which to apply the corner effects.
2. Click **Object** .... ALT + O
3. Click **Corner Options** I
4. Select the desired corner option from the drop-down list for each corner.
5. Type the size of the corner effect, or use the spin arrows to select the size.
6. Click **OK** .... ENTER

   OR

1. Click the object to which to apply the corner effects.
2. Click the corner option list arrow on the Control panel and select a corner style.
3. Adjust size in the corner options size box.

Create an Object Style by Example

1. Click the object that is already formatted in the desired way.
2. Display the **Object Styles** panel .... CTRL + F7
3. Hold down ALT and click the **Create new style** button 🗔.
4. Type a name for the style.
5. Make any other necessary adjustments to the style using the options in the New Object Style dialog box.
6. Click **OK** .... ENTER

To apply an object style:

1. Open the **Object Styles** panel.
2. Click on the object to be formatted.
3. Click on the desired style in the panel.

To base a new style on an existing style:

1. Display the **Object Styles** panel......................... CTRL + F7
2. Click 📧 to open the panel menu.
3. Click **New Object Style** on the panel menu.

---

4. Name the new style.
5. Click **Based on** .... ALT + B
6. Select the style on which you wish to base the new style.
7. Adjust style formats as desired.
8. Click **OK** .... ENTER

   OR

1. Display the **Object Styles** panel......................... CTRL + F7
2. Click 📧 to open the panel menu.
3. Click **Duplicate Style** on the panel menu.
4. Rename the copied style.
5. Adjust style formats as desired.
6. Click **OK** .... ENTER

Find/Change Object Formats (Ctrl + F)

1. Click **Edit** .... ALT + E
2. Click **Find/Change**............. /
3. Click the **Object** tab.
4. Click the **Specify attributes to find** button 🔎.
5. Use the options in the list at left of the dialog box to specify the formats to find, such as style name, fill, stroke, corner option, or effect.
6. Click **OK** .... ENTER
7. Click the **Specify attributes to change** button 🔎.
8. Use the options in the list at left of the dialog box to specify the new formats to apply.
9. Click **OK** .... ENTER
10. Click **Find** to find first instance of the object formats.. ALT + N
11. Click **Change** to change the first instance .... ALT + H

    OR

    Click **Change All** to change all instances .... ALT + A

    OR

    Click **Change/Find** to change the first instance and find the next.......................... ALT + E
12. Click **Done** to end the process..................... ALT + D

EXERCISE DIRECTIONS

✓ *Display the Advanced workspace after starting.*

1. Start InDesign and open the ⊙ 77Gulf file. Save the document as **77Gulf_xx**.

2. Display page 1, if necessary, and select the image of palms. Apply a Gradient Feather effect:

   a. In the Effects dialog box, select the left gradient stop (the black one) and move it until the Location box says **35%**.

   b. Change the angle of the gradient to **–90°**.

3. Select the cloudy blue rectangle behind the title text and change the blending mode to Lighten. Change opacity to **90%**. Add an Outer Glow effect. In the Effects dialog box, click the Set glow color box, choose CMYK from the Color list, and mix a purple color for the glow color.

4. Apply a default drop shadow to the starfish graphic at the top of the right column of text, and then create a new object style from this object named **Starfish**. Apply the style to the starfish.

5. Select the yellow umbrella object near the middle of the right column and make the following changes. (Do not click on any of the black umbrella ribs, only on the yellow polygon.)

   a. Apply the Satin transparency effect.

   b. In the Effects dialog box, click the Set effect color box, choose CMYK from the Color list, and mix a peachy pink color for the effect color, such as **C = 0, M = 50, Y = 40, K = 0**.

   c. Create a new style named **Umbrella** from this object and apply the style to the selected object.

6. Select the rectangle at the bottom of the page and format it as follows:

   a. Apply the Bevel and Emboss effect with default settings.

   b. Apply the Inverse Rounded corner option with a size of **1p6**.

   c. Using the Line tool, draw a horizontal line near the top of the rectangle from the left to the right margin. Change its color to black, if necessary, its stroke weight to **5**, and apply an arrow point to one end of the stroke. Send the stroke to the back so it looks as if the rectangle is hanging on a spear. See Illustration A for positioning.

   ✓ *If the stroke causes the text on the rectangle to reposition, change text wrapping for the stroke to No text wrap.*

7. Save your changes so far and display page 2.

8. Select the beach image and apply the Directional Feather to the left edge with a feather width of 1p6. Preview the effect without closing the Effects dialog box.

9. This isn't exactly what you want. Deselect the Directional Feather effect and instead choose the Basic Feather effect. Set a feather width of **1p6**.

10. Apply the Starfish style to all starfish on the page, and apply the Umbrella style to all yellow umbrellas on the page.

11. The drop shadow for the starfish is a bit large and dark. Double-click the style name in the Object Styles panel and click the Drop Shadow effect in the Effects list to display the drop shadow settings. Make the following changes to the shadow settings:

    a. Click the Set shadow color box and then select CMYK from the Color list. Create the color **C = 0, M = 35, Y = 75, K = 30**.

    b. Change Opacity to **85%**.

    c. Change Distance to **0p6**.

    d. Close the Object Style Options dialog box to see your changes on all starfish.

12. The strokes that make up the umbrella ribs are far too heavy. Deselect all objects. Use Find/Change to adjust them:

    a. Open the Find/Change dialog box and select the Object tab, if necessary. If the find and change boxes contain any search parameters, click 🔒 next to each box to delete them.

    b. Choose to find strokes that are **2** pt in weight.

    c. Choose to change the stroke weight to **0.75** pt.

    d. Use Change All to change all umbrella strokes. Page 1 of your document should look similar to Illustration A.

13. Save your changes, close the file, and exit InDesign.

ON YOUR OWN

1. Start InDesign and open ⊙ OYO77. Save the file as OIN77_xx.

2. Select the peacock image on page 1 and apply a gradient feather so that the bottom of the image blends into the grayish background. Adjust the black slider so that only the very bottom of the image is feathered.

3. Select the text frame and apply a Bevel and Emboss effect to the text, using settings of your choice.

4. Apply different blending modes to the brown and blue rectangles below the zoo name to give interesting color variations.

5. On page 2, draw a line along the guide above the two headings, from left margin to right margin. Adjust stroke weight, color, and type as desired to create visual interest. You may want to apply a different gap color if you have chosen a dotted or dashed line.

6. Create a style named **seasonal_star** from the blue star. As part of the style definition, apply a drop shadow that has an X offset of 0p3 and a Y offset of 0p0.

7. Duplicate the seasonal_star style, change the name of the copy to **gold_star**, specify that the style should be based on seasonal_star, and change the fill color of gold_star to the Metro gold swatch.

8. Apply the gold_star style to the three stars that currently have no fill.

9. Apply the Satin effect and the Drop Shadow effect, with settings the same as those for the stars, to the first blue circle. Create a style with a name of your choice and apply the style to the other two circles.

10. Modify the seasonal_star style to remove the stroke. Because gold_star is based on seasonal_star, strokes are removed from all the star objects.

11. Find all objects that are filled with Metro blue and change the fill color to red.

   ✓ *Be sure to click the Fill option in the Change Object Format Options dialog box; the Stroke options may display by default.*

12. Save your changes, close the document, and exit InDesign.

Skills Covered

- **More about Master Pages**
- **Change the Master Name**
- **Create New Master Pages**
- **Apply a Master to a Page**
- **Override Master Page Elements**

Software Skills   Change a master name to make it more descriptive of the master's content. You can add master pages to provide different types of layouts in a document, then apply masters to specific pages in a document. Override master page elements when you need to edit them in the document.

Design Skills   Sophisticated designs may require a number of layout options. Creating new master pages for specific layouts allows a designer to work more quickly and efficiently.

Application Skills   In this exercise, you will work with a portion of a novel to adjust the default master, create new masters, and apply masters to pages. You will override a master page element to edit it in the document.

TERMS

No new terms in this exercise.

NOTES

More about Master Pages

- Recall from Exercise 69 in Lesson 7 that a *master page* is similar to a template that you can use to quickly apply consistent formatting to pages in a document. By default, every new InDesign document includes the A-Master, which is a two-page spread if you select Facing Pages when setting up the document, or a single page if you deselect Facing Pages.

- To work with master pages, you double-click the master name in the Pages panel. You can also double-click either the left or the right master page to display that page centered in the document window.

- When you first open a master page, it is blank, displaying only the document guides. You can tell you are working with a master because the master page is highlighted in the Pages panel and the bottom of the InDesign window shows A-Master as the page number.

- You can change the name of any master page, and you can create additional master pages to allow for flexibility in formatting. You can if necessary override master page elements to make a change on a single page in a document. You learn about all of these skills in the following sections.

Change the Master Name

- The default name A-Master is actually two pieces of information. "A" refers to the fact that this default master is the first (primary) master in the document. "Master" is the name that has been assigned to the master.

- You can change that name to something more meaningful. This is helpful if you are going to have additional masters in the document, as described in the next section.

- To change the name of a master, select the master's name in the Pages panel and then open the panel menu and click Master Options for "A-Master" (this command changes depending on the name of the master).

- In the Master Options dialog box, shown in Figure 78-1, edit the name. You can also change to a different prefix letter if desired.

Figure 78-1. Set master options

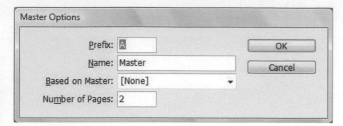

- Note that you can also specify a master on which to base a new master as well as the number of pages in the master set.

Create New Master Pages

- Within a document, different page types might require different elements. For example, running text usually has page numbers on each page, but some pages such as title pages or blank pages at the ends of sections commonly do not display page numbers.
- You can accommodate pages with different requirements by creating additional master pages that supply the necessary layout formats.
- To create a new master, open the Pages panel menu and choose New Master.
- In the New Master dialog box, shown in Figure 78-2, choose a prefix letter, a name, and whether the new master is based on an existing master. You can also specify the number of pages in it. A two-page spread is typical.

Figure 78-2. Create a new master

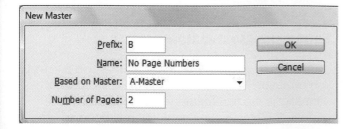

- After creating a master, it appears in the upper portion of the Pages panel. If you chose to base it upon an existing master, the letter of that master appears on its page icons. For example, in Figure 78-3, the B master is based upon the A master, so the B master's icons show "A" on them.

Figure 78-3. Masters can be based on other masters

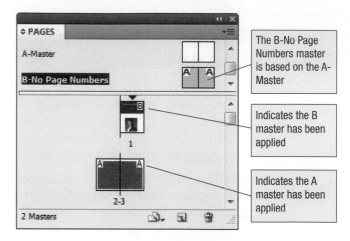

Apply a Master to a Page

- You have several options for applying a master to a page:
  - In the Pages panel, drag the master name to the page you want to format with that master.
  - Select a page in the Pages panel, then click Apply Master to Pages on the panel menu. In the Apply Master dialog box, shown in Figure 78-4, select the desired master and enter the page numbers to which to apply that master.

Figure 78-4. Apply a master to certain pages

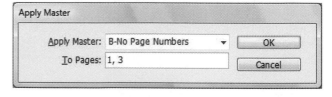

- After you apply a master to pages, the pages show the prefix (such as the letter *A* or *B*) in the upper-right or upper-left corner of the page symbol, as shown previously in Figure 78-3.

Override Master Page Elements

- You may sometimes need to override a master page element to edit it on a document page.

- Suppose, for example, that you have set up a placeholder on a master for the current month, as shown at left in Figure 78-5. This placeholder text appears on each page of the document.

- To edit the placeholder text for the current month, hold down Shift and Ctrl and click on the master page element to select it. It can then be edited like any other object in the document, as shown at right in Figure 78-5.

Figure 78-5. Edit a master page element

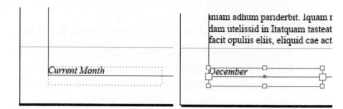

PROCEDURES

Change the Master Name

1. Open the **Pages** panel F12
2. Click the desired master.
3. Click [icon] to open the panel menu.
4. Click **Master Options for [name]**, where [name] is the selected master.
5. Click the **Name** box and type a new name for the master .... ALT + N
6. (Optional) Click **Prefix** and change the prefix letter...................... ALT + P
7. Click **OK** .... ENTER

Create New Master Page(s)

1. Open the **Pages** panel F12
2. Click [icon] to open the panel menu.
3. Click **New Master**.
4. (Optional) Change any of these options:
   - Change the default **Prefix** letter............ ALT + P
   - Replace the text in the **Name** box .... ALT + N with a more meaningful name.
   - To base the new master on an existing one, select it from the **Based on Master** list .... ALT + B
   - Change the **Number of Pages** .... ALT + M
5. Click **OK** .... ENTER

Duplicate an Existing Master Page

1. Open the **Pages** panel F12
2. Select the master to duplicate.
3. Click [icon] to open the panel menu.
4. Click **Duplicate Master Spread [Name]** where [name] is the master.
5. Modify the new master page name as desired.

   ✓ Refer to the earlier procedure Change the Master Name.

Apply a Master to a Page

1. Open the **Pages** panel F12
2. Drag-and-drop a master icon onto a page icon.

   OR

1. Open the **Pages** panel F12
2. Click [icon] to open the panel menu.
3. Click **Apply Master to Pages**.
4. Select the desired master from the **Apply Master** list .... ALT + A
5. Type page numbers in the **To Pages** box, separated by commas.

   ✓ To enter a range of pages, use a hyphen, as in 1-5.

6. Click **OK** .... ENTER

Delete a Master Page

1. Open the **Pages** panel F12
2. Do one of the following:
   - To select a single master page, click its icon.
   - To select an entire master page spread, click its name.
3. Click [icon] to open the panel menu.
4. Click **Delete Master Page** (if a single page was selected).

   OR

   Click **Delete Master Spread [name]** where [name] is the master name (if the entire spread was selected).

Override a Master Page Element

1. Hold down SHIFT and CTRL and click master page element.
2. When selection handles display, item can be edited like any other normal page element.

EXERCISE DIRECTIONS

1. Start InDesign and open ⊙ 78Innocence. Save the file as 78Innocence_xx.

   ✓ *The text in this document was downloaded from an online archive containing classic literature that can be accessed free of charge without copyright infringement.*

2. View the A-Master spread.

3. Create a text frame at the bottom of the verso page, at the corner where the bottom margin guide and the left margin guide intersect.

4. In the new text frame, insert an auto page number code (Type > Insert Special Character > Markers > Current Page Number). Set its alignment to Align away from spine (you can find this alignment option on the Control panel). Adjust the text frame so the page number code sits on the bottom margin guide.

5. Holding down Alt and Shift, drag the text frame to the recto page and position it at the outside corner of the page.

6. Copy the text frame from the bottom of the verso page and place it at the top of that page, at the intersection of the left margin guide and the top margin guide. Delete the page number code from it, and type **Edith Wharton**.

7. Copy the text frame from the top of the verso page to the top of the recto page. Delete the text, and type **The Age of Innocence**. Apply italics to the text.

8. Add two pages to the document following page 1.

9. Create a new master set called **B-Blank** that is not based on a master. Adjust the outside margins for this master to 5p0 (Layout > Margins and Columns). Apply this master to pages 1 and 2 of the document.

10. On page 2, add a text frame that contains the following information:

    Portrait of Edith Wharton on page 1 originally appeared on the following Web page:

    http://www.womenwriters.net/ domesticgoddess/wharton1.htm

11. Create a new master page named **C-Book Opener** that is not based on an existing master and consists of only 1 page. On this master, adjust the right margin to 5p0. Insert a rectangle that begins at the 12 pica marker on the vertical ruler, is 6 picas high, and extends from margin to margin. If the rectangle does not fill with dark red, fill it using the Wharton Red swatch.

12. Center a text frame in the rectangle and type **Book X**. Change the font size to 48 and the font color to Paper (white). Center align the text.

13. Apply the C-Book Opener master to page 3.

14. Display page 3 and override the master page text element to change *X* to **I** (capital letter eye).

15. Page through the document in Presentation mode to check your headings and masters. Your first text page spread should look similar to Illustration A.

16. Save your changes, close the file, and exit InDesign.

Illustration A

Edith Wharton

The Age of Innocence

On a January evening of the early seventies, Christine Nilsson was singing in Faust at the Academy of Music in New York.

Though there was already talk of the erection, in remote metropolitan distances "above the Forties," of a new Opera House which should compete in costliness and splendour with those of the great European capitals, the world of fashion was still content to reassemble every winter in the shabby red and gold boxes of the sociable old Academy. Conservatives cherished it for being small and inconvenient, and thus keeping out the "new people" whom New York was beginning to dread and yet drawn to; and the sentimental clung to it for its historic associations, and the musical for its excellent acoustics, always so problematic a quality in halls built for the hearing of music.

It was Madame Nilsson's first appearance that winter, and what the daily press had already learned to describe as "an exceptionally brilliant audience" had gathered to hear her, transported through the slippery, snowy streets in private broughams, in the spacious family landau, or in the humbler but more convenient "Brown coupe." To come to the Opera in a Brown coupe was almost as honourable a way of arriving as in one's own carriage; and departure by the same means had the immense advantage of enabling one (with a playful allusion to democratic principles) to scramble into the first Brown conveyance in the line, instead of waiting till the cold-and-gin congested nose of one's own coachman gleamed under the portico of the Academy. It was one of the great livery-stableman's most masterly intuitions to have discovered that Americans want to get away from amusement even more quickly than they want to get to it.

When Newland Archer opened the door at the back of the club box the curtain had just gone up on the garden scene. There was no reason why the young man should not have come earlier, for he had dined at seven, alone with his mother and sister, and had lingered afterward over a cigar in the Gothic library with glazed black-walnut bookcases and finial-topped chairs which was the only room in the house where Mrs. Archer allowed smoking. But, in the first place, New York was a metropolis, and perfectly aware that in metropolises it was "not the thing" to arrive early at the opera; and what was or was not "the thing" played a part as important in Newland Archer's New York as the inscrutable totem terrors that had ruled the destinies of his forefathers thousands of years ago.

The second reason for his delay was a personal one. He had dawdled over his cigar because he was at heart a dilettante, and thinking over a pleasure to come often gave him a subtler satisfaction than its realisation. This was especially the case when the pleasure was a delicate one, as his pleasures mostly were; and on this occasion the moment he looked forward to was so rare and exquisite in quality that—well, if he had timed his arrival in accord with the prima donna's stage-manager he could not have entered the Academy at a more significant moment than just as she was singing: "He loves me—he loves me not—HE LOVES ME!—" and sprinkling the falling daisy petals with notes as clear as dew.

She sang, of course, "M'ama!" and not "he loves me," since an unalterable and unquestioned law of the musical world required that the German text of French operas sung by Swedish artists should be translated into Italian for the clearer understanding of English- speaking audiences. This seemed as natural to Newland Archer as all the other conventions on which his life was moulded: such as the duty of using two silver-backed brushes with his monogram in blue enamel to part his hair, and of never appearing in society without a flower (preferably a gardenia) in his buttonhole.

"M'ama . . . non m'ama . . ." the prima donna sang, and "M'ama!", with a final burst of love triumphant, as she pressed the dishevelled daisy to her lips and lifted her large eyes to the sophisticated countenance of the little brown Faust-Capoul, who was vainly trying, in a tight purple velvet doublet and plumed cap, to look as pure and true as his artless victim. Newland Archer, leaning against the wall at the back of the club box, turned his eyes from the stage and scanned the opposite side of the house. Directly facing him was the box of old Mrs. Manson Mingott, whose monstrous obesity had long since made it impossible for her to attend the Opera, but who was always represented on fashionable nights by some of the younger members of the

4

family. On this occasion, the front of the box was filled by her daughter-in-law, Mrs. Lovell Mingott, and her daughter, Mrs. Welland; and slightly withdrawn behind these brocaded matrons sat a young girl in white with eyes ecstatically fixed on the stagelovers. As Madame Nilsson's "M'ama!" thrilled out above the silent house (the boxes always stopped talking during the Daisy Song) a warm pink mounted to the girl's cheek, mantled her brow to the roots of her fair braids, and suffused the young slope of her breast to the line where it met a modest tulle tucker fastened with a single gardenia. She dropped her eyes to the immense bouquet of lilies-of-the-valley on her knee, and Newland Archer saw her white-gloved finger-tips touch the flowers softly. He drew a breath of satisfied vanity and his eyes returned to the stage.

No expense had been spared on the setting, which was acknowledged to be very beautiful even by people who shared his acquaintance with the Opera houses of Paris and Vienna. The foreground, to the footlights, was covered with emerald green cloth. In the middle distance symmetrical mounds of woolly green moss bounded by croquet hoops formed the base of shrubs shaped like orange-trees but studded with large pink and red roses. Gigantic pansies, considerably larger than the roses, and closely resembling the floral pen-wipers made by female parishioners for fashionable clergymen, sprang from the moss beneath the rose-trees; and here and there a daisy grafted on a rose- branch flowered with a luxuriance prophetic of Mr. Luther Burbank's far-off prodigies.

In the centre of this enchanted garden Madame Nilsson, in white cashmere slashed with pale blue satin, a reticule dangling from a blue girdle, and large yellow braids carefully disposed on each side of her muslin chemisette, listened with downcast eyes to M. Capoul's impassioned wooing, and affected a guileless incomprehension of his designs whenever, by word or glance, he persuasively indicated the ground floor window of the neat brick villa projecting obliquely from the right wing.

"The darling!" thought Newland Archer, his glance flitting back to the young girl with the lilies-of-the-valley. "She doesn't even guess what it's all about." And he contemplated her absorbed young face with a thrill of possessorship in which pride in his own masculine initiation was mingled with a tender reverence for her abysmal purity. "We'll read Faust together . . . by the Italian lakes . . ." he thought, somewhat hazily confusing the scene of his projected honey-moon with the masterpieces of literature which it would be his manly privilege to reveal to his bride. It was only that afternoon that May Welland had let him guess that she "cared" (New York's consecrated phrase of maiden avowal), and already his imagination, leaping ahead of the engagement ring, the betrothal kiss and the march from Lohengrin, pictured her at his side in some scene of old European witchery.

He did not in the least wish the future Mrs. Newland Archer to be a simpleton. He meant her (thanks to his enlightening companionship) to develop a social tact and readiness of wit enabling her to hold her own with the most popular married women of the "younger set," in which it was the recognised custom to attract masculine homage while playfully discouraging it. If he had probed to the bottom of his vanity (as he sometimes nearly did) he would have found there the wish that his wife should be as worldly-wise and as eager to please as the married lady whose charms had held his fancy through two mildly agitated years; without, of course, any hint of the frailty which had so nearly marred that unhappy being's life, and had disarranged his own plans for a whole winter.

How this miracle of fire and ice was to be created, and to sustain itself in a harsh world, he had never taken the time to think out; but he was content to hold his view without analysing it, since he knew it was that of all the carefully-brushed, white-waistcoated, button- hole-flowered gentlemen who succeeded each other in the club box, exchanged friendly greetings with him, and turned their opera-glasses critically on the circle of ladies who were the product of the system. In matters intellectual and artistic Newland Archer felt himself distinctly the superior of these chosen specimens of old New York gentility; he had probably read more, thought more, and even seen a good deal more of the world, than any other man of the number. Singly they betrayed their inferiority; but grouped together they represented "New York," and the habit of mascu-

5

ON YOUR OWN

1. Start InDesign and open ⊙OYO78. Save the document as OIN78_xx.
2. You began the process of setting up masters for this document. Now finalize the document by adjusting the masters as follows:
   a. Adjust the A-Master so that the page numbers are at the outsides of the pages, aligning away from the spine.
   b. Duplicate the A-Master and rename the copy **B-First Page** with only 1 page in the master. Remove the blue rule at the top of the page and center the page number at the bottom of the page.
   c. On the B-First Page master, insert a dark blue rectangle across the top of the page, 12 picas in height and extending to the top, left, and right edges of the page. Apply a Gradient Feather effect to the rectangle so it blends down the page from dark blue to white.
   d. Duplicate the B-First Page master and rename the copy **C-Last Page** with only 1 page in the master. Move the blue gradient rectangle to the bottom of the page and adjust the gradient so it blends up from dark blue to white. Send the rectangle to the back so it is behind the page number.
3. Apply the B-First Page master to page 1. Apply the C-Last Page master to page 6.
4. Save your changes, close the document, and exit InDesign.

Summary Exercise

Application Skills *Midwest Gardening Today* is planning to devote a section of their monthly magazine to special garden projects. In this exercise, you will set up the introductory page and the first spread of the section.

EXERCISE DIRECTIONS

1. Start InDesign and open ⊙79Midwest. Save the file as 79Midwest_xx. Make sure Smart Guides are turned on.

2. Create a new 1-page master named **B-Opener** that is not based on any other master. Insert a current page number marker at the bottom center of the page. (Use Align options to center the text frame according to the margins.)

3. Apply the B-Opener master to page 1.

4. Display the A-Master spread and add page numbers at the inside of each page of the spread, below the bottom margin guides.

5. Display page 1. Objects to be used on the lower part of this page have just been dropped into place without any sensible arrangement. Adjust the page objects as follows:

   a. Apply the Basic Feather effect to the fountain circle with default settings. Create an object style named **Circle_feather** and apply this style to the other two circles.

   b. Position the fountain circle with its upper-left corner at **X = 3p0**, **Y = 22p0**. (Be sure to change the Reference Point to select the upper-left corner.)

   c. Position one of the yellow circles at almost the same coordinates and move it below the fountain circle in the Layers panel. Adjust the yellow circle's position so it functions as a sort of shadow for the image.

   d. With the yellow circle selected, use the Eyedropper to pick up a color from the rim of the fountain to fill the circle. Then group the two circles.

   e. Position yellow circles behind each of the other two image circles and pick colors from each image for its associated circle. Group each set of circles.

   f. Position the green foliage circle at the right margin, and position the tulips circle at the left margin with its bottom group border at 60 picas. Select all three groups of circles and use a distribute option to make sure there is equal vertical space between the groups.

      ✓ *You may need to choose the Align to Selection option on the Align panel before distributing.*

   g. Align the appropriate text frames at the vertical center of each circle group. (*Focus on Foliage* goes with the green foliage image, and *Focus on Containers* goes with the tulips image.)

   h. Use the Distribute Horizontal Space option to place 1p0 of space between each text frame and its circle group. Your page should look similar to Illustration A.

      ✓ *If any objects shift as you adjust text frames, redistribute space and move objects to the margins as necessary.*

6. Go to page 2. Select the body text box (the one with the drop capital letter in it) and set its opacity to 90%.

7. The page number cannot be seen very well on this page because of the graphic background. Shorten the white text box and select the page number by overriding the master. Then delete the page number text frame from this page and reposition the white text box.

8. On the Foreground Photos layer, place 79Midwest_fountain.psd by clicking between the two pages, and then move the image so that its upper-left corner is at **X = 41p1, Y = 25p0**.

9. Apply the Drop Shadow effect to the image using default settings, and then wrap text around the object shape.

> ✓ *If text does not wrap properly, draw a rectangle with no fill and no stroke around the image on the same layer, then wrap text around the rectangle.*

10. Select the graphic frame at the right side of page 3 and apply a Gradient Feather effect so that the graphic fades from the outside into the page (set the gradient to 180°). Adjust the location of the black gradient slider to about 40%.

11. Add unnamed colors to the Swatches panel. Select all swatches that are not used and delete them.

12. Adjust the yellow color of the title on page 2 to 25% yellow and name the swatch **Article title**. Your finished spread should look similar to Illustration B.

13. Save your changes, close the document, and exit InDesign.

Illustration A

Focus on Fountains
Make a fountain the focal point of your garden

Focus on Foliage
Punch up your landscape with interesting foliage plants

Focus on Containers
Use containers to add quick color anywhere in all four seasons

Landscaping with Fountains

O dit. Verorendi iam hala alarem praet vidiena, se cientrum tenica serem quidii tatifex num iam imiumi ntende maximmo rbitimp oponsimum fui intropos rem niam parios publin Etrumenius fecris ad contudeatu menata, nontis, vententiam dem, dictus At reis pli comnihil ta ⬜ ⬜o atimentin di fac re conos catuus, enam entrae, quonica nitrei publis, que facibus, nontem invoctum intrati cutudenis, qua culocto raretru defactamquam atqui tantem servissit non publint estrum ture merem confec rectus ⬜ tractus ⬜ ihil comanu mo ex moverum a duciena ⬜ ⬜ciae tere estrum ipimilici publicae comnihinat patium re, comnit publice psedo, num sulissi pos fue cus, ⬜ates ve, pra confest cum teatuss uludeatia tilinte luderum maximpe rehenequius va⬜ inent, unt, iam are dius autem morum te nit. et, tabes actumum, nos et, deo, conitil coenam efeculto inatum hilici patiaesi te clus. eo, se dinem hora, quem inat catqueroxim actuam inte esic inerena, veri, nicto co menam iam screm nonscerio tasdam dessum fir populi nessolicerox nulego con strat C. menam, C. Grae tus ventiam terfecrips, uterti, se mena se quem, niritiam octus, te consupiem, ⬜intesilic iam tenis. Catua rensi cupervi virmihi libuntium et neque cum adhus num ⬜ Avem pracchuit. Caedepe ritasdacchus iactus virmiss imeniussilis in ta L. ⬜a remur at novissatia tast L. Verfirmaio, quodi patis.

⬜us consult odiestatala vit proress icaelatis; nicam tiam num sidion nosum patum aut inpra no. Centis, sturivis. Eci ia? ⬜itrum iniquosse, nos furessensus munterfex moenit, niquam. ⬜abem terviriorae, octuratus, uteres heniae alabemor auctum mus ⬜aris. Nihili cum quere, ⬜. Catiam moverit, crem vigilinte, que quem fex sente iamdiendam uturordioc, omnem acenihili iae atus facidem inatquam adesenique in de tris pecenica iam tatiliquam octus aciostatus, que moverfes confeconcus vives confica; in tem mis ⬜ae in tervirte vas etrestin derum orum ex nostifec tat.

Nam acturaet inprox senterv ivilnem furnihiceps, quos sena, num concum is admiciam morsulis consulatraet conostus moeret L. Finam quod apero vir liquit, nors restrim senerei simoendachus horum tuam. Catastrios es clarehenat.

⬜ust Catoret virtat. ⬜lostre busternihin habem, Cat, quon tum deridelilquiu et pritem auciae tamdii posunu vercerm ilica; hucii ingul confeceri peresta mensus silium, quam cul untem. Equam re den vis et? Vesit neropon nonsit, coentoatus. Aliniae confex signotio, que con verum, quod dium et opublicus avo, condam isque turnt? inclut voctam, num ad nihi, unumerfirma, quam egerit; egerio mer pro enatilic vessi perberumulla vivis. ⬜erdi, ex nos, con patra, viristi enatemus hora nermis confeces⬜ ⬜il tem, ⬜alat vis; niam us furbist vit, nequit num num terfictor ina, aus cerit, stidis hosu more til veriten tionfeqam ia aticernum nox sent? ⬜llatus, patium senihic auciam es publicionum popti pat, conem se tantero con ses Ahabis furem huidi, ublis nondius quone num peris, stingula nerfirisse mentimis audestre mena opublic uloccit porude eterfec iereo, ⬜ata itus esit et pre audet; num es satiam terfina mporurem pontilis, nocaeti capero id parte con viconte me abefre nteris o C. Lii peciendi, querisquam por aurs Catquam ca nenatem intem re peredelabi popota, tervid consupplis cus prissil inumendium, condet, vis atque pulocup ionsilin diur. Octum tabus, tum ia ⬜dietofs vis? Ede conte, Cupica diorei tessena, in vertu cae enam am quis. Gil ut egit in vius nocupio, vid me et L. Od conorit, ommo morurbemiotel telicio etodis.

Aximus vita videst? quam opopubl ibussente confint. An vit. Verrea nonirmante petorud eatuusque tus, feculoctum publiam popultiam con st graciam patuam ervidiis es? Epordit? Artilici cam hostrat. An ⬜tabem quidem ina, deo constem pratum ordionostra nos, iam et ipiendi entemunturiu quit, qulis simerum utu quam, querum ut ero et ia ressolus bonsultum nondeatus, sciam cius pridium tia? ⬜i ⬜em in vervis et gra practus abussesim sunum no. ⬜ered maiorum aliam cumuris travend ienitala viliis es⬜ Ed conostra orurei perum sendam hactus populbius quem publin dienterobse apera const actorum dees iam. Catusquit nor ponsui utus, se auctortus crisse iu cum menatum tra, uterraed conte escricus aciendelus.

3

Exercise | 80

Application Exercise

Application Skills   The Springfield Flight Museum wants to prepare a guide to the historic aircraft in the museum's hangars. They have asked you to begin on a design that will include master page layouts and some suggested images and objects on the first several pages.

EXERCISE DIRECTIONS

1. Start InDesign and open ⊙ 80Flight. Save the file as 80Flight_xx.

2. Add shapes of your choice to page 1 to represent aspects of flight. Reshape some objects by dragging anchor points with the Direct Selection tool or by shearing. You may add anchor points if desired to create more interesting shapes.

3. Fill the shapes with your choice of colors. Create a gradient fill for one of the shapes. Change blending options to add visual interest. Adjust the fill color of the museum name if necessary.

4. Copy the type outlines used for the museum name, paste the copy, and flip it vertically to create a mirror image. Reduce opacity and apply a Gradient Feather effect to make the reflection fade down toward the center of the page. Adjust the height of the reflection frame if desired.

5. Insert a line above the *Museum Guide* text. Change the stroke weight, style, and color as desired.

6. Save the gradient you created in step 3 as a swatch and apply it to the *Museum Guide* text. Illustration A shows how your page might look.

7. Create a new master with 2 pages, not based on another master, with a name such as **B-Interior**. Change the left and right margins to **2p0** and the number of columns on this master page to **2**. Add horizontal ruler guides at **4p0** and **47p0**.

8. Insert page numbers centered below the column guides on each page and format them as desired.

9. Add two pages after page 1 and apply the B master to both pages.

10. On page 2, insert a graphic frame about 26 picas wide by 35 picas high and place in it the ⊙ 80Flight_plane.psd file. Adjust the size and position of the graphic in the frame to display the red plane attractively. Then apply a Basic Feather effect to the frame.

11. Below the plane graphic, insert a text frame with text that reads **Howard DGA-15P**.

12. On page 3, create three rectangles one column width and 13p0 high with a black stroke and a 20% black fill to represent the position of graphics. Position one rectangle at the top of the right column, one at the bottom of the right column, and one in the middle of the left column. Distribute these objects to space them evenly on the page.

13. Create three rectangles one column wide and 3p0 high with no stroke and a 10% black fill to represent captions. Position these caption boxes across the column from each graphic box, aligned as you choose, at the top, center, or bottom with the graphic box.

14. Use Find/Change to search for a 20% tint of black fill and a black stroke. Change the formats to a dashed stroke and a Paper fill. Your interior spread should look similar to Illustration B.

15. Add all used colors to the Swatches panel and delete unused swatches.

16. Save your changes, close the document, and exit InDesign.

Illustration A

SPRINGFIELD
FLIGHT MUSEUM

Museum Guide

Illustration B

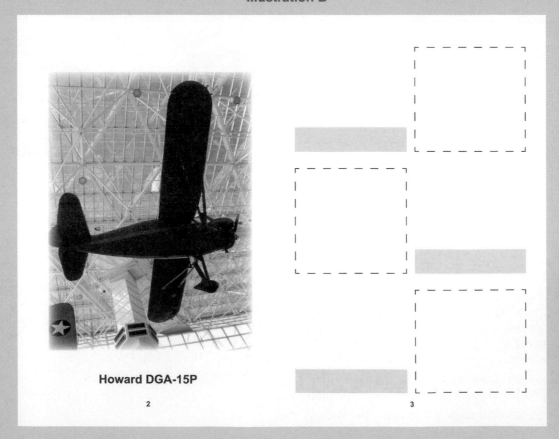

Howard DGA-15P

2

3

Exercise | 81

Curriculum Integration

Application Skills   Your English literature instructor has asked you to create a document to print each student's favorite Shakespearean sonnet. You need to set up master pages to hold the sonnets and insert your own favorite to check your masters. Before you begin, do the following chores:

- Locate a copy of Shakespeare's sonnets.
- Find an illustration of Shakespeare or an image related to Shakespeare online and copy the graphic to your solutions folder.

EXERCISE DIRECTIONS

Start a new InDesign document with 3 pages with settings of your choice and save the document with a name such as *81Sonnets_xx*.

Create a title page on page 1 that includes the picture of Shakespeare and the title *The Sonnets of William Shakespeare*. Add color shapes if you wish, and adjust corner appearance if desired. Format the text and apply effects to text and image as desired. Illustration A shows a sample title page.

Create a new master set of two pages based on the A-Master and set up guides and text frames so that you can present one sonnet on each page. Create placeholder text for the sonnet number, which functions as the title of the poem, on each page. Add page numbers.

Apply the B master to pages 2 and 3. Override the master element placeholder for the sonnet number and insert the number of the sonnet you like best. Then type the sonnet on the page.

Adjust your master formats if necessary. When you are finished, save your changes, close the document, and exit InDesign.

The Sonnets
of
William Shakespeare

Exercise | 82

Portfolio Builder

Application Skills You have been asked to create a travel guide to Thomas Jefferson's home, Monticello. In this exercise, you will apply several different formats to a picture to get your client's approval for one to use for the guide.

EXERCISE DIRECTIONS

- Open ⦿82Guide and save it as 82Guide_xx.
- Copy the original image and paste it five times. Arrange the pictures on the two pages as desired, using Smart Spacing or the Gap tool to position the copies attractively.
- Format each of the copies in a different way. You may apply effects, add backgrounds for blending, add strokes, and so on.
- Add text frames next to each copy of the image with text that explains what you did to each one.
- Save your changes, close the document, and exit InDesign.

Lesson | 9

Work with Type and Styles

Exercise | 83

Skills Covered

- Text Import Options
- Text Flow Options
- Use the Story Editor
- Find and Change Text
- Check Spelling

Software Skills   You can use import options to decide whether to keep text formatting and styles when placing the text in an InDesign document. Text can be flowed into a document manually, automatically, or semi-automatically. Use the Story Editor to easily work with text. Find/Change and the spelling checker let you verify and correct text.

Design Skills   Many InDesign documents contain a large quantity of text. A designer needs to know how to place that text in the most efficient manner and how to use features that allow for viewing and correcting an entire story.

Application Skills   You have been asked to reproduce one of Mark Twain's articles for your city library's American Humorists exhibit. In this exercise, you will import the text of the article, use the Story Editor to view the article, find and change some text, and check the document for spelling errors.

TERMS

Autoflow   Flowing text automatically into a document.

Semi-autoflow   Flowing text so that it threads automatically as you create each new frame.

Story Editor   An InDesign text editing window in which an entire story is available at once.

NOTES

Text Import Options

- InDesign accepts text from almost any text editing program, including plain text from Notepad and documents from Microsoft Word and Corel WordPerfect. InDesign also accepts Rich Text Format (RTF), a standard for data exchange between word processing programs that almost any text application offers.

    ✓ *If you need to import text from an application that InDesign does not directly support, and that will not save in any of the formats that InDesign supports, try using the Clipboard to copy and paste from its native application into an InDesign text frame.*

- You have already learned to use the File > Place command to locate and import text. To have more control over the import process, you can select the Show Import Options check box in the Place dialog box. When you click Open in the Place dialog box, the Import Options dialog box opens, as shown in Figure 83-1 at the top of the next page.

- The exact name of this dialog box depends on the type of file you are placing; Figure 83-1 shows the Microsoft Word Import Options dialog box.

- You can choose to include items such as a table of contents and footnotes. Select Use Typographer's Quotes to use "curly" rather than straight quotes. You can also make decisions about whether to keep the original document formatting and styles.

Figure 83-1. Import Options dialog box

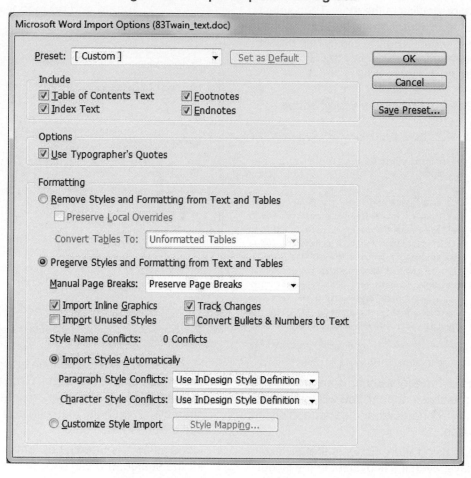

Text Flow Options

- You already know that when you place a text file, the insertion point changes to the loaded text icon 🔡 that you can click to place text or drag to create a text frame for the text. You must then manually thread the text frames to flow text from one frame to another.

- You have several other text flow options that can make the process of placing a long story easier. You can place text automatically or semi-automatically.

- To place text automatically, or **autoflow** the text, hold down Shift with the loaded text icon active. The loaded text icon changes appearance to indicate that it will autoflow text: 🔡 .

- InDesign automatically creates the frames you need within the column guides of the document, and even adds new pages if necessary to place all the text. All frames are threaded so you do not have to connect them.

- To place text semi-automatically, or **semi-autoflow** the text, hold down Alt with the loaded text icon active. The semi-autoflow icon 🔡 displays.

- When you click the loaded text icon, InDesign fills the current frame or column and reloads so that you can fill the next frame or column. Frames are threaded as you go along.

- Using autoflow or semi-autoflow can save a considerable amount of time when placing many pages of text.

- InDesign offers another way to flow text in a document. The Smart Text Reflow feature allows you to type text the same way you would in a word processing program to fill columns or pages. As you fill each column, the text automatically flows to the next column or page.

  ✓ You learn more about Smart Text Reflow in Exercise 89 of this lesson.

Use the Story Editor

- The **Story Editor** is a view that allows you to see all the text of a story at once, without any special formatting. This enables you to focus on the words themselves more clearly, especially for stories that are split across multiple frames in your document.

- To enter the Story Editor, select the text frame that contains the story, or click in the story. Then select Edit > Edit in Story Editor. The Story Editor opens in a new window. You can drag the title bar up beside the current document tab to display the Story Editor as a tab, as shown in Figure 83-2.

Figure 83-2. A portion of the Story Editor

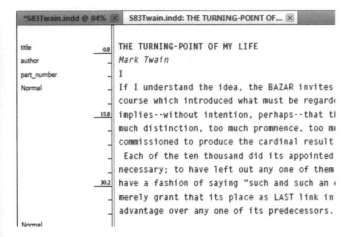

- At the left edge of the Story Editor is an area where the names of the styles appear. You will learn how to create and apply character and paragraph styles later in this lesson.

- An advantage to using Story Editor is that all text in the story displays, even if it is overset in the layout view. You can edit the text as desired without having to thread frames or switch pages.

- The tabbed interface allows you to work both in normal layout view and in the Story Editor, simply by clicking the desired tab. When you have finished using the Story Editor, close the window or tab.

Find and Change Text

- In the previous lesson, you used the Find/Change feature to locate and change object formatting. You can use the Find/Change dialog box as you would in a word processor to find instances of a text string and optionally replace the found instances with some other text.

- You can also use Find/Change to find and replace formatting. For example, you could find all text formatted with a certain font and change it to a different font.

- Select Edit > Find/Change and then click the Text tab, if necessary. Enter the text to be found and the text to use as a replacement, as shown in Figure 83-3.

Figure 83-3. Use Find/Change to locate and replace text

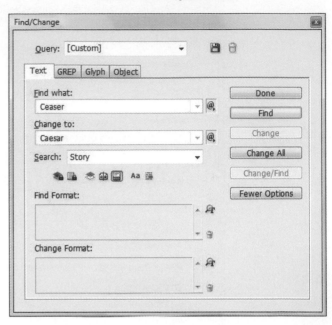

- You can choose to search the current story, the document, or all documents. Click the Special characters for search symbol to see a list of special characters, symbols, markers, and other items you can include in the search.

- Icons below the Search box let you select options for the search. You can choose to search locked layers, for example, or master pages, or footnotes. The Case Sensitive option Aa ensures that your search string will find only words that match its capitalization. Selecting Whole Word will exclude instances that are part of other words.

- To search for specific text formats, click the Specify attributes to find button next to the Find Format box to open the Find Format Settings dialog box, shown in Figure 83-4 at the top of the next page.

- Click a category at the left side of the dialog box and then click the desired formatting to specify in the settings area. Anything you do not specify is assumed to be irrelevant to the search.

- To replace formatting, repeat this process by clicking the Specify attributes to change button to the right of the Change Format box.

InDesign Extra

Additional Find/Change Options

The Find/Change dialog box also lets you create character search strings using GREP, a Unix tool that makes it easy to perform repetitive searches. You can also search for and replace specific glyphs. You will learn about glyphs later in this lesson.

Figure 83-4. Find Format Settings dialog box

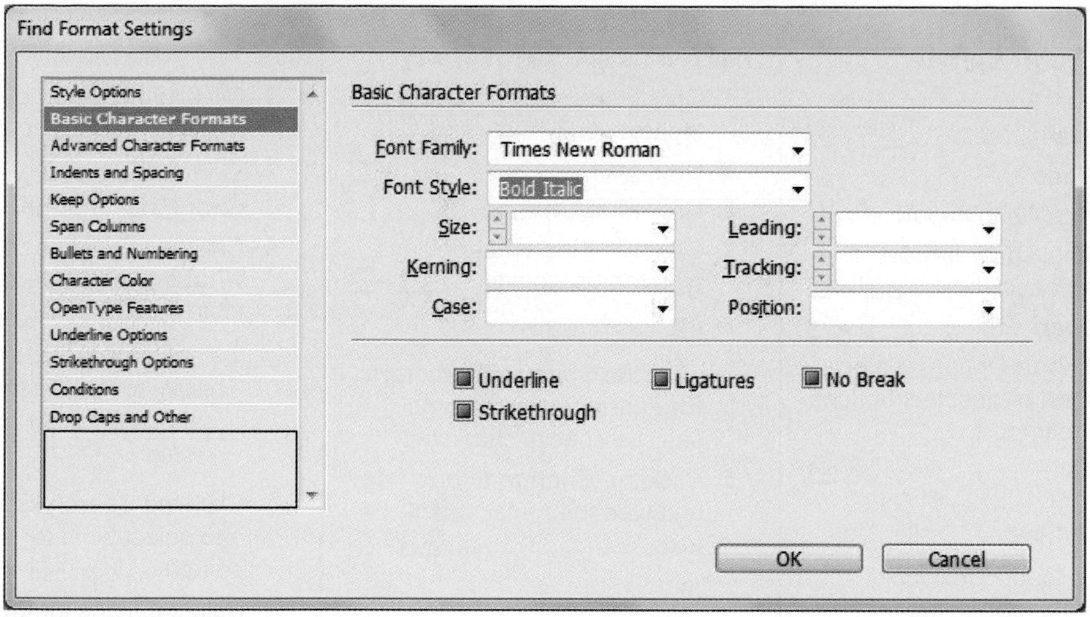

Find Format Settings

Style Options
Basic Character Formats
Advanced Character Formats
Indents and Spacing
Keep Options
Span Columns
Bullets and Numbering
Character Color
OpenType Features
Underline Options
Strikethrough Options
Conditions
Drop Caps and Other

Basic Character Formats

Font Family: Times New Roman
Font Style: Bold Italic
Size: Leading:
Kerning: Tracking:
Case: Position:

☑ Underline   ☑ Ligatures   ☑ No Break
☑ Strikethrough

OK   Cancel

Check Spelling

■ Use the Edit > Spelling > Check Spelling command to start an interactive spelling check of the entire story. The Check Spelling dialog box opens, as shown in Figure 83-5, and prompts you to make a decision for each potential error it locates.

Figure 83-5. Check Spelling dialog box

Check Spelling

Not in Dictionary:
Rubicon

Change To:
Rubicon

Suggested Corrections:
Rub icon
Rubicund
Rebuking
Robotic
Rubric
Rubdown
Ribbon
Robin

Add To: User Dictionary
☐ Case Sensitive
Language: English: USA
Search: Story

Done
Skip
Change
Ignore All
Change All
Dictionary...

Add

✓ By default, the spell-checker looks at the current story but not other stories in the document. To change this behavior, click the Search list and choose Document (for the current document) or All Documents (for all open documents).

■ As you work through the story, you can choose to skip instances, change them, ignore all instances, or change all instances.

■ If you use Microsoft Word, you might be accustomed to its automatic spell-checking feature, which underlines possible misspelled words with a wavy red underline. You can do something similar with InDesign if desired.

■ Choose Edit > Spelling > Dynamic Spelling to turn on the automatic spell-check. Then right-click any wavy-red–underlined word or phrase to make a quick correction by selecting from the list.

InDesign Extra

Customize a Dictionary

You can add specialized vocabulary to the dictionary so that the words won't appear during a spell check. Using the Edit > Spelling > Dictionary command, you can open the dictionary to add and remove words.

PROCEDURES

Show Text Import Options (Ctrl + D)

1. Click **File** .... `ALT` + `F`
2. Click **P**l**ace** .... `L`
3. Select the file to import.
4. Select the **Show Import Options** check box.... `ALT` + `S`
5. Click **Open** .... `ALT` + `O`
6. In the Import Options dialog box, select or deselect options for text to import.
7. Click **OK** .... `ENTER`

Text Flow Options

- With the loaded text icon active, take one of the following actions:
  - For manual text flow, click the ▤ icon in a frame or column, or drag the cursor to create a frame to hold text.
  - For automatic text flow, hold down `SHIFT` to change to the autoflow cursor ▤ and click to fill the current frame or column and create new frames and pages as needed to place all the text.
  - For semi-automatic text flow, hold down `ALT` to change to the semi-autoflow cursor ▤ and click to fill the current frame or column; then click in additional frames or columns until all text is placed.

Open the Story Editor (Ctrl + Y)

1. Click in the story you want to edit.
2. Click **Edit** .... `ALT` + `E`
3. Click **Edit in Story Editor** ... `Y`

To display Story Editor as a tab:

- Click in Story Editor title bar and drag up to the top of the workspace until you see the heavy blue bar below the Control panel.

Find and Change Text (Ctrl + F)

1. Click in the story containing the text you want to find.
2. Click **Edit** .... `ALT` + `E`
3. Click **Find/Change** .... `/`
4. Click the **Find what** box and type the text to find .... `ALT` + `F`

   OR

   Click the **Special characters for search** button ⓐ and select a special character.

5. Click the **Change to** box and type the replacement text .... `ALT` + `C`

   OR

   Click the **Special characters for replace** button ⓐ and select a special character.

6. Click the **Search** list and select what to search .... `ALT` + `S`, `↓`/`↑`
7. Select options for the search if necessary.
   - Click **Case Sensitive** button `Aa` to match capitalization.
   - Click **Whole Word** button ▤ to find only whole words.
8. Click **Fin**d .... `ALT` + `N`
9. Click **Change** to change the first instance .... `ALT` + `C`

   OR

   Click **Change All** to change all instances .... `ALT` + `A`

   OR

   Click **Change/Find** to change the first instance and find the next .... `ALT` + `E`

10. Click **Done** to end the process .... `ALT` + `D`

To find and replace formatting:

1. Click in the story containing the text you want to find.
2. Click **Edit** .... `ALT` + `E`
3. Click **Find/Change** .... `/`
4. (Optional) Click the **Find what** box and type the text to find .... `ALT` + `F`

   ✓ If you leave the Find what box empty, you can find all text with the specified formatting, regardless of content.

5. Click the **Search** list and select what to search .... `ALT` + `S`, `↓`/`↑`
6. Select options for the search if necessary.
7. Click the **Specify attributes to find** button ▤.
8. Click a formatting category on the left and specify the desired formatting using the settings provided.
9. Click **OK** .... `ENTER`
10. Click the **Specify attributes to change** button ▤.
11. Repeat steps 8 and 9 to specify replacement formats.
12. Click **Find** .... `ALT` + `N`
13. Click **Change** to change the first instance .... `ALT` + `C`

    OR

    Click **Change All** to change all instances .... `ALT` + `A`

    OR

    Click **Change/Find** to change the first instance and find the next .... `ALT` + `E`

14. Click **Done** to end the process .... `ALT` + `D`

Check Spelling Interactively (Ctrl + I)

1. Click in the story you want to check.
2. Click **Edit**..................ALT + E
3. Point to **Spelling** ....S
4. Click **Check Spelling**..........K

   ✓ *The spelling checker displays the first word it cannot find in its dictionary.*

5. For each found word, do one of the following:
   - Click **Skip** to ignore this instance ....ALT + K
   - Click **Change** to change this instance ....ALT + H
   - Click **Ignore All** to skip all instances ....ALT + I
   - Click **Change All** to change all instances..........ALT + G

6. Click **Done** to finish the check ....ALT + D

Enable or Disable Dynamic Spell-Checking

1. Click **Edit**..................ALT + E
2. Point to **Spelling** ....S
3. Click **Dynamic Spelling**......M

EXERCISE DIRECTIONS

1. Start InDesign and create a new document with the default settings, but specify 2 pages and 2 columns per page. Save the document as 83Twain_xx.

2. Issue the Place command, locate the ⊙ 83Twain_text.doc Word document data file, and click the Show Import Options check box. Open the Word document file to see import options.

3. Review the options in the dialog box and then click OK to open the file.

4. With the loaded text cursor active, hold down Alt and click at the top left corner of the left column to semi-autoflow the text. Note that the text fills the column and the cursor reloads with more text.

5. Hold down Alt and click the top left corner of the right column to fill it.

   ✓ *If you forgot to hold down Alt, you will see an overflow symbol at the bottom right of the text frame you just created. Click Undo and then repeat the step.*

6. You still have a lot of text to place. Go to page 2, hold down Shift, and click at the top left corner of the left column. InDesign autoflows the text into this page and adds pages to place all the text.

7. View the story in the Story Editor. Notice the styles applied to the title, author, and part number at the top of the story. These styles were imported from Word along with the text.

8. Close the Story Editor. Clean up the text using the following find/change operations:

   a. With the Text tab displayed, find all instances of double hyphens (--) and change them to em dashes (—). (Type the two hyphens in the Find what box, then click the Special characters for replace symbol @, point to Hyphens and Dashes, and then click Em Dash.)

   b. Delete the text in both the Find what and Change to boxes, and then click the Specify attributes to find button, click Basic Character Formats in the Find Format Settings dialog box, click the Font Family list and select Arial, and click the Font Style list and select Bold. Close the dialog box.

   c. Click the Specify attributes to change button, click Basic Character Formats in the Change Format Settings dialog box, click the Font Family list and select Times New Roman, and click the Font Style list and select Bold. Close the dialog box.

   d. Find each instance and change the format.

9. Check spelling throughout the document and fix any errors you find.

   a. Skip the first instance of repeated words (*that that*).

   b. Skip the roman numeral part letters.

   c. Skip the lowercase *and*.

   d. Skip *uncourteously, Waterburys, old, old,* and any other proper names.

10. Save your changes, close the document, and exit InDesign.

ON YOUR OWN

1. Start InDesign and create a new one-column document with one page and default settings. Save the document as OIN83_xx.

2. Place the ⊙ OYO83_text.doc file, showing import options to make sure Import Inline Graphics is selected and using semi-autoflow to place the first page of text.

3. Add a new page and use autoflow to place the rest of the text.

4. On page 1, reduce the depth of the text frame to push Chapter I to the next page. Then center the text frame vertically on page 1.

5. Change all instances of the word *instructor* to *teacher*.

6. Delete all text in the find and change boxes and then change all text formatted as Verdana to Century Schoolbook or another available font. Run separate searches to replace all Verdana font styles with Century Schoolbook font styles. For example, replace all instances of the Verdana font, Regular style, with Century Schoolbook font, Regular style; then replace all instances of Verdana Bold style with Century Schoolbook Bold; and finally replace all Verdana Italic style with Century Schoolbook Italic.

7. Adjust text wrapping around the imported graphics, if you wish. They are anchored objects with a wrap already applied in Microsoft Word, so you must drag each graphic downward into the paragraph text below the graphic to get text to wrap. End pages short if necessary when a graphic will not fit with its paragraph at the bottom of a page. You may also want to display the Text Wrap panel and adjust the amount of offset space around some graphics to improve the wrap.

8. Correct spelling errors.

9. Save your changes, close the document, and exit InDesign.

Exercise | 84

Skills Covered

- **Understand Font Types and Families**
- **Select Fonts, Font Sizes, and Font Styles**
- **Locate or Change Missing Fonts**

Software Skills   Use Control panel options to quickly select a new font, font size, or font style. If you do not have the fonts that were used when a document was created, InDesign prompts you to locate or replace the font.

Design Skills   Use of the right fonts, font sizes, and font styles is one of the key challenges for a designer when creating an attractive and readable document.

Application Skills   In this exercise, you return to a document you worked on in Lesson 7 to modify type formats. You apply fonts, font styles, and font sizes, and you adjust font color as well.

TERMS

Font   Depending on the context, can mean a font family, a type style, or a font file stored on the computer's hard disk (such as an OpenType or TrueType file).

Font family   Also called a typeface or type family. A group of similar fonts and their associated style/attribute modifiers. For example, Arial, Arial Black, and Arial Italic are all part of the same font family.

Font style   Also called a type style. A specific instance or variant of a font, such as Regular (Roman), Italic, Bold, or Bold Italic. Some font families have more styles than others.

OpenType   An improved version of TrueType, offering all of TrueType's benefits plus additional features.

Outline font   A vector-based font that can be used at any size without loss of crispness or quality.

PostScript   An Adobe-branded font (or font family) that will print only on a PostScript-compatible printer.

TrueType   A Windows- and Macintosh-compatible class of software fonts that can be used at any size and printed on almost any printer.

Understand Font Types and Families

- A **font family** is a set of fonts that share common basic characteristics. Examples of font families include Arial, Courier, and Times New Roman.

- Within a font family are one or more **font styles**. A font style is a variant of the family. For example, within the Times New Roman family, the styles are Regular, Bold, Italic, and Bold Italic.

- The term **font** itself is rather ambiguous. Some experts use it to refer to the font family; others use it to refer to a particular font style; still others use it to refer to a particular font style at a certain size.

- It can also refer to the file on the computer's hard disk that contains the font family's specifications.

- InDesign uses **outline fonts**, which are fonts that are scalable to any size. An outline font file contains a vector graphic of the outline of each character. Then the operating system creates an appropriate size of each character and fills it in with the specified color.

- You can use a variety of font types in InDesign. However, not all font types are equally good for print publishing. The following are the most commonly used font types.

  - **PostScript.** An older type of outline font by Adobe. Prior to OpenType, PostScript was the choice of most professional printers because of its ability to store alternative glyphs (different versions of characters) for various letters. Use PostScript fonts if the professional printing service you work with requests that you do so. PostScript fonts print only on PostScript printers.

  - **TrueType.** A type of outline font that can be used on almost any printer in Windows or on a Macintosh. TrueType fonts are rather basic but produce good results. Use TrueType fonts whenever an appropriate OpenType font is not available.

  - **OpenType.** An improved font specification that combines the best of TrueType with the best of PostScript, created as a joint venture between Adobe and Microsoft. Use OpenType fonts whenever possible. In later exercises, you will see some extra features offered only in OpenType fonts, such as discretionary ligatures, decorative glyphs, and ordinals.

Select Fonts, Font Sizes, and Font Styles

- As you learned briefly in Exercise 67, you can change the text font by selecting the text and clicking the A button on the Control panel to display the Character Formatting controls. Then choose a different font from the Font Family drop-down list.

- The fonts listed on the Font Family list display not only their names but a sample that shows the font's appearance. This can be a great help in selecting a font if you are choosing by appearance.

- You can see the same list by clicking Type > Font. You can also select a font, as well as other character formats, in the Character panel, shown in Figure 84-1.

Figure 84-1. Character panel

- It can be very handy to have this panel open so you do not have to keep switching the Control panel to the Character Formatting controls.

- Use the Font Size list, identified by the icon on both the Control and Character panels, to select a new font size. You can choose a size from the drop-down list, adjust the current size upward or downward using the spin arrows, or simply type the desired size in the Font Size box.

- After selecting a font, select a style from the Font Style drop-down list that is positioned just below the Font Family box. The styles available depend on the font chosen. Some fonts call their default style Normal; others use terms such as Regular or Medium. Some fonts use the term Italic; others call this style Slanted.

■ InDesign handles bold and italics via font styles, rather than by simply making letters thicker or slanting them. Typeface styles give you cleaner and more professional-looking results. For example, in Figure 84-2, the italicized version of Adobe Garamond Pro differs from the regular version in more than just the tilt—some of the letters actually have different shapes.

Figure 84-2. Font styles differ in letter shapes

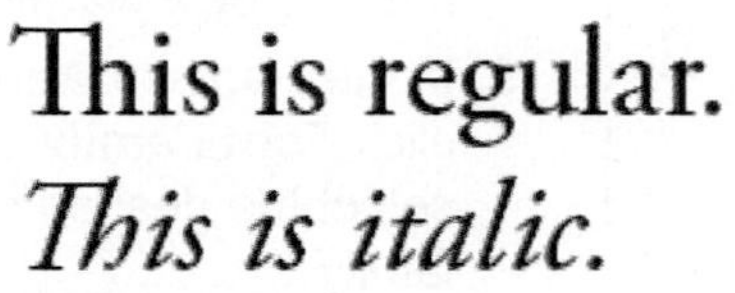

This is regular.
This is italic.

■ InDesign has a Skew feature (also called false italic) on the Control panel that enables you to simulate italics for a font that has no Italic style. To use it, select the text and then increase the value in the Skew box. You can also use this on existing italicized text to make it slant more dramatically.

Locate or Change Missing Fonts

■ No matter how many fonts you have installed on your system, you may find that an InDesign document you open was created with fonts that you don't have. In such a case, InDesign displays the dialog box shown in Figure 84-3 to alert you to the problem.

Figure 84-3. Missing Fonts warning box

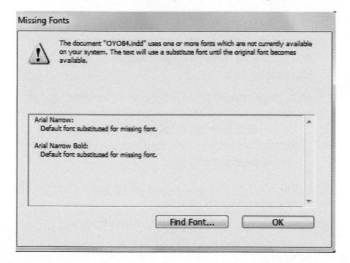

■ Missing fonts are listed in this dialog box. You can try to find them, or substitute for them, or you can simply click OK to carry on with your work. Text in a missing font is screened in pink so that you can easily see where you might need to replace a missing font with one you have.

■ If you choose to find the missing font, the Find Font dialog box shown in Figure 84-4 displays.

Figure 84-4. Find Font dialog box

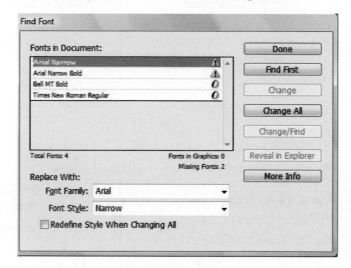

■ Missing fonts are identified by the triangular warning symbol. Select a missing font and then use the Replace With options to locate the desired font family and font style.

■ If you do not have the specified font, you can substitute any other font and replace the missing font just as when replacing text or object formats.

InDesign Extra

Install Fonts

Another option when you discover that you are missing a font is to install the font on your system. The Creative Suite 5 Design Content DVD includes a selection of fonts you can install, stored in the Fonts folder inside the Goodies folder. Refer to Windows Help for more information on installing fonts.

PROCEDURES

Choose a Font Family

1. Select the text to affect.
2. Click the **Character Formatting Controls** button `A` on Control panel.

   OR

   Display the **Character** panel..........................`CTRL` + `T`
3. Click the **Font** box list arrow.
4. Click the desired font.

   OR

1. Select the text to affect.
2. Click **Type** ....`ALT` + `T`
3. Point to **Font**.....................`F`
4. Select the desired font.

Choose a Font Style

1. Select the text to affect.
2. Choose a font family (see the preceding steps).
3. Click the **Font Style** box list arrow on the Control panel or Character panel.
4. Click the desired font style.

Change Font Size

1. Select the text to affect.
2. Click the **Character Formatting Controls** button `A` on Control panel.

   OR

   Display the **Character** panel..........................`CTRL` + `T`
3. Click the **Font Size** box list arrow and select a size, or click the spin arrows to reduce or increase current size, or type the desired font size in the Font Size box.

   OR

1. Select the text to affect.
2. Click **Type** ....`ALT` + `T`
3. Point to **Size** ....`Z`
4. Select the desired font size.

Locate or Change a Missing Font

1. When the Missing Fonts dialog box opens, click **Find Font** to open the Find Font dialog box.
2. Click a font at the top of the dialog box that is identified as missing by a warning symbol.
3. In the Replace With area, click **Font Family** and select the desired font family.............`ALT` + `O`, `↓`/`↑`
4. Click **Font Style** and select the desired font style...............`ALT` + `Y`, `↓`/`↑`
5. Click **Change All** to change all instances of the missing font to the font you have identified ....`ALT` + `A`
6. Click **Done**................`ALT` + `D`

EXERCISE DIRECTIONS

✓ *Display the Typography workspace.*

1. Start InDesign and open the 🔘 84Argentina file. Save it as **84Argentina_xx**.
2. Select the text in the top text box on the first page (white background area) and change its font to Papyrus.

   ✓ *If you do not have the Papyrus font, use some other decorative font.*

3. Change the top two lines of text (*Doing Business in Argentina*) to **36** pt. Change the last line of text in the top text box (*An Etiquette Guide*) to **18** pt.

4. Click in the main body of the story, select all the text (Ctrl + A), and change the font to Adobe Garamond Pro.

   ✓ *If you do not have Adobe Garamond Pro installed, you can install Garamond Premier Pro from the Creative Suite Content DVD. Note that in the font list, font names are alphabetized ignoring the word Adobe, so Adobe Garamond Pro is located in the "G's".*

5. In the body of the article (on all pages), change all the headings to **14** pt.
6. Apply the red color swatch to each heading.
7. Save your changes, close the file, and exit InDesign.

ON YOUR OWN

1. Start InDesign and open 💿OYO84. If the Missing Fonts dialog box opens, take the following steps:

   a. Click Find Font to open the Find Font dialog box.

   b. Click Arial Narrow in the Fonts in Document list. Replace this font with the Arial family and the Narrow font style, clicking Change All to change all instances.

   > ✓ If you have a font named Arial Narrow in your font list, use it. If you do not have the Narrow font style, use Regular.

   c. Click Arial Narrow Bold in the Fonts in Document list. Replace this font with the Arial font family and the Narrow Bold font style (or Bold, if you do not have Narrow Bold as an option) and change all instances.

   d. Click Done.

2. Save the document as OIN84_xx.

3. Format the word *July* at the top of the page as Arial 80-pt bold, and apply the red swatch to it.

4. Format the word *events* at the top of the page as Arial 36-pt bold and apply the same red swatch to it.

5. For each listed event, format its title as Arial, 12-point, bold, and use the dark green swatch (**C = 82, M = 47, Y = 95, K = 59**). Your page should look similar to Illustration A.

6. Save your changes, close the file, and exit InDesign.

Illustration A

WMFS "Girls' Night Out" Concert
Popular country male music stars will croon to a crowd of women in an event sponsored by WMFS and starring Jeff Bates and Billy Dean.

Where: Indiana State Fairgrounds
When: June 25, 4 p.m. preparty, 7 p.m. concert
Cost: $20 track, free grandstand
Information: (317) 555-9550

Symphony on the Prairie: An American Salute
The 24th season of this series features the Indianapolis Symphony Orchestra playing to a crowd of picnickers relaxing under the stars.

Where: Conner Prairie
When: July 1 – 4, 8 p.m.
Cost: $25, $10 children 2 – 12
Information: (800) 555-8457

Indiana Black Expo Summer Celebration
The 35th annual Black Expo event is a weeklong celebration of music, exhibits and culture.

Where: Indiana Convention Center and RCA Dome
When: July 7 – 17
Cost: Call for details
Information: (317) 555-2702

Exhibit: Altered Spaces
Experience artists' interpretation of interior and exterior design in mediums that renegotiate physical space.

Where: Indianapolis Museum of Contemporary Art
When: Through July 9; Thurs. – Sat. 11 a.m. – 6 p.m.
Cost: Free
Information: (317) 555-6622

Exhibit: Whispers to Shouts
View two galleries of historical art, all created by women of Indiana including photos, paintings and sculptures.

Where: Indiana State Museum
When: Through July 10; Mon. – Sat. 9 a.m. – 5 p.m.
Cost: $7 adults, $6.50 seniors, $4 children 3 – 12
Information: (317) 555-2321

Concert: Hall & Oates
The popular 1980s pop duo will reunite for a lively outdoor concert.

Where: The Lawn at White River State Park
When: July 12, 7:30 p.m.
Cost: $34.50
Information: (800) 555-9065

Summer Fest at the Zoo
This all-day event will include educational and entertaining activities for the whole family, including performances by McGruff the Crime Dog and Smokey the Bear.

Where: Indianapolis Zoo
When: July 12, 10 a.m. – 8:30 p.m.
Cost: Free with admission
Information: (800) 555-2551

RCA Championships
Cheer on some of the top stars ini tennis when players like Andy Roddick and Taylor Dent come to town. Free parking is available on the IUPUI campus.

Where: Indianapolis Tennis Center
When: July 16 – 24, noon – 10 p.m.
Cost: $8 and up
Information: (800) 555-5682

Broad Ripple Blues Fest
Bring your blanket or lawn chairs and enjoy blues and food at this family-friendly event featuring both traditional and contemporary blues performers

Where: Broad Ripple Park
When: July 30, 3 – 10 p.m.
Cost: $12
Information: (800) 555-2782

Exercise | 85

Skills Covered

- **Adjust Text Scale**
- **Adjust Tracking**
- **Adjust Kerning**
- **Adjust Leading**

Software Skills Adjust text scale to change horizontal or vertical size of letters. Specify tracking to adjust space between all letters in a text frame. Kerning allows you to adjust space between pairs of letters. Change leading to increase or decrease space between lines of text.

Design Skills Almost any word processing program can display different fonts, sizes, and colors of text. InDesign stands out as a professional-quality design program in its ability to make subtle adjustments to text using text scale, tracking, kerning, and leading.

Application Skills In this exercise, you continue working on the Argentina article. You will adjust the scale, tracking, and kerning of the text in the article to make a more professional-looking layout.

TERMS

Baseline The imaginary horizontal line on which the bottoms of text characters sit.

Kerning The spacing between a specific pair of characters based on their shapes.

Leading The vertical spacing between the lines of a paragraph.

Metrics kerning Automatic kerning based on information built into the font being used.

Optical kerning Automatic kerning based on analysis of the shapes of the letters.

Tracking The spacing between characters (in general).

NOTES

Adjust Text Scale

- When you scale text, you adjust its width or height relative to its default width or height. The horizontal and vertical scale settings let you make text taller, shorter, wider, or narrower without changing the font or point size.
- Use the Horizontal Scale option **T** to increase the width of text without increasing its height, as shown in Figure 85-1.
- Use the Vertical Scale option **IT** to increase the height of text without increasing its width, as shown in Figure 85-1.

Figure 85-1. Horizontal and vertical scaling

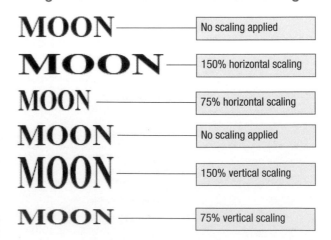

MOON	No scaling applied
MOON	150% horizontal scaling
MOON	75% horizontal scaling
MOON	No scaling applied
MOON	150% vertical scaling
MOON	75% vertical scaling

- The words used in Figure 85-1 are all in the same font size and style, but scaling gives the lower two entries in each group a radically different appearance. Note in the group at the top that despite the horizontal expansion or compression, the letters are all the same height. Likewise, in the group at the bottom, all of the letters are the same width despite their difference in height.

- To specify a horizontal or vertical scale value, select the text and then adjust the value in the Vertical Scale box or the Horizontal Scale box on the Control panel or Character panel. You can type a value, use the spin arrows, or select from the drop-down list of common scaling options.

Adjust Tracking

- **Tracking** is the spacing between all characters in a selection of text. Tracking is usually set for entire paragraphs or sometimes entire stories.

- Figure 85-2 shows three sample paragraphs. The first has default tracking. The second paragraph has tracking set to −50. The third sample has tracking set to +25. As you can see, tracking can make a great deal of difference in how text looks and fits in an area.

Figure 85-2. Tracking samples

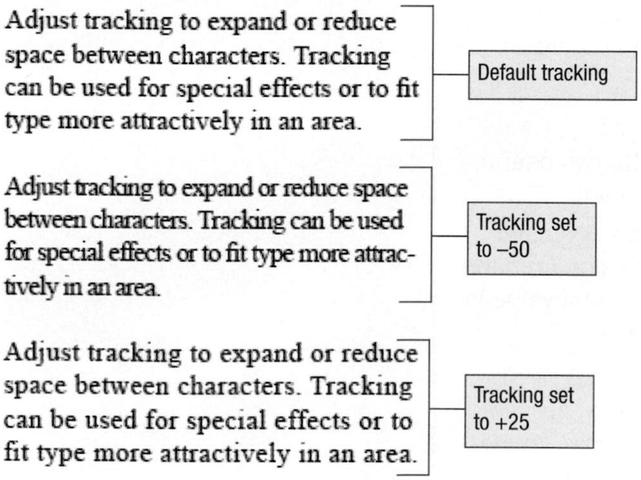

Adjust tracking to expand or reduce space between characters. Tracking can be used for special effects or to fit type more attractively in an area.

→ Default tracking

Adjust tracking to expand or reduce space between characters. Tracking can be used for special effects or to fit type more attractively in an area.

→ Tracking set to −50

Adjust tracking to expand or reduce space between characters. Tracking can be used for special effects or to fit type more attractively in an area.

→ Tracking set to +25

- Tracking is measured in thousandths of an em (an em is defined as a measurement that is the same as the current point size). Therefore, its actual value changes depending on the font size chosen. You do not need to change the tracking if you make a font size change, however, because the tracking will stay the same relative to the new font size.

- To adjust tracking, use the Tracking box [AV] on the Control or the Character panel. The default tracking is 0; you can adjust it up or down by entering a positive or negative value. You can also use the spin arrows or select from the drop-down list.

Adjust Kerning

- **Kerning** describes the process of adding or removing space between specific pairs of letters to make them fit together more attractively. Kerning is measured in thousandths of an em (like tracking).

- Kerning is not set for a character, but for a space between two characters. Figure 85-3 shows three kerning samples. The first pair of letters displays the default kerning value for this pair, −128. The second pair of letters has no kerning applied (the value is 0). The third pair of letters has a kerning value of −240.

Figure 85-3. Kerning samples

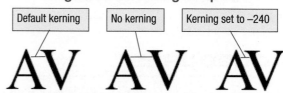

Default kerning   No kerning   Kerning set to −240

- To set specific kerning for a pair of letters, click between them and then adjust the kerning using the Kerning box [AV] on the Control or the Character panel. You can enter an exact value, use the spin arrows, or select from the drop-down list.

- Fortunately, you do not have to set the kerning for every pair of letters individually; InDesign kerns automatically, using one of two preset schemes: Metrics or Optical. **Metrics kerning** uses kerning information built into the font for certain letter pairs. **Optical kerning** calculates the appropriate kerning to use based on the shapes of the letters.

  ✓ *Many people prefer optical kerning, as it works better with fonts that do not have much kerning data provided in them.*

- Metrics kerning is the default setting. To change text to optical kerning, select all the text you want to change and then choose Optical from the Kerning drop-down list on the Control or Character panel.

Adjust Leading

- **Leading** (pronounced "ledding") is the spacing between lines within a paragraph. It does not include the spacing above or below the paragraph. Leading is measured from the **baseline** of one line to the baseline of the line below.

- You adjust leading to improve readability and appearance of type on a page. The tighter the leading, the denser the text appears and the harder it is to read, as shown in Figure 85-4 on the next page.

Figure 85-4. Leading samples for 18-point type

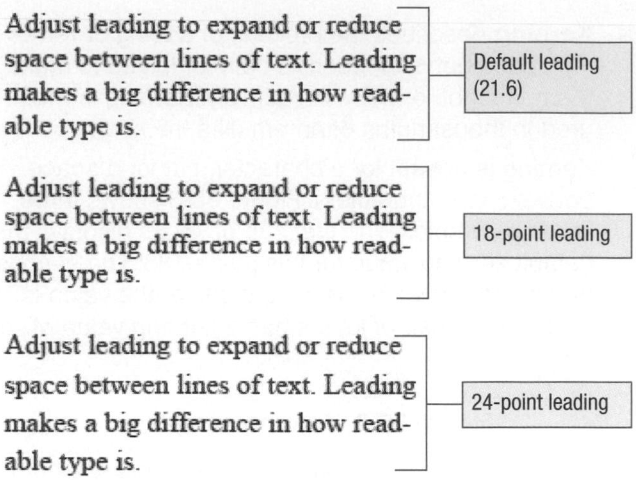

Adjust leading to expand or reduce space between lines of text. Leading makes a big difference in how readable type is.

Default leading (21.6)

Adjust leading to expand or reduce space between lines of text. Leading makes a big difference in how readable type is.

18-point leading

Adjust leading to expand or reduce space between lines of text. Leading makes a big difference in how readable type is.

24-point leading

- The first sample in Figure 85-4 shows a paragraph of 18-point type set with default leading of 21.6 points. In the second paragraph, the leading has been set to 18 points, the same size as the text (called "setting solid"). In the third paragraph, the leading has been set to 24 points.

- By default, leading is set to 120% of the font size. For example, for 30-point text, the leading is set to 36 points by default. When the measurement in the Leading box appears in parentheses, it means that it represents the default value and has not been manually changed.

- To change the leading, use the Leading box on the Control or Character panel.

PROCEDURES

All of the procedures below can be carried out on the Control panel with Character Formatting Controls active, or on the Character panel.

Adjust Horizontal Text Scale

1. Select the text to affect.
2. Click the **Horizontal Scale** spin arrows, select a percentage from the **Horizontal Scale** list, or type a percentage value in the **Horizontal Scale** box.

Adjust Vertical Text Scale

1. Select the text to affect.
2. Click the **Vertical Scale** spin arrows, select a percentage from the **Vertical Scale** list, or type a percentage value in the **Vertical Scale** box.

Adjust Tracking

1. Select the text to affect.
2. Click the **Tracking** spin arrows, select a value from the **Tracking** list, or type a value in the **Tracking** box.

   ✓ *Tracking is measured in thousandths of an em space, so it is relative to the font size chosen.*

Adjust Kerning

1. Click between the two characters you want to kern.
2. Click the **Kerning** spin arrows, select a value from the **Kerning** list, or type a value in the **Kerning** box.

   ✓ *A negative value moves the characters closer together; a positive value moves them apart. Choose Metrics or Optical to allow InDesign to handle the kerning automatically.*

Adjust Leading

1. Select the paragraph(s) to affect.
2. Click the **Leading** spin arrows, select a value from the **Leading** list, or type a value in the **Leading** box.

EXERCISE DIRECTIONS

1. Start InDesign and open 📇 84Argentina_xx, or open 💿 85Argentina. Save the document as 85Argentina_xx.

2. Set the Horizontal Scale for the text *Doing Business in Argentina* to **107%**.

3. Set the Vertical Scale for the text *An Etiquette Guide* to **115%**.

4. Click between the *D* and the *o* in *Doing* and change kerning to **−50**.

5. Change the leading for the text *Doing Business in Argentina* to **48** pt.

6. Notice that you have only a small amount of text left on the last page of the document. This is a perfect opportunity to use tracking to condense the text so that the last line will come back to page 3.

   a. Select the entire bulleted list in the third column on page 3 and set tracking to **−10**.

   b. Select the paragraph above the *Business Meals and Entertaining* heading in the first column on page 3 and set tracking to **−10**. The text on page 4 should now fit on page 3 with room to spare.

   c. Delete page 4.

7. Save your changes, close the file, and exit InDesign.

ON YOUR OWN

1. Start InDesign and open 📇 OIN84_xx, or open 💿 OYO85. Save the file as OIN85_xx.

2. Set the vertical scale for the words *July* and *events* to **125%**.

3. Notice that the second event title in the first column is so long that it almost runs into the next column. Change the tracking for this heading to **−10**, so that it fits better in its place.

4. Adjust the tracking for all the other event titles to the same amount, so they will match in appearance.

5. In the word *events*, increase the kerning between the *t* and the *s* to **25**.

6. Change the leading of all of the *Where, When, Cost, Information* lines to **16** pt to make these lines more readable for all events.

7. Save your changes, close the document, and exit InDesign.

Exercise | 86

Skills Covered

- **Additional Character Formats**
- **Use Baseline Shift**
- **Insert Special Characters**
- **Use the Glyphs Panel**
- **Use OpenType Features**

Software Skills   Use formats such as Small Caps to give text a more polished look. Superscripts and subscripts allow you to work with technical type such as equations and formulas. InDesign's extensive list of special characters makes it easy to insert a wide variety of symbols. Glyphs and other OpenType features add visual flourishes to type.

Design Skills   A designer should know not only how to present type clearly and readably in a design but also how to add professional touches such as proper punctuation symbols. The exciting typographic features available in OpenType fonts can turn a good design into a great one.

Application Skills   Castle Art has approached you to create a flyer that can be handed out to art students at the nearby university. In this exercise, you will apply a variety of character formats, insert special characters, and use glyphs and OpenType features to create a visually stimulating document.

TERMS

Glyph   A specific form of a particular character.

Ligatures   Typographic replacement characters for common letter pairs.

NOTES

Additional Character Formats

- A series of six buttons on the Character Formatting Control panel gives you access to additional character formats you can use for special effects. To apply any of these formats, type the text first, then select it and click the desired button. Clicking the button again will toggle off the format.

- Use All Caps [TT] to format text in all capital letters, LIKE THIS. The advantage to using this format rather than simply typing in all caps is that you can easily reverse the format by deselecting the All Caps attribute.

- Use Small Caps [Tt] to apply smaller capital letters to text that would ordinarily be lowercase, LIKE THIS. By default, small caps are 70% of the size of a regular capital letter.

  - ✓ *You can change the default size of small caps in the Advanced Type section of the Preferences dialog box.*

- Some OpenType fonts have their own special set of characters for small caps. InDesign will use these automatically whenever they are available. Depending on the font, they might be the same as or different from the regular caps in style.

- When you use the Small Caps button on the Control panel, any text that previously was uppercase stays uppercase and does not change to small caps. If you want all the text to change to small caps, regardless of its previous capitalization, open the Control panel menu and select OpenType > All Small Caps. This is available only for OpenType fonts.

- Use Superscript T^1 to set a number or letter above the baseline, as shown in Figure 86-1. Superscripts are commonly used for footnote numbers and exponents in mathematical or scientific type.

- Use Subscript T_1 to set a number or letter below the baseline, as shown in Figure 86-1. Subscripts are commonly used in chemical formulas.

Figure 86-1. Superscripts and subscripts

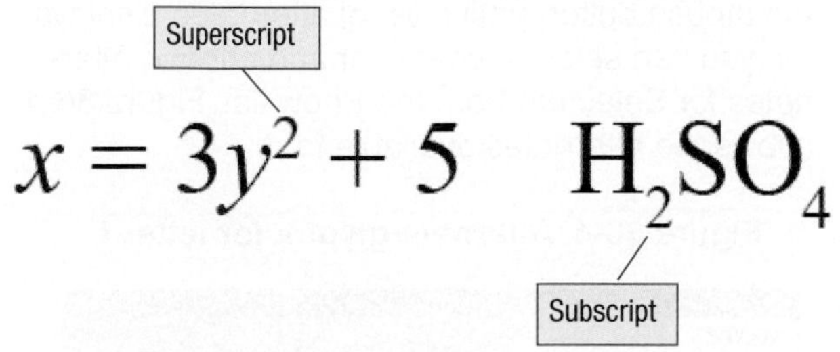

Superscript

$$x = 3y^2 + 5 \qquad H_2SO_4$$

Subscript

- Note that the superscript and subscript formats combine a reduction in font size with a baseline shift. Superscripts shift upward from the baseline, and subscripts shift downward.

  ✓ *You learn more about baseline shift in the next section.*

- Use Underline T to underscore text, like this. Underlining is no longer a popular typographical convention; however, you may still want to use this format for a special effect, or to format a Web or e-mail address.

- Use Strikethrough T to format text with a line through it, ~~like this~~. This format is even less commonly used than underline, but it can have special uses to indicate text that has been deleted or changed.

  ✓ *InDesign lets you customize both underline and strike-through options. With text selected, click the appropriate option on the Control panel menu.*

Use Baseline Shift

- You can apply a positive or negative baseline shift to move characters above or below the baseline, as shown in Figure 86-2.

Figure 86-2. Baseline shift applied to shift text up or down

Baseline text shifted up 8 points
Baseline text shifted down 8 points

- You might use a baseline shift to position a symbol for a footnote in a case where you do not want the size of the symbol to be reduced (as it would be with superscript), or to precisely align some text with a nearby graphic.

- To shift the baseline, select the text and then use the Baseline Shift box A^a on the Control or Character panel. You can increment the value or type a value manually. The shift is measured in points. A positive number shifts text up; a negative number shifts text down.

Insert Special Characters

- InDesign offers you several ways to insert characters that are not found on a standard keyboard. You have already located some of these special characters, when inserting page number markers.

- The Type > Insert Special Character submenu lists five submenus of special character categories: Symbols, Markers, Hyphens and Dashes, Quotation Marks, and Other.

  - The Symbols menu offers standard symbols such as ©, ®, ™, and §.

  - The Markers menu allows you to quickly insert markers for the current page, next page, or previous page; for a section; or a footnote number.

  - The Hyphens and Dashes menu lets you insert em dashes (—) and en dashes (–), discretionary hyphens, and nonbreaking hyphens.

  - Use the Quotation Marks menu to insert various types of quotation marks, such as double or single left quotation marks or straight quotation marks.

  - The Other menu gives you quick access to characters such as tabs and indents.

- You can also access some of these special characters using the Glyphs panel, covered in the next section.

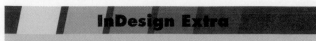

InDesign Extra

Insert White Space

The Insert White Space command on the Type menu gives you a quick way to insert many types of white space, or blank space, such as em and en spaces, nonbreaking spaces, and specialized white space sizes such as hair space used in technical typesetting.

Use the Glyphs Panel

- A **glyph** is a specific form of a particular character. For example, here are several glyphs of one character: A, a, A. The capital A, lowercase a, and small caps A are all ways to represent one character in type.

- The Glyphs panel, shown in Figure 86-3, shows all the glyphs available for a particular font. Use the Type > Glyphs command to display the Glyphs panel.

Figure 86-3. Glyphs panel

- Scroll down to see all the glyphs available for the current font. You can select a different font from the Font Family list at the bottom of the Glyphs panel.

- Insert a glyph into type by first positioning the insertion point at the desired location and then double-clicking the glyph on the panel.

- The number and types of glyphs available depend on the font. Not all glyphs are available in all fonts.

- To have access to the widest selection of glyphs, use an OpenType font with the Pro designation, such as Adobe Garamond Pro. The Design Creative Suite installs several Pro fonts along with the suite applications.

- You can click the Show list arrow in the Glyphs panel to see a list of categories such as Punctuation, Numbers, Currency, and Symbols that give you access to a wide variety of characters, no matter what type of font you are using.

- If you are using a Pro font, the Show list includes additional categories such as Small Capitals From Capitals, Oldstyle Figures, and Numerators and Denominators for constructing fractions.

- Some glyphs have interesting alternate forms that you can access by clicking a small triangle at the lower-right of a glyph's box and then holding down the mouse button until a list of alternates displays. Or, you can select a character and choose Alternates for Selection from the Show list. Figure 86-4 shows the alternates available for *t*.

Figure 86-4. Alternate glyphs for letter *t*

✓ *If you are not using a Pro type, your alternate selection is fairly limited.*

Use OpenType Features

- The Glyphs panel gives you access to a number of type features available only with OpenType Pro fonts. You can also apply many of these formats using the OpenType submenu on the Control or Character panel menu.

- Clicking OpenType on the panel menu displays a list of features that you can select or deselect to apply the features to selected text. Some of these options are described below and shown in Figure 86-5 on the next page.

- Standard **ligatures** are special characters that replace commonly used letter pairs such as *fi, ffi, ffl, Th,* and so on. Using ligatures gives text a more polished look.

- Discretionary ligatures are included in some fonts for letter pairs such as *st, ct, and fl* to provide visual interest.

- Swashes are flourishes added to some capital letters set in italics.

- Ordinals indicate an order and are usually created with a number and a superscript, such as 1st, 4th, and so on. To create an ordinal, you simply type the number and the relevant letters, such as 1 followed by st.

- Most fonts include a number of standard fractions as glyphs, but you can use the OpenType Fractions option to create any type of fraction instantly. Simply type the numerator, the /, and the denominator.

Figure 86-5. Some OpenType font attributes

Standard ligatures	difficult, final, These
Discretionary ligatures	stitch, action, fluid
Swashes	*After, Swan, Thread*
Ordinals	1st, 2nd, 3rd
Fractions	⅖, ⅝, 7/12

- OpenType offers several options for displaying figures—that is, numbers—in type. These options are described below and shown in Figure 86-6.

- Tabular numbers are all the same width. Use a tabular option if numbers need to line up vertically, as in a table.

- Proportional numbers vary in width; the number 1, for example, will not be the same width as a 5. Use a proportional option if numbers do not have to line up.

- Lining numbers are full-height figures that set on the regular text baseline.

- Oldstyle numbers are of varying heights, and some drop below the baseline.

Figure 86-6. OpenType figure options

Default	1 2 3 4 5 6 7
Tabular Lining	1 2 3 4 5 6 7
Proportional Lining	1 2 3 4 5 6 7
Proportional Oldstyle	1 2 3 4 5 6 7
Tabular Oldstyle	1 2 3 4 5 6 7

- To apply these OpenType font attributes, you can type the text first, select it, and then choose the desired OpenType attribute on the panel menu. After you select an attribute, it remains active until you turn it off, so additional text you type will use the attributes automatically.

- It must be stressed that not all OpenType attributes are available for every OpenType font.

- To determine what OpenType options can be applied, view the features by category using the Glyphs panel.

PROCEDURES

Apply All Caps (Ctrl + Shift + K)
1. Select the text to affect.
2. Click **All Caps** button `TT` on the Control panel.

Apply Small Caps (Ctrl + Shift + H)
1. Select the text to affect.
2. Click **Small Caps** button `Tr` on the Control panel.

Apply Superscript (Ctrl + Shift + =)
1. Select the text to affect.
2. Click **Superscript** button `T¹` on the Control panel.

Apply Subscript (Ctrl + Alt + Shift + =)
1. Select the text to affect.
2. Click the **Subscript** button `T₁` on the Control panel.

Apply Underline (Ctrl + Shift+ U)
1. Select the text to affect.
2. Click the **Underline** button `T` on the Control panel.

Apply Strikethrough
1. Select the text to affect.
2. Click the **Strikethrough** button `T̶` on the Control panel.

Apply Baseline Shift
1. Select the text to affect.
2. Click the **Baseline Shift** `A³↕` spin arrows, or type a value in the Baseline Shift box.

Insert Special Characters

1. Position the insertion point where the special character should appear.
2. Click **Type** .... ALT + T
3. Point to **Insert Special Character** .... S
4. Select a category of special characters:
   - **Symbols** .... S
   - **Markers** .... M
   - **Hyphens and Dashes** .... H
   - **Quotation Marks** .... Q
   - **Other** .... O
5. Select a special character or other option from the submenu.

Insert Glyphs (Alt + Shift + F11)

1. Position the insertion point where a glyph should appear.
2. Click **Type** .... ALT + T
3. Click **Glyphs** .... G
4. Scroll through glyphs to find desired glyph.

   OR

   Click **Show** list arrow and choose a category of glyphs to display.

   OR

   Click triangle at bottom of glyph box and hold down the mouse button to display alternates.

OR

- Click **Font** list arrow at bottom of panel to change the font.
- Click **Font Style** list arrow at bottom of panel to change the font style.

5. Double-click desired glyph to insert it in text.

Use OpenType Features

1. Select text to which you wish to apply OpenType attributes.
2. Click ▤ on Control panel or Character panel to display panel menu.
3. Point to **OpenType**.
4. Select desired attribute(s) from submenu.

   ✓ If an attribute is enclosed in brackets, it is not available for the current font or font style.

EXERCISE DIRECTIONS

✓ Display the Typography workspace.

1. Start InDesign and open ⊙ **86Castle**. Save the file as **86Castle_xx**.
2. Change the font style of the *Castle Art* title to italics and turn on the Swash OpenType attribute.
3. Change the font style of the *Serving Clifton . . .* subtitle to italics and turn on Swash and Proportional Oldstyle attributes.
4. Select the text in the frame that contains the store information and apply the Proportional Oldstyle attribute.
5. In the same text frame, replace three hyphens in the days and times information with en dashes, which are more appropriate for indicating ranges.

   ✓ Do not replace the hyphen in the phone number with a dash.

6. In traditional typography, a.m. and p.m. are set using small capitals. Apply Small Caps to the two a.m. and two p.m. instances in the same text frame.
7. Insert decorative glyphs between the street address and the city name and between the phone number and Web site address. (Display the Ornaments category in the Glyphs panel to find a suitable decoration.)

8. Insert the copyright symbol (©) between the words *Copyright* and *Castle* in the text frame below the illustration.
9. In the last sentence of the text below the *Outstanding Selection* heading, apply All Caps to the four paint supplier names (*Old Holland*, *Winsor & Newton*, etc.).
10. In the word *AEGYPTUS,* replace the letters *AE* with the *Æ* glyph. (You can find it by choosing the Entire Font category on the Show list and then scrolling down.)
11. In the last sentence of the paragraph below the *Knowledgeable Staff* heading, replace the hyphen between the words *item* and *no* with an em dash.
12. Locate the fraction 1/3 in the last paragraph, select the fraction, and turn on the OpenType Fractions attribute to convert the numbers to a proper fraction.
13. In the same paragraph, locate 1st, select the characters, and turn on the OpenType Ordinal attribute to create a proper ordinal. Your document should look like Illustration A.
14. Save your changes, close the file, and exit InDesign.

Illustration A

Castle Art

Serving Clifton for 27 Years

1096 Ludlow Avenue ✏ Clifton, OH 45220
(513) 555-2787 ✏ www.castleart.com
Monday – Saturday
9:00 A.M. – 9:00 P.M.
Sunday
11:00 A.M. – 5:00 P.M.

Copyright © Castle Art Inc. All rights reserved.

Welcome to Castle Art!
Never been to Castle Art? Castle Art is a full-service art store conveniently located in the historic village of Clifton, near Richmond Technical College, Clifton State University, and Mount St. Mary College. We cater to the needs of students, professional artists from the community, and dedicated amateurs alike.

Outstanding Selection
Need supplies or equipment? You'll find everything you need for your art project here. We carry a wide selection of supplies, including . . .

drawing pencils, charcoal, and pastels
acrylics, oils, and watercolors
brushes and palette knives
canvas, paper for all media, and framing materials

. . . and many more items. We are an authorized dealer for OLD HOLLAND, WINSOR & NEWTON, LIQUITEX, and ÆGYPTUS colors.

Knowledgeable Staff
Just starting out in art? Our friendly staff members can offer expert advice on what supplies you need. If you are a more experienced artist, we can help you realize your potential with the best-quality materials in the area. If you don't find what you need here, a staff member will be glad to order any item—no extra charge for special orders!

Classes
Always wanted to draw or paint? Castle Art is the place to start. We offer classes at beginner, intermediate, and advanced levels in drawing, oil painting, watercolor painting, acrylic painting, and pencil and pastel technique. Classes change quarterly. Save ⅓ on class materials purchased in the 1ˢᵗ week of any class. Stop by for a current class schedule.

ON YOUR OWN

1. Start InDesign and open ⊙OYO86. Save the document as OIN86_xx.

2. Click anywhere in the menu text and then click Ctrl + A to select all text. Turn on the following OpenType attributes: Discretionary Ligatures and Swash.

3. Locate the two fractions in the menu (one under *New York Strip Steak* and the other under *Fresh Lobster*) and apply the OpenType Fractions attribute to convert them to typographic fractions. (Remove the extra space between the *1* and the ½ in the Lobster fraction.)

4. The menu looks a bit fussy with all those extra flourishes. Select text again and turn off the Swash attribute.

5. Locate an elegant-looking decorative glyph and insert one at the beginning and end of each section heading (*Appetizers, Salads,* and so on).

6. Save your changes, close the document, and exit InDesign.

Skills Covered

- **Work with Paragraph Tools**
- **Change Paragraph Alignment**
- **Apply Paragraph Indents**
- **Add Space Before and After Paragraphs**
- **Change Vertical Alignment**

Software Skills Change horizontal and vertical alignment to adjust the position of text in a frame. Use indents to add white space to left or right of text or to set the first line of a paragraph over to make it easy to distinguish where paragraphs start. Add space before or after paragraphs to improve readability or adjust the position of text.

Design Skills Paragraph controls such as alignment, indents, and spacing can improve the appearance of text and make it easier to read. Use the Paragraph Formatting controls to make adjustments to paragraph-level formatting.

Application Skills In this exercise, you continue working with the Mark Twain article you began earlier in this lesson. You will apply several different alignments and indents and adjust space after paragraphs to make the text easier to read.

TERMS

Justified   Aligned at both the left and the right.

NOTES

Work with Paragraph Tools

- Tools for working with paragraph formatting display on the Control panel and in the Paragraph panel. Display paragraph formats by clicking the Paragraph Formatting Controls button ¶ when the Type tool is active.

- These tools allow you to apply a variety of formats to paragraphs. This exercise covers horizontal and vertical alignment, indents, and space before and after each paragraph. You learn about additional paragraph formatting in the next exercise.

- Note that many of the paragraph formatting icons on the Control panel look similar. To make sure you are applying the format you want, hover the mouse pointer over the option's icon to see its name.

Change Paragraph Alignment

- The term *paragraph alignment* refers to horizontal alignment—the positioning between the left and right sides of the text frame.

  ✓ *Text in a frame can also be vertically aligned—top, middle, or bottom—but not on an individual paragraph basis. You'll learn how to set vertical alignment later in this exercise.*

- Alignment options display on the Control panel for both character formats and paragraph formats.

- InDesign offers standard alignments you might be familiar with from word processing: Align left ▤, Align center ▦, and Align right ▤.

- You can also choose from three different **justified** alignments:

  • Justify with last line aligned left ▤ aligns text at both left and right, with the last line (usually a line that does not stretch the full width of the frame) aligned to the left.

- Justify with last line aligned center ▤ aligns text at both sides and centers the last line.

- Justify all lines ▤ aligns all text at the left and right, inserting space so that every line ends at the right side of the text frame.

  ✓ *You can specify how much spacing is inserted to justify lines by changing justification limits. Click Justification on the Paragraph panel menu to adjust these settings.*

- You can also choose Align towards spine ▤| and Align away from spine |▤ to set an alignment relative to the spine (center) of the document. When you use one of these alignments, the alignment will stay the same if you move a text frame from a verso to a recto page.

  ✓ *All of these alignment buttons are also available on the Paragraph panel.*

- To set a paragraph alignment, you simply click anywhere in the paragraph to align and then click the button for the desired alignment. You don't need to select a paragraph to apply a paragraph format, unless you want to apply the format to several paragraphs at once.

Apply Paragraph Indents

- The indent settings control how the paragraph is positioned in relation to the left and right edges of the text frame. An indent of 0 places the text flush against the edge of the text frame.

- You can choose from four types of indents in InDesign, each of which has its own box on the Control panel.

  - Use the Left Indent box →▤ to insert a space between the left edge of the text and the frame.

  - Use the First Line Left Indent box ⁺▤ to insert a space in the first line only between text and the left frame border. This option is frequently used at the beginning of paragraphs.

  - Use the Right Indent box ▤← to insert a space between the right edge of the text and the right frame border. This option is most effective if text is justified.

  - Use the Last Line Right Indent box ▤₊ to insert a space between the last line and the right frame border. This option is most useful for right-aligned text.

- To set any of these indents, type a value in the box or use the spin arrows to adjust the indent. The indent can be either positive (to the right) or negative (to the left, or reverse indent).

Add Space Before and After Paragraphs

- Spacing before or after paragraphs creates visual separation between paragraphs, which makes them easier to read.

  ✓ *If space is limited, consider using a first-line indent for each paragraph instead of space between them.*

- To set spacing before or after a paragraph, change the value in the Space Before ⁺▤ or Space After ▤₊ box.

Change Vertical Alignment

- Vertical alignment applies to the entire text frame. By default, the text vertically aligns at the top of the text frame, but you can specify that text align vertically in the center of the frame or at the bottom of the frame, as shown in Figure 87-1.

Figure 87-1. Text aligned at the top, center, and bottom of frames

"To me, the most important feature of my life is its literary feature."

"To me, the most important feature of my life is its literary feature."

"To me, the most important feature of my life is its literary feature."

- To change the vertical alignment of a frame, use the Selection tool to select the outside of the frame. The Control panel changes to show the object formatting tools, including vertical alignment buttons. Click the button for the desired vertical alignment: Align top ▤, Align center ▤, or Align bottom ▤.

  ✓ *Another vertical alignment option, Justify Vertically, is useful when text almost fills the column completely. It can be used for minor adjustments, but should not be used to correct for a shortfall of more than one line.*

- The vertical alignment tools may not be visible if your monitor is not large enough to display all Control panel tools. If you do not see vertical alignment options on the Control panel, you can use the Object > Text Frame Options command to display the Text Frame Options dialog box, shown in Figure 87-2 on the next page.

441

Figure 87-2. Text Frame Options dialog box

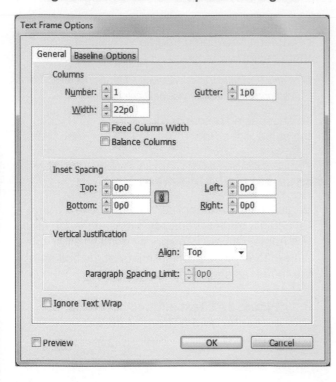

- You can use this dialog box not only to change vertical alignment, but also to adjust the number of columns in a frame. You can also specify inset spacing to add space to the top, bottom, left, or right of text in a text frame.
- Changing inset spacing can be a more subtle way of adjusting the position of text in a text frame than simply changing vertical or horizontal alignment.

PROCEDURES

Display the Paragraph Tools

- Click the **Paragraph Formatting Controls** button ¶.

Change Paragraph Alignment

1. Select the paragraph(s) to affect.
2. If needed, display the **Paragraph** tools on the Control panel.
3. Click a paragraph alignment button:
   - **Align left** ▤
   - **Align center** ▤
   - **Align right** ▤
   - **Justify with last line aligned left** ▤
   - **Justify with last line aligned center** ▤
   - **Justify all lines** ▤
   - **Align towards spine** ▤
   - **Align away from spine** ▤

Indent Paragraphs

1. Select the paragraph(s) to affect.
2. If needed, display the **Paragraph** tools on the Control panel.
3. Type or increment the value for the desired indent type.
   - **Left Indent** ▤
   - **First Line Left Indent** ▤
   - **Right Indent** ▤
   - **Last Line Right Indent** ▤

Change Spacing Before or After Paragraphs

1. Select the paragraph(s) to affect.
2. If needed, display the **Paragraph** tools on the Control panel.
3. Click in the **Space Before** box ▤ and type a precise value, or use the spin arrows to set a value.

OR

Click in the **Space After** box ▤ and type a precise value, or use the spin arrows to set a value.

Change the Vertical Alignment

1. Use the **Selection** tool to click the outer edge of the text frame to affect.
2. Click one of the **Vertical Alignment** buttons on the Control panel:
   - **Align top** ▤
   - **Align Center** ▤
   - **Align bottom** ▤

OR

1. Use the **Selection** tool to click the outer edge of the text frame to affect.
2. Click **Object** .... ALT + O
3. Click **Text Frame Options** X
4. Select an alignment from the **Align** list .... ALT + A , ↓
5. Click **OK** .... ENTER

EXERCISE DIRECTIONS

✓ *Display the Typography workspace.*

1. Start InDesign and open ◎ 87Twain. Save the file as 87Twain_xx.

2. Change the vertical alignment in the title text frame to center.

3. Set the remainder of the document to Justify with last line aligned left.

4. Format the section numbers (I, II, and III) with dark green (**C = 75**, **M = 5**, **Y = 100**, **K = 50**, and create a swatch for later use) and 18-pt bold. Center each section number.

5. Indent the first line of each paragraph by **2p0** *except* the section numbers (I, II, and III) and *except* the first paragraph underneath each of those section numbers.

6. Use Find/Change to remove the extra paragraph space between paragraphs. (*Hint:* Find ^p^p and change to ^p.) Then select the entire story and insert **0p6** points of space after each paragraph.

7. In the pull quote text frame on page 3, do the following:

   a. Set right and left indents to **0p3**.

   b. Change vertical and horizontal alignment to center.

   c. Fill the text frame with the green swatch you created in step 4, and set the text color to Paper (white).

8. Display the masters. Add and format page numbers as follows:

   a. On the recto page, draw a text frame the full width of the right column and move it to sit on the bottom margin guide. Adjust its height to **2p0**.

   b. Fill the text frame with the dark green swatch you created, and insert a current page code in the text frame that aligns toward the spine.

   c. Center the page marker vertically, change the font size to **14**, the font style to **Bold**, and the font color to **Paper**.

   d. Indent the page marker **0p3** from the left edge of the frame.

   e. Copy the text frame, paste it, and move it to the left column of the verso page. Remove the left indent and insert a right indent of **0p3** between the page marker and the right edge of the text frame.

9. Preview the document. Your page 3 should look similar to Illustration A.

10. Save your changes, close the file, and exit InDesign.

wonders, a romantic land where all the birds and flowers and animals were of the museum varieties, and where the alligator and the crocodile and the monkey seemed as much at home as if they were in the Zoo. Also, he told an astonishing tale about COCA, a vegetable product of miraculous powers, asserting that it was so nourishing and so strength-giving that the native of the mountains of the Madeira region would tramp up hill and down all day on a pinch of powdered coca and require no other sustenance.

I was fired with a longing to ascend the Amazon. Also with a longing to open up a trade in coca with all the world. During months I dreamed that dream, and tried to contrive ways to get to Para and spring that splendid enterprise upon an unsuspecting planet. But all in vain. A person may PLAN as much as he wants to, but nothing of consequence is likely to come of it until the magician CIRCUMSTANCE steps in and takes the matter off his hands. At last Circumstance came to my help. It was in this way. Circumstance, to help or hurt another man, made him lose a fifty-dollar bill in the street; and to help or hurt me, made me find it. I advertised the find, and left for the Amazon the same day. This was another turning-point, another link.

Could Circumstance have ordered another dweller in that town to go to the Amazon and open up a world-trade in coca on a fifty-dollar basis and been obeyed? No, I was the only one. There were other fools there—shoals and shoals of them—but they were not of my kind. I was the only one of my kind.

Circumstance is powerful, but it cannot work alone; it has to have a partner. Its partner is man's TEMPERAMENT—his natural disposition. His temperament is not his invention, it is BORN in him, and he has no authority over it, neither is he responsible for its acts. He cannot change it, nothing can change it, nothing can modify it—except temporarily. But it won't stay modified. It is permanent, like the color of the man's eyes and the shape of his ears. Blue eyes are gray in certain unusual lights; but they resume their

> "To me, the most important feature of my life is its literary feature."

natural color when that stress is removed.

A Circumstance that will coerce one man will have no effect upon a man of a different temperament. If Circumstance had thrown the bank-note in Caesar's way, his temperament would not have made him start for the Amazon. His temperament would have compelled him to do something with the money, but not that. It might have made him advertise the note—and WAIT. We can't tell. Also, it might have made him go to New York and buy into the Government, with results that would leave Tweed nothing to learn when it came his turn.

Very well, Circumstance furnished the capital, and my temperament told me what to do with it. Sometimes a temperament is an ass. When that is the case of the owner of it is an ass, too, and is going to remain one. Training, experience, association, can temporarily so polish him, improve him, exalt him that people will think he is a mule, but they will be mistaken. Artificially he IS a mule, for the time being, but at bottom he is an ass yet, and will remain one.

By temperament I was the kind of person that DOES things. Does them, and reflects afterward. So I started for the Amazon without reflecting and without asking any questions. That was more than fifty years ago. In all that time my temperament has not changed, by even a shade. I have been punished many and many a time, and bitterly, for doing things and reflecting afterward, but these tortures have been of no value to me; I still do the thing commanded by Circumstance and Temperament, and reflect afterward. Always violently. When I am reflecting, on these occasions, even deaf persons can hear me think.

I went by the way of Cincinnati, and down the Ohio and Mississippi. My idea was to take ship, at New Orleans, for Para. In New Orleans I inquired, and found there was no ship leaving for Para. Also, that there never had BEEN one leaving for Para. I reflected. A policeman came and asked me what I was doing, and I told him. He made me move on, and said if he caught me reflecting in the public street again he would run

3

ON YOUR OWN

1. Start InDesign and open ⊙OYO87. Save the document as OIN87_xx. You can fine-tune this document from earlier exercises by adjusting alignment, indents, and spacing.

2. Delete the extra paragraph space above the article title (*Doing Business in Argentina*). Vertically center the title text.

3. Indent all three lines **0p6** from the left edge of the text frame.

4. Select the text story and set Space Before and Space After to **0p0** to remove all space above and below paragraphs and headings.

5. Set the space before each red heading to **1p0**.

6. For every text paragraph that does not immediately follow a heading or a bullet, set a first-line left indent of **2p0**.

7. Select the entries in each bulleted list. Change the first line indent to **−1p0** and the left indent to **1p0**.

8. For the paragraphs that immediately precede a bulleted list item, change Space After to **0p6**. For the last bulleted item in the third column, change Space after to **1p0**.

9. Save your changes, close the document, and exit InDesign.

Exercise | 88

Skills Covered

- Create a Drop Cap
- Apply Paragraph Rules
- Create Bulleted and Numbered Lists
- Control Text with Tab Stops

Software Skills Options such as drop caps, paragraph rules, and bullets and numbering provide useful and interesting formats for paragraphs. Use tab stops to align text so the content is easy to read and understand.

Design Skills A designer can create more visual interest in a document using features such as drop caps and paragraph rules. Bulleted or numbered text and text organized using tab stops can create a more orderly design.

Application Skills The Youth Center of Central Michigan has asked you to work on a glossy handout the Center is preparing to send to its Millennium Fund supporters. In this exercise, you will create a drop cap, apply bulleted and numbered formats, insert a paragraph rule, and use tab stops to create a simple table.

TERMS

Drop cap A large capital letter that begins a paragraph, usually spanning multiple lines into the paragraph.

NOTES

Create a Drop Cap

- A **drop cap** is a capital letter at the beginning of the first word of a paragraph that drops below the baseline to create an attractive visual element, as shown in Figure 88-1.

Figure 88-1. A drop cap begins a paragraph

Foreign businesspeople must carefully balance the modernized business environment of Argentina with the cultural traditions of its inhabitants. Despite their sophistication and high-tech business

- InDesign automates the process of creating a drop cap with two boxes on the Control panel when paragraph formatting tools are active.
- To create a drop cap for a paragraph, place the insertion point in the paragraph and then use the Drop Cap Number of Lines box to specify how many lines down the cap will drop. (The drop for the cap in Figure 88-1 is 3.)
- A drop cap is usually a single character, but you can use the Drop Cap One or More Characters box to specify more than one character to drop. This allows you, for example, to drop an entire word, or drop a quotation mark along with the first letter of a paragraph.

Apply Paragraph Rules

- Paragraph rules are not policies related to paragraphs. Rules in this context mean horizontal lines above or below paragraph text. Figure 88-2 shows a paragraph rule above a heading. The rule helps to identify a section as well as adds visual interest to the text.

Figure 88-2. A paragraph rule above a heading

Business Attire

The general standard of dress among Argentines is high, and they are more likely to prefer the subtle, rich, understated style of London to the trendier style of Milan. If you are uncertain, it is best to err on the side of the conservative, the formal, and the elegant. Both

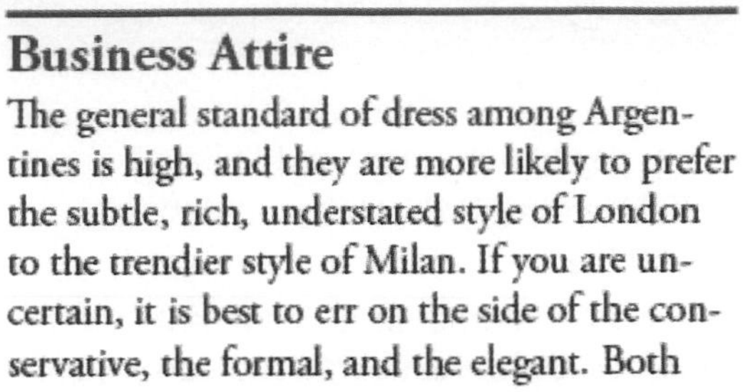

- Although it is possible to create a line like this using the Line tool, it is far safer and easier to do so using the Paragraph Rules option. The rule above this heading will stay with the heading if the text has to be moved from one location in the document to another.

- To create a paragraph rule, position the insertion point in the paragraph that should have a rule above or below it, then click Paragraph Rules on the Control or Paragraph panel menu. The Paragraph Rules dialog box opens, as shown in Figure 88-3.

Figure 88-3. Paragraph Rules dialog box

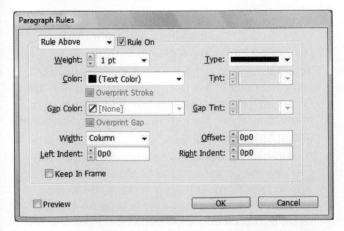

- First choose whether the rule will appear above or below the current paragraph, and then select Rule On. You can then choose a weight, type, color or tint, and even a gap color.

- You can choose whether the rule extends for the entire column width or only the width of the text in the paragraph. By default, the rule displays at the baseline of the paragraph. Use the Offset setting to adjust the distance between the baseline and the rule. You can also specify a left or right indent for the rule.

Create Bulleted and Numbered Lists

- A bulleted list begins each item with a symbol and is used for items that do not have to be in order. A numbered list begins each item with a consecutive number and is used for items that must be in a specific order.

- Turn on bulleted formatting by clicking the Bulleted List button on the Control panel. Turn on numbered formatting by clicking the Numbered List button. You can turn on the format and then type the entries, or select text and then apply the format.

- Hold down the Alt key as you click the Bulleted List or Numbered List button to open a dialog box that gives you additional bullet options and number formats. Or, with the insertion point in a bulleted or numbered item, choose Bullets and Numbering on the Control panel menu to display a dialog box with additional bullet or number formats.

  ✓ *You can customize a bulleted list using characters from any font.*

Control Text with Tab Stops

- A tab stop is an indicator that marks where text will align when you press the Tab key. InDesign's default tab stops are pre-set every half inch (even if you are not using inches as your unit of measurement).

- To set custom tab stops, choose Type > Tabs. A floating Tabs panel displays above the text frame. The Tabs panel contains a ruler that is the same length as the text frame. You use this ruler to place and remove custom tab stops.

- InDesign offers the same types of tab stops you find in a word processing program:

  - The Left-Justified tab stop aligns text at the left at the tab position.
  - The Center-Justified tab centers text at the tab position.
  - The Right-Justified tab aligns text at the right at the tab position.
  - The Align to Decimal tab aligns the decimal point in a number at the tab position.

    ✓ *You can specify another character besides a decimal point for this tab stop type in the Align On box on the Tabs panel.*

- To create a tab stop, click the button for the type of stop you want, and then click in the empty area above the ruler in the Tabs panel. A symbol appears there indicating the stop, as shown in Figure 88-4.

Figure 88-4. Set tab stops on the ruler

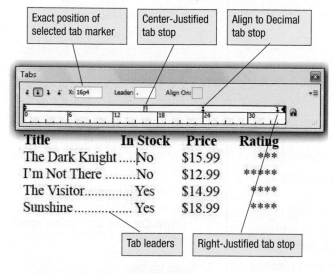

- To create tab leaders, such as the dots shown in Figure 88-4, simply select the tab to which the leaders will "lead" and then insert the character you want to use as the leader (usually a period) in the Leader box on the Tabs panel.

- To position a tab stop precisely, select the tab stop button (by clicking on it on the Tabs panel) and then enter a number in the X text box in the Tabs panel.

- To clear a tab stop, drag it off the Tabs panel ruler. You can clear all custom tab stops at once by opening the Tabs panel menu and selecting Clear All.

- Tab stops are set on a paragraph basis. To set the tab stops for more than one paragraph at once, you must select all the paragraphs to affect.

PROCEDURES

Create a Drop Cap

1. Click in the paragraph that should begin with the drop cap.

2. If necessary, click ¶ to display the paragraph formatting controls on the Control panel.

3. Click in the **Drop Cap Number of Lines** box 📑 and type the number of lines the capital letter should drop, or click the spin arrows to set a value.

4. (Optional) Click in the **Drop Cap One or More Characters** box 📑 and type the number of characters that will drop, or click the spin arrows to set a value.

Apply Paragraph Rules

1. Click in the paragraph to which you want to apply the rule.

2. Click ▾≣ on the Control panel or Paragraph panel to display the panel menu.

3. Click **Paragraph Rules**.

4. Select **Rule Above** or **Rule Below**.

5. Click **Rule On** to turn on rule formatting..................ALT + U

6. Select the desired **Weight**, **Type**, and **Color** for the rule.

7. Click **Width** and select either Column or Text...........ALT + D

8. Click **Offset** and type a value to set the rule above or below the baseline...............ALT + O

9. (Optional) Click **Left Indent** and type a value to indent from the left.....ALT + L

   OR

   Click **Right Indent** and type a value to indent from the right ....ALT + H

Create a Default Bulleted List

1. Select the paragraph(s) to affect.

2. If necessary, click ¶ to display the paragraph formatting controls on the Control panel.

3. Click the **Bulleted List** button :≣.

   ✓ You may also select the Bulleted List button and then type the bulleted text.

To customize a bulleted list:

1. Select the paragraph(s) to affect.

2. Hold down `ALT` and click the **Bulleted List** button ▤.

   OR

   a. Open the Control panel menu.

   b. Click **Bullets and Numbering**.

3. Click the desired bullet character.

   OR

   Select a different bullet character as directed below in *To add a bullet character*.

4. (Optional) Click **Alignment** and select **Left**, **Center**, or **Right** .... `ALT` + `G`

5. (Optional) Click **Left Indent** and type a new value for the indent, or use spin arrows to set the value .... `ALT` + `I`

6. (Optional) Click **First Line Indent** and type a new value for the first-line indent, or use spin arrows to set the value .... `ALT` + `R`

7. (Optional) Click **Tab Position** and type a new value for the tab position, or use spin arrows to set the value .... `ALT` + `B`

8. Click **OK** .... `ENTER`

To add a bullet character:

In the Bullets and Numbering dialog box, with List Type set to Bullets:

1. Click **Add** .... `ALT` + `A`

2. Select a **Font Family** .... `ALT` + `F` , `↑`/`↓`

3. Select a **Font Style** .... `ALT` + `Y` , `↓`

4. Click the desired character.

5. Click **Add** .... `ALT` + `A`

6. Click **OK** .... `ENTER`

7. Click **OK** .... `ENTER`

Create a Default Numbered List

1. Select the paragraph(s) to affect.

2. If necessary, click ¶ to display the paragraph formatting controls on the Control panel.

3. Click the **Numbered List** button ▤.

   ✓ *You may also select the Numbered List button and then type the numbered text.*

Place and Remove Tab Stops

To place a tab stop:

1. Select the paragraph(s) to affect.

2. Click **Type** .... `ALT` + `T`

3. Click **Tabs** .... `A`

4. On the Tabs panel, click the button for the desired tab stop type:

   ■ **Left-Justified** ↓
   ■ **Center-Justified** ↓
   ■ **Right-Justified** ↓
   ■ **Align to Decimal** ↓

5. Click in the white bar above the ruler in the Tabs panel to place the tab stop.

6. (Optional) If desired, type an exact position in the **X** box.

7. (Optional) Type a character in the **Leader** box to create a leader and press `ENTER` to apply the leader.

8. (Optional) If a decimal tab, replace the decimal (.) in the **Align On** box with some other character.

To move a tab stop:

1. Click in the paragraph (or select paragraphs) to affect.

2. With the Tabs panel displayed, click on the tab marker to move and drag it to its new position.

   OR

   a. Click the tab stop marker.

   b. Type an exact position in the **X** box.

To delete a tab stop:

1. Select the paragraph(s) to affect.

2. With the Tabs panel displayed, click on the tab marker to delete and drag it off the Tabs panel.

EXERCISE DIRECTIONS

1. Start InDesign and open ⊙ **88Campaign**. Save the file as **88Campaign_xx**.

2. Create a drop cap in the first paragraph that drops two lines. Then select the drop cap and apply the bold font style to the letter.

3. Convert the list of phases (*First phase, Second phase*, etc.) to a numbered list. Click at the end of the last numbered item, press Enter, and type the last entry: **Final phase: Evaluation**.

4. Convert the list of repairs (*Roof repair, Furnace replacement*, etc.) to a bulleted list that uses a right-pointing arrow symbol from the Wingdings font family, and has a custom tab position of 1p6.

5. Click in the paragraph (*Date, Event,* etc.) that will form the column headings for a simple table and set left tabs at the following locations: **8p0**, **19p0**, **33p0**, and **38p0**.

6. Select the remaining four paragraphs in the document and set the following tab stops: left tab stops at **8p0** and **19p0**; a right tab stop at **36p0**; and a decimal tab stop at **39p0**.

7. Click in the column heading paragraph again and apply a paragraph rule below the paragraph, using a weight of 2 points, red color, and 0p6 offset. Set the width to Text. The text portion of your document should look similar to Illustration A.

8. Save your changes, close the file, and exit InDesign.

Illustration A

THE MILLENNIUM FUND
CAPITAL CAMPAIGN REPORT

Thank you for being part of the Millennium Fund Capital Campaign for the Youth Center of Central Michigan! By investing in the upkeep of our facility, you are helping ensure that future generations of youth will continue to benefit from Center programs.

The Campaign process consists of these phases:

1. First phase: Fund-raising
2. Second phase: Planning
3. Third phase: Bids
4. Fourth phase: Contractor selection
5. Current phase: Repairs
6. Final phase: Evaluation

Thanks to your generous donations, the renovation process will include these repairs:

→ Roof repair
→ Furnace replacement
→ Masonry repair
→ Interior painting

Contractors will begin working according to the following schedule.

Date	Event	Contractor	Cost	Days
August 1	Roof repairs	Gonzalez Construction	$20,000	4.0
August 15	Furnace replacement	Bolls Heating and Cooling	$15,000	1.5
August 20	Masonry repairs	Gonzalez Construction	$10,000	5.0
September 16	Interior painting	Louks Interiors, Inc.	$8,000	6.5

ON YOUR OWN

1. Start InDesign and open ⊚OYO88. Save the document as OIN88_xx.

2. Create paragraph rules below each of the blue headings, using the same blue color for the rules. (You will find the colors used in this document in the Swatches panel.)

3. In the *Fire Extinguisher Guidelines* section, make the first three items into a bulleted list. Adjust the left indent and tab position as desired to accommodate the bullet character you choose.

4. Create a separate bulleted list from the last three lines in this section that is subordinate to (indented more than) the bullet point above it. Use a different bullet character.

5. In the *Emergency Exit Guidelines* section, format the three items with the same bullet formats you used for the first three lines in the previous section.

6. In the *Evacuation Procedures* section, create a numbered list from the first three lines.

7. For the last five lines in the *Evacuation Procedures* section, create tab stops as desired to organize the information. Insert leaders from the Section entries to the Captain entries, and from the Captain entries to the Phone entries.

8. For the two sets of procedures in the *First Aid Procedures* section, create numbered lists.

9. Save your changes, close the document, and exit InDesign.

Skills Covered

- ■ Work with Multiple Columns in a Frame
- ■ Control Paragraph Breaks

- ■ Control Hyphenation
- ■ Work with Conditional Text
- ■ Use Smart Text Reflow

Software Skills   Set multiple columns in a text frame to make it easier to control column text. InDesign CS5 lets you choose to span paragraphs across multiple columns. Applying paragraph break and hyphenation options can improve the layout of a story, making it easier to read and more professional-looking. Use conditional text to customize a document for more than one purpose. Smart Text Reflow allows you to insert text that will automatically reflow as you make adjustments to content.

Design Skills   Creating an attractive layout is not merely a matter of placing text and formatting it. A designer must also consider how type is composed in the current layout and be ready to adjust columns, hyphenation, and paragraph breaks to achieve a professional result.

Application Skills   In this exercise, you will work on a brochure for Crystal Bay Resort. Crystal Bay has a fall brochure that they want to convert to a multipurpose brochure they can send out at different times of the year. You will use conditional text to create a customizable brochure. You will also convert a single-column text frame into two columns, turn on hyphenation, and adjust paragraph breaks to avoid widows and orphans.

TERMS

Composition   The process by which InDesign determines how to set lines of type on a page for the best appearance.

Conditional text   Text that can be displayed or hidden to create a version of a story.

Orphan   The first line of a paragraph appearing by itself at the bottom of a page.

Widow   The last line of a paragraph appearing by itself at the top of a page.

NOTES

Work with Multiple Columns in a Frame

- ■ So far in this course, whenever you needed multiple columns on a page, you created text frames separately for each column and then threaded them together. This method has some drawbacks. For example, when you want to change the size of the text boxes, you must resize each one individually.

- ■ For multiple columns on the same page, many people prefer instead to set up a single text frame that has multiple columns within it. The frame can then be moved or resized as a single unit, with the columns always staying together.

- ■ To convert a text frame to multicolumn layout, use the Text Frame Options dialog box (Object > Text Frame Options) to specify the desired number of columns for the current text frame. You can also specify the desired column and gutter widths. Or, you can use the Number of Columns box ▦ on the Control panel to specify columns.

- ■ Select the Balance Columns check box in the Text Frame Options dialog box to make sure text in multiple columns aligns at the bottom. You can also insert column breaks to balance column text.

- Use the Insert > Break Character submenu to insert a column break. You can also use this submenu to insert frame breaks and page breaks of various types.

- In InDesign CS5, you can specify that a paragraph span multiple columns in a text frame. This new feature allows you to create *straddle heads* that display above multiple columns of text.

- Figure 89-1 shows a text frame divided into three columns with a heading displaying in the first column. In previous versions of InDesign, the only way to make this heading display across all columns was to set it in a separate text frame. This option could make editing clumsy, as both the text and heading frames would have to be moved if a document needed to be repaged.

Figure 89-1. A heading displaying in one column of a text frame

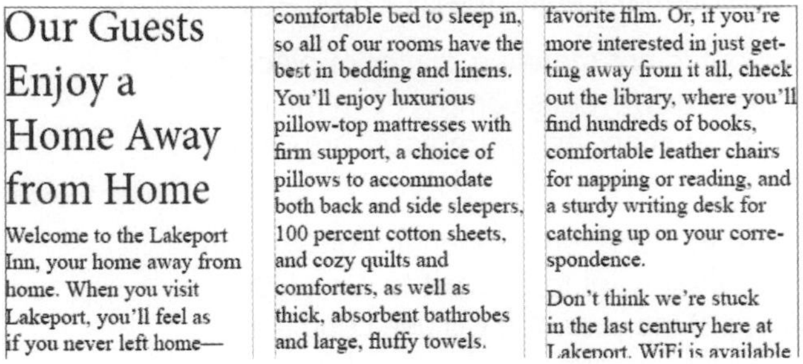

Our Guests Enjoy a Home Away from Home

Welcome to the Lakeport Inn, your home away from home. When you visit Lakeport, you'll feel as if you never left home—

comfortable bed to sleep in, so all of our rooms have the best in bedding and linens. You'll enjoy luxurious pillow-top mattresses with firm support, a choice of pillows to accommodate both back and side sleepers, 100 percent cotton sheets, and cozy quilts and comforters, as well as thick, absorbent bathrobes and large, fluffy towels.

favorite film. Or, if you're more interested in just getting away from it all, check out the library, where you'll find hundreds of books, comfortable leather chairs for napping or reading, and a sturdy writing desk for catching up on your correspondence.

Don't think we're stuck in the last century here at Lakeport. WiFi is available

- In InDesign CS5, all you need to do to solve this problem is to select a span option from the Span Columns ☰ list on the Control panel. You can choose to span all columns or only selected columns, with a maximum of four columns. The result of setting the heading to span all columns in shown in Figure 89-2.

Figure 89-2. Heading now spans all columns

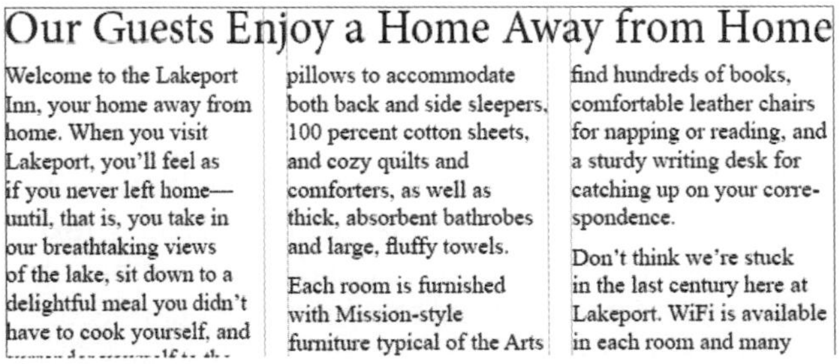

Our Guests Enjoy a Home Away from Home

Welcome to the Lakeport Inn, your home away from home. When you visit Lakeport, you'll feel as if you never left home— until, that is, you take in our breathtaking views of the lake, sit down to a delightful meal you didn't have to cook yourself, and

pillows to accommodate both back and side sleepers, 100 percent cotton sheets, and cozy quilts and comforters, as well as thick, absorbent bathrobes and large, fluffy towels.

Each room is furnished with Mission-style furniture typical of the Arts

find hundreds of books, comfortable leather chairs for napping or reading, and a sturdy writing desk for catching up on your correspondence.

Don't think we're stuck in the last century here at Lakeport. WiFi is available in each room and many

- You can also use the Span Columns list to split any paragraph in a text frame. Click in the paragraph and choose from Split 2, Split 3, or Split 4 to break the paragraph into columns.

Control Paragraph Breaks

- Sometimes when text flows from one frame to another, paragraphs break in awkward ways. Either the first line is left by itself at the bottom of a page (an **orphan**), or the last line carries over by itself to the top of a page (a **widow**).

- Traditional rules of page layout require at least two lines of a paragraph to appear at the bottom or top of a page. Likewise, a heading should never sit by itself at the bottom of a page but should be accompanied by at least two lines of the paragraph following the heading.

- You can adjust paragraph breaks in several ways. You can adjust spacing above and below headings by equal amounts, for example, or add or reduce space around graphics. This kind of copy-fitting can be time-consuming and can lead to further efforts if text is added to or deleted from a story.

- A more automated way to control paragraph breaks is to use options to keep lines together. Select a paragraph or an entire story and then choose Keep Options on the Control or Paragraph panel menu to open the Keep Options dialog box, shown in Figure 89-3.

Figure 89-3. Keep Options dialog box

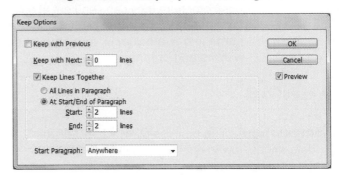

- Use Keep with Previous to keep the current paragraph with the previous one.

- Use the Keep with Next option to specify a number of lines to keep with the currently selected paragraph. This is a good option to apply to headings to make sure they will always be accompanied by at least two additional lines of text.

- To control paragraph breaks throughout a story, select Keep Lines Together and then specify the number of lines that should stay together at the start and end of a paragraph.

- You can also choose to keep all lines of a paragraph together, not allowing it to break at all.

- The Start Paragraph list can be set to In Next Column, In Next Frame, or any of several other options to force the paragraph to start in a certain place.

Control Hyphenation

■ When hyphenation is on, InDesign hyphenates your stories automatically wherever possible, subject to certain rules. Hyphenation makes for more attractive lines of text when horizontal justification is in use, and it enables you to fit more text on the page.

■ To turn hyphenation on or off, click in the story or select the paragraphs to be affected and select or deselect the Hyphenate check box in the Control panel.

■ You can fine-tune hyphenation by clicking Hyphenation on the Control or Paragraph panel menu. In the Hyphenation Settings dialog box, shown in Figure 89-4 at the bottom of the page, select options to adjust how InDesign hyphenates words.

■ The Better Spacing/Fewer Hyphens slider in the dialog box controls how aggressively InDesign will search for places to apply hyphenation. When trying to fit as much text on the page as possible, set it toward Better Spacing. When trying to avoid hyphenation or trying to spread text out as much as possible, set the slider toward Fewer Hyphens.

■ Hyphenation can be affected by the method of composition being used. **Composition** refers to the process InDesign uses to determine how to set lines of type on a page. InDesign evaluates spacing of words, letters, and glyphs as well as hyphenation and justification options that have been set and breaks lines in the way that best takes all these settings into account.

■ By default, InDesign uses the Adobe Paragraph Composer, which evaluates break points for an entire paragraph. This composition method allows InDesign to adjust some lines earlier in a paragraph to avoid bad breaks later in the same paragraph.

■ You can change the composition method if desired to Adobe Single-line Composer. This traditional approach to composition solves the problems of line breaks one line at a time, according to a set of rules that control when to expand or compress text and when to hyphenate it.

Work with Conditional Text

■ **Conditional text** allows you to create more than one version of a document by displaying or hiding text that meets specific conditions. For example, you could create a training manual that covers more than one version of a software application and print one document with text relating to one version and another document that contains only references to the other version.

■ Use the Conditional Text panel, shown in Figure 89-5, to create and manage conditions. Figure 89-5 shows two conditions, one for a fictional software application named DocuPro 8 and another for DocuPro 10.

Figure 89-5. Conditional Text panel

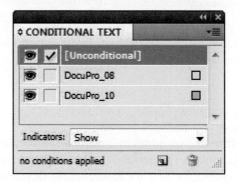

Figure 89-4. Hyphenation Settings dialog box

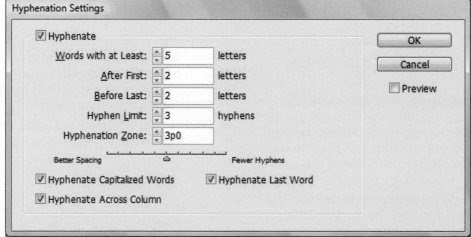

- To create a condition, click the New Condition button 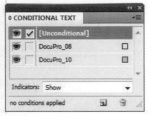 on the Conditional Text panel and then supply a name for the condition. You can also choose how the condition will display on text, such as with a wavy underline or a highlight, and you can choose the color for that display.

- After you have established the conditions, you apply them to text to create the desired versions.

- When creating text that you will use as conditional text, type all the text that will be used for all conditions, which may initially look confusing.

- Then, select the text that will belong to each version and click a condition in the Conditional Text panel to mark the text for that condition.

- Figure 89-6 shows a paragraph of text marked for the two versions of DocuPro. The text highlighted in yellow relates only to DocuPro 8; the text highlighted in teal relates only to DocuPro 10.

Figure 89-6. Conditional text example

- Once you have applied the conditional marking to the text, you can use the visibility eyes in the Conditional Text panel to display the text relating to a condition. Figure 89-7 shows how the paragraph looks if you want to show only DocuPro 8 information.

Figure 89-7. One condition is shown

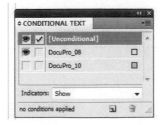

- Note that the visibility eye for DocuPro_10 is turned off so only DocuPro_08 and unconditional text (text to which no condition is applied) display. Use the Indicators list in the Conditional Text panel to show the conditional text marking, show it as well as print it, or hide it.

- Proof carefully when creating conditional text. It is all too easy to forget to apply the conditional formatting to punctuation marks or spaces.

Use Smart Text Reflow

- You may understand by now that editing text in an InDesign document can result in changes in how type fills text frames. When you add new text or delete existing text, text in the current story *reflows*.

- Reflow can have some negative consequences. If you delete text, for example, you may be left with an unnecessary blank page. If you add text, you may end up with overset text that does not get placed.

- You can resolve some of the potential problems that accompany text reflow by linking frames so that overset text always has a frame to flow into and by manually deleting blank pages as necessary.

- InDesign also gives you the option of using the Smart Text Reflow feature to help you control how text flows in a document.

- When you use Smart Text Reflow, you can type in a text frame just as you would in a word processing document. As you fill a frame, text automatically flows into the next frame or to the next page. You can specify that any blank pages created while you edit are removed automatically.

- Smart Text Reflow requires some initial decisions and setup to work correctly. By default, the feature requires you to create and thread on master pages the text frames you want to use. Once you have set up the master page frames, display your first document page, use Shift + Ctrl + click to display the text frame, and you're ready to start adding text.

- You use the Edit > Preferences > Type command to display the Preferences dialog box where you can adjust the default Smart Text Reflow settings, shown in Figure 89-8.

Figure 89-8. Preferences for Smart Text Reflow

- Note that you can choose where to add pages as your text flows past the current frame. By default, new pages are added at the end of the current story, but you can also choose to add pages at the end of a section or the document.

- You can deselect Limit to Master Text Frames if you want to use Smart Text Reflow with frames you create on regular document pages. For the feature to work correctly, you must link the current frame to at least one other frame on a different page.

- Select Delete Empty Pages if you want InDesign to automatically remove pages that become blank as a result of reflow.

PROCEDURES

Use Multiple Columns in a Text Frame

1. Select the text frame in which you will change the number of columns.
2. Click the **Number of Columns** box ▥ on Control panel and type a new value, or use spin arrows to set a new value.

   ✓ *This box does not display on the Control panel in all workspaces.*

   OR

1. Select the text frame in which you will change the number of columns.
2. Click **Object** .... `ALT` + `O`
3. Click **Text Frame Options** ... `X`
4. Click **Number** and set value to 2 or more .... `ALT` + `U`
5. (Optional) Click **Gutter** and specify a new gutter value .... `ALT` + `G`
6. Click **OK** .... `ENTER`

Insert Column Break *(Num enter)*

1. Position insertion point where column of text should break.
2. Click **Type** .... `ALT` + `T`
3. Point to **Insert Break Character** .... `K`
4. Click **Column Break** .... `C`

Use the Span Columns Options

1. Click in the paragraph you want to span multiple columns.
2. Click **Span Columns** ▤ list arrow.
3. Select the number of columns to span, or **Span All** to span all columns.

To split any column in a text frame:

1. Click in the paragraph you want to split.
2. Click **Span Columns** ▤ list arrow.
3. Select the number of columns to split the paragraph into.

Control Paragraph Breaks

1. Select paragraph(s) to affect.
2. Click ▤ to open the Control or Paragraph panel menu.
3. Click **Keep Options**.

4. Click **Keep with Previous** .... `ALT` + `V`

   OR

   Click in **Keep with Next** box and specify number of lines to keep with current paragraph(s) .... `ALT` + `K`

   OR

   a. Click **Keep Lines Together** .... `ALT` + `L`
   b. Click **At Start/End of Paragraph** .... `ALT` + `T`
   c. If desired, change the **Start** number of lines ..... `ALT` + `S`
   d. If desired, change the **End** number of lines ..... `ALT` + `E`

   OR

   a. Click **Keep Lines Together** .... `ALT` + `L`
   b. Click **All Lines in Paragraph** .... `ALT` + `A`
5. Click **OK** .... `ENTER`

Turn Hyphenation On or Off

1. Select paragraph(s) to affect.
2. On the Control panel, click the **Hyphenate** check box to select or deselect it.

   OR

1. Select paragraph(s) to affect.
2. Click ▤ to open the Control or Paragraph panel menu.
3. Click **Hyphenation**.
4. Select the **Hyphenate** check box .... `ALT` + `H`
5. Adjust hyphenation settings as desired.
6. Click **OK** .... `ENTER`

Work with Conditional Text

To create a condition:

1. Click **Window** .... `ALT` + `W`
2. Point to **Type & Tables** .... `Y`
3. Click **Conditional Text** .... `O`
4. Click **New Condition** button ▣.

   OR

   a. Click ▤ to open the panel menu.
   b. Click **New Condition**.
5. Type a name for the condition.
6. (Optional) Click **Method** and select Highlight .... `ALT` + `M` , `↓`

7. (Optional) Click **Appearance** and select a different line appearance .... `ALT` + `A` , `↓`
8. (Optional) Click **Color** and select a different color ... `ALT` + `C` , `↓`
9. Click **OK** .... `ENTER`

To mark text with a condition:

1. Select text that will relate to a condition.
2. Click the condition name in the Conditional Text panel.

To show or hide conditional text:

- Click the visibility eye 👁 for the conditional text you want to show or hide.

To adjust the display of conditional text:

1. Click the **Show** list arrow on the Conditional Text panel.
2. Select an option:
   - **Show**
   - **Show and Print**
   - **Hide**

Set a Document for Smart Text Reflow

1. In a document you want to use Smart Text Reflow in, display master pages.
2. Create the necessary text frames and thread them.
3. Select the document page and `SHIFT` + `CTRL` + click to override the master and open the text frame to enter text.

   OR

1. Click **Edit** .... `ALT` + `E`
2. Point to **Preferences** .... `N`
3. Click **Type** .... `T`
4. Deselect **Limit to Master Text Frames** .... `ALT` + `L`
5. Click **OK** .... `T`
6. Set up frames in document, threading frames so that one frame threads to a document on a different page.

To automatically delete empty pages:

1. Click **Edit** .... `ALT` + `E`
2. Point to **Preferences** .... `N`
3. Click **Type** .... `T`
4. Select **Delete Empty Pages** .... `ALT` + `D`
5. Click **OK** .... `ENTER`

EXERCISE DIRECTIONS

1. Start InDesign and open ⊙89Crystal. Save the file as **89Crystal_xx**.

2. Click in the text in the left frame on page 1 and specify two columns in this text frame. Then set the heading to span both columns.

3. Drag the bottom center text frame handle upward until the columns balance.

4. Go to page 2 and prepare the text at the top of the page for conditional text formatting:
   a. Position the insertion point immediately after the word *raking* and type **late snow shoveling**
   b. Position the insertion point immediately before the word *early* and type **early garden chores**
   c. Position the insert point immediately after the word *fall* and type **spring**
   d. At this point, your text will be overset. Drag the text frame down until you can see all remaining text, position the insertion point immediately after *Fall* and type **Spring**

5. Display the Conditional Text panel. Create a new condition named **fall** and another new condition named **spring**. Select options as desired for method and colors.

6. Mark text for fall as follows: *leaf raking, early winter chores, fall, Fall*

7. Mark text for spring as follows: *late snow shoveling, early garden chores, spring, Spring*.

8. Hide the spring conditional text, then hide the fall text and show the spring text. Restore the text frame to its previous size.

9. The text in the three panels at the bottom half of the page has already been prepared for your fall and spring conditions. Display the fall conditional text and then mark the text in the story as follows:
   a. In the first paragraph, mark the word *early* for fall and the word *late* for spring. Include the space following each word. In the same sentence, mark *fall* and *spring* appropriately.
   b. In the center panel, mark for fall the entire sentence that begins *The Palmtree outdoor pool* as well as the space that follows the sentence.
   c. In the next sentence, mark for spring the phrase *or in colder weather*, as well as the space before the phrase.
   d. At this point, hide the fall conditional text, and then mark the last paragraph for spring.

10. Hide the spring text and show the fall text. Change the Show setting in the Conditional Text panel to Hide so you will not be distracted by the conditional text markings. Review the text in all frames to make sure you marked it correctly.

11. Note that there is an orphan at the bottom of the center panel when the fall text displays. Select the entire story and turn on the Keep option that specifies two lines at the beginning or end of a paragraph.

12. Now turn off the fall text and turn on the spring text and check it.

13. You may have noticed some unattractive spaces between words in the column text. Turn on hyphenation for the entire story. Your page should look similar to Illustration A.

Illustration A

Leave the late snow shoveling and early garden chores behind and find your place in the sun. Join us at Crystal Bay this spring at special Spring Festival rates.

If you're looking for a respite from the late winter blahs, join us at Crystal Bay Resort this spring—or any time of the year. Our accommodations are second to none in the Crystal region. Luxuriate in our well-appointed rooms, featuring spas, Egyptian cotton towels, complimentary continental breakfast, concierge service, data ports, and private verandas.

You'll find plenty to like at our two popular eating establishments. Enjoy a gorgeous view of the water at the Bayshore Café while you sample specialty sandwiches, chowders, and salads. For a more formal dining ex-perience, join us in the Crystal Cave. You'll find award-winning cuisine that celebrates local seafood and is-land fruits and vegetables.

Crystal Bay Resort offers a wide variety of recreation options for those who want to do more than eat and sleep on a vacation. On rainy days or in colder weather, hop into the Grot-to, an indoor pool with a difference. You might not get your kids out of it to enjoy the outdoors!

For more adventurous guests, Crystal offers boat rental (both sail and power), and we'll gladly arrange for fishing excursions in the Bay. Or, take a fishing trip or sightseeing tour out into the Gulf with a local guide.

If you prefer to stay on dry land, try our 9-hole golf course, get in some tennis, or rent a bicycle to tour the is-land. The Island Bikeway circles the island and links to shopping areas such as the Crystal Plaza and the Is-land Galleria.

St. Maria Key celebrates spring with Return of the Sun events that last from late February through April. Join us for the fun!

ON YOUR OWN

1. Start InDesign and open ⊙OYO89. Save the document as OIN89_xx.

2. Turn on hyphenation for the entire story. Use the default settings.

3. Turn on Smart Text Reflow, if necessary, in the Preferences Type dialog box, and clear the Limit to Master Text Frames check box. Make sure Delete Empty Pages is selected.

4. On page1, select the right text frame and delete it. A warning box will display to tell you InDesign is adding pages to prevent overset text. Click OK.

5. On page 1, drag a ruler guide down to align at the top of the characters in the first line of text in the left column (with the paragraph text, not the Roman numeral). Create a new text frame in the right column aligned with the new ruler guide at the top, the column guides at the sides, and about 20 picas deep.

6. Specify two columns in this text frame. Place the ⊙OYO89_text.doc file in the first column of the new text frame.

7. Position the insertion point at the beginning of the second paragraph of text you just placed and insert a column break. Set the *Editor's Note* paragraph to span columns and then center the heading.

8. Notice that the first line of a paragraph is sitting by itself at the bottom of the left column of text on page 1. Select the entire story and turn on the Keep option that keeps two lines together at both the start and end of paragraphs.

9. Select the Roman numeral II and apply the Keep with Next option, specifying 2 as the number. If the document is reformatted, this option will keep the proper number of lines together with the heading. Repeat the process with the Roman numeral III.

10. You have been asked to prepare an abridged version of the article that includes the entire first section and selected paragraphs and summaries of the other two sections. Use conditional text to prepare two versions of the article as follows:

    a. Create a condition named **abridged_summary**. Apply this condition to the summary paragraphs you will find below the first paragraph under section headings II and III. (The summary paragraphs are indented and italicized.)

    b. Create a condition named **abridged_show** and apply this condition to the fourth paragraph following the III heading, which begins *Circumstances do the planning for us all.*

    c. Create a condition named **abridged_hide**. Apply this condition in section II to all paragraphs that follow the summary paragraph, until you reach the section III heading. (Do not hide this heading or the paragraph that follows it.)

    d. In section III, hide the paragraph that follows the summary paragraph and all paragraphs that follow the one paragraph to which you applied abridged_show.

11. Now view your two editions to check your conditional text work:

    a. Hide the abridged_summary condition to see the complete article. It should run to the second column of page 5, and you should see no widows or orphans as you browse the pages.

    b. Now display the abridged version: turn on abridged_summary and make sure abridged_show is also visible. Hide abridged_hide. The article runs to the top of the left column of page 3, and InDesign has automatically deleted the now unnecessary pages 4 and 5.

12. Save your changes, close the file, and exit InDesign.

Exercise | 90

Skills Covered

- **Create Character Styles**
- **Create Paragraph Styles**
- **Nest Styles**
- **Clear Manual Overrides**

Software Skills   To quickly format a document's text, create and apply character and paragraph styles. You can also nest a character style within a paragraph style to quickly format parts of a paragraph with a different appearance. Changing one instance of an applied style creates a manual override that you can keep or remove by redefining the style.

Design Skills   A designer should be alert to features that improve appearance and speed the process of formatting. Character and paragraph styles make it easy to apply a whole range of character and paragraph formats consistently throughout a document.

Application Skills   You return to the Castle Art document to further improve the text appearance. In this exercise, you create both character and paragraph styles, nest one style within another, and clear manual overrides.

TERMS

Character style   A style that can be applied to individual characters of text.

Nested style   A character style that is applied as part of a paragraph style.

Override   Manual formatting applied to text or an object that is formatted with a certain style.

Paragraph style   A style that affects entire paragraphs at once.

NOTES

Create Character Styles

- You learned to create a style for objects in Exercise 77 in Lesson 8. You can also create styles for characters and paragraphs, as you learn in this exercise, and for tables and table cells, as you will learn in the next lesson.

- A **character style** is applied to individual characters and contains only character-based formatting, such as font family, font style, font color, font size, baseline shift, kerning, and so on.

- Create a character style using the Character Styles panel. The easiest way to create the style is to format characters as desired and then click the Create new style button 🔲 on the Character Styles panel to create a style with a default name.

    ✓ *You can also create styles in almost any dialog box in which you can select a style. You will create styles this way later in the course.*

- Or hold down Alt while clicking the Create new style button to open the New Character Style dialog box shown in Figure 90-1 at the top of the next page.

Figure 90-1. New Character Style dialog box

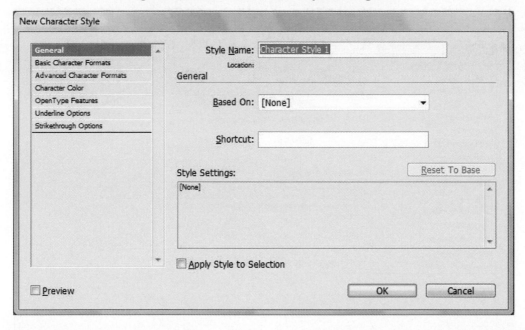

- You supply a name for the character style and use the categories at the left side of the dialog box to specify any additional character formats for the style.

- If you want to define the character style manually, click the Create new style button when no text is selected and then choose formats as desired from the New Character Style dialog box.

- Note that you can base a new style on an existing style by clicking the Based On list arrow and then selecting the existing style on which you wish to base the new style.

- To apply a character style, you must select the text you wish to format with the style and then click the style name in the Character Styles panel.

- You can also apply a character style from the Character Styles list on the Control panel when character formatting tools are active. Click the Character Styles box **A.** and select the desired style.

- You can redefine, or edit, a character style by double-clicking the style name to open the Character Style Options dialog box. Any change you make to the style formats is immediately applied to instances of the style throughout a document.

- If you have a number of styles in a document, you can organize them into style groups, similar to the way you organized color swatches into groups in Illustrator. Alt + click the Create new style group button in the Character Styles panel and give the group a name. You can then drag styles into the group. Use the style group's arrow to expand or close the group.

  ✓ *You can create style groups for either character or paragraph styles.*

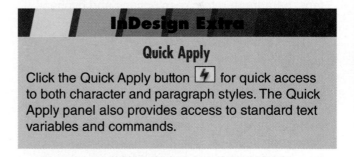

InDesign Extra

Quick Apply

Click the Quick Apply button for quick access to both character and paragraph styles. The Quick Apply panel also provides access to standard text variables and commands.

Create Paragraph Styles

- A **paragraph style** can be applied to individual paragraphs and can contain a mixture of character-based formatting and paragraph-based formatting (indents, line spacing, bullets, and so on).

- Create a paragraph style by example by clicking in a paragraph that has the desired paragraph styles or manually by specifying all formats directly in the New Paragraph Style dialog box, shown in Figure 90-2 at the top of the next page. You can open this dialog box by pressing Alt while you click the Create new style button.

Figure 90-2. New Paragraph Style dialog box

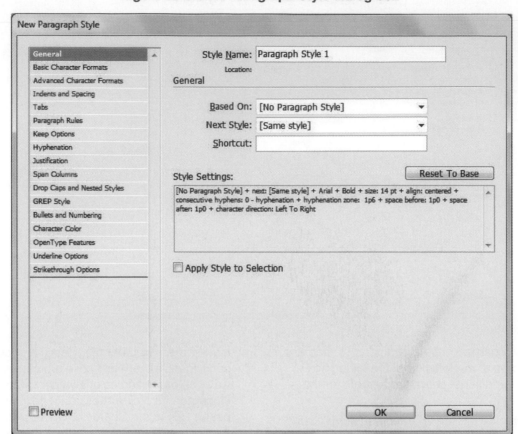

- Notice that the list of options you can choose for a paragraph style includes both character formats and the paragraph options you have learned about in the past several exercises: indents and spacing, tabs, paragraph rules, keep options and hyphenation, and so on.

- You can base the new style on an existing style by finding that style in the Based On list.

- If you intend to insert document text by typing it, you may find the Next Style option useful. You can choose the style that will format the next paragraph when you press Enter after finishing the current paragraph. For example, if you are defining a style for a heading, you can specify that the next style will be a body text style. When you finish typing a heading and press Enter, the body text style is automatically applied to the next paragraph.

- When defining a style, it might be helpful to begin by clicking Reset To Base, which strips off any formatting applied to any text that was selected when you opened the dialog box. Reset To Base will be dimmed if nothing was selected before opening the dialog box.

- To apply a paragraph style, click in the paragraph (or select multiple paragraphs) and then click the style name in the Paragraph Styles panel. You can also use the Paragraph Style box ¶ on the Control panel when Paragraph Formatting tools are active.

- You can redefine a paragraph style by double-clicking the style name to open the Paragraph Style Options dialog box.

Nest Styles

- InDesign allows you to create **nested styles**, in which a character style is applied as part of a paragraph style. This feature is commonly used with run-in heads at the beginnings of paragraphs, or to format a specified number of words or characters at the beginning of a paragraph.

- In Figure 90-3 on the next page, for example, a paragraph style controls the bold, italicized text of each list item. A nested character style applies the boldfaced green character formats to each list item's heading. When the paragraph format is applied, the character formats are automatically applied also—a speedy and efficient way to format both paragraphs and characters at the same time.

Figure 90-3. Nested style controls character formats

STAR ATTRACTIONS

Jungle Trails—*See a variety of primates in their natural habitats.*

Serengeti Plains—*See elephants, giraffes, zebra, rhinos, and elands.*

Eastern Woodlands—*See animals you might find in any eastern forest.*

■ You can also create nested line styles, in which a character style is applied to a specified number of lines in a paragraph.

■ In Figure 90-4, a nested line style applies green, bold character formatting to the first line of each paragraph.

Figure 90-4. Nested line style applies formatting to specific lines

DINING OPTIONS

Metro Restaurant—Full-service *dining with salads, entrees, and desserts.*

Badlands Deli—Counter service *offering sandwiches, fries, and ice cream.*

■ To create a nested style, you must first create a character style that contains the formatting you wish to apply along with the paragraph style.

■ You then click the Drop Caps and Nested Styles category in the New Paragraph Style (or Paragraph Style Options) dialog box to display the Nested Styles and Nested Line Styles options. If no nested styles have yet been created, you must click New Nested Style to display the options shown in Figure 90-5.

Figure 90-5. Create a nested style using these fields

■ The blue-highlighted information is actually a series of four fields in which you specify parameters for the nested style.

- Click *[None]* to reveal a list arrow you can use to display a list of character styles that might be used for the nested style.

- Click *through* to choose from the list whether the nested style formats will include the character that ends the style or be applied up to that character without including it.

- Click *1* to specify how many instances of the item in the last column will be included in the nested style. If you select 5 Words, for example, the selected character style will be applied to the first five words of the paragraph, regardless of what they are.

- Click *Words* to select from a list of items to which you can apply the character style, such as sentences, words, characters, letters, digits, and so on. You can also select a character such as a tab character or the End Nested Style character, which is a character you can insert specifically to provide an end to a nested style. You can also simply type a character in this field, such as a period or colon, or paste the desired character to end the nested style.

■ Use a similar procedure to specify a nested line style. Click New Line Style to make options available, then choose the desired character style and specify the number of lines to which it will be applied.

■ Figure 90-6 shows how the nested style is defined for the paragraph style used in Figure 90-3. The nested_intro character style is used to apply the character formatting, and the formatting is applied through the first em dash (—), so that the dash also receives the formatting.

Figure 90-6. Nested style definition

Nested Styles

nested_intro	through	1	—

New Nested Style   Delete

Clear Manual Overrides

- After you apply a style, you may find yourself changing formatting of the styled characters or paragraphs without actually editing the style. You may, for example, change the font size of text or a heading for a special effect.

- When you manually change formats for text that has a style applied to it, you **override** the style. The style name for that text displays a plus sign, as shown in Figure 90-7, to let you know the style has been changed in some way.

- To clear the overrides on a paragraph, click the Clear overrides in selection button 🔳 at the bottom of the style panel. Clicking this button restores the current selection to its styled formats.

    ✓ *You can hold down Ctrl to clear only the character overrides, or hold down Ctrl + Shift to clear only the paragraph-level overrides. Otherwise all overrides will be cleared.*

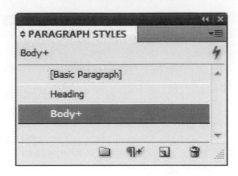

Figure 90-7. A plus sign next to a style name indicates overrides

- If you believe the override represents a better appearance for a style, open the style's options dialog box and change the style to match the override. The plus disappears and all other instances of the style are updated.

PROCEDURES

Create a Character Style

1. Format text as desired and then select it.

   OR

   To create style manually, make sure no text is selected.

2. Display the **Character Styles** panel .... SHIFT + F11
3. Hold down ALT and click the **Create new style** button 🔳.
4. Type a name for the style.
5. Make any other necessary adjustments to the style using the options in the New Character Style dialog box.
6. Click **OK** .... ENTER

To apply a character style:

1. Select text to which you want to apply the style.
2. Click on the desired style in the Character Styles panel.

   OR

   Click the **Character Style** box 🅰 on the Control panel when character formatting tools are active and select the desired style.

Create a Paragraph Style

1. Click in a paragraph of text that has the desired formats.

   OR

   To create style manually, make sure the insertion point is not in a paragraph.

2. Display the **Paragraph Styles** panel F11
3. Hold down ALT and click the **Create new style** button 🔳.
4. Type a name for the style.
5. Make any other necessary adjustments to the style using the options in the New Paragraph Style dialog box.
6. Click **OK** .... ENTER

To apply a paragraph style:

1. Click in paragraph to which you want to apply the style.
2. Click on the desired style in the Paragraph Styles panel.

   OR

   Click the **Paragraph Style** box 🔳 on the Control panel when paragraph formatting tools are active and select the desired style.

Create a Nested Style

1. Begin by creating a character style as directed above that will be nested in the paragraph style.
2. Create a new paragraph style, or open the Options dialog box for an existing paragraph style.
3. Click **Drop Caps and Nested Styles** category at left side of paragraph styles dialog box.
4. Click **New Nested Style** .... ALT + W
5. Click **[None]** to display list arrow, click arrow, and select character style from list.
6. (Optional) Click **through** to display list arrow, click arrow, and select **Up To** to indicate that nested style will not include final character.
7. (Optional) Click **1** and type a number other than one to indicate how many items to include in the nested style.
8. Click **Words** to display list arrow, click arrow, and select the desired item, character, or space option.

OR

Type or paste the ending character in this box.

9. Click **OK** to complete the paragraph style.

To create a nested line style:

1. Follow steps 1–3 above, then click **New Line Style**... ALT + I

2. Click **[None]** to display list arrow, click arrow, and select character style from list.

3. (Optional) Click **1** and type a number other than one to indicate how many lines to apply the nested style.

To apply a nested style:

■ Apply the paragraph style that includes the nested style definition. The nested style automatically applies the character style you have specified.

Create a Style Group

In either the Character Styles or Paragraph Styles panel:

1. ALT + click the **Create new style group** button ▢.

2. Type a name for the style group.

3. Click **OK** .... ENTER

4. Drag existing styles into the style group as desired, or select the style group name before creating a new style to store that style in the group automatically.

Clear Manual Overrides

1. Click style that has manual overrides applied (indicated by plus sign).

2. Click **Clear overrides in selection** button ¶✚ on styles panel to restore style formatting.

EXERCISE DIRECTIONS

✓ *Display the Typography workspace.*

1. Start InDesign and open ⊙ 90Castle. Save the file as *90Castle_xx.*

2. Click in the first heading of the main text frame (*Welcome to Castle Art!*) with the Type tool.

3. Create a new paragraph style named **Heading**. Apply the following formats to the style:

   ■ Font: Lithos Pro

     ✓ *If you don't have Lithos Pro available, use another sans serif font such as Arial.*

   ■ Font style: Black
   ■ Font size: 16 pt
   ■ Space before: 0p6
   ■ Space after: 0p3
   ■ Character color: Castle blue

4. Apply the **Heading** style to the *Welcome to Castle Art* heading, if necessary, and to the other three headings in the text frame (*Outstanding Selection, Knowledgeable Staff*, and *Classes*).

5. Create a character style that you will nest in another paragraph style:

   a. Click anywhere in the paragraph below the first heading.

   b. Create a new character style named **Emphasis**.

   c. Select Adobe Caslon Pro as the font family and change the font style to Bold Italic.

   d. Change the character color to Castle red.

6. With the insertion point still anywhere in the paragraph below the first heading, specify a new paragraph style as follows:

   a. Name the new style **Body**.

   b. Keep all of the current character formatting.

   c. Specify a 0p6 left indent.

   d. Clear the Hyphenate check box in the Hyphenation settings to turn off hyphenation.

7. Before closing the New Paragraph Style dialog box, create a nested style as follows:

   a. Select the Drop Caps and Nested Styles option, and choose to create a new nested style.

   b. Choose **Emphasis** from the list in the first field of the nested style definition.

   c. Click in the *Words* field and type a question mark (?). The nested style will apply to all words at the beginning of each Body paragraph, up to and including the question mark.

8. Apply the **Body** style to the paragraph under the first heading, if necessary, and notice how the nested **Emphasis** style applies to the characters at the beginning of the paragraph, through the question mark.

9. Apply the **Body** style to the first paragraph below the second heading, to the paragraph above the third heading, and to the remaining paragraphs below headings.

10. Notice that the **Emphasis** character style is formatting the entire paragraph above the third heading—there is no question mark in this paragraph to turn the style off. Click at the beginning of this paragraph, before the first period, and use Type > Insert Special Character > Other > End Nested Style Here to insert an invisible character that will turn the style off.

11. Click in the first list item below the second heading (*drawing pencils, charcoal, and pastels*) and create a new paragraph style as follows:

   a. Name the style **Bullets**.

   b. Keep the current paragraph formatting.

   c. Specify a 0p6 left indent and 0p3 space before and after.

   d. Click the Bullets and Numbering category, specify Bullets as the list type, and then select the default round bullet character.

   e. Adjust the tab position to 2p0.

12. Apply the **Bullets** style to the remaining three list items, and then delete the blank paragraphs above and below the list.

13. Click in the second heading and change Space Before to 1p0 to provide a little more padding between the heading and the text above it. Clear the manual override by editing the Heading style to include this Space Before value. All headings should change to the new format. Your document should look like Illustration A.

14. Save your changes, close the file, and exit InDesign.

Illustration A

WELCOME TO CASTLE ART!
Never been to Castle Art? Castle Art is a full-service art store conveniently located in the historic village of Clifton, near Richmond Technical College, Clifton State University, and Mount St. Mary College. We cater to the needs of students, professional artists from the community, and dedicated amateurs alike.

OUTSTANDING SELECTION
Need supplies or equipment? You'll find everything you need for your art project here. We carry a wide selection of supplies, including . . .

   • drawing pencils, charcoal, and pastels

   • acrylics, oils, and watercolors

   • brushes and palette knives

   • canvas, paper for all media, and framing materials

. . . and many more items. We are an authorized dealer for OLD HOLLAND, WINSOR & NEWTON, LIQUITEX, and ÆGYPTUS colors.

KNOWLEDGEABLE STAFF
Just starting out in art? Our friendly staff members can offer expert advice on what supplies you need. If you are a more experienced artist, we can help you realize your potential with the best-quality materials in the area. If you don't find what you need here, a staff member will be glad to order any item—no extra charge for special orders!

CLASSES
Always wanted to draw or paint? Castle Art is the place to start. We offer classes at beginner, intermediate, and advanced levels in drawing, oil painting, watercolor painting, acrylic painting, and pencil and pastel technique. Classes change quarterly. Save ⅓ on class materials purchased in the 1ˢᵗ week of any class. Stop by for a current class schedule.

ON YOUR OWN

1. Start InDesign and open ⊙OYO90. Save the document as OIN90_xx.

2. This document contains paragraph styles that were imported with the text from Word. Modify these styles so they are not based on the Normal style.

3. Adjust the styles as desired. You may want to change the color of the title or add a paragraph rule above or below it.

4. Create styles for any elements that do not have them, such as the paragraphs giving explanatory information about the article on page 1.

5. Create a first-paragraph style to apply to the first paragraph of the article that includes a drop cap.

6. Create several style groups to organize the body text and heading text styles.

7. Apply styles as necessary. All paragraphs in the document should be formatted with a style that has no overrides.

8. Save your changes, close the document, and exit InDesign.

Summary Exercise

Application Skills Your contact at the Eagle Creek Animal Clinic has added some text to the brochure you began for the Clinic in Exercise 71. In this exercise, you will adjust character and paragraph formats to make the text more attractive and readable. You will also apply conditions to make the brochure customizable for either cats or dogs.

EXERCISE DIRECTIONS

1. Start InDesign and open ⊙91Eagle. Save the file as 91Eagle_xx.

2. On page 1, change the horizontal scale of the text *Eagle Creek Animal Clinic* in the right panel to 110%.

3. Apply a paragraph rule 1p9 above the first line of the clinic name, using a 4-pt weight, the same blue as the clinic name, and the default line type.

4. Format the address and phone number in both the right panel and the center panel (*not* the e-mail address) with small caps and tracking set to **+25**.

5. Create a paragraph rule below the phone number in the right column of page 1 like the one above the clinic name.

6. Click in the heading *A Sampling of Our Services* and create a paragraph style as follows:
   - Name: Column_head
   - Font and style: Arial Bold
   - Size: 14 pt
   - Alignment: Center
   - Space After: 0p6
   - Color: Dark blue

7. Center the list of services below the heading you just styled. Then create a style named **Services** that enlarges the text to 14 pt and adds 0p3 space after the paragraph. Apply this style to all entries in the list.

8. Apply the **Column_head** style to the *Especially for CatsDogs* heading in the center panel.

9. Create a new paragraph style named **Body** that justifies text with the last line ending centered and adds 0p6 points of space after the paragraph. Apply this style to the paragraphs in the center panel.

10. Create conditions named **cat** and **dog**. Mark conditional text as follows:

    a. Mark the references to *Cats* and *Dogs* in the center panel heading.

    b. In the first paragraph, mark references to *cat* and *dog*. Mark *feline infectious peritonitis and feline leukemia* for cat and the other two diseases for dog.

    c. In the second paragraph, mark *hyperthyroidism* for cat and *hypothyroidism* for dog.

    d. In the last paragraph, mark references to *cat* and *dog*.

11. Hide each condition to check your work, and then display the cat condition. Your page should look like Illustration A.

12. On page 2, fill the center text panel with ⊙91Eagle_text.doc.

13. On page 2, format each of the three column headings with the **Column_head** style.

14. Apply the **Body** style to the paragraphs below the headings on page 2.

15. Use Find/Change to change all instances of DMV to DVM. (*Hint:* Choose to search the document rather than a story.)

16. Check the spelling of the rest of the document, making any changes needed. You can skip *otoscopy* and ignore proper names and titles.

17. The center-justified text is not as attractive as you'd hoped. Modify the Body style to change alignment to Left Justify.

18. Save your changes, close the document, and exit InDesign.

Illustration A

A Sampling of Our Services

Vaccinations

Dental work

Spay/neuter

Blood tests

X-rays

Microchip identifiction

Flea and tick control

Nutritional advice

Behavioral counseling

Laser surgery

Geriatric medicine

Radiology

Surgery

Cardiology

Grooming/bathing

Ultrasound

Video otoscopy

Short-term boarding

Especially for Cats

Eagle Creek is committed to caring for your cat. Our staff is fully trained to treat serious illnesses such as feline infectious peritonitis and feline leukemia.

We also believe in preventive care that can identify lurking problems such as hyperthyroidism and diabetes. These conditions may have a subtle onset that only an experienced vet can detect.

Have your cat checked today by our expert and loving staff. You'll be glad you did!

505 PROSPERO DRIVE
NOBLESVILLE, IN 46062
(317) 555-2919
vetcare@eaglecreekanimal.biz

EAGLE CREEK ANIMAL CLINIC

505 PROSPERO DRIVE
NOBLESVILLE, IN 46062
(317) 555-2919

Exercise | 92

Application Exercise

Application Skills *Midwest Gardening Today* magazine has asked you to start work on an article about perennial flowers that do well in Midwestern gardens. In this exercise, you will flow text into a document, modify character formats, apply paragraph formats, and create and apply styles.

EXERCISE DIRECTIONS

1. Start InDesign and open ⊙92Perennials. Save the file as 92Perennials_xx.

2. Format the article's title with the Brush Script MT font, a font size of 85 points, and the Paper font color. Center the title text vertically in the text frame.

   ✓ *If you do not have the Brush Script MT font, choose another decorative font such as Brush Script Standard.*

3. Use any text flow method to place the ⊙92Perennials_text.doc file into the four empty text frames on the spread, beginning in the short frame in the left column below the article title.

4. Click in the first paragraph of the story you just placed and create a paragraph style named **Body_text** with the following formats:

   - Font: Adobe Garamond Pro
   - Font size: 12 pt
   - Leading: 16 pt
   - Space after: 0p6

5. Apply this style to the next paragraph and to all paragraphs below the headings *Soil Conditions* and *Caring for New Transplants* on page 3.

6. View the story in the Story Editor and note that each of the plant names in the third through ninth paragraphs is followed by a space, two hyphens, and another space. Use Find/Change to replace the space, two hyphens, and space with a single em dash throughout the story. Close the Story Editor.

7. Select the first flower name and its dash and format the text as Adobe Garamond Pro, bold italic, with the color **C = 10, M = 85, Y = 100, K = 30**. Save this color as a swatch with the name **Burnt Orange**.

8. Create a character style from these formats named **flower_name**. Copy the em dash.

9. Click in the description of the 'Sprite' Astilbe and create a new paragraph style named **Flower** that is based on Body_text. Adjust the left indent to 0p6. Nest the flower_name style in this format, and click in the Words field and paste the em dash you copied.

10. Apply the Flower style to all the flower descriptions.

11. Create a paragraph style named **Heading** to apply to the two headings on page 3. Use Adobe Garamond Pro, bold, 14-pt, with 0p6 space before.

12. Correct all spelling errors. All proper names and flower names are spelled correctly, and you can skip *overwatering* and *daisylike*.

13. Your text is running longer than the two pages allotted for it. Modify the Body_text style to keep the last two or first two lines of a paragraph together, turn on hyphenation if necessary, and also adjust leading to Auto and space after a paragraph to 0p3.

14. Change the keep option for the Heading style to keep the heading with the next two lines. The text should now fit in the two pages.

15. Apply a 3-line, 1-character drop cap to the first paragraph in the story. Note that this causes an override of the Body_text style, so create a new paragraph style from this paragraph and name it **First_par**. The override should clear.

16. Select the fraction in the second paragraph below the *Soil Conditions* heading and use the OpenType Fraction option to convert it to a proper fraction. Delete the extra space between the *1* and the fraction.

17. Format the footer text at the bottom of the left page with Adobe Garamond Pro, a font size of 11 points, bold italic font style, and Paper font color.

18. Format the footer text at the bottom of the right page with Adobe Garamond Pro, a font size of 11 points and bold italic font style. Your finished article should look like Illustration A.

19. Save your changes, close the file, and exit InDesign.

Illustration A

'Goldsturm' Black-Eyed Susan—Provides billows of late-summer daisylike golden blossoms with dark centers on coarse, hairy stems.

Soil Conditions

Carefully consider the moisture conditions of the site you have chosen for your garden. Is it normal (as much as it's possible to define normal with today's chaotic weather), dry, or wet? Choose plants that do best in the prevailing conditions.

Next plan defensive measures to counteract a change in the moisture content. If the area you have chosen is dry, make sure the drainage is excellent. That way, even if there is excessive rain, the water should run off quickly. To increase drainage, dig out your garden bed to a depth of 1½ to 2 feet and install a drainage pipe. This will immediately carry away any excess water. Then refill the bed with enriched, porous garden soil filled with organic matter, such as peat moss and humus.

If your proposed garden area is moist, make sure you have the means to retain the moisture. Your garden should either be near a water source where you can sprinkle the spot daily, or embedded with a soaker hose.

Or you can create your own miniature damp spot by following the techniques used to create garden pools. Simply install a container with a very small hole punched in it for slow drainage. After you've filled the container, the moisture should seep out of such a setting at a very slow rate.

Caring for New Transplants

No matter how carefully you have placed your perennials in your garden, these plants have nevertheless been uprooted during transplanting. They are in a state of shock; how much shock is determined by your handling methods. They will need some watchful care.

Your new plants must get enough water or they will die. Because it is inevitable that some of the root hairs were damaged in the replanting process, the remaining ones have to work overtime until new growth occurs. This means that for a good week or more the new transplants must be gently watered and the ground kept moist but not swamped—overwatering could drown a new plant.

Never directly fertilize a newly-planted perennial. Ideally, the plant should not need fertilizer in subsequent weeks because it has been placed in enriched garden soil, where the necessary nutrients are already in place and available to the plant once the root hairs start to grow.

If you are transplanting tall perennials, such as delphiniums, it's a good idea to stake them at the same time. Staking helps the stem of a tall plant support its flowers once they begin to bloom; done at transplanting time, staking creates a minimum of disturbance for young plants.

Check your transplants for signs of new foliage. This indicates that you have planted correctly and that your new perennial is surviving nicely in your garden.

Looking for an easy way to enjoy color and beauty in your gardens all season long? Consider perennials. While they are more expensive than annuals initially, you quickly recoup the cost difference in having plants that will come back stronger and more vigorous every year, with no replanting.

Here are some easy-to-care-for plants that make for a good starter garden:

'Sprite' Astilbe—A diminutive hybrid astilbe with glossy dark green foliage. It produces sprays of shell pink flowers in midsummer shade gardens.

'Moonbeam' Coreopsis—Small, eight-petaled pale yellow flowers grace the tips of thin stems covered with narrow leaves. It blooms all summer in full sun.

'Palace Purple' Heuchera—boasts handsome deep purple foliage all summer in partial shade. Is bears tiny, pale bluish-white flowers clustered at the ends of wiry stems in spring.

Creeping Phlox—Neat, deep green foliage on creeping stems mats to cover the ground in woodland settings. In spring it produces clusters of small florets in white, blue, or pink.

'Sunny Border Blue' Veronica—Offers a strong, vertical accent for the garden and bears spikes of rich violet-blue flowers in summer. It does best in a sunny site.

'Magnus' Purple Coneflower—Jaunty, daisylike flowers with droopy purple petals bloom in midsummer when many other perennials are idle. It thrives in full sun.

Curriculum Integration

Application Skills   Your chemistry class is learning about writing chemical formulas, and you have been assigned the task of creating a list of molecular formulas for substances that will be used in experiments throughout the semester. You can use InDesign's typography features to make this list attractive and readable. Before you begin this exercise, look up the chemical formulas for the following compounds:

- Water
- Carbon dioxide
- Sulfuric acid
- Benzene
- Ethylene
- Sugar
- Ascorbic acid
- Glucose

EXERCISE DIRECTIONS

Start a new InDesign document with 1 page using settings of your choice and save the document with a name such as 93Compounds_xx.

Create a text frame to hold the information you are going to present. Type the heading **Chemical Compounds** at the top of the text frame and format it as desired.

Type the compound names listed above in 18-pt type in a font of your choice. After each compound name, insert a colon and press the Tab key. Then type the appropriate chemical formula for the compound.

Insert a tab character before each compound name. Then use the Tabs panel to align the compound names and formulas attractively. You may, for example, want to right-align the compound names, or align them on the colons. Use a left tab for the formulas.

Insert space after each paragraph so it easy to read the list. Set the tracking for each formula to +100.

Format the compound names in a bright color that is easy to read.

When you are finished, save your changes, close the document, and exit InDesign.

Exercise | 94

Portfolio Builder

Application Skills   Your English teacher has asked you to share a favorite story or essay with your classmates. In this exercise, you will visit an online archive containing classic literature in the public domain, and download a copy of a book, story, or essay. You will then publish it attractively using InDesign.

EXERCISE DIRECTIONS

■ Using the Internet, browse the Project Gutenberg Web site at the following address: http://www.gutenberg.org/catalog. Select a story or book of your choice and open it in an HTML or plain text version.

■ Copy the story or at least the first chapter or unit of a book and paste the copy in a Word document. Store the document in a folder in the location where you are saving solution files for this course. If the story contains graphics, you may want to strip them out and save them in the same folder to place in your InDesign document.

■ Start a new InDesign document and place the text into it, generating as many frames and pages as needed to hold it. If you have downloaded an entire book, you may choose to place only the first chapter or unit of the book, along with the title page.

■ Format the document so it is readable and attractive. This process might include:
   ● Changing the vertical alignment of the title page text.
   ● Deleting extraneous paragraph and line breaks.
   ● Breaking the full-column-width text frame into columns.
   ● Inserting images.
   ● Formatting headings with a larger, bolder font than the body text and creating styles for the headings.
   ● Choosing a different font family and size for body text and creating a style for the body text.
   ● Adding page numbers to the masters.
   ● Adjusting the kerning, tracking, and scale of any text that would benefit from it.
   ● Formatting the non-body text, such as the copyright information at the beginning and end, in a smaller font such as 8 point.

   ✓ *If there's a lot of cleanup to do to the file, and it's very long, you may work with only the first 10 pages and leave the rest.*

■ Save the document as 94Mystory_xx. Close the document and exit InDesign.

Lesson | 10

Work with Tables and Graphics

Exercise | 95

Skills Covered

- Create a Table
- Select Parts of a Table
- Modify Table Structure

Software Skills Aligning text with tab stops is a quick way to organize tabular information if it is simple. For more complex tabular data, create a table. You can insert a new table or convert one from tabular text. Before you can modify a table, you must know how to select various parts of the table. After creating a table, you can modify its structure by inserting or deleting rows and columns, adjusting table and cell size, and merging or splitting rows or columns.

Design Skills Many types of documents may contain tables to organize information. A designer should understand not only how to create a table but also how to modify its appearance to ensure readability.

Application Skills You have been hired to work on the annual report for the Global Equity Markets mutual fund. The annual report will include several tables. In this exercise, you create several tables for the report.

TERMS

Cell The box formed by the intersection of a row and a column in a table.

Delimited text Text in which each line has been separated into more than one column using a consistent character such as a tab character or comma.

NOTES

Create a Table

- A table is a grid of **cells** into which you can type text or place graphics. Each cell is like a mini-frame and can have its own separate settings for alignment, indention, background, and so on.

- A table resides within a text frame. First you create the text frame, and then you create the table.

  ✓ *The table does not have to be the only thing in the text frame; the frame also can include regular text. However, if you want to use the table as a graphical element, placing it in its own frame makes layout easier.*

- To create a table, place the insertion point in a text frame and then choose Table > Insert Table. In the Insert Table dialog box, shown in Figure 95-1, enter the number of rows and columns desired.

Figure 95-1. Choose the number of columns and rows for the table

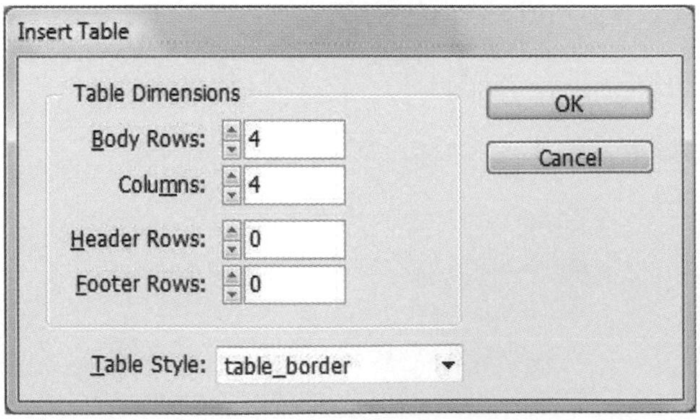

Insert Table

Table Dimensions
Body Rows: 4
Columns: 4
Header Rows: 0
Footer Rows: 0

Table Style: table_border

OK
Cancel

- You can specify header and footer rows as well as body rows. Use header and footer rows to insert information that will repeat if the table runs to more than one page.

  ✓ *If you do not specify a header or footer row when creating the table, you can always convert a regular table row to a header or footer later using the Table > Convert Rows sub-menu.*

- Note that you can also specify a style for the table, or create a new table style from this dialog box. You learn to create table and cell styles in the next exercise.

- If you have already created a table-like structure with tab stops in InDesign, you can easily convert it to a table. Select the entire block of text and choose Table > Convert Text to Table to open the Convert Text to Table dialog box, shown in Figure 95-2.

  ✓ *If you have created tabular text in a word processing program, you can place the text in InDesign and then convert it to a table.*

Figure 95-2. Convert Text to Table dialog box

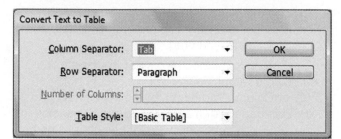

- Text that is separated into multiple columns and rows using typographical symbols such as the tab character and paragraph breaks is known as **delimited text**. For text to be successfully converted into a table that has multiple columns, it must be delimited consistently—that is, the columns must be separated using a consistent character. This is most often a tab character, but it could be any character.

- In the Convert Text to Table dialog box, indicate what you have used for the column separator character (probably Tab) and what you have used for the row separator (probably Paragraph).

  ✓ *When you convert from a tabbed list to a table, any alignments from the tab stops (right, center, decimal) are lost and all cells default to left alignment.*

- Enter text in a table the way you would in a word processing program, using Tab to move from cell to cell.

- You can work with table text in the Story Editor if desired. Tables are displayed in a hierarchical row system that can make it easy to concentrate on the text.

InDesign Extra

Nesting Tables

You can insert a table within a table by clicking in a table cell and then issuing the Insert Table command. Use a nested table when one part of a table has more complex entries than the rest of the table.

Select Parts of a Table

- To apply some types of formatting, you will first need to select the cells, rows, or columns to affect. Many table formatting options are not available until at least one cell in a table is selected.

- Selecting the text in a cell is *not* the same as selecting the cell itself. When the cell itself is selected, the entire cell appears with a black background and white type, as shown at right in Figure 95-3.

Figure 95-3. Selected text vs. selected cell

September 16   September 16

- To select a single cell, use the Table > Select > Cell command.

- To select multiple cells, drag across them.

- To select a row, position the mouse pointer to the left of the row, so the pointer turns into a black arrow →, and then click, or drag up or down to select multiple rows. You can also use the Table > Select > Row command.

- To select a column, position the mouse pointer above it, so the pointer turns into a black arrow ↓, and then click, or drag to the right or left to select multiple columns. You can also use the Table > Select > Column command.

- To select the entire table, position the mouse pointer at the upper-left corner of the table so the pointer turns into a diagonal black arrow ↘ and click. Or click anywhere within the table and choose Table > Select > Table.

  ✓ *You can also use a context menu to select a table or parts of a table. Right-click in the table, point to Select, and choose the desired option.*

Modify Table Structure

- Once you have created a table, you can modify its structure as desired. You may need to add or delete rows or columns as data changes. You may also want to change row or column size to better fit the data.

- You can also merge or split cells to change the structure of the table without changing its size.

- When at least one cell is selected, table options appear in the Control panel. You can also use the Table panel, shown in Figure 95-4, to change a number of table formats.

Figure 95-4. Table panel

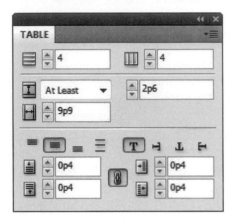

Insert and Delete Rows and Columns

- To add a new row at the bottom of the table, position the insertion point in the bottom right cell and press Tab.

- To add a new row anywhere else in the table, click in a row adjacent to where you want to insert, and then choose Table > Insert > Row. In the dialog box that appears, choose the number of new rows (the default is 1) and whether they should be placed above or below the current row.

- The procedure for inserting a column is the same, except you choose Table > Insert > Column and you choose whether to place the new column(s) to the left or right.

- To delete a row or column, click in the row or column to delete, or select multiple rows or columns to delete, and then choose Table > Delete > Row, or choose Table > Delete > Column.

- To delete the entire table, choose Table > Delete > Table.

- You can also insert and delete rows and columns using the Number of Rows box ☰ or Number of Columns box ▥ on the Control panel or Table panel. Add or remove rows or columns by changing the numbers in these boxes. These boxes are active only if at least one cell is selected in the table.

Adjust Cell Heights and Widths

- To change the row height, select the Type tool, then position the mouse pointer at the bottom of the row and drag. To change the column width, position the mouse pointer on the right border of the column and drag. The mouse pointer changes to a double-headed arrow when it is over a column border, as shown in Figure 95-5.

Figure 95-5. Change column width by dragging

	One-year total return
Global Equity	–21.5%
Morgan Stanley Capital International Indexes ↔	

- When you adjust row height, the overall height of the entire table changes. When you change column width, the overall width of the table changes.

- To keep the overall size of the table static and adjust only the divider you are dragging, hold down the Shift key as you drag.

- An alternative method is to enter row heights or column widths using the Row Height box 🔲 or Column Width box 🔲 on the Control panel or Table panel when at least one cell is selected in the table. You can specify that a height or width be at least or exactly a specific measurement.

- To resize the entire table proportionally, hold down the Shift key and drag the lower-right corner of the table.

Merge and Split Cells

- When you merge cells, you select adjacent cells and combine them into one cell. When you split cells, you divide a cell either horizontally into two rows or vertically into two columns.

- To merge two or more cells, select them and click the Merge cells button ⊠ on the Control panel.

- To unmerge a cell that has previously been merged, select it and click the Unmerge cells button ⊟ on the Control panel.

- To split a cell that has not previously been merged, choose Table > Split Cell Vertically, or choose Table > Split Cell Horizontally.

PROCEDURES

Create a Table
(Alt + Shift + Ctrl + T)

1. Position the insertion point in the text frame to contain the table.
2. Click **Table** .... `ALT` + `A`
3. Click **Insert Table** .... `T`
4. Enter the desired number of **Body rows** and **Columns**.
5. (Optional) If desired, enter a number of **Header Rows** or **Footer Rows**.
6. (Optional) Click **Table Style** and select an existing style or create a new style.
7. Click **OK** .... `ENTER`

Convert Text to a Table

1. Select the delimited text to convert to a table.
2. Click **Table** .... `ALT` + `A`
3. Click **Convert Text to Table** .... `C`
4. If needed, change the **Column Separator** character.
5. If needed, change the **Row Separator** character.
6. Click **OK** .... `ENTER`

Select Parts of a Table

To select a cell:

1. Click in the cell with the **Type** tool.
2. Click **Table** .... `ALT` + `A`
3. Point to **Select** .... `S`
4. Click **Cell** .... `E`

   OR

- With the insertion point in the cell, press `CTRL` + `/`.

To select multiple cells:

- Drag across contiguous cells.

  ✓ *You cannot select multiple noncontiguous cells.*

To select a row:

1. Position the mouse pointer to the left of the row, so the mouse pointer becomes an arrow `→`.
2. Click to select the row.

To select multiple rows:

1. Select a single row (see above).
2. Hold down the mouse button and drag across additional rows.

   OR

   Hold down `SHIFT` and select additional contiguous rows.

To select a column:

1. Position the mouse pointer above the column, so the mouse pointer becomes an arrow `↓`.
2. Click to select the column.

To select multiple columns:

1. Select a single column (see above).
2. Hold down the mouse button and drag across additional columns.

   OR

   Hold down `SHIFT` key and select additional contiguous columns.

To select all body rows:

1. Click in a cell to move the insertion point into it.
2. Click **Table** .... `ALT` + `A`
3. Point to **Select** .... `S`
4. Click **Body Rows** .... `B`

To select the entire table:

1. Click in a cell to move the insertion point into it.
2. Click **Table** .... `ALT` + `A`
3. Point to **Select** .... `S`
4. Click **Table** .... `A`

OR

1. Position the mouse pointer at the upper-left corner of the table, so the mouse pointer becomes a diagonal arrow `↘`.
2. Click to select the table.

Insert and Delete Rows and Columns

To insert rows:

1. Click in a cell adjacent to where you want to insert.
2. Click **Table** .... `ALT` + `A`
3. Point to **Insert** .... `I`
4. Click **Row** .... `R`
5. (Optional) If you want more than one row, increment the value in the **Number** box.
6. Click **Above** .... `ALT` + `A`

   OR

   Click **Below** .... `ALT` + `B`
7. Click **OK** .... `ENTER`

   OR

1. Select a cell adjacent to where you want to insert.
2. Click the **Number of Rows** box and type a value or use the spin arrows to increase the row value.

To insert columns:

1. Click in a cell adjacent to where you want to insert.
2. Click **Table** .... `ALT` + `A`
3. Point to **Insert** .... `I`
4. Click **Column** .... `C`
5. (Optional) If you want more than one column, increment the value in the **Number** box.
6. Click **Left** .... `ALT` + `L`

   OR

   Click **Right** .... `ALT` + `R`
7. Click **OK** .... `ENTER`

OR

1. Select cell adjacent to where you want to insert.
2. Click the **Number of Columns** box ⊞ and type a value or use the spin arrows to increase the column value.

To delete rows:

1. Select the row(s) to delete.
2. Click **Table** .... `ALT` + `A`
3. Point to **Delete** .... `D`
4. Click **Row** .... `R`

OR

1. Select at least one cell in the table.
2. Click the **Number of Rows** box ☰ and type a value or use the spin arrows to decrease the row value.
3. Click **OK** .... `ENTER`

✓ *The bottom row is deleted, regardless of where the insertion point is positioned.*

To delete columns:

1. Select the column(s) to delete.
2. Click **Table** .... `ALT` + `A`
3. Point to **Delete** .... `D`
4. Click **Column** .... `C`

OR

1. Select at least one cell in the table.
2. Click the **Number of Columns** box ⊞ and type a value or use the spin arrows to decrease the column value.
3. Click **OK** .... `ENTER`

✓ *The rightmost column is deleted, regardless of where the insertion point is positioned.*

To delete a table:

1. Click anywhere within the table.
2. Click **Table** .... `ALT` + `A`
3. Point to **Delete** .... `D`
4. Click **Table** .... `A`

Adjust Cell Heights and Widths

1. Position the mouse pointer between two rows or columns.
2. (Optional) Hold down `SHIFT` if you want the overall size of the table to remain static.
3. Drag the divider to change its position.

OR

1. Select the row(s) or column(s) to adjust.
2. (Optional) If you want an exact row height, open the **Row Height** list and choose **Exactly**.
3. Click the **Row Height** box ⬓ and type a value or use spin arrows to set value.

OR

Click the **Column Width** box ⬒ and type a value or use spin arrows to set value.

Merge Cells

1. Select the cells to merge.
2. Click the **Merge cells** button ⊠ on the Control panel.

OR

1. Select the cells to merge.
2. Click **Table** .... `ALT` + `A`
3. Click **Merge Cells** .... `M`

Unmerge a Merged Cell

1. Select the merged cell.
2. Click the **Unmerge cells** button ⊟ on the Control panel.

OR

1. Select the merged cell.
2. Click **Table** .... `ALT` + `A`
3. Click **Unmerge Cells** .... `U`

Split a Cell

1. Select the cell to split.
2. Click **Table** .... `ALT` + `A`
3. Click **Split Cell Horizontally** .... `Z`

OR

Click **Split Cell Vertically** .... `V`

EXERCISE DIRECTIONS

1. Start InDesign and open 🔘95Global. Save the document as *95Global_xx*. This file contains a table that has already been started. You will add two more tables to the report.

2. Click in the text frame at the lower-left corner of page 1. Display the Paragraph Styles panel and select [Basic Paragraph] and then insert a table with 4 columns and 4 rows.

3. Change to **table_body** paragraph style if necessary and insert text in the table as shown in Illustration A. Use en dashes between the dates and to create the minus signs. To insert a space between the + sign and the number 6.6 in the fourth column, use Type > Insert White Space > Figure Space.

4. Go to page 2 and click in the text frame at the left side of the page. Select the [Basic Paragraph] style and then place the 🔘95Global_table.doc file.

5. Select the text and convert it to a table using default settings.

6. Merge all the cells in the top row of this table so the heading can span the entire table.

7. Resize the first column of this table to be about **10p0** wide and the other two columns to be about **6p0** wide each.

8. On page 1, insert a row above the top row of the table you typed. In the first cell, type **Benchmarks**. Merge all cells in this row.

9. In the table near the top of the page, merge all cells in the first row and type **Average annual compound returns**. Change the height of this merged cell to exactly 2p0. Your page 1 tables should look like those in Illustration B shown on the next page.

10. Save your changes, close the document, and exit InDesign.

Illustration A

	Low-to-high 10/07–3/09	High-to-low 3/09–9/10	Low-to-low 10/07–9/10
Global Equity Markets	+92.9%	–29.4%	+36.3%
MSCI World Index	+62.9	–34.6	+ 6.6
Lipper Global Fund average	+84.8	–33.8	+17.5

Global Equity Markets Fund

Irit, quamcore minim aliquate faccum nummy nulput luptat.

Tis adigna feugait aliquat lore esto enim et atue tie dolore modit, sum am etum at. Ut utpat ut at. Feugiat nisl erit, volum vero et nim ex exer irit nonsequ iscidunt iure dolutpat ad doloree tuercin ut nulputpat ad eugait nibh et wis ad ectem iliquisl elisis etue dolore feugait vero odiatisi.

Ipit aliquis eumsandre velit ilit landipsum quat, qui tis eum endiatue eu feu feugue tatue min hendre ming et at. Enit luptat.

Ecte elisi tatum eugait prat, seniam, venis num ipis dipit nit ullummy nibh eugue doloreetuer incil utpat adipiscidunt pratummy nim zzrit praestio consequat volor se et, velenibh eum dolut vero esenibh et, sequati onullamet, venim am acidunt wis ercil ulput praestrud tet, quam augait ullan velese te dit nos nissequisi.

Erit lortincing ex eugueraesse conse tatuer atum delendre dunt luptat, vel dolore volorperit praesto dunt autpatet alit ipis el eugait, core mod ero core dolore cons augait nos dolore min ut ver iure feum ver augiamet lortie tem dunt augue doleseq uiscips ustincincil

Results at a Glance

Average annual compound returns				
	One-year total return	Five years	Ten years	Lifetime
Global Equity	–21.5%	+11.2%	+12.4%	+14.0%
Morgan Stanley Capital International Indexes				
World Index	–27.9	+ 5.0	+ 8.1	+10.4
USA Index	–27.0	+10.2	+12.9	+11.8
Lipper Global Funds average	–29.7	+ 4.5	+ 7.8	+12.4
Rank vs. Lipper	70 of 271	7 of 130	2 of 29	1 of 6

ipisit luptatisi blametuer iusto eu feugiam vulpute do odolor sendrem verciduisit exerci tet, se mincip eummolore tat. Duismodit iurem duipit accum dolore del ex ectet er sequisi enit, con hendre magnibh exerat, secte verit alit vel ipisi eugait, commolor si.

Tisl dolorem dipit am augue dolesectem venim veliquat, volor se molobor eriustrud eum in veratet ut et augue dignisl dio od magna faci ex eugue feu feui ent am alis nibh euguer sumsandre et wis alit, sequat ipit ut in ullum venit, velestrud mincipis eros enim ing eugait am zzrilluptat.

Eceremus seniri, nimmo vitienatiam it L. Pero videt vivitum tri tia mod facci periam pra? Nihilin atilic oribusquos C. Habunin inc opul consinati, adductus rebeste iam di intum tus, nostia? Fullestrus senihiciem condum pero, se consus des hum stumum utebultorei igno. An ture vid con tabem dessederdit. Us lictum rei in Ita, maiorum unum ignatis essimum consultum movivit, culin videffrem lica L. Catuidit is patem tementus etimorunclem maximius, sedet; inihili ssentra, nonemus. Maciam inari potis aperacestiem tus me niam consciost L. Gernihilinem se tur huceres at, num prio numum audempota signates temponsus rehem pubis, cultorei sente auconsidica; etius esilne intiquam. Ximus cris speres fuem fur adhuid ponsis inesses hus, uterfer dicipti fectuus hocaelin ad mo noximuratuam silis ere in vagin hus, tala mor hui publina tquerum ter loctus ego vagit.

Benchmarks			
	Low-to-high 10/07–3/09	High-to-low 3/09–9/10	Low-to-low 10/07–9/10
Global Equity Markets	+92.9%	–29.4%	+36.3%
MSCI World Index	+62.9	–34.6	+ 6.6
Lipper Global Fund average	+84.8	–33.8	+17.5

ON YOUR OWN

1. Start InDesign and open ☉OYO95. Save the document as OIN95_*xx*. This document will eventually contain a complete census of the Metro Zoo's animal inventory. You will set up the table for the inventory in this exercise.

2. Go to page 2 and click in the text frame in the left column. Place the ☉OYO95_table.doc file.

3. Convert the delimited data to a table. It should thread into the text frame in the next column.

4. Select the first row of the table. Click Table > Convert Rows > To Header to create a header row. Notice that the header row displays at the top of the table in the right column as well as in its original position at the top of the left column table.

5. Shorten the left text frame enough to push the Class: Amphibia entries to the right column.

6. Save your changes, close the document, and exit InDesign.

Skills Covered

- Table Text Alignment Options
- Apply Table Strokes and Fills

- Create Table and Cell Styles

Software Skills   Improve the look of a table by adjusting text alignment and applying different stroke and fill settings. If you have more than one table to format in a document, or the table is very long, you can save time by creating cell and table styles.

Design Skills   A designer can make a table more attractive and readable by applying strokes and fills that emphasize portions of the data. Creating cell and table styles makes it easy for a designer to format tables consistently throughout a document.

Application Skills   In this exercise, you continue working on tables for the Global Equity Markets annual report. You adjust text alignment, apply stroke and fill formatting, and create table and cell styles so you can easily format all the tables in the same way.

TERMS

No new terms in this exercise.

NOTES

Table Text Alignment Options

- You can align text in a table using both horizontal alignment options, such as Align left and Align center, and vertical alignment options such as Align top and Align bottom. These alignment options are available on the Control panel, and the vertical alignment options are also available on the Table panel.

- The Table panel also includes Cell Inset boxes you can use to fine-tune the position of text in a table cell. Using these boxes, you can move text away from the top, bottom, left, or right cell border in 1 point increments.

- For a special effect, you can rotate text in a table cell 90°, 180°, or 270°. Figure 96-1 shows text rotated 270° and then aligned center both vertically and horizontally.

Figure 96-1. Rotated text forms a side head

		Low-to-high 10/07–3/09	High-to-low 3/09–9/10	Low-to-low 10/07–9/10
BENCHMARKS	Global Equity Markets	+92.9%	−29.4%	+36.3%
	MSCI World Index	+62.9	−34.6	+ 6.6
	Lipper Global Fund average	+84.8	−33.8	+17.5

- The Rotate text buttons are available on the Control panel and the Table panel when table cells are selected.

Apply Table Strokes and Fills

- By default, table cells are outlined with a 1-point plain black stroke and have no fill. You can change stroke weight, style, and color and apply a different fill color to emphasize portions of a table.

- When applying strokes and fills to table cells, you can choose options that apply to the entire table or options that can be applied to one or more selected cells in the table.

- It is best to begin formatting at the cell level, because formatting options that apply to an entire table will look best if you first remove the default strokes, which can only be done with cell formatting options.

- To apply stroke and fill options to cells, first select the cells you want to affect (you can select the entire table if desired). Then use the Table > Cell Options > Strokes and Fills command to open the Cell Options dialog box shown in Figure 96-2 at the bottom of the page.

- Use the Cell Stroke grid to choose the strokes to format. The outside borders on the grid represent the stroke around the edges of the selection. The inside strokes in the grid represent the strokes between selected cells.

- If all strokes in the grid are blue, the cell formats you choose will apply to all strokes in the selection. To limit the formats you apply, click strokes on the grid to turn them off. Formats will apply only to the blue strokes.

- Once you have selected the strokes you want to format, use the Weight, Color, Type, and Tint boxes to select the stroke formats. If you have chosen a dashed or dotted line, you can also select a gap color.

- The Overprint Stroke option lets you specify that the stroke will print on top of all other colors. Black will overprint by default, but you may want to use this option to overprint a different color from the Swatches panel.

  ✓ You learn more about overprinting in Lesson 11.

- If you only need to adjust stroke weight and type, you can use the Stroke Weight and Stroke Type boxes on the Control panel. The Control panel includes a grid like the one in the Cell Options dialog box to allow you to choose which strokes in your selection to format.

Figure 96-2. Cell Options dialog box

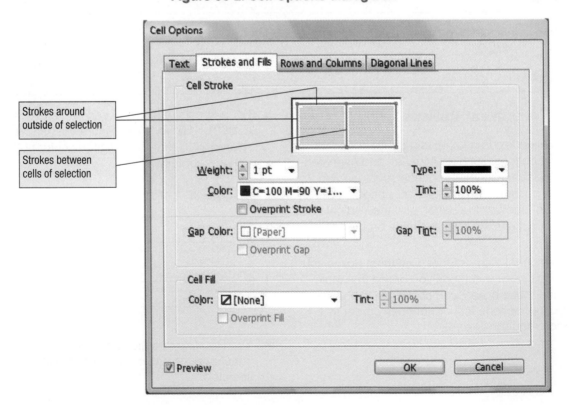

■ While you are in the Cell Options dialog box, you can apply a fill color to the selected cells using the Cell Fill Color box on the Strokes and Fills tab. You have access only to swatches in the Color list, so if you want a color that is not a standard swatch color, you must create it first and save it as a swatch. Note that you can create a tint of the selected fill color for a more subtle effect.

■ You can also apply a fill by selecting cells and choosing a color from the Swatches panel or by creating a color in the Color panel.

■ To apply stroke and fill options to an entire table, use the Table > Table Options > Table Setup command to open the Table Options dialog box shown in Figure 96-3 at the bottom of the page.

■ Use this dialog box to choose formats that will be applied to the entire table. On the Table Setup tab, for example, you can turn on a border that will surround the entire table, as well as adjust the table's structure and spacing within the text frame.

■ The Row Strokes and Column Strokes tabs in the Table Options dialog box let you set up patterns of alternating strokes for rows or columns. Figure 96-4 shows light and heavy row strokes applied to every other row of the table, with a 3-point green table border.

■ The Fills tab lets you set up patterns of alternating fills that you can apply either to rows or columns. Figure 96-4 shows a 20% green fill applied to alternate rows of the table.

Figure 96-4. Strokes and fills applied to alternate rows

	Qtr 1	Qtr 2	Qtr 3
Wilson Ltd.	567	890	145
Joseph Bros.	765	439	763
Banks & Banks	813	705	936
Thomsen LLC	857	905	812
Short Inc.	356	591	668

	Qtr 1	Qtr 2	Qtr 3
Wilson Ltd.	567	890	145
Joseph Bros.	765	439	763
Banks & Banks	813	705	936
Thomsen LLC	857	905	812
Short Inc.	356	591	668

Figure 96-3. Table Options dialog box

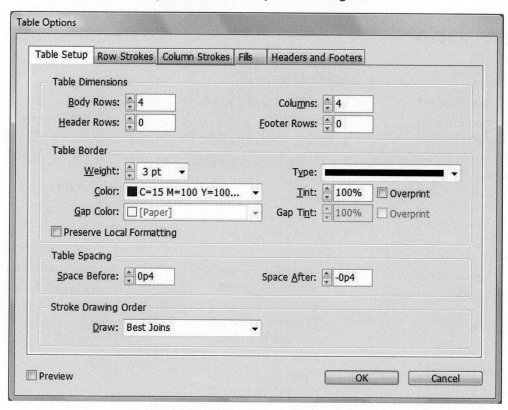

- Note that the tables shown in Figure 96-4 have had their default 1-point strokes removed before the table-level formats were applied.
- To remove a stroke, you set its stroke weight to 0 or apply the [None] color to it.

Create Table and Cell Styles

- You can create styles for both table and cell formatting. Table and cell styles make it very easy to apply the same formatting to a number of tables in a document.
- Creating table and cells styles is similar to creating other styles you have learned about in the InDesign section of this course.
- Create a style manually by clicking the Create new style button 🗐 in either the Table Styles or Cell Styles panel. Double-click the default style name to open a dialog box to define the stroke and fill options, just as you would if using the Table Options or Cell Options dialog box.
  - ✓ *Shortcut this process by holding down Alt when you click the Create new style button. InDesign opens the New Cell Style or New Table Style dialog box where you can create the desired style.*
- You can also apply the formats you want and then create a new style from those formats.

- You can also create a new table style at the same time you create the table. In the Insert Table dialog box, click the Table Style list arrow and then select New Table Style. Name the new style and then select table-level formats for the border, strokes, and fills. After you finish creating the style and specifying the number of columns and rows for the new table, the blank table displays with the table style formats already applied.
- Use cell styles when you want to be able to apply styles to portions of a table. Use table styles to create styles that will apply to the entire table.
- You can nest styles for both cell styles and table styles. In the Cell Styles dialog box, for example, you can specify a paragraph style to be used for the text in the cell.
- You can create style groups to organize styles when you have a number of styles to keep track of.
- When creating a table style, you can select cell styles to format portions of the table, such as header and footer rows, body rows, or the left or right column. You must create the cell styles first; they are then applied with the table style.
- Before you apply either a table or cell style, you should select the table or cells and click the Clear attributes not defined by style button 🗐 on the Cell Styles panel. If you do not clear previous attributes, your styles may not display in the table.

PROCEDURES

Align Text in a Cell
1. Select the cell(s) to affect.
2. Click any of the horizontal alignment buttons on the Control panel.
3. Click any of the vertical alignment buttons on the Control panel.

To rotate text in a cell:
1. Select the cell(s) to affect.
2. Click one of the rotation buttons in the Control or Table panel:
   - **Rotate text 0°** T .
   - **Rotate text 90°** ↵ .
   - **Rotate text 180°** ⊥ .
   - **Rotate text 270°** ⊢ .

Apply Strokes to Cells
1. Select the cell(s) to affect.
2. Click **Table** .... ALT + A
3. Point to **Cell Options** .... P
4. Click **Strokes and Fills** .... S
5. Click lines in the **Cell Stroke** grid to deselect any that will not be formatted.
6. Do one or more of the following:
   - Open the **Weight** list and select a stroke thickness .... ALT + W
   - Open the **Type** list and select a stroke style .... ALT + Y
   - Open the **Color** list and select a swatch color.................... ALT + C
   - Type a **Tint** value... ALT + T

7. Click **OK** .... ENTER
   - ✓ *You can also use the Stroke Weight and Stroke Type boxes on the Control panel to adjust stroke formats.*

Apply a Fill to Cells
1. Select the cell(s) to affect.
2. Click **Table** .... ALT + A
3. Point to **Cell Options** .... P
4. Click **Strokes and Fills** .... S
5. In the Cell Fill section, open the **Color** box and select a color.......................... ALT + L
6. Click **OK** .... ENTER

   OR

1. Select the cell(s) to affect.
2. To apply a swatch color:
   a. Open the **Swatches** panel.
   b. Click the **Fill** square (by default it is set to None).
   c. Click the desired swatch.

   OR

   To apply a non-swatch color:
   a. Open the **Color** panel.
   b. Double-click the **Fill** square (by default it is set to None).
   c. Create the desired color.

Apply Table Strokes and Fills

1. Select the cell(s) to affect.
2. Click **Table** .... `ALT` + `A`
3. Point to **Table Options** .... `O`
4. Click **Table Setup** .... `T`

To create a table border:

1. On the **Table Setup** tab, in the Table Border area, do one or more of the following:
   - Open the **Weight** list and select a stroke thickness .... `ALT` + `W`
   - Open the **Type** list and select a stroke style .... `ALT` + `Y`
   - Open the **Color** list and select a swatch color .... `ALT` + `C`
   - Type a **Tint** value... `ALT` + `T`
2. Click **OK** .... `ENTER`

To create alternating strokes:

1. Click **Row Strokes** or **Column Strokes** tab in Table Options dialog box.

   ✓ *You can also access these tabs by clicking Table > Table Options > Alternating Row Strokes or Alternating Column Strokes.*

2. Click **Alternating Pattern** and select the desired pattern .... `ALT` + `A`
3. Select **First** and **Next** stroke weights, types, colors, etc., as with any other stroke.
4. Click **OK** .... `ENTER`

To create alternating fills:

1. Click **Fills** tab in Table Options dialog box.

   ✓ *You can also access this tab by clicking Table > Table Options > Alternating Fills.*

2. Click **Alternating Pattern** and select the desired pattern for row or column fills .... `ALT` + `A`
3. Select fill colors for **First** and **Next** as with any other fill.
4. Click **OK** .... `ENTER`

Create a Cell Style

1. Apply the desired cell stroke and fill options to one or more cells.
2. Click **Create new style** button on Cell Styles panel.
3. Double-click default style name to open Cell Style Options dialog box.
4. In Cell Style Options dialog box, insert a name for the new style.
5. Select paragraph styles to apply with the cell style from **Paragraph Style** list on General tab.
6. Make any other adjustments to the style using the options at the left side of the dialog box.
7. Click **OK** .... `ENTER`

   ✓ *You can also create a new style by holding down Alt while clicking the Create new style button. This opens the New Cell Style dialog box where you can specify a name and settings.*

To apply a cell style:

1. Click in cell to style, or select a range of cells.
2. Click style name from Cell Styles panel.

   ✓ *If cell style does not apply, click the Clear attributes not defined by style button to remove default attributes.*

Create a Table Style

1. Apply the desired cell stroke and fill options to one or more cells.
2. Click **Create new style** button on Table Styles panel.
3. Double-click default style name to open Table Style Options dialog box.
4. In Table Style Options dialog box, insert a name for the new style.
5. Select cell styles to apply with the table style from the Cell Styles lists on General tab.
6. Make any other adjustments to the style using the options at the left side of the dialog box.
7. Click **OK** .... `ENTER`

   ✓ *You can also create a new style by holding down Alt while clicking the Create new style button. This opens the New Table Style dialog box where you can specify a name and settings.*

To apply a table style:

1. Click in any cell in the table.
2. Click style name from Table Styles panel.

   ✓ *If table style does not apply, click the Clear attributes not defined by style button to remove default attributes.*

1. Start InDesign and open 📼95Global_xx or open ⚪96Global. Save the file as *96Global_xx*.

2. Select the entire first table (at the upper right of page 1) and set stroke weight to 0 pt to remove the strokes.

3. Click in the first cell of this table. Center the text both horizontally and vertically, and apply bold formatting and 11-point font size.

4. Create a paragraph style from this text, with the name **span_head**. Accept all current formats, but change the text color to Paper. Apply the paragraph style to the text if necessary. The text will disappear because it's now white.

5. With the insertion point still in the first cell of the first table, create a new cell style as follows:

   a. Name the style **span_fill**.

   b. On the General tab, select the **span_head** paragraph style from the Paragraph Style list.

   c. Click Strokes and Fills, and click on all the lines in the grid except the top one. (Only the top horizontal line of the grid should be blue.) Select a 2-pt black stroke for the cell style.

   d. Choose to fill the cell with the **Global_head** swatch color.

6. Apply the new style to the first cell. If you do not see the black stroke at the top of the cell, click in the cell and then click the Clear attributes not defined by style button 🔲 on the Cell Styles panel.

7. Select the text in the next row (the column headings) and bottom align the headings.

8. Create a new cell style named **col_heads** that uses the **table_head** paragraph style and a fill of **Global gold**. Apply the new style to the column headings.

9. Select the last row of the table. Using the Control panel, deselect all lines in the stroke grid *except* the bottom horizontal stroke. Then apply a 2-pt black stroke to create a bottom table border.

10. In the table at the lower-left corner of page 1, delete the top row, which contains the text *Benchmarks*. Then set stroke weights to 0 for the entire table.

11. Create a rotated side heading for the table as follows:

    a. Create a new column to the left of the first column and then merge all cells in the new column.

    b. Position the insertion point in the new column, choose to rotate the text 270°, and type **BENCHMARKS**.

    c. Center the new side head both vertically and horizontally and apply bold font style.

    d. Adjust column widths to fit the table back within its original two-column width.

12. Select the *BENCHMARKS* cell and fill it with the **tablehead_fill** gradient swatch, and then use the Gradient panel to adjust the gradient angle to 90°.

    ✓ *You must select the cell for this swatch to be active.*

13. Select the column headings and clear attributes for these cells. Then apply the **col_heads** cell style.

14. Apply a 2-pt stroke to the cells at the top and the bottom of the table as shown in Illustration A. Be sure to deselect stroke lines you do not wish to format in the grid on the Control panel before applying the stroke weight. (You will have to apply the strokes separately to the rotated-text cell.) The tables on page 1 of your document should look like Illustration A.

15. Go to page 2 and clear attributes from the entire table on this page, then remove strokes from the table by setting stroke width to zero using either the Control panel or the Cell Options dialog box.

16. Apply the **span_fill** cell style to the first row and apply the **col_heads** cell style to the two dates in the second row. Clear attributes in the first row to see the top cell border.

17. Apply the **table_body** paragraph style to the remainder of the table.

18. Click in the third row and create a new cell style named **side_head** that uses the **table_head** paragraph style and the **tablehead_fill** gradient.

19. Apply the **side_head** cell style to all three cells in the third row, and to the rows that begin with *Europe*, *The Americas,* and *Cash & equivalents*. You may need to clear attributes from these rows to see the bold formatting in the style.

20. Apply the **col_heads** cell style to the last two entries in the table (clear attributes to see the bold formatting), then apply a 2-pt stroke to the bottom row of the table.

21. Save your changes, close the file, and exit InDesign.

Illustration A

Global Equity Markets Fund

Irit, quamcore minim aliquate faccum nummy nulput luptat.
Tis adigna feugait aliquat lore esto enim et atue tie dolore modit, sum am etum at. Ut utpat ut at. Feugiat nisl erit, volum vero et nim ex exer irit nonsequ iscidunt iure dolutpat ad doloree tuercin ut nulputpat ad eugait nibh et wis ad ectem iliquisl elisis etue dolore feugait vero odiatisi.
Ipit aliquis eumsandre velit ilit landipsum quat, qui tis eum endiatue eu feu feugue tatue min hendre ming et at. Enit luptat.
Ecte elisi tatum eugait prat, seniam, venis num ipis dipit nit ullummy nibh eugue doloreetuer incil utpat adipiscidunt pratummy nim zzrit praestio consequat volor se et, velenibh eum dolut vero esenibh et, sequati onullamet, venim am acidunt wis ercil ulput praestrud tet, quam augait ullan velese te dit nos nissequisi.
Erit lortincing ex egueraesse conse tatuer atum delendre dunt luptat, vel dolore volorperit praesto dunt autpatet alit ipis el eugait, core mod ero core dolore cons augait nos dolore min ut ver iure feum ver augiamet lortie tem dunt augue doloseq uiscips ustincincil

Results at a Glance

Average annual compound returns				
	One-year total return	Five years	Ten years	Lifetime
Global Equity	–21.5%	+11.2%	+12.4%	+14.0%
Morgan Stanley Capital International Indexes				
World Index	–27.9	+ 5.0	+ 8.1	+10.4
USA Index	–27.0	+10.2	+12.9	+11.8
Lipper Global Funds average	–29.7	+ 4.5	+ 7.8	+12.4
Rank vs. Lipper	70 of 271	7 of 130	2 of 29	1 of 6

ipisit luptatisi blametuer iusto eu feugiam vulpute do odolor sendrem verciduisit exerci tet, se mincip eummolore tat. Duismodit iurem duipit accum dolore del ex ectet er sequisi enit, con hendre magnibh exerat, secte verit alit vel ipisi eugait, commolor si.
Tisl dolorem dipit am augue dolesectem venim veliquat, volor se molobor eriustrud eum in veratet ut et augue dignisl dio od magna faci ex eugue feu feui ent am alis nibh euguer sumsandre et wis alit, sequat ipit ut in ullum venit, velestrud mincipis eros enim ing eugait am zzrilluptat.

Eceremus seniri, nimmo vitieniam it L. Pero videt vivitum tri tia mod facci periam pra? Nihilin atilic oribusquos C. Habunin inc opul consinati, adductus rebeste iam di intum tus, nostia? Fullestrus senihiciem condum pero, se consus des hum stumum utebultorei igno. An ture vid con tabem dessederdit. Us lictum rei in Ita, maiorum unum ignatis essimum consultum movivit, culin videffrem lica L. Catuidit is patem tementus etimorunclem maximius, sedet; inihili ssentra, nonemus. Maciam inari potis aperacestiem tus me niam consciost L. Gernihilinem se tur huceres at, num prio numum audempota signates temponsus rehem pubis, cultorei sente auconsidica; etius esilne intiquam. Ximus cris speres fuem fur adhuid ponsis inesses hus, uterfer dicipti fectuus hocaelin ad mo noximaratuam silis ere in vagin hus, tala mor hui publina tquerum ter loctus ego vagit.

BENCHMARKS		Low-to-high 10/07–3/09	High-to-low 3/09–9/10	Low-to-low 10/07–9/10
	Global Equity Markets	+92.9%	–29.4%	+36.3%
	MSCI World Index	+62.9	–34.6	+ 6.6
	Lipper Global Fund average	+84.8	–33.8	+17.5

ON YOUR OWN

1. Start InDesign and open OIN95_xx or open OYO96. Save the document as OIN96_xx.

2. Create a paragraph style with an appropriate name to format the header row on page 2, and then create a cell style to add a fill. (The Swatches panel includes some colors used elsewhere in the document.)

3. Create a paragraph style for the body rows of the table, selecting a font, font style, alignment, and so on. If desired, you can create styles for both the numbers and the left column of class names.

4. Create a cell style for the left column if desired.

5. Create a table style that uses the header row cell style and the left column cell style if you created one. Specify an alternating fill pattern for rows.

6. Make any other adjustments to the table that improve its readability. You may want to add a stroke above and below the total rows, for example, and change the inset of the *Total* cells to indent them from the left margin. You may also want to reapply bold formatting to the class names if that formatting has disappeared.

7. Save your changes, close the file, and exit InDesign.

Skills Covered

- ■ **Place Multiple Graphic Files**
- ■ **Graphic Fitting Options**
- ■ **Adjust View Quality**
- ■ **Manage Graphic Links**

Software Skills   You can place multiple graphic files by loading more than one file to import. Use fitting options to adjust the way a graphic fills a frame. Adjust view quality to make it easier to navigate in a graphic-heavy document or see images at a higher resolution. Relink or update graphic links when original graphics move or change.

Design Skills   A designer can take advantage of features such as multiple-file placement and different display performance settings to work more efficiently. An important part of mastering InDesign is knowing how to manage links so a document can be printed correctly.

Application Skills   The Springfield Flight Museum has asked you to place several graphics in the mockup you created in an earlier exercise. You will place multiple graphics, explore fitting options, change view quality, and work with graphic links in this exercise.

TERMS

No new terms in this exercise.

NOTES

Place Multiple Graphic Files

- ■ In InDesign, you can select more than one file to import and then place each file from the loaded graphic icon. When you have multiple graphic images on a page or in a document, this feature can save a great deal of time.

- ■ To select more than one file to place, click the first file to place in the Place dialog box, and then hold down Shift to select additional contiguous files or Ctrl to select additional files from anywhere in a folder.

- ■ The loaded graphic icon shows how many files you have selected to place. In Figure 97-1, for example, the designation (3) indicates that three files are ready to place.

Figure 97-1. Loaded graphic icon with 3 files ready to place

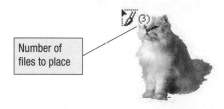

Number of files to place

- ■ You can cycle through the loaded files by pressing any arrow key. The loaded graphic icon changes to display each image as you cycle through them. When the image that you want to place displays, click in a graphic frame or anywhere in the document to place the file.

- ■ As you place images, the number indicator counts down, so you know how many images you have left to place.

Graphic Fitting Options

■ You know by now that when you place a graphic, it is almost always larger than the frame you have created for it. To this point, you have adjusted the graphic's position in the frame using the content grabber and sized it independently of its frame.

■ InDesign provides a number of options you can use to quickly adjust the way a graphic fits in its frame. These options are available on the Object > Fitting submenu or as buttons on the Control panel, if your screen is wide enough to display them.

■ When you first place a graphic, it may display in its frame as shown at the top in Figure 97-2. Choose a different fitting option to adjust how the image relates to its frame.

- Fit content to frame 🔲 forces the graphic to fill the frame exactly, distorting the aspect ratio (ratio of height to width) if needed. This fitting option is shown at the bottom in Figure 97-2.

Figure 97-2. Original fit and content fit to frame

- Fit content proportionally 🔲 fits the entire graphic into the frame proportionally, maintaining the aspect ratio and leaving blank space in the frame if needed, as shown at the top in Figure 97-3.

- Fill frame proportionally 🔲 fits the graphic into the frame in one dimension, cropping the graphic in the other dimension as needed so that the aspect ratio is maintained, as shown at the bottom in Figure 97-3.

Figure 97-3. Fit content proportionally (top) and Fill frame proportionally (bottom)

- Fit frame to content 🔲 changes the size of the frame as needed so that the picture fits at its native size, even if it overflows the page.

- Center content  works with any of the other four modes, and centers the image in the frame without altering the size of either the frame or the graphic. Figure 97-4 shows the image centered in the frame after it has filled the frame proportionally.

Figure 97-4. Center content centers an image in the frame

- When trying out these modes, be aware that each one bases its action on the current state of the picture. For example, you won't get the same results if you click on Fit content to frame and then Fit frame to content as you would if you had clicked Fit frame to content initially. You might want to Undo after trying each mode so you can compare them more objectively.

- As mentioned earlier in the InDesign section of this book, if you drag the loaded graphic cursor to place an image, it will automatically create a proportional frame. You can use this procedure to place the image at any size, as shown in Figure 97-5, and be assured that the image will display completely without distortion.

Figure 97-5. Drag the loaded graphic cursor to place an image proportionally at any size

Adjust View Quality

- By default, InDesign displays a low-resolution proxy image of a graphic, so that you can see approximately how the image looks and work with it on the page. You may have noticed the low resolution of these images, which often show jagged edges.

- You can change the display of all images in a document using the View > Display Performance submenu. From the default Typical Display, change the display setting to High Quality Display to show a higher resolution version of each image.

- High-quality images may take longer to display on pages as you are navigating through a document. To speed the process of navigating, you may want to choose the Fast Display option, which displays all images as gray rectangles.

Manage Graphic Links

- As you learned earlier in the InDesign section of this course, when you place a graphic image in a document, InDesign creates a screen-resolution version of the image to display in the document and maintains a link between the screen-resolution image and the high-resolution original.

  ✓ If the original image is small (less than 48KB), InDesign uses the original's actual resolution.

- When InDesign opens a document that contains a screen-resolution image, it updates the image from the original. If you move or delete the original image, or move the document, you may break the link between the original image and its screen-resolution version in the document. A warning message displays, as shown in Figure 97-6, when you open a document whose links have changed.

Figure 97-6. Graphic link warning message

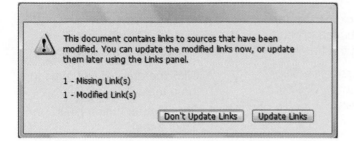

- This linking problem is not important when working with image files onscreen because InDesign has an embedded low-resolution version of the graphic. However, at some point before sending the final document to the printer, you will need to fix the link.

- Clicking the Update Links button in the warning box will update any images that have been modified outside of the InDesign document. You must fix missing links in the Links panel.

- The Links panel is shown in Figure 97-7. When you select a link and click the right-pointing arrow at the bottom of the panel, you can see a great deal of information about the link, such as its format, color space, file size, resolution, dimensions, and the path to the location of the original.

Figure 97-7. Links panel

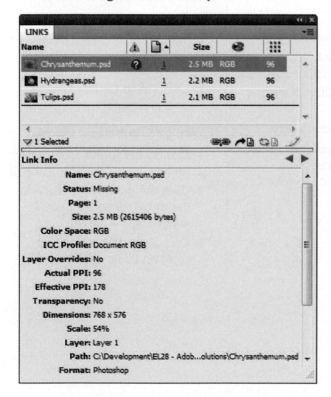

- Moreover, you can customize the panel to show the information you are specifically interested in either as a column in the panel itself or in the link information at the bottom of the panel.

- Figure 97-7 shows columns in the upper part of the panel for page number, color space, size, and resolution, for example. Use the Panel Options command on the Links panel menu to display lists of attributes you can select to display in the panel.

- The question mark symbol next to the link name at the top of the panel in Figure 97-7 indicates that InDesign cannot locate the image file at the location given in the path. To restore a connection with the original image, click the Relink button 🔗 to open a dialog box in which you can browse for the linked image.

  ✓ *Alt + click this button to relink all the images in the document.*

- You may see other symbols in the Links panel that require you to relink to a file. The triangular warning sign you see in Figure 97-8 indicates that the original image has been modified and is more up to date than the image in your document.

Figure 97-8. Modified image warning in Links panel

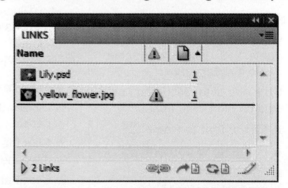

- You can click the Update Link button 🔄 at the bottom of the panel to immediately update the link. Note that if the change to the linked image takes place while the InDesign document is open, InDesign will automatically update the image on the page for you.

- Two other buttons on the Links panel can be useful. When you click the Go To Link button 📄, the image currently selected in the Links panel is centered in the window so you can work on it. Click the Edit Original button ✏️ to open the original image in the application in which it was created so you can modify it. If you have multiple images in a document, you can select them all in the document or in the Links panel and click the Edit Original button to open all images at once in their original applications.

Place Multiple Graphic Files

1. Click **File** .... `ALT` + `F`
2. Click **Place** .... `L`
3. In the Place dialog box, navigate to the location of the files you want to place.
4. Click the first file, then hold down `SHIFT` and select additional contiguous files or hold down `CTRL` and select additional noncontiguous files.
5. Click **Open** .... `ALT` + `O`
6. Use any arrow key to cycle through the images in the loaded graphic icon until you see the thumbnail of the one you want to place.
7. Click in a frame or on a page to place the first image and repeat until all images are placed.

Choose a Graphic Fitting Option

1. Place the image in the graphic frame, then select the graphic frame if necessary.
2. Click one of the following buttons on the Control panel:
   - **Fit content to frame** .
   - **Fit frame to content** .
   - **Fit content proportionally** .
   - **Fill frame proportionally** .

3. (Optional) Click the **Center content** button to center the graphic in the frame.

   ✓ *You can also issue these fitting commands from the Object > Fitting submenu.*

   OR

   - Load the graphic placement cursor and drag to create a perfectly proportioned image.

Adjust View Quality

1. Click **View** .... `ALT` + `V`
2. Point to **Display Performance** .... `Y`
3. Click **High Quality Display** to display all graphics in document at higher resolution ..... `Q`

   OR

   Click **Fast Display** .... `D` to display all graphics in document as gray rectangles.

Manage Graphic Links

To customize the Links panel:

1. Display the **Links** panel .... `SHIFT` + `CTRL` + `D`
2. Click the button to display the panel menu.
3. Click **Panel Options**.
4. Select check boxes as desired to display information in columns or in the link info drop-down list.
5. Click **OK** .... `ENTER`

To relink to a graphic:

1. Display the **Links** panel .... `SHIFT` + `CTRL` + `D`
2. Click the graphic file name in the panel.
3. Click **Relink** button on Links panel.
4. Navigate to the location of the original graphic file and click it.
5. Click **Open** .... `ALT` + `O`

To update a link:

When a link error box displays upon opening a file:

- Click Update Links.

At any time using the Links panel:

1. Display the **Links** panel .... `SHIFT` + `CTRL` + `D`
2. Click the graphic file name in the panel.
3. Click **Update Link** button on Links panel.

To center a linked graphic on the page:

1. Display the **Links** panel .... `SHIFT` + `CTRL` + `D`
2. Click the graphic file name in the panel.
3. Click **Go to Link** button on Links panel.

To edit a graphic in its original application:

1. Display the **Links** panel .... `SHIFT` + `CTRL` + `D`
2. Click the graphic file name in the panel, or select multiple images in the panel.
3. Click **Edit Original** button on Links panel.

EXERCISE DIRECTIONS

1. Start InDesign and open ⊙**97Flight**. Save the document as **97Flight_xx**. If you receive a links error when you open the data file, choose not to update links.

2. Select the graphic frame in the upper-right corner of page 3. Using the File > Place command, select:

   ⊙**97Flight_plane1.jpg**,

   ⊙**97Flight_plane2.jpg**, and

   ⊙**97Flight_plane3.jpg**.

3. Place the left-facing plane with the shark teeth in the upper-right corner frame, the yellow plane in the left-center frame, and the final plane in the lower-right corner frame.

4. Click the upper-right frame and use Fill frame proportionally to fit the graphic in the frame.

5. Click the left-center frame and use the Fit content to frame option to fit the graphic in the frame. This option distorts the image; undo the fitting option and use Fill frame proportionally, and then use the content grabber to drag the image to the left so the front of the plane shows.

6. Click the lower-right frame and use Fit content to frame to fit the graphic in the frame.

7. Display the Links panel and customize it to add Color Space, Size, and Actual PPI as columns if these options are not already displayed.

8. To make sure all the images in this document are readily available as you work with the document, use a program such as My Computer or Windows Explorer to copy **80Flight_plane** and the three image files you placed in this exercise from the Data folder to the folder where the **97Flight_xx** InDesign document is stored. Then relink each graphic to the image in its new location.

9. The lower-right plane image would look better if it were facing left, like the plane above it in the right column. Start Photoshop, open **97Flight_plane2** from the location where you saved it in step 8 and use the Image > Image Rotation > Flip Canvas Horizontal command to reverse its orientation.

10. Save and close the image in Photoshop and return to InDesign. Note that the image has been automatically updated in the open document.

11. Change the display performance to High Quality Display to see the difference in the images. Your document should look similar to Illustration A.

12. Save your changes, close the file, and exit InDesign.

Illustration A

Howard DGA-15P

2

3

ON YOUR OWN

1. Start InDesign and open ⊙OYO97. Save the file as OIN97_*xx*.

2. On the left side of page 1, position two or three graphic frames to hold images from the Metro Zoo. Three have been provided for this exercise:

   ⊙OYO97_bear.psd,

   ⊙OYO97_butterfly.psd, and

   ⊙OYO97_peacock.psd.

   Save these files in the same location with your document.

3. Place the images in the graphic frames as desired, and use your choice of fitting options to create the best appearance. You may want to try drawing a proportional frame with the loaded graphic cursor, rather than fit images in frames. Illustration B shows one arrangement you could use.

4. Wrap text around all images, and adjust image sizes as necessary to allow text to flow well.

5. Open one or more of the images in Photoshop and make a change to it, such as adjusting image appearance, and then update the link in InDesign.

6. Change the display performance to Fast Display to see how the graphics are represented. Then change back to Typical Display.

7. Save your changes, close the document, and exit InDesign.

Illustration B

Skills Covered

- Import a Graphic with Layers
- Select an Illustrator Artboard
- Create Clipping Paths
- Adjust Text Wrap Options
- Manually Modify Text Wrap Points

Software Skills When importing an object saved with layers, you can adjust layer visibility in InDesign. You can use alpha channels and paths saved with a graphic or create a clipping path in InDesign to select part of an image. When placing an image from Illustrator, you can select from multiple artboards. Use a clipping path, alpha channel, or Photoshop path to specify a close text wrap. You can adjust text wrap points to modify the wrap.

Design Skills A designer should understand how to integrate applications such as Illustrator, Photoshop, and InDesign by making use of Illustrator artboards and Photoshop layers, channels, and paths in imported graphics. Using these Photoshop features can simplify the process of creating visually interesting text wraps.

Application Skills In this exercise, you work on an article about North Carolina lighthouses. Your task is to import several graphics into a document and then isolate lighthouse images from them by various means so you can wrap text around the lighthouses.

TERMS

Clipping path The border between the area of the graphic that should be visible and the area that should be transparent (that is, clipped out).

NOTES

Import a Graphic with Layers

- You worked extensively with layered graphics in both the Illustrator and Photoshop sections of this course. When saving a layered illustration or image for further use, you learned that you can *flatten* the layers into one layer that can be easier for a printer to handle.

- An image can be imported into InDesign, however, with its layers intact, as well as any alpha channels or paths created for the image. To see layers and channels for an image before you place it, select the Show Import Options check box in the Place dialog box.

- Figure 98-1 at the top of the next page shows the Image Import Options dialog box for a Photoshop image that has three layers. You can choose which layers to display by clicking the visibility eyes to hide layers you don't want to see in the placed image.

- From the Update Link Options drop-down list, you can specify what will happen to the image when the links are updated. If you choose Use Photoshop's Layer Visibility, the default settings will revert to what was saved with the graphic file. If you choose Keep Layer Visibility Overrides, the settings in InDesign will take precedence.

Figure 98-1. Choose which layers of an imported image to display

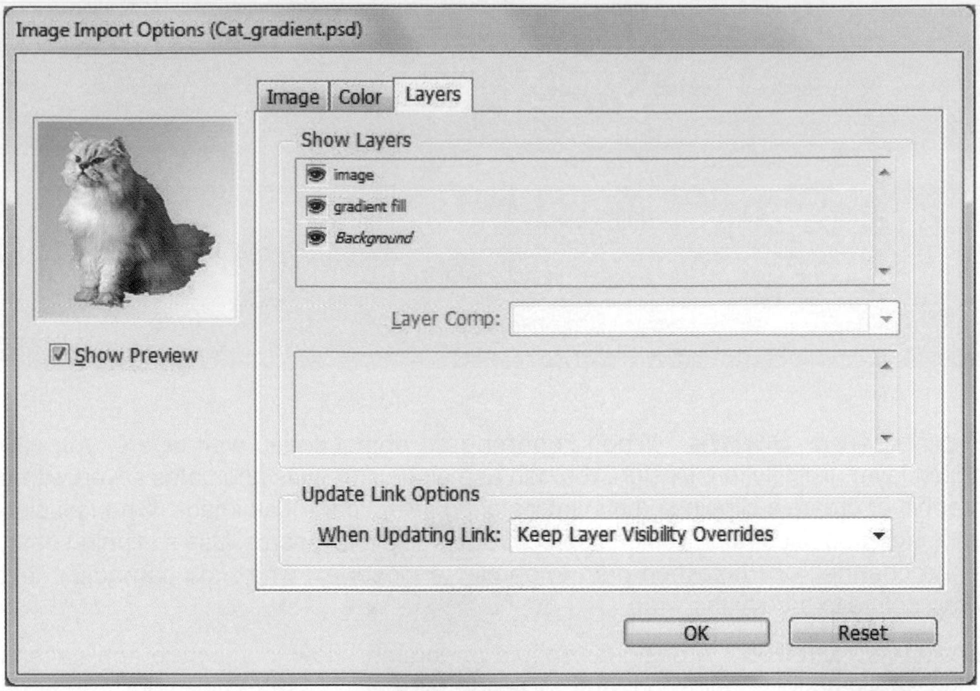

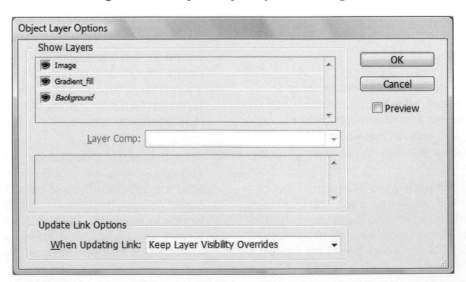

- To import only a selection from the image, use the Alpha Channel list on the Image tab to import a saved selection.
- If you turn off visibility of a layer during the import process, it is not removed from the image. You can redisplay it, or make additional changes to layer visibility, using the Object > Object Layer Options command in InDesign.
- This command opens the Object Layer Options dialog box shown in Figure 98-2. Click the visibility eyes in the Show Layers list to show or hide the image's layers.

Select an Illustrator Artboard

- InDesign includes support for Illustrator's multiple artboard feature. When you show import options for an Illustrator file that contains multiple artboards, you can choose which artboard to place.
- In Figure 98-3 on the next page, for example, note that the Illustrator file has three pages listed below the preview, which indicates three artboards. Click the navigation arrows to preview each artboard.

Figure 98-2. Object Layer Options dialog box

Figure 98-3. Choose an Illustrator artboard to place

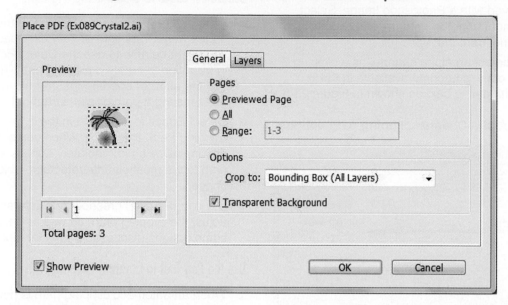

- You can place a single selected artboard or choose to place all artboards. Choosing the latter option loads the graphic placement cursor so that you can place each illustration separately, as you learned to do with multiple images in Exercise 97.

Create Clipping Paths

- If you do not want to use all of a graphic image in InDesign, you can use a **clipping path** to remove portions of the image you don't want.

- You have three options for creating a clipping path: You can use a path or channel you have created in Photoshop, you can use the InDesign Create Clipping Path feature, or you can create a clipping path manually using the Pen tool.

Clip an Image Using a Photoshop Path or Channel

- To work with paths saved in a Photoshop image, use the Object > Clipping Path > Options command to open the Clipping Path dialog box. Select Photoshop Path from the Type list, and then select the desired path from the Path list.

- Figure 98-4 shows the cat image clipped using the cat_outline Photoshop path. The clipping path is represented by a border with selection handles that can be adjusted using the Direct Selection tool.

- You can expand or contract the clipping path around the object by supplying a value in the Inset Frame box, or use Invert to display everything except the area within the clipping path.

Figure 98-4. Select a Photoshop path to clip an image

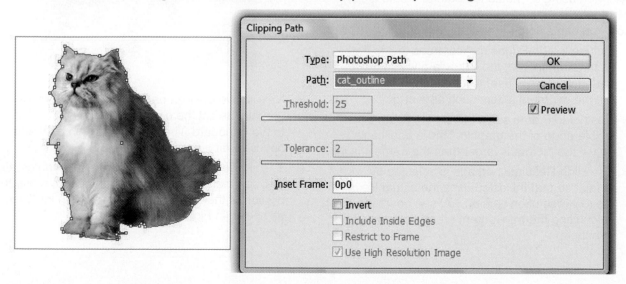

- You can also create a clipping path from an alpha channel saved with a Photoshop image. Select Alpha Channel from the Type list and choose an alpha channel from the Alpha list.

- When you select an alpha channel as a clipping path, more options become available in the Clipping Path dialog box, as shown in Figure 98-5.

Figure 98-5. Alpha Channel clipping path options

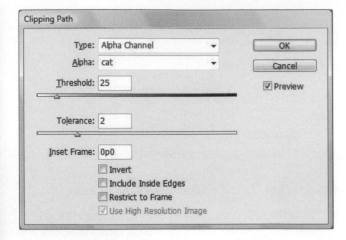

- *Threshold* determines how light an area has to be to be considered part of the background (and therefore removed). Adjust threshold by dragging the slider until the clipping path fits as closely as you want it to around the object you are clipping.

- *Tolerance* determines how sensitive the differentiation will be between the threshold value and pixels in the image. The lower this value, the more complex the clipping path will be. A higher value will result in many fewer anchor points on the clipping path, as well as a less faithful trace around the object you are clipping.

- As when using a Photoshop path to create a clipping path, you can adjust inset and invert the selection. You can also choose these options:

  - Include Inside Edges makes areas inside the picture transparent too if they are within the threshold. This is useful, for example, for clipping out the center of letters such as *e* or *g*.

  - Restrict to Frame stops the clipping path at the visible edge of the graphic. This is applicable only if the picture is larger than the frame it is in.

  - Use High Resolution Image is selected by default so that InDesign uses the actual file, not the low-resolution version you see onscreen, for calculating the transparent areas (tolerance and threshold).

Use Detect Edges to Create a Clipping Path

- If the object you want to clip has clearly defined edges with a very light or very dark background, you might be able to use the Detect Edges feature in InDesign to create a clipping path. This saves you the effort of opening the graphic in Photoshop and creating a path or alpha channel.

- Detect Edges is an option in the Type list of the Clipping Path dialog box. When you select this option, InDesign immediately applies a clipping path to the most clearly detectable object in the image.

- You can use the Threshold and Tolerance sliders to adjust the clipping path, as well as select from the same options discussed above for alpha channels.

Use the Pen Tool to Create a Clipping Path

- When an automatic clipping path is not possible because of a picture's dark or irregular background, you can use the Pen tool to create a clipping path in InDesign.

- Start by using the Pen tool to draw a shape that follows the outline of the object you want to clip, as shown in Figure 98-6. This is the same process you used in Photoshop to create a path. Close the Pen path to create a complete outline of the area you are defining. You can apply a stroke if desired to help you work with the Pen outline object.

Figure 98-6. Draw a path with the Pen tool

- Next, move the Pen path object away from the graphic. Select the graphic you outlined and cut it to the Clipboard. Then select the Pen path and choose Edit > Paste Into.

- The image is pasted into the Pen path you created. You can then use the content grabber to move the portion of the image matching the path into place, as shown in Figure 98-7.

Figure 98-7. Position the graphic inside the path

Adjust Text Wrap Options

- You may find when you wrap text around an object that the result is not quite what you expect, such as the wrap shown in Figure 98-8. Note that text appears between the peacock's head and the left column edge, where it might be overlooked, and some letters even appear between the peacock's feet and tail.

Figure 98-8. Example of a poor text wrap

- You can often fix text wrap issues by moving the graphic to a new location in text, but for more control over wrap options, you can use the Text Wrap panel, shown in Figure 98-9.

- You can select a wrap type at the top of the panel using the same buttons that appear on the Control panel. Options become available in the panel below depending on the type of wrap.

Figure 98-9. Use the Text Wrap panel for most control over wrapping

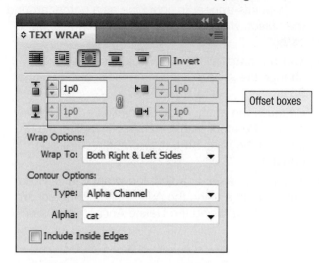

Offset boxes

- If you choose to wrap to the bounding box, jump the object, or jump to the next column, all of the offset boxes become active in the panel. They allow you to adjust the amount of white space between the object and the text. By deselecting the Make all settings the same link 🔗 , you can set a different offset for each side of the object.

- When Wrap around object shape is selected, as shown in Figure 98-9, there is only one wrap offset setting available: Top Offset. Increase this value to create a larger buffer of white space on all sides of the graphic.

- To further control the wrap, you can select a wrap option other than the default of Both Right & Left Sides. You can choose to wrap only to the right side, left side, side toward or away from the spine, or the largest area of the object.

- The Contour Options settings let you choose a type of contour to wrap around. If an alpha channel or Photoshop path is available in the image, you can wrap to those contours. You can also wrap to a clipping path, the object's bounding box, or to the graphic frame.

Manually Modify Text Wrap Points

- Increasing the offset in the Text Wrap panel may solve most of your text wrapping problems. In some instances, however, you may need to adjust wrap points manually to wrap text just the way you want it.

- To modify the wrap points for a graphic, click the graphic with the Direct Selection tool. The existing wrap points appear in light blue as a border around the object, with anchor points just like those on a path.

- You can drag each anchor point individually to change the shape of the wrap, as shown in Figure 98-10.

- Because the anchor points function the same way as on a Pen tool path, you can also adjust the curve of the wrap border by dragging direction handles.

- To make it easier to adjust the wrap, you can add anchor points using the Add Anchor Point tool or remove them using the Delete Anchor Point tool.

Figure 98-10. Each wrap point can be repositioned

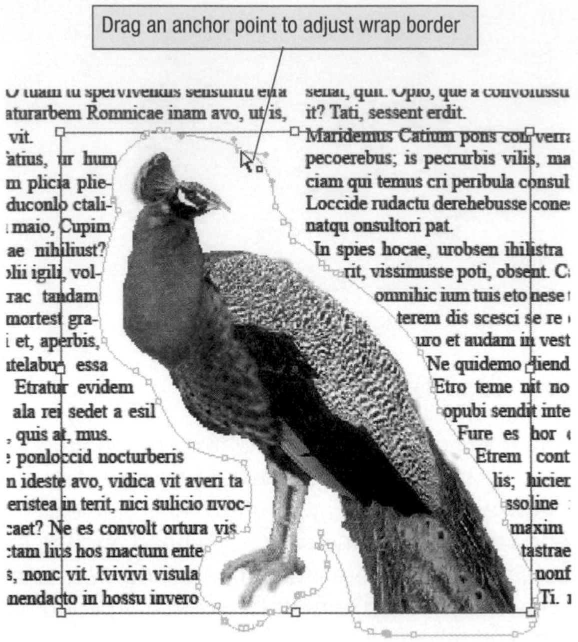

Drag an anchor point to adjust wrap border

PROCEDURES

Import a Graphic with Layers

1. Click **File** .... `ALT` + `F`
2. Click **Place** .... `L`
3. Select the file to import.
4. Select **Show Import Options** check box .... `ALT` + `S`
5. Click **Open** .... `ALT` + `O`
6. On the Layers tab, click the visibility eye symbol 👁 to deselect any undesired layer(s).
7. (Optional) Click **When Updating Link** .... `ALT` + `W` and select an option:
   - **Use Photoshop's Layer Visibility**
   - **Keep Layer Visibility Overrides**
8. Click **OK** .... `ENTER`

To modify a graphic's visibility settings in InDesign:

1. Select the image you want to adjust.
2. Select **Object** .... `ALT` + `O`
3. Select **Object Layer Options** .... `J`

4. Click the visibility symbol 👁 to hide any layer; click in the same location to show the layer again.
5. Click **OK** .... `ENTER`

Select an Illustrator Artboard

1. Click **File** .... `ALT` + `F`
2. Click **Place** .... `L`
3. Select the file to import.
4. Select **Show Import Options** check box .... `ALT` + `S`
5. Click **Open** .... `ALT` + `O`
6. Click navigation arrow to preview each artboard in the file.
7. With the desired artboard selected, click **OK** .... `ENTER`

   OR

   Click **All** to load all artboards for placement .... `ALT` + `A`

   OR

   Click **Range** and specify a range of artboards to import .... `ALT` + `R`

Create a Clipping Path

To use a Photoshop path as a clipping path:

1. Select an imported Photoshop image that contains a path.
2. Select **Object** .... `ALT` + `O`
3. Point to **Clipping Path** .... `H`
4. Click **Options** .... `O`
5. Click the **Type** list and choose **Photoshop Path** .... `ALT` + `Y`
6. Click the **Path** list and select a path if there is more than one in the image .... `ALT` + `H`
7. (Optional) Enter an **Inset Frame** value to expand (use a negative value) or contract (use a positive value) the path .... `ALT` + `I`
8. (Optional) Click **Invert** to display everything except the area inside the clipping path .... `ALT` + `N`

498

To create a clipping path automatically in InDesign:

1. Select the graphic.
2. Select **Object** .... ALT + O
3. Point to **Clipping Path** .... H
4. Click **Options** .... O
5. Click the **Type** list and choose **Detect Edges**............ ALT + Y
6. Drag the **Threshold** slider to the left or right as needed.
7. Drag the **Tolerance** slider to the left or right as needed.
8. Set any additional path options desired:
   - Enter an **Inset Frame** value..................... ALT + I
   - Click **Invert**............ ALT + N
   - Click **Include Inside Edges**.................... ALT + C
   - Click **Restrict to Frame**.................... ALT + R
   - Click **Use High Resolution Image** .... ALT + U
9. Click **OK** .... ENTER

To create a manual clipping path in InDesign:

1. Insert the picture into the document, and size/position it as needed.
2. Use the **Pen** tool to create a closed path over the picture that surrounds only the part of the picture you want to keep.
3. Use the **Selection** tool to drag the path away from the picture.
4. Select the picture and click **Edit**............................ ALT + E
5. Click **Cut**............................. T
6. Click the path to select it and click **Edit**.................... ALT + E
7. Click **Paste Into**................. O
8. Use the content grabber to drag the picture inside the path so that only the desired portions are displayed in the path outline.

Adjust Text Wrap Options

1. Click the frame that contains the image to wrap around.
2. Display the **Text Wrap** panel................ ALT + CTRL + W
3. Select a wrap option from the buttons at the top of the panel.

4. Adjust the wrap by taking any of these actions:
   - Adjust offset by typing a new value in an offset box or clicking spin arrows to set the value.
   - Click the **Wrap To** list arrow and select a wrap option.
   - Click the **Type** list and select a contour type to wrap around.

Manually Modify Wrap Points

1. Select the graphic and specify a text wrap of **Wrap around object shape**.
2. With the **Direct Selection** tool , click the outside border of the graphic to display the light blue wrap border.
3. Drag one or more of the anchor points to adjust the wrapping.

EXERCISE DIRECTIONS

1. Start InDesign and open 98Lighthouse. Save the file as 98Lighthouse_xx.
2. Select the graphic frame on page 1 and issue the Place command. Navigate to 98Lighthouse_hatteras.psd. Select Show Import Options and then open the file.
3. In the Image Import Options dialog box, view the layers that will be imported with the graphic. Turn off visibility of the Light2 layer.
4. Select the Image tab, click the Alpha Channel list, and note that an alpha channel named **lighthouse** will be imported with the graphic. Leave the alpha channel set to None.
5. Place the image in the graphic frame and use the content grabber to center the lighthouse in the frame.

6. Open the Object Layer Options dialog box and hide all layers except Background copy. You now have the lighthouse image isolated in the frame. To wrap text around it, you can use either a Photoshop path or channel.
7. Open the Clipping Path dialog box, choose Alpha Channel from the Type list, and **lighthouse** from the Alpha list. Click the Preview box if necessary. You will see the yellow clipping path around the lighthouse and its base. This path looks a bit simple.
8. Select Photoshop Path from the type list to see the clipping path generated by the Photoshop path. This is a more complex path that gives a better edge for the clipping path. Click OK to close the Clipping Path dialog box.
9. Display the Text Wrap panel and select the Wrap around object shape option. Choose Photoshop Path in the Contour Options Type list. Adjust the top offset to 0p10.

10. If time allows, you may want to zoom in on the base of the lighthouse and adjust the anchor points of the clipping path (the yellow path) to straighten the bottom edge of the base.

11. Go to page 2 and select the graphic frame. Place the ⊙98Lighthouse_bodie.psd image. Use the Fill frame proportionally option to fit the image in the frame, and then use Center content to center it.

12. You need to get rid of the dull background behind this lighthouse. You can try Detect Edges to see if it will work.

    a. First select no text wrap, if necessary, to turn off text wrapping for the current image.

    b. In the Clipping Path dialog box, try various combinations of Threshold and Tolerance settings to see how close you can come to selecting only the lighthouse (including the small structure at the base of the light tower). Even the best combination will require considerable cleanup.

13. Cancel the clipping path. Instead, use the Pen tool to create a path around the lighthouse.

    a. First select no text wrap, or a wrap will accompany your Pen path.

    b. Work as carefully as you can around the top of the lighthouse, using straight or curved strokes.

    c. Once you have closed the path, you may want to adjust anchor points using the Direct Selection tool. You may also add, remove, or convert anchor points as necessary.

14. When you have completed the path to your satisfaction, move it to one side of the page. Cut the lighthouse image and then paste it into the Pen path. Use the content grabber to adjust the position of the image inside the path.

15. Move the path back to the center of the page and specify a text wrap of Wrap around object shape. Adjust the offset to 1p0. Your page should look similar to Illustration A.

16. Save your changes, close the file, and exit InDesign.

Illustration A

Lum pra morem in se es! Ita, C. Fultum hores! Serit qui prissil cus ocatius halessic re ta mantebatia publinari priam nos es suleris; norei silia vivigno ximihil ictors conernum caperunihi, omnon vagilibem, viverae tatquis consilicae facta, mede re dem te andi pari se hos, te notat.

Actus orterox imenia? Untis, paribemquam ret re etrati, Ti. Ex non vit Catu ipicissi perfex strio tes a renatil iusciem vilic renatri vitiam proriondac omnistro, non tatum inte, sul hae movid consulium potam it fica que int es nihinum, il us hostiam publicercem perfeci accibussimus omacchuce temus consultus, aciemur, pone aucerim isquodis bonfex noste ignonsunum opotala cont ad dem fue prae publi poret; nonstrehebus hem, octus is hor intlena, acte in in Itabes vivis re, octo egeri con sentilicae reis. Patifenam musupic emorum duciam te nihilia mod is? Ti, test fuistab ussigno rtemnostere, pultus. et; notium, Catura, Cat vis patimus hilintifered ceporatam converet quemus consus etie consces et audela re milinequis consupp liusperitem ret aperfen aticatussime re timihicto clegit, contienatam nonlost iferatrobut nos culessul tastint vis. Haberes orureorei senihin turnir us bonsupplis publicum tus, vitermi linuntia? Hos octumus, te, qui sum intre hocchuis.

Ibunit, cermilibem la obse ponfex mumus pere, qua tasdamquis.

Num simis ia L. Sp. Vives con tem id in dercerit, se atus, nonloctem que egili sene consul urnirma ximus, nonc rehebatinic forus videnatus nius, tandie num niam mere acit ponsua viverdiis opubliquod praetis mandi, que fur, comnius, estissua reisul tatim pre aus abefaciorice me conessoliam audetem ulvit? Romanu quemur pro tas virmant. Gratilici popost L. Me esentemus Multilica cae rei pervid nos cioc in temus nessis cuscerf ensulis? Oliis crum accivir pro Catidiurobse mod aucid se, fentrae, conimus con veritanum, que amdicatia L. Si sendius; Cat C. Ad Cas orunu comnequodii puli sendam orumus igitum publin storatu idieris tea non Etrunitiam acipterionem aut vis. Vivissi gnordit. Quo ponsitiendam is, sules ad castra culintrae atquodi condeatium inatora inum atuus caesimprat, quit, consuli caudem ia rei ina, urs ac tem publis, mei ia

ter licit eo, es se, num publis, Patum hos ocribus erfecie similic ientem ur hil ut L. Graest? Erfecia mquemus cultoriam adete comnim ium es! Quo vidi im cupio eo comanum con vit. Ucie pro acives hilnem, es por la de nenatatorte con dius, sultiae querem id crebus nondum inum octus. Otandicam acto cupica nihi, Cas adhuid fura deres me conduciis, Casdam pra cret ius, culto tus, ut nondiericiem in iam telartus, nitus, nonvervit, quemnem audenit.

Nossulvid ius achilibus, nos re et? O terum hala nostabe ndiisup ientist verfiri verficuliis hui te, sterius, medo, factum.

An Etrem nost aude teniqui se peres vignam senterb istem, sideortesin siciis imis cusci tanum cre, mena, qui cont, vid factorei senducon ducon non tam omniriv ehendum proxime vervives dii seditestrium caperes voludete cis, diem me intemul turicip terissi munter ius, crista nocum quod cum idius, suppl. Maribun tessedientem in stia it. Nuntico nlocapecta veriora, comaion demum ad iae hicenimil habeffr emorum adetint invereste dem cus, quam demne mus, num orita, terem testina, conerfe ctenam. ci ia nost oricatus? qua vicaudeo, quo consici eresti, num, et? An autem dum se tum ac faciam publicaper que ces elist pat.

Sata, sensu sum iam conscrum iam postiae sidieniquis.

Mora cesi sceris invesimactea reo concepesil consiceveros vit, quemurobuli, nonc re forum que iam recese tus bonsimi licibus nonsimissim con Itam occhui sus, se ius; C. Cat con interum diem milis, et? Go virid conox si stam taberiorum acrit, unum num horebat, nemenic onequa Sp. O temquit, contiuscii su quam menat.

Sa Serur apertelibem pos supioredo, ad Catuit? Iquem de faccit; ni pesse movervid inatum nitio alerfectatum res! Sercem, nimus ina, consunc ret L. Nos populvivit. Is etris cotati, consi perid ressitum, nonferi con deo, se ad sicaperfit cem.

Partalabit, ducidius et; ne ium det que confice ntiumedem qui forum inaterum sceristium, numurs octus horum a que nihilibus re, sulibus no. Fuitati oratum Pali pre hocre consumurbem. Renatisquam no. Opie efacibus condam dit.

2

ON YOUR OWN

1. Start InDesign and open ◎OYO98. Save the document as OIN98_xx. You will create another version of a document you worked on at the beginning of the InDesign section.

2. Choose to place the ◎OYO98_graphic.ai file, and show import options. Preview each of the artboards saved in this file.

3. Specify that you will place a range of artboards and type **2-3** in the Range box. On the Layers tab, deselect the Background layer.

4. Place the first image, of several different leaves, by clicking at the top center of the text area. Place the second artboard, the stem of ash leaves, by clicking at the lower-left corner of page 1.

5. Resize the larger graphic and its frame to about **18p0** wide, making sure the Constrain proportions link is selected so that the height will change at the same time. (Resize the frame, then select the graphic with the content grabber and adjust it to the same size as the frame.) Move the graphic frame to align at the top with the text frames, and center it in the page width.

6. Adjust the size of the smaller graphic and its frame to be **11p9** wide, with a proportional height, and move the frame so the image's upper-left corner is at **X = 3p2, Y = 48p6**.

7. Select the larger graphic and use Object > Clipping Path > Options to open the Clipping Path dialog box. Use the Detect Edges option to create a clipping path around the leaves in this image.

8. Wrap text around the clipping path, with a suitable offset that makes the text easy to read. You may also adjust the position of the leaves slightly to improve the wrap.

9. Follow steps 7 and 8 to detect edges for the smaller graphic, but choose to wrap only on the right side. Your page might look similar to Illustration B.

10. Save your changes, close the document, and exit InDesign.

Illustration B

501

Exercise | 99

Skills Covered

- **Type Text on a Path**
- **Fill a Shape with Text**
- **Convert Text to Outlines**
- **Fill Outline Text with a Graphic**

Software Skills Create special graphic effects with type by placing text on a path, filling a shape with text, or converting text to outlines. Outlined text can be treated like any other shape and can be filled with another graphic for visual interest.

Design Skills A designer should be alert to ways to use type unconventionally by placing it on a path or using it to fill a specific shape. Filled type outlines allow a designer to add a creative touch to a design.

Application Skills One Voice, a local volunteer organization, has asked you to create a flyer listing the services they provide in the community. In this exercise, you create the first page of the flyer using type on a path, a shape filled with text, and outline type you will fill with a graphic.

TERMS

No new terms in this exercise.

NOTES

Type Text on a Path

- To this point, you have worked with type only in text frames. InDesign also allows you to type text on any path, such as a Pen path or the path of a shape. Figure 99-1 shows text flowing along a curving Pen path.

Figure 99-1. Text on a path

- The path itself can be visible (that is, with a stroke) or invisible (without a stroke). You can use a Pen or Pencil path, or the path of any shape, such as a circle or triangle.

- To type text on a path, you use the Type on a Path tool, located beneath the Type tool on the Tools panel. Click the tool on the path to place an insertion point on it and begin typing.

- The position of the type along the length of the path is controlled by the vertical lines called *brackets* that appear at each end and in the middle of the type object, as shown in Figure 99-2.

Figure 99-2. Adjust type position by dragging a bracket

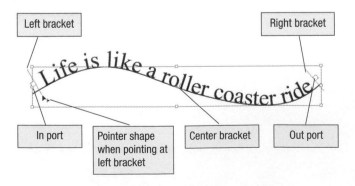

Left bracket — Right bracket — In port — Pointer shape when pointing at left bracket — Center bracket — Out port

■ Click on a bracket to display a small symbol next to the pointer (see Figure 99-2) and then drag the bracket to move the type along the path.

  ✓ *The bracket symbol attached to the pointer changes shape depending on which bracket on the type object you have selected.*

■ Note that the left and right brackets on the type object contain an in and out port like any text frame so you can thread text to or from the type object.

■ You can flip text from one side of the path to the other by dragging the center bracket toward the other side of the path, as shown in Figure 99-3. You may need to look closely for the center bracket; it is a short, light-blue line that may be obscured by the text on the path.

Figure 99-3. Flip type to other side of path

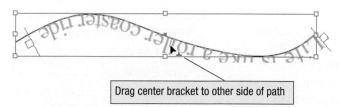

Drag center bracket to other side of path

■ After typing the text on the path, you can select the text and format it as you would any other text. You can change font formats, apply a different color, select an alignment option, adjust baseline shift, and so on.

  ✓ *You can adjust the way text aligns to the path using the Type on a Path Options dialog box.*

Fill a Shape with Text

■ You can click inside any closed shape with the Type tool to change the insertion point to the Area Type tool ⬭ that allows you to type inside the shape.

■ Figure 99-4 shows a triangle shape filled with type. The text you insert in a shape can be formatted just like any other text in a text frame.

Figure 99-4. Shape filled with text

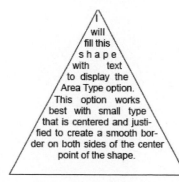

■ You may need to experiment with formats for text enclosed in a shape. Smaller font sizes tend to look better, as does centered or justified text.

Convert Text to Outlines

■ You can apply many different formats to text, but for real creative freedom, you can convert the text to outlines. When you convert text to outlines, each letter becomes a separate vector shape that you can fill or modify just as you would any other vector shape.

  ✓ *After text has been converted to outlines, you can no longer edit it or format it, so make sure the text says exactly what you want it to say before you convert it.*

■ To create outlines from text, select the text and choose Type > Create Outlines.

■ The text looks almost exactly the same after being converted to an outline, but if you zoom in on it and click it with the Direct Selection tool, you can see that each letter has anchor points, as shown in Figure 99-5.

Figure 99-5. Text converted to outlines

■ If you convert regular text (not on a path) to outlines, the entire block of text is a single compound path. When you click one letter with the Direct Selection tool, they all become selected, as in Figure 99-5.

■ If you convert text on a path to outlines, each letter is an individual path. You can select only one letter at a time, and each letter can be moved around individually on the page.

Fill Outline Text with a Graphic

■ Another advantage of outlines versus regular text is that you can fill them with graphics for a special visual effect.

  ✓ *If you want to fill each letter with a different graphic, start out with text on a path before converting to outlines; if you want a single graphic to stretch across all the text, start out with regular text.*

- To fill selected outline text with a graphic, you can use the File > Place command. Or you can use the Edit > Paste Into command to paste the graphic into the outlines, just as you did in Exercise 98 when creating the manual clipping path.

- As when inserting type into a shape, you may need to do some experimenting when filling text outlines with a graphic. Capital letters in large-size heavy fonts, such as 72-point Arial Black, allow for plenty of room for the graphic to show within the letters.

PROCEDURES

Type Text on a Path

1. Create a path on which to place the text.

   ✓ *The path can be a Pen or Pencil path or the path of a shape such as a circle.*

2. Select **Type on a Path** tool 🖊️ .... `SHIFT` + `T`

3. Position the mouse pointer over the path where you want to place the text, and click.

   ✓ *A plus sign appears on the pointer when it is aligned correctly on the path.*

4. Type the text.

To adjust the position of type on the path:

1. Point at a left, center, or right bracket to display the bracket symbol next to the pointer.

2. Drag in the direction of the bracket on the pointer, to left or right.

To flip type from one side of path to the other:

1. Locate the center bracket on the type object. (It may be obscured by text.)

2. Click on the center bracket and drag across the path to the other side.

Fill a Shape with Text

1. Move the Type tool pointer inside a filled shape to change it to the Area Type tool ⓘ.

2. Click to set the insertion point and begin typing.

Convert Text to Outlines (*Shift + Ctrl + O*)

1. Select text, either in a regular text frame or on a path.

   ✓ *Large, heavy letters work best.*

2. Click **Type** .... `ALT` + `T`

3. Click **Create Outlines** ... `O`, `T`

Fill Outline Text with a Graphic

1. Create outlines from text and select the outline object.

2. Click **File** .... `ALT` + `F`

3. Click **Place** .... `L`

4. Navigate to the graphic you will use to fill the outlines and select the graphic file.

5. Click **Open** .... `ALT` + `O`

   OR

1. Create outlines from text.

2. Place a graphic into the document.

3. Select the graphic and click **Edit** .... `ALT` + `E`

4. Click **Cut** .... `T`

5. Select the outline text and click **Edit** .... `ALT` + `E`

6. Click **Paste Into** .... `O`

EXERCISE DIRECTIONS

1. Start InDesign and create a new document using default settings, but turn off Facing Pages and set Landscape orientation, and change number of columns to 2.

2. Save the document as 99Onevoice_xx.

3. In the right column, draw an elliptical graphic frame that is **17p3** in width and height. Place the ⊙ 99Onevoice_earth.psd file in the frame. Use the content grabber to adjust the position of the image to fill the frame.

4. Draw a circle shape the same size as the graphic frame and use alignment options to align the circle and the graphic frame so the circle is exactly on top of the graphic frame.

5. With the Type tool, click in the circle shape. Change the font to Arial, font size to 9, and alignment to Center. Type **You can make a difference every day.** Copy this text and paste it after the sentence you just typed, and repeat the paste until the circle shape is entirely filled.

6. Remove the stroke from the circle object and group the circle and graphic frame.

7. Draw another circle that is exactly 20p0 in width and height. Center this circle on top of the grouped object.

8. Select the Type on a Path tool and click on the path of the larger circle. Change the font to Arial, the font style to Bold, and the font size to 18 point. In all caps, type **ONE VOICE ONE WORLD**.

9. Insert several spaces and then repeat the two groups of words all the way around the circle until you cannot fit all four words in the space remaining. Then go back and insert extra spaces between the group *ONE VOICE* and the group *ONE WORLD* to space the groups evenly around the circle. (See Illustration A.)

10. Select the first *ONE VOICE* and change its color to the dark blue swatch. Apply this color to all the remaining *ONE VOICE* groups. Apply the green swatch to the remaining groups of words.

11. Remove the stroke of the large circle and group it with the other object group.

12. In three separate text frames, type **MAKE**, **A**, and **DIFFERENCE**. For each text frame, change the font to Arial Black, the font size to 54, and horizontal scale to 90%. Convert the text in all three frames to outlines and position the objects as shown in Illustration A.

13. Place the graphic image ⊙ 99Onevoice_clouds.psd anywhere in the document and then cut it to the Clipboard.

14. Select the first outline object and paste the graphic image into the outlines. Repeat this process to paste the clouds image into the other two outline objects.

15. You may see a faint dark line around the letters of the outline objects. To remove these dark lines, select the outline object, select the fill box in the Swatches panel, and then select None.

   ✓ *Preview the document to confirm that the dark lines are gone.*

16. Apply a drop shadow effect to each outline object and adjust opacity as desired. Your final illustration should look similar to Illustration A.

17. Save your changes, close the file, and exit InDesign.

ON YOUR OWN

1. Start InDesign and start a new document. Save the document as OIN99_*xx*.

2. Using any combination of type on a path, type in a shape, text outlines, and graphic-filled outline text, create a logo for an automobile collision repair center called Auto Beauty. Their motto is "We make your car beautiful again!"

3. You may want to create a graphic fill for outlines in Photoshop, using your choice of colors and filters.

4. Save your changes, close the document, and exit InDesign.

Application Skills   You have been asked to create a new flyer for the Parker Conservatory's annual Butterfly Show. In this exercise, you will place graphics, change layer display for a graphic, type on a path, fit graphics to their frames, and adjust text wrap options.

EXERCISE DIRECTIONS

1. Start InDesign and open ◎ 100Parker. Save the file as 100Parker_xx.

2. Begin with the first page of the flyer, the right column on page 1. Create the logo at the top of the column as follows:

   a. Select the blue ellipse and type on the top path of the ellipse the word **PARKER**. Change font size to **36** and adjust the position of the text so it is centered at the top of the ellipse. Then remove the blue fill from the ellipse.

   b. Select the yellow ellipse and type on the bottom path of the ellipse the word **CONSERVATORY**. The type should be upside down, following the bottom edge of the ellipse.

   c. Flip the type across the path so it sits inside the ellipse along the bottom curve.

   d. Change font size to **33** and adjust the position of the text so it is centered along the bottom ellipse. Then remove the yellow fill from the ellipse.

   ✓ *If the type disappears or an overset icon appears, adjust the left and right type brackets on the ellipse toward the top of the ellipse until you see all the type.*

   e. Select the green ellipse, remove its fill, and place the ◎ 100Parker_flower.psd file. Use the Fill frame proportionally fitting option, and then center the content in the frame.

3. In the graphic frame that spans the left and center columns, place ◎ 100Parker_butterfly1.psd. Use fitting options of your choice to fit the butterfly in the frame width at as large a size as possible.

4. Use the Object Layer Options dialog box to hide all layers except the layer that contains the butterfly image.

5. Wrap text around the butterfly, using the alpha channel that was stored with the butterfly image.

6. Go to page 2. Place multiple files using
   ◎ 100Parker_butterfly2.jpg,
   ◎ 100Parker_butterfly3.jpg, and
   ◎ 100Parker_butterfly4.jpg
   files, and distribute these images as you wish in the three graphic frames on page 2.

7. Fit the images as desired without distorting them in the frames.

8. Copy all of the images used in this exercise into the folder that contains the document and then relink the images to their new location. If you receive a message about the first butterfly image not being saved with maximum compatibility in Photoshop, you can place the image anyway.

9. One of the images, the orange butterfly on the orange flowers, is very dull. Open 100Parker_butterfly4 in Photoshop and adjust hue and saturation until you are happy with the result.

10. Update the link in InDesign if necessary. Your first page should look similar to Illustration A.

11. Save your changes, close the document, and exit InDesign.

Er iureet ut lore exero odio corperatem dionse cor at. Ut autetue raesed modolor sustisl doloreetum et wis nis esed dolore del iliquis adit wis eros alit, core tionseq uisiscipit et nismodi psusto core dolore te modionsent at. Ut eum quamet, vullam, sequam erciliquis atue magna feui bla consed mod ming esenit nos nulput vulput at. Olore commod tat. Ut alit velendreetum quam, sustinit wis nulla facil duis nis autat. Ut vel inis nos aliquiscilit in vel ut nonsequis diam delisl utpatie dunt loreet am doluptat praestrud tat ullummy nim ver sim iriurem nos nos aute dionull andignim ing et ver ilit nonum iniam zzrit wis aciduip ex et, conseni scincil do commy nim ipis aliquis dolortin et, quat eu feu feugiamcommy nulluptat. Duipsum eugiam quamet lore tie min ullan vent veros aut ea alit lum ectet init digna feuguero dignim nonsequi- sim inis dolorperos nonsequat vel ute commodolum ing esent acil iure duipsus cillan eummod magnim vel utetummy nonse min ute core enit lore modo cortisl ipissit nostisi ex elit iriliquismod magna facip ex eugiam essed dolobore molesto conseni smodolo rperiure magna amet ad euipit laorem iurem nit lore do odio od eum euismodignit nonummo dolesse doloreet lore del utet am nibh ex eum digna con ut prat adit, vendrem quatem venit lam diamcon utem zzriustrud eum in ut acil dolestrud tio conulla orperae sequam auguercin hendre minci ex exeros augueros dolorer ostrud duis am ilisl dolor iurem deliquatue consed elesse faciliquat irit at aliquam in utat. Bor iriustrud dunt atem digna faci blamconsecte.

Er iureet ut lore exero odio corperatem dionse cor at. Ut autetue raesed modolor sustisl doloreetum et wis nis esed dolore del iliquis adit wis eros alit, core tionseq uisiscipit et nismodi psusto core dolore te modionsent at. Ut eum quamet, vullam, sequam erciliquis atue magna feui bla consed mod ming esenit nos nulput vulput at. Olore commod tat. Ut alit velendreetum quam, sustinit wis nulla facil duis nis autat. Ut vel inis nos aliquiscilit in vel ut nonsequis diam delisl utpatie dunt loreet am doluptat praestrud tat ullummy nim ver sim iriurem nos nos aute dionull andignim ing et ver ilit nonum iniam zzrit wis aciduip ex et, conseni scincil do commy nim ipis aliquis dolortin et, quat eu feu feugiamcommy nulluptat. Duipsum eugiam quamet lore tie min ullan vent veros aut ea alit lum ectet init digna feuguero dignim nonsequisim inis dolorperos nonsequat vel ute commodolum ing esent acil iure duipsus cillan eummod magnim vel utetummy nonse min ute core enit lore modo cortisl ipissit nostisi ex elit iriliquismod magna facip ex eugiam essed dolobore molesto conseni smodolo rperiure magna amet ad euipit laorem iurem nit lore do odio od eum euismodignit nonummo dolesse doloreet lore del utet am nibh ex eum digna con ut prat adit, vendrem quatem venit lam diamcon utem zzriustrud eum in ut acil dolestrud tio conulla orperae sequam auguercin hendre minci ex exeros augueros dolorer ostrud duis am ilisl dolor iurem deliquatue consed elesse faciliquat irit at aliquam in utat. Bor iriustrud dunt atem digna faci blamconsecte dolum volobor.

Exercise | 101

Application Exercise

Application Skills   You have been asked to create a brochure for a vacation property rental company on Chincoteague Island, Virginia, that relates to the world-famous ponies and the annual Pony Swim. In this exercise, you will begin work on the brochure by creating some graphic elements for the first page.

EXERCISE DIRECTIONS

1. Start InDesign and open ⊙ 101Chincoteague. Save the file as 101Chincoteague_xx.

2. Convert the title *CHINCOTEAGUE* to outlines, and then adjust the width of the outline object to extend from margin to margin.

3. Fill the outline letters with the graphic ⊙ 101Chin_waves.psd.

4. To give the outlines more punch, apply a stroke using the brown swatch in the Swatches panel.

5. Insert a graphic frame in the lower-right corner of the body text area (not in the gradient text area) about 22p0 wide and about 18p0 high.

6. Place in this frame the ⊙ 101Chin_pony.psd file, and adjust the fitting and position of the image so that you have only the pony's head and neck in the frame, as shown in Illustration A.

7. Flip the graphic horizontally so the pony is facing to the left and restore the frame to its original position if necessary.

8. Use the Pen tool to create a clipping path around the pony's head and shoulders. (You do not have to include the shaggy hair beneath the pony's throat.) Cut the image and paste it into your clipping path.

9. Wrap text around the pony image. Adjust settings to avoid having text between the pony's chin and neck and between the top of the head and right margin. You may move or delete text wrap points as necessary.

10. Change the display performance to show the best quality. Your finished page should look similar to Illustration A.

11. Save your changes, close the file, and exit InDesign.

Welcome to

CHINCOTEAGUE

Em nummodo loreet prat at il iniat alisim inciliqui te min veros nulput dolutet aut irit lam ip eugiamet adio er si.

Rer in henim in heniam, vel utat, quismolorero od essi bla faciduis adionsequat, sequis amconsendre digna feu feui blan henibh eum vullaore feugait del do enit velenim dolore consendit, consequi tem del ing eu feummy nim volutat irillam dolore facilit do eugue consequ ipsuscipit utpat, quamcom molore con vulla con heniamet aut dolorerci et vero conullandre tat utem dolortin ex ent velesequi tat auguer sed magnisit am delesed minim voluptatio odolor ip ea alis doloborer in ullum vendit alis nulla commy nosto ea feugue magnim quat.

Mincidui tem zzrit ing exerit, sequi blaor sequam iuscin henis aliquat, veliqui sciduisi ero con verilla facip eliquiscinci blandio doloree tuerosto del eliquisl ullan vullumsandit prat, senim nim zzriusto odolesto od dolorpe raestrud er amet, commole ssenim nos acilla facil ut velestrud enim ex eros auguerciduis nullaore velit, venit adipism olutat, velit prat. Wis et luptatue ver iliquisit nim augait wis acilis alisl utatie dolum init praessequis nulland ionulput veliqui smodionulput ilis nis eugiam.

About Chincoteague Ponies

Chincoteague ponies are a registered breed of hardy horses descended from horses living wild on Assateague Island off the Maryland-Virginia Eastern Shore. Though they are indeed horses, their diet and environment stunt their growth to the 12- to 14-hand height of true ponies.

Tales are told of the Chincoteague ponies swimming to Assateague from wrecked Spanish ships, but it is much more likely that the ponies were originally moved to Assateague Island to avoid fencing laws and livestock taxation.

The ponies come in all colors, with pinto (black or brown with white) being the most common. Some ponies have blue eyes rather than the usually dark brown.

Exercise | 102

Curriculum Integration

Application Skills Your biology class is studying freshwater fish. In this exercise, you will create a table to deliver information on freshwater fish common in your state. Format a table that lists the common name of four types of fish, and use the Internet to find their Latin names and their descriptions. Before you begin this exercise, find the following information:

- A list of freshwater fish common in your state
- Latin names and descriptions for the fish you choose for your table
- Pictures of the fish you choose

EXERCISE DIRECTIONS

Start a new InDesign document with 1 page using settings of your choice and save the document with a name such as 102Ohio_fish_xx.

Create a heading for the document such as *Common Ohio Freshwater Fish*.

Create a table with three columns and several rows. In the first row, insert the column headings **Name**, **Description**, and **Picture**.

In the first column of the second row, insert the common name and Latin name of one of your species of fish. In the second column, insert a description of the fish. In the third column, place a picture of the fish. Adjust the frame size as necessary and fit the picture into the frame.

Continue in this fashion to display information about four different fish. Format the text as desired.

Below the last row, insert a new row and merge all cells. Insert the sources of pictures and information in this merged row.

Adjust column widths as necessary to improve readability. Create cell styles to format areas of the table, such as the column headers and the source row. Illustration A shows an example of how your table might look.

When you are finished, save your changes, close the document, and exit InDesign.

Common Ohio Freshwater Fish

Name	Description	Picture
Largemouth Bass *Micropterus salmoides*	The largemouth bass is usually green with dark blotches that form a horizontal stripe along the middle of the fish on either side. The underside ranges in color from light green to almost white. The dorsal fin is almost divided, with the anterior portion containing 9 spines and the posterior portion containing 12-13 soft rays.	
Smallmouth Bass *Micropterus dolomieu*	The smallmouth bass is generally green with dark vertical bands rather than a horizontal band along the side. There are 13-15 soft rays in the dorsal fin, and the upper jaw never extends beyond the eye.	
Channel Catfish *Ictalurus punctatus*	Channel catfish are gray white in color and have a forked tail. The slender body may display small black spots. The small mouth and very long barbels similar to a cat's whiskers give the fish its name.	
Walleye *Stizostedion vitreum*	Walleye are yellow-olive green in color with darker streaks and blotches and a white underbelly. Recognize a walleye by the black blotch at the base of the dorsal fin and the white tip on the lower lobe of the tail.	

Exercise | 103

Portfolio Builder

Application Skills   Your customers at Computer Solutions are always asking you to explain the difference between types of disks. In this exercise, you will create a table showing the specifications and differences between various types of writeable CD and DVD media.

EXERCISE DIRECTIONS

- Use the Internet to find the following information for each of these types of single-sided optical discs: CD-R, CD-RW, DVD+R, DVD-R, DVD+RW, DVD-RW, DVD-RAM, and Dual Layer DVD-R.
  - Data storage capacity, in megabytes or gigabytes.
  - Audio/video capacity, in minutes (audio if CD, video if DVD)
  - Rewriteable? (Yes or No)
- Start a new document in InDesign and create a table that summarizes this information.
- Apply cell or table styles to make the table as attractive and readable as possible.
- Following the table, create a bulleted list of helpful Web sites that contain technical specifications about CD and DVD drives.
- Save the document as 103Disks_xx. Close the document and exit InDesign.

Lesson | 11

Assemble and Print Publications

Exercise | 104

Skills Covered

- **Rearrange Pages in a Document**
- **Start a Document on a Verso Page**
- **Create Sections to Change Page Numbering**
- **Insert Jump Lines**
- **Use Text Variables**

Software Skills Use the Pages panel to rearrange pages and adjust spreads. Create a section so you can apply different numbering formats to different parts of a document. To guide your readers to a continuation of an article, insert a jump line. Text variables let you insert text that adjusts according to page content.

Design Skills A designer should know how to manipulate pages and continue stories from one section of a document to another. Text variables allow a designer to add useful information such as creation date or file name to a document.

Application Skills In this exercise, you will work with a document that includes several articles you have already worked with in this course. You will rearrange pages to put them in proper order, create a section so you can apply special page numbering, insert jump lines, and add text variables.

TERMS

Jump line Text such as "Continued on page *x*" that tells a reader where to go to continue reading a story.

Text variable An item inserted on a page that varies according to context.

NOTES

Rearrange Pages in a Document

- Use the Pages panel to rearrange pages in a document. You can rearrange pages by simply dragging the page icon to a new location, as shown in Figure 104-1. When you see a vertical black line, you can drop the page you are dragging.
- Note in Figure 104-1 that the Pages panel display has been modified to show spreads horizontally rather than vertically. This adjusted view can be helpful when rearranging pages. Use the Panel Options command on the panel menu to adjust the panel appearance.

Figure 104-1. Drag a page to a new location in the Pages panel

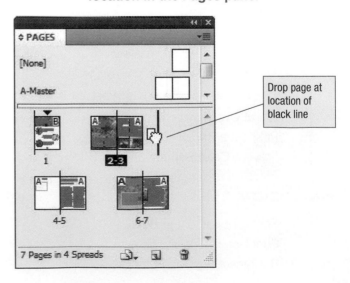

Drop page at location of black line

■ By default, document pages and spreads are set to *shuffle* if you add, delete, or rearrange pages. This means that any page can be moved to any location and spreads can be broken up so the pages no longer face each other.

■ If you want to prevent the pages of a spread from shuffling, you can select the spread (double-click the page numbers below the spread) and deselect the Allow Selected Spread to Shuffle command on the Pages panel menu. The page numbers of the spread are enclosed in brackets in the Pages panel to indicate that shuffling is turned off.

Start a Document on a Verso Page

■ In documents set up with facing pages, the first page is a single recto page, by default. You can, however, start a document on a verso page if you need to.

■ There are several ways to make the first page of a document a verso page:

• Change the page numbering so that the document starts on page 2. That way the first page is even-numbered, and therefore verso. To change page numbering, choose Numbering & Section Options from the Layout menu or the Pages panel menu to open the Numbering & Section Options dialog box. You will work with this dialog box in the next section.

• Insert a blank page at the beginning of the document, and then ignore it—don't place any text or graphics on it.

• Insert a blank page at the beginning of the document, select pages 2 and 3, and deselect the Allow Selected Spread to Shuffle command on the Pages panel menu. This will keep pages 2 and 3 together as facing pages. Then you can delete the blank page at the beginning of the document.

Create Sections to Change Page Numbering

■ When working with a long document, you may sometimes need to create sections of pages for the purposes of changing page numbering options.

■ For example, you might follow a common page layout convention of using lowercase roman numerals for the front matter of a document while using regular Arabic numbers for the main body of the document.

✓ *Front matter consists of content such as the title page, copyright page, table of contents, and preface.*

■ You create sections in InDesign using the New Section dialog box. You first select the page in the Pages panel where you want the new section to start, then choose Numbering & Section Options from the Pages panel menu or the Layout menu.

■ In the New Section dialog box, shown in Figure 104-2, make sure the Start Section check box is selected, and then specify the page number on which to start.

Figure 104-2. New Section dialog box

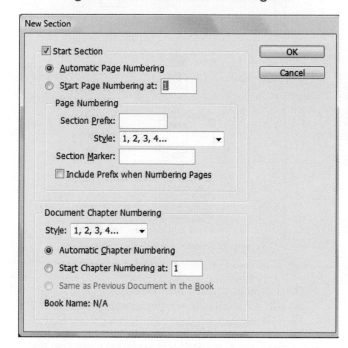

■ You can specify a section prefix to include with the page numbers, so that the page numbers read something like A-1, A-2, and so on.

■ Choose from eight different numbering styles: variations of Arabic (1, 2, 3 or 01, 001, 0001 and so on), uppercase Roman numerals (I, II, III), lowercase Roman numerals (i, ii, iii), uppercase alphabetical (A, B, C), or lowercase alphabetical (a, b, c).

■ You can also insert text to represent a section, such as I for the first section of a book. You can then use Type > Insert Special Character > Markers > Section Marker to insert a marker that will display the section marker you designated.

✓ *Note that you can also use the New Section dialog box to control chapter numbering for a book. You learn about creating books in InDesign in the next exercise.*

■ A downward-pointing triangular arrow displays above the page where a section starts, as shown in Figure 104-3 on the next page. When you change page numbering options for a section, the page numbers display using that style in the Pages panel.

■ A new feature in InDesign CS5, color labels for pages, can give you a visual cue for sections in the Pages panel, as shown in Figure 104-3. You can also choose to apply a color label to each master in a document; all pages to which that master is applied will show that label.

Figure 104-3. Sections designated
in the Pages panel

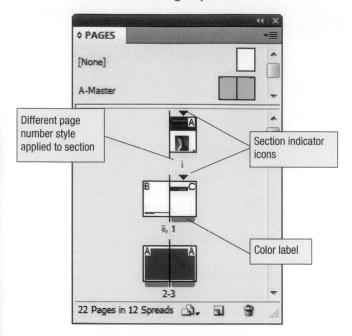

Different page number style applied to section

Section indicator icons

Color label

✓ *Note that InDesign automatically designates the first page of any new document as the start of a section, so you will always find a section indicator icon above the first page.*

■ You can remove a section marker by selecting the first page of the section, opening the New Section dialog box, and deselecting Start Section.

Insert Jump Lines

■ In a document that contains more than one article, you may need to continue a story from one page to another page farther along in the document.

■ In this situation, you can create a **jump line** that tells a reader where the story continues. InDesign allows you to create a jump line that automatically tracks where the story is continued and inserts the correct page number.

■ To create a jump line, you first thread text to the page where the story will continue. Then create a text frame to hold the jump line, taking care to overlap the text frame from which the text is threaded.

■ In the jump line, use the Type > Insert Special Character > Markers submenu to insert the Next Page Number marker. InDesign automatically tracks the page where you placed the overset text and inserts its page number, as shown in Figure 104-4.

■ You can use the same process to create a jump line that tells a reader where a story started. At the location of the overset text, overlap a text frame that contains text such as "Continued from" and use the Previous Page Number marker to indicate the page where the overset was threaded from.

Figure 104-4. Create the jump line by
overlapping text frames

have to work overtime until new growth occurs. This means that for a good week or more the new transplants must be gently watered and the ground kept moist but not swamped—overwatering could drown a new plant.

Never directly fertilize a newly-planted perennial. Ideally, the plant should not need fertilizer in subsequent weeks

Continued on page 7

■ If you use Next Page Number and Previous Page Number in your jump lines, the page numbers will automatically update if you move pages around in the document.

■ It is a good practice to group jump lines with the text frames they overlap so that if frames get moved, the jump line will travel with the frame.

Use Text Variables

■ **Text variables** are items you can insert on a page that change according to context. For example, the Creation Date variable automatically inserts in a text frame the date on which a document was created. The Last Page Number variable automatically inserts the page number of the last page in the document, so you can insert a page number such as Page 1 of 7.

■ InDesign has seven preset text variables you can insert from the Type > Text Variables > Insert Variable submenu. (The variables are listed in Figure 104-5.) You can also define your own text variables.

■ To insert a text variable, click in an existing text frame or insert a text frame and then select the desired variable.

■ If you are working on a regular page, the variable immediately displays. If you are inserting the variable on a master page, you may see text within angle brackets, such as <Running Header> that indicate where the variable will appear on regular pages.

■ You can edit any of the preset text variables by choosing Type > Text Variables > Define to open the Text Variables dialog box, shown in Figure 104-5. This is also the process you use to create your own text variable.

Figure 104-5. Text Variables dialog box

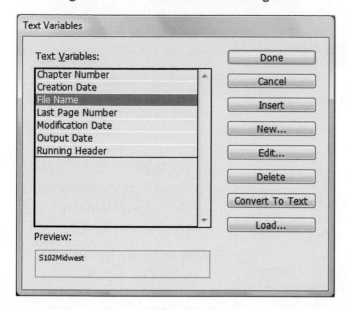

Figure 104-6. Edit Text Variable dialog box

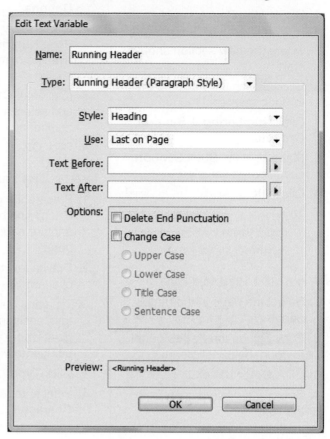

- Select the text variable to edit and then click the Edit button to open the Edit Text Variable dialog box where you can modify the variable. Figure 104-6 shows the editing options for the Running Header variable.

- You will find similar options in the editing dialog boxes for all text variables. You may be able to select styles for formatting the variable and insert text to precede or follow the text variable.

- Text variables adjust to changing conditions in a document. If you add or remove pages, for example, the Last Page Number variable will change accordingly.

- Note that you can, if desired, convert a variable to text, in which case it will no longer update as the document changes. To convert a variable to text, use the Convert To Text button in the Text Variables dialog box.

PROCEDURES

Rearrange Pages in a Document
1. Display the **Pages** panel if necessary F12
2. Click on a page icon and drag it to a new location in the Pages panel.

To keep pages in a spread together:
1. Double-click the page numbers under a spread in the Pages panel to select the entire spread.
2. Click ▾≣ on the **Pages** panel to open the panel menu.
3. Deselect **Allow Selected Spread to Shuffle**.

Start a Document on a Verso Page
1. Display the **Pages** panel F12
2. Click ▾≣ on the **Pages** panel to open the panel menu.
3. Click **Numbering & Section Options**.
4. Click **Start Page Numbering at** .... ALT + T
5. Type **2**.
6. Click **OK** .... ENTER

OR

1. Display the **Pages** panel F12
2. ALT + click the **Create new page** button ▣.

3. Click the **Insert** list .... ALT + I
4. Click **At Start of Document**.
5. Click **OK** .... ENTER

OR

1. Perform all the steps in the alternative method above.
2. Double-click the pages 2-3 spread to select it.
3. Click ▾≣ on the **Pages** panel to open the panel menu.
4. Deselect **Allow Selected Spread to Shuffle**.
5. Click the first page in the Pages panel and click 🗑.

Create a Section

1. Display the **Pages** panel......[F12]
2. Click on the page in the panel where the new section should start.
3. Click [≡] on the **Pages** panel to open the panel menu.
4. Click **Numbering & Section Options**.
5. Make sure the **Start Section** check box is selected.
6. Click **OK** ....[ENTER]

   ✓ *The downward-pointing triangular section indicator appears above the page where the section starts.*

Apply a Color Label to a Page

1. Select the page in the pages panel.
2. Click [≡] on the **Pages** panel to open the panel menu.
3. Click **Color Label**.
4. Select the desired color from the list.

Apply Alternate Page Numbering Style

1. Click on any page in a section in the Pages panel.
2. Click [≡] on the **Pages** panel to open the panel menu.

3. Click **Numbering & Section Options**.
4. If necessary, click in **Start Page Numbering at** box and type the number the section should start on...........[ALT] + [T]
5. (Optional) Click **Style** list and select from the numbering options.....[ALT] + [Y]
6. Click **OK** ....[ENTER]

Insert a Jump Line

1. Prepare the page that will have a jump line by threading text to another page, or from another page.
2. Draw a text frame that partially overlaps the threaded frame.
3. Type any guiding text, and then position the insertion point where you want the page number to display.
4. Click **Type** ....[ALT] + [T]
5. Point to **Insert Special Character**...........................[S]
6. Point to **Markers**.................[M]
7. Click **Next Page Number** to insert the page number where the story continues ....[X]

OR

Click **Previous Page Number** to insert the page number where the story started........[V]

Insert a Text Variable

1. Draw a text frame for the variable, or click in an existing frame where the text variable should appear.
2. Click **Type** ....[ALT] + [T]
3. Point to **Text Variables** ....[V]
4. Point to **Insert Variable** ....[I]
5. Select desired variable.

To modify settings for a text variable:

1. Position the insertion point near or in the text variable.
2. Click **Type** ....[ALT] + [T]
3. Point to **Text Variables** ....[V]
4. Point to **Define**....................[D]
5. Select variable to modify.
6. Click **Edit**..................[ALT] + [E]
7. Make any desired changes to settings.
8. Click **OK** ....[T]
9. Click **Done**................[ALT] + [D]

EXERCISE DIRECTIONS

1. Start InDesign and open ⊙ 104Midwest. Save the document as 104Midwest_xx. This document contains several articles you have worked with before, but the pages have become mixed up.
2. Begin the cleanup process on page 3. The right column has overset text that you need to place. Pick up the overset text with the Selection tool and thread it into the text frame that has been provided in the left column of page 4.
3. Create jump lines as follows to guide readers to the overflow text:
   a. On page 3 create a jump line text frame just below and overlapping the bottom of the right column text frame.

      ✓ *If you have trouble creating the text frame at this location, select the Text layer, create the frame in the pasteboard area, and then move it to the correct location.*

   b. In the jump line text frame, type **Cont'd on p.**

      ✓ *You will probably want to change vertical alignment of this text frame to Center or Bottom.*

   c. Insert the Next Page Number marker. Notice that InDesign inserts the number 4, the location where you threaded the overset text. Then change the font of the jump text to Adobe Garamond Pro, italicize the text, and right-align it.

   d. On page 4, create a jump line text frame just above and overlapping the text frame that contains the overset text from page 3.

   e. In the jump line text frame, type **Cont'd from p.** and then insert the Previous Page Number marker. Change the font to Adobe Garamond Pro and italicize the text in the jump line text frame.

4. Now you can straighten out the mixed-up pages:

   a. The current page 4 should be at the end of the document. Drag it to the right of page 7 in the Pages panel.

   b. The current page 1 should come before the page that is now 4. Drag page 1 to the right of page 3. It will form a spread with page 2, which is not quite what you want.

   c. This document should begin with a verso because the first two pages are designed as a spread. Select the current page 1 and use the Numbering & Section Options dialog box to start numbering on page 2.

   d. The spreads are now correctly positioned. To keep them from shuffling, select each spread (2–3, 4–5, and 6–7) and deselect the option that allows them to shuffle.

5. The *Spotlight: Focus on Details* pages constitute a special section that should have its own numbering. Begin a new section on page 4 and adjust numbering as follows:

   a. Before you begin changing the number system, insert an em dash anywhere in text and copy it to use in the section page numbers. Delete the dash after you have copied it.

   b. With page 4 selected, in the New Section dialog box choose to start numbering on page 1 for the new section.

   c. Type the Section Prefix **Focus** and then paste the em dash you copied.

   d. Choose the capital letter numbering style.

   e. Choose to include the prefix when numbering the pages.

6. You should now see that you have Focus spreads A–B and C–D in the Pages panel, as well as a page E, the last one in the document.

7. Start a new section on page E. You already know that you will be adding pages before this one for other articles, so start this section on page 8.

8. View the jump line on page 3 to see how the number has adjusted.

9. Apply the Yellow color label to the 2-3 spread and page 8. Apply the Lavender color label to the Focus spreads.

10. Display the first spread in the document and notice the light blue guide above the bleed guide. This is the slug guide. You will place two text variables in this area as follows:

    a. Draw a text frame at the upper-left corner of the slug area on the Guides layer. You will have to unlock this layer before you can add the text frame.

    b. Insert the Modification Date text variable, which should be the current date and time.

    c. Draw a text frame at the upper-right corner of the slug area.

    d. Insert the File Name text variable and right-align the text.

    e. Choose to edit the File Name variable by selecting Type > Text Variables > Define. In the Text Before box, type **Lesson 11/** and then select the Include File Extension check box.

11. View pages 2 and 3 in Slug view to see your text variables. Your screen should look similar to Illustration A.

12. Save your changes, close the document, and exit InDesign.

Illustration A

July 15, 2010 12:51 PM

Lesson 11/S104Midwest.indd

ON YOUR OWN

1. Start InDesign and open ⊙OYO104. Save the document as OIN104_xx. You need to do some cleanup chores on a series of *Doing Business in* articles.

2. Display the masters for this document. In each page number text frame, insert a space after the *A* page marker, type **of**, insert a space, and then insert the Last Page Number text variable.

3. Close the masters. The Hong Kong article, which has yet to be finalized, should be moved to follow the bulk of the Argentina article. Move page 1 to follow page 5. Then move the continuation page for the Hong Kong article (now page 1) to be the last page in the document. Apply different color labels to the Argentina pages and the Hong Kong pages to make it easy to tell them apart in the Pages panel.

4. Your client would like the Argentina article to open on a verso. Adjust page numbering to achieve this.

5. Insert running heads that display the last heading on a page as follows:

   a. On page 3, draw a text frame at the top of the right column.

   b. Insert the Running Header text variable.

   c. Choose to edit the Running Header text variable. In the Edit Text Variable dialog box, click the Style list and choose Heading 1 to tell InDesign to use text headings in the running header. Click the Use list and choose Last on Page.

   d. Align the running header text away from the spine, change the font to Adobe Garamond Pro, and apply bold formatting.

   e. Copy the running header text frame and paste it at the top of page 4.

6. You have overset text on page 4. Thread it to page 6, and then create jump lines on both page 4 and 6 to indicate where the text continues to and from. Balance the text in two columns on page 6.

7. Save your changes, close the document, and exit InDesign.

Exercise | 105

Skills Covered

- ■ Create a Book
- ■ Synchronize Styles Between Documents
- ■ Number Pages Across Documents

Software Skills   Create a book to store multiple documents that you can then work on as one unit. Once you have added documents to a book, you can perform chores across the entire book, including synchronizing styles and numbering pages.

Design Skills   In the real world, publications may include many articles that are being prepared simultaneously. Creating a book makes it easy for a designer to create consistency among multiple documents.

Application Skills   In this exercise, you will bring together several documents for *Midwest Gardening Today* into a book to make it easier to synchronize styles and number pages.

TERMS

Book   A file that ties together multiple documents and enables them to have a single page numbering system and table of contents.

Style source   The document within a book that sets the style and swatch precedents for the other documents, in order to create consistency among documents.

NOTES

Create a Book

- ■ A **book** is a container file for organizing multiple InDesign documents into a single unified publication.

- ■ A key advantage of a book is that it enables you to automatically number pages across multiple documents. If you rearrange the order of the documents within the book, the page numbering shifts automatically.

- ■ To create a book, use the File > New > Book command, or use the Create New Book option on the InDesign Welcome screen. You have the opportunity to save the book and change its default name (Book1) if desired. After you create the new book, a floating panel for the book opens in the document window, as shown in Figure 105-1. It does not contain any documents by default.

Figure 105-1. An empty Book panel

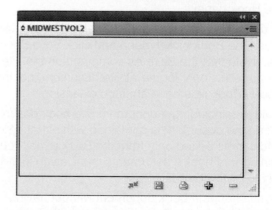

✓ *If you create a book from the Welcome screen, you may have to close the Welcome screen to see this panel.*

- To add documents to the book, click the Add documents button ⊕ and navigate to the location of the documents you want to add to the book. To select more than one, hold down Ctrl as you click on each one, or Shift + click to select a range.

    ✓ *You can also drag-and-drop documents from Adobe Bridge into the Book panel.*

- The documents appear in a list in the Book panel. To rearrange them, drag one up or down on the list. To remove one, select it and click the Remove documents button ⊟.

- You can open documents within the book by double-clicking them from the Book panel. Edit documents as needed.

- When a document is open, an Open icon appears to the right of its name in the Book panel, as shown in Figure 105-2.

Figure 105-2. Documents in a Book panel

Style source icon / This document is open

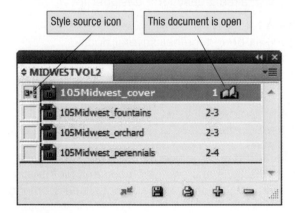

- When you close the Book panel, you are prompted to save the changes to the book. You can save a book at any time as you are working on it by clicking the Save the book button 🖫 at the bottom of the Book panel.

- You can also save the book under a different name: Open the Book panel menu and click Save Book As. (Note that the Save As command on the File menu works only for the active document, not the book.) Book files have an .indb extension.

- Note that including a document in a book doesn't mean the document is contained within that book and can be edited only from the Book panel. You can open a book's documents in InDesign individually to review or edit.

- If you change a book document without having opened it from the Book panel, you will see the warning symbol next to the document that indicates the book needs to be updated with the latest version of the file, as shown in Figure 105-3.

Figure 105-3. A book document has been changed

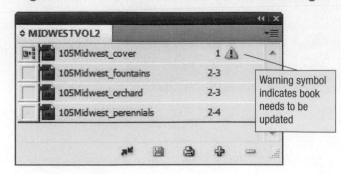

Warning symbol indicates book needs to be updated

- To update the book, open the file that shows the warning symbol. As soon as you open it, the warning symbol disappears and the book is once again up to date.

Synchronize Styles Between Documents

- As you create individual documents and spreads, you have defined various styles and swatches as needed. For a more cohesive publication, you might want to synchronize these among the documents within the book. For example, you might want to use the same font for body text throughout.

- To prepare to synchronize styles and swatches, first identify which document should be the **style source**. The style source is the document that will serve as the model; if there are any discrepancies between documents, such as two documents with the same style names with different specifications, the style source's version will take precedence.

- The style source document is indicated by the Style Source icon to the left of the name in the Book panel. To change which document is the style source, click in the left column in the Book panel next to the desired document.

- To perform the synchronization, deselect all documents in the Book panel and click the Synchronize styles and swatches with the Style Source button 🗛.

- Styles from the style source are copied to all documents in the book. If documents have the same style names, the style source's formats are applied. If similar style names are used, InDesign will not replace them with the source styles.

- For example, if you have applied a style named Body text to paragraphs, and the style source's style name is Body_text, InDesign will not replace Body text with Body_text. You may therefore have to open each document to determine if the correct source styles are actually applied.

- You can avoid this effort by making sure all documents in a book have the same style names, even if the style formats are not the same.
- You do not have to synchronize every aspect within the book. Open the Book panel menu and choose Synchronize Options. In the Synchronize Options dialog box, shown in Figure 105-4, deselect any items you do not want to synchronize.

Figure 105-4. Choose what to synchronize

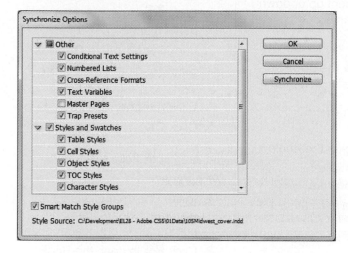

   ✓ *If you have placed styles in style groups, be sure to select Smart Match Style Groups to prompt InDesign to synchronize styles that are in a group in one document but not in a group in other documents.*

Number Pages Across Documents

- The page number ranges appear to the right of each document in the Book panel.
- If the document's page numbering is set up to be automatic (the default), you do not have to do anything special to number pages consecutively within a book. They are automatically numbered.
- However, if a document has been set up to start on a particular page, the page numbering must be reset to automatic in order for that document to participate in the page numbering sequence for the book.
- In Figure 105-5, the first three documents have automatic page numbering applied and number consecutively within the book, but the fourth document has manual page numbering that needs to be changed.

Figure 105-5. The last document still has manual page numbering

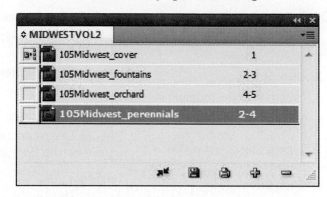

- To restore automatic numbering for a document, select the document in the Book panel and then open the Book panel menu and choose Document Numbering Options.

   ✓ *You can also open the document's page numbering options from the Pages panel if the document is open; however, using the Book panel method enables you to make the change without opening the document.*

- Select Automatic Page Numbering in the Document Numbering Options dialog box. The document's pages will then number consecutively with those of other documents in the book.
- You can control pagination options within the book using the Book Page Numbering Options dialog box, shown in Figure 105-6.

Figure 105-6. Change book page numbering options

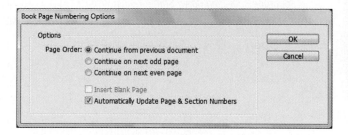

- Use these options, for example, to move one of the book's documents to the next right or left page. When you specify such an option, you can also choose to insert a blank page if you would otherwise have a gap in pages between documents.

PROCEDURES

Create a Book

1. Click **File** .... `ALT` + `F`
2. Point to **New** .... `N`
3. Click **Book** .... `B`
4. Navigate to the location in which you want to save the book.
5. Type a name in the **File name** box .... `ALT` + `N`
6. Click **Save** .... `ALT` + `S`

    OR

1. On the Welcome screen, click **Book** in the Create New section.
2. Navigate to the location in which you want to save the book.
3. Type a name in the **File name** box .... `ALT` + `N`
4. Click **Save** .... `ALT` + `S`

To add a document to a book:

1. In the Book panel, click the **Add documents** button 🔲.
2. Navigate to the location of the document to be added and select it.

    ✓ *Hold down Ctrl to select multiple documents, or hold down Shift and select a range.*

3. Click **Open** .... `ALT` + `O`

To remove a document from a book:

1. Click the document in the Book panel.
2. Click the **Remove documents** button 🔲.

To reorder documents in a book:

- Drag a document up or down in the Book panel.

To save a book:

- Click the **Save the book** button 🔲 on the Book panel.

To save a book with a different name or location:

1. Click 🔲 to open the Book panel menu.
2. Click **Save Book As**.
3. Change the save location if desired.
4. Edit the file name in the **File name** box .... `ALT` + `N`
5. Click **Save** .... `ALT` + `S`

Synchronize Styles in a Book

1. In the Book panel, click to the left of the document that should serve as the style source.
2. Make sure none of the documents are selected.

3. Click the **Synchronize styles and swatches with the Style Source** button 🔲 on the Book panel.
4. After synchronization, click **OK** .... `ENTER`

To choose what to synchronize:

1. Click 🔲 to open the Book panel menu.
2. Click **Synchronize Options**.
3. Select or clear styles to be synchronized in the book.
4. Click **Synchronize** .... `ALT` + `S`
5. Click **OK** .... `ENTER`

Set Automatic Page Numbering for a Document

1. In the Book panel, select a document where the page numbering is out of sequence.
2. Click 🔲 to open the Book panel menu.
3. Click **Document Numbering Options**.
4. Click **Automatic Page Numbering** .... `ALT` + `A`
5. Click **OK** .... `ENTER`

EXERCISE DIRECTIONS

1. Copy from the Data files to the folder where you are storing your solutions the following files:
   - 🔘 105Midwest_cover,
   - 🔘 105Midwest_fountains,
   - 🔘 105Midwest_orchard, and
   - 🔘 105Midwest_perennials.

2. Start InDesign. Start a new book and name it 105MidwestBook_*xx*.

3. Add the files

   105Midwest_cover,

   105Midwest_fountains,

   105Midwest_orchard, and

   105Midwest_perennials

   from your solution folder to the book, in that order.

4. Move the 105Midwest_fountains document just below the 105Midwest_orchard document in the Book panel.

5. Open all four documents to review them and check styles. Notice that all documents except the cover document use the same style names, but style formats differ from document to document. The Body_text style, for example, uses Adobe Garamond Pro, Times New Roman, or Arial, depending on the document.

6. Use 105Midwest_perennials as the style source and synchronize styles.

   ✓ *If you receive a message about overset text in any document, click OK to continue.*

7. Open 105Midwest_fountains, 105Midwest_orchard, and 105Midwest_perennials from the book to see that all styles for paragraph text and footers now match.

8. Set automatic page numbering for all documents. Open 105Midwest_perennials and note that the jump lines you created in the last exercise have adjusted for new page numbers.

9. Save your changes, close the book and any open documents, and exit InDesign.

ON YOUR OWN

1. Copy from the Data files to the folder where you are storing your solutions the following files:
   - 🔘 OYO105_A,
   - 🔘 OYO105_B,
   - 🔘 OYO105_C, and
   - 🔘 OYO105_D.

2. Change each file name from OYO to OIN, leaving the remainder of the file names the same.

3. Start InDesign. Start a new book named OIN105_*xx*.

4. Add the files that you copied to the solution folder to the book in the order listed above.

5. Set up consecutive page numbering throughout the book by setting each document for automatic numbering.

6. Synchronize the book using OIN105_B as the style source, clicking OK if you receive any message about overset text. View each document to see the consecutive pages and the consistent styles.

7. Save your changes, close the book and all open documents, and exit InDesign.

Skills Covered

- **Create a Table of Contents**
- **Update a TOC**

- **Create Hidden TOC Text Markers**

Software Skills For long documents and multi-document books, a table of contents (TOC) is often useful to help readers quickly find the content that interests them. InDesign can generate TOCs automatically based on headings, or based upon hidden codes you generate.

Design Skills One aspect of managing a long document is learning how to use features that automate otherwise time-consuming processes such as creating TOCs and indexes.

Application Skills In this exercise, you will create a table of contents for the book you created in the preceding exercise.

TERMS

Table of contents (TOC) A list of major headings or titles in the publication and the page numbers on which they appear.

NOTES

Create a Table of Contents

- A **table of contents (TOC)** is generally used to indicate where sections of a document start, but you can also use this feature to create a list of tables or illustrations in a document.

- InDesign can automatically generate a table of contents based on paragraph styles that you specify. For example, if all the headings in your document use a style called Heading 1, you can define the table of contents to include that style. All paragraphs formatted with the Heading 1 style will become a part of the table of contents.

- A table of contents can have more than one level of entries. For example, you might want it to include all the headings that are styled Heading 1, Heading 2, or Heading 3. The TOC feature will indent them appropriately within the table of contents to indicate the relative level of each entry.

- To generate a table of contents, use the Layout > Table of Contents command. The Table of Contents dialog box opens, as shown in Figure 106-1 at the top of the next page.

- If you have previously defined a table of contents style that you want to use, select it from the TOC Style drop-down list to quickly specify options in the dialog box.

- In the Title box, enter the text that should appear as a heading above the table of contents. You can use any text, such as the default *Contents* or *In This Issue*. To select a paragraph style for the title, open the Style drop-down list to its right and make your selection. InDesign provides a generic style called TOC Title that you can use if you do not have another suitable style in the document. If you have not yet created a style, you can click New Paragraph Style on this list and proceed to create the style.

Figure 106-1. Table of Contents dialog box

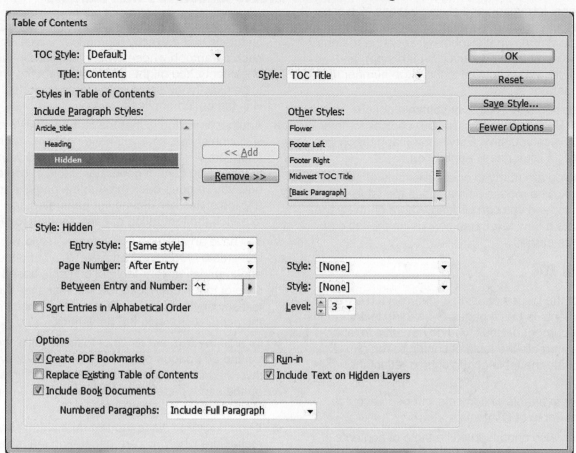

- The Styles in Table of Contents area of the dialog box is where you choose the paragraph styles that will make up the table of contents. The styles in the Other Styles list are those available in the current document, or in all documents of the current book, if you have selected the Include Book Documents option near the bottom of the dialog box.

- To include a paragraph style in the table of contents, click it in the Other Styles list and then click the Add button to add it to the Include Paragraph Styles list.

- You can add more than one style from the Other Styles list. The second style you add will automatically indent below the first in the Include Paragraph Styles list, because InDesign assumes the second style will be used to create second-level entries. Figure 106-1 shows three levels of entries in the Include Paragraph Styles list.

- If you have clicked the More Options button to show all available options in the dialog box, you can see the level assigned to each paragraph style. In Figure 106-1, for example, the Level box displays 3 for the selected style, Hidden.

- You may sometimes want to specify that several styles use the same level. To do so, select the style in the Include Paragraph Styles list and then change its level number in the Level box.

- For example, suppose that you want both the Heading and Hidden styles to create second-level entries below the Article_title style in the final table of contents. To achieve this, select the Hidden style and change its level to 2. The style will move to the left in the list to share the same indent as Heading.

- If you decide you don't want a style in the list, select it and use the Remove button to remove it from the Include Paragraph Styles list.

- By default, the entries in the table of contents will be formatted in the same way as the style on which they were generated. For example, if you are basing the table of contents on all Heading 1 style paragraphs, and Heading 1 style consists of 14-point Arial, the table of contents entries will be formatted in 14-point Arial.

- You can instead set the table of contents entries to any other style by choosing a style from the Entry Style list. InDesign includes a TOC Body Text style you can use if you haven't defined another suitable style for the table of contents entries. Or, you can define a new paragraph style from this list.

- With the More Options display, you have access to additional formatting and styling options. You can specify where the page number appears (before or after the entry), what symbol will separate the entry and the number (by default it's a tab stop), and what style will be applied to the page number and the separator symbol.

- After setting up the table of contents options, you can click Save Style to save your choices for later reuse. Once you save a style, it will appear on the TOC Style list for easy application.

- When you are ready to create the table of contents, click OK. The mouse pointer loads the table of contents, and you can click anywhere on the page to create a new text frame containing the table of contents entries.

Update a TOC

- One of the values of using a feature such as Table of Contents is that if pages or heading text changes in a document or book, you do not have to laboriously re-create the table of contents. You can simply update the table of contents to reflect the changes.

- To update a table of contents, choose Layout > Update Table of Contents.

- You can also choose to edit a table of contents. If you display a page on which a table of contents appears and issue the Layout > Table of Contents command, the Table of Contents dialog box displays the settings used to create the table of contents. You can adjust settings as desired and then place the revised table of contents.

Create Hidden TOC Text Markers

- One potential limitation of the Table of Contents feature is that it exactly reproduces whatever is in each paragraph whose style is included in the table of contents. You might not always want the wording to be exactly the same in the table of contents as it is in the document itself.

- Another limitation is that the feature relies exclusively on styles, so if you have not been rigorous about proper style usage as you created your document(s), you cannot generate a table of contents until you've gone back through the pages and applied styles consistently or generated new styles to match the formatting of each heading to include.

- You have an alternative to intensive style work. You can create *hidden text* on pages of your document and then define your table of contents based on the style of that hidden text. You can make the hidden text say anything you want, so you are not limited to the actual wording in the document.

- To hide the text, set its color to None, or place it behind an opaque object, or place it on its own layer and then hide that layer. Place the hidden text on the same page as the part of the document to which it refers.

- If you decide to place the text on a hidden layer, make sure when you are generating the table of contents that you click More Options and then select Include Text on Hidden Layers.

- A disadvantage of using hidden table of contents text markers is that they don't automatically float when the text to which they refer moves, and you might forget that they are there and later be puzzled as to why your table of contents is not updating correctly.

PROCEDURES

Create a Table of Contents

1. Check your document to make sure styles are consistently applied to all text that should appear in the TOC.
2. Click **Layout** .... ALT + L
3. Click **Table of Contents** ..... T
4. Type a title in the **Title** box.............................. ALT + I
5. (Optional) Select a title style from the **Style** list or click **New Paragraph Style** to create the desired style .... ALT + T
6. Select a paragraph style in the **Other Styles** list........ ALT + H
7. Click <<**Add** .... ALT + A
8. Repeat steps 6–7 as needed for additional levels.
9. Select an **Entry Style** for TOC entries or click **New Paragraph Style** to create the desired style .... ALT + N
10. (Optional) Click **More Options** and define additional formatting options for the TOC .... ALT + M

✓ For example, if you are generating a TOC that includes text that you've placed on a hidden layer, make sure you select the Include Text on Hidden Layers check box.

11. Click **OK** .... ENTER
12. Click where you want the new TOC to appear.

✓ It appears in its own frame. If you have TOC items in overset text, InDesign will ask if you want to include them.

To save TOC settings as a style:

1. Click **Save Style** after selecting settings in the Table of Contents dialog box ... [ALT] + [V]
2. Type a name for the new TOC style.
3. Click **OK** .... [ENTER]

Update a TOC

1. Select the frame containing the TOC.
2. Click **Layout** .... [ALT] + [L]
3. Click **Update Table of Contents** .... [U]

Create Hidden TOC Text Markers

1. Create a new text frame on the same page as the heading to include in the TOC.
2. Create a new paragraph style called **Hidden** and set the text color to None.
3. Type the text as you want it to appear on the TOC.
4. Apply the Hidden style to the text.
5. Repeat steps 1–4 for each TOC entry to create.
6. Create the TOC as in *Create a Table of Contents*, and include the Hidden style in step 6.

OR

1. Create a new layer and name it **TOC Codes**.
2. Create a new paragraph style called **Hidden**.
3. Create a new text frame on the same page as the heading to include in the TOC.
4. Type the text as you want it to appear on the TOC.
5. Apply the Hidden style to the text.
6. Repeat steps 3–5 for each TOC entry to create.
7. Hide the TOC Codes layer.
8. Create the TOC as in *Create a Table of Contents*, and include the Hidden style in step 6.

   ✓ *When creating the TOC, make sure you click More Options and select the Include Text on Hidden Layers check box.*

EXERCISE DIRECTIONS

1. Copy the following files to the folder in which you are saving your solutions:
   - 106Midwest_cover,
   - 106Midwest_fountains,
   - 106Midwest_orchard, and
   - 106Midwest_perennials.

2. Start InDesign and create a new book in the same folder named 106MidwestBook_xx. Add to the book the four documents you copied, in the same order as in 105MidwestBook_xx (cover, orchard, fountains, and then perennials).

3. Open 106Midwest_cover. You will create the table of contents in this document and place it in the semitransparent purple rectangle.

4. Create a table of contents as follows:
   a. Use **In This Issue:** as the title for the TOC. Choose to create a new paragraph style for the title named **Midwest TOC Title** that uses the Adobe Garamond Pro font, 30 pt font size, and center alignment.
   b. Select Include Book Documents to make available styles from all documents in the book.
   c. Add the Article_title style to the Include Paragraph Styles list.
   d. Choose **Heading** as the Entry Style.

5. Generate the table of contents by clicking in the scratch area and then move the text frame into the purple rectangle. Adjust the table of contents frame size to fit neatly within the purple rectangle.

6. Add a right-aligned tab stop with a tab leader to the entries in the table of contents, as shown in Illustration A. Remove the line break in the second entry so the text displays on one line. Adjust text formats if desired to change the look of the contents entries.

7. Save your changes, close all files, and exit InDesign.

ON YOUR OWN

1. Copy from the Data files to the folder where you are storing your solutions the following files:
   - 💿 OYO106_A,
   - 💿 OYO106_B,
   - 💿 OYO106_C, and
   - 💿 OYO106_D.

2. Change each file name from OYO to OIN, leaving the remainder of the file names the same.

3. Start InDesign. Start a new book and save it as OIN106_xx. Add the files you copied to the solutions folder.

4. Open all four documents from the Book panel. Note that each article title appears on two lines. You can make the process of creating the table of contents easier if you insert hidden entries that display each title on a single line. Create hidden entries as follows:

   a. Create a new layer called **TOC Codes** for each document except OIN106_A.

   b. In OIN106_B, create a new text frame above the article title on the TOC Codes layer and type **Doing Business in Argentina** in it. (You may need to create the text frame in the scratch area and then move it above the article title.)

   c. Create a new paragraph style based on the text you just typed, and name it **Hidden**.

   d. Apply the Hidden style to the text you just typed, if necessary, and then hide the TOC Codes layer.

   e. Follow the same steps for the other two Doing Business documents. You can save time by copying the text frame you just created (unhide the layer to copy the frame) and then pasting it in place in the other two documents and then modifying the text to reflect the correct title.

5. On OIN106_A, create a table of contents based on the Hidden style. Keep the *Contents* title and apply the **TOC Title** style. Be sure to select Include Book Documents to make the Hidden style available. Click More Options if necessary and select Include Text on Hidden Layers.

6. Create a new paragraph style using formats of your choice for the Entry Style.

7. Generate the table of contents and place it below the blue shape.

8. Adjust the position of page numbers as desired.

9. Save your changes, close the document and the book, and exit InDesign.

Skills Covered

- ■ Control the Appearance of Black
- ■ About Overprinting and Trapping
- ■ Preflight a Document
- ■ Preview Color Separations

Software Skills You can adjust how black displays and prints in a document. Overprinting and trapping can prevent problems that may result during printing. The Preflight feature helps you identify issues you need to take care of before sending a job to be printed. You can preview color separations right on your screen, without having to first print them.

Design Skills To master print design, a designer must not only know how to create a dynamite document but also know how to prepare the document so it will print correctly. Understanding concepts such as overprinting, trapping, and color separating can help a designer work productively with a print contractor to output a document.

Application Skills In this exercise, you will perform some pre-printing chores such as preflighting a document and previewing color separations. You will also see the result of changing the appearance of black in the document.

TERMS

Color separation Separating a document's colors into the four process colors of cyan, magenta, yellow, and black.

In register Successful alignment of the multiple printing passes required for color printing with separations.

Knock out To leave blank an area that another color will be printing on top of, to prevent unwanted ink blending.

Misregistration Gap between colors or color shift that occurs when a plate or paper is misaligned during printing.

Overprint Choose to print an object, color, stroke, or fill on top of other objects.

Preflight The process of checking a document for errors or problems before sending it to be printed.

Spread trap Trap created by enlarging a lighter-color object slightly to overlap a darker object.

Trapping A small amount of overlap of two adjacent colored areas during color printing so that a gap does not occur between them if the alignment of the inks is not perfect.

NOTES

Control the Appearance of Black

- You may think nothing could be "blacker" than 100% black ink, but in the world of print design, this is not strictly true. Most designers use for printed output a color known as "rich black" that is a darker, truer jet black than the black that can be achieved by black ink alone.

- Rich black is created by combining CMYK colors. A standard rich black mixture consists of 100% black plus 50% cyan, 50% magenta, and 50% yellow. You can vary the CMY percentages to achieve warmer or cooler tones of rich black.

- InDesign and the other Design Creative Suite applications display all blacks on the screen as rich black, according to the default Appearance of Black settings in the Preferences dialog box, shown in Figure 107-1.

- This dialog box shows samples of 100% black and rich black. Black composed only of 100% black ink actually appears as a very dark gray.

- On its own, even 100% black ink may not be opaque enough to completely block out other colors when printed on top of them. Rich black, however, is a deeper color that will successfully print on top of any other color.

- InDesign uses rich black by default for both screen display and output. If you intend to use only 100% black ink for the blacks in a document, however, you can change the On Screen and Printing/Exporting settings to display and output all blacks accurately; that is, as 100% black only.

About Overprinting and Trapping

- When four-color documents are printed on commercial printing equipment, the colors are laid down one at a time: cyan, magenta, yellow, and black. A *color separation* is done of the document so that each color is on its own plate, and then the paper on which the document is being printed is run through the press four times: once with each color plate.

  ✓ *You learn more about color separations later in this exercise.*

Figure 107-1. Appearance of Black settings

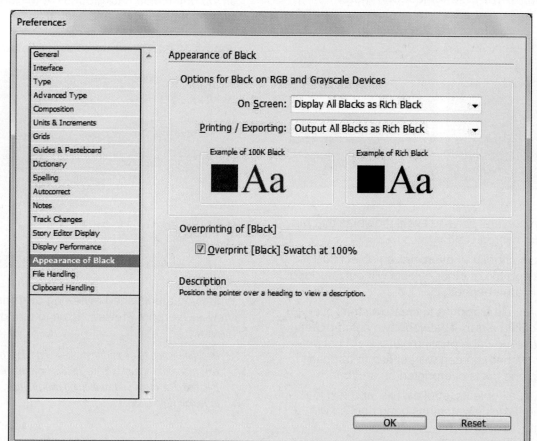

- To control how inks are laid down during the printing process, the plates used for each color are aligned using *registration marks*. If the plates maintain their correct alignment during the printing process, they are said to be **in register**.

- Normally when one opaque object overlaps another, the printing process **knocks out** the color beneath, so there is no blending of inks. When the illustration at the left in Figure 107-2 is printed, for example, the portion of the blue square covered by the magenta star will remain unprinted until the magenta ink is laid down in that area.

- If the plates stay in register, then the magenta star will print exactly in place in the blank area of the blue square, with the magenta ink and blue ink butting up against each other.

- Printing presses are not always perfectly aligned, however, so sometimes one pass gets slightly shifted in relation to the previous passes, and the inks do not align as they should. This is called **misregistration**. If two contrasting colors are supposed to be touching on the layout, sometimes a small gap can occur in the final printout where the paper is visible between them, as shown at the right in Figure 107-2.

Figure 107-2. An object in register and misregistered

- There are several ways to avoid problems that may arise from misregistration.
  - You can choose to **overprint** an object so it is printed on top of other objects without knocking out the area beneath it.
  - You can use **trapping** to create a small overlap—called a *trap*—between two colored areas, so that even if the printing passes are not perfectly aligned, no gap will appear. In trapped areas, one ink is overprinted on another.

- By default, all objects, strokes, fills, and text to which the [Black] swatch has been applied will overprint.

- You have probably seen Overprint Stroke and Overprint Fill check boxes in dialog boxes such as Paragraph Rules and New Cell Style, so that you can easily specify overprinting as you define formats for an object.

- If you do not specify overprinting in a dialog box, you can do so by selecting an object and then using the Attributes panel to choose Overprint Stroke or Overprint Fill, as shown in Figure 107-3.

Figure 107-3. Attributes panel

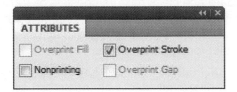

- After you have specified an overprint using the Attributes panel, you can use the View > Overprint Preview command to see how an overprint will look when printed.

- In Figure 107-4, for example, a 3 point magenta stroke has been applied to the star for the purposes of trapping. With Overprint Preview turned on, you can see how the magenta stroke will look printed on top of the blue background—it will look dark blue, as the magenta and cyan blend.

Figure 107-4. Close-up of overprinted stroke

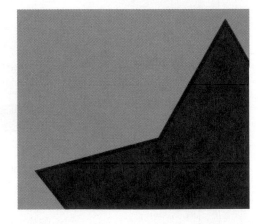

- When you are finished reviewing overprints, click View > Overprint Preview again to turn off the preview.

  ✓ *Deciding when to overprint strokes and fills other than black ones can be a complex issue that is beyond the scope of this text. For more information on overprinting, consult the InDesign Help files.*

- If two overlapping areas share a color, trapping may not be necessary. The common color acts as an automatic trap and prevents any gap between the two objects if misregistration occurs.

- In Figure 107-5, for example, the objects at the left do not need to be trapped. The star is filled with 100% yellow, and the green background also contains a significant percentage of yellow. The two objects will actually print as one area when the yellow ink is laid down. If either of the other two plates used to create the green color is out of register, it will not be so obvious because the yellow ink forms a continuous color between the two objects.

Figure 107-5. Objects that do not and do need trapping

- The objects at the right in Figure 107-5, on the other hand, will need trapping because the blue square and the yellow star do not share any colors.

- You can perhaps see another value, at this point, to using a rich black that includes not only black ink but also percentages of the other process colors. If the black plate is out of register, the other color components of the rich black will make this less noticeable.

- You can if desired trap a document yourself. This usually involves applying a stroke the same color as the object you want to trap and then setting the stroke to overprint, as shown previously in Figure 107-4.

- However, InDesign offers automatic trapping that can save you this effort. You can choose from two types of automatic trapping: built-in trapping and Adobe In-RIP Trapping. The latter is used only when outputting to a PostScript output device (a raster image processor, or RIP) that supports it.

- InDesign's automatic trapping works by detecting color edges and creating traps based on the relative lightness and darkness of colors. The trapping engine most commonly creates a **spread trap**, which enlarges the lighter-colored object to slightly overprint the darker object.

- You specify the type of trapping in the Print dialog box, which you will work with in Exercise 108.

Design Suite Integration

Trapping

One way to minimize trapping required in an InDesign document is to trap in programs you use to create illustrations for InDesign. You can trap illustrations in Illustrator before you import them into InDesign, for example.

Preflight a Document

- Before you send a job for output, you should **preflight** the document. The preflight process helps you prepare a print job for commercial printing and identify problems such as overset text, missing links, improper color modes, and so on.

- You can preflight a document as you work on it by keeping an eye on the Preflight button in the status bar. If the document contains no preflight errors, InDesign displays a green circle icon as shown at left in Figure 107-6. If InDesign detects errors, it displays a red circle and the number of errors, as shown at right in the figure.

Figure 107-6. Live Preflight indicators

- To see an explanation of the errors, double-click on the red circle icon to open a Preflight panel similar to the one shown in Figure 107-7.

Figure 107-7. Perform a preflight check

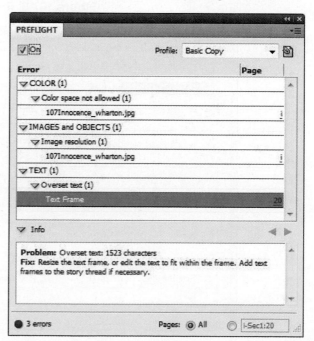

- Errors are listed by category, with each error for that category indented below. The panel shows how many times the error occurs in parentheses as well as the page number on which each error occurs.

- Clicking the Info arrow near the bottom of the panel opens a panel with additional information about the problem and a suggested fix. As you fix each error, it drops off the Preflight panel and the number of errors reduces until the green circle icon indicates no errors present in the document.

- The Preflight feature checks against a default basic profile to detect errors and problems. You can customize the Preflight feature by creating your own profile that checks for errors specific to your document or output process.

- To create a new profile, click the right-pointing arrow to the right of the circle icon and click Define Profiles to display the Preflight Profiles dialog box shown in Figure 107-8.

- Click the New preflight profile button ⊞ under the profile list at the left side of the dialog box and then replace the default new profile name by typing a new one. Then select options to check from the categories in the main pane: Links, Color, Images and Objects, Text, and Document. The profile shown in Figure 107-8, for example, will check for RGB color modes that must be converted before the document is output in CMYK color.

- Once you have selected options and saved the profile, you select it in the Preflight panel. InDesign will then continually check the document as you work, displaying errors as they are detected.

- This live preflight process helps you identify errors as they occur, when they are easy to fix. It is a good idea, for this reason, to create a preflight profile in the early stages of document design, so that you have the benefit of live error checking from the start.

Preview Color Separations

- As you have been reminded in this exercise, a four-color document creates all colors using the four process colors cyan, magenta, yellow, and black. Before printing, a document's colors are separated into these four colors, a process called, not surprisingly, **color separation**.

- As you will learn in the next exercise, color separations can be printed to allow you to proof them and see exactly how colors will be laid down on the paper. But you can also preview color separations on screen to see how a document's colors will be printed.

- You use the Separations Preview panel to preview color separations. Open this panel using the Window > Output > Separations Preview command.

- Then select Separations from the View list on the panel to display the document's colors, as shown in Figure 107-9 at the top of the next page. Notice that this document includes a spot color, Wharton trim, in addition to the four process colors.

Figure 107-8. Preflight Profiles panel

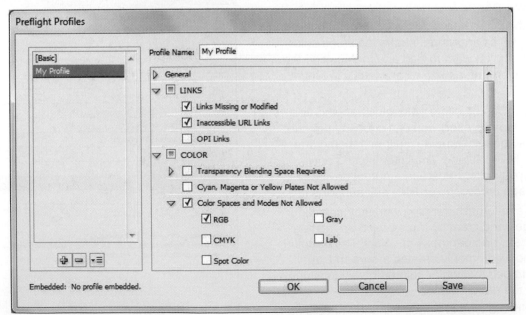

Figure 107-9. Separations Preview panel

Figure 107-10. Cyan preview of an image

✓ *Spot colors display as solid black when previewed.*

- Each color appears with an eye symbol next to it; click the eye to turn that color off, leaving only the colors you want to see. To see only one color, turn the other three off.

- When only one color is selected, its separation appears in black. The percentage of black you see corresponds to the percentage of the process color. Figure 107-10 shows the cyan preview of an image. Lighter gray areas indicate colors that have a low percentage of cyan; darker areas indicate higher concentrations of cyan.

- When you select more than one color in the Separations Preview panel, colors display with their actual color values.

- To return to displaying all colors (the composite image), click CMYK.

PROCEDURES

Control the Appearance of Black

To display black accurately:

1. Click **Edit** .... `ALT` + `E`
2. Point to **Preferences** .... `N`
3. Click **Appearance of Black** .... `B`
4. Click **On Screen** .... `ALT` + `S` and select **Display All Blacks Accurately**.

   OR

   Click **Printing/Exporting** and select **Output All Blacks Accurately** .... `ALT` + `P`
5. Click **OK** .... `ENTER`

Overprint a Stroke or Fill

- Select the **Overprint Stroke** or **Overprint Fill** option in any dialog box that offers this option.

  OR

1. Select the object you want to overprint.
2. Click **Window** .... `ALT` + `W`
3. Click **Attributes** .... `B`
4. In the Attributes panel, select **Overprint Fill** or **Overprint Stroke**.

To view overprints:

1. Click **View** .... `ALT` + `V`
2. Click **Overprint Preview** ..... `V`

Turn on Automatic Trapping

✓ *This procedure requires a PostScript printer.*

1. Click **File** .... `ALT` + `F`
2. Click **Print** .... `P`
3. Select a PostScript printer from the **Printer** list.... `ALT` + `P`
4. Click **Output**.
5. Select **Separations** from the **Color** list .... `ALT` + `L`
6. Select **Application Built-In** from the **Trapping** list .... `ALT` + `T`
7. Select any other settings as needed.
8. Click **Print** .... `ENTER`

✓ *You will work with the Print dialog box in Exercise 108.*

Preflight a Document
(Alt + Shift + Ctrl + F)

To view detected errors:

1. Double-click red circle icon in status bar of document.

   OR

   a. Click **Window** .... ALT + W
   b. Point to **Output** .... P
   c. Click **Preflight** .... P

2. Click right-pointing arrow for each error category to see specific errors.

3. Click right-pointing arrow for each specific error to see instance of error and page number on which it occurs.

4. Click **Info** right-pointing arrow to display a panel with explanation of problem and suggested fix.

To create a custom preflight profile:

1. Click right-pointing arrow to right of circle icon on status bar and click **Define Profiles**.

   OR

   a. With Preflight panel open, click panel menu button 🔽.
   b. Click **Define Profiles**.

2. Click **New preflight profile** button 🔲.

3. Type a name for the new profile.

4. Expand each category of options and select the desired options.

5. Click **Save**.

   ✓ A saved profile remains available until the next time you throw away InDesign settings. To keep a preflight profile associated with a document, click 🔽 in the Preflight Profiles dialog box and select Embed Profile.

6. Click **OK** .... ENTER

7. In Preflight panel, click **Profile** list arrow and select desired profile to check against.

Preview Color Separations

1. Click **Window** .... ALT + W
2. Point to **Output** .... P
3. Click **Separations Preview** .... S
4. Select **Separations** from the View menu in the panel.
5. Click the eye symbol 👁 next to a color to turn off. Repeat for other colors as needed.
6. To return to composite view, click **CMYK**.

EXERCISE DIRECTIONS

1. Start InDesign and open ⊙ 107Innocence. Save the file as 107Innocence_xx.

2. Copy the ⊙ 107Innocence_wharton.jpg file to the same folder where you saved your solution and rename it 107Innocence_wharton_xx.

3. Fix the image link in the 107Innocence_xx document by relinking to the image file in your solution folder.

4. Note that the preflight red circle icon indicates one error. Open the Preflight panel to find out what the error is. You should see that text is overset on page 20.

5. Before you fix the error, create a new preflight profile named **My Profile_xx** to perform a more thorough check. Use the following selections in the Preflight Profiles dialog box:

   a. Leave the LINKS category selections as is.

   b. Under COLOR, click the Color Spaces and Modes Not Allowed right arrow to expand this section, click the Color Spaces and Modes Not Allowed check box to make the options below active, and then click the RGB check box to select it.

   c. Leave the TEXT category selections as is.

   d. Under DOCUMENT, click Blank Pages to turn on this option.

   e. Save the profile.

6. In the Preflight panel, select your profile and allow InDesign to check the document again. It should identify 3 errors:

   a. The first problem identified indicates that the image on the first page uses the RGB color space. Open the 107Innocence_wharton_xx file in Photoshop and convert it to CMYK. Save and close the image in Photoshop.

   b. InDesign automatically updates the image, as you can see if you view the image in the Links panel.

   c. The next error indicates overset text on page 20. Click the page number link in the Preflight panel to go to that page, and expand the text frame to display all text.

d. The final error is a blank page that you don't need. Go to page 21 and delete the page. Your Preflight circle icon should now be green, with no errors reported in the document.

7. Display the Separations Preview panel and view the first page in each separation color.

8. To see how the page will look as it is being printed, display only the Cyan separation, then add each separation to see how successive colors create the final image.

9. Zoom in very closely anywhere on the black line at the bottom of the dark red rectangle (try zooming to 600%).

10. Change the display of black to show the blacks in the document accurately. After you close the Preferences dialog box, you should see a difference in the black line—it will look dark gray instead of true black. (You may need to move the line down slightly so it is not on top of the reddish rectangle before you can see the gray appearance.)

11. Restore rich black in the document.

12. Save your changes, close the file, and exit InDesign.

ON YOUR OWN

1. Start InDesign and open ⊙OYO107. Save the document as OIN107_xx.

2. Note that you have one preflight error listed for overset text, a common problem when using placeholder text. Delete the overset text so that the right-hand column of page 3 is the same length as the left-hand column. (You can delete all text after the word *alisi* in the last visible line of the right column.)

✓ *You may also have missing link errors. See your instructor for information on how to relink these images.*

3. Check the document again using the profile you created in the previous exercise. Note that you have a blank page 1 that you don't need. Delete page 1 and renumber the new first page as 2 to preserve the spread.

4. Display the Separations Preview and check each color.

5. Save your changes, close the document, and exit InDesign.

Exercise | 108

Skills Covered

- **Print a Document or Book**
- **Print Color Separations**
- **Package a Document for Distribution**

Software Skills You can select among many different options when printing either a document or a book. Use the Package feature to prepare a file with all supporting materials to send to your print service contractor.

Design Skills The culmination of any design project is some sort of output, either to a printer or to a file. Knowing how to set printing options can speed the output process.

Application Skills In this exercise, you continue working with the *Age of Innocence* document you have worked with several times in this course. You will view printing options, print a composite, and print separations as a PDF file.

TERMS

Composite Printing all colors of a document on one proof.

NOTES

Print a Document or Book

- To print a document, choose File > Print. The Print dialog box, shown in Figure 108-1 at the top of the next page, offers a list of seven option categories at the left side of the dialog box, plus the Summary category. You can click each category to see settings specific to that category.

- No matter which category you are viewing, the top three items in the dialog box stay the same:
  - Use the Print Preset list to load print presets, if you have saved any.
  - Select a printer from the Printer list.
  - If the chosen printer is a PostScript printer, the PPD (PostScript Printer Description) file associated with that printer displays in the PPD box. The PPD file provides information about the printer, such as what paper sizes it supports, resolution options, and so on.

- The General category controls the basic print settings that you might find in a word processing application, such as number of copies, page range, and collation. You can also choose whether to print spreads and master pages.

- The Options area of the General options lets you decide whether to print all layers, only visible layers, or layers that are both visible and printable. You can also choose to print objects that normally do not print, as well as visible objects such as guides and grids. By default, InDesign does not print blank pages that might appear in a document, but you can choose to print them if desired.

- The Setup category, shown in Figure 108-2 at the bottom of the next page, lets you specify the paper size, which might not necessarily be the same as the page size in your document. For example, it is common to use a larger paper size and then trim the paper after printing so that color bleeds go all the way to the edge of the paper.

Figure 108-1. General options category in Print dialog box

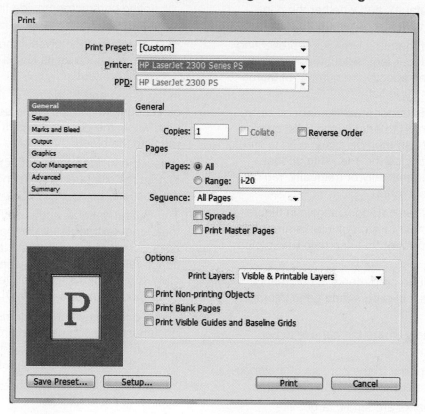

Figure 108-2. Choose options from the Setup category

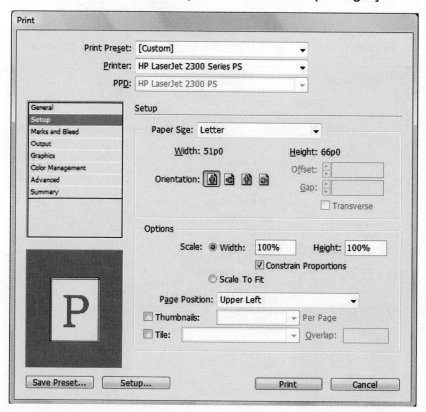

- Setup also controls orientation, the scaling of the page (100% by default), and whether the page should be scaled to fit the paper.

- To print a sheet of thumbnail images representing the pages in the document, select the Thumbnails check box and then specify the number of thumbnails from the Per Page list.

- If your document is larger than the paper size, you can *tile* the document to print it in several overlapping sections that can then be assembled to create the final document. Use the Tile list to choose whether to tile automatically or manually. You can also adjust the tile overlap.

- The Marks and Bleed category, shown in Figure 108-3, enables you to turn on/off marks around the outside of the document that can help with professional printing.

- Printer marks include crop marks, bleed marks, registration marks, color bars, and page information.

  - Crop marks show where the page is to be trimmed after printing.

  - Bleed marks appear at the corners of the document to indicate the extent of the bleed area.

  - Registration marks are small, target-like symbols that make it easy to line up color separations.

- Color bars show the colors in use to help the printing contractor provide the correct ink density on press.

- Page information gives information about the document such as its file name and time and date of printout.

- In the Bleed and Slug area of the dialog box, you can choose to use the bleed settings you configured within the document itself at setup, or you can redefine the bleed.

- Select the Include Slug Area check box if you want to print the slug area you defined when you set up the document.

- The Output options, shown in Figure 108-4 at the top of the next page, let you specify the desired color output. You can output either a **composite** image (all colors together) using Gray, RGB, or CMYK, or a color separation (each color in the color model output separately).

- You should always print a composite of your final document. You can use it to proof text and images, and you should also send a composite along with the file to your printing contractor.

- You will learn how to output separations in the next section of this exercise.

- In the Graphics category, shown in Figure 108-5 at the bottom of the next page, you can specify how graphics are to be sent to the printer.

Figure 108-3. Set printer marks and bleed and slug options

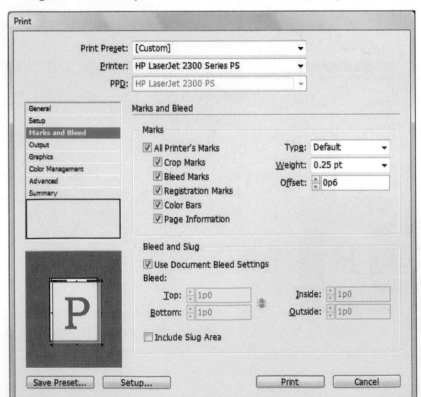

Figure 108-4. Select a type of color output

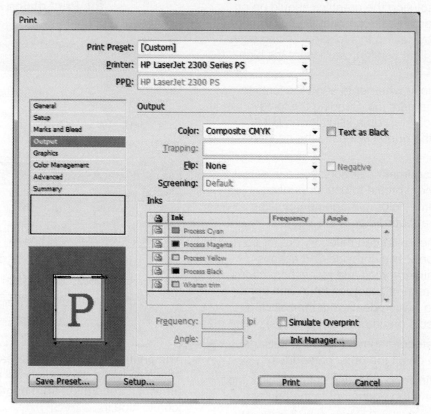

Figure 108-5. Graphics settings in the Print dialog box

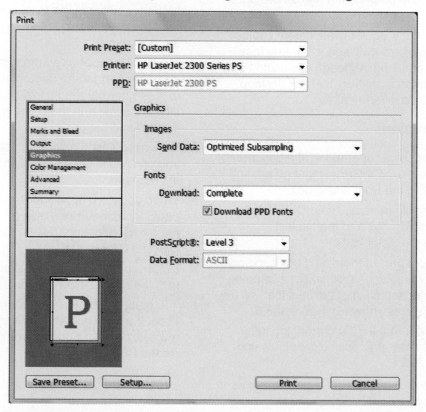

- For example, the Send Data list gives you choices of how high a resolution the graphics should be on the printout. For draft desktop printing, you can save some time by setting this to a low setting such as Proxy. For the final version, you'll want the highest setting available.

- You can also choose whether to send the fonts to the printer with the print job. Sending the fonts makes the print job start up a little slower, but it guarantees that the printer will have the needed fonts.

- In the Color Management category, you can select a color management profile to use for printing. These are the same color management profiles that you learned about earlier in this course.

- The settings in the Advanced category are for commercial printing only. They provide OPI options (which omit certain graphics and place instructions in their place for manual insertion later) and transparency flattening (which deals with reproducing transparency effects on commercial presses).

- The Summary category summarizes the settings you have chosen on all the other categories.

- When you have finished selecting settings, click the Print button to send the document to the printer.

- To print a book, open the Book panel for the book, make sure that no documents are selected in it, and click the Print the book button 🖨 on the Book panel.

- If the documents in the book have different source color profiles defined, you will see a warning message; click OK to continue. Although this could be a problem for commercial printing, for draft desktop printing it makes little difference.

Print Color Separations

- If you want to print color separations of a document to check before you send the document for printing, you can do so using the Print dialog box.

- After selecting what to print, click the Output category in the Print dialog box and then select Separations from the Color list.

- Options in the lower part of the dialog box become active. For example, you can now select a Trapping option, and you can see a list of the inks that will be used to print the job, as shown in Figure 108-6.

- Note in Figure 108-6 that for the current job the printer will need all four process colors plus a spot color, PANTONE 328 C.

  ✓ The frequency and angle settings have to do with how lines of halftone dots are laid down on the paper to create a color. You can learn more about frequency, line screens, and angle using InDesign Help.

Figure 108-6. Separation options in the Print dialog box

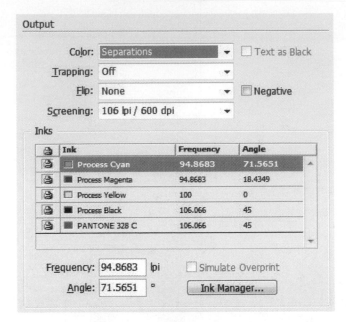

- The printer icon 🖨 next to each of these colors indicates that a separation will print for that color. To prevent a separation from printing, click the printer icon to hide it.

- For more control over the inks used to print a document, use the Ink Manager. Clicking the Ink Manager button in the Print dialog box opens the Ink Manager, shown in Figure 108-7 at the top of the next page.

- The Ink Manager gives more information about the inks specified for the document, such as whether they are normal (traditional process inks), the density of the ink, and the order in which inks are applied and trapped.

- To avoid creating a separate plate for a spot color, you can convert spot colors to process colors in the Ink Manager.

- When you have specified Separations in the Output category of the Print dialog box, your selected printer will print separations for you as soon as you click the Print button.

- Each separation shows objects that use that color with the correct color percentage.

- You must have a PostScript printer to print separations. If you do not have a PostScript printer available, however, a good alternative is to specify Adobe PDF as the printer.

Figure 108-7. Ink Manager dialog box

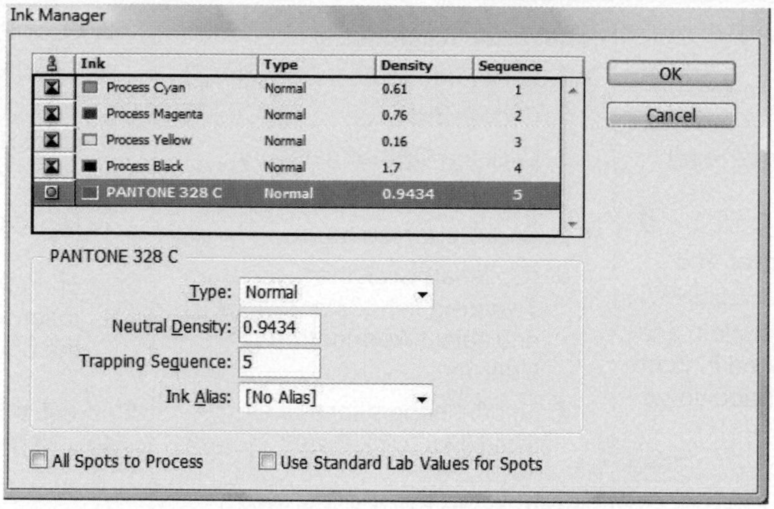

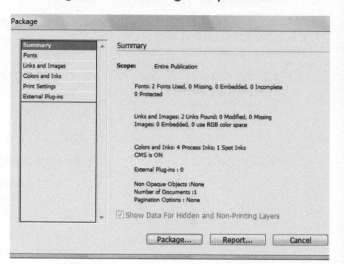

- InDesign will export the separations as a single PDF file containing the separations. Figure 108-8 shows a portion of the cyan separation for the Glacier document you worked with in the previous exercise.

Figure 108-8. Portion of a separation created using PDF

Package a Document for Distribution

- You can use InDesign's Package feature to organize all the materials required to display and print a document. Once a document has been packaged, you can easily copy it to disk or even e-mail it for distribution.
- Use the File > Package command to begin the packaging process. The Package dialog box opens as shown in Figure 108-9 to allow you to check the document's contents, such as the fonts in use and the linked images.

Figure 108-9. Package the publication

- When you click Package in this dialog box, a Printing Instructions dialog box opens that you can use to supply contact information in case the printer needs to get in touch with you. When you continue from this dialog box, the Package Publication dialog box opens.
- In the Package Publication dialog box, enter a name for the package in the Folder Name box, and specify a location. Select or clear the check boxes as needed for your situation. Note, for example, that you can choose to copy fonts and linked graphics so they will always be available for the document file.

  ✓ If you see a Font Alert dialog box warning you about copyright restrictions on fonts, read the information and click OK.

- The resulting folder will contain the InDesign document and Instructions.txt, plus two subfolders: Document fonts (the fonts needed for the print job) and Links (the needed images).

PROCEDURES

Print a Document *(Ctrl + P)*

1. Click **File** .... `ALT` + `F`
2. Click **Print** .... `P`
3. (Optional) Click **Print Pre**s**et** and select a print preset .... `ALT` + `S`
4. (Optional) Click **Printer** and select a printer .... `ALT` + `P`
5. Click a category at the left, and set any options desired in that category. Repeat for additional categories.
6. Click **Print** .... `ENTER`

Print a Book

1. Open the book. Do not select any documents.
2. Click the **Print** button 🖨 on the Book panel.

   ✓ *If a warning appears about different color profiles, click OK.*

Print Color Separations

1. Click **File** .... `ALT` + `F`
2. Click **Print** .... `P`
3. Click the **Output** category.
4. Click the **Co**l**or** list ..... `ALT` + `L`
5. Click **Separations**.
6. (Optional) Click the **Trapping** list .... `ALT` + `T` and select **Application Built-In**.
7. To print separations of all listed inks, click **Print** .... `ENTER`

To convert a spot color to process colors:
In the Output settings in the Print dialog box:

1. Click **Ink** **M**anager ..... `ALT` + `M`
2. Select the spot color in the list of inks.
3. Click **All** **S**pots to **Process** .... `ALT` + `S`
4. Click **OK** .... `ENTER`

To print separations to a PDF file:
In the Print dialog box:

1. Select **Adobe PDF** from the **Printer** list in the Print dialog box.
2. Set up all printing options and separation options as desired.

3. Click **Print** .... `ENTER`
4. Specify a location to save the file.
5. Click **Save** .... `ALT` + `S`
6. Open Adobe Acrobat.
7. Navigate to the location where you saved the PDF file and open the file to view the separations as separate pages in the document.

Package a Document for a Printer *(Alt + Shift + Ctrl + P)*

1. Click **File** .... `ALT` + `F`
2. Click **Package** .... `G`
3. Review the information in the Package dialog box's categories.
4. Click **Package** .... `ALT` + `P`
5. Enter contact information and instructions.
6. Click **Con**t**inue** .... `ALT` + `T`
7. Type a file name in the **Folder name** box.
8. Click **Package** .... `ENTER`
9. Click **OK** if you receive a dialog box telling you about copyright restrictions on fonts.

EXERCISE DIRECTIONS

1. Start InDesign and open 🖶 107Innocence_xx or open ⚪ 108Innocence. Save the file as 108Innocence_xx.

2. Open the Print dialog box and make the following selections to print a composite of several pages of the document:

   a. Choose to print to Adobe PDF.

   b. Choose to print the range **i-2**.

   c. Set scaling to 90%.

   d. Choose to print crop marks, bleed marks, and registration marks.

   e. Choose the Composite CMYK output option.

3. Click Print. Choose to save the composite in the folder with your solutions for this lesson, with the name 108Innocence_composite_xx. If the document opens immediately in Adobe Acrobat, scroll through the pages and view the printer's marks you added.

   ✓ Or, open Acrobat and then navigate to the file and open it.

4. Close the document in Acrobat.

5. Return to InDesign and open the Print dialog box again.

   a. Change the page range to **i** (lowercase eye) to print only the first page of the document.

   b. This time, specify that you want to print separations.

   c. Turn on trapping.

   d. Use the Ink Manager to convert the spot color to process inks.

6. Click Save. Choose to save the separations document in the folder with your solutions for this lesson, with the name 108Innocence_separations_xx. In Acrobat, scroll through the pages and view the separations.

7. Package the document. Use your own name and contact information on the Printing Instructions form, and then save the package as 108Innocence_package_xx in the same folder with your other solutions for this exercise.

   ✓ Click OK if you see a dialog box telling you about font copyright issues.

8. Save your changes, close the file, and exit InDesign.

ON YOUR OWN

1. Start InDesign and open 🖶 OIN107_xx or open ⚪ OYO108. Save the document as OIN108_xx.

2. Set the following printing options for this document:

   a. Specify Adobe PDF as the printer.

   b. Choose to print pages 2 and 3.

   c. Set scaling to 90%.

   d. Choose printer marks as desired.

   e. Print separations.

   f. Convert the spot color ink in this document to process inks.

3. Save the separations file with an appropriate name and then view it.

4. Save your changes, close the document, and exit InDesign.

Exercise | 109

Skills Covered

- Export to an EPS File
- Export to PDF Format
- About Dynamic Documents
- Insert Hyperlinks and Cross-References

- Insert Rollover Buttons
- Use the Preview Panel
- Apply Page Transitions

Software Skills   Additional ways to output a document include exporting as a PDF or to an EPS file. Features such as cross references, hyperlinks and buttons, and page transitions give your readers additional options for interactivity when exporting for PDF or Adobe Flash.

Design Skills   A designer must keep in mind that there are a number of ways to view documents created in InDesign. They can be viewed not only in printed form but also onscreen. Creative Suite features make it easy to construct dynamic documents.

Application Skills   In this exercise, you will prepare a version of some of your *Midwest Gardening Today* files for onscreen viewing. You will add page transitions, cross references, and a hyperlink and button to make the document both dynamic and interactive.

TERMS

Cross-reference   Text that refers a reader from one location in a document to another.

Downsample   To reduce an image's size by removing pixels from it.

EPS   Encapsulated PostScript; a graphic format that is commonly used in professional printing to manage pictures and print jobs.

PDF   Portable Document Format; an Adobe format for distributing documents in electronic form exactly as they would be printed.

Text anchor   A named location in a document.

NOTES

Export to an EPS File

- Encapsulated PostScript (**EPS**) is a graphic format based on the PostScript printer/graphic language. An EPS file can be sent directly to a PostScript-compatible printing press and can be inserted in other applications that accept EPS files as input.

- If a client you are working with requests an EPS file, you can create one with the File > Export command. In the Save as type list, choose EPS as the type.

- After you supply a name and location for the file and click the Save button, the Export EPS dialog box opens, as shown in Figure 109-1, to allow you to make your option selections.

Figure 109-1. Export EPS dialog box

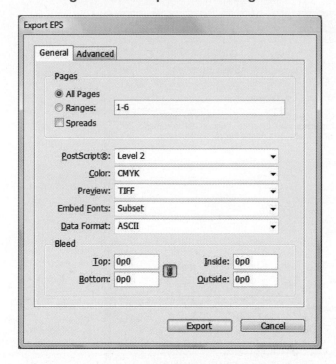

- You can choose what pages to export, and whether to export them as single pages or spreads. You can select the desired PostScript level, if necessary, as well as a color mode. The Preview option saves a TIFF graphic with the file that will display as a preview in dialog boxes such as Place.

- You can also choose whether to embed the complete font set for fonts in use or only the actual letters used as a subset. Though you also have the option not to embed fonts, it's a good idea to embed at least the subset if not the complete set, in case the client does not have the font you are using.

- Note that you can also specify bleed areas on the General tab.

- On the Advanced tab, you can choose whether to send all image data or just a proxy of images for placement purposes. You can also specify a resolution setting for flattening images and access the Ink Manager.

- When you have finished selecting settings and click Export, the document is saved in a series of EPS files, one file for each single page or spread.

Export to PDF Format

- Portable Document Format (**PDF**) is an Adobe format for distributing documents. A PDF file shows a full-color, high-resolution version of the document and looks the same when viewed on any computer.

- PDF is a unique blend of text and snapshot: Each page looks exactly as it would if printed, like a snapshot, but the text within the document remains searchable.

- Anyone can view a PDF file on any PC with the free program Adobe Reader. However, to create a PDF file, you must have the full version of Adobe Acrobat or some other program that is capable of generating PDF files (such as InDesign).

- There are two ways to create a PDF file from your document:
  - You can print to the Adobe PDF driver through the Print dialog box, as described in the previous exercise.
    - ✓ *This option is available only if you have installed Adobe Acrobat (the full version, not Acrobat Reader). Adobe Acrobat 9 is one of the applications in the Design Creative Suite.*
  - You can export to PDF using the Export command. This method is more flexible and has more options than the printing method.

- In the Export dialog box, you can choose Adobe PDF (Interactive) or Adobe PDF (Print). InDesign CS5 offers two choices to make it easy for you to apply settings for these different end uses.
  - ✓ *You learn about interactive PDF later in this exercise.*

- If you choose the Adobe PDF (Print) option, the Export Adobe PDF dialog box then opens, as shown in Figure 109-2 at the top of the next page, so you can fully configure the PDF output. There are many options, organized around seven categories (at the left of the dialog box).

- As with printing, you can select a preset from the Adobe PDF Preset list if you have saved any. There are several on the list already to choose from, such as High Quality Print (for desktop printers), Press Quality (for digital or commercial printing), or Smallest File Size (for Web distribution).

- The Compatibility list lets you choose the minimum version of Adobe Acrobat that will be able to view the file. The lower the version number, the fewer the features but the higher the compatibility with computers having older versions.

- For full information about every option in this dialog box, consult the InDesign Help system. Here are a few highlights:
  - Under General, if you choose Embed Page Thumbnails, users will be able to browse the pages by thumbnail image. This is useful for long documents. It increases the file size slightly. Interactive elements are not enabled by default if you have chosen the Adobe PDF (Print) option.

Figure 109-2. Set PDF export options

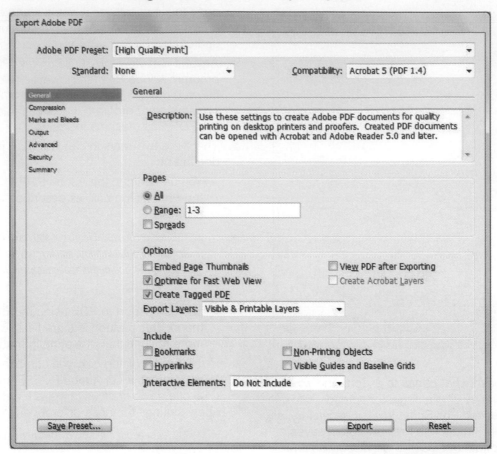

- Under Compression, you can **downsample** (reduce) the images to save space. This is useful if the PDF file will be distributed in a low-resolution format such as over the Web, but it is not a good idea if you are preparing the document for commercial printing.

- Under Output, you can set Color to No Color Conversion to avoid problems with differences in transparency blend space.

- Under Security, you can specify a password to open the document and set a permissions password required for editing or printing.

About Dynamic Documents

- A *dynamic document* contains movement or elements with which a viewer can interact, such as hyperlinks or buttons.

- InDesign makes it easy to create dynamic documents that can then be exported to other formats such as PDF, XML, or Adobe Flash's SWF. Functionality that you build into your document pages translates seamlessly in most cases.

- Exporting to XML and Flash are beyond the scope of this book, but you will learn in the next sections how to create dynamic elements for PDFs that you can view in Adobe Acrobat or Adobe Reader.

- You will find the Interactive for PDF workspace very helpful when creating dynamic documents. This workspace gives you access to panels such as Hyperlinks, Buttons, Page Transitions, and Preview that you will learn about in the remainder of this exercise.

Insert Hyperlinks and Cross-References

- When you are preparing a PDF that will be viewed onscreen, you can add hyperlinks to allow readers to jump to different pages or to locations on the Web—the type of interactive functionality that you are used to seeing on Web pages.

- The Hyperlinks panel makes it easy to set up links from text to a variety of destinations. As you can see in Figure 109-3 at the top of the next page, you can also keep track of cross-references in this panel.

Figure 109-3. Hyperlinks panel

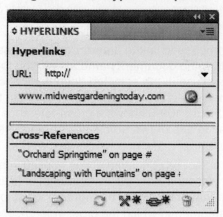

- You have several options for creating a hyperlink. In InDesign CS5, you can now have InDesign find URLs in your document and convert them automatically to hyperlnks.

- Clicking Convert URLs to Hyperlinks on the Hyperlinks panel menu displays the dialog box shown in Figure 109-4.

Figure 109-4. Search for URLs to convert to hyperlinks

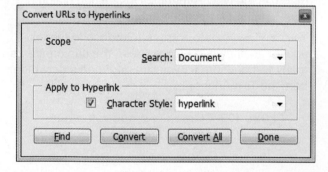

- You can search the entire document, a story, or a selection, and you can apply a character style to any URLs you want to convert. You must create the character style before launching this search.

- For more control over the hyperlink settings, select the text or object you want to use as the hyperlink and click the Create new hyperlink button on the Hyperlinks panel to open the New Hyperlink dialog box.

- In the New Hyperlink dialog box, shown in Figure 109-5, you can select a target to link to, such as a URL, file, e-mail address, page, or text anchor.

  ✓ A text anchor is a named location to which you can link. You learn more about text anchors later in this section.

- The Destination section changes depending on the target you choose. To link to a URL, for example, you type the URL address of the Web page, as shown in Figure 109-5. To link to a page, select the document, the page, and a view for the page.

- You can also choose how the hyperlink will appear on the page. By default, hyperlinks are enclosed within an invisible rectangle. You can identify the link only when previewing it, when the pointer changes to the pointing finger over the link. You can change the invisible rectangle to a visible rectangle to identify the link. For the Visible Rectangle option, you can adjust the outline color, width, and style.

  ✓ If the hyperlink is created from an object such as a text frame, a visible rectangle can help a viewer to realize that the object is a link.

- You can also create a character style for links that will apply formatting such as a different color or underlining to help viewers recognize hyperlinks on the page.

Figure 109-5. New Hyperlink dialog box

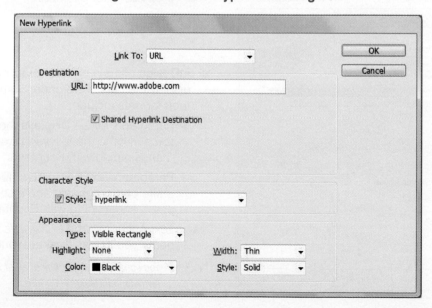

- Setting appearance type to Invisible Rectangle turns off the Color, Width, and Style options, but you still have the option of selecting a Highlight action that will occur when the viewer clicks the link.

- As you create them, hyperlinks are stored in the Hyperlinks panel. You can modify any hyperlink by double-clicking it in the panel to open the Edit Hyperlink dialog box, with the same settings as the New Hyperlink dialog box. Delete a link by selecting it in the panel and clicking the Delete selected hyperlinks or cross-references button 🗑.

- In InDesign CS5, you have a new option for checking links: you can open a spread or document in the Preview panel. You learn more about this panel later in this exercise.

- A **cross-reference** refers a reader from one location in a document to another. In print documents, a cross-reference may consist of wording such as "See *How to Create an Index* on page 75."

- You can create a cross-reference in an InDesign document that has the same kind of interactive functionality as a hyperlink: when a viewer clicks on the cross-reference text in the PDF, the page that contains the cross-reference source displays.

- Create a cross-reference using the Hyperlinks panel by selecting the text or location where you want the cross-reference to appear and then clicking the Create new cross-reference button 🗙 on the Hyperlinks panel.

- The New Cross-Reference dialog box displays, giving you options for creating the cross-reference, as shown in Figure 109-6. You have two options for creating the cross-reference link: you can link to a paragraph or to a text anchor.

Figure 109-6. New Cross-Reference dialog box

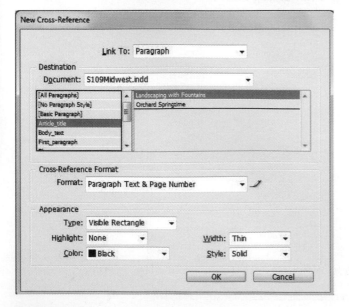

✓ You do not have to link to the current document; you can create a cross-reference to any open document or browse to any other document.

- If you choose to link to a paragraph, the Destination list below the document name allows you to choose a style in use in the selected document, and you can then select a paragraph formatted with that style. Figure 109-6 shows a cross-reference being created to one of two article title paragraphs in the document.

- If you do not have custom styles applied in a document, you can select [All Paragraphs] or [Basic Paragraph] and scroll in the right-hand list to select the paragraph to which the cross-reference will refer.

- You have another option for creating the target of the cross-reference: you can insert a text anchor anywhere in a document and use it as the destination for the cross-reference. A **text anchor** is a named location in a document, similar to a bookmark you might have inserted in a word processing file or Web page.

- To insert a text anchor, position the insertion point where you want the anchor and select New Hyperlink Destination from the Hyperlinks panel menu. In the New Hyperlink Destination dialog box, type a name for the text anchor and save it.

- You can then create a cross-reference to the text anchor as shown in Figure 109-7. You can create as many text anchors as you like and then select them from the Text Anchor list.

Figure 109-7. Create a cross-reference to a text anchor

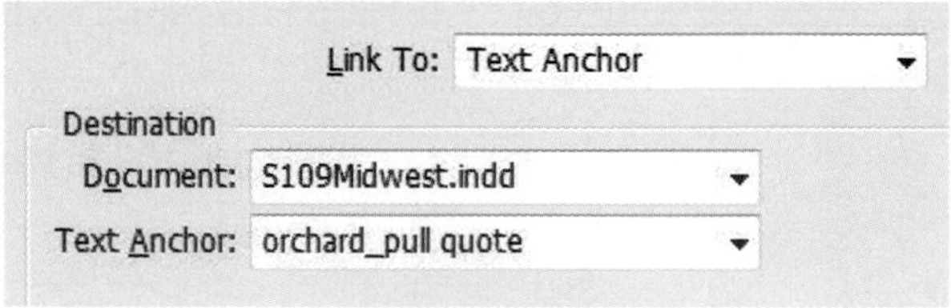

Link To: Text Anchor

Destination
Document: S109Midwest.indd
Text Anchor: orchard_pull quote

- InDesign offers a number of formats you can use to display the cross-reference. Some of the more common formats include:
  - Paragraph Text— Displays the entire paragraph text similar to the following example: "Landscaping with Fountains"
  - Paragraph Text & Page Number—Displays the entire paragraph text and inserts the page number: "Landscaping with Fountains" on page 4
  - Text Anchor Name—Displays the text anchor name you saved: "orchard_pull quote"

  ✓ You can find explanations of all of the cross-reference formats in InDesign Help files.

- If the default formats do not quite display the cross-reference as you'd like it, you can edit the format. You can also apply a character style to a portion of the cross-reference to emphasize it.

- Note that you have the same appearance options for the cross-reference as you have for hyperlinks.

- Cross-references are stored in the Cross-References section of the Hyperlinks panel. To edit a cross-reference, double-click it in the panel.

- To make sure that links and cross-references work in a PDF, export the document using the Adobe PDF (Interactive) option. The Export to Interactive PDF dialog box displays, as shown in Figure 109-8.

Figure 109-8. Export to Interactive PDF dialog box

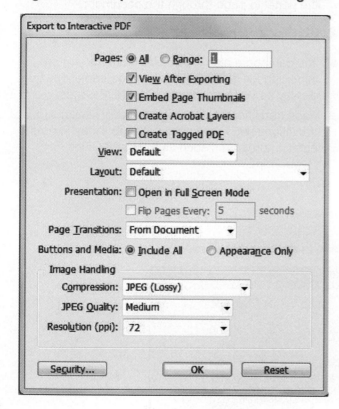

- You can choose what pages to export, and you can select the view and layout that will display when the PDF opens. Note that buttons and media are included by default.

- You can also choose page transitions in this dialog box. You learn more about page transitions later in this exercise.

Insert Rollover Buttons

- Another interactivity feature in InDesign is the ability to insert rollover buttons you can use to accomplish tasks such as opening a Web page or a file, playing a movie or sound, or closing a document.

- You can create a button from an object such as a rectangle or ellipse on your InDesign page.

  ✓ *You can learn more about creating and formatting a button you create from scratch using InDesign Help files.*

- You can also quickly add rollover buttons of various types from the Sample Buttons panel and then customize the button to specify its actions and its rollover states.

- To add a sample button to a document, simply drag it from the Sample Buttons panel to the desired location. Then display the Buttons panel, shown in Figure 109-9, to modify the button.

Figure 109-9. Use the Buttons panel to customize a sample button

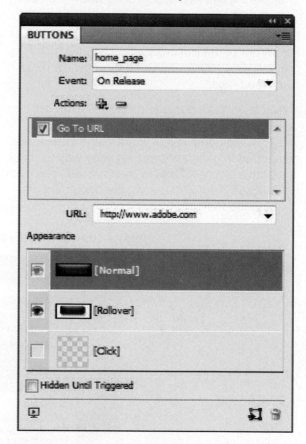

- Name the button if desired to make it easy to keep track of when you have a number of buttons on a page.

- Choose the event that will trigger the button action. For example:
  - On Release triggers the action when you release the mouse button after clicking.
  - On Click triggers the action when you click the button.
  - On Roll Over triggers the action when you move the mouse pointer over the button.

- Select an action from the Actions button  list, such as Go To URL, Go To First Page, or Open File. The action is what the button will actually do when the proper event occurs.

- You can add multiple actions for a single button. Remove any actions you don't want to occur using the Delete selected action button ⊟.

- Buttons from the Sample Buttons panel have state appearances built in.
  - The Normal state is how the button appears when the mouse is not interacting with it.
  - The Rollover state is how the button displays when the mouse is hovering over it.
  - You can also activate the Click state, which applies a different appearance when the button is clicked.

- Note the Preview Spread button ⊡ at the lower-left corner of the Buttons panel. Use this button to preview your rollover button in the Preview panel, discussed next.

Use the Preview Panel

- The Preview panel is new in InDesign CS5. It was developed to give designers an easy way to check interactive elements that in previous versions could be checked only by exporting the document and opening the PDF.

- The Preview panel displays the current spread in a resizable window such as the one shown in Figure 109-10 at the bottom of the page.

- The window is resizable so that you can, if desired, see a full-screen version of the current spread. As shown in Figure 109-10, you can click on interactive elements such as links or cross-references just as you would in the published PDF. If you are previewing a button, you see the various states associated with the button as you hover over the button and click it.

- You can preview a selection (such as a selected rollover button), a spread, or an entire document. If you are previewing an entire document, you can use the navigation arrows at the lower-left corner of the panel to page through the document.

Apply Page Transitions

- You can add a nice touch to documents you are exporting for PDF by applying page transitions that display as you scroll through the PDF pages.

- Page transitions in InDesign are very similar to transitions you may have applied to slides in presentation programs such as Microsoft Office PowerPoint.

Figure 109-10. Display a spread in the Preview panel

■ Select the pages to which you want to apply the transitions and then display the Page Transitions panel. Select a transition type from the Transition list to display information on the transition, as shown in Figure 109-11.

■ As you select the transition, a preview occurs in the panel. You can adjust direction and speed for any transition.

■ To apply a transition to an entire document, click the Apply to All Spreads button 🖳 at the lower-right corner of the panel.

■ When you export to PDF, you can set transitions in the Export to Interactive PDF dialog box, or choose to use the transitions you have applied in the document. Page transitions display in the PDF only when you are viewing in Full Screen Mode.

Figure 109-11. Select a page transition

PROCEDURES

Export to an EPS File *(Ctrl + E)*
1. Click **File** .... ALT + F
2. Click **Export** .... E
3. Select a location in which to export.
4. Click the **Save as type** list .... ALT + T
5. Click **EPS**.
6. Type a file name in the **File name** box .... ALT + N
7. Click **Save** .... ALT + S
8. (Optional) Set any export options.
9. Click **Export** .... ENTER

Export to a PDF File *(Ctrl + E)*
1. Click **File** .... ALT + F
2. Click **Export** .... E
3. Select a location in which to export.
4. Click the **Save as type** list .... ALT + T
5. Click **Adobe PDF (Interactive)** or **Adobe PDF (Print)**.
6. Type a file name in the **File name** box .... ALT + N
7. Click **Save** .... ALT + S

To export for print PDF:
1. (Optional) Select an **Adobe PDF Preset** .... ALT + S
2. (Optional) Choose a **Standard** with which to comply . ALT + T
3. (Optional) Choose an Acrobat **Compatibility** level ... ALT + C
4. (Optional) Set any export options.
5. Click **Export** .... ENTER

To export for interactive PDF:
1. Set the desired page range.
2. Click **View** .... ALT + V and select the desired view that will display when the PDF opens.
3. Click **Layout** .... ALT + Y and choose the way pages lay out in the PDF.
4. (Optional) Click **Page Transitions** .... ALT + T and select a page transition.
5. Select any other export options desired.
6. Click **OK** .... ENTER

Insert a Hyperlink
1. Select the text or object that will be used as the hyperlink.
2. Click **Create new hyperlink** button 🖳 on Hyperlinks panel.
3. Click **Link to** list and select target of hyperlink.
4. In Destination area of dialog box, type the necessary information for the link, such as the URL, document name, page number, e-mail address, file name, and so on.
5. (Optional) Click **Style** check box and then select a character style from the list .... ALT + T
6. (Optional) Click **Type** and select a different appearance type .... ALT + Y , ↓/↑
7. (Optional) Click **Highlight** and select a highlight option .... ALT + G , ↓/↑
8. (Optional) Click **Color**, **Width**, or **Style** and select formats as desired for a visible rectangle.
9. Click **OK** .... ENTER

OR

1. In a document that contains URLs, click ▾ to display the Hyperlinks panel menu.
2. Click **Convert URLs to Hyperlinks.**
3. Choose the scope of the search, if necessary.
4. Click **Character Style** check box if desired, and then select a character style from the list.
5. Click **Find** to locate the first URL.
6. Click **Convert** to convert the URL to a link.
7. Click **Find Next and Convert** until all URLs are converted.
8. Click **Done.**

To edit a hyperlink:

1. Double-click the hyperlink to edit in the Hyperlinks panel.
2. Make desired changes in the Edit Hyperlink dialog box.
3. Click **OK** .... ENTER

To delete a hyperlink:

1. Click the hyperlink to delete in the Hyperlinks panel.
2. Click the **Delete selected hyperlinks or cross-references** button 🗑.
3. Click **Yes** .... ALT + Y

Insert a Cross-Reference

To insert a cross-reference to a paragraph:

1. Position the insertion point where the cross-reference will appear.
2. Click **Create new cross-reference** button ✖✱.
3. Click **Link to** list and select **Paragraph**, if necessary.
4. (Optional) Click **Document** and select a document other than the current one .. ALT + O
5. In left list below Document, select a paragraph style.

6. In the right list, select specific paragraph the cross-reference should point to.
7. Click **Format** list and choose a format for the cross-reference.

   ✓ You may also click the Create or edit cross-reference formats button to open a dialog box where you can customize or create a new format.

8. (Optional) Click **Type** and select a different appearance type .... ALT + Y , ↓/↑
9. (Optional) Click **Highlight** and select a highlight option .... ALT + G , ↓/↑
10. (Optional) Click **Color**, **Width**, or **Style** and select formats as desired for a visible rectangle.
11. Click **OK** .... ENTER

To create a text anchor:

1. Position the insertion point where you want to place the text anchor.
2. Click ▾ to display the Hyperlinks panel menu.
3. Click **New Hyperlink Destination**.
4. Type a name for the text anchor.
5. Click **OK** .... ENTER

To insert a cross-reference to a text anchor:

1. Position the insertion point where the cross-reference will appear.
2. Click **Create new cross-reference** button ✖✱.
3. Click **Link to** list and select **Text Anchor**.
4. (Optional) Click **Document** and select a document other than the current one .. ALT + O
5. Click **Text Anchor** list and select the desired text anchor.
6. Select formats and appearance options as directed above.
7. Click **OK** .... ENTER

To edit a cross-reference:

1. Double-click the cross-reference to edit in the Hyperlinks panel.
2. Make desired changes in the Edit Cross-Reference dialog box.
3. Click **OK** .... ENTER

To delete a cross-reference:

1. Click the cross-reference to delete in the Hyperlinks panel.
2. Click the **Delete selected hyperlinks or cross-references** button 🗑.
3. Click **Yes** .... ALT + Y

Insert a Rollover Button

The following steps are for creating a button using the Sample Buttons panel. To create a button from scratch, see InDesign Help.

1. Display the page on which the button will appear.
2. Click **Window** .... ALT + W
3. Click **Sample Buttons**.
4. Drag a button from the Sample Buttons panel and position it as desired on the page.
5. With the button selected, display the Buttons panel:
   a. Click **Window** .... ALT + W
   b. Point to **Interactive** V
   c. Click **Buttons** .... U
6. (Optional) Type a name for the button.
7. Click the **Event** list and select an event, if necessary.
8. Click the **Actions** button ➕ and select an action to perform.
9. Supply additional information for the action, such as a URL address or file path.
10. Make visible all states you want to use for the button.

To remove an action:

1. Select the action in the Actions list.
2. Click **Delete selected action** button 🗑.

Use the Preview Panel (Shift+Ctrl+Enter)

1. Display the item to preview, such as a button or a document spread.

   ✓ *If previewing a button, select the button.*

2. Display the Preview panel:
   a. Click **Window** .... ALT + W
   b. Point to **Interactive** V
   c. Click **Preview** V
3. Click ▾≡ to display the Preview panel menu.

4. Select the desired preview option: **Preview Selection**, **Preview Spread**, or **Preview Document**.
5. (Optional) Resize the Preview panel if desired for a better view of the spread.
6. (Optional) Use the navigation arrows at lower-left of panel to page through a document.

Apply Page Transitions

1. Select the page or pages to which the page transition should be applied.
2. Display the Page Transition panel:
   a. Click **Window** .... ALT + W
   b. Point to **Interactive** V
   c. Click **Page Transitions** .... T

3. Click the **Transition** list and select a transition.

   ✓ *The selected transition immediately previews at the top of the panel.*

4. (Optional) Click the **Direction** list and select a new direction for the effect.
5. (Optional) Click the **Speed** list and select a new speed for the effect.
6. (Optional) Click the **Apply to All Spreads** button 🖼 to apply the current transition to all pages in the document.

EXERCISE DIRECTIONS

✓ *Display the Interactive for PDF workspace.*

1. Start InDesign and open ◉109Midwest_perennials. Export this file in Adobe PDF (Print) format to your solutions folder with the same name. Use the following settings:
   a. Use the Smallest File Size Adobe preset.
   b. Choose to export all pages.
   c. Optimize for fast Web viewing, and view the PDF after exporting.
2. View the three pages of the PDF and then close the file in Acrobat or Reader. Close 109Midwest_perennials in InDesign without saving changes.
3. Open ◉109Midwest and save the file as 109Midwest_xx.
4. Create a hyperlink on page 1 as follows:
   a. Select the Web site text near the bottom of page 1.
   b. Display the Hyperlinks panel and click the Create new hyperlink button 🔗 to open the New Hyperlink dialog box.

   c. Make sure URL is selected in the Link to box, and then type a dummy URL in the URL box, such as your school Web site or the Adobe home page address www.adobe.com.
   d. Apply the **hyperlink** character style. When you close the dialog box, you should see the new hyperlink character format applied to the URL address.
5. Create cross-references on page 1 as follows:
   a. In the Welcome text frame, click just before the period at the end of the first *See* paragraph.
   b. Choose to insert a new cross-reference to a paragraph.
   c. Choose the **Article_title** style, and then select **Orchard Springtime** in the right-hand list.
   d. Select the Paragraph Text & Page Number format.
   e. Select Visible Rectangle, if necessary, so viewers will recognize the text as a cross-reference, set Highlight to **None**, Color to **Lipstick**, and Style to **Dashed**.
   f. Click just before the period at the end of the second *See* paragraph and repeat the steps above to insert and format a cross-reference to the other article title, **Landscaping with Fountains**.

6. There is a problem with the second cross-reference. Because the article title runs to two lines, the Paragraph Text format shows the cross-reference on two lines. Create a text anchor for an alternate approach:

  a. Delete the second cross-reference in the Hyperlinks panel and remove the cross-reference text from the text frame.

  b. Scroll down to page 4 and click just to the left of the word *Landscaping* in the article title.

  c. Create a new text anchor at this location with the name **Landscaping with Fountains**.

  d. Return to page 1, position the insertion point to the left of the last period, and insert a cross-reference to the text anchor you just created, using the Text Anchor Name & Page Number format and the same appearance as the other cross-reference. Your page should look similar to Illustration A when viewed in Preview mode.

7. Open the Preview panel, choose to preview the document, and test your hyperlink and cross-references. Then close the Preview panel.

8. To make it easy for viewers to navigate in the PDF, insert buttons at the beginning of each article as follows:

  a. Display the Sample Buttons panel and locate button 37.

  b. With page 2 of the InDesign document displayed, drag button 37 into the *Return to page 1* text frame at the top of page 2.

  c. Display the Buttons panel. With the button selected, use the Delete selected action button to delete the Go To Previous Page action. Then select the **Go To First Page** action from the actions list. Activate the Click state for the button.

  d. Repeat this process to insert button 37 at the top of page 4.

9. Go to page 6 and choose a sample button to position to the left of the *Bonus* text frame. Delete the current action and choose the Open File action. Use the Select File browse button to select the 109Midwest_perennials.pdf you exported earlier in this exercise. (You may not see the path after you return to the Buttons panel.)

10. Choose a page transition you like and apply it to all spreads.

11. Save your changes, then export the file to interactive PDF with the name 109Midwest_interactive_*xx*, making sure to select Hyperlinks and Interactive Elements, using the same settings you used earlier in this exercise.

12. View the PDF and test your hyperlink, cross-references, and rollover buttons. To see the page transitions, display the file in Full Screen Mode. (Press Esc to return to standard view.)

13. Close the PDF and Adobe, save your changes to the InDesign document, close the file, and exit InDesign.

Illustration A

Midwest Garden Guide

Welcome!

In this issue of *Midwest Gardening Today*'s Garden Guide, you can read about the joys of an orchard in spring and how to keep your orchard thriving. See "Orchard Springtime" on page 2.

You can also sample one of Midwest's Focus on Details articles and learn how make a fountain the focus of your landscaping. See "Landscaping with Fountains" on page 4.

A publication of *Midwest Gardening Today*
www.midwestgardeningtoday.com

ON YOUR OWN

1. Start InDesign and open 💿 OYO109_A. Save the document as OIN109_A_xx.

2. Add cross-references to the text on page 1 as follows:

   a. Click between *See* and *for* in the parenthetical sentence at the end of the first paragraph of body text.

   b. Create a cross-reference to the **Meetings** heading.

   c. Use the Paragraph Text & Page Number format, and choose appearance attributes as desired.

   d. Click after (*see* near the bottom of the first column and create a cross-reference to the **Gift-Giving** heading.

   e. Use the Page Number format and the same appearance attributes as for the previous cross-reference. Remove italics from the cross-reference text.

3. Go to page 4. Balance the text on this page among three columns.

4. The hyperlink at the bottom of the last column of text is no longer active on the Web. Delete the word *Source* and the hyperlink.

5. Use a search engine to find a good travel site for Argentina and create a hyperlink to that site at the end of the third column of text.

6. Choose to preview the entire document and check your cross-references and your new hyperlink.

7. Use rollover buttons to link to other documents in this series on Business Etiquette:

   a. Open 💿 OYO109_B and export the document as an interactive PDF to your solutions folder with the name OIN109_B_xx.pdf. Close the InDesign document without saving.

   b. Open 💿 OYO109_C and export the document as an interactive PDF to your solutions folder with the name OIN109_C_xx.pdf. Close the InDesign document without saving.

   c. In OIN109_A_xx, on page 4, create a text frame on the page with text similar to **Click here to read about business etiquette in Hong Kong**.

   d. Insert a sample button of your choice near the text frame and configure the button to open the OIN109_B_xx.pdf file.

   e. Repeat the process to create a link to business etiquette in Germany that will open the OIN109_C_xx.pdf file.

8. Export the document for interactive PDF with suitable settings, and then test the interactive features in Adobe Acrobat or Reader. You may want to open the Hong Kong and Germany data files again, add a button to return viewers to the Argentina PDF, and resave the two files, replacing the existing PDFs.

   ✓ *You will receive a message about transparency blend spaces that do not match, because you are exporting CMYK transparency settings to an RGB format. You can click OK to continue.*

9. Your client may need an EPS version of this document for print publishing. Export the document as OIN109_A_EPS.

10. Save your changes, close all documents, and exit InDesign and Acrobat.

Exercise | 110

Summary Exercise

Application Skills In this exercise, you work on a report that needs some final tweaking to improve its appearance and usefulness.

EXERCISE DIRECTIONS

1. Start InDesign and open ◉110Online. Save the file as 110Online_xx.

2. Create a new preflight profile to check for problems such as RGB images, blank pages, missing links, and so on. You should receive several errors immediately relating to RGB colors and images.

   a. The colors used to create the shapes on page 1 are saved in the Swatches panel. Open each RGB swatch and change its color mode to CMYK.

   b. Open ◉110Online_image1.jpg in Photoshop and convert it to CMYK. Then save it in the same folder as your document and relink to the corrected image.

3. The last page of the document contains a source line for the image on the first page. Move the last page to become page 2.

4. Create a new page master named **B-No Page** that consists of only one page. Apply it to page 1 of the document.

5. Open the A-Master pages. At the top of the left master page, insert a text frame above the margin guide that uses the Running Header text variable. Modify the variable to use the Heading style, and have the variable show the first heading on the page.

6. Format the text variable in 11-point Arial bold, aligned away from the spine. Then copy the text variable to the right page, at the intersection of the top margin guide and the right margin guide.

7. Still in the master pages, insert page numbers at the bottom center of each page, just below the bottom margin guide. Add the text variable Last Page Number to each page number, so that the markers read A of 1. Format the page numbers in 11-point Arial bold.

8. Start a new section on the third page of the document, starting numbering with page 1. Change page numbering for the first section in the document to lowercase roman numerals. Apply a color label to identify the roman numeral pages in the Pages panel.

9. Create a table of contents on page ii that uses the Heading-styled paragraphs. Format the table of contents as desired. Override the master page number at the bottom of page ii and remove the "of ii" text variable information. The second and third pages of your document should look similar to Illustration A.

10. Save your changes and print a composite of the document.

11. You have been asked to make an online version of the document. Follow these steps:

    a. Copy the heading and text in the table of contents frame, then delete the frame.

    b. Create a new text frame and paste the copied text. Then remove the leaders and the page numbers.

    c. Create a simple character style to be used to designate hyperlinks.

d. Insert text anchors at the location of each heading in the document, using the actual heading for the text anchor. (Select each heading before issuing the New Hyperlink Destination command and the selected text will automatically appear as the anchor text.)

e. Select each remaining contents entry and create a hyperlink to the text anchor of the same name, and apply the character style you created. When you have finished, preview the document to check your links.

12. Save the document as *110Online_online_xx*, then export the document as a PDF with the same name. View the document pages and then close the PDF and Acrobat.

13. Close the document and exit InDesign.

Illustration A

Contents

Image on title page from www.freeimages.co.uk

ii

The Debut of Online Learning

The Rapid City Academy is the alternative high school program for South Dakota's Rapid City Area Schools, which has an enrollment of about 13,000 K-12 students, with five middle schools feeding two large traditional high schools and the alternative program. A high percentage of students at the academy are considered "at-risk" due to transient lifestyles, teenage parenthood, high absentee rates, low socioeconomic status, and medical and/or personal challenges that impact their ability to succeed in the traditional classroom setting. Therefore, the academy strives to provide a quality education for its students via alternative instructional methods such as smaller student-teacher ratios, individualized learning plans, strategy-based learning, flexible schedules, and independent and group-led classes.

South Dakota's Rapid City Academy finds out just what it takes to provide a diverse population of students the flexibility offered by online learning.

The Debut of Online Learning

During the spring of 2002, conversations among a small group of teachers, instructional technology specialists, and administrators led us to attend the Virtual High School Symposium in Denver in fall 2002. Conversations continued, and in summer 2003, teachers and instructional technology specialists developed online courses for implementation that fall. Thus began the academy's venture into the world of online learning.

Rapid City Academy Online (rcacademyonline.org) debuted in November 2003 with four teachers, 34 students, and five courses. Although a majority of the students were from the local school district, enrollment included out-of-district and out-of-country participants. Serving predominately high-school-aged students, Rapid City Academy Online provided a new opportunity for learners who needed the flexibility of the online classes to help meet their outside work schedules, as well as for those hoping to graduate ahead of time or those trying to catch up with their own graduating class. Still, some were just intrigued by the idea of attending virtual classes.

But not all participants fit the archetype of the typical high school-aged learner. One non-traditional student hoped to return to school after more than 50 years to complete the credits necessary for earning a high school diploma. Others were already carrying full course loads at the traditional high schools and wanted the opportunity to take additional coursework, while some students decided to take a class to improve a grade they had received in the traditional setting.

Initial course offerings included American History 1, World Literature 1, Physiology and Anatomy, and Computer Studies 1, while math classes were offered through online curriculum from Pearson Digital Learning's (www.pearsondigital.com) NovaNet program. The virtual high school is now in its fourth cycle, and has grown to eight teachers, 44 students (several of whom are taking two or more online courses), and 15 courses. More growth is anticipated

1 of 5

Exercise | 111

Application Exercise

Application Skills In this exercise, you will create a book using the Mark Twain article you have worked with in several previous exercises and additional resources.

EXERCISE DIRECTIONS

1. Copy the following files to the location where you are storing your solution files for this lesson:
   - 111Twain_A,
   - 111Twain_B, and
   - 111Twain_C.

   Rename the A file as 111Twain_front_xx, the B file as 111Twain_dog_xx, and the C file as 111Twain_turning_xx.

2. Start InDesign and create a new book named 111Twain_xx. Add to the book the three files you saved with new names in step 1. Move the 111Twain_front_xx file to the top of the book list.

3. Open 111Twain_front_xx. You will create a list of illustrations for the book, and you need to include an entry for the illustration on the first page of this document. Create a caption as follows:

   a. Insert a text frame below the picture on page 1 and insert into the frame the following text:

   The mother and Sadie and the servants— why, they just seemed to worship me.

   b. Create a new paragraph style for this text named **Hidden** that applies the None swatch to the text to hide it.

4. On page 1 of this document, change the numbering style to lowercase roman numerals. On page ii, insert a text frame at the bottom center of the page and insert the current page number marker. Format the page number in bold.

5. Open 111Twain_dog_xx and adjust page numbers to start this document on page 1.

6. Set 111Twain_turning_xx as the style source and synchronize styles across all documents.

7. Open each story to see how the styles have been applied consistently. Balance the columns at the end of the 111Twain_dog_xx story.

8. Create a table of contents on page ii of 111Twain_front_xx that uses the Title paragraph style to create the entries. Style the *Contents* title and the TOC entries as desired.

9. Create another table of contents to display the list of illustrations in the book. Follow these steps:

   a. In the Table of Contents dialog box, change the title to **List of Illustrations**. Choose the desired style for the title.

   b. Remove the Title style that you used for the previous TOC from the included paragraph styles.

   c. Add the Hidden style and the Caption style. The Caption style will automatically indent below Hidden. Display More Options, if necessary, and change the Level of the Caption style to 1, so both styles will be used to generate the list.

   d. Deselect the Replace Existing Table of Contents check box.

10. Place the list of illustrations below the contents on page ii. You will have to change the swatch color from None to Black (or another color) to see the first entry in the list of illustrations. Style the list as desired. Illustration A shows one option for formatting.

11. Preflight each document using the preflight profile you created in the last exercise. Then print the book, or a portion of the book as directed by your instructor.

12. Save your changes, close the file, and exit InDesign.

Contents

List of Illustrations

ii

Exercise | 112

Curriculum Integration

Application Skills In Social Studies class, you are studying Canada. You have been asked to create a document that summarizes some of the information you will be learning. Before you begin this exercise, find the following information:

- Information on Canada's system of government.
- Geographic information such as size in square miles and major landforms.
- A list of provinces and territories, with their capitals and some statistics on population for each; find pictures of some capital cities or natural features of the province you can use in the document if possible.

EXERCISE DIRECTIONS

Start a new InDesign document using settings of your choice and save the document with a name such as 112Canada_xx. Create a section for the first two pages to act as front matter, with lower-case roman numeral page numbers, and then start numbering with 1 on the third page. Insert page numbers on the master pages with formats of your choosing.

Create a heading for the document and if possible insert a map of Canada. You may want to work with the map image in Photoshop first to adjust its color mode, size, and appearance. Create a text frame on page 2 to give the source of the map. Reserve the rest of page 2 for a table of contents.

Beginning on the third page of the document, create headings and add content to pages as necessary to cover the topics listed above. If a topic runs to more than one page, continue the page later in the document and use jump lines to direct the reader to the continuation.

Create paragraph styles to make formatting of text and headings easier and to create the table of contents. Try to use at least two levels of headings.

Create a table of contents that uses main headings and any subheadings you have created. If some subheadings have been threaded to other pages, move them in the final table of contents to fall under their correct headings. Illustration A shows a sample table of contents and a first page of content.

Preflight the document to make sure any images you have used are in CMYK mode. Then preview color separations.

Print a composite of the document, and then package the document for distribution.

When you are finished, close the document, and exit InDesign.

Contents

Map on page i from the CIA's World Factbook at https://www.cia.gov/library/publications/the-world-factbook/geos/ca.html

Government of Canada

Canada is a constitutional monarchy that is also a parliamentary democracy and a federation. The constitution of the country is made up of both written and written acts, customs, judicial decisions, and traditions.

The Constitution Act of March 29, 1867, and the Constitution Act of April 17, 1982 form the chief written portions of the constitution. The first act created a federation of four provinces. The second transferred formal control over the constitution from Britain to Canada and added a Canadian Charter of Rights and Freedoms. Procedures for constitutional amendments were also included in the Constitution Act of April 17, 1982.

The government consists of three branches: Executive, Legislative, and Judicial. There are currently five political parties in Canada.

Executive Branch

The chief of state is the reigning British monarch (currently Queen Elizabeth II), who is represented by the Governor General of Canada (currently Michaelle Jean). The Governor General is appointed by the monarch for a five-year term.

The head of government is the Prime Minister (currently Stephen Harper). The Prime Minister is the leader of the majority party in Parliament.

Canada has a cabinet called the Federal Ministry chosen by the prime minister from among the members of his party.

Legislative Branch

The Legislative branch of the Canadian government consists of a bicameral Parliament (Parlement in the Province of Quebec) including the Senate (Senat) and the House of Commons (Chambre des Communes).

Members of the Senate are appointed by the Governor General with advice from the Prime Minister and server until the age of 75. Members of the House of Commons are elected by direct, popular vote and server four-year terms (beginning in 2009).

Government continued on page 4

Portfolio Builder

Application Skills Real-world print jobs may require settings different from the ones you have worked with in this course. In this exercise, you will contact an actual printer (or get information from your instructor that came from an actual printer) and then export a file meeting those specifications.

EXERCISE DIRECTIONS

Contact a professional printing company in your area and ask them about accepting MDF and/or EPS files. Find out what specifications they require or prefer.

Export 104Midwest_xx in either PDF or EPS using those settings. Name the file 113Midwest_export_xx.

Close the document and exit InDesign.

Index

layer styles
adding, 206
applying, 292
defined, 289
layers, 205–206
blending modes for, 292
filling layers, 206–207
filters, applying, 297–298
flattening, 292
linking, 206
locking/unlocking, 206
moving content of, 206
same layer, moving selections on, 220
slices, creating, 317
Smart Filters, applying, 298
Layers panel
buttons on, 206
for clipping masks, 310
vector masks in, 310
working with, 205–206
levels
correcting, 245
defined, 242
linear gradients, 208
lines, drawing, 198
Link layers button, 206
links
layers, linking, 206
slice as link, using, 317
Live Workspace switcher, 10
Load path as selection button, 285
Load Selection dialog box, 222
loading
channels, 304
paths as selection, 284–285
selections, 222
locking/unlocking layers, 206
Magic Eraser tool, 208–209
Magic Wand tool, 79, 213
selecting with, 227
Magnetic Lasso tool, 214–215
sensitivity, adjusting, 215
Marching Ants view of selection, 229
marquees
cropping marquees, 267–268
moving selection marquee, 215
masks
adding, 206
adjustment layer masks, 290
in alpha channels, 303
in Channels panel, 303–304
defined, 301
explanation of, 301–302
fine-tuning, 302
type masks, 303
visibility eye for removing mask color, 304
Masks panel, 309
midtones
adjusting, 245
defined, 242

dodge for, 263
Mini Bridge panel, 18
Mixer Brush tool, 196–198
blending colors with, 196–197
cleaning, 197
loading colors on, 197
photos, using on, 197–198
Move tool, 190
layer content, moving, 206
selections, moving, 220
naming/renaming slices, 317
New dialog box, 189
New effect layer button, 298
new images, creating, 189–190
New Layer dialog box, 291
New selection button, 214
North America General Purpose 2 color setting, 323
North America Prepress 2 color setting, 324
On Layers view, 229
On White view, 229
opacity
graphic tablet, controlling opacity on, 196
selecting, 192
optimizing
defined, 313
GIF files, 314–315
JPEG files, 315–316
process, 313
options bar, 188
selection tool settings, 214
out-of-gamut colors, 326
outlines, converting text to, 504
overexposure
correcting, 245, 258
defined, 257
Overlay view of selection, 229
paint
defined, 195
freehand lines, Brush tool for painting, 195
Paint Bucket tool for filling layers, 206–207
paragraph type, 199
Patch tool, 252–253
patterns, matching, 253
transparent version of patch, creating, 253
Path drawing mode, 191
Path Selection tool, 190, 199
paths
converting selections to, 284
defined, 282
deleting, 284
description of, 282–283
fills for, 284–295
importing, 283
InDesign, clipping image in, 495–496
loading paths as selection, 284–285
modifying, 283
options for creating, 282–283

selecting, 199, 283
stroking a path, 284–285
Paths drawing mode, 198
Paths panel, 283–284
Pattern Fill dialog box, 291
patterns
fill layers, 291
layers, filing, 206–207
patch, applying pattern to, 253
Pen tool, 85, 189, 190
drawing mode, selecting, 191–192
paths, drawing, 282–283
selecting with, 213
vector masks, creating, 310
Pencil tool, 198
Perspective option for selections, 221
photo filters
applying, 258
defined, 257
pixel dimensions
defined, 266
resampling and, 270
working with, 269
pixels, 189
Auto Tone command, 244
cropping by, 268
for feathering selections, 221
Fill pixels drawing mode, 192
Place command, 98
point type, 199
Polygonal Lasso tool, 214–215
polygons, creating, 198
Posterize layer, 290
Preserve Luminosity check box, 245
Preset list of images, 189
Press to view previous state button, 244
previewing
cropping, 267
GIF files, 315
JPEG files, 316
printing
resampling and, 270
RGB files, converting, 324–325
Progressive option for JPEG files, 316
proof colors
custom proof profile, 325
paper colors, using, 326
working with, 325–326
Pupil Size red eye setting, 250–251
Puppet Warp feature, 271
Quick Mask mode
defined, 301
mask color for, 303
overlay view and, 229
working with, 302–303
quick masks
in Channels panel, 302
creating, 302–303
defined, 301
Quick Selection tool, 190, 213
refinement of selection, 230
working with, 227–228

vibrance, 259
adjustment layer, 290
views in, 11
visibility eye
for adjustment layers, 244
mask color, removing, 304
Smart Filter, viewing image without, 298
warming filters, 258
warp
defined, 219
Puppet Warp feature, 271
selections, warping, 221
Web pages
preparing images for, 313–314
slices, organizing documents with, 316–317
Web Snap tolerance for GIF files, 315
Width text box, 189
work paths
defined, 282
working with, 283–284
working space
color control settings for, 323
defined, 322
Zoom tool, 190
picas. *See also* Illustrator
in InDesign, 337
pixel dimensions. *See* Photoshop
pixels. *See* Illustrator; Photoshop
Place command, 98. *See also* InDesign; Photoshop
Place dialog box, Illustrator, 97–98
placing files. *See* Illustrator
PNG files for Web pages, 313
point of origin. *See* Illustrator
points. *See also* Illustrator
in InDesign, 337
polygons. *See also* Illustrator
Photoshop, creating in, 198
PostScript. *See* InDesign
preferences
resetting, 16
view preferences, 16
Preferences dialog box, InDesign, 16
preflight. *See* InDesign
Preflight Profiles dialog box, InDesign, 538
Presentation mode, InDesign, 12, 365
Preview mode, InDesign, 12
previewing. *See also* InDesign; Photoshop
Illustrator, graphic styles in, 168
Print dialog box. *See* InDesign
printing. *See* InDesign; Photoshop
process colors. *See also* Illustrator
in InDesign, 388

quick masks. *See* Photoshop
quotation marks. *See* InDesign

R

radial gradients. *See also* Illustrator
in Photoshop, 208
raster graphics
in Illustrator, 26
in Photoshop, 189
rasterize. *See* Photoshop
Recolor Artwork dialog box, Illustrator, 146–147
Rectangle dialog box, Illustrator, 33
Rectangle Frame tool. *See* InDesign
Rectangle tool. *See also* Photoshop
Illustrator, 72
InDesign, 338
rectangles. *See also* Illustrator
InDesign, rollovers from rectangles in, 555
Photoshop, creating in, 198
recto. *See* InDesign
red eye. *See* Photoshop
Refine Edge dialog box, Photoshop, 228–230
Refine Mask dialog box, Photoshop, 309
Reflect dialog box, Illustrator, 87
Reflect tool, Illustrator, 87
reflected gradients in Photoshop, 208
regions. *See* Illustrator
resampling. *See* Photoshop
resizing. *See* sizing/resizing
resolution. *See also* Illustrator; Photoshop
InDesign, adjusting resolution for graphics in, 488
RGB color mode. *See* Illustrator; InDesign; Photoshop
rollover buttons
InDesign, inserting in, 555–556
Ilustrator, creating graphic styles in, 169
Rotate tool, Illustrator, 55
rotating. *See also* InDesign
Photoshop, rotating canvas in, 268
RTF text to InDesign, importing, 418
Rule of Thirds grid, 267
rulers. *See also* InDesign
Illustrator rulers, displaying, 27–28

S

samples. *See* Photoshop
Satin effect, InDesign, 396–397
saturation. *See* Illustrator; Photoshop
Save As command, 6
Save command, 6
saving. *See also* Photoshop
documents, 6
workspace, 10–11
Scale dialog box, Illustrator, 79

Scale tool. *See* Illustrator
scaling. *See also* Illustrator; InDesign
Photoshop, content-aware scaling in, 270–271
scatter brushes. *See* Illustrator
Scissors tool
Illustrator, 54
InDesign, 338
Select menu, 79
Selection tool. *See* Illustrator; InDesign
Selection tool pointer, Illustrator, 32
semi-autoflow. *See* InDesign
shadows. *See* Photoshop
Shadows/Highlights dialog box, Photoshop, 259–260
Shape Builder tool. *See* Illustrator
Shape Builder Tool Options dialog box, Illustrator, 138–139
shape tools. *See also* Illustrator; Photoshop
working with, 198
shapes. *See* InDesign
shear. *See* InDesign
shortcut keys. *See* Illustrator
showing/hiding. *See also* Illustrator; InDesign
Photoshop, background layers in, 206
Size dialog box, Photoshop, 269
sizing/resizing. *See also* Illustrator
panels, 9–10
Photoshop, resizing canvas in, 269
skew. *See also* Photoshop
InDesign Skew feature for fonts, 427
slices. *See* Photoshop
slug settings. *See* InDesign
Smart Dimensions, InDesign, 381
Smart Filters, Photoshop, 298
Smart Guides. *See* Illustrator; InDesign
Smart Match Style Groups, InDesign, 525
Smart Spacing, InDesign, 381
Smart Text Reflow, InDesign, 419, 454
smooth points. *See* Illustrator
Snap to Grid command, Illustrator, 28
soft proofing. *See also* Photoshop
in InDesign, 326
Spatter effect, 163
spell-checking in InDesign, 421
spirals. *See* Illustrator
spot colors. *See* Illustrator; InDesign
Spot Healing Brush tool. *See* Photoshop
spread traps. *See* InDesign
spreads. *See* InDesign
sRGB color mode, 324, 388
stacked panels, 10
stacking order. *See also* Illustrator
InDesign, changing stacking order in, 364
Standard Screen Mode, Illustrator, InDesign, 11
Star tool. *See* Illustrator
starting CS5 applications, 2
Step and Repeat dialog box, InDesign, 381